Equality
and Authority

S Encel

Equality and Authority
a Study of
Class, Status
and Power
in Australia

Cheshire

SBN 7015 0133 2 (cased edition)
SBN 7015 1193 1 (limp edition)
© 1970 S. Encel
First published 1970
Printed in Australia for
F. W. Cheshire Publishing Pty Ltd
346 St Kilda Road, Melbourne
142 Victoria Road, Marrickville, NSW
at The Griffin Press, Marion Road, Netley, SA
Registered in Australia
for transmission by post as a book

by the same author
Cabinet Government
in Australia
Australian Society:
A Sociological Introduction
(joint ed.)

Contents

Part One   Introduction

1 Scope and Purpose   3
  Sociology and Social Comment   4
2 The Natural History of Class   6
  Some Basic Issues   9
  The Upper Class   16
  Varieties of Class-Consciousness   19
3 Class, Status and Power   27
  Levels of Theory   29
  Three Dimensions of Social Inequality   31
  Social Relations and the Dimensions of Inequality   42

Part Two   An Egalitarian Society?

4 The Paradoxes of Equality   49
5 The Bureaucratic Ascendency   58
  Bureaucracy and the Economy   62
  The Historical Background   65
  The Bureaucratic Revolution: 1939 and After   66
  The Bureaucrat and Society   71
  Courts, Commissions and Policemen   74
  Bureaucracy and Equality   78
6 Class, Status and Power in Australia   80
  Travellers' Tales   81
  From Literature to Science   87
  The Australian Class System: A Model   101
7 Aspects of Social Stratification (1)   109
  Income   109
  Occupation   115
  The Honours System   123
  Clubland   131
  Divers Groups   135

8 Aspects of Social Stratification (2): Education and Religion   143
     Education and Society (1)   143
     Education and Society (2): *The Private Schools*   152
     Religion   164
9 Aspects of Social Stratification (3): Australia in Perspective   184
     The Anglo-Australian Relationship   184
     Anglo-American Society   189

Part Three   Political Authority

10 The Political System   199
     Romantics and Realists   199
     Politics and Bureaucracy   204
     Social Change and Politics   207
11 The Political Class (1): The Politicians We Deserve   210
     Political Leadership   215
12 The Political Class (2): The Called and the Chosen   223
     The Aspirants   223
     The Parliamentarians   227
     Cabinet Ministers   234
13 The Bureaucratic Structure (1)   242
     The Predominance of the Expert   249
     Professional Syndicalism   256
     Conclusion   257
14 The Bureaucratic Structure (2): The Rise of the Meritocracy   258
     The Public Service Personnel System   258
     An International Perspective   263
     The Triumph of the Meritocracy   268
15 The Bureaucratic Structure (3): The New Elite   275
     Recruitment and Careers   275
     The New Elite   280
     The Bureaucratic Elite in the States   281
     Religion and the Public Service   284
     Night on Black Mountain   287

Part Four   Economy and Society

16 Broad Acres   293
    A Pastoral Aristocracy   294
    The Family Nexus   303
    Pastoral Empires   307
    Land and Politics   314
17 Capitalism in Australia (1)   318
    Government Intervention and 'Free Enterprise'   319
    Ownership and Control   326
    Mergers and Takeovers   332
    Restrictive Practices   332
    Overseas Ownership   335
18 Capitalism in Australia (2): Wealth and Power   340
    The Attack on 'Money Power'   341
    Capitalism and the Middle Classes   346
    Money and Politics   349
    The Lobbyists   351
19 Capitalism in Australia (3): Feet Under the Table   357
    Government and Business   357
    'Pantouflage'   364
20 The Business Elite (1): Family Affairs   376
    The First Family   378
    Other Family Groups   384
21 The Business Elite (2): Directors and Managers   390
    The Men on the Boards   390
    Managers and Executives   397
    The Stock Exchange   409
    The Business Way of Life   411

Part Five   Nationalism, Imperialism and Militarism

22 Australia and the Outside World   419
    Australia and Japan   422
    Australia and Indonesia   427
    Australia and the United States   428

23 A Military Tradition   430
24 World War and Cold War   437
    Two World Wars   437
    Defence Policy Since 1945   444
25 The Officer Corps   447
    The Regular Army   450
    The Armed Services Since 1945   462
26 Cincinnatus at Home   464

Acknowledgments

The writing of this book took a long time and was made possible by the help of many people.

For assistance in collecting survey material, I have to thank Mr Arthur Gardner, Auditor-General of the State of Victoria, Mr Harold Dickinson, of the New South Wales Public Service Board, and Sir William Dunk, former chairman of the Commonwealth Public Service Board; the Australian Institute of Management and the Industries Division (as it then was) of the Department of Trade and Industry; the Commonwealth Department of Primary Industry; the Departments of the Navy, Army and Air; and Mr A. D. Brett and his staff of the Beacon Research Company.

I owe a special debt to the various research assistants who helped me to collect information over the years, especially Mrs Naomi Caiden, Mrs Marjory O'Dea, and Miss Digna Smit. To the successive typists and secretaries who have typed and retyped drafts I owe an equal debt for their patience and diligence—Mrs Rubina Evans, Mrs Patricia Coulthard, Mrs Winifred Kieweg and Mrs Patricia Trivière. I am indebted to a number of individuals for information and ideas about the subject, including Dr Charlotte Erickson, Mr Geoffrey Tebbutt, Mr George Munster, Dr Gerald Caiden, Professor Geoffrey Blainey, Mr T. M. Fitzgerald, Dr Stephen Murray-Smith, Dr Alan Barnard, Dr Alan Hall and Mrs Shirley Cass. Others are acknowledged in the text. The late Mr Gavin Long, Mr David Sissons, and Dr Eric Dowling kindly read sections of the manuscript.

My former colleague, Professor L. F. Crisp, encouraged and assisted me in various ways over the years of our association. To another former colleague, Mr Allan McKnight, I am indebted for help at various stages of this enterprise, and to him and his wife Marion I also owe thanks for their kindness to me while I was completing the manuscript. Dr Andrew Fabinyi helped me through a very trying period and for his encouragement and assistance in finishing the book I owe more thanks than I can express. To Miss Anne O'Donovan, of the London office of the Cheshire Group Publishers, I am grateful for much assistance.

The research connected with the book was greatly assisted by grants from several sources. The Royal Institute of Public Administration gave me initial support, followed by the Social Science Research Council of Australia. To Professor Herbert Burton, formerly principal of the School of

General Studies, Australian National University, I also owe thanks in this matter. The Rockefeller Foundation provided a grant which enabled me to extend my researches considerably, and to Dr Gerald Freund, of the Foundation's Division of the Social Sciences, special thanks are due.

To the University of Sussex, where I completed the manuscript in 1968-9, I am indebted for its hospitality, and especially to Mr Christopher Freeman of the Science Policy Research Unit. To Lyndal and Ingwald Kraft, I am indebted for their great friendship and hospitality during my stay in England.

There are many others who could be mentioned. To all of them I express my heartfelt appreciation.

Part One
Introduction

1: Scope and Purpose

The genesis of this book lay in the work done by the author as a post-graduate student, while employed as a junior clerk in the Commonwealth public service in Canberra. In writing my master's thesis, it became apparent to me that the government bureaucracy was, in fact, a complex status system which operated in ways that threw serious doubt on the egalitarian picture of Australia on which I had been brought up. It was this experience that first sensitised me to the growth of stratification in post-war Australia, and started me looking for more evidence of it. I began to collect such evidence systematically in 1956 by carrying out a detailed survey of the social origins and careers of government officials in the Commonwealth and the two largest states, New South Wales and Victoria. This was followed up by similar surveys in other fields where I expected to find comparable situations—politics, business, and the armed services. At that stage, my interest in the subject was confined to making comparisons between these areas of social stratification (or elite formation) and putting them also in an international perspective.

This stage had been reached, and I had published some of my findings in a fragmentary way, when I found myself, in 1960, on study leave at the London School of Economics and Political Science, where Professor David Glass suggested that I should incorporate the material in a book. This entailed more research and much more consideration of a theoretical framework into which to fit the material I had collected. Not long after returning to Australia in 1961, I was asked by the student ALP Club at the University of Melbourne to deliver the annual Chifley Memorial Lecture, in memory of the former Labor prime minister who had died while I was a young public servant. I was to discuss the question, 'Is there an Australian power elite?' This problem had recurred to me a number of times in the course of my work, which had been influenced in various ways by the work of C. Wright Mills, and both in the lecture and in subsequent researches I tried to find a satisfactory answer. The difficulties which I encountered in doing so made me look for a different style of analysis, and led me to think increasingly about *classes* rather than *elites*. Gradually, I formed the view that Mills' concept was inadequate because he had attempted to separate the notion of power from that of class, and that neither could be discussed in isolation from the other. This finally led me to the ideas expressed in the two following chapters, where I have attempted to relate the three notions of class, status and power and to link them with every-day aspects of experience. The discussion in these chapters is no more than a preliminary sketch, which has enabled me to put in order the material I have collected over a period of years. There is no shortage of works on the subject of social class, and I have not aimed to write another one, although it is impossible to avoid retracing well-trodden ground as in these chapters. This is a book about a particular country and its social structure, and the framework of ideas I have chosen is the one which appears best suited to the task of explaining it.

In doing this, however, I have done my best to write about Australia in an international perspective, and to treat it as a special case of contem-porary, affluent, urban, industrial, white society. If, for instance, one is to answer the question whether there is a power elite in Australia, it can only be answered by putting the question in such perspective, and inquiring what this notion means in any country where it might be asked. It will then, I think, become apparent that Wright Mills' use of the term reflects a specific situation in the United States arising from the overwhelming power of great wealth in that country, controlled by a large number of giant corporate enterprises, linked with a war economy and the relative weakness of certain checks and balances which apply in other societies. In a sense, every country is bound to have a power elite, but the explanatory value of the term is limited, although it is tempting to apply the notion to a country like the Soviet Union, which may fit the description even more accurately than the USA.The sociology of power is still in a primitive state, and only crude comparisons are possible between various countries while it remains so. Thus, it is still more accurate to describe Britain as having a 'ruling class' rather than a 'power elite', whose position depends on what Antonio Gramsci called 'hegemony', i.e. the dominance of a social bloc, not simply by force or wealth, but by a social authority sanctioned and expressed through cultural supremacy. In Australia, there is neither a ruling class in this sense nor a power elite in Mills' sense, but a loose collection of elite groups linked together by what may be called a *governing consensus*. It is this consensus which maintains the existing structure of class, status and power and the settled policies of the country on which that structure depends, including the 'white Australia' policy, the system of industrial arbitration, the balance between urban and country interests, the educational compromise, the primacy of government action in many fields, the Protestant ascendency, and the special status and privileges of various groups.

Sociology and Social Comment

Sociology, like politics and economics, should be an opinionated study and the sociologist should have definite views about the matters he is describing. In this book, I have touched upon a wide variety of social issues in contemporary Australian life and politics, and my personal opinions should be clear to the reader. The period with which the book is concerned may be known to future historians as the 'Menzies era', the period from 1949 to 1966 which witnessed the unbroken reign of Sir Robert Menzies as prime minister. This was a period of rapid social change in which economic, social and political transformation constrained many people to question traditional assumptions about the nature of their own society. By a nice piece of historic irony, the man whose name will be linked with it was himself an arch-conservative whose refusal to question traditional values provides a striking example of continuity between the old and the new. During this period, a large number of political decisions were made which I regard as pernicious. Many of these represent the diseases of the affluent society which J. K. Galbraith summed up, mordantly, as 'private affluence and public squalor'. There was also a failure to review Australia's relations with the rest of the world and a determination to cling, instead, to the role of a colonial outpost of a great power. Australia's size and geographical position do, indeed, compel a degree of economic and political dependence on more powerful nations, but a more adventurous spirit would be concerned to minimise rather than accentuate the colonial element in this situation. The strength of bureaucratic conformism in Australian social life was underlined by the repression of dissent on political issues, paralleled by a grotesque censorship in cultural matters, especially books and films. The growth of affluence was accompanied by increases in social and economic inequality and an enhancement of the privileges of already privileged groups.

But the object of this book is not to act, primarily, as a source of social commentary or a guide-book to the class structure of the Australian community. The contemporary issues just mentioned are the outcome of the long-term character of class, status and power in Australia. In order to construct a meaningful model of the Australian class system, it is essential to clarify the meanings which I attach to these three related terms, and this I have endeavoured to do in the two succeeding chapters. The general reader may find this discussion of comparatively little interest, in which case he is free to leave it alone. The student of society will, I hope, appreciate that I have tried to make a contribution to sociology, and this is how I should like the book to be judged.

2: The Natural History of Class

Rousseau began his inquiry into the nature of the social contract with a paradox: man is born free, yet everywhere he is in chains. He was unable to say how this had come about, but believed he could explain what could make it legitimate. He returned to the subject in his *Dissertation on Inequality*, where he argued that natural or physical inequality had no necessary connection with moral or political inequality, which is established by human action. Sociology begins with a similar paradox: men are born equal, yet human society divides them. Common humanity far outweighs individual differences, yet social relations establish and magnify inequalities of physical and mental capacity, of property, power, and esteem. Historically, asserts Ralf Dahrendorf, the origin of inequality was the first question asked by sociology, which 'lies neither in human nature nor in dubious historical factors such as private property', but is the result of social norms backed up by sanctions to enforce them. This is what generates inequality of rank among men.[1]

The two great products of eighteenth century Europe, rationalism and industrial capitalism, took it as self-evident that men were created equal, or as Nietzsche wrote in the *Genealogy of Morals*, 'the masters have been abolished; the morality of the common man has triumphed.' Yet the unending movement of industrialisation repeatedly generates new forms of differentiation and, in consequence, new attempts to resolve the paradox of their existence. The task of the social sciences, and especially of sociology, begins with the exploration of the social division, cleavage and conflict arising from the tension between natural equality and established social inequality.

The systematic investigation of social division begins with Marx and Engels, who assimilated and transformed a number of ideas about man and society which date from the English political debates of the seventeenth century. The utilitarian picture of economic man, engaged in the 'rational' pursuit of satisfying his material wants, provided the model for the bourgeois entrepreneur, intent on accumulating capital by exploiting the labour of others, and the ownership and control of productive resources became the sole or at least overriding cause of social division. In *The*

[1] Ralf Dahrendorf, 'On the Origin of Social Inequality', in P. Laslett and W. G. Runciman (eds.), *Philosophy, Politics, and Society*, Cambridge, 1962, p. 104

Poverty of Philosophy Marx wrote that 'with the moment in which civilisation begins, production begins to be based on the antagonism between accumulated and direct labour.' In his last statement on the subject, contained in the unfinished Chapter 52 of the third volume of *Capital*, Marx repeated this argument at greater length: 'It is the permanent tendency and law of development of the capitalist mode of production to separate the means of production increasingly from labour, and to concentrate the separate means of production more and more in large groups— in other words, to transform labour into wage labour, and the means of production into capital.'

The corollaries of this theory are that all other bases of social division are of secondary and/or transient importance; that the abolition of the private ownership of the means of production will put an end to class divisions; and that the existence of class differences depends on class conflict arising from private ownership. 'Individuals form a class only in so far as they are engaged in a common struggle with another class.' (*The German Ideology*)

Like other heroic achievements of system-building, the Marxian synthesis began to disintegrate almost as soon as its creator had left the scene. The history of social thought since Marx's death has been dominated by attempts variously to re-create, transcend, or refute the synthesis, or alternatively to establish a genuinely non-Marxian theory of classes. The result is a spread from the 'revolutionary cosmology' of Marxism to the 'middle-class, status-involved, and ethnocentric'[2] categories of W. Lloyd Warner. Each variety of class theory, in its turn, depends on moral assumptions about the inevitability and/or justifiability of social inequality. Every theory, observes Reissman, must take an explicit or implicit stand on 'the character, the form and the necessity of such divisiveness.'[3] This echoes Lenin's dictum that no social science is possible without moral assumptions. Not all social scientists accept this position, and insist that they are merely describing the moral assumptions of the people they are studying. Yet, as Runciman argues, no account of social inequality is possible without evaluation of people's feelings towards equality and inequality, and especially the feeling of 'relative deprivation' which remains even when the physical circumstances of life have improved greatly. 'The notion of social justice is somewhere implicit in every account of how people feel about social equality . . . [and] only a theory of justice can provide an adequate assessment of relative deprivation.'[4]

Outside Marxist fundamentalism, it appears that present-day sociology has arrived at a broad consensus which regards social division in terms of three related dimensions of analysis—class, status and power. The dissolution of the original Marxist system into these three categories is usually

[2] Leonard Reissman, *Class in American Society*, London, 1960, p. 44

[3] ibid., p. 38

[4] W. G. Runciman, *Relative Deprivation and Social Justice*, London, 1966, pp. 247-51

attributed to Max Weber, whose work, as Joseph Schumpeter once observed, consists of deductions from the original Marxian theorems. Kurt Mayer, attributing the threefold approach to Weber, argues that 'only a class theory which recognises these three vertical dimensions as analytically distinct and which intends to trace their inter-relationships can provide a realistic understanding of the class structure of complex, industrial societies.'[5] A similar attribution is made by Runciman, who praises Weber for avoiding the confusion of 'class' with 'status', and for establishing the separate validity of the 'power' dimension of stratification, particularly by his emphasis on the role of bureaucracy in an affluent industrial society.[6]

It is doubtful whether Weber, who can rarely be accused of excessive precision, had arrived at this clear-cut position. The main evidence for his contribution is the essay 'Class, Status, Party', first published in full in English in 1944. In it, Weber formulates the well-known distinction between class as based on 'market situation' and status as based on 'work situation' and prestige, but he makes no similar analysis of the origins of power, or of its exact relation to the other two notions. The section on 'party' in this essay is the shortest and least systematic, and is mainly concerned to distinguish party membership, as a form of group affiliation, from membership of a class or status group. Elsewhere, Weber appears to assimilate his view of class into a more inclusive concept of power as the most fundamental of all social relationships. In one of his numerous accounts of 'domination' (*Herrschaft*), Weber describes it as having two aspects; economic, arising from constellations of economic interest, and authoritative, arising from the need for an established order in society.[7]

The conception of power as a separate dimension of inequality (as against the treatment of power in purely political or legal terms) owes much to Weber, but probably even more to a directly Marxist source. Already at the turn of the century there were heretical Marxists who foresaw a society stratified on the basis of control by bureaucrats, technicians and managers, like the eccentric Pole, Machajski.[8] The most important contributor to this current of thought, however, was Trotsky, whose account of the bureaucratic deformation of Russian society in *The Revolution Betrayed* and elsewhere has had a major influence, directly or indirectly, on a host of writers about the 'managerial revolution'. Detached from their particular historical context, these unorthodox extensions of Marxist thought have given a powerful stimulus to the picture of a bureaucratised industrial society where, in direct contrast to classical Marxist theory, material wealth and social status are dependent upon

[5] Kurt B. Mayer, 'The Theory of Social Classes', *Transactions of the 2nd World Congress of Sociology*, London, 1954, vol. 2, p. 332
[6] W. G. Runciman, *Social Science and Political Theory*, Cambridge, 1963, ch. 8
[7] Max Rheinstein (ed.) *Max Weber on Law in Economy and Society*, New York, 1957, p. 324
[8] For an account of Machajski see Max Nomad, *Aspects of Revolt*, New York, 1959

position in a political and administrative hierarchy. In combination with Weber's account of bureaucracy, and tributary influences such as the writings of Pareto and Michels on the elite, the effect was to establish power as a dimension of social analysis alongside class and status. But this has happened by a process of slow accretion rather than by conscious, large-scale attempts at systematisation, which are still rare. I shall endeavour, on a small scale, to examine the relations between these three dimensions and to arrange them in some kind of logical system.

Some Basic Issues

Despite enormous confusion over definition, relevance, and interpretation in the study of social division, a number of consistent strands may be identified within it. An attempt to list these, made some years ago by a group of American sociologists, comprises ten headings.[9]

(i) Should social strata be regarded as part of the natural order, or as subject to human action and policy? (or both, perhaps?)

(ii) The relation between power and prestige, and their relation in turn to 'observable phenomena' like occupation (prestige and power being regarded as 'intervening variables').

(iii) Do national patterns of stratification exist, or only collections of local and regional patterns?

(iv) The moral status of class divisions: are they a remediable defect of mass society, *or* a reflection of differential rewards for merit and effort, *or* an expression of the evil in human nature?

(v) Is class a matter of objective rank or dependent on class-consciousness?

(vi) Is there a single system or a multitude of overlapping systems?

(vii) Do classes form definable groups, or is there only a long continuum of gradations? The number of classes, the sharpness of the distinctions between them, and similar questions, are 'not given in the world of events, but are artifacts of the operations employed and purposes intended by the investigator . . . the issue of classes versus continuum cannot be settled in the final analysis by an appeal to public opinion.'

(viii) Is information about classes to be gained by collecting the views of participants or by detached outside observation?

(ix) Should class analysis be static or dynamic?

(x) Should mobility and change be measured by examining individual mobility or group advancement?

This list, though open to criticism on the grounds of both omission and commission, does identify a wide range of basic questions. The most important omission is the failure to deal with the argument, deriving from Marx, that class divisions are an expression of conflict, which underlies the contention that class is an 'illegitimate' phenomenon and not part of a natural order. Conflict arises, according to T. H. Marshall, because of the

[9] N. N. Foote, et al, 'Alternative Assumptions in Stratification Research', *Transactions of the 2nd World Congress of Sociology*, vol. 2, pp. 380-89

division of labour, because of competition between classes, and because of differences over the nature of the system itself, and even social groups which differ in other ways become united into classes because of their common position in relation to economic institutions.[10]

The most ambitious attempt in recent years to restate the conflict theory of social division is due to Dahrendorf. 'Change and conflict', he suggests, 'have to be assumed as ubiquitous, all elements of social structure have to be related to instability and change, and unity and coherence have to be understood as resulting from coercion and restraint.'[11] Social classes, therefore, are to be understood always as conflict groups, in which common interests arise out of, and in relation to, the authority structure of 'imperatively co-ordinated associations'. The latter phrase, deriving from Parsons' ungainly though accurate translation of Weber's *Herrschaft*, reflects Dahrendorf's attempt to synthesise Marx and Weber and to incorporate the Marxian conception of *class* conflict as a special case of a general theory of conflict arising from the universal problem of authority. 'Conflicts are ultimately generated by relations of authority, i.e. by the differentiation of dominating and subjected groups.' Economic changes alone will not affect this situation. 'The fact that economic demands may provide the substance . . . of manifest interests must not give rise to the erroneous notion that satisfaction of these demands eliminates the causes of conflict. Nor does the replacement of capitalists by managers remove the basis of industrial class conflict. 'The replacement of functioning owners or capitalists by propertyless functionaries or managers does not abolish class conflict, but merely changes its empirical patterns.' It is the distribution of authority which is crucial, making social conflict 'as universal as the relations of authority and imperatively co-ordinated associations.'[12]

Another recent restatement of the conflict approach is due to John Rex. All social systems, he argues, are marked by conflict at key points, ranging from peaceful bargaining to open violence. In the resulting class society, relations between the classes (each of which is a social system in itself) depend on the conflict situation. The balance of power is unequal; the dominant class constantly seeks to legitimate its position, the subject class to deny this claim and to give visible evidence of its denial. A basic change in the social situation may, however, enable the subject class to effect a revolutionary destruction of the power of the ruling class, and the revolutionary class will then itself become subject to internal conflicts.[13]

Class theories based on conflict were originally an instrument of radical criticism of the social order, and retain this character. The development of sociology has been marked by the rise of 'functional' theories of social

[10] T. H. Marshall, 'Class Conflict' in Marshall (ed.), *Class Conflict and Social Stratification,* London, 1938, pp. 97-101
[11] Ralf Dahrendorf, *Class and Class Conflict in Industrial Society*, Stanford, 1959, p. 237
[12] ibid., pp. 253-54
[13] John Rex, *Key Problems of Sociological Theory*, London, 1961, pp. 129-30

stratification which suggest that class divisions are necessary and natural. Schumpeter wrote, for instance, that 'every class has a definite function, which it must fulfil according to its whole concept and orientation, and which it actually does discharge as a class and through the class conduct of its members. Moreover, the position of each class in the total national structure depends on the one hand on the significance that is attributed to that function, and, on the other hand, on the degree to which the class successfully performs the function.'[14] Schumpeter goes so far as to assert that classes do not come into existence because of their possession of certain means of production; it is the function of the class which leads to the possession of these means. The survival of a class depends upon the success with which members 'fulfil their characteristic function, and according to the rise and fall in the social significance of this function, or of those functions which the class members are willing and able to accept instead.'[15]

At the present day, the word 'functional' refers most commonly to the work of Parsons and his school, which owes something to Weber and more to social anthropology. In the Parsonian system, as in Malinowski's theory of culture, every individual has drives and needs, the satisfaction of which depends on social structure and its hierarchy of values. Hence stratification, which implies a system of social ranks in line with the value hierarchy; in Parsons' words, 'the ranking of units in a social system in accordance with the standards of the common value system.'[16] *Units* include such variables as occupation, religion, and racial origin. Ranking is also possible on the basis of *qualities*, which refers to individual attributes like intelligence; *performances*, involving judgments of a person by others, e.g. ranking on a scale of occupational prestige; and *possessions*, including not only wealth but skills, official positions, and the like. Parsons' propositions are expressed less grandiloquently and more pithily in a well-known paper by Davis and Moore. 'As a functioning mechanism a society must somehow distribute its members in social positions and induce them to perform the duties of these positions.'[17]

The acceptance of inequality as the natural order of things is lubricated by the assumption that society operates by the distribution of rewards according to ability. Differential rewards account for the existence of stratification. The system depends on the functional importance of various status positions, and the ability and talent needed to fill them. This kind of stratification theory embodies the perfect bourgeois dream of a society where virtue and hard work are appropriately rewarded, and the distribution of rewards is governed by an invisible hand. The comparison with classical economics is irresistible, and indeed Reissman notes that Adam

[14] J. A. Schumpeter, *Social Classes*, New York, 1955, p. 137
[15] ibid., p. 159
[16] T. Parsons, *Essays in Sociological Theory*, New York, 1954, p. 388
[17] A. Davis and W. E. Moore, 'Some Principles of Stratification', *American Sociological Review*, vol. 10, no. 2, 1945

Smith, by similar reasoning, reached similar conclusions on the need for different pay for different occupations.[18] Moreover, by excluding institutional structures from consideration, particularly those involving power and authority, Parsons and his fellow-writers discreetly avoid the really awkward and important questions about the methods used by society to 'induce its members to perform the duties of their positions'. Power and conflict appear almost as accidental factors which do not shape the value hierarchy but have an incidental bearing upon it.[19]

The logical extension of this kind of theory into empirical investigation is to be found in the work of Lloyd Warner, where social stratification is taken for granted, and is assumed to arise from a consensus within the community regarding the criteria for placing individuals within one stratum or another. The task of the investigator is to decipher these criteria, to analyse the symbols of class membership, and to identify the occupants of the various strata. Following his earlier studies, Warner attempted to systematise his methods by inventing two indices of class and status—the Index of Status Characteristics (isc), based on occupation, source of income, type of house, and dwelling area, and the Evaluated Participation method (ep), based on judgments of a person's class position given by informants in the same community. A social class, writes Warner, 'is to be thought of as the largest group of people whose members have intimate access to one another. A class is composed of families and social cliques. . . . A person is a member of a social class with which most of his participation, of this intimate kind, occurs.'[20] It is not difficult to argue that Warner's work has little to do with the traditional subject-matter of theories of social class; it contains much information about the behaviour of individuals and small groups, but little or nothing about the structure of society. Many writers have criticised Warner on these grounds and also because his methods of collecting information are suspect. It will be sufficient to cite one representative critic, Kurt Mayer.[21] Warner's methods and assumptions, observes Mayer, are popular and influential because they provide an apparently simple and ideologically sound method of studying class, which has the advantage of being unhistorical and therefore avoids some awkward questions. In practice, the simplicity of approach turns out to be deceptive and the apparently objective standards of measurement to have some highly subjective features. To define classes by association, and then to examine association in order to discover class affiliation, is simply a tautology. Warner's static picture of the social structure 'neatly bypasses the possibility of clashing economic interests which, under given circumstances, may lead to organised class action and fundamental changes

18 Reissman, op. cit., p. 86; cf. M. M. Tumin, *Social Stratification*, New Jersey, 1967
19 Reissman, op. cit., p. 81
20 W. L. Warner, methodological note in Horace Cayton and St Clair Drake, *Black Metropolis*, New York, 1945, pp. 772-73; cf. Warner, Meeker and Eells, *Social Class in America*, New York, 1949
21 K. Mayer, loc. cit.

of the class structure.' In this world, the class structure is simply the collective way of life with which the individual is required to cope by personal adjustment and self-improvement.

Another recurrent problem in the study of social division is the relation of 'class' to other forms of social grouping about whose reality there is little argument, such as occupation, religion, racial origin and 'culture'. The tendency of a monistic theory like Marxism is to assimilate these into one inclusive scheme. 'On the different forms of property and the social conditions of existence a whole superstructure of various and peculiarly formed sentiments, illusions, modes of thought, and conceptions of life is built. The whole class creates and forms these out of its material foundations and the corresponding social relations.'[22] Theories of stratification, on the other hand, tend to emphasise the complexity and many-sidedness of social division and to treat religion, occupation, income, education etc. as *real* categories; class is largely a matter of self-identification. In between these two positions are writers who treat class as a particular form of social relationship comparable with the others mentioned. Schmoller, in defining class, began by excluding groups which were *not* classes. His example is followed by Marshall, who argues in favour of the term 'social class' because it is more specific and less ambitious than 'class' sans qualification. Occupation, political power and property are excluded as the basis of class differentiation, and the residue is 'social class', which is hierarchical, socially recognised, and relatively permanent. A social class is 'a group of persons with similar life chances . . . the essence of social class is the way a man is treated by his fellows (and reciprocally, the way he treats them).'[23]

Marshall is right to reject the notion that class is purely subjective, and right also to argue that it is not the same as occupation, wealth, and so forth. But his account is rather baffling because he does no more than hint at the nature of the relation between class and these other categories, and he spreads the confusion by speaking, for instance, of the 'class structure' of the legal profession, which persists despite the growth of the impartial administration of justice. The central problem in a systematic theory of class, status and power is to establish a logical relationship between the two sets of notions. As Reissman observes, 'though there are close resemblances and interlocking consequences between institutions and their ability to confer status and power, each institution maintains some autonomy not directly affected by the others. The problem for a theory of class becomes one of bringing order to the variety of effects that are exerted by institutional segments of the social order.'[24]

The most ambitious recent effort to 'bring order to the variety of effects' is Lenski's *Power and Privilege*, which endeavours to subsume them under the heading of power and also to combine conflict and integration

---

[22] Karl Marx, *The Eighteenth Brumaire of Louis Bonaparte*
[23] T. H. Marshall, *Citizenship and Social Class*, Cambridge, 1950, p. 92
[24] Reissman, op. cit., p. 41

theories. Hence he introduces the notion of a 'power class', i.e. 'an aggregation of persons in a society who stand in a similar position with respect to force or some specific form of institutionalised power.' The term 'class' on its own should be used to describe any aggregate of people ranked according to a particular criterion. The structure of power and privilege is the result of struggles between these classes. In general, the products of men's labour are distributed according to need and to power; the latter is the main principle which regulates distribution in societies with a surplus, while more primitive societies, characterised by scarcity, operate on the basis of need, which determines the structure of privilege.[25]

Lenski's argument, although it is an impressive attempt to unify conflict theories with integration theories, suffers from important defects which render its wide application doubtful. His historical evidence is interesting, but not convincing, and he hedges on the role of power in primitive societies where need is supposed to be dominant. There is no logical necessity to construct one structure of privilege linking wealth and power, which can be treated as independent phenomena each of which gives rise to a distinct structure of privilege.

Marshall's insistence that class is both objective and subjective naturally recalls the classic Marxian distinction between a class *in itself* and a class *for itself*. Class consciousness, bred in the process of class conflict, transforms the former into the latter. 'The domination of capital created the common situation and common interests of [the workers]. Thus, this mass is already a class in relation to capital, but not yet a class for itself. In the struggle . . . this mass unites and forms itself into a class for itself. The interests which it defends become class interests.'[26] Similarly, the bourgeoisie first formed itself into a class under the feudal system and absolute monarchy, and then, formed into a class for itself, overthrew feudalism and monarchy and transformed society into bourgeois society.[27] And again, speaking about the peasantry, Marx asserts that 'in so far as millions of families live under economic conditions of existence that separate their mode of life, their interests, and their culture from those of the other classes, and put them in hostile opposition to the latter, they form a class.'[28] This combination of class position and class-consciousness provides the basis for the contention that class is an 'actual empirical entity'. As against this, a number of sociologists have argued that class is, and cannot be more than, a construct in the mind of the observer, a social map which he needs to make sense of the social territory beyond his immediate range of observation. Dowling[29] has suggested two reasons why this objection may be justified. The first is that the vagueness and

[25] G. E. Lenski, *Power and Privilege*, New York, 1966, pp. 75-82
[26] Karl Marx, *The Poverty of Philosophy*
[27] Ibid.
[28] Marx, *The Eighteenth Brumaire of Louis Bonaparte*
[29] R. E. Dowling, 'Are Social Classes Hypothetical Constructs or Actual Empirical Entities?', paper delivered to the Australian Political Studies Association, 1962

disputability of the notion of class-consciousness are as pronounced as the similar vagueness and disputability surrounding the notion of class position. The second is a logical difficulty. The emphasis on class-consciousness gives it a special import denied to such characteristics of class membership as occupation, power, prestige, and the like. Class-consciousness, he argues, 'has the peculiar function of endowing the class with "existence", a function that is neither demanded of nor accorded to the other defining characteristics . . . there would seem no reason for regarding a particular defining characteristic as having an existential import which is denied to the remaining characteristics, and we may regard the argument from class consciousness as inadequate.'

A denial of the reality of class is sometimes linked with the contention that there are no clear boundaries between classes, but only a continuous gradation of social groups. (This assumption seems to underlie studies of occupational prestige.) This view is strongly contested by Marshall, who attacks the idea that 'because classes are hard to identify class is non-existent, and that, because the possible bases of classification are numerous, therefore they are infinite and lead into a morass from which no traveller can hope to extricate himself.' On the contrary, he asserts, class is a basic social institution which 'presses behaviour into socially determined moulds and produces uniformities of conduct in those who conform to custom.' A recognition of this will prevent an underestimation of the importance of class in a society which appears to be without definable classes, and prevent futile arguments about the true lines of social division. On the other hand, in Marshall's scheme, unlike Marxism, it is assumed that classes exist on the basis of their internal characteristics, and not because of an inherent conflict relationship.[30]

The ideological character of the 'gradation' theory of social differences, popular in the United States, is discussed at length by Ossowski. The notion of 'gradation', which he distinguishes from that of 'polarised' classes, is rooted in the democratic optimism of American folklore, transmitted to American students of society. The theory of gradation permits the concept of a 'classless but inegalitarian' society.[31] Ossowski divides this concept into four components:
(1) Social and economic status is not determined by descent, and all may aspire to the highest position.
(2) The status scale is a continuous gradation and not broken up by barriers.
(3) No special privileges are attached to social groups, and there are no permanent conflicts of interest between groups higher or lower on the scale.
(4) No separation or restriction is practised in social contacts.
Ossowski noted, ironically, that there was a strong element of this theory in official Soviet accounts of social life in the USSR.

[30] Marshall, *Citizenship and Social Class*, op. cit., pp. 106-13
[31] Stanislaw Ossowski, *Class Structure in the Social Consciousness*, New York, 1963

The Upper Class

A recurring problem in the study of social division is that of identifying an upper class. In the nineteenth century, various writers found no difficulty in describing the upper class, or upper classes, even if they meant rather different things by it. Perhaps the most important link between all theories which postulate the existence of an upper class, a ruling class, or a power elite is their perception that the concept always involves the elements of political authority and cultural domination. Marx and Engels wrote in the *Communist Manifesto* that 'each step in the development of the bourgeoisie was accompanied by a corresponding political advance of that class . . . the bourgeoisie has at last, since the establishment of modern industry and of the world market, conquered for itself, in the modern representative State, exclusive political sway. The executive of the modern State is but a committee for managing the common affairs of the whole bourgeoisie.' And in *The German Ideology*, they extended this to culture. 'The ideas of the ruling class are, in every age, the ruling ideas; i.e. the class which is the dominant material force in society is at the same time its dominant intellectual force. The class which has the means of material production at its disposal has control at the same time over the means of mental production. . . . In so far, therefore, as they rule as a class and determine the whole extent of an epoch, . . . [they] rule also as thinkers, as producers of ideas, and regulate the production and distribution of the ideas of their age.'

The theory of the ruling class deriving from the work of Mosca, Pareto and Michels rests on entirely different premises, but it shares with Marxism an emphasis on the political character of the upper class. Mosca's political class 'performs all political functions, monopolises power and enjoys the advantages that power brings . . .'.[32] In addition, as Mosca noted later, the political class represents the interests of economic and social groups.[33] The value of these concepts is shown by the repeated attempts to link them with the Marxian analysis by a succession of writers including Harold Lasswell, Raymond Aron and C. Wright Mills. Because the objectives of these writers are primarily political, they can accommodate the concept of a ruling group without theoretical strain. The study of social stratification, in which politics plays only a minor role, has little use for the concept of an upper class. Perhaps the principal reason is that studies of stratification rely heavily, and on the whole uncritically, on the identification of social classes by the 'man in the street'. In a democratic country, at any rate, the man in the street does not provide the investigator with a usable concept of an upper class. As a result, social investigators of all kinds use scales of social class which begin with the 'upper middle' class. One notable exception is Lloyd Warner, who discovered both

[32] G. Mosca, in A. Livingston (ed.), *The Ruling Class*, New York, 1939, p. 50
[33] For a discussion of these views see T. B. Bottomore, *Elites and Society*, 1967, ch. 1 and J. H. Meisel, *The Myth of the Ruling Class*, University of Michigan, 1958

'upper upper' and 'lower upper' groups in Yankee City; but one of the main criticisms of his work is precisely that although these findings may be valid for the small community which Warner studied, they cannot be extrapolated to a national class structure.

An account of this problem, at once entertaining and extremely perceptive, is given by the English writer Michael Frayn.[34] In his weekly column in the London *Observer*, Mr Frayn described an argument with his wife, who was studying sociology and showed him three standard scales which make no provision for an 'upper class'—the classification used by the Registrar-General for England and Wales, the Hall-Jones scale of occupational prestige, and the alphabetical scale used by the Institution of Practitioners in Advertising (IPA).

It's a difficult subject all right, class. (*Mr Frayn continues.*) Last week Anthony Powell was on television, and the *Radio Times* described him as a novelist who 'satirises the upper-middle classes with a brilliant sense of social nuance.'

The Upper-middle classes? The Earl of Warminster, Sir Gavin Walpole-Wilson, General Conyers, Sir Magnus Donners-Brebner, Lady Ardclass, Lady Molly Jeavons, Prince Theodoric, and all the rest of those magnificent characters, *upper-middle* class?

Well, stap me! I thought they were the *upper* classes! I suppose that just shows my embarrassing lower-middle class naivety. The *Radio Times* with its brilliant sense of social nuance, saw immediately that all Powell's earls, courtiers, and great industrialists were really horribly bourgeois. And indeed, the whole upper class recedes like the horizon as you approach it. What could be more middle class than an earl or a newspaper proprietor, when you come to think about it? Except perhaps a royal duke or an oil millionaire?

Indeed, as my wife pointed out when I raised the matter at my next tutorial, for sociological purposes the upper classes simply don't exist. The Registrar-General's classification and the Hall-Jones scale both start with the professional classes; the IPA grading with Group A, the upper-middle class.

'But look,' I protested, 'the middle classes must be in the middle of something. They can't just be sandwiched between the lower classes and God.'

'*Lower* classes?' said my wife. 'What are they? You don't mean the working classes, do you?'

'What I'm getting at is, are you trying to tell me that you and your professional pals are higher up the social scale than earls and kings and so on?'

'It depends how the earls and kings spend their time, Michael. If they just inspect their troops and supervise the running of their estates I suppose they come in the Inspectional and Supervisory category along with you.'

'What? You honestly think a doctor's daughter's higher up than a fully-blown belted earl!'

'This is a surprisingly reactionary attitude you're taking up, Michael.'

Well, for heaven's sake! I mean, one does know certain things instinctively. I mean, well, for heavens' sake!!

[34] *Observer*, London, 16 January 1966

An American sociologist argues that no theory of social division makes sense unless it provides for an upper class. 'The fact that the lower classes may not distinguish between an upper and an upper-middle class does not necessarily signify that this distinction is not both meaningful in a social-psychological sense and distinctly functional in life chances and social interaction at the level at which it is recognised. Does everyone in the forest have to hear the tree fall before we are allowed to conclude that it is truly on the ground?'[35]

Social surveys indicate that working class respondents are much more responsive to the notion of an upper class, cut off from them by the possession of power in such spheres as economic relations, the control of the mass media, and the ability to manipulate legal and political institutions for its own benefit. This will hardly come as a surprise to anyone with even a tincture of Marxism, but it seems to cause difficulties for a number of sociologists and other middle class observers. The editor of a recent British symposium on the subject falls into a logical (and sociological) morass with a reference to 'the middle class, by definition the controller of most of our important institutions.'[36] One of these institutions turns out to be the English public-school system, and the confusion is extended when another contributor refers, more accurately, to the 'upper class education' given by Eton.[37]

The social role of the upper class is complicated by the fact that it has two distinct relationships with the middle and working classes. In terms of social prestige, income, education and style of life, there is a considerable overlap between the upper class and the upper-middle class, and the main distinction resides in the possession of power. This is the kind of distinction made by Mosca and Pareto, who separated the 'governing elite' from the elite as a whole. The circulation of the governing elite which Pareto, Mosca and others described means, in practice, the continuing recruitment of individuals and groups from other social strata, but above all from the upper-middle class. For the upper-middle class, the governing class is only a few steps away; its social status is not significantly different; and even the power which its members possess does not put them out of reach. In a democratic country, where social status is clearly separated from power, the working classes have no need to regard the middle classes as being *above* them in any more elaborate sense than possessing more money. Conversely, the upper class is unlikely to regard the middle classes as being significantly *below* them. This triangular relationship complicates both the nature of class-consciousness and the problems of measuring it; by definition, its nature will differ from one class to another. In practice, the complications of the situation lead to the observation commonly made by investigators, that 'everybody' describes themselves as middle class. But the simple conclusion that this indicates

35 M. M. Gordon, *Social Class in American Sociology*, New York, 1958, p. 121
36 Richard Mabey, in Mabey (ed.), *Class: A Symposium*, London, 1966, p. 7
37 Dennis Marsden, in ibid., p. 33

a continuum of class-consciousness, dominated by middle class assumptions and attitudes, entails both a large logical fallacy and an abdication of the investigator's responsibility to construct his own hypothesis.

Varieties of Class-Consciousness

The social event that made the strongest impression on Marx and Engels was the formation of an urban working class which had never existed in previous history. The reverberations of this spectacular historical change echo throughout Marxism, accounting for the special character of the Marxian theory of class, including its emphasis on class-consciousness and 'false consciousness', its prediction of the inevitability of a revolutionary confrontation between classes, and its insistence on the absorption of the lower-middle class into the proletariat. The historical fact is that since Marx's death there has been an unbroken growth in the size and importance of the middle classes which makes the orthodox Marxist conception of class relationships of only limited, though indispensable, value in the comprehension of social differences and social conflict. (The historian A. J. P. Taylor once observed that Marxism was to social theory as alcohol is to beverages: an essential ingredient of any good drink, but poison if taken neat.) A critical Marxist who recognised the possibility of an independent role for the middle classes at an early stage was Georges Sorel, who noted in *Reflections on Violence* that the elementary Marxian picture of class conflict applied only when economic conditions approximated the competitive market model. Under these conditions 'all the actors walk straight before them like veritable automata, without taking any notice of the great ideas of the sociologists; they are subject to very simple forces, and not one of them dreams of escaping from the circumstances of his condition. Then only is the development of capitalism carried on with that inevitableness which struck Marx so much, and which seemed to him comparable to that of a natural law.' However, if the middle class, especially when 'led astray by the chatter of the preachers of ethics and sociology', found themselves able to assert a separate role and tried to 'correct the abuses of economics', the relationship between classes would become complicated and unpredictable: 'one part of the forces which were to further the development of capitalism is employed in hindering it, an arbitrary and irrational element is introduced, and the future of the world becomes completely indeterminate.'[38]

A more recent critical Marxist, Karl Korsch, has also observed that the ups and downs of Marxist theory reflect changes in the social situation to which Marxism cannot intellectually accommodate itself.[39] According to Merleau-Ponty, philosophical and dialectical Marxism corresponds to periods when the revolution appears to be at hand. When this prospect recedes, Marxism becomes less philosophic, more dogmatic and afflicted

[38] Georges Sorel, *Reflections on Violence*, Glencoe, 1950, p. 182
[39] Karl Korsch, *Karl Marx*, London, 1938

by scientism. It becomes apparent that the economic and social 'infra-structure' is more solid than the dialectical method assumes, for instance when capitalism became stabilised at the end of the nineteenth century, or when the intractable difficulties of economic planning in the USSR underlined the persistence of factors not taken account of in traditional Marxism.[40] The Marxist insistence on the unity of theory and practice becomes difficult to maintain, and the opposition between them is clearly evident. 'Le savoir et la pratique affrontent la même infinité du réel historique, mais ils répondent de deux facons opposées: le savoir en multipliant les vues, par des conclusions provisoires, ouvertes, motivées, c'est-à-dire conditionnelles, la pratique par des decisions absolues, partiales, injustifiables.'[41]

The rise in political, social and cultural influence of the lower-middle class is one of the outstanding features of social life in the industrial societies of the twentieth century, often described and implicitly recognised as important, but never accommodated in any systematic theory of class, status and power, perhaps because of the abiding influence of Marxism. Yet the rise of a number of political movements since the turn of the century has depended upon lower-middle class support. Gerth analysed the preponderantly lower-middle class origins of the Nazi leadership.[42] Lasswell and Sereno made a similar study of the Italian Fascist movement,[43] and Lasswell, in an early contribution on the role of the 'authoritarian personality' in politics, also described the psychological appeal of Nazism to the German lower-middle class.[44] Students of the 'radical right' in the United States have shown the great prominence of lower-middle class groups, especially small businessmen, in supporting McCarthyism and its residuary legatees, the John Birch Society, Senator Goldwater et al.[45] The Poujade movement in France was a similar phenomenon, and lower-middle class support was of crucial importance for General de Gaulle. Much of the work done on the psychology of politics, which has led to a series of overlapping formulations of character traits variously called the authoritarian personality, dogmatism, extra-punitiveness, intolerance of ambiguity, and ethnocentrism,[46] entails little more than the description of lower-

40 Maurice Merleau-Ponty, *Les Aventures de la Dialectique*, Paris, 1955, pp. 87-88
41 ibid., p. 17
42 Hans H. Gerth, 'The Nazi Party; its leadership and composition', *American Journal of Sociology*, vol. 56, no. 2, 1940
43 H. D. Lasswell and Renzo Sereno, 'The Changing Italian Elite', in H. D. Lasswell, *Political Behaviour*, London, 1948
44 H. D. Lasswell, 'The Psychology of Hitlerism', *Political Quarterly*, vol. 4, no. 4, 1933
45 Daniel Bell (ed.), *The Radical Right*, New York, 1963, provides the most comprehensive account
46 See, inter alia, T. W. Adorno, et al, *The Authoritarian Personality*, New York, 1950; H. J. Eysenck, *The Psychology of Politics*, London, 1954; M. M. Rokeach, *The Open and Closed Mind*, New York, 1960; R. E. Lane, *Political Ideology*, New York, 1962

middle class illiberalism as perceived by upper-middle class, liberal social scientists.

The studies just mentioned relate mostly to pathological or at best reactionary political manifestations. In reality, the political role of the lower-middle class is more varied. The resurgence of nationalism in a variety of forms also owes much to the lower-middle class; indeed, nationalism may be the prime expression of its class-consciousness. The political posture of labor and socialist parties, especially under parliamentary regimes, has been profoundly influenced by lower-middle class support, especially from the white-collar 'salariat'. Complexities in the political role of the salaried lower-middle class, reflecting the discrepancies in its relation to the three major axes of social division—class, status and power—first attracted serious attention in the 1930's, but largely from a more or less orthodox Marxist standpoint which assumed that the only political alternatives were support of Fascism or alignment with the labor movement.[47] Traces of this view may be found in C. Wright Mills' *White Collar*, published in 1951, which recognised that the bureaucratisation of society stimulates the rapid growth of the salariat, but regarded support for right-wing political movements as a rearguard action in support of traditional middle-class individualism. David Lockwood's *The Blackcoated Worker* (1958) also recognises the effects of bureaucratisation, but simply regards the situation of the white-collar worker as different from that of the manual worker, and justifies this on the basis of a multi-factor theory of class position.

The significance of bureaucracy in promoting this major shift in the class structure has received less attention than the emergence of bureaucratic elites and speculation about their role in the power structure of modern communities. Yet this may be the greatest social consequence of bureaucratisation—the large growth of a virtually indestructible lower-middle class whose economic and social situation has strong affinities with that of the industrial proletariat, but perhaps even greater dissimilarities. Because of the comparatively large size of this group and its economic importance as a consumer of goods and services, it exercises a profound influence on the social, cultural and political norms and values of affluent industrial societies. An Australian social scientist, who has attained high rank in the public service, observes that the culture of the public service is marked by a 'pervasive pressure to conform to the value systems, attitudes and behaviour which might be broadly described as belonging to Anglo-Saxon middle-class morality of a generation ago. . . . The civil servant, both in his official and unofficial capacity, is expected to observe what is regarded as conventional morality . . . [and] to conform to certain standards of dress. . . . Extreme or radical opinions on contemporary political or social issues are not encouraged. Much emphasis is placed on such respectable

[47] An influential example was Lewis Corey, *The Crisis of the Middle Class*, New York, 1935

virtues as punctuality, adherence to routine and orderliness.'[48] The great stress on the reality of 'status', as distinct from 'class', which has marked the past generation, largely reflects the social aspirations of the growing lower-middle class, rather than the working class affluence to which it is frequently attributed, especially in Britain.[49]

The development of new forms of social division since the earlier phases of industrial capitalism has also had its effects on the class-consciousness of the upper-middle class. In particular, the growth of professionalism has stimulated theories about the special role of the professional man in a society where the division of labour grows ever more elaborate. Marx was acutely aware of the dynamic character of mechanised industry in promoting specialisation of tasks. In Chapter 13 of the first volume of *Capital*, he wrote:

Modern industry never looks upon or treats the existing form of a production process as final. The technical basis of industry is therefore revolutionary, while all earlier modes of production were essentially conservative. By means of machinery, chemical processes, and other methods, it leads to continual changes not only in the technical basis of production, but also in the function of the labourer, and in the social combinations of the labour process.

He recognised, moreover, that technical training became essential in these circumstances, but he regarded it, oddly enough, as a 'concession wrung from capital', and concluded that 'such revolutionary ferments, the final aim of which is the abolition of the old division of labour, are diametrically opposed to the capitalist mode of production.' Twenty years earlier, in *The German Ideology,* he had painted a romantic picture of work in communist society: 'nobody has one exclusive sphere of activity but each can become accomplished in any branch he wishes, production as a whole is regulated by society, thus making it possible for me to do one thing today and another tomorrow, to hunt in the morning, fish in the afternoon, rear cattle in the evening, criticise after dinner, in accordance with my inclination, without ever becoming hunter, fisherman, shepherd or critic.' The romantic belief of Marx's youth that the division of labour, and consequently the alienation of the worker from his work, could be abolished if the means of production were transferred to common ownership, blinded him to the technological, economic and social factors which press specialisation forward irrespective of the structure of ownership. Indeed, the private capitalist frequently sees specialisation as a nuisance, since it regularly involves an increase in labour costs. (In no country has specialisation of labour been organised more elaborately than in the Soviet Union, where higher education is geared extremely closely to the

[48] P. H. Cook, 'Psychologists in the Australian Civil Service', paper read to the British Psychological Society, Australian branch, Canberra, 1956
[49] For a destructive analysis of the alleged effects of affluence on the working class and an examination of different attitudes towards unionism among white-collar and manual workers, see D. Lockwood, et al, *The Affluent Worker*, Cambridge, 1968

production of specialists for industry and the government bureaucracy.)
The advance of specialisation is attested particularly by the growth of
professionalism since the middle of the nineteenth century. The progressive
differentiation of techniques, and of those who practise them, appears
likely to continue indefinitely. 'Science advances and techniques multiply.
In the long run, technical advance implies an increase in the numbers of
those doing more or less specialised intellectual work relative to the
number of those who are engaged in manual labour or in an unspecialised
intellectual region.' As a by-product, management and administration
assume, or aspire to, professional status. With the growth of large-scale
organisation, 'all those who occupy the important positions will gradually
come within professional positions, or at least under professional
influence.'[50]

Professional people, who for the purpose of this discussion may be taken
to include managers and officials of big organisations, now form the
largest and most important section of the upper-middle class. Their
common interests, work situation, and style of life form the basis of a
distinct pattern of class-consciousness, which assumes that social distinctions are inescapable, but tolerable if they can be rationalised in terms of
the necessary division of labour in an industrial community. Class differences, in other words, depend upon occupational differences and are
correspondingly legitimate. This is very much the kind of class-
consciousness or class ideology manifested, in a high-falutin form, in
Parsonian functionalism, whose political tendency is conservative. But
similar arguments have been put forward from a liberal-radical standpoint,
whose political intent is to attack private capitalism on the grounds that
the profit motive is immoral and that capitalist society has a cock-eyed
set of values leading to an unjust distribution of rewards. Before the First
World War, Veblen in America and the industrialist, Walther Rathenau, in
Germany had emphasised the economic importance and social value of
the manager and the technician as against the property-owner, the rentier,
and the speculator. Rathenau and his associate Moellendorf foresaw the
need for a planned economy (*Planwirtschaft*) in which the capitalist owner
would play no significant part, but decisions would be made jointly by
industrial technicians and government officials. To Rathenau, the character
of modern society was due to the extension of mechanisation from the
industrial sphere to all areas of social life. The division of labour based
on mechanisation led, among other things, to an impersonal structure of
authority in which the modern industrial worker was reduced to a more
oppressive condition of dependence on his superiors than the independent
craftsman of the past. Mechanisation, however, also contained the promise
of solving these problems, partly through the continued increase of material
wealth, and partly through the emergence of a new type of manager,
dissociated from ownership and impelled by disinterested creative

[50] A. M. Carr-Saunders and P. A. Wilson, *The Professions*, London, 1933, p. 491-93

motives.[51] Veblen, like many other middle class radicals (including his latter-day disciple Wright Mills)[52] accepted the 'revisionist' critique of Marxism which perceived that capitalism would not be destroyed by the action of the proletariat, but would be forced to change its spots because of its inherent inefficiency. The real threat to private capitalism would come from the key men of industry, the 'engineers' upon whom its operations depended. They had become, wrote Veblen, 'keepers of the community's material welfare' and were no longer content to provide unearned income for the 'kept' classes. Because of their role in industry, and also as a relatively compact and increasingly class-conscious group, they were in a position to become 'arbiters of the community's material welfare'.[53] The apotheosis of this argument came thirty years later with James Burnham's *The Managerial Revolution*, which assimilated Veblen's contentions into the Trotskyist theory of bureaucratic collectivism. The political intent of Burnham's book is neatly epitomised by the title of the destructive review—'A Marx for the Managers'—written by Gerth and Mills[54] who stress the basic fallacy in Burnham's argument: 'The chance of political power for those filling technically indispensable roles is not a function of their technical roles but of their class position and political affiliations.' Gerth and Mills go on to note that at least three contrasting political deductions had been made by writers who were impressed by the rise of the technician in industry. Veblen sought the support of the workers for his 'engineers'; the English guild socialist, G. D. H. Cole, sought *their* support for the workers;[55] and another American, Alfred Bingham, predicted that the technicians would support Fascism (a prediction exemplified by the history of Albert Speer, the organiser of Hitler's war machine, convicted as a war criminal at Nuremberg).[56]

Cole is not the only social-democratic writer who attempted to deal with the class problems of industrial capitalism by invoking the disinterested expertise of skilled professional and managerial groups. R. H. Tawney, his close contemporary, condemned the profit motive in industry in his early book *The Acquisitive Society* (1920), and looked forward to its transformation from a mere vehicle of gain into a profession directed to the service of the public. The only criterion of industry under private capitalism was 'the financial return which it offers to its shareholders', whereas the essence of a profession was that 'though men enter it for the sake of livelihood, the measure of their success is the service which they perform, not the gains which they amass'. A similar view about the role

51 Ralph Bowen, *German Theories of the Corporative State*, London, 1947, pp. 167-70
52 C. W. Mills, 'Letter to the New Left', reprinted in I. L. Horowitz, (ed.), *Power, Politics and People*, London, 1963
53 Thorstein Veblen, *The Engineers and the Price System*, New York, 1963, p. 74
54 H. H. Gerth and C. W. Mills, 'A Marx for the Managers', *Ethics*, Vol. 52, no. 2, 1942
55 G. D. H. and M. I. Cole, *The Condition of Britain*, London, 1937
56 Alfred Bingham, *Insurgent America*, New York, 1935

of the professions was expressed by another socialist, Graham Wallas, in
Our Social Heritage, published in 1921.

It is not only among the middle classes that the complexity and ambiguity
of class-consciousness manifests itself. The dominance of Marxism in the
study of social division has been responsible for a long-standing neglect of
internal differences of class-consciousness within the working classes.
However, the relative absence of class conflict in the affluent industrial
societies of Western Europe and the English-speaking world since 1945
has made it both intellectually respectable and politically profitable to
explore differences in working class consciousness. The Marxist attitude to
the worker, observes Lockwood, is based on the essential characteristic of
propertylessness, but this 'fact' is not a simple one and means different
things to different people. Writing in the Marxist tradition, Halbwachs
contends that the essential basis of working class consciousness is wages.
'It is the attitude of workers towards their employers or employers' groups,
in fact their collective behaviour, that really gives a clue to what determines the most important thing in the worker's life: the amount of his
wages and the quantity of work he gives for them.'[57] As against this,
Lockwood argues that variations in class consciousness arise from the fact
that 'class position' is an amalgam of several factors, of which he
enumerates three: market situation, work situation and status situation.
Hence, differences in class-consciousness among workers are not, following
Marx, to be attributed to 'false consciousness', but to the discrepancies
between these three factors. 'Variations in class identification have to be
related to actual variations in class situations and not attributed to some
kind of ideological aberration or self-deception.'[58] Too much emphasis on
the egalitarian sentiments of the working class obscures and falsifies actual
divisions of interest and outlook among working men. The differences are
strikingly reflected in the varying relations between unionism and class-
consciousness, and Lockwood suggests various indices for measuring the
relationship.[59] These ideas have been taken further by Blackburn in his
studies of 'union character'.[60]

Runciman makes a similar point in describing the concept of 'relative
deprivation'. As a result of post-war affluence, he argues, working class
aspirations became 'less a common resentment of the subordinate position
of manual work as such and more an individual pursuit of middle class
prerogatives. This pursuit did not have to be motivated by a deliberate
imitation of non-manual workers; but it was accompanied by an increasing
detachment from the lateral loyalties of a proletariat still resentful of its
powerlessness as well as its poverty or its lack of social esteem.'[61] A

[57] Maurice Halbwachs, *The Psychology of Social Class*, London, 1958, pp. 70-71
[58] D. Lockwood, *The Blackcoated Worker*, London, 1958, p. 203
[59] ibid., p. 137-38
[60] R. M. Blackburn, *Union Character and Class-Consciousness*, London, 1968
[61] Runciman, *Relative Deprivation and Social Justice*, p. 135

recognition that the outlook of groups such as manual workers and white-collar workers is best described in terms of feelings of relative deprivation will enable the restatement of the 'false consciousness' argument in an appropriate form.[62]

Lockwood also notes that working class consciousness can restrict the influence of dominant status values because not all classes accept these values. An example is the study of occupational prestige, which appears to provide an unbroken scale for measuring social differences. However, as at least one English study has shown, the reaction of manual workers to such a scale reveals a wide area of disagreement with the essentially middle-class assumptions on which the scale is based.[63] Conversely, as Lockwood again notes, status distinctions can aggravate or mollify class-consciousness. Democratic manners, as in the United States or Australia, dilute class hostility because they deprive it of the social distance which supports it. Students of industrial relations in Britain have commented on this factor in the success of the productivity agreements made at the oil refinery at Fawley, where an important factor was the willingness of the American management staff to work long hours 'in shirt sleeves' side by side with the industrial workers, as compared with the caste-like aloofness of the British managers.[64]

[62] ibid., p. 251
[63] Michael Young and Peter Willmott, 'Social Grading by Manual Workers', *British Journal of Sociology*, vol. 7, no. 3, 1956
[64] Allan Flanders, *The Fawley Productivity Agreements*, London, 1964

3: Class, Status and Power

The study of social inequality by sociologists and social philosophers is influenced by the constant search for higher orders of explanation and more inclusive systems of classification. The existence of concepts such as class, status and power, side by side with observable phenomena such as occupation, income, education, property, ethnic origin, religion and the like, which divide people in their daily lives and interpersonal relations, generates a search for theoretical frameworks that will contain all these categories in a logically consistent form which corresponds to life experience as well as permitting broad generalisations. Marx, in the unfinished Chapter 52 of the third volume of *Capital*, was evidently playing with the problem, for he not only refers to 'classes' but to social distinctions derived from source of income and occupation. The classes, he wrote, are

three great social groups whose components, the individual members, live from wages, profit and rent respectively, that is, from the utilisation of their labour power, capital, and landed property. However, from this point of view, doctors and officials would also form two distinct classes, for they belong to two different social groups, and the revenues of the members of each group come from the same source. The same would also be true of the infinite distinctions of interest and position which the social division of labour creates among workers as among capitalists and landowners; in the latter case, for instance, between owners of vineyards, farms, forests, mines and fisheries . . .

At this point he stopped. Dahrendorf's imaginative reconstruction of this chapter as it might have been completed[1] is undoubtedly accurate in emphasising the basic role of conflict in Marx's theory of class. He does not, however, inquire whether Marx thought that the concept of class could be built up from the components of occupation, income, inherited social rank and so forth, or whether it represented a more fundamental form of social inequality based on conflict which, through the operation of class-consciousness, would override these less important forms of distinction between men. The whole drift of Marx's work throughout his lifetime suggests the latter, whereas the tendency of modern sociology, once it addressed itself seriously to the detailed examination of class divisions,

[1] Ralf Dahrendorf, *Class and Class Conflict in Industrial Society*, ch. 1

has been to emphasise the former. This is due, among other things, to the process of model-building which is inherent in the methodology of the social sciences. The building up of a concept of class which subsumes and relates the visible distinctions of income, occupation etc., follows what are taken to be the mental processes of the thinking individual, who builds up for himself 'class maps' and 'class models' which can be identified by the investigator. Kahl argued some years ago that survey research had identitfied four such models which combine 'power' and 'prestige':

(i) A two-valued model based on power;
(ii) A three-valued model based on prestige;
(iii) A many-valued model based on prestige;
(iv) A model combining power and prestige.

The choice of one of these models by any individual depends on his social position as he conceives it. The task of the scientific observer, asserts Kahl, is to 'abstract fundamental similarities in perception among wide groups of people by using a scheme . . . which simplifies but does not deny the differences in modes of perception.'[2] Elizabeth Bott, in a detailed and subtle investigation of class maps and models among a group of families in London, uses similar language to explain her conclusions. 'When an individual talks about class, he is trying to say something in a symbolic form about his experiences of power and prestige in his actual membership groups and social relationships both past and present.' This symbolic picture of a class system develops gradually as the individual learns to place himself in relation to a series of reference groups at different stages of his life—groups defined in terms of material possessions, religion, residence, speech, occupation, appearance, etc. When the individual needs to place himself in the widest social context, he 'manufactures a notion of his general social position out of these segregated group memberships. He reduces them all to a sort of common denominator . . . [which] is accurate enough for orientating him in a complex society.' This means that, although the individual will use varying and sometimes disconnected standards of reference in particular contexts, 'there will be a strain of consistency and continuity running through each person's usage at different times.'[3] A similar process is described by Lasswell, who asserts that every individual has a need to make sense of society by endowing it with a structure which goes beyond the direct reference groups described by Bott and many others. The result is the construction of 'mass stereotypes', which he links with the need for widely intelligible symbols used by the mass media. An illustration of the use of a wide range of reference group material to build up a mass stereotype is Lasswell's own account of the 'Cadillac-urbanity-power-leisure syndrome' used to identify the upper class, and its opposite, the 'stupidity-immorality-filth-disease syndrome'.

[2] Joseph A. Kahl, *The American Class Structure*, New York, 1953, p. 180.
[3] Elizabeth Bott, *Family and Social Network*, London, 1957, pp. 59-91

'Any American movie, television, or comics fan is well acquainted', continues Lasswell, 'with the mass indicators of social class. . . . By means of mass stereotypes, socialised persons know how fictional characters must act and what they must say in order to reveal their class. The playwright or novelist may be judged by how precisely and artfully he can humanise mass stereotypes.' The existence of these mass stereotypes is compatible with, and distinct from, the use of direct reference group norms, which govern direct intercourse between individuals.[4]

Levels of Theory

Some philosophers dispute the need or value of going beyond the accurate exploration of what Nagel calls 'empirically ascertainable regularities', whose examination requires only the 'explicit formulation of determinate relations between a set of variables'.[5] A similar point is made by Dowling, who agrees that the work of Bott and Lasswell demonstrates the existence of mass stereotypes, backed by a wide area of agreement about constructs like the 'middle class', but asserts that these stereotypes, although *recognised* by the more sophisticated, are also *rejected* by them, and he suggests that social scientists—presumably included among the more sophisticated—should also avoid the use of class as an analytical category. In the classification of social data, he argues, 'it would seem highly desirable that the term "social class", or, specifically, the term "class" should never be used . . . simply because of its liability to misunderstanding. There would seem no reason why this sort of work should not proceed easily without reference to "classes", and indeed there has already been a lot done in terms of "strata", "levels", and so forth.' In dealing with the common usage, moreover, the social scientist should confine himself to an account of this usage. 'To say that social scientists can and should give an account of popular uses of the term "class" is not to say that that account itself should use the term "class".'[6]

The most extended statement of the methodology underlying the work of Bott, Lasswell, and others was given by Alfred Schutz. The basis of meaning in any science, he declares, is the 'pre-scientific life-world' of everyday experience, and the task of the observant, reflective individual is to build up the meaning of the phenomenon he observes (in the words of Husserl, to 'measure the life-world for a well-fitting garment of ideas'). The scientist, as a disinterested observer, creates different categories from those used by the 'naive' observer of the life-world, and in doing so he must modify references whose meaning is self-evident to the naive observer. This modification is the analogue, in the social sciences, of mathematical

[4] T. E. Lasswell, *Class and Stratum*, New York, 1965, pp. 146-47
[5] Ernest Nagel, in American Philosophical Association, *Science, Language and Human Rights*, Philadelphia, 1952, p. 46
[6] R. E. Dowling, 'Are Social Classes Hypothetical Constructs or Real Empirical Entities?', loc. cit.

treatment of physical phenomena, but it requires the construction of a typology rather than rigorous mathematical analysis, which goes far beyond the possibilities of everyday observation. Such typologies, however, must be considered as 'methods' rather than 'true being'. Constructs designed to bring order to complex material are not simply referable to specific individual acts.[7]

In a further paper, Schutz went on to answer the views of Nagel and C. G. Hempel.[8] The logic of their position, he contends, makes possible only an 'ideally refined behaviourism', and could not explain the outlook of the observing behaviourist, but only the behaviour of those he is observing. Yet such an explanation is essential because the same overt behaviour seen by the observer may have an entirely different meaning to the performers. And he continues:

The observational field of the social scientist—social reality—has a specific meaning and relevance structure for the human beings living, acting, and thinking within it. By a series of commonsense constructs they have pre-selected and pre-interpreted this world which they experience as the reality of their daily lives. It is these thought objects of theirs which determine their behaviour by motivating it. The thought objects constructed by the social scientist, in order to grasp this social reality, have to be founded upon the thought objects constructed by the commonsense thinking of men, living their daily life within their social world. Thus, the constructs of the social sciences are, so to speak, constructs of the second degree, i.e. constructs of the constructs made by the actors on the social scene, whose behaviour the social scientist has to observe and to explain in accordance with the procedural rules of his science.

Schutz agrees with Hempel and Nagel that the social sciences must be objective and susceptible to controlled verification; indeed, the object of his 'second order constructs' is to make it possible to test the subjectivity and consistency of the abstractions which are used by the commonsense observer in making and interpreting his observations.[9] The constructs of the social scientist must therefore be logically consistent, capable of subjective interpretation, and adequately referable back to commonsense reality.[10]

The failure of many sociologists engaged in research on social stratification to appreciate the methodological procedures advocated by Schutz is strikingly exemplified in the work of Lloyd Warner and his school. Warner's conception of class, and his indices for measuring it, represent nothing so much as the criteria of the man in the street, quantified and elaborated, with no real attempt to establish a wider theoretical framework within which data about income, occupation, family, style of life and community

[7] Alfred Schutz, 'Phenomenology and the Social Sciences', in Maurice Natanson (ed.), *Alfred Schutz, Collected Papers*, The Hague, 1962, vol. 1, pp. 120-38
[8] C. G. Hempel, American Philosophical Association, op. cit., pp. 76-81
[9] Schutz, 'Concept and Theory Formation in the Social Sciences', in *Collected Papers*, pp. 51-64
[10] ibid., 'Commonsense and Scientific Interpretation of Human Action', p. 36

participation can be interpreted. According to Hempel, the 'explicative re-interpretation' of a concept like that of class has two stages. First, the reformulation in precise terms of 'at least a large part of what is customarily expressed by means of the terms under consideration.' Second, the use of these reconstructed concepts to develop a 'comprehensive, rigorous, and sound theoretical system.'[11] The Warner approach assumes that meeting the first of these requirements is in itself sufficient. It reflects the dependence of American sociology on the survey technique, which relies entirely on the accurate transcription of common usage: whatever the man in the street regards as significant (especially if it is statistically significant) becomes the subject matter of the survey.

The social scientist's model of class is, then, a counterpart of the 'class maps' which he finds by observation among Schutz's 'naive observers'. 'Class-consciousness' acquires a double significance; it denotes the acceptance of a particular class map by the class-conscious individual and an act of self-location. The social scientist must construct a set of categories which, as Schutz remarks, should be determined by the nature of the scientific problem, but must also correspond to the reality of class-consciousness which he finds in a particular situation. He also needs to recognise the question-begging nature of the conventional titles for class divisions, which are a mixture of occupation, status, and power. The mixture varies, however; the term 'working class' is occupationally loaded, whereas 'middle class' is status-loaded. A working man who is well-paid and well-trained may—and often does—prefer to call himself 'middle class' because he perceives the status questions involved in this terminology. As some investigators have found, the size of the working class ebbs and flows in survey research as the possibilities for identification are manipulated, and the 'class-consciousness' of the research worker is itself at work in these cases. Class-consciousness is at once a social image, an ideology which shapes conduct, and an aspect of interpersonal relations and behaviour. It is not a description but an interpretation of social differences and social inequality—the legitimation which Rousseau thought he could provide.

Three Dimensions of Social Inequality

The broad acceptance of class, status and power as three distinct dimensions of inequality, of comparable analytical validity, has already been mentioned in the previous chapter. It will be argued here that these are 'second order constructs' of the kind postulated by Schutz. They are built up from the 'actual social relationships or membership groups' described by Bott, although, following Schutz, these should be regarded as 'first order constructs'. The epistemological questions involved here need not detain us. (But we should at least note that Schutz, who set out

[11] C. G. Hempel, 'Fundamentals of Concept Formation in Empirical Science', *International Encyclopedia of Unified Science*, Chicago, 1952, vol. 2, no. 7, p. 11

to resolve the ambiguities inherent in Weber's methodology of ideal types, was moved to lament Weber's lack of interest in epistemology, which led him to ignore the philosophical underpinning of the analytical tools he developed.[12])

In various writings, Runciman has strongly maintained the need to use class, status and power as a tripartite system of analysis, in spite of the difficulties of doing so. In his most recent essay on the subject, he looks at the objections to the use of the three categories. The first objection is that they are unnecessary, since measures like socio-economic status, based on occupation, income and education, may be more useful and revealing (cf. the argument of Dowling). Secondly, this style of analysis leaves untouched a number of important questions in the study of social differentiation. Thirdly, the logical and experimental difficulties are such as to make the system unusable. Despite these objections, he maintains, the arguments in favour are stronger. In the first place, class, status and power, which may be expected on various grounds to fit closely together (thus supporting single-factor theories), often do not fit closely in actual cases, and these are of critical importance. Discrepancies such as 'wealth accruing to members of despised but essential professions, the rejection of economic gain by the ruling elite in favour of martial glory, or the refusal of commensurate reward to highly esteemed occupations' are particular instances.[13] In addition, the role of racial differences in the twentieth century creates a discrepant factor of the greatest significance, practical as well as theoretical.

Secondly, Runciman continues, comparative studies of social differentiation acquire much more meaning if it is recognised that the criteria of inequality interact differently in different national communities. How far, for instance, does public ownership of the economy in the Soviet Union diminish or abolish class differences; what is meant by speaking of an egalitarian society in the United States where economic differences are so enormous? Other questions demanding investigation include assumptions about the 'convergence' of national societies; the meaning of working class *embourgeoisement*; the nature and role of elites in modern society; and the impact of industrial growth on inequality. 'It is precisely', he concludes, 'because the distinction between the three dimensions of stratification has often been neglected that the discussion of these topics has often been unnecessarily confused . . . the researcher who ignores the distinction between the three . . . must show good reason for doing so.'[14]

To Runciman's list of relevant topics we may add the broad question of social change, which alters the significance of 'objective' criteria of stratification and their relation to one another, and exposes discrepancies

[12] Alfred Schutz, *The Phenomenology of the Social World*, tr. G. Welsh and F. Lehnert, Chicago, 1967, p. 7
[13] W. G. Runciman, 'Class, Status and Power?' in J. A. Jackson (ed.), *Social Stratification*, Cambridge, 1968, p. 57
[14] ibid., pp. 60-61

between class, status and power relations which were either ignored or minimised in the conventional wisdom of the past. Politics is another highly relevant subject, since class-consciousness and political allegiance are so highly correlated, and the complexity of the political changes which have taken place in many countries since 1945 demands this kind of analysis.

The distinction between class, status and power, Runciman suggests elsewhere, is tantamount to the distinction between economic, social and political inequality. Inequality under the heading of class includes not only income and occupation, but also different opportunities for upward mobility, advantages in kind, provisions for retirement and security of employment. Class situation is itself 'a complex phenomenon which embraces aspects of a person's economic situation in society which need not be in strict correlation with each other. They all, however, reflect inequalities directly derived from the productive system.'[15] Status also derives from economic factors, but not from the same ones as class. 'Inequality of status, not class, is at issue when a clerical worker looks down on an artisan because he works with his hands, or a middle-class father does not want his son to marry a working-class girl. Very often, relative deprivation of status rather than of class lies at the root of what is termed "class-consciousness".'[16]

Historically, it could be argued that the 'original' or 'natural' form of social inequality took the form of status, and although Lenski does not explicitly make this point, it emerges by implication from his treatment of 'primitive' societies where *need* is regarded as the prime factor in establishing a social hierarchy.[17] Every society, no matter how simple, develops a status system as the product of interaction between necessity and human nature.[18] Status provides a framework for regulating the normal intercourse of individuals and groups. The stratification system of a society, remarks Shils, is 'the product of imagination working on the hard facts of the unequal allocation of scarce resources and rewards.' Deference—the visible manifestation of status differences—is not merely a reflection or epiphenomenon of other forms of stratification, but is itself responsible for the formation of strata.[19] Eisenstadt has explored the role of prestige—another synonym of status—in determining the distribution of wealth and power in a number of empires of the past, and contends that a strongly established prestige system, sustained by a strong central authority or an accepted value system (as in India) can be the major factor in establishing an economic and political structure.[20] The importance

---

[15] Runciman, *Relative Deprivation and Social Justice*, p. 38
[16] ibid., p. 40
[17] Lenski, *Power and Privilege*, loc. cit.
[18] An entertaining description of the development of a status hierarchy is given by J. K. Galbraith in his account of the 'men of standing' in the small Scotch-Canadian community where he grew up. *The Non-potable Scotch*, London, 1967
[19] E. A. Shils, 'Deference', in Jackson, op. cit., pp. 130-32
[20] S. N. Eisenstadt, 'Prestige, Participation and Strata Formation', ibid.

of status in contemporary sociology derives, as is well known, from the work of Weber. There is not, however, a unique meaning attached to the term throughout Weber's work. In the essay 'Class, Status, Party' he appears to distinguish between *class* as based on 'market situation' and *status* as based on 'work situation', prestige, and material style of life or 'acquisition'. Later, in *Wirtschaft und Gesellschaft*, he attempts to assimilate class into an all-embracing concept of status which includes distinction in the ownership and provision of goods, the external conditions of life and the subjective satisfactions or frustrations experienced by an individual or a group. Not only does this lead Weber to talk of the 'class status' of a social group, but also to describe status groups as distinct 'communities'.

Insofar as Weber regards status as distinct from class, his conception of it has been clearly reformulated by Reissman. Status is the result of 'social differences based on life-chances and life-styles and the product of community relationships. The status-structure, no matter how closely it might be tied to and determined by market relationships, was planted firmly in the social life of the community rather than in the impersonal and rational affairs of the economy. The social power that derived from these status relationships had its own sphere of operation and its own reality, just as did the economic power that derived from economic organisation.'[21]

In the long history of social differentiation, status may therefore be regarded as anterior to class,[22] which derives from the market economy, and more fundamental than power, which becomes a factor of distinctive importance only when the size and complexity of organised communities passes beyond a certain point. According to Marshall, there is a hierarchy of status whose divisions are enshrined in established customs and/or legal rights; 'it is endowed with meaning and purpose and accepted as a natural order.'[23] In a rigidly stratified society, like that of feudalism, the development of contractual relations took place within the status framework, and those contracts which could be made only enhanced the structure of inequality.[24] The spread of contractual relations in modern times meant that economic factors ceased to be dominated by the status hierarchy; the latter did not disappear, however, but took new forms. In a later discussion, Marshall notes that whereas stratification has, in past generations, meant the social order by which men's lives were properly governed, contemporary difficulties of analysis arise from the replacement of this 'simple, clear and institutionalised structure by a complex, nebulous and

---

[21] Reissman, *Class in American Society*, p. 104

[22] Anthropological studies, such as Linton's account of the Tanala, or the Lynds' two books on Middletown, sometimes take this view.

[23] Marshall, *Citizenship and Social Class*, p. 30

[24] Marshall is referring here to Sir Henry Maine's distinction (in *Ancient Law*) between 'status' as the basis of legal relations in medieval society and 'contract' in modern society.

largely informal one'.[25] The emergence of the centralised national state, and of class relations based on a market economy, stimulated the conservatism of Burke, de Maistre and others who looked back to the ordered, 'simple status society of the Middle Ages'.[26] Social differentiation may adequately be explained, in concrete instances, in terms of status and power. The social and political structure of imperial China, for instance, is explicable in this way, and the role of the imperial bureaucracy exemplifies the operation of both factors. So closely were status and power intermeshed, that this is probably one of the major reasons for the failure of an industrial economy to develop, despite the advanced state which science and technology had reached long before the Middle Ages in Europe.[27] In India, the role of status, in the form of caste, long provided a source of social stability of far greater importance than a centralised power structure, which has only existed fitfully throughout the history of the sub-continent. Other instances where the growth of class relationships lagged behind the onset of industrialisation are provided, in very different ways, by Russia and Japan.

Bernard Shaw once remarked (in *The Apple Cart*) that the Soviet Union was based on British history, written in London by Karl Marx. Practical ends, as so often, were attained on intellectually unsound premises. Without his British experience, Marx might never have gained his insight into the nature of capitalism; the price he paid was to minimise other, related phenomena and to misstate the historical circumstances in which class relations were able to develop. It was the existence of a particular kind of status system, *and* of an effectively centralised national power structure, *and* the advent of machine technology, which made possible the rapid growth of capitalism in Britain and with it the emergence of a national class system.

A somewhat similar picture of the historical transition from status to class is given by Macpherson in terms of three models.[28] These are: (a) customary, or status society; (b) simple market society; (c) modern or 'possessive' market society. In the first, social relations have four main aspects:

(i) authoritative allocation of duties for groups, ranks, and individuals, enforced by law or custom;

(ii) each group is confined to its manner of work and the appropriate rewards, both being determined by consensus or by ruling authority;

(iii) possession of land and property is not unconditional, but rests on performance of the authoritatively allocated functions;

[25] T. H. Marshall, 'Social Stratification in the 20th Century', *Transactions of the 3rd World Congress of Sociology*, London, 1956, vol. 3, p. 5
[26] See Karl Mannheim's essay on conservative thought in *Essays on Sociology and Social Psychology*, Oxford, 1953.
[27] The nature of this puzzle is discussed by Joseph Needham in M. Goldsmith and A. Mackay (eds.), *The Science of Science*, London, 1964.
[28] C. B. Macpherson, *The Political Theory of Possessive Individualism*, Oxford, 1962, pp. 46-51

(iv) there is no free market in labour, which is tied either to the land, to functions, or to masters.

Mobility, in other words, is exceptional, although those with power may attempt to enlarge their power or perquisites, sometimes to the extent of civil war. From this, society moves to a 'simple' market situation, where goods and services, but not yet labour, are dealt with in a free market. Macpherson appears to regard this as a transitional stage between 'status' and 'class' society, differing less for economic than for political reasons which restrict the emergence of the cash nexus as the characteristic social relationship. This is reached in possessive market society, which again has four major features:

(i) labour becomes an alienable commodity;

(ii) land and resources are owned by individuals and are also alienable;

(iii) individuals aspire to more than they have;

(iv) some people have more skills, possessions or energies than others.

As a result of (iii) and (iv) above, some people will accumulate capital and power, while others will accept wages because they lack the personal resources to gain more.

Macpherson's work, ostensibly a critique of Hobbes and Locke, has the effect of linking them with Marx, and incidentally of underlining the dependence of class conflict (and class relationships in general) on the prior existence of bourgeois individualism. Class becomes a major and distinctive category only with the advent of industrial capitalism—or at least with the accumulation of capital on a large scale—and the quality of class relationships in any particular community is strongly influenced by the strength of bourgeois individualism in that community.

It will be apparent that the relations between class, status and power can be the subject of many permutations and combinations, and sociologists have produced a wide variety since Weber. The Danish sociologist Svalastoga postulated three main classes (upper, middle, working) and added four types of status—economic, political, intellectual, and 'general social acceptability'. These criteria made it possible to divide each of the three main classes into three subdivisions. There is a positive association, asserts Svalastoga, between 'a person's social status or class position and his major specific statuses (economic, political, intellectual, cultural, physical).' On the other hand, 'political status is probably the only important specific status of a person that evidently may hold a negative relation to general social status over a considerable period.'[29] This is a rather leaden-footed recognition of the fact that political identification (e.g. voting) is frequently out of step with apparent class interests or status position; more generally, that class, status and power do not fit perfectly together.

Another attempt to systematise the categories of social differentiation is made by Gordon, who endeavours to extract a consensus from the vast

[29] K. Svalastoga, *Prestige, Class and Mobility*, Copenhagen, 1959, p. 204

literature of American sociology. He distinguishes three 'stratification variables': economic power, status ascription and political power. *Economic power* may be dissected into income, wealth, access to credit, control of employment, the control of wages and prices; *political power* into formal governmental authority, informal control and influence in the political process, and influence over public opinion; *social status* into a variety of segmental status judgments arising from a variety of social roles, which can be combined into a general social status description.[30] Gordon's concept of general social status is derived from the well-known account by Goldhamer and Shils, which also contends that status is derived from the three types of power—force, domination and manipulation.[31] The social class system, according to Gordon, arises from the 'complex and innumerable interweavings of economic factors with politico-community power, with the status structure, with occupational pre-emption, with cultural attributes, and with group-life divisions.'[32]

Gordon's account (and others like it) fails to recognise that concepts like class, status and power are logically different from 'actual social relationships' like occupation, education, wealth, religion and so forth. The confusion of ideas is often due to ideological motives on the part of the writer. Nowhere is this more apparent than in controversies over the relation between class and status. The controversy goes back to the writings of Marx and Engels on 'false consciousness', which is integral to the Marxian distinction between a class 'in itself' and a class 'for itself'. For sociologists who do not accept the political implications of the notion, it has acted as an irritant, stimulating a closer examination of the relation between class and status. The common sociological viewpoint is that stated by Geiger, who observed that 'differences in the class consciousness of members of the same class are facts that simply exist; logically they can be neither true nor false.'[33]

Lockwood's study of clerical workers, which is devoted to an analysis of false consciousness, argues that the problem disappears if we recognise the distinct but interdependent evidence of both class and status. (Unfortunately, Lockwood sometimes uses 'class' as an inclusive term of which 'status' is one component; at other times, he appears to use the two words as alternatives.) Class position is a compound of market-situation and work-situation, and 'focuses on the divisions which result from the brute facts of economic organisation'. Status divisions are more subtle; they stem from 'the values that men set on each other's activities'. Class divisions emphasise disagreement; status judgments require a certain level of agreement. In practice, the distinction is less clear. 'A dominant class has never existed which did not seek to make its position legitimate by placing

30 M. M. Gordon, *Social Class in American Sociology*, p. 239
31 H. H. Goldhamer and E. A. Shils, 'Types of Power and Status', *American Journal of Sociology*, vol. 55, no. 2, 1939
32 Gordon, op. cit., p. 234
33 Quoted by D. Lockwood, *The Blackcoated Worker*, p. 200

highest value on those qualities and activities that came closest to its own.' Theoretical agreement on the nature of the status system is therefore limited by differences of class attitudes. Similarly, status differences can influence the nature of class-consciousness. Sombart, noting the acceptance of manual labour as a normal activity by all social groups in the United States, and contrasting this with the situation in Europe, found in it a good reason for the failure of socialism to develop in America. Class division, concludes Lockwood, is 'never a simple matter of opposition of interest but is also inextricably bound up with the notions of social superiority and inferiority current in the society.'[34]

Lockwood's account exposes the ideological distortion which denies the reality of status differences. The opposite distortion, which asserts that the prosperity of the advanced capitalist countries has largely dissolved class differences and made status the really important axis of social division, is strongly entrenched in contemporary social discussion. Prandy suggests that this ideological emphasis on status is due to the implication that it entails an assured set of authority relationships. 'Sociologists', he continues, 'have accepted the ideology and built it into surveys so that their respondents, also, are constrained to emphasise status in their replies.'[35] However, he then goes on to assert a further ideological proposition: 'Status, which is based on the differential distribution of honour and prestige, arises out of the pre-existing class situation. It derives from the attempt of those with power to legitimise their position.'[36]

Whatever the differences of opinion about the relation between class and status, they are commonly regarded as logically similar. So far, few people have been willing to treat power in the same way. Runciman, for instance, observes that no one has attempted to treat social inequality on the basis of this tripartite distinction. Inequality of power, he maintains, is not necessarily co-extensive with inequality of class or status, though the connection between class-situation and power-situation is usually demonstrable enough. One of the difficulties is that there is a lack of equivalent terminology; 'we speak of a "low-status" occupation, but not of a "low-power" one.'[37] A distribution of rankings on the basis of power would be very difficult, because it tends to be a function of personality, of circumstances, of numbers, or of organisation. The notion of power creates theoretical problems, 'not because we cannot isolate inequalities of power from inequalities of class and status but because having done so it is virtually impossible to make the kinds of comparison and measurement which would be necessary to justify it.'[38]

Nevertheless, Runciman believes in the necessity of constructing such a tripartite analysis. It is made all the more necessary because of the

---

[34] ibid., pp. 208-10
[35] K. Prandy, *Professional Employees*, London, 1965, p. 38
[36] ibid., p. 174
[37] Runciman, *Relative Deprivation and Social Justice*, p. 41
[38] Jackson (ed.), *Social Stratification*, p. 53

importance of elites in modern industrial society. Jackson notes that traditional theories of stratification are 'inappropriate for the analysis of the competing interests of power elites in a situation where access to power is not necessarily dependent upon either the ownership of property or the "value" of the performance of needed tasks to the society.'[39] The concept of elite is not a substitute for the concept of class, but an addition to it which is a necessary part of the conceptual apparatus for examining the structure of inequality in modern industrial societies. Indeed, the concept is an illustration of the separateness of the three dimensions of class, status and power, for the description of the composition, role and function of elite groups requires the use of all three dimensions. The Marxist assertion that the state was an executive committee for managing the affairs of the bourgeoisie rested on the postulate that class was the universal basis of social inequality; the assertion that the distribution of wealth, power and prestige in a modern society is related to the existence of elite groups is, in effect, based on the postulate that status and power have an existence of their own side by side with class. Ideological differences between elites, for example, are an important source of information about the general social structure and the processes of social interaction. Weber's comparative studies of power structures showed how the ideology, recruitment, organisational structure, and effective sphere of influence of elite groups could be related to the economic institutions of different societies. As Aron has written, each national community has a characteristic set of elites, whose structure embraces 'the relation between the groups exercising power, the degree of unity or division between these groups, the system of recruiting the elite and the ease or difficulty of entering it.'[40]

The solution to Runciman's problem may lie in treating all three dimensions of social inequality as functionally different aspects of a complex phenomenon. Status, for instance, is different from class and power in that it does not involve the gaining of ends against opposition. Logical tidiness is less important here than meaningful analysis.

The relation between class, status and power may be summarised for analytical purposes as follows:

class refers to superior/inferior access to and control over the processes of production and distribution of material goods;

status refers to superior/inferior position in an accepted or established hierarchy of social roles and functions;

power refers to superior/inferior access to and control over the political, legal, and coercive mechanisms of influence and authority.

The way in which class, status, and power are related to one another will vary considerably from one society to another; indeed, the relationships will be characteristic of the society and of the period. In working out these relationships, at least six points need to be taken into consideration.

---

[39] ibid., p. 3
[40] Raymond Aron, 'Social Structure and the Ruling Class', *British Journal of Sociology*, no. 1, 1950

1 In each case, the relative importance of class, status and power will vary, and different weights will have to be attached to each factor. Class, for instance, has only limited separate relevance to a pre-industrial community, even a large one.

2 The closeness (or 'covariance') of the three variables will also differ from one specific case to another. Class, status and power can be either divergent or cumulative. In the United States, where economic differentiation is enormous, the existence of status divisions is strongly denied on ideological grounds. The frequent use of the term status in academic sociology and also in pop sociology (e.g. Vance Packard's *The Status Seekers*) illustrates both ideological and methodological confusion, which reaches its acme in the title and subtitle of the book published in 1949 by Warner, Meeker, and Eells; entitled *Social Class in America*, it is subtitled *A Manual for the Measurement of Socio-Economic Status*. In the sense of an established hierarchy of social roles which governs the growth of different life styles and invidious social distinctions, the concept of status is less applicable to the United States than perhaps any other society. The use of 'status' is largely an attempt to escape from 'class'. In Britain, on the other hand, the effect of class, status and power is cumulative, but the enormous visibility and pervasiveness of status distinctions (such as speech) creates a situation where people regularly use them to illustrate the importance of 'class' in English society.

3 In a particular society, the balance between class, status and power is strongly influenced, if not determined, by the relative importance of 'actual social relationships'. A society which attaches particular significance to age is more likely to be a status society. Social division by religion is also likely to contribute to the strength of the status dimension. Racial difference operates similarly. In the USA, an analysis of the position of the negro has constrained a number of writers to apply the notion of caste, which may be regarded as a special case of status. Much of this writing arose from the assumption that the social structure of the American South was different from that of the rest of the USA, being a mixture of class *and* caste (e.g. Dollard's *Caste and Class in a Southern Town* or Davis and Gardner's *Deep South*). Now that the focus of the struggle over the position of the negro has shifted to the big centres of urban America, the limitations of the earlier analysis have become evident. Questions of class, status and power are involved in the situation wherever it occurs, although their relative importance is different in Birmingham, Alabama and Newark, New Jersey.

Again, public office has a widely different significance from one case to the other. In the Soviet Union, not only does membership of the Communist Party appear to be the greatest single index of social position, but the very existence of class and status differences is denied by the official ideology. If our analysis has any general validity, it must be applicable to the Soviet Union. In other words, it should establish that although party office is of enormous importance, it does not therefore override all the other relationships described; and secondly, that in Communist society, as elsewhere, the variety of forms of social division may be reduced to a three-dimensional analysis in terms of class, status and power. Obviously, this involves a denial of the orthodox Marxist-Leninist claim that the abolition of the private ownership of the means of production leads to the disappearance of class conflicts, leaving only 'non-antagonistic contradictions'. Apart from the fact that official Communist propaganda does not require to be treated as serious sociological analysis, such a denial is clearly inherent in the argument so far. There is no shortage of evidence to show that social differentiation in the USSR encompasses a wide range of distinct relationships. Racial and national differences have not disappeared: African students complain about discrimination, anti-Semitism occurs both officially and unofficially, and the problem of nationalism recurs periodically in constituent republics such as the Ukraine and Georgia. Religion as such is prevented by official action from being socially influential, but its role has been largely taken over by tests of orthodoxy derived from party doctrine. Occupation, education and income form a cluster of factors as they do in any other industrial community, and in some ways their incidence is even sharper than in capitalist countries. Access to the party hierarchy is increasingly influenced by social position, both achieved and inherited.

An observation of Marshall's has some relevance here. Noting the enlarged influence attached to forms of social division other than class, he suggests that this is due 'not merely to the growth of more dimensions of stratification, but also to the emergence of more dimensions of social grouping of all kinds than the compelling class loyalty of the mid-capitalist phase of social history.'[41] Additionally, although class remains the expression of conflicts of economic interest, these no longer revolve exclusively around the private ownership of the means of production. This point, originally made by Theodor Geiger, has become even more pressing with the continued growth of affluence in the advanced capitalist countries. This means that economic conflicts come to centre increasingly on the distribution of the surplus. A similar process is evidently at work in the Soviet Union. The consolidation of the Communist regime, and the ending of 'primary socialist accumulation', involve the re-emergence of other forms of social division to modify the orthodox picture of a society whose structure is entirely dependent on the political role of the ruling party.

4 Social differentiation exists in every community, and in all communities which have undergone industrialisation it takes the form of class, status and power in combination. However, the steepness of the gradient varies a great deal from one community to another, and even within a single community there will be differences between one dimension and another. The huge spread of incomes in the United States gives material wealth a

41 Marshall, in *Transactions of the 3rd World Congress of Sociology*, vol. 3, p. 7

quite unparalleled importance, and with great wealth goes great power. Status differences in America are less solid and less elaborate, because they lack the support of inherited social position derived from aristocratic traditions. It is this discrepancy which generates the intensity of the search for status distinctions, so that Warner and Vance Packard have a point after all. In Australia, with a relatively small spread of income differentiation by American standards, the weight of class distinctions and of the power structure is also relatively small; on the other hand, the egalitarian ideology which supports and is supported by this situation results in the undervaluing of status distinctions.

5 A famous remark in the literature of class is that made by the English social philosopher Morris Ginsberg, who asserted that he did not know what he was supposed to be conscious of when he was class-conscious. The answer may be briefly stated: the forms of 'class-consciousness' which exist in any given society are products of the actual structure of class, status and power in that society, shaped and coloured by prevailing ideologies. The task of the social investigator is to examine the extent to which class-consciousness corresponds to and/or distorts the nature of class, status and power. The investigator is neither constrained to accept the prevailing models of social inequality nor able to ignore them, but his own model should be able to account for their origins and significance.

6 Political action by parties and interest groups represents, among other things, an attempt to modify or in extreme cases to overthrow the existing structure of class, status, and power. It is the nature of the latter which determines the character of parties and interest groups in any given political system. As Weber observed in his essay *Class, Status, Party*, political parties live in a 'house of power', i.e. their activities depend on the permanent social framework within which they operate. Parties expressing broadly similar group interests will, in different societies, vary in regard to social composition, ideological character, and political effectiveness. The structure of class, status and power also defines the valuation placed on political activities within the society. In Britain, for example, political activity continues to be defined in terms of party, parliament and Cabinet, and the activities of interest groups attract only occasional scrutiny (much of it from Americans); in Australia, politics has mostly been regarded as the interplay of pressure groups, and the permanent social framework on which they depend is either ignored or taken for granted.

Social Relations and the Dimensions of Inequality

The building up of an analytical framework of class, status and power from the components which, following Bott, I have called 'actual social relationships', is a complex process where arbitrary and speculative criteria must be applied, since no precise ones exist. No amount of theoretical discussion is a substitute, in this case, for the attempt to apply such criteria to an actual instance, and such an attempt is made in the ensuing chapters of this book. It remains to give a list of the social relationships which are regarded as relevant and to make a few comments on their relation to the analytical framework I have chosen.

The list is conventional:

Income and wealth
Occupation
Education
Family and kinship
Racial origin
Religion
Public rank
Age
Sex

We may remark first on the significance of family and kinship, whose contribution to class, status and power has long been recognised. Inherited social position plays some part in all societies and has many ramifications. Schumpeter observed that the history of social classes was the history of the rise and fall of families.[42] Habakkuk has compared the effects of different systems of inheritance of family property on economic change in Britain and France. Capitalism in England grew rapidly for a number of reasons, one of which was the fact that family fortunes could be transmitted intact because younger children had no claim at common law on their father's estate. Also, the development of marriage settlements which provided capital sums for the daughters contributed greatly to the growth of the mortgage market in the seventeenth century.[43] Bell carries this point further by stressing that changes in the class system involve changes in the role of the family. Without this emphasis, 'one cannot understand the peculiar cohesiveness of dominant economic classes in the past, or the sources of the break-up of power in contemporary society.' The linkage of family and property systems meant that 'people met at the same social levels, were educated in common schools appropriate to their wealth, shared the same manners and morals, read the same books and held similar prejudices . . . in short, created and shared a distinctive style of life.'[44]

Barber uses Schumpeter's point to define a class as 'a set of families that share equal or nearly equal prestige according to the criteria of evaluation in the system of stratification.'[45] Marriage is a crucial test of social equality and of social intimacy, of particular interest because ideologies of social intimacy may be used to conceal social inequalities [e.g. 'but I wouldn't let my daughter marry one'].

[42] J. A. Schumpeter, *Social Classes*
[43] H. J. Habakkuk, 'Marriage and Economic Change', *Journal of Economic History*, vol. 15, no. 1, 1955
[44] Daniel Bell, 'The Break-up of Family Capitalism', in *The End of Ideology*, New York, 1962, p. 37
[45] Bernard Barber, *Social Stratification*, New York, 1957, p. 73

Parsons takes up Schumpeter's hint by putting family and kinship on a comparable level of importance with occupation. Class, he argues, depends on these two phenomena, and may be defined as 'a plurality of kinship units which, in those respects where status in a hierarchical context is shared by their members, have approximately equal status. The class status of an individual, therefore, is that which he shares with the other members in an effective kinship unit.'[46] Marshall reformulates Schumpeter in these terms: 'Social class reproduces the quality of the family as a form of association for the satisfaction of non-specialised social ends.'[47]

These observations also relate to power, or at least the attainment of public office, which can be strongly influenced by family connections. Political families, judicial families, civil service families, military families, all attest to the part that kinship can play in widely differing political systems.

The connection between religion and class is more controversial. To Marx, religion was merely the moral sanction of an inverted and unjust social system. Proudhon, brought up within the Catholic Church, attached more importance to religion as a distinct support for the established order. The Mass and other religious ceremonies, he wrote, strengthen the feeling of a hierarchical order. Religious practice 'disciplines the masses through continuous pressures of which they are scarcely aware'.[48] In more recent years, the clustering of religion with other indices of social position has been observed in a number of studies, the most extensive of which is Lenski's *The Religious Factor*. Another American study has established high correlation between religion and occupation, income, education, and ethnic origin.[49] In Western Europe, Dogan has used survey data to show how religious membership forms part of the relation between social class and political affiliation,[50] and Alford has shown similar relationships in four English-speaking countries, including Australia.[51]

The significance of distinctions arising from racial origin is another area of controversy. Again, Marxism has been important in fostering the view that racial distinctions are incidental to economic conflicts and will lose their force if the latter are resolved. Although Marx wrote little on the subject, his early essay on the 'Jewish question' (in the *Deutsch-Französische Jahrbücher*, 1844) states his essential position, which has had a wide influence on many people who do not regard themselves as Marxists. A recent Marxist writer, Oliver Cox, argues that racial prejudice is the result of capitalist or imperialist exploitation, and is 'propagated

[46] Talcott Parsons, 'Social Classes and Class Conflict', in *Essays in Sociological Theory*, New York, 1954, p. 328
[47] Marshall, *Citizenship and Social Class*, p. 97
[48] Quoted by Halbwachs, *The Psychology of Social Classes*, p. 128
[49] B. Lazerwitz, 'A Comparison of Major US Religious Groups', *Journal of the American Statistical Association*, vol. 56, 1961, pp. 568-79
[50] M. Dogan, 'Le Vote Ouvrier', *Revue Francaise de Sociologie*, vol. 1, no. 1, 1960
[51] R. R. Alford, *Party and Society*, New York, 1963

among the public by an exploiting class for the purpose of stigmatising some group as inferior, so that the exploitation of either the group itself or its resources or both may be justified.'[52] As Banton observes, this view of race relations is only one of three possible models: the *ideological* model, derived from Marxism, the *prejudice* model, derived from psychology, and the *discrimination* model, which depends on the concept of social distance.[53]

The converse of the Marxist view is that industrialisation, even if it has the initial effect of stimulating racial antagonism, will ultimately lead to the dissolution of social differences based on racial origin. Blumer describes this as the 'conventional' view, and restates it as follows:

The logical imperatives of industrialism move to the elimination of race as a factor in the industrial order. . . . Since industrialism necessarily places its supreme premium on economical productivity and efficient operation all usable elements are ultimately chosen in terms of such standards . . . in the impersonality of these transactions non-industrial factors such as . . . racial makeup become irrelevant.[54]

As against this, Blumer argues that racial divisions have an independent and stubborn reality.

The conventional view depends heavily on the picture of rational man (more specifically, economic man) derived from liberal individualism. Blumer continues:

While industrialisation may alter greatly the social order, it may leave the racial system that is embedded in that order essentially intact . . . the entrance of industrialism may undercut and transform much in traditional life and social structure . . . yet amidst such transformation the framework of the established racial system may be retained . . . when introduced into a racially ordered society industrialisation conforms to the alignment and code of the racial order.[55]

Blumer's essay reflects the reaction among American sociologists, at least since R. E. Park, against the naive individualism of the 'melting pot' theory.[56] The more general use of the word 'race' is perhaps symptomatic, following the odious implications of racialist theories like those of the Nazis. Although the term remains scientifically suspect, its widespread use in the social sciences may be due to an awareness of the sad reality that 'race prejudice' is a pervasive social fact, for which it is pointless to seek euphemisms. In Shils' words, 'the coincidence of colour with inferior positions in the various distributions in colonial societies, in predominantly white societies, and in the world society reinforces—some would say generates—the interpretation of "colour identity" as a variant of "class identity".'[57]

52 Oliver C. Cox, *Caste, Class and Race*, New York, 1959, p. 393
53 Michael Banton, *Race Relations*, London, 1967, pp. 237-38
54 Guy Hunter (ed.), *Industrialisation and Race Relations*, Oxford, 1965, pp. 237-38
55 ibid., pp. 234-35
56 R. E. Park, *Race and Culture*, New York, 1950
57 E. A. Shils, in *Daedalus*, Spring 1967, p. 281

The notion of 'public rank' as a category of social relationships is based on the obvious fact that urban industrial society is characterised by the enormous growth of formal organisations in which human relations are regulated hierarchically by established systems of authority, deference, responsibility, influence and differential rewards. These relationships are 'public' in the sense that, even when they operate in 'private' organisations like business firms, they are based on formal rules which can be enforced according to established procedures. As Aristotle noted, the public sphere of social life is distinct in that it is concerned with the exercise of power. The growth of this sphere at the expense of private social relations is examined at some length by Hannah Arendt (in *The Human Condition*). An analysis of the role of public rank as an agent of stratification was made some years ago by Form, who showed how 'organisational affiliation and participation' can act as the focus of an elaborate structure of status differences.[58] The role of stable authority patterns in maintaining an established system of values and methods of making policy has been examined by Spiro, who notes the growth of 'procedural' as well as 'substantive' sources of authority in a highly organised society.[59] The importance of elites in urban industrial society rests, to a large extent, on this growth of what C. Wright Mills called the 'command posts'. Mills argued that the nature of capitalist industry had not changed fundamentally merely because large corporations were now controlled by managers (the 'corporate rich') instead of owners. The emergence of a managerial elite adds a new dimension to the class structure of capitalist society, but does not necessarily mean that society at large is better understood in terms of 'elites' rather than 'classes'. Rather, it may be said that no description of the structure of class, status and power in a modern community is possible without taking account of the growth of elite groups, which is closely linked with the extension of formalised procedures, such as higher education, in determining the social position of individuals.

Age and sex are two categories which differ from the rest in being 'natural' rather than 'conventional' (as Rousseau put it). Nevertheless, their contribution to social hierarchies changes as social patterns change. In a highly organised society, age acquires a specific economic significance through formal retirement rules; at the other end of the age scale, the expansion of education gives a specific character to adolescence and youth for ever-growing numbers of young people. Similarly, the position of women in any society is a sensitive index of class and status differences and the strength of the values which sustain them.

From this general discussion we may now turn to the examination of these issues in the context of a specific society.

58 W. H. Form, 'Status Stratification in a Planned Community', *American Sociological Review*, vol. 10, 1945, pp. 604-18
59 H. J. Spiro, 'Authority, Values and Policy', in C. J. Friedrich (ed.), *Authority*, Cambridge, Mass., 1958, pp. 49-57

Part Two
An Egalitarian Society?

4: The Paradoxes of Equality

This is a true republic—the truest, as I take it, in the world. In England the average man feels that he is an inferior, in America that he is a superior; in Australia he feels that he is an equal. . . . Here the people is neither servile nor insolent, but only shows its respect of itself by its respect for others.

Francis Adams, *Australian Essays* (1886)

The explorer of social inequality in Australia makes his way through unfriendly territory. The natives worship at the shrine of egalitarianism, and their beliefs have been fortified for more than a century by travellers' tales. 'Rank and title have no charms at the Antipodes', wrote an English gold-digger in the 1850's.[1] A succession of literary gents—Trollope, Froude, Siegfried, Leroy-Beaulieu, Bryce, D. H. Lawrence—drew essentially the same conclusion. Lawrence noted the absence of that 'distinction in the very being' between the proletariat and the ruling classes which he had left behind in England. An Australian contemporary saw it as a community 'intolerant of special privileges . . . with no aristocracy of birth, of talent or of skill.'[2]

As in North America, the strength and pervasiveness of egalitarianism are often attributed to the 'frontier ethos' common to the lands colonised by British settlers. As Porter remarks about Canada, the persistent image of a country with no classes is sustained by the rural environment and the pioneer way of life imposed by it.[3] Unlike North America, however, the rise of a strong Labor movement in the late nineteenth century gave the drive for equality a characteristically political and institutional form. The Labor publicists of the generation before the 1914-18 war, inspired by a mixture of class and nationalist emotions, were insistent that a new social pattern was to be established in which the class divisions of the old world should have no place. The Australian working class would be unlike its docile counterpart in England, 'content to labour on and permit the upper classes to think and act for them.'[4] Henry Lawson's oft-quoted poem

[1] G. B. Earp, 'The Gold Colonies of Australia', quoted in R. N. Ebbels, *The Australian Labour Movement 1850-1907*, Melbourne, 1956, p. 37
[2] C. H. Northcott, *Australian Social Development*, New York, 1918, p. 17
[3] John Porter, *The Vertical Mosaic*, Toronto, 1965, p. 3
[4] From a speech by the chairman of the Trades Hall Committee, Melbourne, in

'For'ard' (1893) saw a time when 'the curse of class distinctions from our shoulders shall be hurled', and the novelist Joseph Furphy wrote in *Such is Life* (1903) that human equality was 'self-evident . . . and impregnable as any mathematical axiom'.

Two generations of writing in this vein were summed up by Hancock when he wrote that the crucial assumption of Australian society, expressed in the fixing of the first basic wage in 1907, was that of 'fair and reasonable' standards for everyone, a notion in which was expressed 'the decision of a people to seek general well-being rather than special excellence'.[5] In his classic work, *Australia*, first published in 1930, Hancock did for Australia what de Tocqueville had done for America a century earlier, and traced the influence of the egalitarian outlook through economics, government, culture and manners. No other book about Australia has had a comparable influence, and one unfortunate result is that many inferior imitations have been produced. Frequent repetition makes even the most brilliant generalisations look jaded. It is impossible to avoid quoting Hancock, but much more relevant at this later date is to show the limitations and shortcomings of his analysis in the Australia of the 1950's and 1960's.

The pervasiveness of the egalitarian ideology has always depended heavily on a shortage of labour which, as Manning Clark notes, gives special strength to the working-class movement. 'The labour shortage corroded the centuries-old fear of the employer, and with it one of the pillars of inequality. Thus the labour market, not the gold diggers or the Chartists, was one of the great creators of social equality in Australia.' Moreover, as the shortage was mainly one of unskilled labour, the gap between the wages of skilled and unskilled workers was smaller than in Europe or North America, and by reducing economic distinctions within the labour movement added to its solidarity and effectiveness. In addition, the relative absence of an entrenched upper class, secured in its position by a history of feudal privilege and aristocratic domination of political and cultural life, meant that there were only tenuous obstacles to the advancement of 'the frugal, the industrious, and the talented'.[6] As a popular nationalist weekly wrote, 'the masses . . . recognise no natural nobility in the new order of plutocrats which warrants their eminent fortunes . . . when they perceive great wealth to be often the direct result of selfish insensibility, and to be frequently coupled with a brutal arrogance, . . . they deny that Providence can have had any hand in it.'[7]

Similar arguments have been advanced by American writers concerned with a similar question of historical explanation. America, writes Hartz,

1859; quoted R. A. Gollan, *Radical and Working Class Politics*, Melbourne, 1960, p. 69

[5] W. K. Hancock, in *Cambridge History of the British Empire*, Cambridge, 1933, vol. 7, pt. I, p. 510

[6] C. M. H. Clark, *Select Documents in Australian History*, Sydney, 1955, vol. 2, p. 660

[7] *Bulletin*, 21 July, 1883; quoted Clark, pp. 559-60

represents the 'liberal mechanism of Europe functioning without the European social antagonisms.'[8] Liberalism, in the countries of European settlement, was a successful reaction against feudal conservatism, and an assessment of its influence requires a 'comparative study of new societies which will put alongside the European institutions left behind, the positive cultural concepts brought to the various frontier settings'.[9] Among these positive concepts Hartz includes the aims of the Chartist movement, whose influence on Australian political history has been exaggerated by many historians, and only demolished in fairly recent years by the new school of postwar Australian historiography. Veblen had a similar point in mind when he wrote that the United States had enshrined the eighteenth century doctrines of natural liberty in its political institutions, whereas other ex-colonial countries had inherited later radical doctrines which undermined the faith in natural rights and natural law.

Inasmuch as this is true, the effective doctrines were those of the collectivist liberals and Fabian socialists of the late nineteenth century, which found their institutional embodiment in Australia in public enterprise and compulsory wage-fixing, whose effects on the character of Australian society are examined in later chapters.

The most recent discussion of these questions from an American stand-point is to be found in the work of Lipset, many of whose generalisations can readily be extended to Australia.[10] Lipset observes that the value system of American society is to be explained, to a large extent, by opposition to the imposition of an elite culture, which implies that a large part of the population is required to accept a negative concept of its own worth, so that low status becomes a form of punishment. There are three common adaptive mechanisms in this situation: religion, a drive for social mobility, and political action.[11] Religion has been less important in Australia, but the other two mechanisms are of the greatest consequence.

Lipset also addresses himself to the paradox that, although social mobility in the USA does not appear to be significantly higher than in other societies, belief that a high level does exist is profound. For this he suggests five reasons: (1) the absence of feudal survivals; (2) a high degree of educational opportunity; (3) special opportunities for enrichment in business; (4) special career opportunities for different ethnic groups; (5) a consumer society with a high working class standard of living. These factors support an ideology which means, in practice, that 'people continue to believe in the "equalitarianism" of American society despite their daily experience of status differences.'[12] The 'mythology of the spectacular

[8] Louis Hartz, *The Liberal Tradition in America*, New York, 1955, p. 16
[9] ibid., pp. 20-21
[10] Lipset's most systematic attempt to do this is his article on 'Anglo-American Society' in the *International Encyclopedia of the Social Sciences*, New York, 1968.
[11] S. M. Lipset, *The First New Nation*, London, 1964, pp. 271-72
[12] S. M. Lipset and R. Bendix, 'Ideological Equalitarianism and Social Mobility in the US', *Transactions of the 2nd World Congress of Sociology*, London, 1954, vol. 2, pp. 36-37

career' is of particular importance in sustaining the ideology, and it is aided by the 'frequency with which the sons of manual workers and farmers have become engineers, teachers, government administrators, businessmen, and occasionally corporation executives.'[13]

The growth of egalitarian sentiment in Australia can be described in similar terms, although the emphasis differs. The mythology of the spectacular career is much less resounding; 'from telegraph messenger to director-general' is a low-keyed theme compared with 'rags to riches'; and neither Samuel Smiles nor Horatio Alger were popular authors in Australia. Hostility to noble pretensions, however, is just as strong. 'We, as free-born Australian, will not have our liberties trifled with for the benefit of privileged sprigs of "nobility", who with their arrogant assumption of superiority are not wanted in Australia.'[14] William Westgarth, merchant, social commentator, and politician, wrote in 1857 that ambition could rear its head from any social grade: 'there is not the political monopoly—the impenetrable adamantine front presented by an old society to the industrial masses of its people.'[15] The historian Russel Ward links hostility to aristocratic pretensions with hostility towards established authority and both with anti-British sentiment. In this reaction a key role was played by the Irish, whose attitudes found a famous historical expression in the open letter written by the outlaw Ned Kelly in 1878 when his gang held up the small town of Jerilderie in southern New South Wales.[16] In this case, religion also played an important part, and adds the final element to a syndrome which gives the Irish-Catholic minority its special place in the social pattern, making it one of the significant exceptions to the received picture of a socially homogeneous, egalitarian, prosperous community, where there is 'a general equality of opportunity, increased by a liberal scheme of education, that opens a career to ability, initiative and merit . . . (and) religious hatreds, racial prejudices, social inequalities and great industrial wrongs never seem to have influenced the corporate governing life of the new nation.'[17]

Hostility towards aristocracy, authority and privilege has its less admirable side in distrust of special excellence and unorthodox tastes or opinions. The connection between egalitarian sentiments and anti-intellectualism in American history has been thoroughly explored by Hofstadter in a study devoted mainly to the development of educational thought and policy. Anti-intellectualism, he asserts, is a pervasive factor in American society. 'It made its way into our politics because it became associated with our passion for equality. It has become formidable in our

[13] ibid., p. 38
[14] Letter in the *Age*, Melbourne, 14 March 1887, quoted Clark, op. cit., p. 42
[15] Quoted, Ebbels, op. cit., p. 42
[16] Russel Ward, *The Australian Legend*, London, 1958, ch. 3
[17] Northcott, loc. cit. The author, who was a tutor in sociology for the WEA in Sydney, is typical of many other writers in underrating the force of the exceptions to his generalisations, but perhaps with less excuse in his case.

education partly because our educational beliefs are evangelically egalitarian.'[18] As a result, preponderant power in most spheres of public education has been exercised by opponents of the intellectual life. Hofstadter also examines, at length, the hostility of organised religion, both evangelical Protestantism and Catholicism, to intellectual activity. The aggressively anti-intellectual posture of American Catholicism, analysed in detail in a well-known article by Monsignor J. T. Ellis in the American Jesuit magazine, *Thought*, in 1955, was largely due to the 'harsh Puritanism and fierce militancy' of the Irish clergy, whose close identification with the working class has always fed their hostility to the Protestant Establishment. Cardinal Cushing of Boston observed in 1947 that every bishop known to him was the son of a working man, and not one was a college graduate.[19]

Hofstadter's analysis fits the Australian scene in many ways, and his complaint about egalitarian resentment of the intellectual has been echoed by a number of Australian writers. Hancock devotes a chapter to the impact of an egalitarian society on arts and letters, although he was less concerned with the stultification of intellectual life than with the search for a literary expression of egalitarian and humanitarian values in the work of representative writers of poetry and fiction. Manning Clark makes much the same point as Hofstadter when he writes that Protestant Christianity and Irish Catholicism strengthened the grasp of the puritan and the philistine, and industrialisation added a habit of conformity and uniformity, leading some writers, artists and philosophers to adopt a Nietzschean philosophy of culture for the great souls.[20] Hofstadter's attack on American education is echoed by McLaren, who writes sardonically that 'the practice of Australian schools has been heavily influenced by the values of a society which likes to imagine that it is egalitarian. . . . Australian traditions leave their mark on the schools in a distrust of individual excellence, except in the approved form of piling up marks, an aversion towards heterodox behaviour, and a disliking for any intellectual enthusiasm. Finally, this depressing jelly of philistinism is set in its mould by moral overtones of loyalty to queen and country, worship of the flag, and reverence for the pioneers, the diggers and the sportsmen.'[21] The difference between America and Australia in educational philosophy lies in the acceptance of 'progressive education' in the former as compared with a rigidly academic, examination-bound system in the latter. Both countries, however, have solved the problem of reconciling anti-intellectualism with the demands of industrial society for trained intellects by elevating the practical 'expert' rather than the uncomfortable 'intellectual'.[22]

[18] Richard Hofstadter, *Anti-Intellectualism in American Life*, New York, 1963, p. 23
[19] ibid., pp. 136-39. The subject is also explored by G. E. Lenski, *The Religious Factor*, New York, 1961, esp. at p. 278
[20] C. M. H. Clark, *A Short History of Australia*, London, 1964, pp. 226-27
[21] John McLaren, *Our Troubled Schools*, Melbourne, 1968, p. 2
[22] Hofstadter, op. cit., ch. 13

Lipset and Bendix note the paradox that a community whose emphasis on equality means a lack of recognition of intellectual attainment is none the less ready to accord high status to university professors. The latter is attested by the high scores obtained by professors in American surveys of occupational prestige, where they normally rank just behind doctors. A similar situation exists in Australia, as shown by Congalton's surveys of occupational prestige.[23] The solution of the paradox may be that professors are regarded as successful professional men, in a desirable and socially valuable occupation; the survey situation does not arouse the suspicion which the word 'professor' obviously does on other occasions. Lipset and Bendix suggest that Americans (and Australians too) may 'esteem the attainments of a man and recognise his high position, but they will not defer to him.'[24] As de Tocqueville said many years earlier, democratic communities are ready to use great talents, but do not stand in awe of them. However, this is too simple, and it overlooks the limitations and inconsistencies of egalitarianism in practice. In Australia at least, and perhaps in America too, people do not *only* esteem the attainments of professional men (doctors above all); direct deference is readily observable as well. Another kind of inconsistency was remarked by the French socialist, Métin, in the 1890's, when he saw the trade union movement issuing a reproof towards a British socialist visitor who had declared, during Queen Victoria's diamond jubilee, that he could not see why the workers should feel indebted to her.[25]

Egalitarianism is limited not only by deference, but also by restricted coverage. Some men are less equal than others, for instance the American negro; as Myrdal saw in the 1940's, the strength of the doctrine of equal opportunities in the USA actually imposes special burdens on negroes. In Australia, women, aborigines and foreigners have found themselves less esteemed than white Australian males. 'Socialism', wrote a trade union paper in 1892, 'is being mates',[26] but as Clark comments, 'mateship' did not extend to Asian immigrants.[27] A recent writer on rural life also questions the traditional emphasis on mateship, portrayed in a great deal of writing about the 'outback'. 'The romantic picture sometimes painted of life in the outback as a classless companionship among mates and "characters" does not often correspond to the facts. However much masters and men may help each other in those periods of stress and crisis which occur so much more frequently under conditions of extreme isolation, in their normal lives there is a fairly strict social hierarchy. Managers and overseers have their meals at the homestead (or in their own cottages); station hands and stockmen eat "outside"—i.e. in separate quarters. . . .

---

[23] A. A. Congalton, *Status and Prestige in Australia*, Melbourne, 1969
[24] Lipset and Bendix, loc. cit., p. 51
[25] Albert Métin, *Le socialisme sans doctrines*, Paris, 1901, p. 272
[26] *The Hummer*, 16 January 1892; quoted in Clark, *Select Documents*, p. 588
[27] ibid., p. 788

Again, in many parts of the outback, the stock work is done by aborigines who are not usually included in the mateship group of the whites.'[28]

One of the strongest limitations on egalitarian sentiment is the long-established hostility of Australians towards Asians, which finds its political expression in the so-called White Australia Policy. The demand for a white Australia in the last two decades of the nineteenth century was a principal factor in the federation of the Australian colonies, and one of the first legislative acts of the new federal parliament was the Immigration Restriction Act of 1901. The *Bulletin*, mouthpiece of the radical nationalism of the period, carried on its masthead the motto 'Australia for the White Man', which it discarded only in 1961 after a change of ownership. The Brisbane *Worker* hailed the legislation as saving Australia from 'the coloured curse', and in 1905 the federal conference of the Australian Labor Party declared that its policy was 'the cultivation of an Australian sentiment based upon the maintenance of racial purity'. Officially, the Labor movement was in favour of White Australia because an influx of Asian labour was a threat to the living standards of Australian workers; unofficially, the economic motive and the racialist motive were inextricably interwoven. In the words of Manning Clark, 'the believers in the brotherhood of man and equality of all in the sight of God were silent. So the men who believed that the unity of labor was the hope of the world united with the apostles of Christian civilisation to preserve Australia for the white man.'[29]

As Yarwood has pointed out in a careful study of the period, a mixture of racialist and utilitarian attitudes was common to members of all parties, and was fully exposed during the debates on the 1901 Act.[30] The Prime Minister, Edmund Barton, quoted at length from *National Life and Character*, written by C. H. Pearson, a former minister for education in Victoria who had warned Australians about the dangers of being swamped by an inferior race. Isaac Isaacs, later to be Chief Justice and Governor-General, warned against the 'contamination and the degrading influence of inferior races'. (Did Isaacs, one may wonder, ever reflect during the 1930's and 1940's—he died in 1950—on his choice of words when the Nazis destroyed millions of Jews in the name of this doctrine?) The Labor leader, J. C. Watson, declared that his objection to coloured immigration, although influenced by 'considerations of an industrial nature', was mainly due to the 'possibility and probability of racial contamination'. The statistician and economic historian, T. A. Coghlan, wrote in the London *Times* in 1908 that the 'ethnical' objection to the coloured races was the most important, and that 'the economic objections might perhaps be waived were the other non-existent'. The Brisbane *Worker* called for a state composed of a 'multitude of perfect human units' (the drawbacks to

[28] F. H. Gruen, 'Rural Australia', in A. F. Davies and S. Encel (eds.), *Australian Society*, Melbourne, 1965, pp. 266-67
[29] Clark, *Short History*, p. 193
[30] A. T. Yarwood, *Asian Migration to Australia*, Melbourne, 1964, pp. 22-35 passim

perfection being obvious), and the *Bulletin* played on race prejudice constantly by its use of words such as 'mongrelisation' and its cartoons, which depicted the coloured man as a grinning caricature of humanity. In the context of this discussion, perhaps the most revealing sentence was uttered by Barton in a speech in parliament in September 1901, after the Immigration Restriction Act had become law: 'I do not think that the doctrine of the equality of man was really ever intended to include racial equality.'

With the passage of the years, the stridency of these racialist sentiments has been softened by a number of factors, including the realisation by many articulate Australians that the price of egalitarianism within Australia is a negative form of colonialism, exclusion rather than exploitation, isolationism rather than apartheid. During the 1939-45 war, when the implications of racial doctrine were being spelt out by Hitler for all the world, Labor politicians were ready to declare that Labor's support for White Australia was economic, not racial. The claim was historically inaccurate. Racial prejudice has always been an element of the policy since the 1850's, although the balance of ingredients within it has varied from generation to generation.[31] Opposition to Asian immigration remains the settled policy of the country, tempered since 1945 by a growing sensitivity among educated people towards its racialist elements and their incompatibility with egalitarian pretensions.

In sum, the conception of equality which prevails in Australia is one which places great stress on the enforcement of a high minimum standard of material well-being, on the outward show of equality and the minimisation of privileges due to formal rank, and almost by implication restricts the scope for the unusual, eccentric, or dissenting individual. Métin asserted in the 1890's that the forward march of the working class consisted of attaining the same level as the bourgeoisie, and that the Australian worker had 'assured himself of the prestige of outward appearances, . . . more and more one can observe the external difference between the worker and the bourgeois diminishing except during working hours.'[32] The objection to this form of egalitarianism, as Isaiah Berlin has noted, is that a commitment to the philosophy of equal treatment tends to breed rigid rules for equal treatment which deal with all cases, 'whether individual characters or moral situations or moral actions, that are necessarily unique and incommensurable, under the umbrella of some universal formula' which forces human activity into a 'Procrustean bed of symmetrical sets of moral rules'.[33] Again, Australian egalitarianism insists that only those should be admitted to Australia who can become good Australians. In addition to excluding coloured people, this means that European immigrants are expected to become good Australians and abandon their own

31 David Johanson, 'History of the White Australia Policy', in K. Rivett (ed.), *Immigration: Control or Colour Bar?* Melbourne, 1962, pp. 25-27
32 Métin, op. cit., pp. 267-70
33 Isaiah Berlin, 'Equality', *Proceedings of the Aristotelian Society*, 1955-6, pp. 310-11

group characteristics as rapidly as possible; immigration and 'assimilation' go together. The same assumption, as embodied in the American civil rights movement, is criticised by a political philosopher who argues that the white supporters of the movement require the negro to give up his group identity in order to achieve public equality. Constitutional liberalism, which thinks in terms of uniform general laws, would create a set of bureaucratic rules to enforce equal treatment. Bureaucracy 'is the very model of the regime which acts by the rule of equality.'[34] Herein lies the paradox of egalitarianism in Australia: the search for equality of the redistributive kind breeds bureaucracy; bureaucracy breeds authority; and authority undermines the equality which bred it.

[34] John H. Schaar, 'Some Ways of Thinking About Equality', *Journal of Politics*, vol. 26, no. 4, 1964

5: The Bureaucratic Ascendency

'Bureaucracy is a bad European system of government, created by the use of permanent public officials, a system that does not, should not, and cannot exist in England.'—Palmerston to Queen Victoria, 1837

The bureaucratic quality of social and political organisation in Australia colours the whole pattern of social relations. It arises partly from the special problems of settlement in a large, remote, and inhospitable country, and partly from the deliberate use of bureaucratic institutions to satisfy the social demands of an egalitarian society. The most famous statement of the relationship between bureaucracy and egalitarianism was made by Hancock in 1930, and as it has never been improved upon it remains the most frequently quoted example. State action, he asserted, was the result of egalitarian pressure which was, in its turn, the local version of nineteenth century British individualism. To the Australian, he wrote, 'the State means collective power at the service of individualistic "rights". Therefore he sees no opposition between his individualism and his reliance upon Government.' Every citizen claims his rights—'the right to work, the right to fair and reasonable conditions of living, the right to be happy—from the State and through the State.' In consequence, he concludes, 'Australian democracy has come to look upon the State as a vast public utility, whose duty it is to provide the greatest happiness for the greatest number.'[1]

Hancock's ideas about the role of state action were strongly influenced by the writings of Sir Frederic Eggleston, who asserted that the scope and importance of state action in Australia was unparalleled outside the Soviet Union. 'State socialism', he declared, 'has been the result of a demand that the State shall definitely be used to secure social and economic objectives. Whether from the lack of the usual equipment of more mature communities, or from an impatience at the slow progress of liberalism in remoulding "this sorry scheme of things", Australian democracy has called in the State whenever there was a demand for any advanced policy.'[2] A similar observation had been made a number of years earlier by the Australian correspondent of the London *Times*, A. W. Jose, who wrote that Australians had become 'inured to a habit of regarding their own State as a

[1] W. K. Hancock, *Australia*, London, 1930, pp. 61, 65
[2] F. W. Eggleston, *State Socialism in Victoria*, London, 1931, p. 24

material power outside themselves which held the keys of failure or success, and which each interest must capture or conciliate for its own purposes lest others should capture it for theirs.'[3]

More recently, Davies has remarked that 'the characteristic talent of Australians is not for improvisation, nor even for republican manners; it is for bureaucracy.'[4] He notes that even in rural areas, where the traditions of self-help and individualism are strong, the habit of leaning on the bureaucracy is too deeply embedded to be resisted. 'The characteristic political form of the countryside is not the local committee of management, but the deputation. . . . There is a decided preference for waiting your turn with the bureaucracy, rather than making your pace by voluntary effort.'[5] During the depression years of the 1930's, this led to a proliferation of bureaucratic agencies to help the farmers, whereas a similar situation in the Canadian prairie provinces led to the creation of a network of self-help agencies staffed by elective officials—one such post for every three farmers, according to Lipset's estimate.[6]

This enormous and pervasive insistence upon authoritative action to deal with economic and social demands is one of the pillars of the bureaucratic ascendency in Australian life. Instead of collective bargaining, public debate, or direct action, the characteristic style of decision-making, firmly established in Australia since the turn of the twentieth century, rests on a broad public willingness to delegate the power to decide to rule-making bodies of an administrative or quasi-judicial character. Some of these are what Miller calls 'organs of syndical satisfaction', set up to provide a legal-administrative framework for adjudicating and enforcing the demands of organised interest groups which Miller prefers to describe as 'syndicates', i.e. 'people whose economic and vocational interests have induced them to band together for action to their common advantage, such as trade unions, associations of manufacturers and traders, farmers and graziers' unions.' Hence the Australian political system is one in which 'a variety of syndicates are struggling to enjoy the favours of government.'[7] A prime example is the Tariff Board, sustained by the ideology of government protective action, established by law in 1921 and operating in a semi-judicial manner, which exercises a determining influence on the structure of Australian industry. Another area where this legal-bureaucratic system operates, with profound consequences for the whole pattern of social relations in Australia, is that of industrial arbitration, where the processes of collective bargaining and employer-employee confrontation over the distribution of rewards are replaced by a legal-bureaucratic hierarchy of tribunals. This system, also, became entrenched at the turn of the century,

---

[3] *The Times*, London, 1 August 1908
[4] A. F. Davies, *Australian Democracy*, Melbourne, 1964, p. 1
[5] A. F. Davies, in E. L. French (ed.), *Melbourne Studies in Education 1958-59*, Melbourne, 1960, p. 157
[6] S. M. Lipset, *Agrarian Socialism*, New York, 1950
[7] J. D. B. Miller, *Australian Government and Politics*, London, 3rd ed., 1964, ch. 1

and in 1907 the corner-stone was laid by the introduction of the principle of the basic wage. In that year, Henry Bournes Higgins, President of the Commonwealth Arbitration Court and the greatest figure in the history of industrial arbitration, delivered the famous 'Harvester Judgment' which laid down a 'fair and reasonable' standard for a minimum wage, determined according to the needs of Walt Whitman's 'divine average'. In his writings, Higgins described the role of arbitration as a 'new province for law and order'. The province has grown steadily since his lifetime to become the heartland of the Australian system of social values, in which the demands of an egalitarian social philosophy are canalised and enforced by a network of authoritarian, legal-rational controls. The modern prince, wrote Gramsci, can only be an organisation in which a collective will is cemented.

The absence of serious racial, religious or economic conflicts in Australia gives this authoritarian framework a relatively non-repressive character, so that it sits lightly on the shoulders of the citizenry and is not unduly difficult to tolerate. The comparative social and political homogeneity of the community also makes it fairly easy to enunciate general rules and to enforce them through a rational-legal bureaucratic system. Its maintenance is further assisted by certain processes of positive feedback generated by the system itself. Because disputes about the social allocation of values, both material and non-material, are so readily directed into bureaucratic channels, public controversy over such issues is effectively damped, and the need for interest groups to present a convincing case in public is correspondingly reduced. Whereas the British community depends heavily on 'government by committee', the Australian community depends even more heavily on recommendation by royal commission. In the eighty years up to 1939, royal commissions were in session in Australia at an average rate of six or seven per year, and although the rate has slowed down since then, they are still a notable part of the legal-bureaucratic apparatus. It was entirely in character with this tradition that the federal government should investigate the circumstances surrounding the defection of a Soviet Embassy official, Vladimir Petrov, in 1954, by assigning the task to a royal commission.

The strength of egalitarian sentiment is closely linked with the strength of the trade union movement, and this, combined with the great importance of public enterprise in the Australian economy, provides another feedback mechanism to strengthen the bureaucratic ascendency. This point has been convincingly argued by Lockwood, who notes that bureaucratisation is greatest where an industry is monopolised by one big employer who brings it under centralised and unitary control, as is the case with the large public utilities in Australia.[8] 'To the degree that a field of employment is subject to such bureaucratic rules, administrative particularism will be replaced by the standardisation of working conditions.' Unionisation, Lockwood contends, is very closely associated with the growth of

[8] David Lockwood, *The Blackcoated Worker*, London, 1958, pp. 141-43

standardised, bureaucratic rules, which provide a situation extremely favourable to the growth of collective action. The relationship is reciprocal. 'Just as bureaucratisation provides fertile ground for unionisation, so unionisation, once established, leads to further bureaucratisation by its demands for uniformity of working conditions.' Bureaucratisation and unionisation have, to borrow a phrase from Myrdal, been 'mutually cumulative' in their effects.[9]

Although Lockwood is referring specifically to white-collar workers, his generalisations are broadly applicable to the relation between unionism and bureaucracy. Compulsory arbitration for industrial disputes was not originally sought by the trade union movement, but devised by middle class radical lawyers like W. P. Reeves in New Zealand, C. C. Kingston in South Australia and H. B. Higgins in Victoria. Kingston was largely responsible for the federal Conciliation and Arbitration Act of 1903, and Higgins, as President of the Arbitration Court, established the principle of the national minimum which was even then, in England, being pursued energetically by Sidney and Beatrice Webb on the Royal Commission on the Poor Law.[10] Once the arbitration system was in operation, it became part of the settled framework of trade unionism. Although the unions recurrently chafe against arbitration, and 'left-wing' postures within the union movement are frequently associated with expressions of hostility towards the system, outbursts are usually associated with dissatisfaction at particular awards made by tribunals, or with the slowness of the machinery, rather than pointing to any fundamental disaffection towards the principle of arbitration. One of the great advantages of the system for the unions is that it stimulates union membership by making awards which, being of a judicial or quasi-judicial character, are meant in principle to apply to the parties to the 'dispute', real or fabricated, on which arbitration has been made. Indeed, in some cases unions have been able to use the arbitral machinery to impose sanctions on their own errant members.[11]

Awards made by the Commonwealth Arbitration Commission (as it became in 1956) are frequently attacked on the grounds that they constitute

[9] Gunnar Myrdal, *An American Dilemma*, New York, 1944, appendix 3, 'Methodological note on the principle of cumulation'

[10] The concept of the national minimum was embodied in the famous Minority Report of the Poor Law Commission, and later in the first manifesto of the British Labour Party, *Labour and the New Social Order*, in 1918. Personal contacts played a part in these events. The Webbs visited Australia in 1898-9 and Reeves, who was in London as Agent-General for New Zealand, became an active Fabian and director of the London School of Economics and Political Science, established by the Webbs.

[11] Some interesting examples are quoted by J. S. Hagan, *Printers and Politics*, Sydney, 1966, and the general legal situation is set out by J. H. Portus, *The Development of Australian Trade Union Law*, Melbourne, 1958. General discussions of the arbitration system are numerous, but particular mention may be made of M. Perlman, *Judges in Industry*, Melbourne, 1954; Kingsley Laffer, 'Industrial Relations' in A. F. Davies and A. G. Serle (eds.), *Policies for Progress*, Melbourne, 1954; K. F. Walker, *Industrial Relations in Australia*, Melbourne, 1956; G. W. Ford and J. E. Isaac (eds.), *Australian Labour Economics*, Melbourne, 1967.

decisions about economic policy which are made by judges innocent of economics. The common recipe prescribed by the critics is to put economists on the bench or to supply the judges with a bureau of economic advice. Many of these criticisms miss the point that the social role of the system depends on its legal-bureaucratic character and the use of judicial authority to procure and enforce its decisions. The original Harvester Judgment was itself a remarkable example of this process, and an equally remarkable one was the 10 per cent all-round cut in wages decreed by the Court in 1931, at the trough of the great depression, which demonstrated the extraordinary strength and effectiveness of the bureaucratic ascendency and its ability to impose discipline in a situation which, in many other countries, led to political crisis, violence, and Fascism.

Bureaucracy and the Economy

For many years, economic writing was dominated by assumptions that treated the economic history of Australia as an illustration—albeit an eccentric one—of the growth of competitive capitalism. The role of government, though important, was treated as a background factor. Since the 1950's there has been a decisive shift from this interpretation, aided by similar shifts in economic thought throughout the world. Recent writing in economic history has underlined the steady expansion of state inter- vention since the middle of the nineteenth century, and demonstrated that it was a key factor in the economy even during the 'pastoral ascendency', when the economic, social and political dominance of the wool interests went side by side. State action, especially in capital formation, was at least as important as the export of wool. Economic development was the result of a special form of public-private relations in which the former was the senior partner, where the common pattern was one of 'positive government intervention with the central feature of large scale outlays for capital formation'.[12] It is this which Eggleston described as 'state socialism', but was described by W. P. Reeves at the time as 'colonial governmentalism' and more recently by Butlin as 'colonial socialism'.

Hartshorne has distinguished eight factors in economic growth: transport, capital goods, power resources, raw materials, entrepreneurship, money, labour, and markets for finished products.[13] In Australia, govern- ments played a key role in each of these in the nineteenth century, and have continued to do so in the twentieth, with some changes of emphasis. In North America and Great Britain, the relative unimportance of the government as an entrepreneur was due, according to Mathews, to five main factors: a prosperous agricultural sector; the acceptance of large inequalities of income; the acceptance of low standards of personal

[12] N. G. Butlin, 'Colonial Socialism in Australia' in H. G. J. Aitken (ed.), *The State and Economic Growth*, New York, 1959, p. 27
[13] R. Hartshorne, in ibid., ch. 11

consumption and a high rate of personal saving; cheap transport; and ready access to imports of necessities, which in Britain meant cheap food and in the US a plentiful supply of overseas investment capital, especially from Britain. When some or all of these conditions did not exist, the state was forced to accept major responsibilities, and most of them did not exist in Australia.[14]

According to Butlin's estimates, government intervention was responsible for about one-half of all capital formation in the nineteenth century, and the pastoral ascendency itself depended heavily on government action. Government construction and operation of railways was a major aspect of the development process, and Butlin demonstrates that this occurred not only because private railways were unprofitable, but through the ability of governments to raise capital and find entrepreneurial ability.[15] These activities took place against prevailing *laissez-faire* attitudes, such as those expressed in an official inquiry which, noting that expenditure on 'extra-ordinary' matters such as public works and social services was double the amount spent on the 'ordinary' functions of government, regarded this as a 'necessary incident of the imperfect stage of development that pertains to a very young country', whereas 'private enterprise or local exertion' would be the agents in more advanced countries, and looked forward to the day when a 'normal' pattern would prevail.[16]

The link between the nineteenth and twentieth century patterns of government economic initiative has been forthrightly stated by McFarlane:

From the very earliest days . . . a public sector has been crucial in setting the pace, atmosphere, and social investment 'infrastructure' essential to economic development. With the coming of federation and the growth of a tariff system the government was virtually taking the risk out of capitalism —helping to underwrite risk, to build up guaranteed markets for the products of domestic private enterprise. Industrialisation was not achieved by a thrifty, development-orientated aggressive middle class. What happened rather was that the public sector or government regulation became substitutes for the normal functions of the middle class and capitalist groups as agents of economic development. Inevitably there followed the growth of a bureaucracy to run a network of regulation agencies.[17]

In the decade 1881-90, according to Butlin's estimates, the public sector contributed 40 per cent to gross domestic capital formation; in the depression decade of 1891-1900, 54 per cent and in 1901-10, 42 per cent. In 1896-67, public expenditure was 18.6 per cent of the gross national product, and in 1911-12, 37.5 per cent.[18] At a similar period, public investment in Britain rose from 9 per cent of GNP in 1890 to 12 per cent in 1905 and 13 per cent in 1910. Before 1910, the statistician Robert

14 Russell Mathews, *Public Investment in Australia*, Melbourne, 1966, ch. 1
15 Butlin, loc. cit., pp. 38-42
16 *Report of the Royal Commission on the Civil Service of Victoria*, 1859, p. 8
17 Bruce McFarlane, *Economic Policy in Australia*, Melbourne, 1968, p. 69
18 N. G. Butlin, *Australian Domestic Product, Investment and Foreign Borrowing 1861-1938/9*, Cambridge, 1962, pp. 6-7, 16-17

Giffen was thought to be extreme in suggesting that 10 per cent of national income was a reasonable level of public expenditure in peacetime.[19] American figures were similar (9 per cent in the decade 1902-12), and a little earlier President Cleveland had written in a veto message that 'the lesson should be constantly enforced that, though the people support the government, the government should not support the people.'[20]

Since 1914, differences in the incidence of public expenditure between Australia and other countries have become relatively small, although defence spending is a much less important factor in Australia. Ratchford concluded, after a careful series of comparisons, that the rate of public expenditure in Australia remained one of the highest in the world. According to his calculations, public investment grew tenfold between 1946 and 1957, while private investment grew fivefold, giving a high rate of capital formation in relation to GNP, the second highest in the world during that period, and predominantly attributable to public investment.[21]

The extent of government activity may also be judged from the range of enterprises established by colonial, state and federal governments, mostly in the form of public corporations. Fields of public enterprise, past and present, have included the following:

Acquisition and export of farm products
Air transport
Aluminium production
Bakeries
Banking
Brick and pipe making
Broadcasting
Clothing manufacture
Coal mining and briquette manufacture
Electricity generation and supply
Fisheries
Home building
Insurance
Manufacture of engineering equipment
Meat production and distribution
Oil refining
Port administration
Postal communications
Railways
Shipping and shipbuilding
Telecommunications

[19] A. T. Peacock and J. Wiseman, *The Growth of Public Expenditure in the United Kingdom*, Princeton, 1961, p. 66
[20] S. Fabricant, *The Trend of Government Activity in the United States Since 1900*, New York, 1952, p. 7. Cleveland wrote this in a veto message on an appropriation of $25,000 to buy seed corn for farmers in Texas, ruined by drought.
[21] B. U. Ratchford, *Public Expenditures in Australia*, Durham, NC, 1959, pp. 285-88

Timber milling
Tourism
Urban transport
Whaling

The Historical Background

To say that bureaucracy is a major force in Australian society is, in a sense, to say only that Australia is like the rest of the world, and that any historical differences in the growth of bureaucratic institutions have been eclipsed by world-wide developments since 1929, the year of the great depression. But this understates the extent of the bureaucratic ascendency in Australian society and blurs some of the specific historical and social aspects of the phenomenon.

The historical evolution of bureaucratic institutions and influences in Australia is strikingly different from its parallels in other societies. Weber was the first to appreciate the connection between bureaucratic administration and the growth of imperial power. In various ancient empires, bureaucracy was used by autocratic rulers to create a centralised, unified governmental system under their direct control, and to counteract the power of aristocratic, theocratic and other groups with separate claims to authority.[22] The rise of national states in Europe was followed by the deliberate use of bureaucracy as an agent of political and social centralisation. The Prussian bureaucracy was built up by Frederick William, the 'Great Elector', and his successors as the 'rock of bronze' on which the autocratic Prussian state was founded. In post-revolutionary France, the republican government and later Napoleon set out to create a new official elite, bureaucratically recruited and trained, to replace the aristocratic ruling class of the *ancien régime*.

Similarly, the movement towards political centralisation in Great Britain in the nineteenth century soon led to the establishment of the new civil service recommended by the Northcote-Trevelyan report of 1854. On the one hand, centralisation was due to urban growth at home and the consolidation of the empire overseas; on the other, it marked the coalescence of the aristocracy and the rising upper-middle class into a new governing elite. 'Imperial responsibilities, trade growth, and a rising population helped create the need for a central bureaucracy, characterised by . . . methods stressing merit as much as birth.'[23] As Laski wrote in 1943, the civil service was an expression of the 'compromise between capitalism and democracy which is the outcome of the last century or so of our history', and an agent of 'that powerful combination of landed aristocracy, professional men, and industrialists who have ruled Britain since 1832.'[24]

[22] S. N. Eisenstadt, *The Political Systems of Empires*, London, 1963, and *Essays on Comparative Institutions*, New York, 1965, ch. 8
[23] Rupert Wilkinson, *The Prefects*, London, 1964, p. 175
[24] Harold Laski, 'The Education of the Civil Servant', *Public Administration*, UK, vol. 21, no. 1, 1943

In Australia, however, the bureaucratic ascendency was established well before the real impact of political centralisation, which came with the 1939-45 war. Its characteristic features were laid down when Australia consisted of six scattered colonies, and even after federation in 1901 the central government played a comparatively restricted role. While the colonies were establishing their own methods of dealing with domestic problems, the British home government retained responsibility for defence, external relations and other central government functions, shedding them only gradually since federation. These influences contributed to the growth of a loosely articulated, decentralised structure of administration, aided by the political instability which was typical of colonial, state and federal politics alike until the 1920's.

The Bureaucratic Revolution: 1939 and After

The Second World War marked a watershed. For the first time, a national bureaucratic machine began to emerge in the shape of the Commonwealth Public Service, and to overshadow the dozens of semi-detached bureaucratic satrapies which had given Australian public administration its distinctive flavour for half a century.

Until the outbreak of the 1939-45 war, the spirit of the federal compact of the 1890's dominated the activities of the Commonwealth. Under that compact, the federating colonies gave away as little power as they could to the new central authority. For the first ten years of federation, the so-called 'Braddon clause' of the constitution, which required the federal government to return at least three-quarters of its revenue to the states, largely prevented the growth of administrative services. Subsequently, a combination of inter-state jealousies and the rigidity of the constitutional amendment procedure made it virtually impossible to enlarge the legal powers of the federal government. As a result, the unavoidable growth of central government authority which did take place was forced into extra-constitutional channels, and the net effect was to enhance the importance of bureaucratic devices in bringing about political change. Given the bureaucratic cast of Australian society and politics, this might well have happened anyway; still, it is remarkable how the actions of politicians conspired to stimulate it.

Until 1939, however, the progress of events was fitful and erratic. The conservative coalitions which dominated federal politics between 1916 and 1941 showed little inclination to interpret their powers broadly. In consequence, Hancock could write in 1930 that 'the average citizen looks more frequently to the Government which sits in Melbourne or Adelaide than to the Government which sits in Canberra. It is this closer, more intimate Government which . . . performs all those functions which seem to affect most nearly his economic and social well-being.'[25]

A temporary enlargement of Commonwealth activities occurred during

[25] W. K. Hancock, op. cit., pp. 64-65

the 1914-18 war and in the years immediately afterwards, especially under the influence of Prime Minister W. M. Hughes, but the political and economic stagnation of the period between the wars, which afflicted Australia as it did other countries, was also reflected in the administrative sphere. In the 1920's, the size of the Commonwealth service remained static, and its functions were extended only gingerly in one or two directions such as health, the overseas marketing of primary products, and scientific research. (The Institute for Science and Industry, modelled on the British DSIR, was set up in 1921, and was succeeded in 1926 by the Council for Scientific and Industrial Research.) The depression of the 1930's found the Commonwealth government with virtually no machinery of its own for planning or executing measures to deal with unemployment and social distress. Policy was made in a curiously decentralised fashion by bodies like the Arbitration Court, the Commonwealth Bank and the Premiers' Conference. The Lyons government, in office from 1932 to 1939, was notoriously *fainéant* and ineffective. Although it appointed one of its members, Frederick Stewart, to deal specifically with unemployment in 1934, he was given the status of 'Under-Secretary', which has no real place in the Australian Cabinet system. With no staff, and without even the right to answer questions in parliament, Stewart's position remained anomalous and uncomfortable, and he resigned after sticking it out for a year.[26] Commonwealth administration began to expand in the late thirties under the combined influence of unemployment, social unrest and the gathering storm of war, but this growth was quite eclipsed by the unparalleled expansion of functions that came as the result of total war. Although the checks and balances imposed by a federal constitution continued to operate, the Commonwealth moved into a position of comprehensive control over the life of a virtually unified state. After the war, moreover, this great enlargement of the Commonwealth bureaucracy became a permanent feature of the political and social scene. It is a major component of the 'changed balance of the constitution' which was lamented for years by conservative politicians, judges and writers, just as it was welcomed by the radical intelligentsia and the Labor movement.[27] Before 1939, the federal government had not employed its superior financial resources to prod the states towards policies of economic expansion or administrative improvement. On the contrary, it had refused approaches from the states for financial support in such projects. In 1936, for example, the Commonwealth turned down a scheme of assistance to technical education put forward jointly by all the states. After 1939, and especially as a result of the policies of the Curtin and Chifley governments, the Commonwealth became directly or indirectly responsible for policy in most areas of government—foreign affairs, defence, public works, economic planning, taxation, social security, health, immigration, industrial relations,

[26] S. Encel, *Cabinet Government in Australia*, Melbourne, 1962, pp. 272-73
[27] E. J. B. Foxcroft, 'The Changing Balance of Government in Australia', *Public Administration*, vol. 6, no. 4, 1946

long-distance transport, etc.—leaving the states largely dependent upon decisions by the Commonwealth for the execution of their own positive functions.[28]

The quantitative impact of these changes may readily be illustrated. Table 5·1 illustrates the growth of Commonwealth functions since federation.[29]

Table 5·1 Growth of Commonwealth Activities

Date	Number of Departments	Number of Public Corporations	Total Employees	Total Outlay (£m)
1901	7	—	11,000	4
1939	14	4	68,000	83
1946	25	8	150,000	391
1965	25	15	350,000*	2,015

* Includes defence forces and territorial services.

Table 5·2, on the other hand, shows the different pattern of growth at the state level, including the greatly increased dependence of the states on federal grants and income tax reimbursements.

Table 5·2 Growth of State Government Activities

Date	Total Expenditure (£m)	Total Employment	Federal Payments (£m)
1901	29	75,000	7
1939	136	276,000	15
1946	181	326,000	72
1965	1,001	550,000	494

In proportionate terms, Commonwealth employees constituted less than one-fifth of all government servants in 1939, and were considerably fewer in number than the employees of the NSW state government. By 1946, they accounted for almost one-third of all government employment, and the proportion has declined only slightly since then (30 per cent in 1967). Between 1939 and 1946, in other words, Commonwealth employment increased by 220 per cent, and it continued to climb at a comparable rate until 1951, when it reached 206,000, i.e. an increase of 300 per cent over

---

[28] For an analysis of the expansion of Commonwealth functions since 1939, see S. Encel, et al, 'Papers on Commonwealth Machinery of Government', *Public Administration*, vol. 17, no. 4, 1958; A. F. Davies, *Australian Democracy*, pp. 4-14; R. S. Parker, 'Structure and Functions of Government', in R. N. Spann (ed.), *Public Administration in Australia*, Sydney, 1959; G. E. Caiden, *The Commonwealth Bureaucracy*, Melbourne, 1967

[29] The figures given in Tables 5.1 and 5.2 are derived from the Commonwealth Year Book and the annual Australian National Accounts. State expenditure figures also include local government activities.

1939. (In the same period, the Australian population increased by about one-third.) After 1951, the rate of growth tapered off to a secular increase averaging 4 per cent per year. In 1967, there were 290,000 civilian Commonwealth employees in Australia, representing 7·5 per cent of the total Australian work force.

These figures refer to *total* Commonwealth employment, which embraces the 'public service' proper as well as the employees of the various public corporations and statutory commissions who are not, technically, 'public servants'. Following the universal Australian pattern, the existence of the Commonwealth Public Service depends on a statute, the Public Service Act, which establishes a unified civil service under the control of a central personnel authority, the Public Service Board. This is composed of three members appointed for statutory terms, with jurisdiction extending to all departmental employees. Public corporations and statutory commissions have control over their own staff, except that since 1947 their personnel codes have required Public Service Board approval. Although there has been a large increase in the number of boards and commissions since 1939, the growth of the Commonwealth Public Service is more remarkable. In 1939, the CPS numbered 47,000, of whom no less than 35,000 were employed by one department, the Post Office. In the peak year of 1951, its numbers were 156,000; after a temporary recession, growth resumed, and in 1967 the number was 203,000. The Post Office's share has dropped from three-quarters of the CPS before the war to a little over half in the post-war period. Other sectors of administration where notable expansion has occurred are defence, where employment grew from 1300 in the single Defence Department of 1939 to 24,000 persons (other than military personnel) in five separate departments in 1967; finance, where the Treasury, the Taxation Department and the Bureau of Census and Statistics employed almost 15,000 persons in 1967 as compared with a little over 2,000 in 1939; Civil Aviation, which accounted for 240 persons in 1939 compared with nearly 7,000 in 1967; and External Affairs, which grew from a tiny office with a staff of 30 in 1939 to an establishment of over 1800 in 1967.

These figures represent a 'bureaucratic revolution'. On a smaller scale, the phenomenon may be compared with the enormous impact of the New Deal on American government and society. Like the New Deal, it arose from the practical application of ideas about government intervention in social and economic affairs, worked out between 1890 and 1920 by liberal and socialist thinkers and brought together in the great Keynesian synthesis. As in Britain, it was the shock of total war and the needs of reconstruction which brought about the swift and spectacular readjustment of attitudes that made this revolution possible. A decision of the High Court in 1942, giving the Commonwealth a virtual monopoly of income taxing powers, and a constitutional amendment of 1946, which provided the legal basis for a wide range of 'welfare state' legislation, were landmarks in this process. Even more important was the adoption, as the settled policy of the country, of a program of full employment and economic expansion, enshrined in a White Paper published a few weeks after the end of the war in Europe. The philosophy of this White Paper was expressed by one of its principal authors, Dr H. C. Coombs, in an address given in 1944. 'The principle upon which a full employment economy can be built is the replacement over a substantial field of economic activity of individual decisions by social decisions. Decisions as to how labour, materials, equipment are to be used will be made or influenced increasingly by public authorities rather than by individuals even though those resources and equipment may continue to be owned and operated by private enterprise . . . [there will be] an increasing responsibility on the Government for the allocation of resources, the prime purpose of which will be the achievement of social objectives, of a high and stable level of employment, of rising standards of living for all people, of the development of our national resources and security and opportunity for the individual.'[30]

The adoption of policies of economic growth, full employment, and large-scale immigration did not come about without some painful readjustments of outlook at the political level. Indeed, it could be argued that politicians as a whole have never readjusted themselves to the activities of the politico-social situation in Australia since 1939, and that the social revolution initiated during the war has remained an essentially bureaucratic one. One important exception is the case of immigration policy, which gradually became an article of faith among a variety of groups for whom its implications were originally uncongenial. The trade union movement and the Labor Party, traditionally suspicious of large-scale immigration as a threat to the living standards of the working class, came to accept immigration policy as a guarantee of economic expansion. The Liberal Party and its middle class supporters, while not hostile to immigration *per se*, were uncomfortable about some of its economic concomitants and the high level of government intervention required to maintain them. Supporters of all parties were reluctant to accept the conclusion, which became evident at an early stage after the war, that a high rate of immigration could only be maintained by an active policy of seeking migrants outside the British Isles, from which 90 per cent of pre-war migration had come. The result of this policy is that only one-third of postwar migration has come from Great Britain and Ireland, bringing a significant shift in the ethnic and social composition of the Australian community.

The impact of the bureaucratic revolution and its consequent social changes on the structure of administration is discussed at greater length in a subsequent chapter.[31]

[30] H. C. Coombs, 'The Economic Aftermath of War' in D. A. S. Campbell (ed.), *Post-War Reconstruction in Australia*, Sydney, 1944, pp. 97-99
[31] See below, ch. 12

The Bureaucrat and Society

'They lurk in every Gov'ment lair,
'Mid docket and dusty file,
Solemnly squat in an easy chair,
Penning a minute of rare hot air
In Departmental style.'

C. J. Dennis, *The Glugs of Gosh*

In France, another country where the disjunction between politics and bureaucracy takes extreme forms, it is proverbial that the most important member of the government is a certain 'M. Lebureau'. In Australia, as in France, the importance of the same gentleman helps to generate a persistent ambiguity about the bureaucratic career and the influence of permanent officials on policy and administration. This ambiguity, reinforced by vulgar prejudice, has also influenced a great deal of writing in history, economics, and politics, so that the contribution of individual officials towards the shaping of Australian society and some of its major institutions is widely under-estimated. Noel Butlin has observed that economic history would read very differently if it were written to take proper account of the part played by officials. A similar judgment is expressed by a student of public administration who speaks of the 'tribe of selfless devoted public servants which has existed throughout Australia's administrative history, men eminently capable of handling crises, domineering towards intellectual inferiors, and used to thinking ahead, to creating models, and to evolving principles.'[32]

The history of administration in the states is punctuated by the careers of such outstanding individuals who have become identified in the public eye with the policies which they administered and usually created. Thus, educational policy in Victoria is identified with the name of Frank Tate[33] and in NSW with those of Peter Board and Harold Wyndham. The building of railways, of great bridges, of water supply projects, electricity generating enterprises and the like is associated with names like Speight, O'Connor, Bradfield, Hudson and Monash. In other cases, leading officials have become dominant figures over the whole range of state administration, occupying positions of much greater political importance than their transient political superiors, like J. D. Story, in Queensland, and Wallace Wurth in NSW. Wurth, in particular, who occupied the key post of chairman of the Public Service Board for over twenty years, was known in his lifetime as the uncrowned king of NSW. He served under six premiers and was principal adviser to each of them in turn, his closest relationship being with W. J. McKell, Labor Premier from 1941 to 1946, who wrote of him as 'an inspiration to a remarkable group of public servants.'[34] A less

[32] G. E. Caiden, *Career Service*, Melbourne, 1965, p. 72
[33] J. O. Anchen, *Frank Tate and his Work for Education*, Melbourne, 1956, esp. ch. 6
[34] *Public Administration*, Wurth memorial issue, vol. 20, no. 1, 1961

flattering picture of Wurth's personality and methods was given in the fortnightly review *Nation* two years after his death:

As a career man, a typical public servant feels about a politician somewhat as a man of property about a huckster, or a rentier about a speculator; he has no need to go into the open market. Taking advantage of his special prerogatives at the Public Service Board, Wurth showed the others how to put politicians in their place. Politicians found more than once that transfers of medium grade public servants from one department to another or promotions within their own ministries were turned into the subject of bargaining by this supreme arbiter. . . . Wurth said he had discovered that Ministers are often out of step with the policies of their own government, and the thing to do was to complain to the head of the government. For his own part, Wallace Wurth put it on record that the head of the government had always agreed with him against a minister.[35]

The economic policies adopted by the federal Labor governments of 1941-49, which formed the basis of the post-war economy, were worked out entirely by official advisers, some of whom, especially during the war, were academic economists working in temporary capacities. The process began at the state level, when several state governments looked for ways of relieving unemployment during the 1930's. The Premier of NSW, Bertram Stevens (himself a former Treasury official), recruited several economists both as full-time officials and part-time advisers; most of them worked for the Commonwealth government during the war. In South Australia, economic recovery was initiated by a government official, J. W. Wainright, who held the rather surprising office of Auditor-General. In his first annual report (1935), Wainright used his introductory remarks to assert that the predominantly agricultural economy of the state could recover from the blight of unemployment only if the government embarked on a policy of industrialisation, and he continued to use his annual report as a platform from which to exhort the government. The message was quickly taken up, and in 1937 the Premier, Sir Richard Butler, announced that he was examining the possibility of appointing Wainright as an economic adviser. 'We would rather', he declared, 'have Mr. Wainright in that position than many professors of economics' (a reference to both NSW and Queensland, the latter having appointed first Professor J. B. Brigden and then Colin Clark to head its Bureau of Industry). In the event, an Industries Assistance Corporation was set up with Wainright as government representative.[36]

The most fertile source of ideas and policies during this period was the Department of Post-War Reconstruction, which existed from 1942 to 1950 and was staffed by a remarkable mixture of talents. At its peak of activity, it contained some thirty people concerned with research and policy, most of whom had subsequent careers of distinction either in the public service or

---

[35] *Nation*, 22 September 1962
[36] T. J. Mitchell, 'J. W. Wainright: The Industrialisation of South Australia 1935-40', *Australian Journal of Politics and History*, vol. 8, no. 1, 1962

the universities.[37] From this department came schemes for immigration, housing, health, social welfare, higher education, research, town and regional planning, agriculture, government support of the arts and many other matters. The department was, naturally and inevitably, derided by the press and by the Liberal opposition in parliament as a home for long-haired professors and doctrinaire socialists, many of whom, nevertheless, became senior public servants under a Liberal government. Its most important product was probably the aforesaid White Paper on Full Employment, tabled in Federal parliament on 30 May 1945. The preparation of this document was centred in the Department of Post-War Reconstruction, although it involved the combined labours of some twenty economists from various departments, and required eight drafts before it was published. This document laid down the policy of economic expansion, fed by industrialisation and immigration, and depending upon government initiative, which has been the motor of social change in Australia since 1945.

The importance of the bureaucrat in the political process is affected, among other things, by the number of officials who have moved from the bureaucratic to the political spheres. This movement is rendered easier by legislation, operative in the Commonwealth and some states, which makes it possible for government officials to stand for parliamentary election without losing their official status. The majority of these men have been officers of public service unions, such as the Amalgamated Postal Workers' Union or the Federated Clerks Union, who naturally find themselves in the Labor Party, but there has always been a proportion of senior officials who move into politics, most of them on the Liberal side. Sir Bertram Stevens, Premier of NSW from 1932 to 1939, was a former head of the state Treasury Department. W. R. Lawrence, deputy Police Commissioner in NSW, was a Liberal member of the state Legislative Assembly from 1952 to 1961; his successor, G. L. Smith, stood (unsuccessfully) as a Liberal candidate in 1962. In the Liberal governments of the 1950's and 1960's there were two former senior Commonwealth officials. Paul Hasluck, originally a diplomat, became a minister in 1951 and completed the circle by becoming Minister for External Affairs in 1965; Leslie Bury, a senior Treasury official and a director of the International Monetary Fund, resigned to enter politics in 1956 and became a minister in 1961. From 1939 to 1965, a total of sixty-seven former officials sat in the Federal parliament, forty-six from state government service and twenty-one from the Commonwealth service. Fifty-six of these belonged to the Australian Labor Party, sixteen to the Liberal Party (or its predecessor, the UAP), four to the Country Party, and one was a former ALP man who had joined the Democratic Labor Party after the Labor split of 1955.[38]

The general tone of the press and of public comment about 'bureaucracy', 'red tape', and the 'government stroke' (the latter derived from the

[37] See below, ch. 13
[38] G. E. Caiden, *The Commonwealth Bureaucracy*, ch. 7

habits of day labourers on public construction jobs) suggests that Australians are hostile to bureaucracy and its works. It would be nearer the truth to say that the prevailing attitude is one of ambiguity. As Davies remarks, although Australians have a talent for bureaucracy, they are a bit shamefaced about it. The results of public opinion polls illustrate some of these ambiguities and contradictions. In July 1948 the Australian Gallup Poll (APOP) asked respondents: 'If two jobs had the same wages and conditions, but one was with the Government and the other in a private business, which would you choose?' Private employment was preferred by 47 per cent, public by 44 per cent, and 5 per cent saw no difference. Manual workers and Labor voters preferred public employment; Liberal and Country Party voters favoured private (ALP, 57 per cent in favour of public; Liberal-CP, 63 per cent in favour of private). These figures underline the division of opinion and certainly do not suggest an overwhelming antipathy to bureaucracy. Another poll, taken ten years later, used a somewhat different version of the question. In April 1958 respondents were asked: 'Which career would you recommend to your son?' The professions were favoured by 36 per cent, skilled trades by 29 per cent, farming by 13 per cent, the Commonwealth public service by 9 per cent, and the state public services by 3 per cent. The relatively low preference for the public services is not, however, as straightforward as it may appear, as the most important characteristic sought in these careers was security, by an overwhelming 72 per cent (against 16 per cent who designated 'future income')—in other words, the very characteristic which makes government employment attractive to so many.

Courts, Commissions and Policemen

The bureaucratic ascendency is supported by the social role of the law and the judiciary. The development of the legal profession in Australia has yet to be the subject of scholarly investigation, and in the absence of such study only fairly general remarks can be made. It is clear, however, that the universal prestige of the law, which is as strong in Australia as elsewhere, is consolidated and intensified by certain features of Australian society. Its historical and institutional character is, of course, an extension of the English common law system. To this are added the special politico-legal consequences of written constitutions in the states and the Commonwealth, including the complications of federalism. As the English constitutional authority, A. V. Dicey, wrote many years ago, federalism means conservatism and legalism; and both predictions have been amply verified in Australia. The federal constitution, and especially its notorious Section 92, has proved a gold-mine to the legal profession and given judges recurring opportunities to act as legislators, especially in defence of private property. The American constitutional lawyer, E. S. Corwin, wrote some years ago that the constitution of the United States had become what the judges of the Supreme Court say it is.[39] The same has been largely true of

[39] E. S. Corwin, *The Twilight of the Supreme Court*, New York, 1938

Australia since the early years of judicial interpretation of the constitution. As early as 1935, for instance, Sir Owen Dixon, later Chief Justice from 1952 to 1964, gave a dissenting judgment which meant that the real import of Section 92 was the protection of private property from government interference, and this became the prevailing doctrine of the High Court from 1947 onwards.[40]

The relation between the political and legal systems thus takes on a special significance. As we shall see in Chapter 10, lawyers in parliament have by far the best chance of becoming cabinet ministers. But even a minister, especially if he becomes Attorney-General, may continue his career on the bench, and some lawyer-parliamentarians proceed straight to the bench without holding a portfolio. Others may be appointed as a reward for political activity, e.g. in standing for a parliamentary seat without success.

J. D. Playford has endeavoured to collect a comprehensive list of judges in various jurisdictions who had been involved in politics.[41] Altogether, he found eighty cases over a period of a century, twelve before 1900, thirty-two between 1900 and 1930, and thirty-six since 1930. Forty-two of them had gone on to the bench directly from a parliamentary seat and/or a ministerial portfolio. A further eighteen had been unsuccessful candidates for parliament or for parliamentary selection, just half of these in the Labor interest, and one had been chairman of the party organisation in South Australia. Thirteen had been appointed to the High Court of Australia, thirty-nine to state Supreme Courts, and thirteen to industrial benches; twenty-three were chief justices or presidents, including all but two of the seven chief justices of the High Court between 1903 and 1965.

The High Court has, indeed, the most political character of all courts. Of the twenty-two justices who sat on the bench from 1903 to the end of 1964, one was a former Prime Minister (Barton); one, a former colonial premier (Sir Samuel Griffith, first Chief Justice); and six had been Attorneys-General, four in the federal government. The most political of all judges was the late Dr H. V. Evatt, who was a Labor member of the NSW state parliament in the 1920's, a judge from 1931 to 1940, and a member of the federal parliament from 1940 to 1960, during which time he was Attorney-General and Minister for External Affairs from 1941 to 1949, and leader of the Parliamentary ALP from 1951 to 1960, when he became Chief Justice of NSW. The court has been dominated by the NSW and Victorian Bars. Eleven judges during this period came from NSW, eight from Victoria, and three from Queensland. However, it is socially the most heterogeneous of all higher courts in Australia. Unlike the legal

[40] Geoffrey Sawer, 'The Constitution and its Politics', in Henry Mayer (ed.), *Australian Politics*, 1st ed., Melbourne, 1966
The political role of the High Court is also discussed by E. G. Whitlam, *Labour and the Constitution*, Melbourne, 1965
[41] John Playford, 'Judges and Politics in Australia', APSA *News*, vol. 6, no. 3, 1961 and vol. 7, no. 2, 1962

profession as a whole, which has a strongly hereditary character and is dominated by the exclusive Protestant private schools, the social background of its members is much more varied. Less than one-half of the twenty-two judges attended schools of this type; three were products of the oldest-established state school in NSW, Fort Street Boys' High School —Sir Edmund Barton (1903-20), Dr Evatt and Sir Garfield Barwick (Chief Justice since 1964). Two were Catholics. Three came from old-established legal families (Gavan Duffy, Owen, Windeyer), and two others have helped to establish legal dynasties—Evatt and Menzies.

The superior courts as a whole, i.e. the state Supreme Courts plus the High Court, reflect the upper-middle class, Protestant, establishment character of the Bar in general. Douglas, in a brief analysis of the Supreme Court of Victoria during the ten years 1958-68, found that of twenty-two judges, twelve had attended Headmasters Conference schools; four had been to other Protestant private schools; four to Catholic schools; one to a state secondary school.[42] A similar picture emerges from an examination of the seven superior courts. Details were obtained about 104 judges who had sat on the bench from 1930 to 1962. Of these, eighty had attended Protestant private schools, sixty-five of them HMC schools; thirty-two, Catholic schools; twenty-four, state secondary schools. Fourteen were the sons of judges. Fifty-four had held commissioned rank in the army. All but six of the Catholics came from NSW and Queensland, where the long predominance of the Labor Party has given it many opportunities to appoint judges. In NSW, and to a lesser extent in Queensland, there are significant Catholic sections of the legal profession, and Catholic lawyers have figured in NSW Labor politics for many years.

Lawyers have also figured prominently in the working of royal commissions. From 1930 to 1960, for instance, no less than forty-five royal commissions and special committees of inquiry were appointed by the Commonwealth, eleven by NSW and ten by Victoria, covering six main fields—industry, the working of government bodies, finance, constitutional and political questions, legislation, and the affairs of special groups of people. Altogether, 128 men sat on these bodies, of whom nineteen were judges and fourteen were lawyers either in private practice or employed by governments. The other large group were public officials (including eight lawyers), forty in all. Thus, sixty per cent of the men charged with using the investigatory powers of the state were judges, lawyers or bureaucrats who in their turn would be required to interpret, administer and adjudicate the policies which evolved from their investigations.

The system of industrial arbitration has a similarly legalistic and judicial character, which has been discussed at length by many students of the subject. Here, we shall content ourselves with noticing how the legalism of the system is bound up with its personnel. From 1905 to 1961, the Commonwealth Arbitration Commission (Court until 1956) operated

[42] R. N. Douglas, 'Courts in the Political System', *Melbourne Journal of Politics*, no. 1, 1968

through a total of fifty-three judges and commissioners. Of these, twenty-one came from the bench, eleven from the bar, and fourteen had been state or Commonwealth government officials.

Finally, we may reflect briefly on Australian attitudes to the police, the most junior and yet for people at large the most familiar and the most threatening aspect of official authority. There is a widespread view in Australia that relations are especially bad. 'Relations between the police and the public', writes an Australian journalist, 'are probably worse in Australia than anywhere else in the world.'[43] The implicit comparison in this and similar statements is traditionally with Britain, and is probably correct, although in the present generation one must also allow for the effect of television programs in generating an 'image' of the British police which is not necessarily accurate in all particulars. It would be difficult to sustain the comparison in detail if one chose, instead, the police forces of the United States, France, or Germany. It is perhaps more relevant to note that the police themselves have a conception of their role which extends beyond the elementary one of maintaining order. A British visitor, himself an ex-police inspector, was struck by this. 'I said at a public meeting in Melbourne,' writes Mr C. H. Rolph, 'that the police, in every country I had seen, had lost essential contact with the law-abiding public and were least loved where the laws they had to enforce were the most unpopular. You could hardly be more platitudinous. But the next day I was slapped down in a press statement by Mr Arnold, the Commissioner of Police for Victoria, and Sir Arthur Rylah, Chief Secretary to the Government. Police-and-public relations in Victoria, they said, were fine. I wish they could have heard public comment on that.'[44] An illustration of the broad view of police functions was provided by the secretary of the Police Association in Victoria, who contended in a published article in 1967 that the police had a right not only to interpret the law on obscene literature but to make the law. Police, he declared, were better equipped than other people to assess the average tastes of the average citizen because they rubbed shoulders with him constantly, and should therefore be represented on a proposed new literary censorship board.[45] In another instance, where the case of an aborigine named Stuart, condemned to death for murder, was being investigated by a royal commission in South Australia, various policemen made public statements attacking the motives of Stuart's lawyers and supporters. The premier of South Australia, defending the police while the case was still being heard, declared in parliament that 'no honourable member would accept that . . . a man had been forced to confess . . . by having a confession bashed out of him.'[46]

Police attitudes towards censorship are clearly similar to those of the Customs officials who are concerned with examining imported books to see

[43] Craig McGregor, *Profile of Australia*, London, 1966, p. 81
[44] *New Statesman*, 10 January 1969
[45] *Australian*, 7 April 1967
[46] K. S. Inglis, *The Stuart Case*, Melbourne, 1961, p. 161

if they are obscene. An obsession with 'purity' has led, in this case, to a number of bizarre incidents which are difficult to believe unless one allows for the strength of the bureaucratic ascendency which makes this kind of paternalist authoritarianism possible. H. G. Wells, visiting Australia in 1938, was struck by the vigilance of the 'barrier of illiterate policemen' who were fondly protecting their countrymen from obscenity.[47] Wells, however, was mistaken. Vigilance in this case is due to zeal and a conviction that people in legal authority have a social duty to preserve moral standards.[48] This zeal is fed by Catholic puritanism, particularly strong in the Customs Department where there is a large number of Catholic officials, but other religious groups have similar attitudes. The magazine *Playboy* is not banned as such, but individual issues are banned when they contain nude pictures which are regarded as offensive. Clearly, the responsible officials have a strong sense of duty which compels them to read each issue of *Playboy* with great care.

The following letter, apparently from a retired Customs official, was published in the daily press in 1968. The writer declared that

We, who support our leaders' wise provisions to prevent the pollution of this country . . . do not do this for ourselves . . . it is for the young, to keep them in their innocence, that we have laboured and will continue to expose ourselves to temptation. . . . How many of your readers have actually felt the blood pounding to their heads, the trembling of their hands, the shortening of their breath, all the painful excitement that pornography would induce in them if they were permitted to see it? . . . As a young man and new to the job (fresh from a good church school) I was often obsessed and unhealthily excited for days . . . if we, now mature and one would hope inured against their vile charms, should still be disturbed by 'frank' films and provocative advertisements for feminine undergarments, how can the young (whose blood is more tempestuous than ours) cope with real pornography?[49]

Bureaucracy and Equality

The ambiguity of Australian attitudes towards authority, and bureaucratic authority in particular, is itself a reflection of the paradox that the quest for equality has been satisfied to such a large extent by the establishment of bureaucratic institutions. Equality and authority, egalitarianism and authoritarianism, are twin sides of one coin. In some situations, the show of authority is resented and informal manners are at a premium; in others, formality, deference, and badges of authority are essential. McCallum asserts that Australians have a generally authoritarian outlook, manifested in repressive attitudes towards children, ambivalence towards the police,

---

[47] H. G. Wells, *Travels of a Republican Radical in Search of Hot Water*, London, 1939

[48] McGregor, op. cit., ch. 3, gives a detailed account of police and customs activity in the field of censorship.

[49] *Australian*, 9 February 1968. The letter was signed 'James Flanagan, customs officer, retired', and gave a Melbourne address.

and generalised deference towards superiors or hostility towards inferiors.[50] Informality in general social relations does not extend to the conduct of public authority, which is one of the obvious differences between Australia and the United States. In government offices, formality of dress and demeanour has always been essential and has yielded only slightly to the general increase in permissive behaviour. By contrast with policemen in many large American cities, the police in Australia place great emphasis on a military style of smartness and discipline. The influence of militarism on society, discussed in later chapters of this book, denotes a much greater acceptance of formal, regimented authority than the conventional stress on egalitarianism would suggest. The persistence of the honours system, also discussed in a later chapter, bears witness to a widespread craving for an ordered system of rank and deference. Australians are great wearers of badges, as if the outward show of membership in some organisation or other helps to establish a visible identity. The price of institutionalised equality is institutionalised authority.

[50] D. M. McCallum, in P. Coleman (ed.), *Australian Civilisation*, Melbourne, 1962, pp. 33-34

6: Class, Status and Power in Australia

It is sometimes said that in Australia there are no class distinctions. It would probably be truer to say that in no country in the world are there such strong class distinctions in proportion to the actual amount of difference between the classes . . . the snobberies and meannesses of old-world society do not perish in the fierce southern sunlight.

P. F. Rowland, *The New Nation*, 1903

The conventional wisdom which, until recently, interpreted Australian social history as the working out of the egalitarian radicalism of the nineteenth century, came under sustained attack from a number of writers in the 1950's and 1960's. The historians were first in the field. This 'dead level' theory, writes one of them, 'although supported by the democratic cast of Australian institutions and by a relatively mediocre achievement in the life of the spirit [is] based on two misconceptions, that Australian history was unrelievedly democratic, and that democracy was necessarily hostile to distinction.'[1] Another historian, Hartley Grattan, contends that the part played by oligarchic and authoritarian elements was consistently undervalued for many years and that Australia is, in most respects, a representative creation of nineteenth century capitalism, peculiar in that a relatively small part was played by the middle class in the shaping of its institutions, which were the result of conflicts between the working class and various oligarchic groups.[2]

A similar point is made by another American, the sociologist Kurt Mayer, who visited Australia in the 1960's. Comparing the two countries, he points out that American society was characterised, from the outset, by the predominance of the middle classes. 'In comparison with contemporary European societies America's early social hierarchy appeared like a truncated pyramid; lacking both an hereditary aristocracy and a peasantry in the European sense, the broad middle class of independent producers was the dominant stratum socially and economically, if not politically. . . . It was this middle class society which gave birth to democratic political institutions and to a philosophy of equalitarianism . . . the image of America as a society where "everybody is middle class"

[1] R. M. Crawford, *An Australian Perspective*, Wisconsin, 1960
[2] C. Hartley Grattan, *The Southwest Pacific to 1900*, Ann Arbor, 1963, ch. 17; and see also his earlier essay in Grattan (ed.), *Australia*, Berkeley, 1947, at pp. 273-75

persisted through periods when it was no longer in accordance with economic and social reality.'[3] By contrast with the US, he concludes, the beginnings of Australian society were not formed by a rural middle class, and its 'militant egalitarianism' is the result of working-class predominance at the crucial stages of social development. The difference between the United States and Australia in the nineteenth century was noticed by that astute observer Sir Charles Dilke, who thought that 'the line between classes, as regards social intercourse, is somewhat more sharply drawn than in the newer parts of British America or of the United States.'[4] Untypically, Dilke concluded that there was *less* egalitarianism in Australia than in the back country of Canada and the US. Francis Adams saw the middle class as doomed to be crushed between the contending forces of capital and labour: 'The trend of things is relentlessly towards huge monopolies of capital and labour, and these petty intermediate classes, striving to combine a little of both, are foredoomed to failure and ultimate extinction.'[5] Another Englishman, R. E. N. Twopeny, made a more searching comment when he noted that, within the middle classes, lower-middle and upper-middle were much less distinct than in England. 'They come more freely and frequently, indeed continually, into contact with each other. This is excellent for the former, but not so good for the latter.'[6]

Travellers' Tales

The conventional wisdom about class and status in Australia is to be found in a long succession of one-volume studies, mostly written by visitors from abroad, who aspired to sum up the essence of a complex community in an array of more or less subjective assessments. 'Simple census data, select political trends, "common knowledge" and a little participant observation were thought enough to establish a country's class structure.'[7] The visitors were no doubt influenced by the views of local worthies, as de Tocqueville was by Judge Story, but the reciprocal influence was probably even greater. Apart from asserting the relative weakness of the middle classes, the received version contains two other elements: (i) the dominant role of wealth as the denominator of class position; (ii) the great strength of class-consciousness despite (or perhaps because of) the plutocratic nature of the class system. The most systematic of these accounts was given by Lord Bryce, who visited Australia shortly before the 1914-18 war. Bryce was famous for having produced, in his major work *The American Commonwealth*, the successor to de

---

[3] Kurt B. Mayer, 'Social Stratification in two Equalitarian Societies: Australia and the US', *Social Research*, vol. 31, no. 4, 1964
[4] Sir Charles Dilke, *Problems of Greater Britain*, London, 1890, vol. 2, p. 232
[5] Francis Adams, *The Australians*, London, 1893, p. 164
[6] R. E. N. Twopeny, *Town Life in Australia*, London, 1883, p. 90
[7] A. F. Davies, *Images of Class*, Sydney, 1967, p. 1

Tocqueville's classic, and his slighter account of Australia contains a number of comparisons, explicit and implicit, with North America. For one thing, there was no populist movement aimed at great concentrations of wealth. 'The fortunes of the rich are not sufficient either to sharpen the contrast between social extremes or to make possible those vast accumulations of capital which are in the United States denounced as a political danger. Neither does wealth flaunt itself: no stately mansions in the country, no sumptuous palaces in the cities, and as the wealth is all new, it has not had time enough to turn itself into rank.'[8]

Reflecting on the paradox of intense class-consciousness in a community where social differences were smaller than either Western Europe or North America, Bryce ascribed this to the jealousy aroused by the passion for equality, which was actually stimulated by the relative weakness of forms of social inequality other than wealth. Precisely because there was nothing but a cash nexus between the employer and the working man, there was less social intercourse between them than in Britain. 'The sentiment of social equality is extremely strong, for there were hardly any distinctions of rank to begin with, and such habits of deference as had belonged in Europe did not attach themselves to those whose only claim was a more rapid rise towards wealth. . . . The passion for equality has induced social jealousy. There is no such deep gulf fixed between classes as that which divides "bourgeoisie" and "proletariat" in France, but there is a feeling of latent antagonism or suspicion, an apparent belief among the workers that the interests of the richer and those of the poorer must be mutually opposed. No similar feeling has existed in Great Britain or in the native population of Canada or of the United States.'[9] Only in France, in fact, did class antagonism have a more potent effect in dividing the community into warring sectional groups. 'Where other distinctions are absent', Bryce concluded, 'and a few years can lift a man from nothing to affluence, differences in wealth are emphasised and resented . . . the more because they often seem . . . due to no special merit in their possessor.'[10]

Bryce then proceeds to construct a map of the class system, in which he distinguished three tiers:
(i) Wage-earners and poorer people
(ii) Landowners and the wealthier members of the commercial class
(iii) Professional men
Among these three groups, Bryce discerned some interesting qualitative differences in class-consciousness. Class (i), 'the mass', were unconcerned with long-term issues of a political or economic character, and were 'content to fall in with views that seem to make for the immediate benefit of their class.' Class (ii), the 'richer people', were 'more sharply cut off from the wage-earners than is the like class in Switzerland or Canada or Norway.' Like the masses, however, they 'contributed little to the practice

8 James Bryce, *Modern Democracies*, London, 1921, vol. 2, p. 186
9 ibid., pp. 197-98
10 ibid., p. 273

or the theory of statesmanship.' About his third class—the men 'occupied in study, thinking, and teaching'—he seems to have had some doubts. Despite their different role in society, they 'belonged socially to the mercantile class', and their influence on public affairs and the formation of a national opinion was less than might be expected.[11]

Bryce's account is memorable for two reasons. He was perceptive enough to notice the special status of professional men in Australia but failed to realise that it did not square with his picture of a class structure based only on pecuniary differences. It is also surprising, in view of his American experiences, that he says so little about the influence of religion. His other contribution was the attempt to resolve the paradox of intense class-consciousness in an egalitarian community where social differences were allegedly so small. The paradox was less troublesome to another English visitor of the same period, P. F. Rowland, who recognised that egalitarianism applied more strongly in some areas of social life than in others. Despite the fact that class distinctions were drawn on 'more purely plutocratic lines than is the case either in England or America', they were a fact to be reckoned with in everyday life. 'The fact that in Australia "sir" is seldom heard, that a "lady" does the washing, and a "gentleman" is behind the bar, does not in the least mean that class distinctions are non-existent. The "classes" cannot extract deference from the "masses"; but neither can the "masses" exact social recognition from the "classes".' The middle classes, he thought, were remarkable for their dislike of the masses, and he attributed the relative failure of voluntary social welfare work to make headway in Australia because of the antipathy of the professional and commercial classes to this kind of contact with the poor and deprived.[12] Twopeny had earlier deplored the 'utter selfishness' of the plutocracy, which did not interest itself in the social duties that were proving 'so effectual a prop to the nobility and landed gentry of England'.[13]

These views were echoed in one of the early attempts at a social profile to be written by an Australian, C. H. Northcott's *Australian Social Development*. Northcott, a tutor in sociology for the Workers' Educational Association who later emigrated to the United States, links plutocracy and class-consciousness in the same way as Bryce. 'The line of social division', he wrote in 1918, 'is constituted by the possession of wealth. In one class, solidified politically, are to be found those who possess wealth and prestige; in the other, where even more solidarity has been realised, remain those who obtain only enough wherewith to live and rear a family in an ordinary degree of comfort. . . . Class bias blinds the eyes of both groups to their common interests and their mutual social responsibilities.'[14] He added, for good measure, that class-consciousness was 'fomented' by

[11] ibid., pp. 268-71
[12] P. F. Rowland, *The New Nation*, London, 1903, pp. 120-25
[13] Twopeny, op. cit., p. 111
[14] C. H. Northcott, *Australian Social Development*, New York, 1918, pp. 21-22

trade unions, where the preponderance of the unskilled workers had prevented the formation of an 'aristocracy of labour'.[15]

Perhaps the best statement of this viewpoint is to be found in a series of articles written for the London *Times* in 1908 by its Australian correspondent, A. W. Jose, who agreed with his contemporaries that the coin of egalitarian sentiment was two-faced.

Australians often claim with pride that they are free from class distinctions and class prejudice. They are so in a sense. Feudal notions of graded rank are almost extinct, and every man is as good as any other man in his own conceit. In another sense, however, class distinctions are real enough in Australia. An Australian working man may not touch his cap to his employer, who, like himself, can only eat one dinner, wear one hat, and vote one vote, and who, in other important respects, is a social and political unit of no greater weight than any of the workmen he employs; but that working man is, I think, far more conscious than an English one of separate class notions and incompatible class interests. He divides the world into two portions, working men and capitalists. There is, he thinks, a more or less definite amount of wealth which the two have to divide, and he is quite convinced that the proportions in which that division is now made are indefensible and iniquitous.[16]

This kind of class-consciousness was greatly stimulated by the remarkable solidarity of the working class, which Jose compared to the Macedonian phalanx. It was, he declared, 'altogether beyond that existing in other countries. The average Australian workingman accepts the *status* of "worker" as his place in life. In the conditions surrounding him he believes that loyalty to his organisation and his class will in itself secure him a position of moderate comfort and ease quite as satisfactory to his mind as any he could secure by personal effort in the pursuit of individual gain. It follows that he thinks less as an individual than as a member of his class.'[17]

Like Bryce, Jose lamented the failure of the educated classes to contribute to the political life of the country. They were, he declared, 'preoccupied with their own concerns to the exclusion of all other interests . . . this state of affairs produces quite as one-sided and stereotyped an attitude to the questions of the day as, in its own sphere, the class-consciousness of the working man . . . only a very few squatters or professional and business men take any serious interest in public questions.' And he quoted the colonial politician Henry Parkes, who attributed this failing to the absence of a 'leisured class trained to the study of political questions . . . [whereas] . . . in a colony like ours every man has to struggle for existence.'[18]

In the period before the 1939-45 war, only one overseas student of Australian society seems to have queried this simple picture of social differences. This was the German sociologist Pfeffer, who visited Australia

15 ibid., p. 245

16 *The Times*, London, 26 September 1908. Some of Jose's material is reproduced in his book *Australia: Human and Economic*, London, 1932. His papers are in the Mitchell Library, Sydney.

17 ibid., 8 August 1908

18 ibid., 26 September 1908

in the early 1930's. Pfeffer's detailed account of society and politics is, understandably, informed by a degree of theoretical sophistication lacking in most of his predecessors. Egalitarianism, he asserted, had the role of a secular religion, derived from the evangelical Christian doctrine of the brotherhood of man. The ethos of 'mateship' lay behind the emphasis on material equality. 'What foreigners miscall "materialistic trade union sentiment" is the true offspring of evangelical brother-love. Each citizen is entitled to a minimum of happiness, of authority, of economic well-being, of education.'[19]

Pfeffer goes on, however, to expose a large number of divergences from the egalitarian ideal, and to demonstrate that society is riddled with social tensions, class feelings, and inter-group rivalries. He perceived a community divided by ethnic origin, religious belief, education, wealth, and occupation, and to this list he added three other forms of differentiation reflecting his own Germanic outlook: 'recreation'; 'public service' (Dienst) which marks off people in official authority; and 'authority', by which he evidently means class structure interpreted as relation to the means of production. Using these criteria, it was possible to construct a three-class model:[20]

(i) *Lower class*—predominantly Irish in ethnic origin, Catholic by religion, educated at Catholic schools, without inherited wealth, manual workers, given to drink and sport, and holding no high offices of state.

(ii) *Middle class*—British or NW European origin, dissenting in religion, medium income level, small proprietors or salaried workers, moralistic in social outlook, given to playing cricket and tennis, the source of 'middle officials' and the citizen militia, educated at state schools.

(iii) *Upper class*—British in origin, Presbyterian or Anglican in religion, educated at private schools, possessing inherited wealth and landed property, working in highly paid occupations, source of the officer class and senior officials.

Pfeffer is quick to point out that this hypothetical, ideal-type construction is quite at variance with everyday reality in Australia. 'In spite of hierarchical features Australian society is not hierarchical, in spite of class tendencies it is not a pure class society.' The major reason for this is political democracy. In the process of gaining an electoral majority, class divisions are blurred, the ideological zeal of the proletariat is blunted, and the Labor Party becomes opportunist. Although Pfeffer at times expresses admiration for the egalitarian ethic, at other times his reactionary political stance impels him to caustic comments on the lack of social and national responsibility which he found in Australia. 'In this wilderness of parliamentary democracy, the three divisions of society gradually lose their sense of social responsibility, and become merely interest groups.' In particular, the upper class had no social responsibility and was concerned mainly to act as a brake on the Labor movement.[21]

[19] Karl-Heinz Pfeffer, *Die Bürgerliche Gesellschaft in Australien*, Berlin, 1936, p. 446
[20] ibid., part 2, ch. 10
[21] ibid., p. 435

The economic and social changes of the period since 1939 are reflected in a different tone among the overseas visitors who have continued to record their impressions of social differences in Australia. The elements of inequality treated as subsidiary by Pfeffer, and ignored by many others, are now seen as significant and deep-seated. Depending on one's previous assumptions, class, status and power have been 'discovered' or 'rediscovered'. According to Mayer, there is 'definite evidence that the middle class is expanding and playing a more important role than previously. . . . Industrialisation has brought about a rapid expansion of the Australian middle class and has also strengthened the small but influential urban upper class. The Australian stratification system is now becoming increasingly complex.'[22] The journalist, John Douglas Pringle, in an outstandingly perceptive and entertaining account, declares on the other hand that the simple picture given by writers like D. H. Lawrence was always too simple. 'Australian society is much more complicated than Lawrence thought, and beneath the democratic surface a surprising number of class distinctions do exist.' In effect, there were two systems of class distinction superimposed on one another. The older system was essentially English, with the private schools at its core, and strongly evident in the urban centres of Melbourne and Adelaide. The Anglocentric upper class, 'extremely conservative in politics—as in everything else—have an infinite contempt for Australian politics and politicians . . . [they are] *emigrés* who have never left their country, lamenting an *ancien régime* which never quite existed.'[23] But working class people, also, are more status-conscious than the conventional wisdom makes out. 'Their ideal', says Pringle, 'is in many ways that of the middle class . . . this is natural enough. Every class unconsciously admires and imitates the class immediately above it.' The rise of a class of *nouveaux riches* since 1939 has strengthened the influence of materialism, but the working man does not resent the new upper class based on money because social mobility in Australia is such that working men may themselves attain this degree of wealth and status in their own lifetimes. Class distinctions and internal strains, he concludes, exist within 'the powerfully democratic structure of Australian society. So far democracy has always conquered in the end, and is likely to go on doing so, though it may be modified, as American democracy has been, by the new class system based on money.'[24]

Another English visitor concluded, after living for a year in Australia, that the simple-minded conclusions of so many overseas writers were due to a confusion between the absence of *any* distinctions and the absence of those with which they were familiar. Behind the egalitarian facade, 'there is hidden in private relations a fairly well defined status scale. . . . Every community, whether it is a suburb or a small town, has its recognised pecking order, in which professional people rank very high; it has its

[22] Kurt Mayer, loc. cit.
[23] J. D. Pringle, *Australian Accent*, London, 1958, p. 98
[24] ibid., pp. 100-111

prestige symbols in the types and furnishings of the home or of the school which the children attend. It has its tendency to put people of one occupation or religion on key committees and to leave others off. . . . The difference between Britain and Australia is not so much the absence of status distinctions as that status which can be acquired is, in Australia, more significant than the social position which is inherited.'[25]

The same kind of 'double take' is reported in a letter to the press by an English migrant, who wrote:

About ten years ago, when I wanted to migrate to Australia, I was told by a well-meaning selection officer that Australia was a country without social classes; in Australia everybody was the same. After I had arrived in this country I found that although there were large differences between people in almost every respect, there was a deeply rooted attitude of equalitarianism.

However, this attitude has been changing rapidly, partly, perhaps, because of the influx of many migrants with different traditions and ideas. The learned and the rich, and also others, today expect to be treated according to their respective rank and status. Doctors, not medical doctors, are popping up everywhere now and you have to call them 'doctor' if you do not want to run the risk of being 'reminded' by a secretary.

On balance, the return to a more realistic attitude as regards differences between people seems a healthy development. After all, differences are there and cannot be eliminated by ignoring them.[26]

From Literature to Science

How accurate is the literary picture of class-consciousness which we have just examined? Until the 1950's, only one serious attempt had been made to produce a systematic analysis using the survey techniques developed in the United States in the 1930's, but since then the growth of academic social science has produced a continuing trickle of studies which have tried to probe, extend and refine the received wisdom of the preceding century.

The exception was the study undertaken in the city of Melbourne in 1949 by a team from the University of Melbourne, under the leadership of S. B. Hammond, which was co-operating in a worldwide survey of social attitudes and social structure promoted by UNESCO.[27] Hammond found that most of his respondents were prepared to agree that there were class differences in Australia and to identify their position in a class hierarchy. In his own words:

A surprising degree of uniformity in the naming of social strata has been demonstrated and also a very high degree of consistency with relatively few frames of reference. This commonness of responses must be due to common influences such as political propaganda, education and interests. It seems likely that such overall uniformity could emerge only if many

[25] Jeanne MacKenzie, *Australian Paradox*, Melbourne, 1961, pp. 130-31
[26] Letter in the *Canberra Times*, 19 February 1966
[27] O. A. Oeser and S. B. Hammond (eds.), *Social Structure and Personality in a City*, London, 1954, part 5

cases had been given these frames of reference almost ready made by one or another source.[28]

Hammond gave his respondents the opportunity to indicate their own conceptions of the class hierarchy, and found that 81 per cent of the replies could be reduced to a three-class scheme. Fifty-five per cent described themselves as middle class, and 37 per cent as working class. The 'middle class' respondents were divided almost equally between the group who described the classes as upper, middle, and working (29 per cent of the sample), and upper, middle, and lower (26 per cent). The 'working class' respondents mostly saw the divisions as upper, middle, and working (26 per cent of the sample), but a significant minority (11 per cent) divided the world between workers and capitalists. Only 8 per cent had no class scheme.

Similar proportions have been found in subsequent studies. A by-election survey in the Victorian electorate of La Trobe produced a 'working class' proportion of 37 per cent, identical with Hammond's results, but the 'middle class' had shrunk to 44 per cent; most of the absconders preferred other labels which were described by the investigators as 'evasive/anti class' (9 per cent), 'non-class groups' (8 per cent), and 'other class' (2 per cent). Hammond's capitalist-worker scheme had almost disappeared. Those who preferred to use labels other than class were mostly churchgoers (like the respondent who described his class as 'Anglican').[29] Respondents who reject class labels are not sufficiently numerous to be analysed in detail, but a clearer picture emerges of the 'evasives'. In the La Trobe study, they tended to be either young people (whose concepts were presumably fluid) or housewives (who presumably had to ask their husbands). In a later survey in Melbourne, conducted by Davies, evasiveness was more likely if the respondent was a Catholic (a point discussed in more detail in Chapter 8), or lived in a socially hetero-geneous district, or was a middle child.[30] In this latter case, middle-aged people were more likely to be evasive than young people.

Fixed-choice questions give a somewhat different result. Hammond's sample identified themselves as 58 per cent middle class, 36 per cent working class. In 1961, the Australian Gallup Poll carried out a national survey which yielded the following results:

	%
Upper middle	5·5
Middle	44·0
Lower middle	12·0
Working	38·5

[28] ibid., p. 285
[29] Creighton Burns, *Parties and People*, Melbourne, 1962, part 2; A. F. Davies, 'Politics in the New Suburb', *Australian Journal of Politics and History*, vol. 8, no. 2, 1962
[30] A. F. Davies and S. Encel (eds.), *Australian Society*, p. 34. The significance of position in the family for the prediction of class identification is discussed by Davies in *Images of Class*, ch. 5.

In 1965, however, a further national survey was carried out by the Gallup Poll on behalf of Broom and his colleagues,[31] using only male members of the work force as respondents, which produced the following breakdown:

	%
Upper middle/upper	11
Middle	28
Lower middle	11
Working	44
Lower	4
No reply	2

The differences between these two surveys are probably an artifact arising from differing techniques of questionnaire construction, plus the male character of the respondents in the second survey. The latter distribution is undoubtedly the more meaningful of the two.

The differences between the two methods of self-rating indicate that, given the chance to avoid self-identification, many people will avoid putting themselves into any social class. But this is not a distinctively Australian characteristic. In Denmark, a country with a hereditary aristocracy and other historically-rooted forms of social distinction which are less important in Australia, Svalastoga found a similar phenomenon. Given a free choice, 24 per cent of his sample identified themselves as working class, compared with 50 per cent using the fixed-choice method; 36 per cent, given a free choice, did not identify themselves with any class, compared with 2·5 per cent on the fixed-choice question. (Middle class identification was similar in both cases.)[32] The Australian data show similar discrepancies, but even so about two-thirds of respondents will readily accept the opportunity to identify themselves with a class, and a further group of about one-quarter will accept it with some reluctance. Hesitancy about class is thus a minority trait and does not particularly distinguish Australia from other countries; rather, it is characteristic of most urban industrial societies.

Broom has tried to give precision to the relation between self-rated class position and 'objective' class position.[33] He constructed a scale of 'social rank' based on Gallup Poll results, which combined occupation with the judgment of social position made by interviewers for the poll organisation, which is based on economic indices, apparent educational level, etc. This gave a system of three ranks, which was compared with self-rated class. Agreement between the two measures was high. Thus, 20 per cent of rank 1 identified themselves as upper-middle class, and 70 per cent as middle

[31] L. Broom, F. L. Jones, J. Zubrzycki, 'Social Stratification in Australia', in J. A. Jackson (ed.), *Social Stratification*, Cambridge, 1968
[32] Kaare Svalastoga, *Prestige, Class and Mobility*, Copenhagen, 1959, pp. 185-86
[33] Leonard Broom and R. J. Hill, 'Opinion Polls and Social Rank in Australia', ANZ *Journal of Sociology*, vol. 2, no. 1, 1965

class. Expressed alternatively, 58 per cent of those who identified themselves as middle class were in rank 1, compared with 86 per cent of those who identified themselves as upper-middle. Again, 82 per cent of rank 3 identified as working class; 35 per cent of rank 2 identified as middle class; and 60 per cent of those who identified as lower-middle class were in rank 2. Broom then went on to examine a number of items taken from twenty-one Gallup surveys between 1951 and 1961, and found that there was a significant association between social rank, voting, life style and social awareness ('strata correlates') and politico-economic awareness ('class interests').

The association between free choice and fixed choice was also tested by Broom and his collaborators in the 1965 study. The most significant correlations were as shown in Table 6·1, where the ratios between free and fixed choice are expressed as a percentage.

Table 6·1 Free and Fixed Choice of Social Class Position

I *Free Choice*	II *Fixed Choice*	I/II%
Upper	Upper	67%
Upper Middle	Upper Middle	89%
Middle	Middle	52%
Average	Working	50%
Lower Middle	Lower Middle	69%
Working	Working	89%
Poorest, lowest	Working	89%

It is also relevant to notice that, given a free choice, 42 per cent of the sample chose to call themselves middle class (fixed choice was 28 per cent); 6 per cent called themselves average; 2 per cent called themselves upper or upper-middle (fixed choice 11 per cent); and only 1 per cent could bring themselves to choose the label lower-middle.

The most elaborate attempt at the use of survey data has been made by Broom and his colleagues. Using five criteria—occupation, education, income, subjective social class and interviewer's assessment—they constructed a composite index of 'social rank', which has affinities to the *Index of Status Characteristics* used by Warner and the *Index of Social Position* used by Hollingshead. Their justification for this procedure is that it provides a more refined measure of stratification than the conventional 'socio-economic status' index of occupation, income, and education. It is useful, they claim, to 'regard each of these five measures of social rank as contributing *some* information about a given individual's position in the national stratification system, and to treat them as a set of interdependent variables whose joint effect determines an individual's social rank position . . . if meaningful social strata do exist, in the sense that certain patterns of scores and associated levels of social rank position occur more frequently than others, then it should be possible to determine what these major strata are by examining the distribution of individual scores on the Index of Social Rank.'[34]

Having constructed the index, Broom and his colleagues divided it into eight strata using the statistical technique of multivariate analysis; this gives the minimum of variance within each stratum, and the maximum of variance between them. The eight divisions were used by Jones in a survey of residential areas in the city of Melbourne to determine a rank order of preferences between suburban areas. Jones' eight-group ranking used twenty-four objective criteria including occupation, religion, age, etc., and produced a clear-cut hierarchy of residential areas, similar in character to the subjective hierarchy of 'desirable' residential areas in Sydney found by Congalton in an earlier study.[35] Jones related his hierarchy with a socio-economic status scale (SES) and also with class identification as found in the Broom survey; in both cases the correlations were high. Jones' conclusion was that the eight-group division used by Broom and his colleagues could meaningfully be combined with residence, as done by Warner and Hollingshead.

It is also of interest that Jones tried to test the significance of immigrant status on his classification, by comparing the SES scale with an alternative SES/ETH (ethnicity) scale. The differences were not statistically significant; if ethnicity does have an influence, it appears to work in the same direction as other variables.

The technique developed by Broom and his co-workers is undoubtedly valuable and should produce a useful tool of analysis for investigating a range of phenomena related to stratification. From the viewpoint of this book, however, it has a number of shortcomings which apply generally to methods of this kind, based on the Warner approach to the study of social differences. The combination of self-rated 'class position' with socio-economic status indices entails logical assumptions about the relation between objective and subjective measures which are highly disputable. The evidence of political surveys shows, for instance, that subjective class identification is closely related to politics, and that the two are reciprocally influential. A statement about class position is, as I have argued in earlier chapters, a statement about the three dimensions of class, status and power, and its relation to objective indices of social position is confirmed but not explained by the existence of statistical associations. Again, the use of the index is clearly based on the assumption that a stratification system exists, in some objective sense, and can be measured by the construction of suitable indices. This is also disputable; the very notion of a stratification 'system' is based on a particular interpretation of social reality, and the incorporation of a subjective measure in the index means that the index itself, instead of being homogeneous, is likely to reflect more than one 'system'. The use of the term 'rank' is questionable because it implies

---

[34] F. L. Jones, 'A Social Ranking of Melbourne Suburbs', ANZ *Journal of Sociology*, vol. 3, no. 2, 1967
[35] A. A. Congalton, *Status and Prestige in Australia*, Melbourne, 1969

the existence of a particular kind of system, and the word itself is an uneasy one to use in the context of an egalitarian society.

Different class schemes like those described above (and in the study by Davies, mentioned below) indicate the range of conceptual systems about social differences. It is remarkable that Broom and his colleagues do not reflect on the discrepancies between their data about class identification and those found in other surveys. Thus, their finding that 44 per cent of respondents described themselves as working class in answer to a fixed-choice question is at variance with other studies where the proportion ranges between 35 per cent and 40 per cent. Even so, they noted that a high proportion of skilled workers identify themselves as middle class (39 per cent in their survey), much higher than in recent American and British studies. Their conclusion is that 'the absorption of skilled workers into the middle class may have proceeded more rapidly in Australia than in these other countries.' This merely begs the question: what does 'absorption into the middle class' mean? The question can be answered either by inventing a special definition of the middle class, or by noting that the apparent 'embourgeoisement' of the skilled workers is not reflected in their voting patterns, which throws doubt on the nature of the identification. As Lockwood and his collaborators have argued, embourgeoisement is a process with a variety of effects, the principal one being to develop a more 'privatised' style of existence, but its influence on class-consciousness and political posture is much more ambiguous.[36]

It is also well known that the wording of questions in surveys can have a considerable effect on the answers. Svalastoga divided his working class into upper, middle and lower, and the combined identifications with these three levels gave him a total of 50 per cent of 'working class' respondents, which is higher than one would expect from his other data. In effect, what he had done was to introduce a status component into the conventional situation where 'working class' people are confronted with an occupational label, while the middle classes are given a more complex set of clues including a range of levels. A similar effect has been observed in an Australian survey. The audience research service of the Australian Broadcasting Commission, using a sample of 414 persons in Melbourne, gave them the opportunity to identify with two 'working class' levels, and raised the proportion to 48 per cent. Significantly, whereas the Gallup Poll found that 15 per cent of those who had completed a secondary education rated themselves as working class, and Broom's survey yielded 30 per cent, the ABC poll gave a result of 36 per cent.[37]

More evidence about the attitudes of skilled workmen is found in the work of Lafitte, who studied a group of employees in a factory in Melbourne, predominantly skilled and semi-skilled men.[38] Responses to

[36] D. Lockwood, et al., *The Affluent Worker*, Cambridge, 1968
[37] A. Kondos, 'The Application of Self-Rating Techniques to the Study of Social Class in Australia', unpublished M.S. thesis, School of Sociology, University of NSW
[38] Paul Lafitte, *Social Structure and Personality in the Factory*, London, 1958

questions about class and politics, he noted, were affected in distinct ways by work situation and social situation, and concluded that the worker's attitude to life is family-centred or self-centred, rather than work-centred. 'Work', he writes, 'can only be the means of earning a living', and social attitudes and values are largely formed outside the work situation.[39] (This is, of course, consistent with the findings of Lockwood and his co-workers, and also with the observations of Zweig[40] that many working men tend to think of themselves as working class in the factory and middle class outside. Zweig's study was also biased towards relatively well-paid working men in skilled or semi-skilled jobs.)

Lafitte analysed the situation by dividing responses under three headings: recognition of peers, class preference, and class identification. Consistent working class response under all three heads came from less than half the sample (54 out of 127); another eleven identified themselves as working class but expressed a preference for a middle class position. At the other end of the scale, seventeen identified consistently with the middle classes, and forty-five exhibited confused patterns of identification, which Lafitte attributed to social mobility or at least the feeling of being mobile. Another instance of confusion came over attitudes to unionism and politics. Although eighty-one of the sample were unionists, only fifty-four thought unions were a good thing; seventy-three were derogatory about politics, and among them sixty-three described all politicians as crooks. Although eighty-nine were Labor voters, twenty-three were evasive or undecided. On the other hand, class-consciousness among them was decidedly sharper than in Hammond's survey, to which Lafitte's was a sequel. Lafitte invited his respondents to construct their own class schemes and compared them with the four schemes identified by Hammond. Three-quarters of Hammond's working-class respondents used a three-class scheme, and one sixth divided the world between capitalists and workers. Lafitte's group chose similarly, but the distribution of three-class schemes was different. Among Hammond's respondents, 58 per cent preferred an upper-middle-working classification, and only one saw the world as divided between rich, middle and poor. Among Lafitte's subjects, 46 per cent chose the upper-middle-working scheme, 20 per cent the upper-middle-lower scheme, and 9 per cent the rich-middle-poor scheme. Evidently the factory situation had the effect of intensifying consciousness of managerial authority and its consequent pecuniary advantages. Similarly, Lafitte's respondents were more willing to identify themselves as working class—72 per cent as against Hammond's 64 per cent. (This was very close to the proportion found by Centers[41] among American working men in 1945, where 77 per cent identified as working class.)

The most penetrating study of class-consciousness yet made in Australia is that of Davies, based on two intensive surveys carried out in Melbourne

[39] ibid., p. 180
[40] Ferdynand Zweig, *The Worker in an Affluent Society*, London, 1961
[41] R. Centers, *The Psychology of Social Classes*, Princeton, 1949

in 1960 and 1962.[42] Davies was concerned to show how models, schemes, or maps of class are built up as abstractions using material drawn from actual social experiences. He concluded that there were five principal 'maps' of the class structure used by the 146 respondents in the sample, as described in Table 6·2.[43]

Table 6·2 Models of the Class System

I Key word was *ordinary*, as contrasted with *wealthy*, *lower*, and *upper*, mostly in the form of *ordinary-lower-upper*. In effect, a denial of class differences. (26 cases)

II Key concept was a *large middle class*, mostly at the centre of a *middle-working-top* scheme. Essentially a middle class viewpoint, stressing fine distinctions. (19 cases)

III A *large working class*, accompanied by a small *middle class* and a still smaller *top class* or *wealthier class*. Marked by indignation over inequality. (32 cases)

IV A two-class system, with a large *working class* and a small *top class*. Also marked by indignation but with additional denial of social gradings. (21 cases)

V Key concept is *middle class*, distinguished from *upper* and *lower*; commonest scheme was *middle-lower-upper*, also with stress on grades, but moralistic rather than analytical distinctions. (31 cases)

In addition, six respondents had idiosyncratic schemes and eleven had none. The schemes were built up from a small number of common ingredients, of which money was by far the most important. 'Scale of expenditure' was nominated by 32 per cent of the sample as the outstanding index of class; combined with snobbery (9 per cent) and with education (8 per cent), money accounts for one-half of the responses. It was almost the prerogative of 'working class' respondents to say that class differences depend on power and privilege (10 per cent) and snobbery (9 per cent), and middle-aged people in the 'working class' group were likelier to use these than younger people. Altogether, 'behaviour' in some form accounted for 40 per cent of responses, but it was a predominantly 'middle class' choice, with restricted intercourse, manners, low behaviour, and education as particular distinguishing marks.

'Upper classes' of three sorts cropped up in the descriptions—a 'wealthy' class designated by conspicuous consumption, an 'upper' group marked by snobbery and social exclusiveness, and a 'boss' group wielding economic and political power. Contrary to Hammond's findings, the 'working class' respondents who chose the two-class scheme (no. IV in Table 6·2) did not describe the 'top class' in the sense of the 'bosses'—a reflection of thirteen intervening years of affluence and the recession of the class-war climate of

[42] A. F. Davies, *Images of Class*; 'Politics in the New Suburb', loc. cit.; 'Social Class in the New Suburb', *Westerly*, no. 3, 1961. These studies are also reported in Davies and Encel, op. cit., pp. 33-40.
[43] Davies, *Images of Class*, ch. 2

the 1930's and 1940's. The working class were distinguished variously as the backbone of society (by 'working class' respondents), as 'battlers', as 'labourers', and as no-hopers or drifters (where *lower* rather than *working* is the key word). The 'middle class' respondents distinguished themselves from the snobs and money-grubbers, and from the less enterprising or shiftless working men. Those using scheme III were, in Davies' words, denoting themselves as a cut above the workers, and those who preferred scheme V saw themselves as the backbone of society.

Recurrent references used to indicate social position included ownership of land, executive or directorial posts in business, quality of housing, inherited wealth, and invitations to 'royal turnouts'. The notions of control and command appeared in a number of interviews, sometimes through pejorative synonyms including rob, scorn, exploit, ignore, and order. Davies found, in other words, wide variety and richness of illustration of actual social relationships focused on inequality. He also found, like Elizabeth Bott, a well-developed mechanism for incorporating these familiar reactions into a symbolic structure of class, status and power, coupled with large-scale denial of the existence or at least importance of such differences. But, as we have already noted, this denial is not peculiar to Australia. It is, however, of special interest that religion, whose significance in the class structure is demonstrated in various sections of this book, was hardly mentioned by Davies' respondents. The Catholic wife of a public servant, living in the new suburb of Ringwood, did say that 'in my own personal experience class doesn't matter, the only discrimination I ever strike is religious',[44] but she was a rare bird. The consensus which impels people to mention some things and to omit others is not in itself sufficient evidence; the investigator must still accept responsibility for his own symbolic framework.

An entertaining illustration of evasiveness about class was provided by a television program broadcast in November 1966.[45] The program was built around a discussion of Craig McGregor's book, *Profile of Australia*. The speaker is a doctor's wife who comes from a landed family. The mixture of recognition and evasion is exemplary:

I think that we are naturally placed there by the circumstances of our birth, by the structure that we live within and those with whom we mix. But I don't think that I've ever thought of myself belonging to a class, but others put me into a class . . .
Interviewer What do you think places you in the upper classes?
Mrs H. You've placed me in it, I haven't. But I think possibly the fact that I belong to that group of people who are usually placed there—that is I come from a long line of landholders, and I happen to be married to someone attached to the medical profession with the magical title of 'Doctor' . . .

[44] ibid., p. 13
[45] I am indebted to the Australian Broadcasting Commission for a transcript of this program.

Mrs H. then went on to remark upon the 'extraordinary effect that magical word "Doctor" has on what we would call the lower middle class mind.' Picked up on this by one of the other participants, she attempted to sidestep by declaring that she had merely acquired the phrase that very day from Mr McGregor's book. At a later stage of the discussion, she was able to block in a wide range of class relations very rapidly, while continuing to deny their significance:

I think there's a very great affinity between the educated people and the working class. Possibly a very much greater affinity than there is with the pretentious middle class . . . I have always felt a tremendous warmth and friendship for what is known as the ordinary working man, because he's completely without any pretensions . . . I don't believe there is such a thing as snobbery, and snobbery is a sense of insecurity . . . really we are placed into classes by other people, not by our own wishes . . . basically we all love someone who is unpretentious . . . as a child growing up my father taught me that I must be able to walk into a fettlers' camp or into a blackfellows' camp and be able to drink out of a pannikin no matter how dirty it is, and take a piece of damper and eat it with them as happily as I would if I was . . . in Government House [replying to an interpolation] it isn't condescending. I would prefer that any day to the lace cloth across the kitchen table and iced cream cake and little paper doilies and things for morning tea. I call that pretentious.

Mrs H. would clearly be at home in the household of Nancy Mitford's 'Uncle Matthew'. In the same discussion, a taxi driver was asked to comment on the existence of classes:

Interviewer What sort of people do you find are in classes that you don't feel you belong to?
Mr S. Well, I don't think there's anyone in a class that I don't belong to.

Having wiped the floor with the subject, so to speak, Mr S. nevertheless was able to find some illustrations of class behaviour.

Interviewer When someone gets into your taxi, what do you look for?
Mr S. His dress.
Craig McGregor What else apart from dress?
Mr S. His speech.
McGregor Yes, accents . . . it's a very clear one, isn't it?
Mr S. My word it is.
McGregor There is a big difference between the way in which different classes in Australia speak, wouldn't you say?
Mr S. Yes, I can imagine . . .

The correspondence between class identification and voting is so close in the survey results that the two may be regarded as largely alternative measures of the same general social outlook. The 1961 Gallup survey produced the result shown in Table 6·3.

Table 6·3 Class and Vote, 1961

	UM (5·5%)	M (44%)	LM (12%)	W (38·5%)
LCP	66	61	42	25
ALP	16·5	29	45	65
DLP	2	5	7	5
DK	15·5	5	6	5
	100	100	100	100

Note LCP—Liberal or Country Parties; ALP—Australian Labor Party; DLP—Democratic Labor Party; DK—Don't Know

Similar results have been found in other surveys. The La Trobe by-election study found that two-thirds of the 'middle class' voted Liberal, just as two-thirds of the 'working class' voted Labor. In Davies' 1962 Melbourne survey, 80 per cent of the 'working class' voted Labor, and just over half the 'middle class' voted Liberal. (The discrepancy is readily attributable to an anti-Liberal swing at the previous federal election.)

By combining the 1961 poll figures for subjective class and occupation, we can obtain a clearer picture of the 'cross-class' voters. 'Middle class' manual workers were the largest group; 50 per cent voted ALP, 35 per cent Liberal or CP, Don't Know/Other 15 per cent. This confirms the views of Lafitte and Zweig about the separation of work-situation from general social stance. Next came non-manual workers who identified as 'working class'; voting was ALP 53 per cent, Liberal-CP 32 per cent, DK/Other 15 per cent. Even here, one-third kept voting separate from general social stance. The two smallest groups were those with congruent class and occupation but eccentric voting behaviour; the larger of the two was the non-manual, 'middle-class', Labor voter, who accounted for 15 per cent of the whole 'cross-class' group. In the La Trobe survey, the 'working class' Liberal voters had more skilled jobs, more concern with religion, and more political awareness than the 'working class' group as a whole. In a third of these cases, social mobility had cut their previous Labor allegiance, but among wives the aberrant voting was often due to a refusal to break allegiance with family tradition (a point also noted by Hammond). The 'middle class' Labor voters were similarly better educated, union conscious, and more politically aware; their middle class style of life was combined, apparently without strain, with political allegiance to a 'working class' position. Family loyalty was again important, especially among wives and young men.

The most recent attempt to test these relationships was made by S. O. D'Alton in a sample survey of voters in Sydney. (The survey, with 1289 respondents, was carried out in 1968, and was unpublished at the time this book went to press. I am indebted to Mr D'Alton, of the School of Sociology at the University of New South Wales, for permission to quote these results.) D'Alton tested Davies' list of indices of class, with results as shown in Table 6·4.

Table 6·4 Indices of Class, 1962 and 1968

	Davies 1962 %	D'Alton 1968 %
Scale of expenditure	32	16
Restricted intercourse	12	8
Power and privilege	10	4
Snobbishness	9	11
Snobbishness and money	9	9
Education	4	5
Education and money	8	6
Other	16	41
	100	100

Davies' results led him to conclude that for almost half of his respondents, 'class is primarily a matter of money', but D'Alton's results reveal a more confused situation in which status has greater importance. D'Alton tested this further by using an alternative set of indices, which gave the results shown in Table 6·5.

Table 6·5 Indices of Class, 1968

	%
Money/income	30
Snobbery/actions	20
Neighbourhood of residence	12
Consumer expenditure	10
Education level	10 ⎫ 14
Place of education	4 ⎭
Ethnic origin	9
Occupation	7
Wealth	5
Other	30

Note Respondents were able to choose more than one criterion, hence the total is over 100 per cent. Under 'other' were criteria such as privilege, religion, intelligence, hobbies, clubs, leisure, speech and dress.

Table 6·5 suggests that although economic factors continue to provide the most important single criterion, they operate in a more complex way than shown in Davies' table (which was derived from a much smaller sample). Class may be 'primarily' a matter of money, but class maps are not necessarily coloured in primary tints.

On the basic question whether classes exist in Australia, D'Alton obtained a positive response from 79 per cent of his sample. Like Svalastoga he found that about half of his respondents preferred not to identify themselves with a class label (58 per cent in this case) but that they were fully able to distinguish class groupings when required. Of the 42 per cent who identified with a class, 22 per cent said they were middle class and 11 per cent working class; others described themselves as poor, professional, or even Gentile. When asked to describe the Australian class system, however, 79 per cent were prepared to identify classes; 42 per cent perceived three classes, 26 per cent perceived two, and 11 per cent had other schemes. Only 7 per cent refused to answer, and 14 per cent said there were no classes. When presented with a fixed-choice question on class identification, the results were as shown in Table 6·6.

Table 6·6 Class Identification, 1968

	%	
Upper	1	
Upper Middle	10	
Middle Middle	32	47
Lower Middle	5	
Upper Working	11	
Middle Working	32	47
Lower Working	4	
Refusal to identify	5	
	100	

Table 6·6, with its bi-modal distribution of responses, reveals how a wider choice of possibilities, far from blurring the picture of class differences, actually encourages the widest degree of polarisation. The link between class and politics is demonstrated in Table 6·7, which divides respondents according to their belief that class differences do exist in Australia.

Table 6·7 Reality of Class Differences, 1968

Class Identification of Respondent	*Liberal Voters %*		*Labor Voters %*	
	(1) Yes	(2) No	(3) Yes	(4) No
U	2	1	1	—
UM	15	8	5	3
MM	43	44	19	19
LM	5	3	5	3
UW	8	9	14	9
MW	22	28	45	47
LW	2	1	5	6
N/A	3	6	6	12
	100	100	100	100

The percentages in columns (1) and (3) coincide precisely with the breakdown of Liberal and Labor voters (i.e. respondents who said they *usually* voted for either of these parties) according to class identification. It may be inferred that those who answered 'Yes' to the question 'Do you feel that there are class differences in Australia?' were more positive at once about their political and their class identifications.

D'Alton also endeavoured to test 'affect' towards class position by combining the results of all the answers to questions about class identification, e.g.:

Do you yourself feel that you belong to a definite social class?

If yes, what would you call your social class?

In what social class would you put (1) your closest friends, (2) most people in this district?

From these and other questions, D'Alton constructed tables which showed whether respondents aspired to belong to other class levels. In many American surveys, it is apparently taken for granted that upward class aspirations are normal and that most people would prefer to identify themselves as middle class. The same assumption was made by Broom and his collaborators when they remarked that Australia was 'the most middle class country in the world'. As with everything else, it depends on what you mean by middle class. The main piece of evidence on which Broom *et al* appeared to be relying was their finding, already quoted, that a high proportion of skilled workers identified themselves as middle class. D'Alton's findings, and those of the ABC survey, illustrate how artificial this conclusion may be. This applies particularly to the questions on affect. The results were as follows:

Upward class identification Positive, 28 per cent; negative, 22 per cent; neutral, 50 per cent

Downward class identification Positive, 21 per cent; negative, 26 per cent; neutral, 51 per cent (2 per cent were not meaningful)

The breakdown of these answers according to self-rated class position shows the bi-modal pattern already noticed.

Table 6·8 Affective Responses towards Class Identification

Self-rated class position	Upward Identification	Downward Identification
U	—	—
UM	6	6
MM	33	33
LM	6	6
UW	8	8
MW	40	41
LW	7	6
	100	100

(N.B. Results were obtained for 75 per cent of the sample.)

The remarkable thing about this table is that the two most class-conscious groups, 'middle middle' and 'middle working', are as likely to identify downwards as upwards. The 'middle middle' group also showed the highest proportion who were neutral on this point, i.e. lacking any clear drive for upward mobility; they were closely followed by the 'middle working' group. The breakdown is similar to that in Table 6·6, except that the 'middle working' group is more important.

D'Alton's results show the effects of a methodology which, like Svalastoga's, is designed to achieve concordance between class and status. As a result, it achieves a much clearer differentiation between the 'working class' and the 'middle class' than most other surveys carried out in Australia or the USA. On the other hand, the social investigator is bound to query the significance of the finding that people prefer to cluster in the middle of both class groups. The distribution so produced shows little correspondence with observable forms of social differentiation like income, occupation, and education; on the other hand, it chimes closely with political consciousness. Class and status may be successfully combined for survey purposes, but their independent significance does not thereby disappear; and their relation to the dimension of power remains obscure.

To sum up: class-consciousness in Australia is real, complex and pervasive. Whatever it was like in Bryce's day, its most notable characteristic in the past twenty years is its essential similarity to the phenomena found in other industrial societies. In the subsequent chapters of this book, the subjective and objective aspects of class, status and power will be explored in detail. Before this exploration, however, it will be expedient to formulate a model which endeavours to place this variety of data in a framework as orderly as the confused nature of the subject will allow.

The Australian Class System: A Model

In pre-industrial societies, and in the early years after the industrial revolution, the 'class structure' was relatively simple and unified. Wealth, power, legal authority, social status and cultural predominance were largely coincident. The growth of industrial society saw the breakdown of this unity and the growth of overlapping and intersecting systems of class, status and power. The disjunction of these systems has proceeded furthest where the general social situation favours an egalitarian social ethic, as in North America and Australasia. The more closely linked they are, the more 'class-bound' does society appear, as in England. Germany, however, has stronger claims to the description if we think of *class* and *power* rather than *status*, which attracts exaggerated attention in England. German society, much more coercive and repressive in nature, is more accurately described as 'class-bound'.[46] Because of the openness of Australian society, it is easy to contrast it with such cases by declaring that it has *no* 'classes'. This conventional view is in fact a subjective reaction to the quality of social life in Australia, masquerading as an analysis of social structure. It is true neither in the structural sense nor as an evaluation of what the mass of citizens actually feel. The following attempt at a model of the 'class system', or rather the structure of class, status and power in Australia, consists of a series of propositions which distil the accumulated evidence of the rest of this book.

I General

(a) The three dimensions of class, status and power are not closely articulated.

[46] The repressive nature of the German social system is examined at length by Ralf Dahrendorf, *Society and Democracy in Germany*, London, 1968.

(b) Although the normal components of a 'class system' exist, their effect on daily social relations is less obtrusive, and the actual range of differentiation is smaller, than in many other industrial communities.

(c) Geographical dispersion inhibits the growth of national hierarchies. It also contributes to the partial detachment of the landowning and farming groups from the class and status systems, and their peculiar role in politics.

(d) The nature of social differentiation is strongly influenced by the prevailing ideology of egalitarianism, which emphasises redistribution and a high general level rather than opportunity for the ambitious. Hence, for example, the role of legal-bureaucratic methods of allocating material rewards and less tangible values, and the relative lack of interest in education as a vehicle of social mobility.

II The Hierarchy

(a) There is no independent base for an 'upper class' such as hereditary aristocracy, feudal privilege, military autocracy, political monopoly, or mandarin bureaucracy. The economic base, such as that which exists in North America, is attenuated by geographical dispersion, the large role of foreign ownership, and the relatively small scale of much of industry. In addition, a colonial type of cultural dependence weakens the intellectual and cultural influence of the most privileged groups.

(b) Nevertheless, no industrial society can operate without some kind of 'upper class', and to work effectively this group must occupy positions at the top of each of the three axes of stratification. To identify the components of the 'upper class' we should therefore look for groups within the social system who occupy such positions. Four groups clearly do so: (i) Professional men—especially doctors and lawyers; (ii) Judges and arbitrators; (iii) Old-established pastoral families; (iv) Old-established business families.

In addition, there are two other groups whose status is more ambiguous— politicians and public servants. Although politicians clearly have power, they lack status because of the disinclination of the community to accord much prestige to politics as an occupation, and they are rarely wealthy. Nor are their links with private business particularly close; politics and the boardroom are not connected as in some other countries. The position of Labor politicians is particularly ambiguous. One reason, which they hold in common with labor and socialist parties elsewhere, is their opposition, at least in principle, to the existing distribution of rewards and their anti-establishment posture. In Australia, the case is accentuated by the widely-held assumption that members of parliament are 'delegates' of the Labor movement rather than 'representatives' in the sense described by Edmund Burke in his address to the electors of Bristol; it is further accentuated by the special position of Catholics in the ALP and the ability of the Catholic church to exercise influence on Labor politics. The position of government officials is also complicated by the lack of prestige accorded to them by the community, which is strongly at variance with the real authority and influence exercised by senior officials; by the very different roles of federal and state officials; and by the effect of professional status. In the latter case, a state-employed professional man can rotate his social position through 180 degrees by identifying himself as an 'engineer' rather than a 'public servant' (and three-quarters of engineers are in fact both).

(c) The line between the 'upper class' and the 'upper-middle class' is relatively faint. In the countries of Western Europe (including Britain) the 'upper class' is not a simple outgrowth of the 'upper-middle class' whereas in Australia the two shade into one another fairly readily. This gives a special significance to the social position of professional groups, particularly lawyers and doctors, who naturally form hierarchies spanning the two levels.

(d) The growth of distinctions between the 'upper-middle' and 'lower-middle' classes has been a major feature of social changes since 1945. The growth of professional and managerial occupations is one reason; another and related factor is the expansion of higher education and the increased influence of education on social position. A distinctively upper-middle class style of politics has been emerging, focused on 'conscience' issues and taking its most active form in various protest movements and student agitation, as in other parts of the world. Religion has lost much of its unifying role at these levels, and in some ways has even tended to sharpen differences in social and political consciousness; the prime examples are to be found among Catholics, who have become increasingly divided over their church's policy on education, international affairs, and of course the whole process of 'aggiornamento' initiated by Pope John XXIII.

(e) Distinctions within the 'middle classes' have long been recognised, but the 'working class' has been treated as one entity. This was always an exaggeration, especially if social mobility and class-consciousness are taken into account. In the post-1945 period, the differences have become clearer and sharper, and given the chance, skilled workers and their families will differentiate themselves from the rest of the 'working class' which may as reasonably be divided into upper and lower as the middle class.

III Lines of Division

(a) In terms of our analytical framework, 'class' may be taken as the strongest of the three axes of social inequality, 'power' (especially in the form of bureaucratic rule-making) as the second, and 'status' as the weakest, but growing in significance.

(b) Class, status and power interlock closely in the case of the professions, especially law and medicine, with high correlation between income, education, social role, and occupational prestige. The professional aura also extends to professionally qualified businessmen and government officials, where formal power and command of resources are added to the other variables. Otherwise, occupation, education, and income do not correlate as well as they appear to do in the United States or, in a different form, in Great Britain. This appears in the case of the old-established business and pastoral families, for instance, whose potential role is also modified by their very limited participation in politics.

(c) Religious affiliation, especially the Protestant-Catholic division, is a particularly effective agent of differentiation because it is closely linked with politics, with education, and with occupation. Thus, Roman Catholics are disproportionately strong in Labor politics and disproportionately weak in the higher levels of business, the professions, and the public services; the Catholic educational system, moreover, ensures a lifetime form of social segregation and group-consciousness. Only Anglicans and Presbyterians are evenly distributed throughout all social strata, unlike Jews and the more evangelical Protestant groups.

(d) The evidence presented in this book and in other studies suggests that the various 'objective' categories of social differentiation contribute to the structure of class, status and power in the following probable order of importance: (i) Occupation; (ii) Ownership and control; (iii) and (iv) Education, religion; (v) Public rank; (vi) Ethnic origin; (vii) Family; (viii) Sex; (ix) Age.

IV Class-consciousness

(a) It is a long time since reluctance to admit the existence of a class system or to identify with anything other than an all-embracing 'middle class' has been accepted by social investigators as 'proof' of a society without classes. In the most professedly egalitarian of communities, it is possible to get nearly all people to construct maps of the class system and to locate themselves thereon. The task of the investigator then becomes one of probing the quality of varying forms of affirmation or denial of the reality and significance of particular aspects of social differentiation. 'Class-consciousness' is the established term, but only the very bored reader of this book will be at a loss to imagine why it is avoided as much as possible.

(b) Denial of the existence of an 'upper class' is a particularly notable aspect of the Australian situation, reflecting both the relatively limited span of social inequality and also a general unwillingness to acknowledge the importance of differentiation by status and power as well as class. The visibility and influence of an 'upper class' depend largely upon the convergence of these three axes, the clustering of certain groups along them, and broad social awareness of this situation. In Australia, the existence of these axes can be demonstrated both by objective and subjective methods, but the effects of clustering and convergence are slight, and social behaviour which presumes upon them may rebound. When the proprietor of a daily newspaper in Sydney peremptorily sacked a messenger for presuming to use the executive lift in the newspaper building, he was met by a strike and forced to withdraw his action.

(c) Australia gives an example of the effect of politics upon society, a phenomenon which runs counter to the assumptions alike of liberal individualism and Marxism, but which is more common than these dominant philosophies would have us suppose.[47] The history of France, with its deliberate creation of new elites after the Revolution, and of Russia, with its recurrent cycles of attempts to remake society by state action, have more relevance for Australia than might appear on the surface. The bureaucratic ascendency is a direct result of the weakness of social groups able to wield certain kinds of influence. One of the most reflective of Labor politicians, W. A. Holman, remarked in a parliamentary debate in 1900 that official organs of arbitration and rule-making were forced upon the community because of the relative absence of an educated upper-middle class. 'It is almost impossible to find men who have no connection with either side who are of sufficient public prominence, unless we take them from the ranks of the professions. . . . We find in Australia no class corresponding to the leisured, cultured middle class of England. We turn, then, to the best available substitute that we have—official life.'[48] A similar analysis of Russian society was made only a few years later by Trotsky, who warned about the danger of 'substitutism' through government action because of the weakness of the Russian middle classes.[49]

The paradoxical reluctance of Australians to recognise this situation and to incorporate it into their image of the social structure has already been commented upon. One reason for this reluctance is the high general level of material well-being, which undermines deference for authority. Henry Lawson observed in one of his short stories that the bushman's lack of deference was related to the universal possession of horses in country districts, which removed one of the crucial distinctions of aristocratic societies. The elite of the Australian army in the 1914-18 war was the Light Horse, but it was recruited from bushmen and not from an equestrian squirearchy. (In Ireland, an impoverished squireen who could not afford a horse was known contemptuously in the eighteenth and nineteenth centuries as a 'walking gentleman'.) A second factor is the relative weakness of status obstacles, such as education and family, to political advancement. Thirdly, the elaborate development of institutions for moderating conflict over the distribution of rewards gives political and economic authority a bureaucratic face which does not inspire deference.

(d) The skilled workers are a key group in this situation, and the influence of their outlook reaches into many corners of society. Skilled workers are relatively mobile, as shown by evidence in other parts of this book. Mobility has been open to them through the Labor movement, through industry, where many entrepreneurs have graduated from their ranks, and

[47] T. H. Marshall, 'Changes in Social Stratification in the 20th Century', *Transactions of the 3rd World Congress of Sociology*, London, 1956, vol. 3, pp. 15-16
[48] Quoted by Alan Barcan, 'The Development of the Australian Middle Class', *Past and Present*, no. 8, 1955
[49] Isaac Deutscher, *The Prophet Armed*, London, 1954, pp. 187-91. Trotsky also noted the fallacy of applying European models to countries of European settlement when he wrote, 'there is no historical analogy, though there is a deep internal connection, between, for example, England and the modern colonies.' (Irving Howe, (ed.), *The Basic Writings of Leon Trotsky*, London, 1963, p. 55)

through the recruitment of their children into the public services and the professions. By contrast, the craftsman-turned-industrialist has tended to remain outside the English 'upper classes' because of status barriers, and in Western Europe the obstacles to social mobility have generated a corresponding radicalism.[50] The arbitration system depends heavily on the notion of 'work value' as a basis for establishing the payment of 'margins' for skill, and until the 1960's the fixing of margins for all kinds of occupations (including university professors) was based on the amount awarded to the A-grade fitter.

(e) Resistance to the idea of an 'upper class' is also conditioned by middle-class prejudice, derived from the liberal individualism which regards government activity beyond a certain minimum as wasteful and unproductive. The development of these attitudes in nineteenth century Britain is mirrored in the literature of the period. As George Orwell observed in his famous essay on Dickens, government is caricatured in Dickens' novels in terms of the Eatanswill election, or the activities of grotesques like Major Bagstock, Lord Coodle and Sir Thomas Doodle, or the Circumlocution Office. The persistence of these attitudes may be traced in Galsworthy, whose Forsytes have no contact with governmental circles. When Fleur Forsyte becomes engaged to Michael Mont, her father Soames is perturbed by this alliance with the governing classes, whose seriousness of purpose he suspects. These attitudes have been effectively transplanted to Australia, and the closeness between the middle classes and the governing groups, already noted, means that the latter are strongly influenced by the same outlook. On the other hand, it has been traditional to ascribe Australian hostility to governmental authority to the anti-authoritarianism of the working classes, and although this is undoubtedly a contributing factor it is only one-half of the story—perhaps even the smaller half.

V Summary

We may summarise these observations by constructing a threefold analysis of class, status and power according to the assumptions set out in the first three chapters of this book.

(a) Class (i.e. superior/inferior access to and control over the processes of production and distribution of material goods).

This is clearly the most important axis of social inequality in Australia, and the most readily separable into stratified levels. The following real-life categories of differentiation have been treated as significant (in roughly descending order): (i) Ownership and control; (ii) Occupation; (iii) Education; (iv) Ethnic origin.

This leads to a six-class system—

Class I ('upper')—comprising large business proprietors and directors, large landowners, the elite of the medical and legal professions, and the heads of large public enterprises.

[50] S. M. Lipset and R. Bendix, *Social Mobility in Industrial Society*, New York, 1959, ch. 2

Class II ('upper middle')—professional men and women, managers and administrators (private and public), proprietors of medium-sized businesses and landholdings.

Class III ('lower middle')—the white-collar majority, small shopkeepers, teachers, small farmers, technicians and some skilled workers.

Class IV ('upper working')—skilled workers and some technicians and white-collar workers.

Class V ('lower working')—unskilled workers, seasonal rural labourers, barmaids and domestics.

Class VI ('depressed')—most aborigines and part-aborigines, lumpen-proletariat, chronic unemployables, pensioners with no other means.

N.B. The word 'depressed' has been chosen here because of the invidious connotations of the term 'lower class'. The group is heterogeneous, but its members would all score low on the real-life categories listed immediately above. The situation of pensioners is occupationally and hence economically depressed. The situation of aborigines is depressed on every count, as is that of chronically unemployable white Australians. Moreover, the operation of the arbitration system provides legal and bureaucratic sanctions which help to legitimate the depressed position of these groups.

(b) Power (i.e. superior/inferior access to and control over the political, legal, and coercive mechanisms of influence and authority).

This is second in importance after class (in Australia), but is not susceptible to the same, relatively clearcut division into strata. Power, in David Riesman's words, is 'situational and mercurial', and is best represented by a system of overlapping and interlacing hierarchies, differentiated by the span of authority of their leading members, the exclusiveness of membership, and the scope of social action to which they aspire. In this case, four real-life categories of differentiation are regarded as significant, again in roughly descending order: (i) Ownership and control; (ii) Public rank; (iii) Occupation; (iv) Religion. (Sex could be added, as a factor which effectively eliminates one-half of the population from the domain of power.)

Along the power axis, we may distinguish at least five of the hierarchies just mentioned, in a rank order which corresponds to the general argument of this book.

(I) (a) and (b) Directors and managers of large companies (which includes a large component of overseas influence), and ministers in the federal government.

(II) Judges, arbitrators, and senior Commonwealth government officials.

(III) Leaders of organised interest groups—trade unions, occupational associations, industrial associations, and special-status groups such as ex-servicemen's organisations.

IV (a) and (b) State government ministers and heads of large state enterprises.

(V) Religious leaders (especially Catholic) and other manipulators and leaders of opinion.

The linkage of these five groups by what I have described in Chapter 1 as a 'governing consensus' gives Australia its nearest approach to a power elite. The form and content of these linkages is explored in detail in parts 3, 4 and 5 of this book.

(c) Status (i.e. superior/inferior position in an accepted or established hierarchy of social roles and functions).

In Australia this comes third in order of importance, and is principally affected by the following categories of differentiation, again in roughly descending order of importance: (i) Occupation; (ii) Public rank; (iii) Ownership; (iv) Education; (v) Religion; (vi) Ethnic origin; (vii) Family; (viii) Sex; (ix) Age.

For reasons examined in the earlier chapters, it is even more difficult in this case to devise an ordinal system of ranks; status is very much an attribute of the individual and a product of overlapping group memberships (Simmel's 'web of group affiliations'). It is, however, possible to point out where rankings on a status dimension differ from those on the two other dimensions. For instance, the highest status can be assigned with confidence to judges and arbitrators, doctors, and other professionals, whose positions on the two other dimensions are significantly different in relation to one another and to other groups. Another high-status group is the 'man on the land', especially the stock breeder, whose position on the class dimension would be lower and on the power dimension lower still. A special aura attaches to the status of the ex-serviceman, reflected in the influence enjoyed by the major ex-service organisation, the Returned Services League, but this does not carry over into the class and power dimensions. Conversely, the status of the government official is not high (unless he also wears a professional man's hat), but he is near the top of the power domain and of only slightly less importance on the class scale. Descent and kinship have status significance but little on either the class or power axes. The businessman's status is well below that of the professional man (and as we shall see in a later chapter, businessmen themselves make this evaluation), but in a capitalist society he appears inevitably at the top of the class and power dimensions. These contradictions illustrate some of the complexities entailed in the relationships between the three dimensions of inequality. It is because of these complexities that I have not attempted, in this chapter, to give a single list of 'class' categories of the kind employed in opinion surveys. Such lists may be regarded as shorthand versions of the more complex schemata which govern individual attitudes. Up to this point, we have been concerned with the general character and possible validity of these schemata. In subsequent chapters, the social structures which exemplify the nature of class, status, and power relationships will be explored at some length.

7: Aspects of Social Stratification (1)

Up to this point, I have endeavoured to set out a theoretical framework for the study of our theme. In parts 3, 4, and 5 of this book, we shall be concerned with the detailed examination of some major hierarchies of class, status and power in Australia. First, however, it will be expedient to look at some of the important influences on stratification, both tangible and intangible, and to suggest how they contribute to the model of class, status and power described in Chapter 6. The next three chapters do this.

Income

Income distribution is a test of the real strength of egalitarian values in any community. On this test, Australia is markedly more egalitarian than most other industrial societies, but it still exhibits extremes of wealth which make possible widely differing styles of life at various levels.

No fully accurate picture of income distribution can be given because sources of information are incomplete. In the USA, incomes are included in the decennial census, but not in Australia (although it is understood that the 1971 census will carry an income question). Sample surveys of households, carried out by official bodies or private research organisations, are comparatively rare. Income tax statistics remain the only real source, and are subject to well-known drawbacks resulting from avoidance in the form of capital gains, expense accounts, profits retained by companies, income splitting by wealthy families, and so on, as well as outright tax evasion.

The reports of the Commissioner of Taxation show a fairly constant profile over the period since 1950, with a large bunching of incomes in the middle ranges. In 1964-65, for instance, this range was between $1,800 and $3,399, taking in 56·5 per cent of all taxpayers and 47·6 per cent of taxable income. This corresponds roughly to manual workers with their wages fixed by industrial tribunals. The next highest group, with taxable incomes between $3,400 and $7,999, accounted for 20 per cent of taxpayers who earned 31 per cent of taxable income, and the higher-income group ($8,000 plus) encompassed 2·43 per cent of taxpayers who earned 11·71 per cent of taxable income.[1]

[1] A detailed discussion of income and taxation figures is given by Bruce McFarlane, *Economic Policy in Australia*, Melbourne, 1968, pp. 201-10. See also P. A. Samuelson, Keith Hancock, Robert Wallace, *Economics*, Sydney, 1969, ch. 6.

An attempt to look further into the taxation figures has been made by Keating in an examination of 'factor income', i.e. income broken up according to sources.[2] In Table 7·1, Keating compares factor income with disposable income, i.e. after taxation.

Table 7·1 Income Distribution, 1953-54

Deciles	Factor Income %	Disposable Income %
10	30·2	25·0
9	13·9	13·3
8	11·5	11·9
7	10·5	9·9
6	9·6	9·2
5	8·2	8·7
4	6·6	6·9
3	4·9	5·5
2	3·3	4·6
1	1·3	5·0
	100·0	100·0

This table indicates the limited amount of redistribution actually achieved by income taxation. Keating notes that the figure of 5 per cent of total disposable income received by the lowest tenth is probably meaningless because it reflects the operation of pensions and other welfare payments; it is much larger than the proportion in the first column because most people at this level are pensioners and have no taxable income. He also suggests that the low proportion of dependants shown on tax returns by wealthy people (1·07 dependants per taxpayer) is a sign not of small families but of large-scale income splitting (largely achieved by setting up private companies with dependants as shareholders). Keating found that salaries and wages were the most equally distributed form of income; the most unequally distributed was farm income, where the 'wealthy grazier' remains an important factor. His table shows that the upper 30 per cent of taxpayers received more than half of total factor income, and he also found that the top 1 per cent, i.e. people with actual incomes of £4,000 ($8,000) or more, received 9 per cent.

A more detailed examination of Keating's top 1 per cent discloses that 3·3 per cent of them (1100 in all) were salaried employees, with an average taxable income of £4,600 ($9,200); the rest, 33,000 in all, derived most of their income from 'personal exertion'. The largest group (11,700) were primary producers, with the highest average income. The situation has changed only slightly in the intervening period. In 1964-65, the highest income group, earning $10,000 or more, included 1·4 per cent of taxpayers and accounted for 8·35 per cent of taxable income. The contribution of salaried managers and professional men, especially doctors, had

[2] M. S. Keating, 'An Experimental Study of the Size Distribution of Personal Income in Australia in 1953-54', B.Com. thesis, University of Melbourne, 1962

risen relative to primary producers, who in 1953-54 were still enjoying the boom in wool prices touched off by the Korean war; nevertheless, wealthy graziers still comprise about half of the highest income group.

The rising trend of salaries among industrial managers has been evident for several years. An international comparison, made in 1962, showed that managers' salaries were rising faster in Australia than in seven other countries—USA, UK, Germany, France, Argentina, Italy, and Mexico.[3] Between 1960 and 1961, the total increase in payments to chief executives in all these countries, apart from the United States, was 9 per cent; the Australian figure was 15·2 per cent. The survey noted, incidentally, that US citizens in the employ of American subsidiaries were paid from one-third to two-thirds more than local managers, which is a direct reflection of the fact that the salaries of chief executives of American companies are 40-50 per cent higher than those of their overseas counterparts. A similar survey made in Australia by a firm of management consultants several years later showed a continuing rise.[4] The survey covered 890 managerial positions in nineteen large firms, eleven American, two British, three Australian, and three jointly owned. During 1967-68, the salaries of chief executives rose by 11·3 per cent, lifting the average base pay from $25,000 to $28,000. 'Middle-rank executives' went up 12·4 per cent, from an average of slightly less than $11,000 to more than $12,000.

A more detailed picture of businessmen's incomes may be derived from a survey of 445 directors and managers made in 1966 by Beed.[5] The results are shown in Table 7·2. Figures relate to taxable income.

Table 7·2 Incomes of Businessmen, 1966

Income Range ($000)	% of Respondents
38 +	10
26 — 38	11
20 — 26	18
14 — 20	30
8 — 14	27
Less than 8	4
	100

Beed found that 65 per cent of his respondents obtained more than half their income from salary; 30 per cent derived as much as 20 per cent of their income from investments, and 14 per cent obtained more than half of their income from this source. These figures illustrate the limitations of taxation figures, especially at the higher income levels, as a source of data,

[3] Arch Patton, 'Executive Compensation Here and Abroad', *Harvard Business Review*, September-October 1962. The article is an examination of an annual survey made by the management consulting firm, McKinsey and Co.
[4] *Australian Financial Review*, 19 June 1968, reporting a survey by the management consulting firm, Hay-MSA Pty Ltd
[5] C. S. Beed, 'Career Structures of Australian Company Directors', M.Com. thesis, University of Melbourne, 1967

since much investment income avoids tax through being treated as capital gains.

The incomes of businessmen have obviously risen much faster than those of people in the lower and middle income groups. Industrialisation has meant that overseas standards of remuneration, as applied by large international companies, have accelerated the rise of managerial salaries. As in other countries experiencing rapid industrial expansion, the demand for managerial personnel has grown faster than the supply, and salary levels and 'perks' have expanded sharply in response. The expansion of professional occupations, and the rising demand for professional services, produces similar effects. Information about professional incomes is available from two surveys carried out in Victoria by the Appointments Board of the University of Melbourne in 1956 and 1964.[6] In this period, average weekly real earnings for all employed males in Victoria rose by 18·3 per cent, compared with increases of real income among professional men in the same period ranging from 63·1 per cent for dentists to 27·6 per cent for lawyers and 28·5 per cent for doctors; other professional groups (engineers, architects, accountants) had increases ranging from 31 to 38 per cent. Table 7·3 gives figures of median income and inter-quartile range, and differentiates between private practitioners and the general body of the profession.

Table 7·3 Professional Incomes in Victoria, 1964

Profession		*Median Income*	*Inter-quartile Range*
		($)	*($)*
1 Medicine	All	8,800	6,000
	Private (58%)	10,600	6,000
2 Dentistry	All	8,160	4,000
	Private (87%)	9,000	4,200
3 Engineering	All	6,180	1,920
	Private (32%)	8,000	6,000
4 Architecture	All	5,700	2,740
	Private (59%)	7,000	5,860

The term 'private' used in the table refers both to self-employed practitioners and to employees of private practitioners. For private practice, the figures are somewhat misleading because earning power varies considerably at different periods of life. Private medical practitioners attain their maximum earning capacity in their forties and retain it for about fifteen years, whereas for architects the peak does not come until ten years later. Lawyers present a somewhat different picture because so few are in public employment (3 per cent of the 1964 survey). In their case, a median figure is of little significance, because the range of earnings at different ages is so wide ($2,600 in the 20—24 age group, reaching $10,800 in the 55—59 age group). Lawyers reached the highest income level of all groups.

[6] K. Gravell, *Professional Incomes in Victoria*, University of Melbourne, 1957 and 1964

Between the ages of 55—59, one-quarter of all lawyers earned more than $16,000. Corresponding figures for the upper quartile of medical incomes were $13,400 (50—54 age group), for dentists $14,300 (50—54 age group), and for architects $10,000 (also 50—54).

This survey is almost certainly biased by a relatively high proportion of people working in the public sector, and by disproportionately few replies from professionals in the highest income ranges. A sample survey of general practitioners in Victoria in 1967 found that 70 per cent had incomes between $8,600 and $15,710, 45 per cent earned more than $11,620, and 14 per cent more than $15,710. The median net income of the sample was $11,620; solo practitioners had the lowest median figure ($10,580) and members of large group practices had the highest ($12,670).[7] Private inquiries from doctors also suggest that medical incomes are somewhat higher than the Victorian survey indicates. According to my informants, the normal range for a general practitioner (in 1968) was from $10,000 to $20,000. Advertisements in the medical press for the sale of practices confirm this estimate. Specialists naturally earn more. Perhaps the highest paid specialists in the age of the motor car, which provides this incidental contribution to medical affluence, are orthopaedic surgeons, whose income was variously estimated as reaching $50,000 to $60,000. Specialist physicians were estimated to earn between $20,000 and $30,000, with neurologists and pathologists somewhere in between the physicians and the specialist surgeons.

Another group affected by these income movements are government officials, whose salaries have risen partly in response to movements in the private sector in conformity with the doctrine of 'fair comparisons' enunciated in Britain in 1955 by the Royal Commission on the Civil Service. In particular, official salaries are influenced by movements in professional employment, since a high proportion of government officials are professional officers. In December 1966, for example, the salaries of the 600 members of the Second Division of the Commonwealth Public Service were fixed at six levels ranging from $9,500 to $14,500, and the salaries of the twenty-five permanent heads in the First Division at $17,500 (Grade A) and $15,000 (Grade B).[8] In the state of New South Wales, top-level salaries in 1967 ranged from $13,000 for permanent heads to $19,000 for the chairman of the Public Service Board, $14,000 for the Crown Solicitor and the Treasury under-secretary, $15,500 for the Auditor-General, $19,100 for the Commissioner of Railways, $19,300 for the Chief Justice, and $17,500 for the puisne justices. Assistant under-secretaries received varying amounts averaging $10,000. Salaries in the other states were similar but lower.

[7] R. B. Scotton and A. D. Grounds, 'Survey of General Practice in Victoria', *Medical Journal of Australia*, 18 January 1969
[8] The salaries of permanent heads were raised in December 1968 to $22,750 + $1,500 allowance for Grade A, and $19,500 + $1,000 allowance for Grade B. A few months later, the salary of the Chief Justice of the High Court was raised to $30,000.

As already observed, income differences in Australia show a smaller spread than in other industrial societies. Mayer has compared the income distribution disclosed in the 1960 census of the United States with corresponding Australian figures. The bunching of incomes in the lower ranges had no counterpart in the United States, where the proportion of incomes in each range of $1,000 was similar, whereas in the Australian distribution 87 per cent of cases fell in the three lowest ranges. In Mayer's comparison, based on 1956-57 figures, the inter-quartile range was $1,300 compared with $5,000 in the US. The top 2 per cent of Australian incomes began at the $4,500 level, the top 2 per cent in the US at the $15,000 level.[9] The inequality of incomes in the United States is demonstrated in detail by Kolko, who argues that a radically unequal distribution of income has existed, with only minor changes, since at least 1910. Throughout the 1950's, the income of the top tenth of income-earners was larger than the total for the bottom five-tenths.[10]

These differences are maintained if we widen the comparison. Kuznets has shown the broad similarity of income distribution in a number of industrial countries.[11] In the United Kingdom, for instance, 18 per cent of taxable income in 1957 went to the top 5 per cent of taxpayers, and 41·5 per cent went to the top 20 per cent. Similar proportions obtained during the 1950's for Germany, Denmark, and the United States. Sweden had a more extreme distribution; 24 per cent of income went to the top 5 per cent and 52 per cent to the top 20 per cent. Holland was at the other extreme, with 13 per cent going to the top 5 per cent and 38·5 per cent to the top 20 per cent. In Australia, in 1956-57, the top 5 per cent earned 16 per cent of taxable income, and the top 20 per cent received 30 per cent. A similar picture is found by looking at the lower income levels. In Germany, the lowest 60 per cent of taxpayers received 34 per cent of taxable income; in Denmark, 32 per cent; in the US, also 32 per cent. In Holland, the figure was 40 per cent and in Sweden only 23 per cent. In Australia, the lowest 60 per cent of taxpayers earned 42 per cent of taxable income.

Since the middle of the 1950's, distribution of income has become more unequal; in particular, the poorest section of the population has received a decreasing share of total income. The very rich, like the very poor, have also received a decreasing share, probably because of a decline in the relative prosperity of primary industry. Between 1952 and 1961, according to Lydall's calculations, the income level of the top 1 per cent of income earners increased from 2·21 times the median figure to 2·55; the income level of the top 10 per cent increased from 1·57 times the median to 1·81. These changes are due partly to the accumulation of private fortunes in

[9] Kurt B. Mayer, 'Social Stratification in Two Equalitarian Societies', *Social Research*, vol. 31, no. 4, 1964

[10] Gabriel Kolko, *Wealth & Power in America*, London, 1962, pp. 13-16

[11] Simon Kuznets, *Modern Economic Growth*, London, 1966, pp. 206-19. See also H. F. Lydall, *The Structure of Earnings*, Oxford, 1955.

industry and partly to increases in differential payments (margins) for skill and responsibility from the middle 1950's onwards.

It should be noted, however, that the distribution of income appears to have remained largely unchanged during this century, and that the share of national income received by the working class, in particular, has remained virtually the same, whereas in Britain and Western Europe the share of the working class in national income has risen appreciably.[12] The rise in professional and business incomes, and the increasing number of large private fortunes made in the post-war industrial boom, are also tending to narrow the difference between Australia and other industrial societies. There is, moreover, considerable evidence of real poverty in Australia, affecting at least 10 per cent of the population,[13] which is rarely taken into account even by those people who favour a more even distribution of income. The neglect of poverty in this connection may be due to the fact that the myth of egalitarianism makes Australians relatively indifferent to the problem of income inequality, as found in attitude surveys conducted by Davies and Collins.[14] Income distribution is largely maintained by the arbitration system, and those in poverty are those who are not in a position to make claims for payment before an industrial tribunal, especially widows, old age pensioners, Aborigines, and chronically unemployable persons. The institutional apparatus of equalising income distribution neglects those whose problems do not fit into the institutional pattern.

The relation between income level and class identification has been studied by Broom and his colleagues on the basis of survey data collected in 1965.[15] Of those with incomes below $1,800, 68 per cent identified themselves as working class, and the proportion fell steadily to 16 per cent in the group with incomes over $5,000. There was a corresponding fall among the 'upper-middle class' respondents, from 32 per cent in the highest income bracket to 3 per cent in the lowest. The 'middle class' respondents peaked in the income range $4,200-$4,999, and the 'lower middle' group in the income range $3,400-$4,199. Peaks of class identification are thus precisely associated with income levels, although the total spread is such as to give a positive correlation of only $0 \cdot 37$. However, this figure is not very different from results obtained in British and American surveys.

Occupation
Individuals form social groupings according to the particular nature of the social activity to which they consecrate themselves. Their natural milieu is

[12] Kuznets, ibid.
[13] John Stubbs, *The Hidden People*, Melbourne, 1966; R. J. A. Harper, 'Survey of Living Conditions in Melbourne', *Economic Record*, vol. 43, 1967
[14] A. F. Davies, 'Politics in the New Suburb', *Australian Journal Politics and History*, vol. 8, no. 2, 1962; J. Collins, 'Social Attitudes & Political Differences', *Australian Journal Politics and History*, vol. 9, no. 1, 1963
[15] L. Broom, F. L. Jones and J. Zubrzycki, 'Social Stratification in Australia', in J. A. Jackson (ed.), *Social Stratification*, Cambridge, 1968, pp. 222-4

no longer the natal milieu, but the occupational milieu. . . . In a general way, classes and castes probably have no origin nor any other nature; they arise from the multitude of occupational organisations.

Emile Durkheim, *The Division of Labour in Society*

The study of occupational differences has been, in Australia as elsewhere, a pillar of the study of social differences in general, especially those grouped under the loosely inclusive title of 'class'. All analyses of class, from Marx onwards, have relied on occupation as a major criterion of 'objective' class position. In the unfinished Chapter 52 of Vol. III of *Capital*, Marx had begun to speculate about the relation between class and occupation. Since then, reliance on occupation has grown, especially in American sociology, as a 'summary indicator for other class characteristics, especially income and education, which in turn also reflect upon other class characteristics such as life styles and attitude patterns.'[16] The study of occupations provides a measure of social differences which is comparatively solid and reliable, which even the unsophisticated can recognise with some precision, which seems to establish a straightforward consciousness of common identity, susceptible to statistical analysis, and capable of experimental replication. Arnold Rose commented that occupation and its two closely related variables, income and education, virtually *are* 'class' so far as the literature of American sociology is concerned.[17] This is a fallacy. Occupation is not a synonym for class differences but an index, and only one of a number of indices whose interrelations are crucial for an understanding of the texture of social inequality in any given society. These relations have at least three aspects. Firstly, changes in the occupational structure provide a convenient way of opening up the general question of structural social change and its effects on the social consciousness of various groups of people. Secondly, the interlacing of occupation with non-economic variables such as ethnic origin, religion and sex helps to build up characteristic structures of social inequality which differ from one society to another. Thirdly, occupational differences contribute to the structure of class, status and power through their relationship to income differentials, economic organisation, the prestige hierarchy of society and the political influence of particular occupational groups.

An early attempt to map the occupational structure of Australia was made by the Commonwealth Statistician's office in 1928.[18] Using categories similar to those of the Registrar-General in England, the Bureau produced a table in which occupation and income were combined to yield four 'classes', as shown in Table 7·4.

At that time, the basic wage of the unskilled worker was approximately £175, so that the spread of occupational and income differentiation was

16 Leonard Reissman, *Class in American Society*, New York, 1960, p. 158
17 Arnold M. Rose, 'The Concept of Class and American Sociology', *Social Research*, vol. 25, no. 1, 1958
18 Commonwealth Bureau of Census and Statistics, *Monthly Bulletin of Employment*, February 1928

narrow in comparison with other countries and with present-day Australia. Since then, the major trends have been a fall in rural employment, which was 26 per cent in 1921, to 14·6 per cent in 1947 and 9·66 per cent in 1966; a growth in white-collar and service occupations; a slow increase in professional and related occupations in the 1940's, and a much more rapid one in the 1950's and 1960's; and, since 1933, a steady climb in the employment of women, among them married women.

Table 7·4 Class, Occupation and Income in 1928

Class	Income (£)	Occupation	Numbers
Upper	1,000 +	Landowner Merchant Wealthy professional Shareholder	52,000 (1·6%)
Upper Middle	800—1,000	Established farmer Successful businessman Public administrator Other professional	650,000 (17·5%)
Lower Middle	400—800	Small farmer Farm worker Office worker Protective services Skilled worker Other services Small business	1,352,000 (34·5%)
Lower		Unskilled Unemployed and 'poor'	2,955,000 (46%)

The study of occupational stratification depends heavily on official statistics, which were collected on a national scale for the first time at the census of 1947, and again at the censuses of 1961 and 1966. Until 1947, the census asked questions only about industry and employment status. In 1947, an occupational scale was introduced with eight categories, based mainly on level of skill, which lumped together a number of occupational groups of diverse character in the same categories (thus, 'domestic and protective' included domestic servants, hairdressers, undertakers, jockeys, policemen and firemen). The 1961 and 1966 censuses are based on the International Standard Classification of 1958.

On the basis of such figures as do exist, Hughes and Rawson estimated that between 1921 and 1947 there were relatively small changes in the work force. Omitting primary industry, the proportion of manual workers remained practically constant from 1921 to 1947, and the growth of white collar occupations was small, enough only to compensate for the falling proportion of employers and self-employed which was noticeable during the same period, and amounting to perhaps 5 per cent.[19] According to the

---

[19] Helen Hughes and D. W. Rawson, 'Collective Bargaining and the White-Collar Pay Structure', *Journal of Industrial Relations*, vol. 2, no. 2, 1960

1928 table, 3·5 per cent of the population were in professional and related occupations, and approximately 4 per cent in administrative, proprietorial or managerial positions. By 1947, professionals accounted for 5·1 per cent, the 'administrative' category (which includes business) for 5·4 per cent, and 'clerical' occupations for 11 per cent. These proportions may be compared with Table 7·5, which shows the extent of changes between 1961 and 1966.

Table 7·5 Occupations in 1961 and 1966

		1961 %	1966 %
Occupational Group			
0	Professional, Technical & Related Workers	8·4	9·3
1	Administrative, Executive & Managerial	7·0	6·3
2	Clerical Workers	13·0	14·7
3	Sales Workers	7·6	7·7
4	Farmers, Fishermen, etc.	11·1	9·6
5	Miners, Quarrymen, etc.	0·8	0·6
6	Workers in Transport & Communications	6·4	6·1
7/8	Craftsmen, Production-Process Workers & Labourers, n.e.c.	36·4	35·5
9	Service, Sport & Recreation	7·0	7·4
10	Armed Services	1·0	1·2
11	Inadequately described or unstated	1·3	1·6
		100·0	100·0

Table 7·5 shows a continuing increase in 'professional, technical and related workers' and clerical workers, and a continuing decrease in rural workers. The fall in the 'administrative, executive and managerial' group is due almost entirely to a fall in the proportion of women; this category accounted for 4 per cent of the female work force in 1961, but only 2·5 per cent in 1966. The reasons for this change are obscure, and may relate to tax avoidance rather than occupational shifts. The male proportion remained almost unchanged. These increases are, of course, linked with the expansion of higher education and the rise of professional and business incomes, discussed elsewhere in this chapter. As Reiss has pointed out, the construction of scales of occupational prestige, which provide one form of social ranking, depends in fact upon the clustering of three variables, which in American studies intercorrelate by a coefficient of at least 0·9.[20] The presence of all three factors is evident in the results obtained by Congalton in a series of studies of occupational prestige. Congalton tested a scale of 134 occupations, first on a random sample of 303 persons in Sydney and then on 1,189 university students in all states, with very high agreement between the two studies.[21] Subjects were asked to rank the

[20] Albert J. Reiss, *Occupations and Social Status*, New York, 1961
[21] A. A. Congalton, *Status and Prestige in Australia*, Melbourne, 1969. A critique of Congalton's methodology is given by J. D. Allingham in the first issue of the ANZ *Journal of Sociology*, 1965, and a reply by Congalton appears in the following issue.

occupations on a seven-point scale. Those most highly regarded were as follows:

1 Doctor
2 University professor
3 Solicitor
4 Architect
5 Professional engineer
6 Director of large enterprise
7 Owner of business worth more than £50,000
8 Dentist
9 Veterinary surgeon
10 Clergyman
11 University lecturer
12 School principal

At the bottom of the list were truck driver, railway shunter, porter, night watchman, waitress, packer, barman, cane cutter, seasonal labourer, wharf labourer, charwoman, and road sweeper. Jobs in the middle ranges, where such studies often encounter wide disagreements, were also placed fairly securely. Most of the twelve highly regarded categories are professional occupations requiring university education.

The relation of occupation and identification with a subjective 'class' label has been investigated in several surveys. The Australian Gallup Poll, in 1961, made a survey of voting intentions before a federal election, and asked a number of related questions at the same time.[22] Unfortunately, the occupational classification used in this survey is too unreliable to show any consistent association between occupation and class identification. Individual associations which are of interest relate to the 'managerial and professional' group (11·9 per cent of the sample) who identified themselves overwhelmingly with the 'middle class' (80 per cent) rather than with the 'upper-middle class' (13 per cent); and the skilled workers (22·5 per cent of the sample), of whom 38 per cent identified with the middle class, 14 per cent with the lower-middle class, and only 46 per cent with the working class. A much more refined survey was carried out by Broom and his collaborators, who proceeded by reducing the census classification of occupations to 100 groups and then to sixteen, with jobs grouped according to the same type of skill.[23] On this basis a prestige hierarchy of six groups was constructed, using American data as well as Congalton's results, which was then tabulated against the social class identifications found in a national sample survey of 1,877 males carried out by the Gallup Poll in 1965.[24]

[22] Detailed breakdowns of this survey are given in A. F. Davies and S. Encel, *Australian Society*, Melbourne, 1965, pp. 110-13.
[23] L. Broom, F. L. Jones and J. Zubrzycki, 'An occupational classification of the Australian work force', ANZ *Journal of Sociology*, vol. 1, no. 2, 1965, supplement
[24] L. Broom, F. L. Jones and J. Zubrzycki, 'Social Stratification in Australia', in Jackson (ed.), *Social Stratification*, pp. 224-26

The six occupational groups were as follows:
I—professional men; graziers, sheep and wheat farmers
II—managerial; self-employed shop proprietors; other farmers
III—clerical and related workers; members of police and armed services
IV—craftsmen and foremen
V—shop assistants; operatives and process workers; drivers
VI—personal, domestic and other service workers; miners; farm and rural workers; labourers
Table 7·6 shows the proportions found in the subjective social classes, as compared with the proportions in these occupational groups.

Table 7·6 Class Identification and Occupational Ranking

	Class Identification		*Occupational Ranking*
	%		%
U	—	I	12·4
UM	11	II	20·5
M	29	III	13·1
LM	11	IV	22·5
W	45	V	18·9
Lower	4	VI	12·6
	100		100.0

Broom and his colleagues found that the correlation between the class scale and the six-point occupational scale was no more than 0·35 per cent. (By using sixteen occupational categories it rose only to 0·36 per cent.) The striking points of association were similar to those in the 1961 Gallup Poll. In occupational group I, 28 per cent of 'upper professionals' identified themselves as upper-middle class and 48 per cent as middle class; the proportions among 'graziers, wheat and sheep farmers' were very similar. Among the 'lower professions' (of whom the largest group are teachers), the distribution of class identification was much more even; 23 per cent identified with the upper-middle class and 20 per cent with the working class. Among the 'other farmers', 40 per cent saw themselves as working class, compared with 27 per cent of clerical workers, 48 per cent of shop assistants, and 26 per cent of those in managerial occupations.[25] 'Craftsmen and foremen', like the skilled workers of the 1961 Gallup Poll, were inclined to identify with the middle classes; 22 per cent identified as 'middle' and 12 per cent as 'lower middle'. Broom *et al,* noting that this proportion is much higher than in American and British studies, suggested that 'the absorption of skilled workers into the middle class may have proceeded more rapidly in Australia.'[26] As pointed out earlier, this depends on what is meant by 'class', and it is more relevant to notice that skilled

[25] The finding concerning working class identification among shop assistants is consistent with the data of Oeser and Hammond in 1949; O. A. Oeser and S. B. Hammond (eds.), *Social Structure and Personality in a City*, London, 1954, pp. 279-80.
[26] op. cit., p. 226

workers (and foremen even more) prefer a status-charged label such as 'middle class' to an occupation-based label such as 'working class'.

The picture of Australia as an open society is linked with the notion of ample opportunities for occupational mobility. Studies of the social background of groups such as government officials, businessmen, etc., reported elsewhere in this volume, suggest that this traditional view is greatly exaggerated, and that its relation to the egalitarian philosophy is also suspect. As Lipset and Bendix have suggested, actual and imagined rates of mobility in industrial societies often differ significantly, and these societies appear to reach a relatively stable level of mobility once their economic development has passed a certain point. Mobility rates seem to be effectively determined by the occupational structure, and influenced only marginally by differing social values.[27] A study by Allingham shows how small the actual rates of mobility may be.[28] Allingham took a sample of 4,548 bridegrooms from 29,328 marriages registered in 1960 with the New South Wales Registrar-General and compared their occupations with those of their fathers.

Table 7·7 Occupations of NSW Males, 1960

Occupation	Sons %	Fathers %
1 Professional and semi-professional	8·7	3·9
2 Administrative, proprietary, managerial	3·8	8·5
3 Clerical and sales	15·9	8·8
Total—'white-collar'	28·4	21·2
4 Skilled and unskilled workers	57·0	57·2
5 Service	5·8	4·9
Total—'blue-collar'	62·8	62·1
6 Rural enterprise	8·4	16·7
7 Not in work force	0·4	—
	100.0	100.0

Although these figures confirm the general picture of an increase in white-collar and professional occupations they suggest that this has not come about through mobility out of manual occupations. On the other hand, Broom and Jones, on the basis of a national sample, argue that 'circulation mobility' in Australia is higher than in the United States, although the latter has a higher general level of mobility. This, they conclude, is due to the high level of 'structural' mobility, which is the result of rapid economic

27 S. M. Lipset and R. Bendix, *Social Mobility in Industrial Society*, London, 1959, pp. 13, 71-74
28 J. D. Allingham, *Occupational Mobility in Australia*, Ph.D. thesis, Australian National University, 1965, and 'Class Regression', *American Sociological Review*, vol. 32, no. 3, 1967

change, whereas circulation mobility involves free choice of occupations. However, even in their study, mobility out of unskilled and semi-skilled occupations is low by comparison with other occupational groups.[29]

The expansion of professional and white-collar occupations has been accompanied by changes in social consciousness, and particularly by assertions on the part of associations of professional workers to a special place in the community. Professionals have successfully claimed increased salary differentials as well as recognition of special status. This has come about, in the established legal-bureaucratic fashion, by decree of industrial tribunals which have been prepared to agree that higher education increases the 'work value' of an occupation.[30] In 1954, the Public Service Arbitrator, who deals with the salaries of Commonwealth government employees, accepted this contention in the case of research scientists, and agreed also that the special character of scientific work merited pecuniary recognition.[31] In 1961 and 1962, the Commonwealth Arbitration Commission extended this principle in the two Professional Engineers' Cases, declaring that 'this is a technological age in which the needs of mankind continue to become more and more complex', that the satisfaction of these needs depended greatly on the skill of the engineer, and that low salaries prevented the professional engineer from occupying the 'honoured place in the community which was his right and entitlement'.[32] The effects of this judgment have encouraged other professional groups to make similar claims, and provided a stimulus to the already apparent trend to raise educational standards among professional and aspiring professional groups. At the same time, the economic and social position of white-collar occupations has undergone large changes which have deprived jobs like that of bank manager of their traditional status and pecuniary value, and led to the growth of white-collar militancy expressed through trade unionism.[33] As two British students remark, the individualism of the white-collar worker has been modified by an attitude of 'instrumental collectivism' which perceives the value of collective bargaining and unionism. 'The development of marked discrepancies between income and status hierarchies tends to be productive of radical attitudes on the part of those who are unable to secure a degree of social recognition commensurate with their economic standing.'[34]

Finally, one should notice the special contribution made by the social standing of particular occupations to the structure of power and authority. This applies with particular force to the role of law and medicine, but

[29] L. Broom and F. L. Jones, 'Father-to-Son Mobility', *American Journal of Sociology*, vol. 74, no. 3, 1969
[30] J. R. Kerr, 'Work Value', *Journal of Industrial Relations*, vol. 6, no. 1, 1964
[31] CPS Arbitration Reports, 1954, determinations 51 and 52
[32] S. Encel, 'Social Implications of the Engineers' Cases', *Journal of Industrial Relations*, vol. 6, no. 1, 1964; Davies and Encel (eds.), *Australian Society*, pp. 30-33
[33] R. J. O'Dea, 'The White-Collar Worker', *Quadrant*, vol. 3, no. 4, 1959; K. F. Walker, in Adolf Sturmthal (ed.), *White-Collar Trade Unions*, New York, 1966
[34] J. H. Goldthorpe and David Lockwood, 'Affluence and the British Class Structure', *Sociological Review*, vol. 11, no. 2, 1963

extends to other professional groups. In subsequent chapters, the special position of professional men in the government service is examined, as well as the contribution of lawyers and doctors to politics. As we have seen, the social position of the medical profession, measured by almost any yardstick, is perhaps the highest of any group in Australia, and it extends into the realm of political decision-making, particularly where matters of health and welfare policy are concerned. The growth of the welfare state, in a number of countries, has brought changes in the position of the medical profession and caused strains in its relationship to governments. Australia is almost unique in that conflicts over policy on medical services have normally resulted in victories for the organised profession, whose political strength is buttressed by its social status. The structure of the national health scheme which has operated since 1950 was virtually dictated by the Australian Medical Association, working in a remarkably direct way through a Minister for Health (Sir Earle Page) who was himself a doctor and was succeeded in office by another doctor. Under this scheme, private medical and hospital insurance organisations play a major role, and have grown immensely wealthy; many of these organisations are presided over by medical men. An interesting subsidiary illustration of the influence of the organised profession relates to the history of bio-medical research under the auspices of the National Health and Medical Research Council, established in 1937, where it was taken for granted for many years that medical opinion should be represented by the AMA and not by medical researchers themselves. It was not until 1963 that this situation began to change, and active researchers were given the opportunity to make policy on research.[35]

The legal profession is, of course, intimately concerned with the structure of authority in many countries. In Australia, its strength is heightened by a written constitution and the intricacies of the federal system, which have provided a goldmine for the profession for two generations. But its distinctive position in the Australian social structure rests, above all, on the complex web of judicial, quasi-judicial and administrative tribunals which constitute one of the pillars of the bureaucratic ascendency—an ascendency which gives an enormous social role to the judge, the lawyer, and the 'bush lawyer' who often fills the role of advocate or adjudicator even in the absence of legal training.

The Honours System

Titles are but nicknames, and every nickname is a title. The thing is perfectly harmless in itself, but it marks a sort of foppery in the human character, which degrades it. It reduces man into the diminutive of man in things which are great, and the counterfeit of woman in things which are little. It talks about its fine blue ribbon like a girl, and shows its new garter like a child.

Thomas Paine, *The Rights of Man*

[35] C. L. Rubenstein, 'The Development of Medical Research in Australia', M.A. thesis, University of Melbourne, 1969

Paine, in 1791, could deride the absurdities of aristocratic titles and use them as an argument for liberal democracy. Like other radicals of the Enlightenment, he regarded the ceremonial display of stars, garters, and ribbons as merely a reflection of the established order of deference, created not by human nature but by human artifice, which democracy would overthrow. Formal titles of deference would have no place in a society where a man's place in the world depended on his own efforts, and not upon inherited rank or royal favour. Sociologists, at least in the United States, have accepted the Enlightenment view and see a decay of formal rank going on *pari passu* with the growth of social democracy. A familiar illustration in such arguments is the decline of ceremonial uniforms and insignia in the armed forces. A recent restatement of this view comes from Edward Shils, who suggests that deference ceases to be concentrated in separate actions but becomes attenuated and fused into a wide range of social interactions. 'Deference survives in attenuation, in a pervasive, intangible form which enters into all sorts of relationships through tone of speech, demeanour, precedence in speaking, frequency and mode of contradiction, etc.'[36] And he asserts that modern Western societies are moving in the direction of attenuation and 'deference-indifference', with the United States, Canada and Australia in the lead. This is no more than extrapolation, a notoriously hazardous and unreliable pastime. Although Canada abolished British honours for its citizens in 1935, it moved back towards an honours system in 1967 with the introduction of national awards to mark the centenary of Canadian federation. In Australia, the proliferation of titles and awards has shown a steady increase since the 1950's. Even in the United States, other trends could be extrapolated to counter Shils' conclusion. For instance, the Purple Heart was actually re-introduced in 1932 after two centuries of desuetude, and Presidential citations have become increasingly common. The Soviet Union, after abolishing titles in 1917, found it necessary to introduce the Order of the Red Flag for its troops in the following year, and the establishment of the Order of Lenin in 1930 was the beginning of a large expansion of awards and prizes for both soldiers and civilians. It is well known that Napoleon established the Legion of Honour in 1802 as a *bourgeois* substitute for hereditary titles, but the red rosette is only the apex of a lesser-known array of awards for Agricultural Merit, Social Merit, Commercial Merit, etc.

It could, in fact, be argued against Shils that the growth of the middle class is a prime reason for the development of the system of official awards. *Bourgeois* society is the world of the *parvenu*, who craves recognition of social status to match his worldly success; like Homais, the pharmacist in *Madame Bovary*, the only character in that tale for whom it ends happily when he is awarded the Legion of Honour. Historically, the rising middle classes were hostile to hereditary titles, but their victory was followed by new forms of honorific symbolism, derived not from hereditary rank but

---

[36] E. A. Shils, 'Deference', in Jackson (ed.), *Social Stratification*, p. 117

from the ancient orders of chivalry, which now acquired a new function. In Britain, for example, most of the orders of merit, both civilian and military, are of comparatively recent origin, created to satisfy bourgeois demands and disdained by the aristocracy, whose attitude was expressed by Lord Melbourne when he praised the Order of the Garter because there was 'no damned merit about it'. One of the more recent is the Order of the British Empire, established in 1917. Many observers have noted the continued use of the word 'empire' in its title (another, less important example is the Imperial Service Order). The empire may have vanished, but its spirit lives on in the honours system, which in Australia depends for its existence on the continuing strength of the British connection and the survival of its colonial aspects.

The growth of the honours system may be gauged from Table 7·8, which covers three periods. The first column is based on the list of knights (and dames) living in 1949, as shown by the 1950 edition of *Who's Who in Australia*. In 1949, the Labor government of Mr J. B. Chifley, which had a very austere policy regarding honours, was replaced by the Liberal government of R. G. (later Sir Robert) Menzies, under whose auspices a large expansion of the system took place. Even the Menzies era, however, divides into two phases which show definite trends. To make these clearer, the ranking of the occupations and activities represented are shown in each column.

Trends in the award of knighthoods, both numerical and qualitative, emerge clearly from Table 7·8. The effects of industrialisation since 1945 are felt in the spectacular increase in the number of company directors knighted, some of them undoubtedly for contributing to Liberal Party funds, but some also for their philanthropic activities. Eight of those knighted between 1960 and 1967 were in the last category. Others have been rewarded not only for their success in business but for service on official boards, committees, and advisory councils. The expansion of higher education is reflected in the growth of awards to academics. Vice-chancellors can now expect to be knighted *ex officio*, as it were, but the increased number of academics in the 1960-67 period also denotes the rise in the prestige of science (some scientists having also been included under the guise of 'government officials'). Medical men have always been a group of particularly high status, and the apparent willingness of an affluent society to spend more and more on health has enriched them, increased their political influence, and raised their status even higher. Politicians have lost pride of place because their numbers are virtually fixed, and so the number of awards varies little. Nor, despite the increase in the size of the federal parliament in 1949, has there been an increase in knighthoods among federal politicians. In state politics, a title remains the emblem of success, a token of elevation from the role of petty colonial politician to that of imperial statesman. In federal politics, a knighthood is commonly a sign that a man has abandoned hope of further advancement. The comparatively relaxed attitude of federal politicians towards knighthoods is exemplified by the story of Sir Arthur Fadden, Federal Treasurer from 1949 to 1958 and briefly Prime Minister in 1941, who remarked on his elevation from KCMG to GCMG, 'Not bad—twice a (k)night at my age.'

Table 7·8 Knighthoods in Australia, 1949-67

Titles held in 1949		*Titles conferred 1949-59*		*Titles conferred 1960-67*	
1 Politicians (state, 25) (federal, 9)	34	1 Politicians (state, 20) (federal, 11)	31	1 Company directors	44
2 Company directors	29	2 Company directors	25	2 Government officials (federal, 28) (state, 9)	37
3 Judges	14	3 Government officials (federal, 17) (state, 6)	23	3 Politicians (state, 18) (federal, 8)	26
4 Medical practitioners	11	4 Judges	20	4 Medical practitioners	22
5 Government officials (federal, 7) (state, 2)	9	5 Medical practitioners	17	5 Judges	15
6 Academics	9	6 Primary producers	9	6 Academics	15
7 Municipal politicians	7	7 Municipal politicians	6	7 Municipal politicians	11
8 Primary producers	3	8 Academics	5	8 Primary producers	8
9 Press proprietors	3	9 Press proprietors	3	9 Welfare workers	6
10 Others	11	10 Welfare workers	3	10 Clergy	2
		11 Clergy	2	11 Sportsmen	2
		12 Others	6	12 Others	18
Sub-total	130		150		206
Soldiers	11		18		7
Total	141		168		213

Another growth area is the honouring of officials of voluntary organisations concerned with sport, social welfare, and above all the affairs of ex-servicemen. Five of the knighthoods awarded during 1960-67 went to officials of ex-servicemen's organisations. Women have figured increasingly, partly through their activity in voluntary organisations, partly as an acknowledgment of their husbands' contribution, personal or financial, to the government parties. Dame Enid Lyons and Dame Zara Holt, both widows of former Prime Ministers, are in this pattern; so are Dame Pattie Menzies and the late Dame Annie McEwen, former wife of the leader of the Country Party.

The inflation of honours can be seen even more strikingly if we move down to the companion level, remembering the advice given to Nancy Mitford's heroine: 'Never look below the OBE's, my dear!' Accordingly, Table 7·9 stops short of the OBE's and includes the CBE, CMG, CB, and ISO.

Table 7·9 Companions in Australia

Occupation or Activity		Awards held in 1949	Awards Conferred 1949-67
1	Government officials	70	203
2	Company directors	23	117
3	Medical practitioners	17	50
4	Politicians	13	26
5	Welfare workers	12	35
6	Academics	9	31
7	Officials of ex-service organisations	9	13
8	Judges	5	13
9	Municipal politicians	3	6
10	Municipal officials	3	5
11	Clergy	2	17
12	Primary producers	1	33
13	Schoolteachers	1	5
14	Sportsmen	—	9
15	Journalists	—	13
16	Political party officials	—	7
17	Others	4	23
	Total	172	606

Table 7·9 shows the extent of the honours inflation even more strikingly than Table 7·8. Military awards have been omitted as they follow a long-established pattern which bears little relation to the trend of civilian awards. The growth points are similar, although rates of increase vary. At the companion level, there has been a particular expansion of awards to company directors, welfare workers, sportsmen, primary producers, clergymen, political party workers, and journalists. There is, of course, an overlap between Tables 7·8 and 7·9, as some of the individuals appearing in the latter were subsequently promoted to the former. This is particularly so in the case of Commonwealth public servants, for whom the *cursus honorum* has become well established: CBE, knight bachelor, KBE. Some graduate from OBE to CBE, but not further, and hardly any from MBE to OBE.

If we disregard the advice given to Miss Mitford's heroine, and look all the way down the list, we can observe how widely, and how rapidly, the practice of awarding honours for the most commonplace 'public services' has spread. The New Year honours list (civil) for 1933 contained just twenty awards, and by 1952 it had grown to only twenty-eight. By 1962, it had climbed to 132—fourteen knighthoods, twenty-two companionages, thirty-two OBE's, fifty MBE's, and fourteen British Empire Medals. All but one of the BEM's went to lowly but faithful servants of the Commonwealth government—cooks in the parliamentary refreshment rooms, typists in the parliamentary typing pool, drivers and attendants. The growth of the MBE reflects the practice of rewarding voluntary welfare work, especially by women, which we have already noticed. In 1962, twenty-five of the fifty MBE's went to Girl Guiders, nursing sisters, Red Cross officials, and charitable workers. Nine of the thirty-two OBE's also went to people in this category, but the general spread of the award is wider.

It need hardly be said that the growth of the honours system does not chime with egalitarian social values. Radical and nationalist sentiment in Australia has, for many years, regarded the honours system as a symbol of colonial dependence on Britain which should be done away with. In Mrs Campbell Praed's novel *Longleat of Kooralbyn*, first published in 1881, the hero is a nationalist politician whose aims include the abolition of titles and the appointment of Australians to the post of colonial governor. On this point, Australian radical opinion has marched closely in step with British radical opinion. Henry Labouchere's famous remark, 'Another bung got a beerage!' on learning that yet another wealthy brewer had been ennobled for contributing to party funds, was popular in republican circles in Australia. Humbert Wolfe's lines would also have been well received:

The House of Lords
is waiting for
the newspaper
proprietor.

Soap! attention!
Listen, beer!
Glory to the
new-made peer.

Hark! the Heralds' College
sings
As it fakes his
quarterings.

The Uncelestial City

In 1891, the *Bulletin* newspaper published a celebrated satire on the Order of St Michael and St George. The two saints, it observed, were both dead and buried, and to be the companion of two corpses was 'about the same as being brother to a quantity of stale fish, or uncle to an ancient egg . . . the whole affair is empty foolishness, inasmuch as nobody cares whether anybody else is the companion of a saint or the grandfather of an umbrella-mender . . . the three letters are sadly misplaced, because most of those who wear them are more in want of a reliable "h" than of any other letter of the alphabet.'[37] O tempora, O mores! The proprietor of the *Bulletin* (since 1961) is Sir Frank Packer.

In 1905, a radical journalist wrote of the award of a knighthood to the

[37] Quoted by C. M. H. Clark, *Sources of Australian History*, London, 1957, pp. 450-51.

semi-literate Premier of Victoria, Thomas Bent, that 'the savage has got his beads and hoop-iron at last.'[38] The London *Times*, in 1903, noted that Australians were 'very suspicious of decorated and betitled politicians', and resolutions opposing the award of honours were adopted by federal conferences of the Australian Labor Party in 1918, 1921, 1930 and 1955. These attitudes have been reaffirmed, both by resolution and by the refusal of awards, on many occasions.[39] Nevertheless, a few Labor politicians accepted awards in the 1930's, among them W. C. Angwin of Western Australia, a former state minister and Agent-General in London (CMG, 1933), and a Labor member of the Tasmanian state parliament, F. McDermott (MBE, 1938). Since 1945, these isolated cases have turned into a steady stream, and despite the party's traditional opposition to the paraphernalia of empire, individual Labor men and women have shown much less disposition to spurn them.[40] The most notable case was the acceptance of a knighthood in 1959 by the former Labor Premier of Tasmania, Robert Cosgrove; his wife had been created a Dame several years previously. Both continued as active members of the party, and no attempt was made to censure them. The former president of the Australian Council of Trade Unions, Mr Albert Monk, who in 1964 upbraided union officials at the May Day celebrations for their ignorance of working class traditions, accepted the CMG in 1966. As R. H. Tawney wrote in 1935, the public could not be blamed for drawing the obvious conclusion that Labor politicians were no different from other politicians, and that their indignation at social inequality was 'vociferous cant'.[41]

There is some evidence that enthusiasm for honours has changed in quality. In 1956, an opinion poll showed that two-thirds of all respondents were in favour of the honours system, and that party differences on the issue were not great.[42] By 1967, a reversal had taken place, and only 24 per cent favoured imperial honours (16 per cent of Labor supporters, 30 per cent of non-Labor supporters). The largest group, 43 per cent, favoured a national system of awards, and the political difference was slight (Labor supporters 46 per cent, non-Labor 42 per cent).[43] The latter poll was evidently influenced by the decision of the Canadian government to institute a national system of awards, and it may also reflect a longer-term decline in the popularity of the monarchy and the attenuation of the Commonwealth of Nations. Nevertheless, the majority of Labor supporters were in favour of an honours system in some form. In the

---

[38] Randolph Bedford, *The Snare of Strength*, Melbourne, 1905. The book is a novel, most of whose characters are thinly disguised portraits of contemporary Victorian politicians.

[39] John Playford, 'The Labour Aristocracy', *Outlook*, February 1968

[40] See Playford for a number of examples; S. Encel, 'The Honours Inflation', *Nation*, 18 June 1962

[41] R. H. Tawney, in *New Statesman* and *Nation*, 22 June 1935

[42] APOP, *Bulletin*, March 1956

[43] ibid., November 1967

affluent society, the widening scope of social differentiation finds one outlet in the thirst for status symbols.

A by-product of this symbolic structure of prestige is the growth of the directory of notable people—the Almanach de Gotha, Debrett and Burke, the *Social Register, Who's Who*. The exact value of the information contained in these publications is difficult to assess, and attempts to use them as a guide to the structure of prestige and status can lead to some comical conclusions. Ambassadors, for instance, are notoriously prone to be misled by using such directories. Wright Mills' chapter on 'The Celebrities' in *The Power Elite* is the least distinguished part of that otherwise compelling book. On the other hand, Baltzell (in *Philadelphia Gentlemen*) has effectively used the history of the Social Register to illustrate the development of the relations between 'old' and 'new' wealth in the United States. A historical examination of *Who's Who in Australia* can be used to trace changes in its standards of selection which are clearly, though imperfectly, related to the growth of an increasingly complex set of social differences. This publication has been issued irregularly throughout the twentieth century by various editors and publishers, until it was taken over in the 1940's by Australia's largest newspaper combine, the Herald and Weekly Times Ltd, which published it at varying intervals until 1959, when it settled down to a regular triennial existence. For the purpose of this study, five issues were examined—1928, 1938, 1947, 1955 and 1965. In the two latter cases, the number of entries was too great for a complete analysis, so a 10 per cent random sample was taken. From a mere 483 entries in 1928, the number had grown to 9,000 in 1965.

Over this period of almost forty years, the strength of the 'bureaucratic ascendency' is reflected in the pages of *Who's Who*. In 1928, 30 per cent of all the entries were state and Commonwealth government officials, and the proportion rose steadily until 1955—31 per cent in 1938, 33 per cent in 1947, 38 per cent in 1955. Thereafter, although the absolute number has continued to increase, the proportion dropped to 24 per cent in 1965 because of growth in other fields, but remains the largest group of all. Politicians, on the other hand, have decreased spectacularly in proportion throughout the whole period because their total numbers are almost static, falling from 28 per cent in 1928 to 8 per cent in 1965. This proportionate fall is even more notable because in 1928 only one-third of all MP's were included, whereas since 1955 the coverage has been complete. Before 1955, only a few judges were thought worthy of inclusion, but since then all judges of the High Court and of the state Supreme Courts have been included, so that in 1965 they formed 2 per cent of the entries.

The inclusion of businessmen has shown some interesting fluctuations. In 1928 they ranked third, after government officials and politicians, with 24 per cent of all entries. This rose to 30 per cent in 1938, 32 per cent in 1947 and 34 per cent in 1955, but in 1965 it had fallen to only 12 per cent. The reason appears to be that *Who's Who* now exercises more rigorous standards for the inclusion of company directors who have no executive functions, especially in smaller companies. Whereas in 1938 two-thirds of the businessmen included had purely directorial functions, by 1955 this was true of only 6 per cent of the entries, and the extension of this criterion into later editions led to a fall in numbers, both absolutely and in proportion.

One of the striking changes after 1955 was the great increase in the representation of the professions. In 1928, 8 per cent of the entries were professional men (including journalists, lawyers, accountants, engineers, medical practitioners, authors and artists). The proportion remained almost static until 1955, when it was 10 per cent, but climbed rapidly thereafter to reach 20 per cent in 1965, when it constituted the second largest group. Medical practitioners, in particular, jumped from 1 per cent of the total in 1955 to 8 per cent in 1965. (These figures do not include government medical officers, who are treated throughout as government officials.) The academic profession, which is not included in the above figures, was almost unrepresented until 1955, when it accounted for 5 per cent, and by 1965 this had grown to 12 per cent. Other groups of special note were artists (especially painters), clergymen, sportsmen, dentists, architects, and scientists, all of them virtually unrepresented up to 1955, but present in appreciable numbers in 1965. The expansion of Australia's international relations is reflected in the increased number of diplomats, who accounted for 4 per cent of entries in 1965 compared with less than 2 per cent in 1955.

Another change, even more striking, is the inclusion of women in significant numbers. Until 1955, only a handful of women appeared in any one edition, but since then the number has risen steadily to 487 in 1965 (over 5 per cent). Among these, the three largest groups were in professional occupations (128), office-bearers in voluntary organisations (115), and artists or authors (105). Education accounted for 101, seventy-six of whom were headmistresses or school principals, and twenty-five were academics.

In earlier years, the editors of *Who's Who* were able to exercise standards of choice which were much more personal and whimsical, reflecting both the comparative smallness of their task and the simplicity and flexibility of Australian social structure before 1939. With a much larger task and the growth of formal criteria the pattern of choice becomes more predictable and easier to relate to broad social changes. The honours list creates a virtually automatic criterion of editorial choice. More important is the expansion of professional, technical and managerial occupations, creating a formalised ladder of social and economic advancement which is increasingly reflected in the pages of *Who's Who*.

Clubland

Bernard Barber has observed that the texture of social stratification depends on a variety of 'accessible associations' whose membership reflects differences based on occupation, income, education, ethnic origin, religion and so on.[44] The prototype of this situation is the club which operates by election, and the extent of status differences in a society can almost be measured by the growth of a hierarchy of 'exclusive' clubs. The role of such institutions in Australia is similar to that of the London clubs (described, e.g. by Anthony Sampson in *Anatomy of Britain*) or those in large American cities (as described by Baltzell in *Philadelphia Gentlemen* and *The Protestant Establishment*), and their criteria for membership are similar—old-established family, wealth, Protestant religion, military rank, and senior status in one of the learned professions. The charter of the Athenaeum Club, Melbourne, defines its purpose as providing 'service and kindly intercourse between persons of kindred tastes and disposition, and to establish common ground on which gentlemen of intelligence and character may meet together, irrespective of class distinction and personal wealth.'[45] In practice, the last injunction is ignored. The early establishment of clubs arose from the needs of the landed gentry or 'squatters' for a residence in the metropolis. The two earliest clubs, the Australian (Sydney) and the Melbourne Club were both founded in 1838 for this purpose, and the latter took over a hotel building with twelve bedrooms to serve its up-country visitors.[46] A century later, a hostile critic observed that the tone of the exclusive clubs was still set by the pastoralists, who graciously allowed 'judges, leading doctors and professors, bankers and a few leading merchants into their sacred halls', shutting out all but a few Catholics and excluding Jews 'silently and hermetically'. The clubs, he declared, had no wish to form 'cultivated communities of "distinguished" men . . . but only to create a carefree atmosphere for people of the "right type". If a man does not belong to this circle, no "distinction" will get him in. . . . People who are uncertain of their chances will prefer not to stand for election rather than risk a blackball.'[47]

Anti-Jewish and anti-Catholic discrimination, although quietly practised by a number of city clubs and select golf clubs, is generally denied in public, but occasionally emerges into full view. The Melbourne Club and the Australian Club (Sydney), both of which customarily extend honorary membership to judges of the High Court of Australia, did so in the case of Sir Isaac Isaacs, who became Chief Justice and later Governor-General, but he refused the invitations because of their general policy of discrimination. At this level, racial and religious discrimination is usually subtle enough not to become public: the members of the out-group which is the object of discrimination are rarely willing to endure the quasi-martyrdom involved in breaking the taboo. In Queensland, however, discrimination against Catholics has resulted in public outbursts. A leading Catholic businessman and civic figure, T. C. Beirne, was blackballed by the Queens-

---

[44] B. Barber, *Social Stratification*, New York, 1957, p. 71
[45] M. H. Ellis, 'A Guide to Clubland', *Bulletin*, 2 April 1961
[46] Margaret Kiddle, *Men of Yesterday*, Melbourne, 1961, p. 79
[47] Karl-Heinz Pfeffer, *Die Bürgerliche Gesellschaft in Australien*, pp. 368-9

land Club; and an even greater uproar was occasioned by the blackballing of his nephew, Chief Justice Macrossan of the Queensland Supreme Court. The club did finally admit Sir William Webb, another Catholic judge who was appointed to the High Court in 1947, but not without obvious discomfort. In 1956, after three businessmen had been blackballed in rapid succession, the Labor government of Mr V. C. Gair, all of whose members were Catholics, put an Act through the state parliament giving the victim of a blackball the right to appeal to a court. One successful action was taken under this Act, but it was soon repealed under the Country-Liberal coalition, led by Mr G. F. Nicklin, which took office in 1957.[48] The Queensland Club, which is effectively the headquarters of the United Graziers' Association of Queensland, is periodically in the news because of its political role, which was well developed in the nineteenth century and has persisted into the twentieth. Its dogged resistance to Catholics is partly due to this political character. Labor politics in Queensland have been dominated for many years by the Australian Workers' Union, representing shearers and other rural workers, many of whose leaders are themselves Catholics. As a result, the professional and businessmen who, in other cities, are well represented in similar clubs, are more likely to be found in the Brisbane Club, Tattersall's Club, or the Johnsonian Club.

In other states, the political role of clubs is largely a thing of the past. In Victoria, accusations were often made in the Legislative Assembly that the colony was governed, or rather that the government of the colony was obstructed, by intrigues hatched at the Melbourne Club. The basis for this accusation was that the conservative members of the upper house were mostly wealthy graziers who resided there.[49] In 1878, the Premier of Victoria, Graham Berry, who was then engaged in a prolonged battle with the upper house, attacked the 'clique or cabal who aspire through the Melbourne Club to rule this colony.'[50] In South Australia, political and social changes in the past generation have diluted the political influence of the Adelaide Club, although it remains considerable.

One of the most celebrated incidents in the history of clubs was the great schism, inspired by a mixture of personal and political antipathies, which led to the establishment of the Union Club in Sydney. After a violent dispute, a number of members of the Australian Club broke away, taking with them records and membership lists, and set up in 1857 as the Union Club, whose title was chosen, as its official historian discreetly observes, to denote 'a place where members of all political parties could meet without any display of the rancour which then undoubtedly existed between "Tory" and "Liberal".'[51] The Australian Club was then a stronghold of 'Toryism', but it would now be difficult to distinguish between the two clubs on these grounds. The main difference is that, while both cater for

[48] *Bulletin,* 8 July 1961
[49] Kiddle, op. cit., p. 478
[50] Ernest Scott, *Historical Memoir of the Melbourne Club,* Melbourne, 1936, p. 61
[51] R. H. Goddard, *The Union Club,* Sydney, 1957, p. 3

squatters, business and professional men alike, the tone of the Australian Club is set by the squatters, and of the Union by businessmen. A list of members of the Union Club shows how the names of a number of well-known business families have remained attached to the club for many years —Knox (since 1857), Baillieu (1918), Fairfax (1863), Hoskins (1904), Lysaght (1929), and Vicars (1921), but a number of well-known pastoral families are similarly represented—Hordern (1913), Dangar (1857), McCaughey (1883), Mackinnon (1900), and Ryrie (1901). The New South Wales Club, somewhat less 'select' than the Union, also caters largely for businessmen, but professional men have in recent years preferred the University Club. In 1968, a new phase in the history of the Australian Club was marked by the announcement that it was combining with the NSW Club and that the two bodies would subscribe jointly to the construction of a new building. The rising value of real estate in central city areas was the main reason for this move. The Pioneers, Imperial Service and Royal Sydney Golf Clubs, and the Royal Sydney Yacht Squadron also have more or less 'exclusive' criteria for membership. The Imperial Service Club has an intermittent reputation as a hotbed of right-wing politics, particularly as it was the centre of the semi-Fascist 'New Guard' in the early 1930's (see below, Chapter 25).

The three leading clubs in Melbourne specialise in a similar fashion. The Melbourne is dominated by graziers, as may be seen from a list of its presidents and vice-presidents.[52] Among them are represented the surnames of a number of old-established pastoral families like Mackinnon, McArthur, Cox, Fairbairn, Officer, Manifold, Niall, and Sanderson. The Australian, partly for geographical reasons, has a large membership of lawyers, brokers, and men connected with the wool and pastoral industries. The Athenaeum, also for partly geographical reasons, caters for business and professional men, especially doctors. Perhaps four other clubs in Melbourne have claims to 'exclusiveness', the Naval and Military, Yorick, Savage, and Tattersalls' Clubs.

Perth, like Sydney, Melbourne, and Brisbane, has three leading clubs— the Weld, West Australian, and Perth Clubs. The Weld, established in 1892, 'was named after a pleasant but quite undistinguished governor of the day, and ever since it has been housed in the secluded building with a high wall at the corner of Barrack Street and Bazaar Terrace. Originally it was composed almost entirely of old Western Australians and was controlled in the most rigid fashion . . . old Western Australians still figure largely on its membership rolls.' This form of exclusiveness was at one time a source of bitterness in Perth society. 'Strong men have died frustrated and chagrined for one reason, and one reason alone. All their wealth and all their power could not buy them membership of the Weld Club. Spoilt wives who had everything their husbands could give them have hung their heads in shame because all their attractions could not make

---

[52] Scott, op. cit., p. 70

them the wives of members of the Weld Club.'[53] Perhaps because of this exclusiveness, the two other clubs have grown up to vie with the Weld, which is now largely a *pied-à-terre* for country gentlemen of the older generation, with various old-world customs such as preparing its own barley-water for elderly members. The West Australian Club is favoured by younger and more active members of the landed gentry, and the Perth Club by businessmen and professionals.

In South Australia, however, one club has succeeded in maintaining an unchallenged position. The Adelaide Club, centre of what is frequently described as the South Australian 'establishment', reflects a remarkably close-knit, complacent and old-fashioned upper class whose ramifications include the land, politics, one or two private schools, commerce and industry; whose solidarity is buttressed by a high degree of endogamy among the 'forty famous families'; and whose values remain strongly coloured by an atavistic attachment to Edwardian England.[54] More than any other, it demonstrates that the exclusive clubs retain a role in the structure of privilege and power, despite a number of changes which have attenuated their pretensions.

Divers Groups

Some social groups defy categorisation, which is probably a good thing for humanity. The student of social reality must resign himself to the existence of difficult cases and the limits imposed by the normal curve and the standard deviation. Not all students of society have been willing to accept these limitations and have worked hard to squeeze complex minorities into their Procrustean taxonomies. The most notorious offenders were Marx and Engels, although their writings about Jews and women, for instance, could charitably be interpreted as lapses. Marx's famous (or infamous) essay on the 'Jewish question', published in the *Deutsch-Französischer Jahrbücher* in 1844, is less open to this charitable interpretation, partly because it is soaked in a familiar brand of 'Jewish anti-Semitism'; partly because the dogmatic attitude of Marxists towards such questions is deep-rooted; and partly because of the actual treatment of Jews by the self-proclaimed Marxists of the Soviet Union and the Communist parties under their control. Engels' treatment of women in his deplorable pamphlet on the *Origin of the Family* may be regarded with more charity, except that it has been used as a scriptural text by successive generations of Marxists.

To describe women as a 'group' is, of course, to strain language beyond reasonable limits, yet the fact that women have certain exclusive roles ('vive la différence', etc.) does give them a special place in the hierarchy

---

[53] V. Courtney, *All I May Tell*, Perth, 1939, p. 181
[54] Katharine West, *Power in the Liberal Party*, Melbourne, 1966, pp. 72-8, examines the political role of the Adelaide Club, whose history is related by E. J. R. Morgan, *The Adelaide Club 1863-1963*, Adelaide, 1963.

of class, status and power. The position of women is itself a contribution to the quality of social hierarchies, and the intersection of their special position with other planes of social division is usually characteristic of any given society. As far as Australia is concerned, certain paradoxical features are worth noting.[55] Legal, civil and political equality was 'granted' (the word, so commonly used, is itself emblematic) to women from an early date, relatively speaking; with only a minor struggle, the right of female adult suffrage was established by the turn of the twentieth century. But, unlike most other countries where there was a struggle, women have made little use of their political opportunities. Perhaps the two are contingent. Since the beginning of the century, fewer than twenty women have sat in state or federal parliaments, and only three have held ministerial office. In other spheres described in this book, such as private business and public administration, women are even more conspicuous by their absence from positions of responsibility, and their role in the professions, the arts and the mass media is also relatively small—relative both to men and to other industrial urban communities with which Australia may reasonably be compared. The marriage bar in public employment began to come down only after the 1939-45 war (in the Commonwealth government service it was not dropped until 1966). The first woman judge was not appointed until 1966, and there are very few female magistrates. It was not until 1966 that a woman teacher was appointed principal of a co-educational high school in NSW.

In general, the ethic of egalitarianism does not extend to women. It can, moreover, be argued that women are able to attain positions of status, influence, and authority much more readily in societies where inegalitarian influences are strongly at work. In England, for example, aristocratic rank has been an important prop for women seeking an influential role in society. The prominence of women in the intellectual life of the country since the middle of the nineteenth century was made possible by the rise of an intellectual aristocracy based on a close network of upper-middle class families, and it was women from this milieu who pioneered the entry of their sex into the professions and fought the battle for political rights.[56] In the United States, the public role of women would not be possible without the existence of a large number of private fortunes in the hands of women, which in its turn helped to finance the establishment of institutions of higher education for women such as Vassar and Radcliffe. Perhaps it is significant that substantial changes in the status of women are occurring in Australia at a time when society is becoming more complex, more stratified, and less egalitarian. These changes include the growth of women in the work force; the rise in the proportion of married women at work until in 1966 it was more than half the female work force; the increase of women's

[55] The position of women is discussed at length by Norman MacKenzie, *Women in Australia*, Melbourne, 1962.
[56] Noel Annan, 'The Intellectual Aristocracy', in J. H. Plumb (ed.), *Studies in Social History*, London, 1955

numbers in the professions; the progressive lowering of the marriage bar in employment; and a generally increased disposition on the part of women to assert themselves.[57]

Women are not separable as a category in terms of class and power, although their position is a most important index of the distribution of status in any community. The Aborigines, on the other hand, who are conventionally ignored in accounts of the Australian social structure, may be fitted into it very readily. They occupy the lowest position on each of the axes of class, status and power, and constitute a powerful argument for the proposition advanced in the previous chapter that an account of social stratification in Australia requires a 'depressed' class to make it complete.

When the first British fleet arrived off NSW in 1788, there were probably something like 300,000 Aborigines in Australia. Through killing, poisoning, disease and ill-treatment their numbers had shrunk, in 1927, to 75,000 (of whom 60,000 were estimated to be full-blooded). Since the 1939-45 war their numbers have increased again to 130,000 at the time of the 1966 census (including 77,000 part-Aboriginals and 8,000 Torres Strait Islanders, who have ethnic links with New Guinea). Until the federal constitution was amended in 1966, Aborigines were not treated as part of the population of Australia. The administration of Aboriginal affairs has remained one of the most backward and unenlightened sections of public administration both in the states and in the Commonwealth. Because Aborigines are largely segregated from the urban white community, living in rural areas of the Northern Territory, Queensland and Western Australia, their problems enter the consciousness of the urban population only fitfully and fleetingly.

Hiatt[58] has classified the relations between Aboriginal and white Australians in geographic and social terms. Geographically, Aborigines come into contact with whites in rural, settlement, and urban settings, and the aims of white people in these three situations are, respectively, to exploit, to reform, and to avoid the Aborigines. Exploitation of Aborigines in the first case is largely connected with the pastoral industry, in which many Aborigines work as stockmen; traditionally, it also meant sexual exploitation of Aboriginal women. In general, Hiatt suggests, Aborigines have fulfilled these demands in order to obtain European commodities, especially food and liquor (although access to the latter has been strictly controlled by law). Treatment of Aborigines on settlements has varied from neglect to strict paternalism in the spirit of the Victorian missionaries who were determined to reform the heathen. Strict social distance has been the rule, although some Christian missions are honourable exceptions. 'Settlement

---

[57] Developments since 1960 are examined in the second edition of MacKenzie's book, N. MacKenzie and S. Encel, *Women and Society: An Australian Study*, Melbourne, 1971.
[58] L. R. Hiatt, 'Aborigines in the Australian Community', in Davies and Encel (eds.), *Australian Society*, pp. 274-95

officers rarely admitted Aborigines to their homes, expected to be addressed as "mister" or "boss", rode in the cabin of the truck with Aborigines in the back, and on visits to town mixed with the local elite.'[59] Justice is sometimes administered in a way which clearly distinguishes the rights of Aborigines from those of white Australians.[60] Settlements, concludes Hiatt, are places 'located away from white communities where Aborigines modify their behaviour in response to reformative pressures . . . the values imposed are characteristic of, though not peculiar to, respectable middle-class whites.'[61]

In urban situations, where Aborigines have settled or been settled by government action in country towns or large cities, white Australians normally do their best to avoid contact, although there has never been an official policy of segregation. Class attitudes show a predictable range of variation; in particular, trade unions have shown little enthusiasm for recruiting Aborigines or championing Aboriginal rights, despite their opposition to cheap coloured labour. In 1968, when the Aboriginal Welfare Board in NSW decided to settle some Aboriginal families in the NSW coastal town of Kempsey, white families in the town unsuccessfully appealed to the Board against this decision. 'I'm not against dark people, but this will devalue our houses', declared a housewife. 'The children will have to be inside by dark. You can't have them playing out there.' And she concluded: 'You wouldn't want your daughter to marry one.'[62] The press report of this interview appeared on the same day as the account of an enthusiastic welcome for the Aboriginal boxer Lionel Rose, who had just returned home after winning a world title.

The situation of the Aborigines is changing as a result of their growth in numbers; an increase among Aboriginal city dwellers; economic developments (including the decision of the Commonwealth Arbitration Commission in 1966 that Aboriginal pastoral workers in the Northern Territory should have equal pay); and the increasingly tender consciences of middle class Australians, stimulated by the world-wide rise of racial consciousness. In 1967, the federal government appointed, for the first time, a minister of state for Aboriginal affairs, who announced on assuming office that he would seek a new deal for Aborigines. Race relations will, in future, assume a new significance as part of the texture of class and status in Australia.

Racial consciousness is also an aspect of attitudes towards the immigrants who have played a major role in post-war social changes. Research on the place of immigrants in Australian society is still at an early stage of its development, and so far there is comparatively little evidence that nationality makes a distinctive contribution to the pattern of class and status. This is only likely to happen through the establishment of immigrant

---

[59] ibid., p. 284
[60] A number of examples are reported by C. M. Tatz, 'Queensland's Aborigines', *Australian Quarterly*, vol. 35, no. 3, 1963.
[61] op. cit., p. 287
[62] *Australian*, 1 March 1968

subcultures, which has not been characteristic of Australia. Although such subcultures do exist, they have so far been on too small a scale to produce anything comparable to the role of ethnic groups in American society and politics, and rapid assimilation into the conventional Australian pattern has been the normal course of events. There is evidence of specific political constellations among migrants,[63] but again their scale is too small to constitute more than a small tributary of the political mainstream. There are signs, however, that the growth of migrant concentrations in particular areas, like the Italian communities in central areas of the cities of Melbourne and Sydney, and the Greek communities in East Sydney and the Melbourne suburb of Prahran, may create specific patterns involving ethnic origin, religion, education, and occupation.

A particular migrant group that traditionally makes a specific and notable contribution to the majority culture is the Jewish community, which persists in being the exception to all rules. The position of Jews in society resists classification because the nature of Jewish identity is itself complicated, disputable and variable; because the Jews have survived as a separate community for so long and through so many tragic episodes; and because the Jewish contribution to European civilisation and European styles of thought is so extensive and so spectacular that it transcends customary standards of assessment. The situation in Australia is rather different, mainly because Jewish numbers have been too small to generate a collective impact on the community. The rate of assimilation and inter-marriage has always been high, and the role played by Jews in various fields has been individual rather than communal. Individual Jews have contributed to the growth of business activity, like Sidney Myer, founder of the largest retail trading enterprise in Australia; the Cohen family of Melbourne, in brewing; the (unrelated) Cohen family of Sydney, in banking, finance, and insurance; and the Michaelis and Hallenstein families of Melbourne, in the leather industry. But these instances do not add up to a Jewish business community like those which exist in New York and London, or used to exist in Western Europe before the Nazi holocaust. Again, several Jews have achieved prominence in the law, notably Sir Isaac Isaacs, who became Chief Justice of the High Court of Australia and first native-born Governor-General. Several other Jews have been appointed to the bench in NSW and Victoria, but there has been no collective Jewish contribution to the law, or indeed to any other profession or branch of learning.

The character of the Jewish community changed as a result of Nazi persecution in the 1930's. In 1933 the community consisted of a large number of anglicised Jews and a small proportion of migrants from Poland and Russia. Subsequent immigration, both before and after the war, created a largely new community dominated by Central and East European migrants and their children. In 1966, this community numbered about

[63] A. F. Davies, 'Migrants and Politics', in Alan Stoller (ed.), *New Faces*, Melbourne, 1967

70,000, only 0·6 per cent of the total population, but it had developed a more strongly marked communal identity which may lead, in turn, to a more specific Jewish contribution to the Australian cultural pattern.[64]

Jewish communities are normally exposed to anti-Semitic prejudice, and Australia is no exception. The manifestations of such prejudice are familiar, such as refusal to admit Jews to membership of exclusive clubs. The depth of prejudice was illustrated by the refusal of the Stock Exchange of Melbourne to admit a well-qualified Jewish applicant. At that time there were no Jewish members of the Exchange, and some members of the committee were reported as expressing their determination to keep them out —so that the Exchange would not be controlled by Jews as it allegedly was in New York.[65] The exposure of the story in the press soon led to a *cause célèbre*, and in the end the committee was forced to give way and admit a Jewish member—but not the original applicant. Prejudice against Jews for their reputed financial skill is not confined to tight little WASP oligarchies like the committee of the Stock Exchange. At an earlier period, it was closely bound up with anti-imperialist sentiment. Before the first world war, the nationalist weekly *Bulletin* invented the composite character of John Bull-Cohen, a British imperialist figure who was the instrument of Jewish financiers. During the war itself, the left-wing Labor MP, Frank Anstey, whose anti-British opinions were reinforced by Irish descent, wrote an anti-war pamphlet entitled *The Kingdom of Shylock*. In more recent years, anti-Semitic propaganda has become the province of extreme right-wing groups who find part of their audience among anti-Communist migrants, especially from southern and eastern Europe, whose anti-Semitism is of a traditional kind.[66]

Last among this collection of divers groups with special roles, we may briefly consider the question of the Australian 'establishment'. The use of this term was taken over, like many Australian intellectual fashions, from the literary world of London, where it became popular during the 1950's. Although nineteenth century English writers had railed against the establishment (or the Thing, as William Cobbett called it), its more recent vogue may usefully be dated from an article by Henry Fairlie in *Spectator* of 25 May 1956. Commenting on C. Wright Mills' book, *The Power Elite*, Mr Fairlie asserted that the two concepts should not be confused. The establishment, he wrote, 'denotes not only the oligarchs, but those who create and the pressures which sustain the climate of opinion within which they have to act . . . the Establishment has a collective opinion which those in positions of power cannot ignore. This opinion is separate from public opinion and, indeed, helps to create it; it is also separate from the opinion of particular and powerful interests. Establishment opinion has its own life and its own resources.' It is doubtful whether Mr Fairlie was wholly

[64] The development of the post-war Jewish community is examined by P. Y. Medding, *From Assimilation to Group Survival*, Melbourne, 1967.
[65] 'A Gentile Rialto', *Nation*, 9 April 1960
[66] K. D. Gott, *Voices of Hate*, Melbourne, 1965

serious, and his choice of the four leading members of the establishment strengthens this suspicion: the Archbishop of Canterbury, the Warden of All Souls, the editor of the *Times*, and the late Lady Violet Bonham-Carter (Baroness Asquith). Moreover, his article was primarily concerned with the BBC and the campaign by the 'establishment' supporters of the BBC against the introduction of commercial television, which may be taken as his serious purpose. His notion of the establishment is less persuasive than Claud Cockburn's invention of the Cliveden Set in the 1930's, which also included the editor of the *Times* and various fellows of All Souls, but was more closely identified with substantive sources of economic and political power.

Although the term 'establishment' quickly gained currency in Australia, few serious attempts have been made to probe either its composition or its scope of operations. By far the most important attempt to do so was made a few years ago by H. A. Wolfsohn, in his paper entitled 'The Ideology Makers'.[67] Wolfsohn contends that there is no such thing as a 'power elite' in Australia, but adopts another of Wright Mills' phrases instead—i.e. the 'higher circles'. His main complaint against the higher circles is their provincial outlook, which he blames for the mediocrity and philistinism of Australian culture. He takes issue with the traditional view that the 'real or alleged mediocrity of Australian society is the faithful reflection of the philistine standards of the Australian working and lower-middle classes.' This, he suggests, is itself a highly provincial view, since there are no societies where the 'working and lower-middle classes are distinguished by intellectual brilliance and cultural tolerance.' Rather, he goes on, the 'institutionally anchored wowserism and provincial conventionalism of the higher circles has so far been able to prevent large sections of the intelligentsia from making contact with the general public and from setting standards countervailing the cramping influence of the "establishment".' Like Henry Fairlie, Professor Wolfsohn has come close to identifying the establishment with the controllers of the mass media, and especially the Australian Broadcasting Commission, whose timidity over the discussion of public issues provides him with several illustrations of his thesis. Another example is the curious episode of the 'Call to the Nation', a manifesto signed by four churchmen and seven judges of state Supreme Courts, which was issued in November 1951 to recall the people of Australia to their duty to 'fear God and honour the King', so that the 'moral order' could be restored and with it 'true social order'. Professor Wolfsohn describes this as a 'third-rate imitation of the paternalistic postures of the nineteenth century British upper class'. (He might have added that the episode of the 'Call' bears a curious resemblance to the fictional account in Robert Musil's novel, *The Man Without Qualities*, of the 'Collateral Campaign' [*Parallel-Aktion*] launched in Vienna on the eve of the 1914-18 war in emulation of German nationalist propaganda.)

[67] Hugo Wolfsohn, 'The Ideology Makers', in Henry Mayer (ed.), *Australian Politics*, Melbourne, 1966, pp. 70-81

Professor Wolfsohn's account of the 'ideology makers' who act as spokesmen of the 'higher circles' is diverting, but no more serious than Henry Fairlie's. To paraphrase Tom Paine's remark about Burke, it concerns itself with the plumage but not the real bird. In particular, it begs the same questions as the 'power elite' theory by using the concept of the 'higher circles', but without trying to identify them. It is, moreover, mistaken in its assumption that the 'unattached intellectuals' have no influence on public policy. (Professor Wolfsohn wants them to gain access to 'some of the key advisory and policy-making positions in the administrative system'.) A number of intellectuals, especially economists, have influenced government policy both from within the system and from outside. W. E. Hearn, who taught political economy (and much else besides) at the University of Melbourne in the nineteenth century, was one such; another was R. F. Irvine, first professor of economics at the University of Sydney.[68] In the 1930's and 1940's, two notable examples were Lyndhurst Giblin and Douglas Copland, both professors of economics at University of Melbourne. The policies of the two federal Labor governments of 1941-49 were largely formulated by 'intellectuals' recruited from the universities and elsewhere. These examples could be multiplied from the fields of economic policy, immigration, external trade, agriculture, education, and welfare. If many intellectuals remain 'alienated', it is not because their views on public policy are disregarded, but because their dissatisfaction with society arises from other causes.[69] Size and geographical isolation are more important here than social structure. To say that Australia is provincial, imitative and colonial is to say that it is a distant and relatively small outpost of European civilisation. As Dan Jacobson, the South African novelist, has written, literary activity in the English-speaking countries of the Commonwealth is hampered by the relative absence of a local literature, the absence of a national intellectual tradition, the absence of established and highly-developed social forms, the absence of a local audience, and the feeling of exile from the metropolis, i.e. England.[70]

These conditions are highly discouraging to the growth of intellectual culture. Professor Wolfsohn is right to condemn the third-rate standards of the 'establishment', but an establishment can only have first-rate standards if it has a first-rate intellectual culture to draw upon.

[68] Irvine's work is described by Bruce McFarlane, 'Professor Irvine's Economics in Australian Labor History', monograph of the Australian Society for the Study of Labor History, Canberra, 1966; Giblin's in Douglas Copland (ed.), *Giblin: The Scholar and the Man*, Melbourne, 1960.
[69] The problems of cultural isolation and provincialism are discussed by Jack Lindsay in his two autobiographical volumes, *Life Rarely Tells* and *The Roaring Twenties*, London 1958 and 1960; and in fictional form by Christina Stead in her novel *Seven Poor Men of Sydney*, London, 1934.
[70] *Encounter*, April 1962

8: Aspects of Social Stratification (2): Education and Religion

Education and Society (1)

Education, which plays a major part in socialising the individual into his role in life, contributes thereby to establishing and perpetuating a hierarchy of social differences. The educational system is a powerful countervailing force against the egalitarian tendencies of Australian society, partly because of its authoritarian temper, partly because it reinforces other hierarchical factors, and partly because of the 'dual system' of public and private schools established between 1872 and 1893.

The authoritarian character of the system has its roots in the original authoritarian structure of the penal colonies which were the first phase of British settlement. Education, according to a Colonial Secretary of the period, had the function of caring for the children of convicts, of rescuing them from the evil influences of their surroundings, and later of developing 'habits of industry and regularity and . . . the principles of the Established Church.'[1] Religious indoctrination, moral regeneration and social control would keep the lower orders in their place and educate them for employment as clerks or mechanics. These attitudes remained entrenched among the upper classes well into the twentieth century. A member of the upper house of the NSW colonial parliament declared in 1880 that the task of education was 'to teach habits of regularity, order and obedience to properly constituted authorities and submission to the law.'[2] Perhaps the crudest formulations in this vein are to be found during the campaign to introduce state education in South Australia, where Low Church obscurantism was strongest. The Minister for Education himself asserted in 1875 that the real motive behind the agitation for free state education was 'continental communism' and that the trade union movement was plotting to use education as a lever to extend state action in other fields. A self-made businessman, Joseph Fisher, was opposed to compulsory education because it would mean wasting money on the instruction of females.

[1] Dispatch from Lord Bathurst to Governor Macquarie, 13 May 1820, *Historical Records of Australia* 1, X, p. 304
[2] Quoted by R. M. Pike, 'The Cinderella Profession: State School Teachers of NSW 1880-1963', Ph.D. thesis, Australian National University, 1965, p. 11

'God forbid', he declared rhetorically, 'that we should have educated women who read Greek authors as a breakfast tonic.' Sir John Downer, a former premier, was still concerned in 1905 with the dire effects of education on the working classes, and told the Legislative Council that 'education spoils good labourers and makes bad scholars.'[3]

Even in 1920, the Director of Education in Victoria found it necessary to make a public attack on 'the hold which deep-rooted prejudices and considerations of caste, alien to the best interests of democracy, have obtained in our state. They make themselves felt in every discussion upon education. They are ever present, working silently in opposition to every proposal to extend the area of public education . . . every attempt to popularise higher education for the mass of the people meets, in Victoria, determined opposition.' This opposition, he noted, came from businessmen and farmers determined to keep taxes low, but also from the churches, content with their own schools and reluctant to see the extension of state secondary education. 'Let us not assume', he concluded, 'that a partial provision for a vital necessity, and that too in the main for the privileged classes of society, is an adequate discharge of an imperative state duty.'[4]

The class character of education is reinforced by the authoritarian structure of the state system itself, which from an early period has been marked by an enormous concern with 'efficiency' and the maintenance of 'standards', achieved by emphasis on examinations. The result is excessive centralisation, which removes responsibility from the individual teacher and headmaster and generates a rigid pattern of advancement by seniority. Responsibility for decisions devolves upon men who have done 'the long crawl up from the classroom through the inspectorial ranks to the remote atmosphere of the administration.'[5] The teachers themselves cling to this system and so, by a familiar paradox, strengthen its authoritarian character. Teachers, most of whom spend their whole lives at school in one capacity or other, become, in the picturesque words of Armytage, 'the Janissaries of the schools: a sturdy helot army, jealous of the degree, and exalters of "method", as opposed to the content of knowledge.'[6]

A senior educational administrator suggests that decentralisation of administration is not welcomed by the teachers themselves because centralisation suits their interest better, guaranteeing as it does a fixed and stable system of promotion and advancement. As a result, the system tends to produce its own type. The 'centrally controlled system of inspection and promotion is . . . leaning to uniformity of thinking in the teaching service by constructing the image of the promotion man, with all kinds of hidden compulsions to conform.' Within the large, centrally controlled system, the various levels of education develop their own syndicalist tendencies, so

[3] Douglas Pike, in E. L. French (ed.), *Melbourne Studies in Education 1957-58*, Melbourne, 1959, pp. 68-82
[4] J. O. Anchen, *Frank Tate and his Work for Education*, Melbourne, 1956, pp. 129-30
[5] John McLaren, *Our Troubled Schools*, Melbourne, 1968, p. 223
[6] W. H. G. Armytage, *Civic Universities*, London, 1955, p. 306

that at the higher levels there is little chance of effective collaboration between them, and in particular, 'the primary and secondary services tend to develop into monolithic structures.'[7] A similar point was made by an American critic, Freeman Butts, who was struck by the situation whereby 'only a few persons within the professional staff are qualified to make real educational decisions . . . professional decisions are basically confined to head office and to the top officials in head office.'[8] Centralisation, according to Butts, owes its strength to two assumptions. The first is that uniform policies are a good thing; secondly, that uniform policies are achievable only by concentrating authority in a few hands. This means, among other things, that the most trivial problem may have to proceed all the way through the official hierarchy before it can be settled. Butts notes ruefully that one of the things he heard almost nothing about was the need for more democracy in education. He was also appalled by the great stress on *correctness*—the correct method, the correct answer. As a result, he inferred that 'orderliness, discipline and development of skills' are the chief goals of primary education in Australia. He found no zest, no enjoyment of doing the thing for its own sake; the important thing was to meet the standards of the inspectors and to win awards which would count towards promotion.[9] Connell, commenting on Butts' observations, points out that all the British and American visitors who have written about Australian education in the course of a generation have been struck by its rigidity, authoritarianism and centralisation. 'This impression which our visitors gain and which they convey in their written observations is one of general rigidity—rigidity of organisation, rigidity of pupil-teacher relationship, rigidity of programming, and rigidity in educational expectation.'[10] Another writer observes that in a period of fifty years there has been astonishingly little change in the authoritarian structure of the typical Australian school. The headmaster and deputy headmaster drink their tea in regal isolation, and the other members of staff retire to departmental staff rooms, which appear to be scattered all over the school building for the express purpose of preventing informal communication, particularly between the sexes. He concludes that centralisation, introduced in the name of equality, has become an end in itself and has brought mediocrity, conformity and rigidity. The result is a suspicion of criticism and a distrust of initiative. When the Australian Council for Educational Research wanted to make a study of methods of school inspection, only one state, Western Australia, was prepared to agree unconditionally.[11] 'From teaching cradle

[7] C. M. Ebert, in E. L. French (ed.), *Melbourne Studies in Education 1961-62*, Melbourne, 1963, pp. 131-3, 148
[8] R. Freeman Butts, *Assumptions Underlying Australian Education*, Melbourne, 1955, p. 15
[9] ibid., p. 47
[10] W. F. Connell, in R. W. T. Cowan (ed.), *Education for Australians*, Melbourne, 1963, p. 83
[11] W. G. Walker, in *Education for Australians*, p. 208

to teaching grave, the department is the Organisation and the teacher is the Organisation Man.'[12]

Social bias in the educational system operates most clearly through the operation of the dual, or rather tripartite system of schools, state, Catholic, and Protestant. The division dates from the 1870's, when the previously existing arrangement by which denominational schools were subsidised by the colonial governments according to the number of their religious adherents was gradually replaced in one colony after another by a system of 'free, compulsory, and secular' education and government subsidies were simultaneously abolished. This three-decker structure was the outcome of an unwritten but firmly rooted consensus which reflected the hierarchy of class and status within the Australian community with remarkable accuracy: 'a working-class content with its education at the State primary schools; a socially conscious white-collar class aware that it was not accepted by "Society", and finally, "Society" itself, composed of higher professionals, top public servants and businessmen who formed a group apart and sent their children to receive primary and secondary education at the numerous independent schools in preparation for a university education.'[13] This account is not quite comprehensive, for it leaves out the landed gentry or 'squatters', whose sons formed a large part of the student body at the private schools, and the Catholic community, who were part neither of 'Society' nor of the state school system. The division of roles between the three sectors has remained fairly stable throughout the twentieth century. In 1966, 78 per cent of primary school children were at state schools, compared with 74 per cent of secondary pupils; 17·4 per cent of secondary pupils attended Catholic schools and 8·5 per cent were at 'other non-government schools'.[14] (The term 'private' is used here in preference to 'public', 'independent', or 'non-government'. The first, used by analogy with England, is misleading; the second, which has become the favoured term used by the private schools is not accurate in the sense that most of them have strong church connections; the third is inelegant, and not strictly accurate for the eight 'grammar schools' established by government action in Queensland. 'Private' denotes the existence of 'private' and 'public' sectors of education.)

The proportions of pupils attending the various types of school have varied only slightly since 1900, the most important trend in the 1960's being the increase in the numbers of secondary pupils at government schools. Throughout the period, the Protestant private schools have produced a disproportionately large share of pupils matriculating and entering university. The Catholic schools have, since the 1920's, produced the second largest group of matriculants, but this masks the fact that Catholic schools vary widely. Those which approximate in type to the Protestant

[12] R. W. T. Cowan, op. cit., p. 279
[13] R. M. Pike, op. cit., p. 13
[14] R. T. Fitzgerald, in *Quarterly Review of Australian Education*, vol. 1, no. 2, December 1967

private schools, and claim the title 'independent', produce similar numbers of matriculants. These schools are generally run by teaching orders. Many Catholic parochial schools, however, produce the lowest proportion of matriculants, giving an average which is higher than the state schools but lower than the non-Catholic private schools.

An analysis of the relative contributions of the three types of school at matriculation level was made by the Australian Council for Educational Research (ACER), which collected data on 114,000 students who left school during 1959-60.[15] Table 8·1 gives the break-up of school leavers at the matriculation level, shown as a percentage of *all* school leavers according to type of school and the state concerned. Figures for male and female school leavers are shown side by side.

Table 8·1 School Leavers at Matriculation, 1959-60

State	Government Schools %		Catholic Schools %		Other Private Schools %		All Schools %	
	M	F	M	F	M	F	M	F
NSW	16	14	32	18	62	44	19	16
Vic	10	7	17	9	48	31	14	10
Qld	9	7	16	16	44	31	13	10
SA	24	16	27	24	67	54	27	19
WA	11	7	28	19	40	34	15	12
Tas	9	7	2	8	41	35	11	9

Despite the wide variations in 'holding power' among different types of schools in different states, the relationship between types of school within each state system is the same, i.e. the holding power of the non-Catholic private schools is greatest among both sexes.

Not all these matriculants go on to universities, and comprehensive figures for university enrolment according to school background are not available. However, the available evidence makes it clear that the proportions are not greatly different, although there has been a significant rise in the proportion of students entering university from state school. In a study at the University of Queensland, it was found that the proportion of first year students entering from state schools was less than 26 per cent of enrolments in 1955, but had climbed to more than 37 per cent in 1961.[16]

The Robbins report on higher education in Britain[17] produced a mass of detailed evidence about the high positive correlation between the educational level of parents, the types of schools attended by parents and the occupation of the father in determining the chances that school pupils would enter university. Similar detailed studies have not been made in Australia, but all the evidence about the occupations of fathers of pupils

15 W. C. Radford, *School Leavers in Australia 1959-60*, Melbourne, 1962
16 F. J. Schonell, E. Roe and I. G. Meddleton, *Promise and Performance*, Brisbane, 1962
17 *Report of the Committee on Higher Education*, Cmnd 2154, London, 1963

at private schools, the schools from which university students come, and the occupations of fathers of university students, shows that similar correlations obtain in Australia, although the extent of discrimination against working class students is not so massive as in Britain. One of the few studies which directly relates parental occupation, education, and attitudes towards higher education was made by R. F. Berdie for the ACER in 1956. Berdie found that the likelihood of a school pupil entering university was influenced by a cluster of factors including parents' education, father's occupation, low educational and occupational aspirations of the parents, and lack of information about higher education—all showing strong positive correlations.[18] He also compared fathers' occupations among students enrolling at university and at teachers' training colleges. The results (slightly adapted) are shown in Table 8·2.

Table 8·2 University and Teachers' College Students in Victoria

Father's Occupation	Male Population 1947 %	First Year University Students 1956 %	First Year Teachers' College Students 1955 %
1 Unskilled or semi-skilled	32	11	12
2 Skilled workers	18	12	25
3 Sales	4	6	3
4 Clerical	11	12	8
5 Small businessmen & farmers	14	16	26
6 Professional			
(a) University educated	} 3·5	13	2
(b) Others		11	15
7 Proprietors, managers, graziers	7	8	4
8 Other	10·5	11	5
	100	100	100

Table 8·2 shows how the children of unskilled or semi-skilled workers have only one chance in three of entering either a university or a teachers' college, compared with the four-to-one chance of the children of university-educated professional men doing so. It also illustrates the great difference between the life chances of a skilled worker's children and those of the unskilled or semi-skilled worker, a point which is noticed elsewhere in this book. The role of the teaching profession as an avenue of social mobility is also clearly illustrated. From the table, it appears that teaching recruits disproportionately from among the children of skilled workers, small businessmen, farmers, and minor professionals (mostly teachers). Studies by Bassett and Pike confirm this deduction. Bassett studied entrants to Armidale Teachers' College, NSW. He found that the great majority of entrants (varying from 69 per cent to 78 per cent) were the children of small shopkeepers, manual workers and farmers, and that teachers' children had a strong propensity to become teachers—25 per cent of sons, and 38·4

[18] R. F. Berdie, *Manpower and the Schools*, Melbourne, 1956, ch. 4

per cent of daughters. Pike studied entrants to Sydney Teachers' College over a ten-year period and found that 50 per cent to 60 per cent of the entrants came from the homes of manual and white-collar workers, shop-keepers and farmers; 10 per cent were the children of teachers.[19]

These relationships were demonstrated on a larger scale in the ACER study[20] of school leavers during 1959-60, as shown in Table 8·3. This deals with students who enrolled as *full-time* entrants to universities during this period, whereas Table 8·2 covers both full-time and part-time university students. The presentation is again adapted.

Table 8·3 Full-Time University Enrolments, 1959-60

Father's Occupation	Proportion Among School Leavers %	Proportion Among Male Students %	Proportion Among Female Students %
Unskilled or semi-skilled	33	8	7
Skilled manual	21	14	12
Skilled supervisory	3	4	3
Sales	3	3	1
Sales supervisory	9	18	13
Farmer	14	5	9
Clerical	5	7	6
University-trained professional	2	13	17
Other professional	5	17	22
Higher administrative	1	4	4
Other supervisory	4	7	6
	100	100	100

The figures show a generally similar profile to Berdie's study, and the differences may be attributed partly to sampling error in his study, and partly to differences between the various states reflected in the aggregate figures. The impact of father's occupation may be shown even more dramatically from Table 8·4, also derived from the ACER study, which shows what proportion of school leavers from each occupational group enrolled at universities in 1959-60.

In other words, only 1·5 per cent of the sons of unskilled or semi-skilled workers entered universities, compared with 35·9 per cent of the sons of university-trained professional men and 29·8 per cent of those whose fathers were engaged in 'higher administration'. The pattern among girls was similar, except that daughters of professional men of all types pre-dominated over the daughters of men in 'higher administration'.

These figures were analysed further for the Martin Committee on

---

[19] G. W. Bassett, 'The Occupational Background of Teachers', *Australian Journal of Education*, vol. 2, no. 2, 1958; 'Teachers and their Children', in ibid., vol. 5, no. 1, 1961; R. M. Pike, op. cit.
[20] W. C. Radford, op. cit.

Tertiary Education by M. L. Turner of the ACER, who extended the analysis to take in entry to teachers' colleges and technical colleges as well as universities.[21] In this case, 4·4 per cent of the sons of unskilled and semi-skilled workers entered tertiary institutions, where they represented 13 per cent of all male entrants. Of this group, 30 per cent entered technical colleges, 36 per cent teachers' colleges and 24 per cent universities. By comparison 44·8 per cent of the sons of 'university-trained professionals' entered tertiary institutions, where they represented 8 per cent of all entrants. Thirteen per cent entered technical colleges, 7 per cent teachers' colleges, and 80 per cent universities.

Table 8·4 Occupational Groups Represented Among University Entrants, 1959-60

Father's Occupation (O)	Male Students (M) as Proportion (M/O%)	Female Students (F) as Proportion (F/O%)
Unskilled or semi-skilled	1·5	0·7
Skilled manual	4·1	1·9
Skilled supervisory	7·9	3·4
Sales	6·6	1·5
Sales Supervisory	13·0	5·0
Farmer	2·4	2·2
Clerical	10·7	4·2
University-trained professional	35·9	23·7
Other professional	20·9	14·7
Higher administration	29·8	14·2
Other supervisory	10·4	5·2

It is difficult not to accept Bassett's conclusion that the secondary school operates as 'a vast sorting machine fashioned to the specifications of the social class structure of society itself . . . its dominant role is that of an agent of social selection and our psychological knowledge of the adolescent, particularly of individual differences, has been used rather more to assist this role than to advance the education of this age group.'[22] The three-decked structure of the school system strongly reinforces this process and gives impetus to the working of what Robert Merton calls the 'Matthew principle', i.e. that 'to him that hath, shall be given; and he shall have more abundance', as declared in St Matthew's Gospel. The working of the Matthew principle is illustrated by Fensham's study of the award of scholarships by the Commonwealth government.[23] In 1964, scholarships were awarded for the first time to secondary school pupils, and 9 per cent

[21] *Report of the Committee on the Future of Tertiary Education*, Canberra, 1965, vol. 1, pp. 43-4, appendix on 'Tertiary Education and Socio-Economic Class'. This is perhaps the first time that the existence of social class has been explicitly acknowledged in an official government report in Australia.
[22] G. W. Bassett, 'The Social Role of the Secondary School in Australia', *Australian Journal of Education*, vol. 1, no. 1, 1957
[23] P. J. Fensham, 'The Distribution of Commonwealth Scholarships in Victoria', *Australian Journal of Education*, vol. 9, no. 3, 1965

of fourth form pupils in Victoria gained scholarships. At government schools, the proportion was 7 per cent; at Catholic schools, 10 per cent; at non-Catholic private schools, 16·5 per cent. (The differences were less marked at the fifth and sixth form levels.) As Butts observed, the existence of different types of schools helps to create and perpetuate class, religious and economic divisions, to separate children in a way which strengthens feelings of superiority and inferiority and to encourage sterile competition based on examination performance and prizes. Within the state system, it leads to the creation of a hierarchy of secondary schools so that those at the top can claim to be effectively 'competing' with the private schools.[24] In the process, as McLaren points out, they adopt the inegalitarian values embodied in the private school system.[25]

The impact of education on class identification has been examined in two national surveys. The first of these, a pre-election poll, was carried out by the Australian Gallup Poll in 1961.[26]

Table 8·5 Class Identification and Education, 1961

	Primary *(30%)*	*Some Secondary* *(30%)*	*Higher Secondary* *(30%)*	*Tertiary* *(10%)*
UM	2	6	6	17
M	30	37	60	58
LM	11	13	11	14
W	57	44	23	11
	100	100	100	100

A somewhat different set of relationships was found by Broom and his colleagues as the result of a survey of adult males in 1965, again carried out by the Australian Gallup Poll.[27] They found that 25 per cent of those with a tertiary education identified as 'upper-middle' or 'upper' class, compared with 17 per cent in Table 8·5, and 45 per cent identified as 'middle', compared with 58 per cent in Table 8·5. In the case of those who had completed a secondary education, 18 per cent identified as 'upper-middle class' (6 per cent in 1961) and 18 per cent as 'middle class' (60 per cent in 1965), but 30 per cent as 'working class' (23 per cent in 1961). Otherwise the distribution was similar. The different figures in 1965 are probably related to the fact that 11 per cent of the total sample identified as upper-middle, compared with only 5·5 per cent in 1961, and 29 per cent as middle (44 per cent in 1961). Allowing for differences in execution of the two surveys, there seems to have been a development towards a

24 Butts, op. cit., pp. 21-2, 31-3
25 McLaren, op. cit., ch. 1
26 A breakdown of the survey results is given in A. F. Davies and S. Encel (eds.) *Australian Society*, pp. 110-13.
27 L. Broom, F. L. Jones and J. Zubrzycki, 'Social Stratification in Australia', in J. A. Jackson (ed.), *Social Stratification*, Cambridge, 1968, p. 227

more sophisticated form of class-consciousness, with education as a factor. The correlation between the two variables is not high (0·35), especially as compared with Europe and the US, but it appears to be rising, particularly at the higher educational levels. Other evidence suggests strongly that it would be higher still if the differences between state and private schooling were taken into account.

Education and Society (2): The Private Schools

If he'll only turn out a brave, helpful,
truth-telling Englishman, and a gentleman,
and a Christian, that's all I want.

Tom Brown's Schooldays

The WASP character of the privileged classes in Australia is fostered, as it is in England and the United States, by a network of private schools founded, *mutatis mutandis*, on the principles of Dr Thomas Arnold. Education began in this spirit. In the early days of the colony of NSW, the clergy and the government tried to provide a parish school for each church, where the children were instructed in reading and arithmetic, read the Bible, and studied the catechism according to the Church of England. The schools were 'foes to vice and wickedness and, at the same time, centres of proselytism for the Anglican Church.'[28] In 1823, the Reverend Thomas Scott recommended to Lord Bathurst, the Colonial Secretary, that this system should be extended and that a secondary school should also be provided. As a result, the Church and Schools Corporation, established in 1825, gave the Anglican clergy a monopoly of education, which was fashioned 'to serve the interests of a society in which economic and political power was concentrated in the officials, the large proprietors of land, and the wealthy merchants.'[29] Scott's successor, Reverend W. G. Broughton (later the first bishop of NSW) recommended in 1830 that colleges should be opened to teach the young landed proprietors to 'exercise their powers of reason and to encourage habits of patient investigation by steeping them in a classical education and by providing a general instruction in the chief articles of the Christian faith. In these king's schools, as they were to be called, the sons of the squatters were to be groomed as a governing class.'[30] The first such institution—The King's School, Parramatta—opened in 1832, but the projected chain of schools did not materialise, and it was not until 1857 that Sydney Grammar School, a non-denominational institution, was established. It was the small colony of Tasmania which was next in the field with the Hutchins School and Launceston Grammar School (1846), followed by South Australia with St Peter's College (1847) and Victoria with Scotch College (1851), the first non-Anglican school in Australia. The establishment of schools in Victoria and NSW in

---

[28] C. M. H. Clark, *A Short History of Australia*, London, 1964, p. 27
[29] ibid., p. 63
[30] ibid., p. 89

the 1850's and 1860's was the result of new educational policies forced upon the colonial legislators by pressure from Catholics and Nonconformists, who had long chafed under the Anglican monopoly but could do little about it while the colonies remained under the autocratic rule of governors. Unable to adjudicate between the many jarring sects, the colonial governments decided on a Solomon's compromise: the government provided funds for education, to be shared out between the denominations through a board on which they were represented. Scotch College, originally known as Melbourne Academy, was the first school established under this policy by the Presbyterian church, followed in 1857 by Geelong Grammar School (Anglican) and Melbourne Grammar (also Anglican) in 1856. The Methodists came into their own in the 1860's with the establishment of Newington College, Sydney (1863), Wesley College, Melbourne (1866), and Prince Alfred College, Adelaide (1869). These schools were all 'corporate' in the sense that they were governed by a council with corporate legal identity, which had been wholly or partly responsible for the establishment of the school. The corporate schools were of three types. In one, the property was vested in a church or congregation, as with Geelong Grammar School, Melbourne Grammar, Bishop Hale's Grammar School, Perth (established in 1858), and Sydney Church of England Grammar School ('Shore'), set up in 1889. A second and rarer type was the state-subsidised secular or 'undenominational' school, of which Sydney Grammar, set up under a special Act of the NSW parliament, was the first example. In 1860, the Queensland parliament passed the Grammar Schools Act, which enabled the setting up of eight such schools, the first at Ipswich, near Brisbane, in 1863, and the second in Brisbane itself in 1867. A third type was the 'private' or 'grammar' school (using the English style of distinction between 'public' and 'grammar' schools), many of which went out of existence when the colonial governments assumed the major responsibility for education in the 1870's and 1880's, and a fourth type— the state school—became the commonest variety.

These schools offered a broader education than the Arnoldian public schools of England on which they were modelled. In a colonial society lacking the sharp class divisions of England, the schools were more alike and gave much the same kind of education; there was no pre-eminent group like the English 'big six' or the rather larger 'Clarendon' group. 'The monied section of colonial society which could afford a secondary education for its sons and daughters was lacking in the sharp social divisions which would conceivably have supported strongly contrasted types of secondary education.'[31] The uniformity of the Australian schools was buttressed by the centralised authority established over examinations, compared with the variety of examining bodies in England. The result was an amalgam of aristocratic and middle class British influences, strengthened by the character of the student body. French has analysed a random sample of parents'

[31] E. L. French, 'Secondary Education in the Australian Social Order', Ph.D. thesis, University of Melbourne, 1958

occupations among pupils of Brisbane Grammar School for the period 1867-1881. Thirty-two per cent of parents were farmers and graziers; 27 per cent merchants; 17 per cent professional men; 17 per cent publicans; 5 per cent bank managers; 1 per cent army officers; 1 per cent others.[32] The only surprise in the list are the publicans, which says something about the way to make money in colonial Queensland.

Some of the private schools acquired a distinctive cachet when they became the favoured places for the sons of the landed gentry or 'squatters' (see Chapter 15). The King's School, Parramatta, rapidly established itself as a centre for squatters' sons, which it has largely remained, with two-thirds of its pupils as boarders. Geelong Grammar School developed similarly, largely for geographical reasons. Geelong, situated on an excellent harbour at Corio Bay, was the natural port for a large area of the Western District of Victoria, and rapidly developed into a mercantile and social centre. After a few years it became evident that the majority of the second generation of Western District landowners, for the most part sons of Scots Presbyterians, were being sent to this Anglican school rather than the Presbyterian Scotch College, in Melbourne. Apart from the fact that doctrinal differences were of much less consequence in Australia, the parents of the schoolboys were also influenced by the personality of the first headmaster of Geelong Grammar, Bracebridge Wilson, and the advantage of an Anglican school at the time when many of them intended to send their sons to Oxford or Cambridge, where Nonconformists still laboured under disadvantages.[33] Once established, this pattern became permanent. However, a few Presbyterian squatters and businessmen, not satisfied with this situation, collaborated to establish Geelong College in 1861 as a Presbyterian alternative. This brought to Australia the first of a formidable dynasty of Scottish schoolmasters belonging to the Morrison family. George Morrison was principal of Geelong College from 1861 until his death in 1898, and was succeeded by his son, C. N. Morrison. Another son was G. E. (Chinese) Morrison, for many years Far East correspondent of the London *Times* and confidant of Dr Sun Yat-Sen. George Morrison's brother, Alexander, was principal of Scotch College until 1904.[34]

A rapid glance at the names of Geelong Grammar alumni indicates its long and close connection with the landed gentry during its first century of existence.[35] The names listed in Table 8·6, all belonging to well-known landed families, are strongly represented.

As all these families were settled on the land by the middle of the nineteenth century, it is clear from the list that the fashion of sending sons to Geelong Grammar has developed in popularity and spread outside Victoria. The strength of the connection is further illustrated by the results of surveys published in the school magazine, *The Corian*, in 1948, 1950,

[32] ibid., p. 156
[33] Margaret Kiddle, *Men of Yesterday*, Melbourne, 1961, pp. 486-90
[34] B. R. Keith (ed.) *The Geelong College 1861-1961*, Geelong, 1961
[35] *Old Geelong Grammarians*, centenary list, Geelong, 1957

1955 and 1960, examining the careers intended by school pupils after graduation. In each case, the land was most favoured. In 1955, 41 per cent of the 293 respondents preferred it, and in 1960, 38 per cent out of 396. The other choices were far behind—medicine (15 per cent in 1955, 12 per cent in 1960); engineering (10 per cent in 1955, 12 per cent in 1960); business (9 per cent in 1955, 13 per cent in 1960).

Table 8·6 Family Representation at Geelong Grammar

Angas (SA)	5	between	1918 and	1948
Armytage (Vic)	13	between	1912 and	1953
Beggs (Vic)	10	between	1925 and	1955
Belcher (Vic)	6	between	1893 and	1955
Chirnside (Vic)	5	between	1924 and	1956
Fairbairn (Vic and NSW)	8	between	1906 and	1946
Falkiner (NSW)	11	between	1917 and	1954
Hawker (SA)	8	between	1910 and	1947
Learmonth (Vic)	5	between	1944 and	1954
Law-Smith (SA)	5	between	1891 and	1948
Macarthur-Onslow (NSW)	3	between	1923 and	1951
Mackinnon (Vic)	18	between	1883 and	1952
Manifold (Vic)	10	between	1905 and	1954
Officer (Vic)	6	between	1937 and	1953

If Geelong is pre-eminently the school of the landed gentry, Melbourne Grammar is that of the business elite. In its roll of ex-pupils there appear many names belonging to well-known business families, particularly those of Baillieu (mining, metals, brewing, papermaking etc.); Grimwade (glassmaking, pharmaceuticals, chemicals); Cuming (steelmaking, chemicals and fertilisers); Luxton (Shell Oil); Hallenstein (leather); Were (stockbroking); Derham (food, retailing); Gillespie (flour milling); Kimpton (pastoral products, food).[36] In a study of company directors, reported in Chapter 20, two-thirds of those who had attended Melbourne Grammar were themselves the sons of company directors.

Scotch College, on the other hand, is one of the few private schools with a significant claim to intellectual distinction, established during the head-mastership of W. S. Littlejohn (1904 to 1933). During his tenure, the school grew spectacularly in size and recruited a number of highly qualified senior staff. In 1927, it was 'the largest public school in the British Empire' and the fact was signalised by the school council in raising Littlejohn's salary to the unprecedentedly high figure of £1,250.[37] W. J. Turner, author and critic, who went to Scotch in 1900, refers to it jocularly in his auto-biography as 'Plato's Academy', beside which, he declares, 'the other famous public schools, and also Eton, Winchester, Harrow and Rugby were completely ordinary schools.'[38] The roll of 'old boys' is marked by the names of many outstanding figures in the professions, the universities, the

36 *Liber Melburniensis*, Melbourne, 1960
37 G. H. Nicholson (ed.), *First Hundred Years*, Melbourne, 1952
38 W. J. Turner, *Blow for Balloons*, London, 1935

public services, the armed forces, and also in industry. Business families having a long connection with the school include those of York Syme (shipping, pastoral products, steel), McKay (agricultural machinery) and Robinson (mining and metals). Its alumni include three chiefs of the army general staff, including Australia's most famous soldier, Sir John Monash; a Chief Justice of Australia, Sir John Latham; five university vice-chancellors; and a galaxy of professors in law, science, mathematics, medicine, and engineering. Between 1903 and 1951, ex-pupils of Scotch won seventeen out of a possible forty-eight Rhodes scholarships, and from 1914 to 1950 the school won, on average, one-quarter of the university scholarships given annually by the state government.

Wesley College, Melbourne, has a special record in connection with the public services. In a survey of senior Commonwealth government officials, described in Chapter 13, Wesley came top of the list of schools represented among them, as it did in a parallel survey of senior state government officials in Victoria in 1956. Wesley also had the curious distinction of producing two successive Prime Ministers—Sir Robert Menzies (1949-66) and the late Harold Holt (1966-67). The pupils celebrated by composing a suitable jingle at the expense of their competitors—

When RG was followed by Holt
Scotch and Grammar received quite a jolt,
There's only one college
For 'Liberal' knowledge—
Three cheers for the purple and gold.'[39]

Melbourne Grammar School can, however, claim not only a prime minister —S. M. Bruce (1923-29)—but three British peers, the aforesaid Lord Bruce (d. 1968), Lord Baillieu (d. 1967) of Australia's premier business family, and Lord Casey (appointed Governor-General in 1965).

In later chapters of this book, the distinctive contributions made by various schools to the structure of social differentiation are examined in detail. Generally speaking, nine schools stand out. Four are in Victoria where private education is strongest—Melbourne Grammar, Scotch College, Wesley College, Geelong Grammar. Three are in New South Wales— Sydney Grammar, Sydney Church of England Grammar School (known as 'Shore' because of its location on the northern side of Sydney Harbour), and The King's School. One is in South Australia—St Peter's College, Adelaide—and one in Western Australia—the Hale School, Perth. While Melbourne Grammar contributes largely to the business elite, it also has strong connections with the professions (law and medicine in particular), and with the landed gentry. Scotch College attracts fewer sons of businessmen but contributes strongly to the ranks of industrial managers, and is well represented in the professions, the public services, and the armed forces. Wesley College makes a distinctive contribution to the public

[39] G. Blainey, J. Morrissey and S. E. K. Hulme, *Wesley College*, Melbourne, 1967

services, also to politics, and to the armed forces. Geelong Grammar School, although pre-eminently a school for the sons of squatters, is also well represented in certain spheres of business (e.g. the stock exchange) and in the diplomatic service. It also contributes to politics. J. G. Gorton, who became Prime Minister in 1968, is an old boy, and so were a number of his colleagues in his own and previous governments.[40] An analysis of entries in *Who's Who in Australia* gives some idea of the contribution made by the six leading 'public schools' in Victoria to the elite of the community as defined by the standards of that publication. Mr Ian Hansen, of the School of Education at the University of Melbourne, examined the entries in the 1962 edition, and found that more than one-half of the Victorian entries were products of these six schools, who also accounted for $10 \cdot 5$ per cent of *all* entries. Of the three Sydney schools, King's is notable only for its traditional links with the landed gentry. Sydney Grammar and Shore have similar social profiles, each having significant connections with business and the professions. In the 1965 edition of *Who's Who*, they provided 16 per cent of the NSW entries. Sydney Grammar is better represented among government officials, and Shore among the squatters. In Adelaide, reflecting the tightly-knit character of wealth and status in South Australia, St Peter's College has long been predominant in many spheres, although this predominance is being diluted by the social changes following upon industrialisation and urbanisation. On a smaller scale, the Hale School plays a comparable but less exclusive part in Western Australia.

Within the private sector, the influence of those schools affiliated with the Headmasters' Conference of Australia is predominant. This association was formed in 1931, at a meeting to which were invited thirteen head-masters who were then actual or presumptive members of the Headmasters' Conference in England. The meeting decided that admission to the Conference should be on the basis of three criteria—independence (i.e. a school council), absence of the profit motive in running the school, and conformity with 'the accepted tradition of public school ideals'. The Conference has grown from the original thirteen schools to a membership of seventy-seven (in 1967), of which twenty-three were in Victoria, twenty in NSW, twelve in Queensland, eight in South Australia, eight in Western Australia, five in Tasmania, and one in the Australian Capital Territory.[41] Altogether, the HMC schools represent one-seventh of the private sector, which had 686 secondary schools in 1967. However, this proportion is not quite what it seems. Of the total number in the private sector 498 were

[40] Sir Alexander Downer, then Minister for Immigration, gave a Speech Day address in 1960 in which he urged a greater contribution to politics from his old school, which should be able to 'produce sufficient men possessing both the willingness and the capacity to inspire our country spiritually or to govern it through Parliament or the departments of State.' The *Corian*, May 1961

[41] These figures are computed from *The Independent Secondary Schools of Australia*, 1968, a directory prepared by the National Fund Raising Council of Australia Pty Ltd.

Roman Catholic schools, of which only twenty-one (4 per cent) were members of the HMC, compared with fifty-six of the 188 other private schools (i.e. 30 per cent). A further eighty-four of the non-Catholic schools (i.e. 45 per cent) were girls' schools affiliated with the Associated Headmistresses of Australia, to which only seven Catholic schools belonged.

Stratification extends beyond this. In both NSW and Victoria there is an inner group of the most 'exclusive' schools, generally the oldest, known in NSW as 'Greater Public Schools' and in Victoria as 'Associated Public Schools'. In NSW there are eight, including five Protestant schools, two Catholic, and oddly, one state school, Sydney Boys' High School, which was admitted to the GPS in 1906 although it is not an 'independent' school. In Victoria there are eleven, nine Protestant and two Catholic. The most important practical function of these associations, and others parallel to them, is to provide a framework for sporting competitions, especially the annual rowing race for the 'Head of the River', but they also carry a definite social cachet. The novelist Martin Boyd, who attended Trinity Grammar School, Melbourne (a member of the Associated Grammar Schools), writes tartly in his autobiography about the 'trade union of public schools' in Victoria, which made it impossible for any more recently founded school, 'though its constitution may be the same, and however good its "tone", to achieve recognition, as these six will have none of it.'[42] A more florid justification for exclusiveness is given in a report, written for a client school, by one of the professional fund-raising organisations which collect donations for the private schools. 'The boy in the Great Public School', it declares, 'is trained for leadership from earliest youth, through service and the acceptance of responsibility. Based on right thinking and right doing, his gospel is *noblesse oblige*. He is proud of his caste. He carries its special cachet, which is "the law and the prophets" to him, throughout life.'[43] As the education correspondent of the *Sydney Morning Herald* commented, the fund-raising firm was presumably telling its clients what they wanted to hear. 'Some readers of the report may have winced as such words as "noblesse", "caste", and "special cachet". One suspects, however, that the school council was not embarrassed, and that the fund-raiser's description rang a bell.'[44]

The claim that private schools generate qualities of leadership—sometimes camouflaged as 'service to the community'—is one that recurs throughout their history. The two notions are compounded in the words of a leading Methodist clergyman on the occasion of the centenary of Newington College, Sydney: 'The students [have shown] a capacity for service which has made so many Old Boys of the school outstanding leaders in their day, and a strong sense of duty which led to a fine record in respon-

[42] Martin Boyd, *Day of My Delight*, Melbourne, 1965, p. 6
[43] *Sydney Morning Herald*, 6 August 1962
[44] ibid.

sible citizenship and in service to their country in two world wars.'[45] 'When our boys go out into the world', declared the headmaster of The King's School a few years ago, 'and they're asked to do something, they're not afraid. They've had responsibility here.'[46] 'It is often said', writes the historian of Geelong College, 'that Public School education is directed to produce leaders, a statement which has been misinterpreted as a claim to privilege. The real aim is to raise men who will identify themselves with the community, make courageous decisions, and accept responsibility.'[47] The establishment of a new private school in Victoria in 1961 called forth a perfect chorus on this theme, led by a judge of the state Supreme Court. 'A great many leaders of the community have come from church schools and have led the Australian community according to those values which they were taught in their young days at school. The tradition of service which a Church school teaches is something of tremendous value . . . leadership unbeholden to any State system, leadership taught according to the best traditions of the Christian religion.'[48] Or, as a supporter of the school wrote, the object of the new Peninsula School was to produce 'people who will not be afraid to give a lead according to what they will learn here without first looking behind to discover what others are thinking. Of course, all who pass through this school will not necessarily be leaders but, if the majority is able to recognise and support good leadership when it is forthcoming, then this school will be a truly great school, and many people will make sacrifices to send their sons to it.'[49]

This conception of 'leadership' conferred by the special qualities of private school education is intimately intertwined with the Arnoldian image of the Christian gentleman. 'I like Arnold's phrase—the Christian gentleman—there's no better', remarked Mr C. O. Healey, former headmaster of Sydney Grammar, although he hastened to add, as head of a 'non-denominational' school, that he equated the Christian gentleman with the Jewish gentleman.[50] The headmaster of the new Peninsula School declared at its opening ceremony that 'the boys will become not only servants of the Christian Church but also serving citizens of the State. The foundation of this School testifies to the strength of the Christian faith . . . religion becomes uncompromisingly the basis of character building and the means of giving boys values for life.'[51] The historian C. E. W. Bean wrote that the school chapel was the place 'where boys are spoken to about what they themselves, however careless, sense at some time or other to be the most important things in life. Most headmasters feel it to have an influence

[45] Rev. C. F. Gribble, foreword to D. S. MacMillan, *Newington College 1863-1963*, Sydney, 1963, p. vi
[46] *Sydney Morning Herald*, 7 August 1962
[47] B. R. Keith, op. cit., p. 124
[48] Mr. Justice Sholl, reported in the bulletin of the Peninsula School, Victoria, August 1961
[49] ibid.
[50] *Sydney Morning Herald*, 7 August 1962
[51] Rev. D. B. Clarke, reported in the bulletin of the Peninsula School, May 1961

more effective than that of most "uplift" organisations.'[52] Bean also noted that, unlike other upholders of the private school system, headmasters prefer to stress the religious aspect rather than the training of leaders, and quotes an inquiry among forty headmasters of whom all but one described the function of their schools as the production of Christians 'with the standards of gentlemen'.[53]

As many Christians have sadly observed, the pacific teachings of Jesus issued in a church of a singularly warlike nature. If character is indeed formed at school, the Christian gentlemen turned out by private schools may well personify this melancholy paradox. The official history of New-ington College notes the enthusiasm of one of its early heads, Rev. Fletcher, for the school cadet corps, for whose formation he was responsible, and who saw to it that it was the smartest group of cadets in the colony.[54] Another headmaster of note, L. A. Adamson of Wesley College, was also a devotee of the cadet corps and encouraged ambitious youths to serve their country by joining its armed forces.[55] The role of the private school was thrown into sharp relief by two incidents, related to the war in Vietnam, which occurred in Sydney in 1966. In one case, the headmaster of a private preparatory school addressed his 110 pupils, aged between five and twelve, on the occasion of the annual Anzac Day celebration. 'We learn that we must be prepared to offer ourselves to serve our country in war if ever the need arises. At this moment some of our young men are fighting in Viet-nam. They are doing this because our government has seen fit to take part in a small war which should be able to prevent a major war involving Australia. There are, however, a number of people who have sown in weak minds the seeds of anti-Vietnam and anti-conscription. This is mainly because they thrive on being "anti" anything, which assures them the satisfaction of stirring up emotionalism, particularly among pampered young men and their mothers.' Questioned by a reporter, the headmaster, Mr R. H. Morgan, denied that he had been talking 'politics' to his young pupils but had been speaking from a 'national' point of view, and added that the boys' parents appreciated that the 'right attitude' was being inculcated into their sons.[56] In the other incident, a fifteen-year-old boy at a leading private school was denied readmission to the school because of his declared opposition to the war and refusal to join the cadet corps.

In view of all this, it is hardly surprising to find that authoritarian attitudes are well-developed among private schoolboys. In an unpublished report on teaching at Geelong Grammar School, a team of educational psychologists from the University of Sydney concluded, in 1957, that authoritarian and anti-democratic opinions were widely shared by the pupils. They administered a battery of personality and attitude tests to the

[52] C. E. W. Bean, *Here, My Son*, Sydney 1950, p. 114
[53] ibid., p. 144
[54] D. S. MacMillan, op. cit., pp. 24-5
[55] Felix Meyer, *Adamson of Wesley*, Melbourne, 1933
[56] *Sydney Morning Herald*, 23 August 1966

boys, including revised versions of the three scales of authoritarianism developed in the California study of the 1940's—the F-scale (Fascism), the E-scale (ethnocentrism) and PEC scale (politico-economic conservatism).[57] They concluded that 'there is evidence of acceptance of authoritarian, almost anti-democratic values in more than the expected proportions at Geelong Grammar. It is not possible to decide here whether this is a reflection of the social structure beyond the school . . . or whether it goes deeper and is either implicit in or is fostered by the way in which the boys are educated and developed at the school.' This conclusion is over-cautious in view of other evidence. The scores on the three scales were much higher than those obtained with state high school pupils in Sydney, and in particular the PEC scores rose steadily with length of stay at the school, in spite of other results showing rejection of parental values. In the light of this study, it is all the more striking to read Martin Boyd's comments that 'the influence of the public schools has been mostly harmful' and that 'they are Fascist in their philosophy.'[58]

The 'exclusiveness' of the private schools is largely a matter of money. In 1950, Bean noted delicately that 'it is often stated that the corporate schools help to maintain a social division based on wealth.'[59] In 1962, the headmaster of Trinity Grammar School, Sydney, Mr J. W. Hogg, went so far as to admit that the private schools might 'soon be in danger of denying the very purpose of their existence by becoming, in the least desirable sense, exclusive—that is to say, by becoming financially exclusive.'[60] Mr Hogg would qualify as a slow learner, since it is doubtful whether the private schools were ever anything else. What has happened since 1945 is that they have become more and more exclusive with the steady rise in fees, and for many middle class parents, especially those on salaries in the middle ranges, the sacrifices needed to send children to private schools have become progressively greater. In the twenty years from 1945 to 1965, fees rose more than fivefold. At the end of 1968, a further increase was announced by schools in NSW. Whereas in 1962 the maximum fees for day boys at Sydney Grammar School were £186 ($372) and for boarders £471 ($942), in 1969 they rose to $615 and $1,400 respectively; at Cranbrook (one of the Associated Schools) they rose from $360 to $615 for day boys and from $936 to $1,380 for boarders; at Newington College, from $348 for day boys to $555, and from $864 for boarders to $1,300. In 1962, it was estimated that a private school education for a day boy in NSW would cost £1,100 (i.e. $2,200) over five years; in 1968, this estimate (which takes account of the extension of secondary education to six years in NSW) would be in the vicinity of $5,000, allowing for increases in fees during that period. For a boarder, the 1962 estimate was £2,800; in 1969,

---

[57] For details see T. W. Adorno et al., *The Authoritarian Personality*, New York, 1950.
[58] op. cit., p. 156
[59] Bean, op. cit., p. 204
[60] *Sydney Morning Herald*, 6 August 1962

it had increased to about $10,000. In 1950, Bean acknowledged cautiously that the private schools 'draw from the professional and other well-to-do classes a much larger percentage than do the State schools; both draw evenly from the small business class; but the corporate schools draw many fewer . . . from the skilled tradesmen, and hardly any from the labouring class.'[61]

Considering the obvious social role of the private schools, they have received strikingly little attention in the literature of Australian social criticism or, indeed, of education. The situation has begun to change in the 1960's, partly because of a growing awareness of the complexity of social divisions, stimulated by the publicity which the private schools have gained since the dramatic reversal of policy on government assistance to the private sector initiated by Sir Robert Menzies in 1963. A. A. Phillips, himself a senior master at a leading private school, remarks the paradox of the private schools in 'a community so self-consciously proud of its egalitarian values', and attributes it to the imitative habits of Australians impressed by English models. 'The advantages of their existence', he continues dryly, 'are less obvious, but perhaps special prestige is obvious enough. They can hardly fail to deepen the ruts of class distinction, whatever their intention. Today . . . many parents still patronise them from snobbish motives or because of the job-winning properties of the Old School Tie.' He dismisses the claim often advanced on behalf of private schools that they provide a source of variety and experiment in a centralised system. 'Too many of them are content to squat on a pedestal of tradition in self-approving contentment.'[62] Even private school headmasters have recently allowed themselves some public self-questioning. Mr C. O. Healey, for some years headmaster of Sydney Grammar and later of Scotch College, complained to the Headmasters' Conference in 1967 that 'public schoolboys, as a class and on the whole, have, during the past twenty years, shunned the Church, teaching, the army and the civil service, and have not been particularly interested in politics. . . . Of the full range of ways in which democratic man must accept responsibility for the working of society, they are almost entirely ignorant.' And he asked, perhaps rhetorically, 'Why is this, when we claim to be the teachers of religion and service?'[63]

John McLaren, an experienced teacher and lecturer with a Presbyterian background, has outspokenly attacked the private schools on a number of grounds. 'Proud, aloof and privileged, the independent schools remain a series of communities for the status-seekers rather than a part of the overall system of education . . . the independent school system has

---

[61] Bean, op. cit., p. 204; a table of occupations of pupils' fathers is given in appendix III.
[62] A. A. Phillips, 'Education', in Peter Coleman (ed.), *Australian Civilization*, Melbourne, 1962, p. 112
[63] C. O. Healey, in P. J. McKeown and B. W. Hone (eds.) *The Independent School*, Melbourne, 1967, pp. 107-8

developed as an institution for maintaining the privileges and recruiting to the members of the more affluent professional, managerial and rural classes. . . . The people who buy this education are accustomed to insisting on value for money, and they ensure that the schools they support provide it. The value is measured in terms of university places gained, social ease and business connections.' To fulfil these economic and social objectives, the schools have 'subordinated their ostensible religious aims until they have become merely a kind of genuflection in the direction of well-bred decency, a code in which loyalty to the sovereign rates well ahead of any unbecoming concern with the ways of the Almighty . . . on the fringes a chaplain operates a spiritual dispensary which, like the best metropolitan hotels, combines the most elegant of traditions with the slickest of service.' The exclusiveness of the private schools results in a mindless, introverted form of group loyalty which produces self-contained little groups who have only the vaguest notions of their wider social responsibilities. This loyalty is the secret of the success of the private schools, the spirit of corporate identity which enshrines their ultimate values. 'The same noisy loyalty can be heard at football matches and boatraces, at summer beach resorts and in winter ski lodges, in cosy night clubs and opulent passenger-liner lounges. It is the price paid for the best of educations, and the fact that its dominant characteristic is perpetual adolescence is no disadvantage in a country whose leaders show no dissatisfaction with that period of life.' The failure to see beyond the Arnoldian model is, in McLaren's words, a mixture of 'pride and folly'. It leads, among other things, to a depressing failure to experiment with new ideas and methods, when the private schools are ideally placed because of their resources and their oft-proclaimed 'independence' to do so.[64]

Many of these criticisms will be familiar to students of the English public schools, the inspiration and still to a large extent the model for their Australian counterparts. Indeed, it is the imitativeness of the Australian schools, and their failure to emancipate themselves from a conception which is rapidly becoming obsolete in England itself, that is one of their most melancholy characteristics. The link with England is maintained by the frequent appointment of Englishmen as headmasters. At Sydney Grammar School, for example, the dominant figure in the school's history was A. B. Weigall, headmaster from 1866 to 1912. Like two of his successors, C. O. Healey (1951-1964) and S. P. Houldsworth (1964 to 1968), he went to Brasenose College. Dr J. R. Darling, headmaster of Geelong Grammar from 1930 to 1962, was another notable instance, among many others. The link was dramatised by the action of Queen Elizabeth in sending Prince Charles to attend Geelong Grammar in 1966. A remarkable spectrum of opinion was evoked by this incident. The publicity officer of the NSW Teachers' Federation suggested that if the aim of the royal family was to acquaint the prince with life in Australia, he should have been sent to a more representative school. His suggestion

[64] McLaren, *Our Troubled Schools*, pp. 5-14, passim

touched off a volley of replies in the correspondence columns of the press. A housemaster at Geelong Grammar declared that 'every walk and station in Australian society' was represented there. The effect of this remark was somewhat spoilt by a letter from the chairman of the school council stating that the school's fees (in 1965) were $1,380 per annum and were about to be increased. A lady in Queensland, noting that Prince Charles was to spend his time at 'Timbertop', a rural branch of the school with emphasis on living off the land, where the boys are required to keep the place clean, asserted sharply that 'the development of Australia today depends no more on this simple-minded "ruggedness" than the victories of England did on the playing fields of Eton. Let us face facts: Australia needs technical excellence, cultural sophistication and personal religion. What has cleaning out latrines to do with this?' A correspondent in South Australia made perhaps the most indicative comment. 'It is refreshing to see that the Palace has recognised the importance of the Prince's learning at first hand something of the Australian people and their way of life. After all, when he ascends the throne, Australia will be the last outpost of colonialism, the only remaining country of the British Commonwealth of Nations.'[65] Perhaps unconsciously, this correspondent revealed the most basic and most objectionable feature of the private school system and its contribution to the structure of social differentiation in Australia.

Religion

We have already noted the WASP character of Australian society. The Protestant ascendency runs alongside, and is interwoven with, the 'pastoral ascendency' of the nineteenth century, when landowners dominated the politics, economy and society of the young colonies, and the 'bureaucratic ascendency' of the twentieth century. Within the Protestant community itself, religion makes differential contributions to social position, as may be seen from the following tables. The figures represent breakdowns of results obtained by the Australian Gallup Poll in a survey of voting intentions before a federal election in December 1961. Respondents were asked to state their religion and to place themselves in one of four 'class' categories

Table 8·7 Religion and Class, 1961

Class Identifi- cation	Catholic (23·6%)	C. of E. (38·6%)	Presbyterian (14%)	Methodist (15·3%)	Other Christian (8·5%)
UM	5·5	5·9	7	4·3	3·8
M	38·8	43·5	50·7	47·4	42·4
LM	11·4	11	11·4	13·7	16·9
W	44·3	39·6	31·9	34·6	36·9
	100·0	100·0	100·0	100·0	100·0

[65] *Australian*, 27 October 1965

—upper-middle, middle, lower-middle, and working. The relationships were as shown.[66]

Neglecting the figures on Catholics for the moment, from Table 8·7 it is evident that there is some differentiation between the major denominations. The Presbyterians, for example, had the highest proportion of respondents who identified themselves as either upper-middle class or middle class; the Methodists, the highest proportion who described themselves as lower-middle class. The largest spread, however, is between the Anglicans and the 'other Christians' (i.e. mainly the smaller evangelical groups like Lutherans, Baptists, Churches of Christ, and Salvation Army), at the lower-middle class level, which corresponds to what is generally known about the social character of these denominations.[67] The relationship may also be shown with the axes reversed, as in Table 8·8.

Table 8·8 Class and Religion, 1961

Denomination	UM (5·5%)	M (44%)	LM (12%)	W (38·5%)
Catholic	23·5	20·8	22·3	27·3
C. of E.	41	38·3	35·4	39·5
Presbyterian	17·6	16	13·1	11·6
Methodist	11·8	16·6	17·8	13·7
Other Christian	6·1	8·3	11·4	7·9
	100·0	100·0	100·0	100·0

If we compare Tables 8·7 and 8·8, it is apparent that the Presbyterians are disproportionately represented among those who identify themselves as upper-middle class, and the Anglicans to a lesser degree. The Presbyterians are also significantly under-represented among the working class, whereas the other denominations appear more or less in proportion.

Interdenominational differences become considerably sharper when we move from class identification to voting intentions, as shown in Table 8·9. These survey results confirm what is generally known about the social profiles of the various denominations. Anglicans, the largest denomination with 34-37 per cent[68] are fairly evenly divided among various social categories. The Presbyterians (9-10 per cent) are biased towards the upper-middle and upper classes, and are disproportionately represented among the professions, the business elite, the landowners, and the government

[66] A. F. Davies and S. Encel (eds.) *Australian Society: A Sociological Introduction*, Melbourne, 1965, pp. 110-13
[67] As shown, for example, in Michael Argyle, *Religious Behaviour*, London, 1958; G. E. Lenski, *The Religious Factor*, New York, 1961; H. R. Niebuhr, *The Social Sources of Denominationalism*, New York, 1929; B. R. Wilson, *Sects and Society*, London, 1961
[68] These proportions are as given in the 1966 census of the Commonwealth of Australia. As the census question on religion is not compulsory, and 10 per cent do not reply or give an indefinite answer, the upper figure is an estimate.

service. The Methodists (10-11 per cent) have a lower-middle class bias and are strongly represented in occupations such as schoolteaching. (Advancement in the administrative hierarchy of the NSW Education Department is traditionally dependent on Methodist affiliations.) Contrary to old-established myths about the 'Nonconformist conscience', they are not notable for their support of the Labor Party. These differences are, however, much less significant than the differences between Protestants as a whole, on the one hand, and Catholics on the other. Although detailed social breakdowns of religious groups in Australia have yet to be made, a number of differences between Catholics and non-Catholics have been examined. The political differences are well known and some aspects are analysed in this chapter and also in Chapter 10.

Table 8·9 Religion and Voting Intention, 1961

Party	Catholic %	C. of E. %	Presbyterian %	Methodist %	Other Christian %	Other %
ALP	50·5	46·5	37·9	39·0	43·1	38·3
DLP	13·8	1·8	1·9	2·4	3·9	5·5
LCP	27·9	46·5	56·0	51·9	46·9	45·2
Ind.	—	—	—	1·2	0·6	—
DK	7·8	5·2	4·2	5·5	5·5	11·0
	100·0	100·0	100·0	100·0	100·0	100·0

Key ALP—Australian Labor Party, DLP—Democratic Labor Party, LCP—Liberal or Country Parties, Ind.—Independent, DK—'Don't Know'

Catholics form the second largest religious group, 26-28 per cent of the population in 1966, the highest proportion for a century. This percentage has climbed steadily since the 1930's, partly because of immigration and partly through natural increase. Day[69] has made a detailed study of fertility among Australian Catholics, which demonstrates that, after thirty years of marriage, the median number of children in a Catholic family in 1954 was three, compared to 2·42 among non-Catholic Christians; and the proportion of families with more than five children was 35 per cent among Catholics compared with 25 per cent among non-Catholic Christians. A Catholic priest, Father Ronald Fogarty, has shown how Catholics have been consistently under-represented in higher education.[70] At the 1921 census, 18·7 per cent of university students were Catholics, who formed 21·6 per cent of the entire population, compared with Presbyterians (18 per cent of students, 11·7 per cent of the population); by 1933, the proportion of Catholic students had dropped to 15·7 per cent. Since then, their numbers have risen steadily, but they still appear to be under-represented. Census data on occupations do not suggest any significant differences related to religion, but a finer-grained analysis would undoubtedly reveal

[69] L. H. Day, 'Family Size and Fertility', in Davies and Encel, op. cit., pp. 157-59
[70] Ronald Fogarty, *Catholic Education in Australia 1806-1950*, Melbourne, 1959

them. In this book, for instance, Catholics are shown to be comparatively rare in a number of high-status groups, including landowners, businessmen, army officers, judges and (to a lesser extent) government officials. According to estimates given to me privately by members of the legal and medical professions, about 20 per cent of doctors and 15 per cent of lawyers were Catholics in 1965.

A national sample survey carried out by Mol in 1966 gives further details of differences between Catholics and Protestants.[71] Mol's survey covered a national sample of over 4,000 people and the responses were analysed according to the type of school attended by the respondent— Catholics who went to Catholic schools; Catholics who went to state schools; Protestants who went to Protestant private schools; Protestants who went to state schools. The Protestants who attended private schools had a markedly upper-middle class character; 44 per cent of them had fathers in professional or managerial occupations, or graziers, or self-employed proprietors, compared with 25 per cent of Catholics attending Catholic schools, who were the second highest group in this category. The same Protestant group had the highest incomes and the highest educational standard; 15 per cent had completed a tertiary education, compared with 6 per cent private school Catholics, 5 per cent state school Protestants, and 2 per cent state school Catholics. They were also the most conservative in political allegiance, but the most liberal on non-party political questions. The Catholics who had attended Catholic schools had the highest score on the standard questions denoting rigid sexual morality: 74 per cent disapproved of sexual relations before marriage, and 52 per cent disapproved of the contraceptive pill. Another attitude question on which they had the highest score related to hereditary social status: 'Would you agree that a member of a family of long-established social standing is entitled to respect?' Of private school Catholics, 46 per cent agreed with this; the other three groups hardly differed in their response, with an average level of agreement of 36 per cent. Catholics who had attended state schools tended to fall between the extremes on most questions, except that their socio-economic status was the lowest, and they were the most authoritarian in their attitude towards children, followed by private school Catholics, state school Protestants, and private school Protestants. They were also the most intolerant, except on sexual questions, and the least patriotic. It is evident that working-class Catholics are much less involved with their church than their middle-class co-religionists—a conclusion which will hardly come as a surprise.

It is interesting to compare these data with American figures. An analysis of three national samples, covering almost 6,000 people, was published a few years ago by Lazerwitz.[72] He found that 9 per cent of the respon-

[71] J. J. Mol, 'The Effects of Denominational Schools in Australia', ANZ *Journal of Sociology*, vol. 4, no. 1, 1968
[72] B. Lazerwitz, 'A Comparison of Major US Religious Groups', *Journal of American Statistical Association*, vol. 56, no. 295, 1961

dents had completed a college education—16 per cent among Jews, 12 per cent among the 'no religion' respondents, 9 per cent among Protestants, 5 per cent among Catholics. Income distribution was similarly skewed by religion. The median income for the sample was slightly less than $5,000, with Catholics very close to the general figure. For Jews and Episcopalians, median income was about $1,000 above the general figure, and for Presbyterians it was about 5 per cent above the average. The proportions of religious groups with incomes over $7,500 were 46 per cent among Episcopalians, 42 per cent among Jews, 26 per cent among Presbyterians and 18 per cent among Catholics. The occupational picture was again similar. Forty-two per cent of the sample were manual workers; 12 per cent owners, managers, or officials; 9 per cent were professionals and 9 per cent farmers. Among Episcopalians, the corresponding figures were 22 per cent, 23 per cent, 23 per cent and 5 per cent. Among Presbyterians, the figures were 32 per cent, 20 per cent, 13 per cent and 5 per cent. Of the Catholics, 52 per cent were manual workers; 11 per cent were owners, managers, or officials; 8 per cent were professionals; and 4 per cent, farmers. Lazerwitz suggests that religion may be combined with the other three indices to give a three-class system in which the upper group includes Episcopalians, Jews and Presbyterians; the middle group, Methodists, Lutherans and Catholics; the lower group, white and negro Baptist denominations, of which there are a large number. The main differences from the Australian pattern are that Episcopalians are a comparatively small denomination in America, whereas Anglicans are the largest in Australia and correspondingly heterogeneous; the social profile of Catholics is skewed more sharply towards the working class in the USA; and the large negro Baptist community has no counterpart in Australia.

The position of Catholics in Australian society constitutes the major form of religious cleavage, which penetrates the whole fabric of social stratification and makes its own special contribution to the nature of class-consciousness. From time to time, writes Pringle, anti-Catholic feeling 'bursts out like lava from a sleeping volcano, burning and destroying everything it touches.'[73] Much of this feeling, he asserts, is fostered by the Masonic lodges, many of which are led by men descended from Ulster families. A similar assertion about the role of the Masons was made twenty years earlier by Pfeffer, who described the lodges as auxiliaries of Protestant-capitalist 'legality' and anti-Catholic 'tolerance'.[74]

Pringle blames the Protestant churches for nurturing anti-Catholic prejudices. The Australian Council of Churches, he recalls, declared in 1953 that Rome and Moscow were equal menaces to the world. The Anglican Church is dominated by low churchmen and evangelicals, some of Ulster origins, who add fuel to the fire.[75] The same point is made with

[73] J. D. Pringle, *Australian Accent*, p. 86
[74] K. H. Pfeffer, *Die Bürgerliche Gesellschaft in Australien*, p. 367
[75] op. cit., p. 87. Pringle's description is true of Anglicanism in NSW, but less so elsewhere. Throughout his book, he treats Australia as an extension of Sydney.

greater emphasis by Horne, who declares that the strongest feature of the Protestant churches is their anti-Catholicism. 'Bitter distrust of the Catholic Church is still part of the system of beliefs of most non-Catholic Australians. It is nurtured by the Protestant clergy; it is an article of faith among many intellectuals (anti-Catholicism is the anti-Semitism of the intellectuals); it is a matter of considerable importance in the lower levels of many government departments; there is an anti-Catholic bias in a significant section of the Liberal Party; many business leaders are anti-Catholic; it is a most important factor in the struggle for the Labor movement.'[76]

Pringle balances his attack on Protestant anti-Catholicism with an onslaught on the 'siege mentality' of the Catholic church, which behaves 'as if it were an invading army in a hostile country. Unfortunately it has inherited from Ireland, not only a great deal of the narrowness, Puritanism and bigotry of the Irish Catholics, but also a great deal of their minority consciousness. In spite of its power and numbers, it cannot believe that it is safe. It is always peering suspiciously out of its stockade to see what the hostile natives are up to. In the Catholic schools this mentality is deliberately fostered. I have heard a Catholic bishop preach a confirmation sermon to a boys' school in which he urged them not to mix with non-Catholics when they went out into the world to earn their living.'[77]

The Irish character of Catholicism in Australia has often been remarked, not least by Catholics themselves. The historian Manning Clark qualifies this by pointing out that the aristocratic, intellectual, urbane stream in Irish Catholicism had little influence.[78] The troubled history of the relations between England and Ireland in the nineteenth century was reflected in the anti-British, anti-authoritarian and populist outlook of Irish immigrants and their ecclesiastics. While the political temper of the Irish was democratic and radical, their cultural outlook was lowbrow, indifferent to ideas, coarse and philistine, and encouraged a superstitious and thaumaturgic form of religion. The power and prestige of the Irish priesthood, who identified themselves with the political aspirations of their flock, meant that the priests gained a voice in everything, including the proper hours for dancing and drinking, styles of dress, sporting activities and so forth. This priest-ridden Catholicism is marked by 'excessive concern with attendance at Mass, indulgences for not missing Mass one thousand times, an undue veneration of the priest, and a ready acceptance of the participation of the church in party politics as well as day-to-day political issues.' When Pius IX announced the dogma of the Immaculate Conception, Clark notes, the Catholic community of Victoria had a medal struck out of gold dug on the Ballarat fields.[79]

[76] Donald Horne, *The Lucky Country*, Melbourne, 1965, pp. 54-55
[77] Pringle, op. cit., pp. 87-88
[78] C. M. H. Clark, 'Faith', in P. Coleman (ed.), *Australian Civilization*, Melbourne, 1962, pp. 78-88
[79] ibid., p. 83

The Irish character of the priesthood began to change only in the late 1930's, when the first native-born Australians were appointed archbishops, and even though the majority of priests are now Australians they have often been reared in the Irish-Catholic ambience. A well-known Catholic, Dr Herbert Moran, writes bitterly about priestly influence in his autobiography. 'The priest had no social sense. . . . He contributed almost nothing to the intellectual life of his times. The priests who had any scholarship were few. Most of them distrusted higher education. For one thing it emphasised their own sense of inferiority.'[80] Their theological concerns were simple. 'Ten Commandments there were, but only one sin really mattered—the sin of the flesh. . . . Alcoholic self-indulgence was a minor error of conduct. The priests themselves were much given to it. . . . But the person who sinned carnally was damned—damned irrevocably.'[81] (Clark amends this to suggest that the moral preoccupations of the Catholic Church are mixed marriages, race suicide and divorce, as opposed to the standard Protestant worries about drinking, dancing, and gambling.) Moran goes on to attack the clergy for being venal, materialistic and uncharitable. 'The evil in Australian Catholicism may be summed up in this way: there is an alarming percentage of unedifying failures among our clergy. A commercial spirit pervades many of the secular priests and nearly all the nursing orders. The prelates, who have always been distinguished by virtuous behaviour, have usually a profound distrust of their own laity. In accordance with the Irish tradition the methods employed are those suitable rather for a religious kindergarten. Only two duties are assigned to a layman: those of practising his religion and subscribing liberally to the Church.'[82]

Moran's views of the Irish and of Irish priests were coloured by his period in Dublin as a post-graduate medical student. He was dismayed by the apathy and fecklessness of the Irish. 'Idleness seems to have been made a Christian virtue. They were mumbling the nursery rhymes of the Catholic Church with a great display of devotion to cover their laziness.'[83]

Other students of Irish migration have commented on the tenacity of the Irish-Catholic 'subculture', for which the English writer Bernard Bergonzi suggests the name 'Hiberno-English' (as distinct from Anglo-Irish). It includes, according to Bergonzi, 'the sound of Latin muttered rapidly with a thick Irish accent; Sunday evening Benediction; Catholic Truth Society pamphlets; hymns such as "Faith of our Fathers" and "God bless our Pope"; bottles of Lourdes water; huge gaudy statues, not only of Christ and the Blessed Virgin, but also of a variety of saints (one or two of whom, like St Philomena, have now been officially declared never to have existed); sermons on the evils of mixed marriages and the need to give financial support to the Church; fund-raising parish dances and foot-

80 H. M. Moran, *Viewless Winds*, London, 1939, p. 23
81 ibid., p. 15
82 ibid., p. 326
83 ibid., p. 169

ball pools; and a highly reverential regard for the personality of the priest, and not only in matters of faith and morals.' This Hiberno-English tradition, reinforced by the writings of Hilaire Belloc (who wrote in a letter that heresy was the source of all error), fosters an ingrained anti-Protestantism which will not easily yield to the promptings of the ecumenical movement.[84]

Bergonzi's description is apt for many features of lower-middle class Catholicism in Australia, although the direct influence of recent immigration from Ireland is much less. Another aspect of the Irish-Catholic social pattern which has thrived in Australia is the relation between the sexes. As Jackson remarks of the Irish community in England, church, home and school jointly promote fear and distrust of the other sex and the role of women is clearly subordinate. The sexes remain sharply divided in many functions outside the home and activities such as drinking, racing and gambling are almost exclusively male. This pattern, clearly marked in Ireland, persists in England.[85] Irish writers have frequently made the same comment, both in fiction and in works of social criticism. 'Irishmen', writes Arland Ussher, 'do not treat women coarsely or brutally. They simply try to ignore and forget them.' As far as sexual relations are concerned, the Irishman tends 'to regard procreation as a shameful necessity, and Irish girls grow up to think of sex as something dark, cold and forbidding.' Irish pubs serve largely as a place of refuge from female company. 'Drinking is a pastime in which the women suffer from most of the ills but enjoy little of the refreshment and social recreation. It serves once again as a means of sex segregation and is, I think, leniently regarded for that reason.'[86] A woman writer in the same symposium declares that an Irishman, once 'hooked' by marriage, will neglect his wife, refuse to enter into any real companionship with her, and return to his men friends and the pub. Denied marital affection, the wife placates herself with a stranglehold on the children.[87]

The persistence of these characteristics among Irish immigrants in the United States has also been described by a number of American historians and sociologists. Oscar Handlin, reviewing the history of the Irish-Catholic community in Boston, notes the unassimilability of the Irish immigrants as compared with all other migrant groups during the nineteenth century. Until the 1880's, even negroes were more readily assimilated into the population of Boston than the Irish, who remained strongly resistant to the Yankee religion of self-betterment, and showed their hostility to it by the contemptuous title of 'lace curtain Irish' bestowed on those who did move into the middle class.[88] It was from the lace-curtain Irish that the Kennedy

---

[84] Bernard Bergonzi, 'The English Catholics', *Encounter,* January 1965
[85] J. A. Jackson, *The Irish in Britain,* London, 1963, pp. 35-37
[86] Arland Ussher, 'The Boundary Between the Sexes', in J. A. O'Brien (ed.), *The Vanishing Irish,* London, 1955, pp. 155-61
[87] Mary Keating, 'Marriage-shy Irishmen', in ibid., pp. 165-67
[88] Oscar Handlin, *Boston's Immigrants: A Study in Acculturation,* Cambridge, Mass., 1959

family emerged. John F. Kennedy's first biographer, James Burns, has suggested that the emergence of the Kennedy family, over three generations, from this Boston Irish background gave him a curiously detached character whereby he was not clearly identified with any social group and made him a genuinely all-American man.[89] Another notable American of Irish-Catholic origins, Daniel Moynihan, argues that Kennedy's detachment from this background contributed to his relative unpopularity among the large Irish community in New York, where he was regarded as having sold out to the WASP establishment. Moynihan's analysis of the Irish-Catholic community in New York emphasises the persistence of the characteristics described above and relates it particularly to the pattern of family life.[90] In Australia, there is a certain parallel between the career of John Kennedy and that of J. B. Chifley, Labor Prime Minister from 1945 to 1949. Although the two men were utterly different in a variety of ways, Chifley also possessed the quality of detachment which enabled him to appeal to all sections of the community. Although descended from Irish-Catholic immigrants, he married a Protestant, was lukewarm in his religious attachments, moved easily among middle class intellectuals and was strongly resistant to political lobbying by the Catholic Church or the 'party-line' Catholics on the right wing of his own party.[91]

In Britain, USA and Australia alike, the survival of a separate Catholic community has been possible largely because of a separate school system. In Western Europe and the Anglo-American countries, the move towards universal elementary education in the nineteenth century provoked fears among Catholics that secular state education would undermine the faith and promote intermarriage, modernism and liberalism. Pius IX's encyclical *Quanta Cura* (1864) provided papal authority for a separate Catholic educational system and the attached Syllabus of Errors condemned state schools and enjoined Catholics against sending their children to them. The resulting conflict over education erupted almost simultaneously in a number of countries—in France, over Jules Ferry's policy of secular education; in Germany, where Bismarck took the offensive against Catholic separatism by launching the *Kulturkampf*; in England, with fierce opposition from the Nonconformist Churches (and their principal political spokesman, Lloyd George) to 'putting Rome on the rates' by public support for church schools; and in Australia, where the struggle over state education in the 1870's marked one of the peaks of Protestant-Catholic conflict, equalled only by the struggle over conscription during the 1914-18 war. In most of these countries, the issue has remained alive because of the unremitting attempts of the church to obtain (or, as in Belgium, to preserve) government assistance for church schools; efforts stimulated by the great educational expansion since 1945 and the strain which it placed on the

[89] J. McGregor Burns, *John Kennedy: A Political Profile*, New York, 1959
[90] Nathan Glazer and Daniel P. Moynihan, *Beyond the Melting Pot*, New York, 1963, pt. 5
[91] For a full account see L. F. Crisp, *Ben Chifley*, Melbourne, 1961.

Catholic educational system. The effort to maintain this system often appears to be the main business of the church. 'Making sure that Catholics send their children to church schools, raising money for schools and running an intricate educational system are often the main preoccupations of clerics in a diocese. The flavour of Catholic life cannot be understood except to a background of Communion Breakfast speeches on state aid; raffles, bingo games and other money-raising activities; family obsessions with school fees; political pressures. This atmosphere helps the impression of living in a hostile society and perpetuates clannishness.'[92] In the words of Australia's most famous Catholic prelate, Archbishop Mannix, the school is the antechamber of the church.[93]

The struggle over secular education has been described at length by a number of historians.[94] Here, I shall be concerned with a few observations to underline the divisive effects of the conflict and its lasting contribution to the formation of a particular style of class-consciousness. The conflicts in the various colonies—especially NSW, Victoria and Western Australia—were, in fact, class struggles, involving basic differences of opinion about the nature of the state and its relation to society. The struggle to establish a system of free, compulsory and secular education to replace the patchwork of government-aided church schools was a conflict over the proper allocation of resources; a struggle to establish social equality through state action. In the end, there was a compromise whose unsettled features have provided the continuing basis for social inequality manifested in the private school system, and for the apparently unending efforts of the Catholic Church to obtain public support for a private system.

The conflict came to a head as a result of a Provincial Council of bishops in 1869 following the encyclical and Syllabus of Errors of 1864, which declared that Catholics had a 'right to our just proportion of the public revenues.' Protestant and secularist opinion was further inflamed by Pius IX's declaration of papal infallibility in 1870. Gladstone declared that Catholic doctrines represented a 'perpetual war against progress', and his pamphlet of 1874 accusing the church of subverting civil allegiance was a best-seller in Australia as well as in Britain. Liberal politicians like Henry Parkes (the dominant figure in NSW politics for thirty years, who had compromised with the churches on several occasions) were now pushed into a position of advocating complete abolition of government aid for

[92] Horne, op. cit., p. 58. The Catholic Church's political activity includes a constant effort to relax the gaming laws and thus facilitate gambling at church functions.
[93] Fogarty, op. cit., vol. 2, p. 305
[94] Notably by A. G. Austin in *Australian Education 1788-1900*, Melbourne, 1961. A Catholic account is given by Fogarty, op. cit. and by J. G. Murtagh, *Australia: the Catholic Chapter*, Sydney, 2nd ed., 1959. Particular aspects of the struggle are examined by J. S. Gregory in two articles, one in *Historical Studies*, vol. 6, no. 20, 1953 and one in E. L. French (ed.) *Melbourne Studies in Education 1958-9*, Melbourne, 1959; A. R. Crane, 'The NSW *Public Schools League*', in ibid., 1964, Melbourne, 1965; and Austin, *G. W. Rusden and National Education in Australia*, Melbourne, 1958.

church schools. This was realised in Parkes' Public Instruction Act of 1880, which established the existing state system. During the preceding year, the news of Parkes' intentions had aroused the anger of Catholic leaders and he was attacked in violent terms by Archbishop Vaughan of Sydney. Vaughan, whom Parkes described as 'an audacious prelate', attacked liberalism as 'the great apostasy' and declared that the state schools were 'seed-plots of future immorality, infidelity and lawlessness'. Unless Catholics had their own schools, they would be crushed by 'tyranny'. Parkes, for his part, spoke of the threat of ecclesiastical 'tyranny', accused Vaughan of 'wanton and libellous' attacks, and declared that the immoderation of his language had united all non-Catholics.[95]

There is no doubt that Vaughan and the other bishops overreached themselves, especially in their unbridled condemnation of the state schools. Vaughan attacked secularism as a 'monster cuttlefish' and secular education as a Masonic plot; one of his Anglican opponents, a leading Mason, riposted that Vaughan was disloyal to the Crown because he had sworn allegiance to a foreign potentate. Vaughan's most famous metaphor was to describe the state schools as a torture instrument, a 'scavenger's daughter' for 'squeezing the life and blood out of those Catholics who declined to deny their God . . . [they] are the most effective instrument invented by man for squeezing very gradually and almost imperceptibly the Catholic faith out of a Catholic people.'[96] Bishop Goold, in Victoria, alleged during an election campaign that if the secular party won, Catholic parents would be compelled, on pain of fine or imprisonment, to send their children to these Godless schools.[97] Even in Western Australia, where the conflict did not come to a head until the 1890's, the priests had not learnt the lesson of events in the eastern colonies and described the state schools as 'hotbeds of immorality', whose pupils behaved in a way to make their parents hang their heads in shame.[98]

One result of the conflict was the welding together of anti-Irish and anti-Catholic prejudices into a bond which endured for more than two generations. Protestants were confirmed in their view that Catholicism was the tribal faith of the Irish. This conjunction had its greatest effect in Victoria, where the struggle over state education was longer and more bitter than in any other colony. It crystallised around the figure of Charles Gavan Duffy, Premier of Victoria in 1871-72. Duffy was both a Catholic and an Irish rebel, who had fled from Ireland to avoid arrest. 'It is hard at this distance', comments Austin, 'to appreciate the violence of the emotions Duffy inspired in Victorian society.' Among other reasons for

[95] Austin, *Australian Education 1788-1900*, pp. 208-12
[96] Crane, loc. cit., p. 227. The torture instrument described by Vaughan was invented by Leonard Skevington, lieutenant of the Tower of London in the reign of Henry VIII. It was a press which forced the victim's head against his knees, bringing blood from the nose and ears, jocularly called Skevington's daughter, and hence scavenger's daughter from his role in eradicating Papistry.
[97] Austin, op. cit., p. 205
[98] ibid., p. 213

the defeat of Duffy's government was the accusation that he had used his powers of patronage to favour Catholics. The press declared that 'episcopal dictation' was the real issue in the election of 1872, that Duffy was 'taking refuge behind the altar', and that Catholics must be taught not to permit 'ecclesiastical organisation to bear on political matters'.[99]

To put the matter in perspective, it is essential to point out that ethnic and religious intolerance are not in themselves sufficient to explain the eruption of this issue at that particular time. Demographic and sociological factors were at least as important. The population of Australia rose spectacularly as the result of the gold rushes of the 1850's; one million people entered the country in the decade ending in 1861. The growth of cities was greatly stimulated and by the 1870's the school system could no longer cope with the great bulge of children of school age and the rising demand for secondary and technical education. The complete abolition of government aid to private schools need not have occurred but for the intransigent attitude and violent language of the Catholic priesthood (paralleled, of course, in France, and with similar results). Even this intransigence, however, should be seen in perspective. In 1879, fifteen years after the Syllabus of Errors, and faced by the rapid growth of 'national' (i.e. state) schools, the hierarchy realised that a large proportion of Catholics were not sending their children to church schools. The result was a joint pastoral letter published by the bishops, which declared that Catholics must send their children to church schools unless they had a dispensation from their parish priest.

The effects of this policy on Catholic school enrolment were dramatic. From 1879 to 1890, enrolments at church schools in the diocese of Melbourne increased ten times as fast as state school enrolments. In 1890, about one-half of Catholic children were attending church schools and the proportion continued to increase until it reached two-thirds, remaining stable at that level until the 1939-45 war.[100] The effects of Catholic education, as measured by Mol's survey, suggest that the apprehensions of the bishops were justified. Mol found that 80 per cent of Catholics educated at Catholic schools were regular churchgoers, compared with 48 per cent of Catholics who attended state schools. Again, 80 per cent of private school Catholics were certain about the existence of God, but only 59 per cent of those educated at state schools. Perhaps the most striking case was the question inviting respondents to disagree with the statement that one can be a Christian without churchgoing. Of those who had attended state schools, 27 per cent expressed this disagreement, compared with 43 per cent who had been to private schools. Not even a religious education can persuade the majority of Catholics that churchgoing is important. Without the Catholic schools, the churches would

---

[99] ibid., pp. 204-7. Duffy's own account is given in his autobiography, *My Life in Two Hemispheres*, London, 1898.

[100] K. S. Inglis, 'The Australian Catholic Community' in Henry Mayer (ed.), *Catholics and the Free Society* Melbourne, 1961, pp. 11-12

indeed be empty. The effort of building schools, churches and other institutions seems to have had the effect of leaving little energy for the subtler tasks of inculcating belief. As Bergonzi remarks, the proliferation of Catholic schools has not succeeded in fostering spiritual development and Catholic faith, and the problem of 'leakage' which obsesses the clergy remains insoluble. 'In many cases the cause seems to be an ignorant and unenlightened form of religious instruction that is no better than brain-washing, and often produces a hostile reaction.'[101]

So successful has the pursuit of Catholic education been in Australia that the proportion of Catholic children educated at church schools is far higher than in other countries. According to Catholic educational authorities in Australia, the world average is about 20 per cent, compared with two-thirds in this country. The exact number of schools, or of pupils, is difficult to discover because of the loosely articulated structure of the Catholic educational system, divided between a number of dioceses which operate parochial schools, and teaching orders of nuns and brothers who are not under diocesan control. In NSW there were, in 1962, 668 schools and 167,000 pupils.[102] In 1968, there were 498 Catholic secondary schools in the whole of Australia out of a total of 686 private secondary schools.[103] This expansion of secondary education has come about only slowly. As we have already seen, the early secondary schools were private institutions established by the Protestant Churches, with government support until the secular education struggles of the 1870's. With the slow growth of a Catholic middle class, the demand for Catholic schools of this type was met by the establishment of St Joseph's College, Brisbane (1875), Xavier College, Melbourne (1878), St Ignatius and St Joseph's, Sydney (1880 and 1881). In 1968, out of seventy-seven schools belonging to the Head-masters' Conference, twenty-one were Catholic. A similar but much smaller growth of girls' schools also took place. These were the outgrowth of select convent schools and have remained select, despite attempts to democratise them; and they remain dedicated to turning out suitably accomplished young Catholic ladies.[104] In 1968, only seven of the ninety-one schools affiliated with the Associated Headmistresses were Catholic.

Barcan[105] has noted the slow growth of secondary and higher education among Catholics. The church was concerned with preserving the faith and its emphasis, dictated both by necessity and by Jesuit theories of education, has always been on primary education. It was the emergence of a Catholic middle class that pushed the church into developing secondary education and improving the standard of teaching. The quality of Catholic teachers

101 Bergonzi, loc. cit.
102 *Sydney Morning Herald*, 5 August 1962
103 Computed from *The Independent Secondary Schools of Australia*, 1968, National Fund-Raising Council of Australia Pty Ltd
104 Fogarty, op. cit., vol. 2, pp. 347-50
105 Alan Barcan, 'Education and Catholic Social Status', *Australian Quarterly*, vol. 34, no. 1, 1962

may be gauged from the fact that in 1900 less than 1 per cent of teachers in church schools in NSW held university degrees, compared with more than 10 per cent in non-Catholic private schools. The real spurt in secondary education came after 1930, when there were 55 Catholic boys' secondary schools; in 1950 there were 103 and in 1968, 340.

The expansion of secondary education produced a renewal of church efforts to obtain government assistance for private schools in the 1950's. By 1950, the increase in the proportion of Catholic children attending church schools had reached its peak (in NSW it was 80 per cent) and thereafter began to fall under the combined impact of three factors: a rising proportion of pupils completing secondary school, a steady increase in costs, and a decline in recruiting to the teaching orders (which also increased costs because of the need to employ lay teachers).[106] Catholic efforts to persuade the political parties to commit themselves to support direct financial aid to private schools gradually made headway during the late 1950's and early 1960's. The task was easier because the embittered atmosphere of the 1870's had lost its influence, and also because the Protestant Churches, which had been violently anti-Catholic at that time, were now prepared to accept government assistance for their schools even if it meant the Catholic schools would also benefit. In a remarkable political stroke the Prime Minister, Sir Robert Menzies, committed his party to the provision of Federal government assistance for private schools; to sweeten the pill, the assistance was made available to *all* schools, thus providing a modicum of federal assistance to the state governments in response to repeated demands.[107]

Since 1945, the relation of Catholics to the community at large has been affected by a variety of economic, social and political factors—social mobility resulting from economic growth; the dilution of the Irish pre-dominance by Italian immigration; the movement of *aggiornamento* initiated by Pope John XXIII; the activities of Catholic Action in the trade union movement and the Australian Labor Party; and the changing nature of Australia's external relations. A new breed of Catholic intellectuals has emerged, expressing themselves through a number of periodicals such as the *Catholic Worker*, *Prospect* and *Dialogue*, who are unwilling to take the traditional position of Catholics in Australian society for granted, and who are particularly hostile to the 'ghetto mentality' fostered by Catholic schools. These discussions show an awareness of the fact that much Catholic education is inferior to state education and that this puts many Catholics at a permanent social disadvantage, while the existence of social differentiation among Catholic schools themselves simply repeats the pattern of socio-educational discrimination in the community at large. At the university level, Catholic schools contribute more students than state

[106] *Current Affairs Bulletin*, 'The Catholic School in Australia', vol. 22, No. 9, 1958
[107] A detailed account of these events is given by P. N. Gill in *Melbourne Studies in Education 1964*, Melbourne, 1965.

schools but less than the major Protestant private schools.[108] However, this conceals the fact that the variations in performance between Catholic schools are very wide, that the less select secondary schools are considerably under-represented, that girls in particular do badly at the university, and that the casualty rate among first-year Catholic students is high.[109]

Whatever the virtues or defects of the Catholic educational system, it does appear to contribute to the relative absence of Catholics in most of the elite groups of the Australian community. Discrimination against Catholics in employment, especially in commerce and industry, has a long history. Herbert Moran records that when he was a boy, it was not uncommon to see advertisements reading 'No Catholic need apply'. For fifty years, he declares (i.e. until the outbreak of war in 1914), Catholics 'remained a breed apart, firebranded like travelling stock in a strange country so that all might know whence they came. . . . At the first state school I attended we Catholics used to be sometimes pursued home to the cries of "Protestant, Protestant, ring the bell, Catholic, Catholic, go to hell".'[110] Even today, the suspicion of Catholics in business remains. A letter in the *Sydney Morning Herald* in 1962, evidently written by a Catholic, related that the writer had applied for various jobs and had been asked on the application forms to state his religion. 'I would like to know', he concluded, 'what is the connection between the way you do your job and religion.' He was answered by another correspondent who obviously took him for a Catholic: 'Any business executive who is looking in a prospective employee for initiative, new ideas and capacity to shoulder responsibilities, cannot find these qualities in a person whose religion indicates that he is content to let religious institutions control and mould his intellectual powers, within the limits prescribed by dogmatic theologians.'[111]

In a democratic society, poverty and discrimination can still be countered through political action. As in the USA, the Catholic community became firmly attached to one political party, and for two generations the Australian Labor Party has been identified with Catholic political action. The novelist Helen Simpson writes feelingly about the Irish-Catholic drive for power in the early years of this century in her quasi-autobiographical novel *Boomerang*, published in 1932. Helen Simpson's maternal grandfather, the Marquis de Lauret, left France after the establishment of the July Monarchy, which he opposed, and settled in rural NSW. In the novel, this history is related in fictional form and describes the friction between

---

[108] Figures on Catholic entrance to university are given by D. S. Anderson in E. L. Wheelwright (ed.) *Higher Education in Australia*, Melbourne, 1965.

[109] Some of these points are brought out by Noel J. Ryan in an unpublished Ph.D. thesis, 'Catholic Higher Education in Victoria', University of Melbourne, 1966. Part of Father Ryan's findings are published in 'A Study of Catholic Residences and Tutorials in the University of Melbourne', ANZ *Journal of Sociology*, vol. 3, no. 2, 1967.

[110] op. cit., p. 10

[111] *Sydney Morning Herald*, 24 and 28 November 1962. The common practice of asking applicants for their religion is also inspired by anti-Semitism.

the aristocratic French-Catholic family and the 'vulgarity' of the Irish Catholics around them. The heroine of the book becomes involved in a politico-religious conflict and her childhood dislike of the 'Micks' is reawakened:

It's the Irish that want the power . . . weak people are greedy of power. Oppressed people, too. The only power an Irishman has been able to hold this last three centuries is the spiritual. That's why religion is so important in Ireland; why every family's ambition is to have one member a priest. Political power's denied them there, here it's not. England keeps Home Rule from them there, and lets them get their fingers on it here. They want it, they'll use every means to take it. And they'll hate England the worse when they have it, because it's only Australia they hold, and not Ireland.

It is not necessary to accept this description as wholly accurate, but it testifies to the strength of politico-religious feeling which the authoress experienced among her rather embarrassing co-religionists. The Irish-nationalist sentiments of the Irish-Catholic community, and their concomitant dislike of Britain, remained strong until the establishment of the Irish Free State in 1922, but their major political interest had been guided into other channels long since. The principal agent of this change was Cardinal Moran of Sydney, perhaps the greatest Catholic prelate in Australian history. It was Moran who persuaded Catholics to see in the Labor movement their chosen instrument of political redemption.[112] Under his leadership, the Catholic community asserted its right to a footing of equality and acquired a national character as Moran 'worked deliberately to divert the sentiments of his flock away from the old homeland and towards the new.'[113] As a result, Irish immigrants soon made themselves felt in the Labor movement, especially in NSW and Queensland (where the early leaders were Scots or Welsh Nonconformists). 'It was natural', writes Pringle, 'for them to choose the Labor Party, for they had the most to gain from Labor policy. The Church sympathised with their aspirations, and had no reason to discourage their choice because there were then so few wealthy Catholics in Australia. To the Roman Catholic Church, as to the poor Irish workers, the Labor Party was the gateway to the promised land.'[114]

This proposition was soon tested by the events of 1913, when a body called the Catholic Federation attempted to put pressure on the NSW state Labor government to introduce government assistance for church schools, and one of the leaders of the Federation, Father O'Reilly, campaigned against the Premier, W. A. Holman.[115] The relations between

[112] Murtagh, op. cit., pp. 138-80
[113] K. S. Inglis, 'Catholic Historiography in Australia', *Historical Studies*, vol. 8, no. 31, 1958
[114] op. cit., pp. 54-55
[115] Celia Hamilton, 'Catholic Interests and the Labour Party', *Historical Studies*, vol. 9, no. 33, 1959. See also Patrick O'Farrell, *The Catholic Church in Australia*, Melbourne, 1968, ch. 5.

church and party were put to a far greater test three years later when the Labor Prime Minister, W. M. Hughes, broke with his party and attempted to obtain public approval for conscription, to supply more troops for the Western Front.[116] The great majority of Hughes' supporters in this conflict were Protestants and his principal opponent within the Labor movement was T. J. Ryan, Premier of Queensland, who was a devout Catholic. Until this period (1916-17) Catholic voluntary enlistment had been notably high; according to Murtagh, it was in excess of the Catholic proportion of the population.[117] Feeling among Catholics had been embittered by the Easter rising in Dublin in 1916 and its violent repression by the British government. Hughes put the issue to two successive referenda, both of which were defeated. The real leader of Catholic opposition to the referendum was Archbishop Daniel Mannix of Melbourne, who had come to Australia from Ireland only a few years earlier. Mannix attacked Hughes and his allies in the most outspoken terms and was equally savage in his replies to fellow-Catholics who criticised him for embroiling the church in politics, particularly Mr Justice Heydon of the NSW Supreme Court. The two referenda were defeated and it has been commonly assumed that Catholic opposition was a major factor. This assumption is disputed, among others, by Herbert Moran, who argues that Mannix's campaign may have actually strengthened support for the referendum. Moran, who served in France and was invalided back to Australia, supported the referendum and writes bitterly about the damage done to the Catholic community by Mannix's activities. 'The decision of a religious leader and above all an Irishman to lead the opposition was incredibly foolish. . . . The Archbishop's temerity split the Catholic body into two hostile layers. The upper social classes, strongly loyal, bitterly opposed their own ecclesiastic . . . [Mannix] had assumed the mantle of the Saviour of Australia. . . . He himself suffered no personal injury or discomfort. But after each display of eloquence in every State humble Catholics were discharged from their jobs. Thanks to the Archbishop a system of boycott against Catholic workmen and tradesmen was set up throughout the whole Commonwealth. . . . Nearly every large firm adopted, though they did not publish it, the old formula, "No Catholics need apply" . . . lukewarm Catholics publicly denied their faith. Many who didn't became bitterly anti-clerical, speaking of some of their own priests with crude offensiveness. . . . He penalised severely the poorer Catholics and the little Catholic tradesmen. He caused social ostracism of the professional Catholics.'[118] Moran recalls that, on his return to Australia

---

[116] There are numerous accounts of the conscription struggle, including L. C. Jauncey, *The Story of Conscription in Australia*, London, 1935; Ernest Scott, *Australia During the War* (Official History of Australia in the War of 1914-18, vol. 11), Sydney, 1938; V. G. Childe, *How Labour Governs*, London, 1923; H. V. Evatt, *Australian Labour Leader*, Sydney, 1940. A recent retelling of the story from a contemporary viewpoint is R. K. Forward and R. Reece (eds.), *Conscription in Australian*, Brisbane, 1968.

[117] op. cit., p. 189

[118] op. cit., pp. 156-59

in 1916, he was entertained by a fellow doctor whose wife declared over the dinner table that Ireland should be pushed under the sea.

The influence of Dr Mannix on the role of Catholicism in Australian society is incalculable.[119] As a former principal of Maynooth College, the leading Catholic seminary in Ireland, he exercised great intellectual influence during his long life (he died in 1963, at the age of ninety-three, having been archbishop of Melbourne for forty-six years). He was largely responsible for giving the Catholic community of Victoria a special character which reinforced its inherent tendencies towards separatism and a distinctive style of politico-religious action. It was Mannix again who was responsible for the establishment of the national secretariat of Catholic Action in 1937 and it was he who invited a young lawyer, Bartholomew Santamaria, to become its assistant director. Santamaria, who remained Mannix's protege and political adviser until the archbishop's death, went on to become director of Catholic Action, president of the Catholic Social Movement (founded 1943) and its successor, the National Civic Council (founded 1957).[120] These bodies were responsible for the establishment of Labor 'industrial groups' within the trade union movement and for the development of a remarkable political network which led to the great split within the Labor movement in 1954 and the emergence of a separate party, the Democratic Labor Party, clearly based on a section of the Catholic community.[121]

The Democratic Labor Party, although it has its counterparts in the confessional parties of Western Europe, is a specifically Australian phenomenon. Its persistence since 1955 is testimony to the way in which class, status and power combine to give the Catholic community a special position reflected in the special type of political and social consciousness from which the DLP draws its strength, but of which it is only the most spectacular manifestation. Like an outcrop of jagged, brecciated rock, it denotes the great tectonic unconformity beneath the level, egalitarian surface.

Opinion polls and surveys have revealed a great deal about the social correlates of DLP voting. The most recent of these is Mol's survey, already quoted. Mol found that the proportion of Protestants voting DLP was negligible, compared with 14 per cent of Catholics who had attended

[119] For a generally favourable estimate of the archbishop, see Niall Brennan's biography, *Dr Mannix*, Melbourne, 1965.

[120] A biographical sketch of Santamaria is given by John Hetherington in *Australians —Nine Profiles*, Melbourne, 1965.

[121] The literature of this subject is now enormous. Special mention may be made of T. C. Truman, *Catholic Action and Politics*, Melbourne, 1959; Henry Mayer (ed.) *Catholics and the Free Society*, Melbourne, 1961; James Jupp, *Australian Party Politics*, Melbourne, 1964; Henry Mayer (ed.), *Australian Politics: A Reader*, 2nd ed., Melbourne, 1968. An early and perceptive account is given by J. D. Pringle in *Australian Accent*. Mr Santamaria's own account is given in a collection of essays, *The Price of Freedom*, Melbourne, 1964.

church schools and 7 per cent who had been to state schools. Alford[122] made a study of all voting surveys carried out by the Australian Gallup Poll between 1943 and 1961 (including the poll analysed in Table 8·8, above). He found that the proportion of Catholics voting 'Labor' (which includes both ALP and DLP from 1955 onwards) fluctuated between 68 per cent and 75 per cent from 1951 to 1961. The peak of DLP strength was in 1958, when 23 per cent of Catholics in the sample declared their allegiance to it; at three subsequent polls, the figure fluctuated between 10 per cent and 15 per cent. The most striking aspect of Alford's analysis is the nature of DLP support among non-manual occupational groups. In 1958, the *annus mirabilis* of the party, 26 per cent of Catholic voters in non-manual occupations supported it, but the figure has oscillated violently, reaching a low point of 10 per cent in April 1961; by comparison, ALP support among the same group remained steady, fluctuating only between 35 per cent and 44 per cent. Support for the DLP among manual workers, which was also at its peak in 1958, declined gradually thereafter.

A similar analysis has been made by McCoy,[123] who took actual voting figures for 1958 and 1961 rather than poll results. In Victoria, where the DLP is stronger than in any other state, DLP voting correlated with the Catholic religion to the extent of 0·93 in 1958 and 0·96 in 1961, by comparison with ALP voting, where the correlations were 0·71 and 0·77 respectively. In NSW, where the ALP is stronger and an outright split did not occur in 1954-5, these correlations were 0·4 and 0·37 for the DLP, and 0·55 and 0·45 for the ALP. The embattled nature of the Catholic community in Victoria is indicated by these strong political allegiances.

Alford concludes from his figures that the DLP is the result of tensions arising from social mobility within the Catholic community and that it serves as 'a mechanism for readjusting the class alignment for Australian politics as a whole by severing the religious and ethnic ties of the mobile Catholics to the ALP.' Similar observations are made by other political analysts. Spann describes the DLP as a party of militant Catholics, though not under direct clerical guidance and suggests that it attracts Catholic voters who find in it new communal ties to replace those disrupted by social mobility. 'The party clearly asserts certain anti-rational values (in Max Weber's sense) which Labor, as it has lost its appeal as a movement, does less and less.'[124] Burns, in a by-election study, found that the typical DLP voter was 'the skilled or white-collar worker, younger and better educated than the average and most probably a conscientious Roman Catholic. He tended either to think of himself as middle class rather than working class, or to be so bemused by his own social promotion that he

[122] R. R. Alford, *Party and Society*, Chicago, 1963, pp. 200-17
[123] C. A. McCoy, 'Australian DLP Support', *Journal of Commonwealth Political Studies*, vol. 3, no. 3, 1965
[124] R. N. Spann, 'The Catholic Vote in Australia', in Mayer (ed.), *Catholics and the Free Society*, op. cit.

had lost his earlier sense of working class identity without acquiring any clear substitute.'[125]

A number of these characteristics are brought together in capsule form by Davies, in his detailed examination of a DLP activist to whom he gives the pseudonym of 'Leonard East'.[126] East, by profession a minor public servant, was once a member of the ALP, but never happy in it. The formation of the DLP came as a great liberation, something to which he could devote himself wholeheartedly. Although Davies is more concerned with the psychodynamic origins of East's personal political outlook, the special tensions of a Catholic existence come through clearly in East's own words. East sees all society as repressive, authoritarian and hostile; no political leaders (not even Santamaria) are worthy of confidence; East's own decision to give up training for the priesthood was made because he could not accept the authoritarian demands of the church. East's anti-authoritarianism sometimes assumes a liberal flavour, but 'pseudo-liberalism' is probably a more accurate label. It is this pseudo-liberalism, with its frequent use of the word 'freedom' to rationalise Catholic anti-Communism, the demand for assistance to church schools, and its ambiguity towards internal conflicts within the church, which is typical of the Catholic posture today. The manner in which it can be exploited by the DLP was demonstrated by an incident during 1965, when the daily newspaper the *Australian*, in an analysis of the case for government aid to private schools, pointed out that the poorer Catholic schools were the worst sufferers from overcrowding, understaffing and lack of facilities, and that this constituted a strong argument for assisting them. The result was a barrage of hostile letters, which gave every sign of being an organised campaign, attacking the newspaper for its slur on the church and its schools. In this way does the existence of a specifically Catholic form of class-consciousness continue to manifest itself.

[125] Creighton Burns, *Parties and People*, Melbourne, 1961, p. 93
[126] A. F. Davies, *Private Politics*, Melbourne, 1966

9: Aspects of Social Stratification (3): Australia in Perspective

The Anglo-Australian Relationship

Australian society is the product of British society—to be exact, of English, Scottish, Irish and Welsh society, each with their distinctive contributions. When imperial sentiment was at its peak in the last quarter of the nineteenth century, the closeness of the relationship was taken for granted by a wide variety of people. Sir John Seeley, the historian, wrote a famous book on the empire entitled *The Expansion of England*; Sir Charles Dilke, the politician, wrote of *Greater Britain*; and the humorist, Max O'Rell, described the progress of *John Bull and Co.: The Great Colonial Branches of the Firm*. Their viewpoint was shared by the Australian politician who called his countrymen 'transplanted Australian Britons'. The colonial situation has been a powerful influence on the making of the Australian community and remains so to this day.

Any serious attempt to fathom the character of Australian society must take account of this umbilical relationship, which has been constantly fed by immigration. Before 1939, approximately 90 per cent of migration to Australia was from the British Isles, and even with the great increase of immigration from continental Europe since 1947, almost one-third of immigration to Australia has been British.[1] At the 1966 census, 14 per cent of the population were British immigrants. The links between the two countries may undergo large structural changes, but they remain firmly attached by a multitude of individual kinship bonds. If Australia seems to many British visitors to be even more British than their own country, a large part of the explanation is that many of the Australians they meet *are* British.

The colonial relationship, like the filial relationship, is ambivalent. Australians have been almost equally ready to stress their Britishness and to attack British snobbery, class-consciousness, and imperial arrogance. Until the First World War, British governments did show some disposition to intervene in colonial and Dominion affairs, arousing outcries about 'Whitehall interference'. Australian nationalism, observes one historian, shows many signs of excessive touchiness about the right to be indepen-

---

[1] C. A. Price, 'Overseas Migration to and from Australia, 1947-61', *Australian Outlook*, vol. 16, no. 2, 1962

dent. It was 'bred of ignorance both of Britain and of the outside world,
. . . fostered by pungent criticism, and hammered into shape in the conflicts with the Colonial Office.'[2]

Perhaps the most important contribution of the British-Australian
relationship to the development of class-consciousness is the repeated
insistence of Australians that the class divisions which exist in England
have no place in this country. The attitude is mutual. British visitors have
declared repeatedly that distinctions of rank do not exist in Australia;
similar assertions have been made by Australians; and both have quoted
from one another. It was axiomatic that the development of sociology, one
of whose principal functions, as Karl Mannheim wrote, is to debunk
accepted ideas about social reality, should require it to undermine this
conventional wisdom. In doing so, it is valuable to recognise which aspects
of social differentiation are of British origin, which are largely home-
grown, and which are fed by the British connection, irrespective of origin.
Detailed illustrations of differences and/or similarities in objective social
structure and social attitudes are scattered throughout this book, but some
general points may be made here.

The distinctive character of the Australian working class is one aspect
on which historians, particularly, have concentrated. Russell Ward
describes the mixture of 'Celtic' and 'currency' (i.e. native Australian)
influences which went into the making of the Australian working class,
giving it a characteristic lack of deference for established authority and a
heavily masculine culture based on 'mateship'.[3] This working class culture,
which came into being during the period of urbanisation and early industrialisation in the generation preceding the 1914-18 war, was very different
from the culture of the industrial working class in England described in
Richard Hoggart's *Uses of Literacy*. Ward's book has been supplemented
by the work of a cultural historian, Edgar Waters, who studied the British
origins of working-class songs, folklore, and social values and illustrates
their transformation in the new environment.[4] The growth of distinctive
political attitudes is explored by R. A. Gollan in a history of the Labor
movement before the first world war.[5]

Among the middle classes, British influence has been more direct,
positive, and continuous. British visitors are continually struck by this.
R. E. N. Twopeny, an English journalist who settled in Australia, recalled
his first impressions: 'In one sense the visitor is disappointed with his first
day in an Australian city. The novelties and the differences from the Old
Country do not strike him nearly so much as the resemblances. . . . The
first prevailing impression is that a slice of Liverpool has been bodily

[2] H. L. Hall, *Australia and England*, London, 1934, p. 39
[3] Russell Ward, *The Australian Legend*, London, 1958, esp. ch. 3, 'Celts and
Currency'
[4] E. P. Waters, 'Aspects of Australian Popular Culture 1880-1915', Ph.D. thesis,
Australian National University, 1963
[5] R. A. Gollan, *Radical and Working Class Politics*, Melbourne, 1960

transplanted to the Antipodes.'[6] Twopeny's words are echoed by the historian J. A. Froude, who felt how entirely English it all was. 'There is not in Melbourne, there is not anywhere in Australia, the slightest symptom of a separate provincial originality. . . . There is more provincialism in Exeter or York than in Melbourne or Sydney . . . [society] is like society in Birmingham or Liverpool.'[7] The most heartfelt reaction came from Francis Adams, another journalist who lived in Australia for several years, and was struck by 'the appalling strength of the British civilisation'. Everywhere he saw the thumb marks and toe marks of Matthew Arnold's British Philistine, and the jaws of the great Moloch of Puritanism, as if in London or Edinburgh. Not only the tracks but the raiment of this six-fingered, six-toed giant were the same. 'The same flowing dresses, cumbrous on the women, hideous on the men, that we see in England! . . . the same food, the same over-eating and over-drinking and (observe how careful we are) at the same hours!'[8] Eighty years later, a visiting lecturer could still have the same reaction: 'It's more British than, when you get back, even Britain turns out to be.'[9]

The influence of English upper-class society expresses itself in several ways, the most obvious being the link with the Crown, maintained through the appointment of British governors, the imperial honours system, and the royal garden-party circuit. Another English visitor, P. F. Rowland, poured scorn on this 'colonial fallacy'. There is something anomalous, he wrote, in a community 'essentially democratic, organised on a commercial and not an aristocratic basis, importing an aristocrat and paying him to ask them to social functions, which bore the entertained as much as the entertainers, and yet excite an amount of heartburn and petty jealousy inconceivable to those who have not seen something of the struggle for invitations.'[10] In Australia as in Britain, in the words of Kingsley Martin, the monarchy is 'the secret well from which the flourishing institution of British snobbery draws its nourishment.'[11] The aristocratic connection has been most strongly maintained by the landed gentry or 'squatters', whose life style has, for generations, included visits to London for the season, the cultivation of patriotic sentiments focused on the Crown and the empire, and the sending of sons to be educated at Oxford or Cambridge, especially the latter.[12] The novelist Martin Boyd has recorded these attitudes in his autobiography, *Day of My Delight*. They were instilled into him at his private school, where he was taught that Australians were a finer, more adventurous type of Englishman. The headmaster drenched the boys in the

6 R. E. N. Twopeny, *Town Life in Australia*, London, 1883, p. 1
7 J. A. Froude, *Oceana*, London, 1886, p. 156
8 Francis Adams, *Australian Essays*, London, 1886
9 C. H. Rolph, in *New Statesman*, 10 January 1969
10 P. F. Rowland, *The New Nation*, London, 1905, p. 279
11 Kingsley Martin, *The Crown and the Establishment*, London, 1963, p. 175
12 This aspect of the Anglo-Australian connection is described fictionally in the novels of Martin Boyd, e.g. *Lucinda Brayford*, and in the satirical *Pioneers on Parade*, by Dymphna Cusack and Miles Franklin.

finest sense of patriotism, and 'neither he nor his scholars were afflicted by any doubt that the British Empire was the most beneficent institution the world had yet seen.' Boyd travelled to England to enlist in the British army in 1914, because an uncle had suggested he go there to obtain a commission among people of his own class. He returned to Australia after being demobilised, but found it impossible to stay because it was 'provincial' and he missed the 'antiquity of the buildings and the green of the fields'. Outside his family circle, he felt he was in a foreign country.

The influence of Oxford and Cambridge on the development of education in Australia is yet to be assessed, but it has been profound and continuous, expressed both through the private schools, many of whose masters were, and are, Oxbridge men, and through the universities. The most systematic connection is through the Rhodes Scholarship. Cecil Rhodes' will foresaw the 'extension of British rule throughout the world . . . and colonial representation in the Imperial Parliament.'[13] Lord Elton, reviewing the first half-century of the scholarships, believed that Rhodes' aims had been realised by the 'far-reaching aggregate impact of successive generations of Rhodes Scholars, not only upon their native countries, but upon the Commonwealth as a whole.'[14] This view merely states what requires to be proved, and the proof is difficult to come by. Rhodes scholars have not been notable propagandists for the imperial idea, and their subsequent careers have rarely been in occupations where they were likely to act as propagandists. Before the war, one-third of them settled permanently overseas. Only Kingsley Fairbridge, the South African who established the 'farm schools' at Pinjarra in Western Australia and Molong in NSW (there is also one on Vancouver Island), can be said to have put Rhodes' visions into practice.

What the Rhodes scholarship has done is to consolidate the links between Oxford and certain areas of education and the professions in Australia.[15] These links are, firstly, with a small group of Oxford colleges, since three of them—Balliol, New College, and Magdalen—took 65 per cent of the Australian Rhodes Scholars from 1904 to 1958, with Lincoln, Christ Church, Exeter and Merton taking a further 22 per cent. (The Rhodes scholarship thus contributes substance to the late Viscount Samuel's remark that life was just one Balliol man after another!) At the Australian end, the prominence of certain schools is equally notable; in each state (one scholar being chosen from each state annually) one school stands out as a recruiting ground for Rhodes scholars. In NSW, it is Sydney Grammar School; in Victoria, Scotch College; in Queensland, Brisbane Grammar School; in South Australia, St. Peter's College; in Western Australia, Guildford Grammar School; in Tasmania, the Hutchins School, Hobart. Each of

13 B. Williams, *Cecil Rhodes,* London, 1928, p. 51
14 Lord Elton, *The First Fifty Years of the Rhodes Trust,* Oxford, 1953
15 The analysis which follows is based on Elton, op. cit.; the *Register of Rhodes Scholars 1903-45,* Oxford, 1950; the address list of scholars published by Rhodes House, Oxford, in 1963; and the usual biographical dictionaries and directories.

these is a private school, and private schools have dominated the field. Only in Western Australia has there been substantial recruitment from state schools. For a total of 230 about whom we have information in the period 1904-49, 171 had attended Protestant private schools, forty-four state schools, and fifteen Catholic schools. In return, Oxford has contributed a number of its graduates as headmasters and staff to the private schools. Education is, in fact, the main profession found among Rhodes scholars everywhere. Between 1904 and 1945, one-third of *all* scholars went into education either as schoolteachers, academics, or administrators. In Australia, the proportion was eighty-nine out of 200, of whom seventy-two were academics (including vice-chancellors). Since then, the academic profession has become even more important, accounting for thirty-one out of seventy-nine scholars between 1945 and 1958 for whom information was available. Next came government service, private business, law, medicine, and scientific research, in that order. All of these, except law, figured more prominently than the average among the Australians. The largest single group among the government officials were to be found in the diplomatic service—a phenomenon also noticed in the United States. Dean Rusk, Secretary of State 1961-69, was a Rhodes scholar.

The desire of Australian families to insist on their links with England is manifested by the number of Australians included in Burke's *Colonial Gentry*, published in two volumes in 1891 and 1895. An analysis by Professor G. C. Bolton of the 535 families listed in its pages shows that 61 per cent of all the entries were Australian (and another 19 per cent New Zealanders).[16] 'Many of the Australian upper classes were class-conscious enough to want to bedeck themselves with the feathers of the British gentry.' Even advanced liberals like Australia's second Prime Minister, Alfred Deakin, ensured that their families were included, possibly because they shared the feeling that they were in some way 'superior in birth or breeding to their contemporaries'. However, when local self-interest clashed with imperial interests the colonial gentlemen did not hesitate to put local interest first, and this ambivalence runs throughout the history of British-Australian relations. Bolton concludes that identification as members of the colonial gentry was sought by the newly established upper classes in an attempt to 'express and symbolise [their] dominance through the same forms and media that were used by the ruling elite in the most powerful source from which Australia drew its patterns of behaviour.'

The importance of symbolic links, both positive and negative, should not be overrated. Economic bonds between the two countries have always been of overriding importance, and the readiness of particular social groups, such as landed proprietors, to identify themselves with Britain and British values rests on a solid economic basis. Moreover, economic links remain strong and important in spite of changes in the pattern of inter-

[16] G. C. Bolton, 'The Idea of a Colonial Gentry', *Historical Studies*, vol. 13, no. 51, 1968

national trade and investment. It is the combination of economic, demo-graphic, personal, and cultural links which has given the Anglo-Australian relationship its peculiar strength, even if the changing pattern of inter-national affairs has removed most of the substance from the political relationship. Sir Robert Menzies, who declared that he was 'British to the bootheels' was Warden of the Cinque Ports on his retirement. One of his successors, John Gorton, himself an Oxford graduate, preferred to describe himself as 'Australian to the bootheels'. It remains to be seen whether this latter phrase has any substance beyond empty rhetoric. Among other things, the Anglo-Australian relationship has been a colonial one. The upper classes represented by Menzies and by his successors have rarely shown any strong desire to break this colonial situation. With the decay of political bonds between Britain and Australia, there has been an intensive search for a new form of dependence on the United States, putting Australia among a motley array of client states including Korea, Taiwan, Thailand, the Philippines, and South Africa. This is strange company for a country with egalitarian and democratic traditions and institutions, but is understandable as an index of the desire to replace one form of colonial status by another. The weakening of the Anglo-Australian relationship poses the awkward necessity to choose between colonial dependence, on the one hand, or the maximum degree of social and political independence consonant with Australia's international position on the other.

Anglo-American Society

A book about social differences in Australia is also, by implication, a book about society in other English-speaking countries. Not only is Australian society a product of the expansion of England, but economic, social and cultural links make it directly receptive to the influence of other English-speaking countries, above all the United States. Generalisations about the nature, scope, and intensity of social differences in Australia acquire perspective against the background of Great Britain and North America, and Australians make these comparisons as it were by reflex action. Yet it may be overlooked that students of these other countries have also found it expedient to examine Australian society as a mirror in which they can see more truly the nature of their own society. The idea of a common Anglo-Saxon culture, existing in varied forms all over the globe, was dear to the heart of imperial-minded Englishmen in the generation before the 1914-18 war, some of them quoted in the preceding section of this chapter. Most recently, the idea has been revived by the American sociologist, Seymour Martin Lipset.[17]

---

[17] S. M. Lipset, *The First New Nation*, New York, 1964, chs. 6-7; and article, 'Anglo-American Society', in David L. Sills (ed.), *International Encyclopedia of the Social Sciences*, New York, 1968, vol. 1, pp. 289-300. The two sources overlap considerably, and references are drawn from both without further attribution.

Anglo-American societies (i.e. Britain, the US, Canada and Australia—there are no specific references to New Zealand or South Africa in Lipset's discussion) are, he suggests, regional versions of the one culture, and he presents considerable evidence for this assertion. Unfortunately, the value of the evidence is greatly reduced because Lipset endeavours to squeeze it into the framework of Talcott Parsons' 'pattern variables', a derivative of Parsonian systems theory which is intended, among other things, to provide a method of comparing different 'social systems' on a basis of their dominant values. This method does tell us something about national differences, but it raises many of the comparisons to a level of generality which renders them lifeless and mechanical. The four pattern variables which Lipset chooses are:

(I) elitism—egalitarianism;

(II) ascription—achievement;

(III) particularism—universalism (i.e. differential treatment of groups as against universal standards for the whole community);

(IV) diffuseness—specificity (i.e. individuals regarded as members of groups rather than an all-embracing collectivity).

In Lipset's view, British society is the most ascriptive, elitist, particularistic and diffuse of the four, and the USA is the least, except in the case of elitism-egalitarianism, where Australia is the most egalitarian in opposition to Britain. Otherwise, Canada and Australia are in intermediate positions. It is difficult to decide what these rankings mean. I would assert, for instance, that Australia is more universalistic, in Parsons' sense, than either Canada or the USA, whereas Lipset places it second after Britain on the scale of particularism. His reason for these rankings is that 'mateship', which he uses as a key concept to describe Australia, has a 'particularistic' significance, especially as the basis of relatively low wage differentials and trade union strength. This is again to assert that which needs to be proved. It could as easily be argued that the Australian wage system, enforced through a legal-bureaucratic apparatus, is much more 'universalistic' in its effects than Lipset allows for and that this is a more important factor than mateship in strengthening the unions.

On ascription-achievement, Lipset gives Britain a ranking of 1, the United States a ranking of 4, and Australia and Canada both a figure of 2·5. Such precision seems altogether misplaced, and Porter's work on Canada[18] suggests that it cannot be equated with Australia, if only because of the position of the French-Canadian minority, to which there is no real counterpart in Australia. It is also likely that Australia is closer to the US on this score than it is to Britain, whereas Lipset puts it exactly in the middle.

Stripped of the methodological paraphernalia, Lipset's main point is in fact an attempt to rank the four countries according to the strength of equality and inequality. But this requires much closer attention to the

[18] John Porter, *The Vertical Mosaic*, Toronto, 1965

qualitative and specific aspects of these two phenomena than his procedure allows.

In comparing Australia, Canada, and the USA with Britain, it is useful to recall Walter Bagehot's famous remark that Britain is a 'deferential' society. England, he wrote, is 'the type of deferential countries . . . in which the numerous unwiser part . . . the numerical majority . . . abdicates in favour of its elite, and consents to obey whoever that elite may confide in. It has a kind of loyalty to some superior persons who are fit to choose a good government, and whom no other class opposes.'[19] Glossing these words five years after they were originally written, Bagehot added that the voters 'did not really form their own opinions, and did not exact of their representatives an obedience to their opinions', but were guided in their judgment by the educated classes, by whom they preferred to be represented, and to whom they gave wide discretion.[20] Britain has changed a great deal since Bagehot wrote those words, and his deferential voter, as electoral surveys have shown, is a vanishing relic, but the basic attitude he described has been transmuted rather than destroyed. Philip Toynbee[21] observed a few years ago that to become a member of Cabinet in Britain remained the peak of social as well as political ambition; Bagehot quoted the case of the man who said that for twenty years he wrote books and was nobody, but now that he had been elected to parliament he was somebody. The prestige of the British parliament, and that of its members, continues to correspond with its overwhelmingly upper-middle class character. In both Australia and the United States, the political role of the politician has never corresponded with his social role, and the prevailing assumption remains that legislatures should be 'representative' in a sense that the British parliament never has been since the Reform Act of 1832. Kahl suggests that the experience of colonising a strange country is responsible for lack of deference to authority and social status. The task of working the land produces equality of circumstances and teaches men to pay as little attention as possible to those differences which do exist.[22]

A history of colonisation also generates an atmosphere of approval for the self-made man, which survives in an industrial urban society in the high value placed on social mobility. As Baltzell writes ironically, in modern America 'virtue and social mobility have become synonymous.'[23] Reissman gives several reasons for this stress on individual success, including the frontier psychology which places great value on individualism and achievement, the secularised Calvinism of the Protestant ethic which sees individual success as a sign of grace, and the history of industrialisation in the US which created the 'rags to riches' legend.[24] In Britain, on the

[19] Walter Bagehot, *The English Constitution*, 2nd ed., London, 1872, pp. 354-5
[20] ibid., introduction, p. 12
[21] 'Who Governs Britain?', *Twentieth Century*, special number, November 1957
[22] Joseph A. Kahl, *The American Class Structure*, New York, 1953, pp. 174-8
[23] E. Digby Baltzell, *Philadelphia Gentlemen*, Glencoe, 1958, p. 4
[24] Leonard Reissman, *Class in American Society*, London, 1960, ch. 1

other hand, the parvenu has been a figure of fun since the eighteenth century, and his success remained incomplete until he had acquired the accepted earmarks of social position, especially the linguistic subtleties which occupy so much attention in English life. Bernard Shaw's Professor Higgins was able to make a duchess out of a 'draggle-tailed guttersnipe' by teaching her the vowels of the upper class, as he also did for self-made millionaires. The growth of the nineteenth century 'public school' was, of course, a major element in the assimilation of the parvenu bourgeoisie into the upper classes, and enabled the 'fusion of plutocracy and feudalism'.[25]

This situation has little counterpart in either Australia or North America, but the situation in these countries is nevertheless shot through with ambiguities. For one thing, Australia has no 'rags to riches' myth of any significance, and although the self-made man has little problem of acceptance, his career is likely to earn him much more prestige if it has been made on the land or in the professions rather than in business. Again, the English 'public schools' have important counterparts in Australia whose influence on social inequality is great and persistent, but markedly different from their English models. Baltzell, noting the role of the select 'prep schools' of New England, observed also that prominent public figures had been known to include the names of their prep schools in the biographies which they gave to the British *Who's Who*, but to omit them for *Who's Who in America*. This sort of reverse snobbery, he writes sardonically, is to be expected in a 'country where egalitarianism often is preferred to the truth.'[26] No such reticence about attendance at a private school is to be observed in Australia. Here is a clear instance of an institution which serves similar functions in three different countries, but attended by a quite different cluster of attitudes in each case, and achieving rather different results.

The idea of equality is itself linked with the liberal individualism which pervades all three countries, yet the outcome of individualism is different in each case. Benjamin Constant wrote in 1787 that England was a country where 'on the one hand, the rights of the individual are most carefully safeguarded, and on the other class distinctions are most respected.'[27] The same paradox is examined at length by Samuel Beer, who notes that liberal individualism took the form of insisting on the rights of the middle class.[28] Bagehot also noticed the way in which a deferential society could nevertheless resist authority with great stubbornness; the freedoms of Englishmen were the result of 'centuries of resistance, more or less legal, more or less illegal, more or less audacious, more or less timid, to the executive government.'[29] In the United States, as innumerable commentators have

[25] Henry A. Mess, in T. H. Marshall (ed.), *Class Conflict and Social Stratification*, London, 1938, p. 171
[26] Baltzell, op. cit., p. 394
[27] Quoted by Francesca M. Wilson, *Strange Island*, London, 1955
[28] Samuel H. Beer, *Modern British Politics*, London, 1965, pp. 35-37
[29] Bagehot, op. cit., p. 377

remarked from de Tocqueville onwards, individualism has its outcome in a great stress on conformity to popular opinion, with consequent intolerance of minority viewpoints. Lipset argues that the existence of an 'establishment', sure of its position, accounts for greater tolerance of minorities in Britain, and the same point has been made at length by Shils, who explains the inordinate stress on 'loyalty' in the United States as resulting from the absence of a stable governing class.[30] In Australia, tolerance of minorities is both less and more than in the United States; greater in politics, but less in other areas of social and moral opinion and behaviour. This may be related to the bureaucratic authoritarianism which, in Australia, is the paradoxical outcome of the demand for the use of collective action to advance individual rights. At the same time, informal social pressure to observe community norms appears to be markedly less in Australia than in the USA. In addition, emphasis on the role of collective action provides a favourable climate for the activities of the Labor movement, just as it provides only lukewarm encouragement for rugged individualism. In America, there is no Labor party to represent the interests of the working class, but an Irish Catholic can move from the working class to become a millionaire. In Australia, there are no Irish-Catholic millionaires, but the Irish-Catholic working man can use the Labor Party for collective action.

Another criterion of equality relates to everyday social relations. In England, the operation of an enormous variety of deferential and class-conscious interactions is proverbial. It was this that led George Orwell to condemn it as the most class-ridden country in the world. The assumption that different stations in society warrant different standards of treatment remains part of the English way of life, as the following newspaper item suggests:

At the new police headquarters and courthouse at East Grinstead the toilets are marked Ladies and Gentlemen for the magistrates, Men and Women for the public, and Male and Female for the staff.[31]

On the other hand, the ostentatious use of symbols of equality, especially in direct personal relations, which is frequently remarked in the United States, may readily obscure the reality of a large number of subtle but important gradations of status. William H. Whyte has commented on this in his writings about American business firms, and formulates an axiom to express the relationship: 'The more uniform the trappings of office, the more important the differences between them. Which is a tribute to our national practicality, for thus do we enjoy all the benefits of status symbols while at the same time luxuriating in the warm glow of egalitarianism their modesty gives us.'[32] Two English students of American business, discussing the 'open door' policy found in many big corporations (by which the chief

---

[30] E. A. Shils, *The Torment of Secrecy*, New York, 1958
[31] *New Statesman*, 2 April 1965
[32] *Fortune*, May 1951

executive's door is always open to anyone) point out its value as a counter-balance to the intense competitiveness of American management.[33] In Australia, a generally egalitarian quality of social interaction yet manages to incorporate a considerable degree of deferential formality in social relations without evoking strenuous efforts to disguise the existence of hierarchy. School uniforms, badges of rank, formal attire for police and other public officials, and deference to authority figures (whether judges, doctors, or professors) are only a few instances.

These phenomena are much more important than the 'values' so beloved of American writers. Another recent attempt to use values as a touchstone of comparison is made by Louis Hartz, who tries to fit the countries of European colonisation into a single pattern. Hartz argues that Canada, Australia, South Africa and Latin America represent 'fragments' of the old world culture which have established themselves in these exotic climes. Three kinds of fragmentation patterns were established: feudal, liberal, and radical—the last applying to Australia.[34] This classification is somewhat more meaningful than Lipset's, but by resting too heavily on differences in 'values' it gives them a kind of causal significance which puts the cart before the horse. As a result of this emphasis, it is possible for Lipset to conclude that the Anglo-American societies are moving towards a 'congruence of values' and to imply that this also means a congruence of institutions and social structures. It is undeniable that many aspects of material life in the Anglo-American countries (and indeed all advanced industrial societies) are showing signs of 'convergence', but it does not automatically follow that their values are also converging or that, even if they are, their institutions and social structures are moving in a contingent fashion. The proposition that Anglo-American societies are committed to egalitarian, individualist values is in any case open to question (as Hartz recognises, although Lipset does not). The differences between them are more likely to be presented meaningfully through an analysis in terms of class, status and power. This has been attempted for the United States by Mills, for Canada by Porter, and in Britain by a variety of historians, political scientists and Sunday journalists. Their work suggests that the ability of entrenched patterns of inequality to resist or to absorb change remains the outstanding characteristic of Anglo-American societies, as it does of other industrial societies.

[33] R. Lewis and R. Stewart, *The Boss*, London, 1961, pp. 219-21
[34] Louis Hartz, et al., *The Founding of New Societies*, New York, 1964

Part Three
Political Authority

10: The Political System

In examining the Australian political culture, I shall be concerned particularly to discuss the social norms which affect the role of government in society, their influence upon the structure and function of political institutions, and the way in which the interaction between social norms and political demands produces a characteristic structure of authority and equally characteristic modes of selection of political and administrative personnel.

Romantics and Realists

Political theories in Australia move between two poles of interpretation, the realistic and the romantic, whether in popular discourse or academic writing in history and political science. The realistic interpretation sees political activity and the structure of institutions as the outcome of the interplay of competing groups pursuing their immediate interests. The Australian political system, on this view, is one in which 'a variety of syndicates (i.e. organised interest groups) are struggling to enjoy the favours of government'; the result is 'a constant emphasis upon problems of economic advantage, and the use of government to provide the answer to them.'[1] In the romantic view, politics is the expression of a class struggle in which the Labor movement, representing the egalitarian ethos of the working classes, has set the pace with its radical and nationalist policies. As a one-time Labor man wrote many years ago, the Labor Party, in or out of office, was 'the magnetic pole by which all political ships must set their courses.'[2] By contrast, the non-Labor parties are simply defensive and negative, the 'parties of resistance' as Hancock wrote in the most influential exposition of this point of view.[3] The term appears to have been coined before the first world war by Bryce, who described the Liberals of that era

[1] J. D. B. Miller, *Australian Government and Politics*, London, 2nd ed., 1958, pp. 220, 225
[2] J. A. McCallum in W. G. K. Duncan (ed.), *Trends in Australian Politics*, Sydney, 1935, p. 50
[3] W. K. Hancock, *Australia*, London, 1930, ch. 11

as 'a party of resistance or caution.'[4] It was put more picturesquely in a contemporary novel by the *Bulletin* writer Frank Fox, who portrayed the antagonists as the Stupid Party and the Feverish Party, one without a policy and the other with policies that were extravagant and impractical.[5]

A fictional account of this traditional conservatism by the writer John Dalley (*Only the Morning*, London, 1930) describes the political creed of a conservative financier as consisting entirely of 'hostility to innovations —Irish Home Rule, the Commonwealth Bank, the Australian national feeling which was finding expression in agitation for citizen service and a local navy, and so on. He saw the world, outside England, as a collection of inferior races who should be controlled for their own good by British seapower. Those who argued otherwise were traitors, like the Boers and Irish, or agitators' dupes, like the Labor voters. . . .' Dalley's hero is deeply apprehensive of the 'Unionist class', which he sees as 'a blatant Hercules, low-browed, truculent, heavy-jawed, with an illimitable thirst, a sullen hatred of the British connection, and a lust for the property of others. . . . On the one side the Unionist and Roman Catholic hordes, boiling with envy of the Empire; on the other a little Samurai class of business and professional men, holding back the flood by means of speeches and contributions to party funds.' With a few adaptations, this description still has contemporary relevance.

The 'romantic' view has been put forward many times since the emergence of the Labor Party in the 1890's.[6] Its most impressive exponents are historians with that positivist bias which leads to 'an obstinate craving for unity and symmetry' in the historical process.[7] With the Labor movement as its Good Old Cause, it serves as a 'Whig Interpretation' of Australian history. Butterfield, it may be recalled, ridiculed this style of writing as a 'gigantic optical illusion' in which attention is focused exclusively upon 'the larger questions of public policy' and historical personages are classified only as 'the men who furthered progress and the men who tried to hinder it.'[8] A similar criticism is implied in Rawson's hostile exposition of the romantic view:

In the late nineteenth century, political radicals and trade union leaders saw the unfolding history of their own society as the history of class struggles. This indigenous tradition, picked up and put into a pseudo-Marxist framework, soon became one of the principal themes of Australian historiography . . . the thesis is . . . that the political and social development of Australia in the sixty years after the discovery of gold can best be

[4] James Bryce, *Modern Democracies*, London, 1921, vol. 2, p. 238
[5] Frank Fox, *Beneath an Ardent Sun*, London, 1923
[6] For a list of examples see Henry Mayer, 'Some Conceptions of the Australian Party System', *Historical Studies*, no. 27, 1956
[7] Isaiah Berlin, *Historical Inevitability*, London, 1956, p. 5
[8] Herbert Butterfield, *The Whig Interpretation of History*, London, 1950, pp. 11, 29, 129

understood in the light of the emergence of a distinctive working-class movement . . . the economic and social development of the colonies, including the failures and successes of the radicals themselves, gradually led to the trade unions becoming the principal support of radical policies. These policies, by the time Labour parties were established in the 1890's, included the institution of a socialist society while, for reasons which were also related to the class character of Australian society, radicalism was closely associated with nationalism.[9]

As Rawson goes on to point out, this theory has a corollary dealing with the 'retreat' from Socialism following the attainment of parliamentary majorities by the ALP early in this century. Thus, Gordon Childe wrote that the Labor Party, 'starting with a band of inspired socialists, degenerated into a vast machine for capturing political power.'[10] The introduction of industrial arbitration, writes the official Communist Party historian of the Labor movement, meant class collaboration which strengthened the opportunist tendencies in the ALP.[11] These observations are the Australian counterpart of very similar analyses in works such as Michels' *Political Parties*, Henri de Man's *Psychology of Socialism*, and more recently Ralph Miliband's *Parliamentary Socialism*. The concluding sentences of Childe's book recall a similar peroration by Michels. Labor organs, he wrote, 'become just a gigantic apparatus for the glorification of a few bosses. Such is the history of all Labor organs in Australia, and that not because they are Australian, but because they are Labor.'[12] Rawson argues that such theories of change or degeneration underrate or ignore the continuity of attempts to bring together industrial workers, small farmers, small businessmen, and salaried workers in support of Labor policy. On most political issues, the division between wage-earners and others is an unreal one, and political strategy is bound to stress common factors among these groups. This discovery is not new. Childe himself, writing forty years earlier, contradicts his own thesis by pointing out how Labor had *always* been constrained to seek support from middle-class radicals, small farmers, prospectors, shopkeepers, the Catholic Church and the liquor interests. Similar contradictions and evasions are noted by Mayer.[13]

Rawson's critique of 'pseudo-Marxism' is representative of widespread scepticism about the initiative-resistance picture of politics, and an emphasis instead on the dependence of all parties on interest groups, all of which are capable of initiative in policy-making. Mayer concludes that the initiative-resistance theme is misleading because it 'usually treats both

[9] D. W. Rawson, review of Robin Gollan, *Radical and Working-Class Politics*, in *Quadrant*, vol. 5, no. 1, 1960
[10] V. G. Childe, *How Labour Governs*, London, 1923, p. 209
[11] E. W. Campbell, *History of the Australian Labor Movement: A Marxist Interpretation*, Sydney, 1945
[12] Childe, loc. cit.
[13] ibid., ch. 5; Mayer, loc. cit.; Rawson, 'Labour, Socialism and the Working Class', *Australian Journal of Politics and History*, vol. 7, no. 1, 1961

sides as self-sufficient and pretty isolated entities. . . . The analysis of Australian parties in terms of interest behind them breaks off when it comes to the crucial question of the context of party policy.'[14] A similar point is made by Miller, whose somewhat eccentric use of the term 'syndicate' may reflect the desire to avoid the abusive overtones of the term 'pressure group'. Party differences are to be explained not in terms of initiative and resistance, but of a range of demands for government action slanted in the interests of different syndicates, with differential attachments to the parties. It is for this reason that the Liberal Party of Australia has little affinity with traditional liberalism of the British or Western European variety.[15] The Country Party, for its part, espouses the 'agrarian socialism' which characterises farmers' movements in the Canadian prairie provinces and the American Middle West. The Labor Party, on this view, differs from the others only in that it is the one which is most consistently eager to exploit settled interventionist policies. It is disputable, Miller concludes, 'whether this has given it any claim to represent the most dynamic elements in Australian politics.'[16]

The 'realistic' interpretation, like the romantic, goes back a long way. The first great burst of political writing about Australia occurred in the quarter-century before the first world war, when the early enactment of advanced measures on the secret ballot, universal suffrage, labour conditions, industrial arbitration, old-age pensions and government enterprise had attracted world-wide attention to the Australian colonies as a social laboratory. A number of contemporary observers were quick to seize on the fact that the ideas expressed in social legislation were derived almost entirely from British and European liberalism,[17] and that the only local influence of importance was that of material interest, which was concerned less with the extension of state action as a general principle, than with specific extensions to favour the interests of particular groups.

The French socialist Albert Métin noted, for instance, the absence of ideological questions in disputes over labour legislation.

One could say, rather brutally, that the opposition between the supporters and the opponents of labour legislation is concerned almost entirely with material questions. On either side, the poverty of ideas astonishes those who are accustomed to European polemics. The employers express an intransigent opposition based on the defence of their profits; there are no arguments, but only a declaration of war. The publicists who uphold the capitalist cause restrict themselves to practical matters, and reveal that they are on unfamiliar ground as soon as they venture upon intellectual questions.[18]

14 loc. cit.
15 This is an old observation; cf. the complaint of a Liberal politician, Bruce Smith, in *Liberty and Liberalism*, published in 1887.
16 op. cit., p. 80
17 e.g. W. Pember Reeves, *State Experiments in Australia and New Zealand*, London, 1901
18 Albert Métin, *Le Socialisme sans doctrines*, Paris, 1901, p. 255

Nor, he adds, should one be misled by class-conscious postures assumed by the Labor Party. 'In appearance they (the Labor parties) are what we would call a *Class Party*, carrying on a struggle against the bourgeoisie. In reality, they include employers and salaried workers and are concerned simply with obtaining good working conditions in the world as it is.'[19] As a result, the level of argument was no better than among the employers; indeed, theoretical arguments were ignored or avoided, and a comprehensive program along socialist lines would be regarded as a positive hindrance.

Socialism, whose philosophy appeals to many European reformers, does not attract the Australasian workers and actually disturbs them by the very breadth of its ideas. When I asked a Labour man to outline his program, he replied: 'My program? Ten Bob a Day!' . . . The workers of the antipodes have such a narrow conception of their interests and pursue them so conscientiously that they are afraid of anything which might make them appear less narrow.[20]

A few years later, André Siegfried made a similar diagnosis for New Zealand. It was strange, he said, to find English colonists prepared, under the compulsion of self-interest, to sacrifice some part of their liberty, and 'to see the sons of the men of the Manchester School becoming the most stalwart disciples of State intervention.'[21] This was rendered easier because the government did not appear remote or mysterious. 'It seems that one only has to stretch out one's hand to grasp it, and to dictate to it laws and regulations. . . . [Europeans] laugh at the story which tells of the misadventure of the citizen who wanted to see the State. In New Zealand, nothing is easier. It is enough to find the Prime Minister. If you are an influential elector he can refuse you nothing.'[22] A more recent writer on New Zealand uses the word 'opportunism' to describe this outlook:

The widening of State functions is due primarily to colonial opportunism and freedom from theories. It has little to do with Socialism. Reeves' phrase, 'colonial governmentalism', is a true description. . . . It is 'étatisme' rather than Socialism.[23]

The theory of a political system based on the continuous interaction of groups pursuing their immediate interests has been given much greater sharpness and intellectual depth in recent years by the work of political scientists, notably Mayer. In the article already quoted, Mayer argues that the attribution of a major policy-making role to the parties puts the emphasis in the wrong place; it is a 'confused voluntarist point of view' which suggests deliberate choice by the parties, whereas their policies are

---

19 ibid., p. 74
20 ibid., p. 256
21 André Siegfried, *Democracy in New Zealand*, London, 1906, p. 51
22 ibid., p. 57
23 J. B. Condliffe, *New Zealand in the Making*, London, 1930, pp. 164-65

in reality made *for* them by their supporting interests. Elsewhere, he points out that the apparently 'illogical' character of the federal constitution, and its resistance to change by the prescribed referendum procedure, is due to the fact that interested groups profit from its illogicalities, and if necessary will combine, regardless of formal party considerations, to prevent changes that would interfere with their pursuit of very short-range, bread-and-butter demands. Settled national policies are relatively unimportant in this context; emphasis upon them overrates the extent of consensus and understates the amount of conflict.[24]

Mayer's work acknowledges the explicit influence of the American writer Arthur Bentley, and illustrates the emancipation of political science in Australia from traditional British influences. Bentley's basic argument, originally advanced in 1908, was that ideologies and similar 'spooks' or 'soul-stuff' must be expelled from the study of political processes. Instead, one must 'look for the interest' and the corresponding interest groups. Government, Bentley contended, was the resultant of group pressures, and the law was a statement of 'the equilibrium of interests, the balancing of groups'. The organs of government were to be seen as the outcome of demands from the 'underlying groups'. When the groups were adequately stated, Bentley wrote in his emphatic style, 'everything is stated. When I say everything, I mean everything . . . there will be no more room for animistic "causes".'[25] One of the banished causes is the concept of public interest, which is untenable as an explanation of policy. What appears to be the public interest is simply 'the equilibrium reached in the (group) struggle at any given moment, and it represents a balance which the contending factions or groups constantly strive to weigh in their favour . . . today's losers may be tomorrow's winners.'[26]

Bentley's work is marked by an emphasis on 'realism' in politics, characteristic of the American Progressive era when his book was written. The pragmatism of William James influenced him deeply. His own influence in Australia chimes with that of John Anderson, for many years professor of philosophy at the University of Sydney, also a 'realist' in philosophy and also influenced by James. Political institutions, according to Anderson, are neither 'an expression of the general will nor the instrument of a particular class, but rather an arena within which conflicts are fought out and compromises reached.'[27] We ought not to ask what end a social institution serves, but of what conflicts it is the scene. There is no reality other than that of everyday experience; ethics and morals (and hence politics) must be concerned with facts, and there are no 'values' whose order of reality is higher.

24 Henry Mayer, introduction to D. Carboch and A. Wildavsky, *Studies in Australian Politics*, Melbourne, 1958
25 A. F. Bentley, *The Process of Government*, 1949 ed., pp. 208-9, 261, 274
26 Earl Latham, *The Group Basis of Politics*, New York, 1954, pp. 35-37
27 John Passmore, introduction to John Anderson, *Studies in Empirical Philosophy*, Sydney, 1963, p. xxii

Criticisms of group theory are many and varied. It neglects the role of the state, which has both the capacity and the need to act independently of pressure-group influence; of the individual, especially the outstanding leader-figure who is able to leave his mark on history precisely because he is not identified with group interests; of ideas and settled national policies, which provide a framework for the interplay of interests. Group theories also neglect the social structure, and they treat all groups and interests as if they were on a par, which is to dissolve away such permanent inequalities as class differences. Parker notes the fallacy of 'scientism' in group theory, and argues that the role of the individual cannot be accounted for by the conventional reply that he is merely the product of his group experience and affiliations.[28] Rothman suggests that group theory disposes of 'attitudes' and 'values' by identifying them with interests. This is the approach of classical liberal utilitarianism, which assumes that because there is a permanent clash of interests in society, the 'real' interest of a group 'lies in striving rationally to attain limited ends within the confines of the system'. Such a formulation excludes utopian, charismatic, and absolutist elements from the political system, yet it is precisely a recognition of these forces that has brought forth modern sociology.[29] Crick points out the 'ideological' assumptions of group theory itself, in that it sees politics as 'a contest for marginal privilege by a great many pressure groups, mostly regional and economic rather than primarily ideological and doctrinal. To the student these could all appear as very much equal in their claims . . . they made it easy for the student of politics to think of himself as just the dispassionate observer.'[30]

Dowling, in a sustained philosophic critique, describes group theory as an attempt to achieve a 'Newtonian' level of political science, with the group as the unit of measurement, and 'pressure' taking the place of the physical concept of force or energy. One result is confusion over the nature of 'government'. It appears variously as the tool of the strongest group; as itself the strongest group; as a balancing factor, stronger than all groups but distinct from them; not as a group at all, but a system of interacting groups, the resultant of a parallelogram of forces. In practice, Bentley wavers between the first three alternatives, while his followers, e.g. Latham and Truman, favour the last.[31]

Partridge notes that to do away with the general will, the common good, and majority rule is to create difficulties which group theory cannot solve. Group interests, he suggests, form a sub-system which interacts with other sub-systems, such as institutions, movements, ways of life, and the social

28 R. S. Parker, 'Group Analysis and Scientism in Political Studies', *Political Studies*, vol. 9, no. 1, 1961
29 Stanley Rothman, 'Systematic Political Theory', *American Political Science Review*, vol. 54, no. 1, 1960
30 Bernard Crick, *The American Science of Politics*, London, 1958, p. 118
31 R. E. Dowling, 'Pressure Group Theory', *American Political Science Review*, vol. 54, no. 4, 1960

process of 'discussion'. By playing these down, group theory makes it difficult to identify the social processes by which some common denominator of sentiment and idea is created within a society.[32]

Other critics have drawn attention to the conservative political implications of a theory which shows an implicit acceptance of the social framework within which the conflicting groups operate. C. Wright Mills attacked such theories as 'romantic pluralism' because they failed to take account of the concentration and centralisation of power in the United States. American social science, writes another critic, reflects an ideological acceptance of pluralism as a social norm and not merely as a description of the actual state of affairs. To say that government is nothing but a responsive instrument for stabilising an equilibrium of competing interests is an ideological as well as a factual statement.[33]

Politics and Bureaucracy

Perhaps the most relevant criticism of interest-group theories from our present viewpoint is their failure to take into account the role of the 'bureaucratic ascendency', described in an earlier chapter, which gives political authority in Australia its distinctive character. It is not enough to attribute this, as Miller does, to a general readiness to provide a system of 'ample government' which can satisfy the demands of interest groups. The left-wing position in Australian politics is, most typically, one of commitment to the extensive use of government. It was established during the quarter-century preceding the 1914-18 war. In 1895, for instance, W. P. Reeves declared in a speech at New Plymouth (NZ) that 'the more the State does for the citizen, the more it fulfils its purpose . . . the functions of the State should be extended as much as possible. . . . True democracy consists in the extension of state activity.'[34] Ten years later, the Labor leader W. A. Holman declared his party's views towards state action in a public debate in Sydney.

We regard the State not as some malign power hostile and foreign to ourselves, outside our control and no part of our organised existence, but we recognise in the State, we recognise in the Government merely a committee to which is delegated the powers of the community . . . only by the powers of the State can the workers hope to work out their emancipation from the bonds which private property is able to impose on them today.[35]

From all this we can deduce an operative concept[36] of the state which forms part of the Australian governing consensus. This operative concept

[32] P. H. Partridge, 'Politics, Philosophy, Ideology', *Political Studies*, vol. 9, no. 3, 1961

[33] Henry S. Kariel, *The Decline of American Pluralism*, New York, 1958, p. 130

[34] Quoted, Métin, p. 229

[35] *Socialism*: Official Report of a Public Debate, Sydney, 1905, pp. 62-3

[36] A. D. Lindsay, in *The Modern Democratic State*, London, 1953, describes the task of political theory as the study of 'operative ideals'.

sees the state as an administrative agency at work, variously, for the 'masses' or the 'interests'. It is regarded as a body where the organs of government and their concomitant institutions, like the party system, express national policy insofar as they execute the expressed demands of organised bodies who legitimate their claims by speaking in the name of the general interest. Party differences are less important than internal party conflicts and disagreements between extra-party interest groups. The notion of the state as neutral, as an arbiter holding the ring between competing interests, is inapplicable to this situation; the state is actually required to decide and to enforce its decisions by law or administrative action. As a counter to this requirement, state intervention, whether of a regulatory or operating character, tends to be detached as much as possible from the central apparatus of government, either by dealing with demands in a quasi-judicial or 'non-political' manner (e.g. arbitration tribunals, the Tariff Board, and frequent royal commissions), or by diffusing responsibility among a number of quasi-independent organs with claims to authority in their own spheres.

Australia differs from other democratic countries partly in the earlier historic acceptance of state intervention as the normal means of evolving and implementing social policies, and in its more rapid advance since then; but it is also distinguished by the relative feebleness of alternative methods, and by the remarkable lack of effective channels of public criticism. One of the few accounts which gives proper weight to the central role of bureaucracy is that of Davies. The characteristic talent of Australians, he writes, is for bureaucracy.

We take a somewhat hesitant pride in this, since it runs counter not only to the archaic and cherished image of ourselves as an ungovernable, if not actually lawless, people; but, more importantly, because we have been trained in the modern period to see our politics in terms of a liberalism which accords to bureaucracy only a small and shady place. Being a good bureaucrat is, we feel, a bit like being a good forger. But in practice our gift is exercised on a massive scale in government, economy and social institutions. Of course bureaucracy pervades most modern societies—it is the price of complex organisation—but Australian demands for security and equality have been unusually strong, and much more concentratedly political.[37]

Davies' account of the central role of bureaucracy is, nevertheless, still coloured by some of the traditional fallacies. For instance, he argues that 'the main interest of political parties is their anti-bureaucratic role in the political system . . . the parties' main functions are to collect and absorb the chaotic and irrational demands of a wide selection of primary political groups, to order them, and on gaining office, to impose them as an authori-

---

[37] A. F. Davies, *Australian Democracy*, introduction. The quotation is actually a composite from the introductory passages to the 1st edition (1958) and the 2nd edition (1964). Subsequent references are all to the latter.

tative pattern of policy on the administration. There are, of course, other groups and institutions of an anti-bureaucratic set, but none rivalling the parties in sheer bravado.' The scope and importance of party organisations is proportional to the area of the irrational.[38] This view has a certain dialectical charm, reminiscent of Weber's theory of the opposition of bureaucratic and charismatic forces in history, but it poses a false antithesis between the parties and the state machine. The parties are only marginally concerned with 'irrational' demands; their main function is to recruit the 'political overhead' of the bureaucratic machine. Experienced political operators admit, in their candid moments, that the mainspring of party activity is the apparatus of pre-selection for parliamentary seats. Continuity of membership between party branches, which confers the rights to stand and to vote in pre-selection ballots, is a major preoccupation within the Labor Party, both for individual members and as an issue in organisational conflicts. As Davies himself demonstrates, most public policy is bureaucratic in origin.[39] His remark that the pressure groups behind the parties 'have only a very fitful interest in influencing the policy of any political party'[40] and prefer to work directly through the administration contradicts his own description of the parties imposing 'authoritative patterns of policy', derived from the demands of interest groups, on the administration.

Davies' account also implies that bureaucracy is a 'rational' phenomenon, by contrast with the 'irrational' parties. But if parties are concerned to promote the material interests of their supporters, this is demonstrably rational, at least in the sense of liberal utilitarianism. The rationality of bureaucracy is a suspect notion, in any event, and in Australia its irrational potentialities are compounded by the fragmentation and dispersion of administrative responsibility within the federal system and within the individual states.

These aspects of Davies' presentation may be due to an attempt to mitigate his own obvious feeling that there is little intellectual interest left in politics. Every student of politics has in him something of what Weber called the occasional politician, who seeks by speaking, writing or voting to influence the distribution of power within and between political structures, and requires of professional politicians not only the craft of manipulating possibilities, but also passion, a feeling of responsibility and a sense of proportion.[41] Davies' emphasis on bureaucracy, like the revival of group theory, is an indication of the profound disenchantment with politics, the 'end of ideology', which marks our generation. As he notes himself, party politics 'has never been of less interest . . . duller than at any time since the 1880's . . . few beyond those vocationally involved are much interested nowadays in political affairs'. As a result of the

[38] ibid., p. 123
[39] ibid., Appendix A, 'Who Made the Laws in 1960?'
[40] ibid., p. 133
[41] Max Weber, *Politics as a Vocation*, in Gerth and Mills (eds.), *From Max Weber*, pp. 83, 115

depreciation of politics vis-a-vis administration, we can only look out upon a 'great grey plain of administrative routine'. The bureaucratic mode, 'spreading like a stain from the growing proportion employed in bureaucracies, private and public', has caused 'most of the stuffing to leak out of the old symbols.'[42]

Social Change and Politics

But if party politics, in Australia as elsewhere, has become a lifeless charade, the life drained out of it has reappeared in a number of political movements which operate on the periphery of the party system and have created an intense feeling of involvement among the people who take part in them. From the viewpoint of this book, the most important thing about these movements is their relation to social changes which have produced political effects among a number of social groups. These changes are both internal and external. Internally, the development of a more complex system of social stratification has produced the shifts in class-consciousness and political identification described in Chapters 7 and 8. Externally, the decline of the British empire, the confrontation between black and white in southern Africa, and the ever-increasing preoccupation with Asia and the Pacific, have produced differential effects on a wide range of social groups. John Dalley's conservative financier would be at home in the 'radical right' movements which developed in the 1960's. These movements were described in 1966 as 'the Australian equivalent of the John Birch Society, with doses of crude racism and anti-Semitism added for flavour'. The writer went on to identify other persistent themes, including support for *apartheid* in South Africa and for the Smith regime in Rhodesia; an obsession with 'purity', not only racial but biological, evidenced by attacks on oral contraceptives and the addition of sodium fluoride to the water supply; and a general condemnation of all 'Reds' and 'pinks'.[43] The most remarkable expression of these views appeared in an editorial in the Sydney *Daily Telegraph* in 1967, following disturbances in Detroit and other American cities. After an attack on 'black lawlessness' and the need for firm discipline to restore 'law and order', the editorial continued:

If sharks took fourteen or fifteen people every week-end on Sydney's beaches there would soon be no one surfing. If, every time Negro revolutionaries decided to burn and kill, those maintaining the law killed 500 Negroes, the Negroes might decide to stop burning and looting. Surely the time has come for the American nation to take the kid gloves off and deal drastically with this lawless minority.[44]

---

[42] op. cit., pp. 123-42, passim
[43] Isi Leibler, 'Australia's Radical Right', *Quadrant*, no. 2, 1966; a more extensive exploration of right-wing groups is made by K. D. Gott, *Voices of Hate*, Melbourne, 1965.
[44] *Daily Telegraph*, Sydney, 27 July 1967

A gloss on this statement was published on the following day, to the effect that shooting Negroes was intended to refer only to actual rioters caught in the act, but that 'a country which is involved in a long and arduous war against Communism in Vietnam simply cannot afford to permit little civil wars to break out on the home front'.

In 1966, right-wing groups intervened in a blue-ribbon Liberal electorate in Sydney. They opposed the official Liberal candidate, Edward St. John, a well-known barrister who had been president of the Australian section of the International Commission of Jurists, and as such had become actively concerned in the affairs of the South African Defence and Aid Fund set up to finance legal aid for political prisoners in South Africa. Although the right-wing candidate received a substantial minority vote, a careful study of the election suggests that no more than 5 per cent of the voters supported him because of their sympathy with the right-wing movement itself. The election propaganda used by the supporters of the right-wing candidate (who ran as an 'independent Liberal') stressed the familiar themes of racism, Communism, support for South Africa and Rhodesia, and of course 'cleanliness'.[45]

The extreme right exercises some influence on Liberal members of federal parliament, varying with the issue. In September 1968, for instance, a number of Liberal back-benchers strongly opposed government policy of supporting United Nations sanctions policy against Rhodesia, and some of them urged the government to withdraw from the United Nations itself. One of them condemned the take-over of the United Nations by the black nations, and another attacked the 'double standard' shown by the United Nations Assembly towards South Africa and Rhodesia.[46]

At the opposite end of the political spectrum, activity has been divided between 'moral issues' like censorship, the abolition of capital punishment, Aboriginal rights, educational policy and international issues, especially the war in Vietnam and with it the implications of Australian relationships with Asia. The re-introduction of conscription at the end of 1964, and the subsequent decision to send conscripts to Vietnam, were a powerful stimulus to the various 'peace groups' which had existed for a number of years. According to one of its leaders, the anti-conscription movement was 'one of the biggest and most active pressure-groups in Australia's history.'[47] The increased activity of these and other movements of protest, resistance to authority, and reform in fields outside conventional party politics, has stimulated the growth of a new role for intellectuals in public discussion with little precedent in Australian history. In 1945, the novelist Eleanor Dark published *The Little Company*. Its title, drawn from the *Chanson de Roland*, recalls the conversation at Roncevalles between Roland and

45 R. W. Connell and Florence Gould, *Politics of the Extreme Right*, Sydney, 1968
46 *Australian*, 12 September 1968
47 Chris Guyatt, 'The Anti-Conscription Movement', in R. K. Forward and Bob Reece, *Conscription in Australia*, Brisbane, 1968, p. 178

Oliver, when they looked towards the approaching Saracens and compared their little band with that mighty host. The metaphor was intended to apply to the position of the intellectual in an unfriendly community. The community has changed considerably since then, not entirely for the better, but the intellectuals at least do not need to feel quite so beleaguered. As Wright Mills asserted in 1960, an age of increasing bureaucracy demands a new kind of political opposition which will be based on students and intellectuals rather than industrial workers.[48] The prescience of this view was demonstrated by the student unrest which began on a large scale within three years of Mills' death in 1962. In Australia, where bureaucracy plays such a special role in the social order, the course of events is likely to be rather different, but the growth of a real focus of criticism and opposition to the bureaucratic ascendency will be a major novelty.

[48] C. Wright Mills, 'Letter to the New Left', *New Left Review*, no. 2, 1960; republished in I. L. Horowitz (ed.), *Power, Politics and People*, New York, 1964

11: The Political Class (1):
The Politicians We Deserve

No Ecclesiastic ever boasted of a greater change in his spiritual faculties than these [Ministers] would persuade us to happen in their understandings as soon as they are admitted to the Secrets of Princes. Such as before were thought at most to be only on a level with their neighbours, once they get footing within the Court, become saucy to their Betters, despise their Equals, and trample on their Inferiors. They value themselves above all things on their profound skill in the Arcana Imperii, and though, in the ordinary actions of life, they possess a very moderate share of Reason, yet they pretend to be absolute Masters of what they call Reason of State.

John Toland, *The Art of Governing by Partys*, 1701

Politicians—in office, in opposition, or on the make—remain for most people the symbol of power. It should, then, be one of our prime concerns to examine the individual and collective characteristics of members of the political class[1] and the methods by which they enter it. Equally, we shall be concerned with the expectations and attitudes of the governed towards their governors, with their reflection in the institutional devices of government, and with the continuous interplay between institutions and attitudes which provides the scenario for the never-ending political movie.

Democratic theory has always equivocated about the role of the political leader. The American critic, Eric Bentley, remarks that government on any scale means government by leaders, and that 'finding the best leaders becomes a prime task, as we all acknowledge at every election.'[2] A century earlier, de Tocqueville had argued that democracy was singularly unfitted to carry out this task. Democratic institutions 'awaken and foster a passion for equality which they can never entirely satisfy'. As a result, distinguished talents are not appreciated, and democracy 'awards its approbation very sparingly to such as have risen without the popular support.' In return, outstanding people are 'apt to retire from a political career in which it is almost impossible to retain their independence, or to advance without

---

[1] The term 'political class' is used here in *one* of the senses that its originator, Mosca, employed, i.e. to denote the politically active minority, as distinct from the 'ruling class' or 'elite' or 'intelligentsia' with which he also made play. For a critical examination see J. H. Meisel, *The Myth of the Ruling Class*, Michigan, 1958.

[2] E. R. Bentley, *The Cult of the Superman*, London, 1940, p. vii

degrading themselves.'[3] Thus is set up a familiar tautology: politics and politicians are not highly regarded, *ergo* outstanding individuals do not enter politics, *ergo* politicians are not highly regarded, and so on. Australians have a long tradition of refusing to admit the need for leadership, coupled with inventiveness in creating devices to circumscribe the discretion of the individual politician and to secure accountability to his constituents. Alongside these major themes may be heard the 'persistent descant upon the iniquities of public men' of which William Pitt complained.

Tautological arguments soon reveal their limitations. Australian thinking, writes the journalist Donald Horne, is deeply populist; hence, 'when someone wants to criticise Australia he criticises not the few who run it, but the mass of the people, as if the genius of the nation resided exclusively in them.' But he soon succumbs to the populist illusion. 'The potential for change within the ordinary people of Australia is great; it is their misfortune that their affairs are controlled by second-rate men who cannot understand the practicality of change.' These second-raters are 'racketeers of the mediocre who have risen to authority in a non-competitive community where they are protected in their adaptations of other people's ideas.'[4] Wilfully or unwittingly, he does not draw the obvious inference that the character of the community's leaders is related to the character of the community, although he sometimes appears to agree with de Tocqueville that democracy 'is not only deficient in that soundness of judgment which is necessary to select men really deserving of its confidence, but has neither the desire nor the inclination to find them out . . . hence it often assents to the clamour of a mountebank who knows the secret of stimulating its tastes.'[5]

A similar ambiguity is to be found in the writings of Brian Fitzpatrick, a historian closely identified with the 'populist' interpretation. Australian political society, he asserts, is so organised that 'where general objection is taken to government policy, the objection can be expressed effectually.' The 'continuity, vigour and efficacy of Australian political activity, or readiness for activity, against governments and largely independent of political parties' is basically due to the 'relatively superior position of Australian working people during several generations, better fed and with a stronger sense of self-respect than serfs and slaves and European proletarians.'[6] This account would lead one to infer that the community does its best to limit the powers of government precisely because there is a general recognition that, in a country where large-scale government action is inevitable, governments should be prevented from becoming tyrannical. But the egalitarian theorem does not work out in practice, as Fitzpatrick himself recognised. The Australian people, he

[3] Alexis de Tocqueville, *Democracy in America*, World's Classics ed., pp. 137-38
[4] Donald Horne, *The Lucky Country*, Sydney, 1964, pp. 71-73
[5] loc. cit.
[6] Brian Fitzpatrick, *The Australian Commonwealth*, Melbourne, 1956, pp. 152-53

laments, have shown themselves 'singularly poor hands at furnishing from their number fit persons to rule'. These elected rulers, in their turn, have 'excelled rather at ineffectual repression than at imaginative measures to inspire the people.' Moreover, the gullible Australian electorate has sometimes seemed cowed, or dulled, to a greater extent than voters elsewhere. As a result, members of parliament have become a privileged class, though ostensibly there is no such stratum in Australia whose rights override those of people in general. Lack of standards, or abuse of privilege, are widespread. Political apostasy in times of crisis, though well known in other democracies, seems to have reached the stature of custom only in Australia, where it has been of obvious material benefit to its practitioners. 'It is unlikely', he concludes astringently, 'that any Prime Minister but an Australian Prime Minister, being asked again and again publicly, in parliament and otherwise, to answer accusations of falsehood and bad faith, should simply refrain from answering.'[7]

A low opinion of the capacity, political morality, and attainments of politicians has been characteristic of Australians for many years. George Higinbotham, a radical democrat who played a notable part in the early politics of Victoria and later became Chief Justice of the colony, expressed his own disappointment with democracy when he declared, in a farewell speech to his constituents in 1876, that if ministers were selected by lot the men chosen would be 'quite as well deserving of the confidence of the people of this country as any of those Ministers who have been competing for power for years past.'[8] A generation later a political correspondent, satirically praising politics as the one mirth-provoking attribute of an otherwise dull society, concluded that with good management and a modicum of luck 'almost anyone can rise to Ministerial rank in Australia, or for that matter obtain . . . the Premiership.'[9]

Similar feelings are expressed more pungently in the writings of the late scientist and publicist, Professor A. J. Marshall. Most Australian politicians, he wrote, aspire to parliamentary seats 'to better their salary, to inflate their egos and to feather their nests.' We have incompetent and ignorant cabinet ministers because 'push and talk' will do the trick. 'A tram-guard may become a National Park trustee, a giggling bush doctor may be placed in complete charge of the finances of the nation. A few years ago a museum of scientific specialists found themselves under the jurisdiction of an ex-coalminer.'[10] But the only explanation he can give for the failure of the public who suffer under these incompetents to choose

---

[7] ibid., chs. 7-8, passim
[8] E. E. Morris, *Memoir of George Higinbotham*, London, 1895, p. 198
[9] Alfred Buchanan, *The Real Australia*, London, 1907, pp. 79-80, 90
[10] A. J. Marshall, *Australia Limited*, Sydney, 1942, pp. 86-87. The doctor referred to is Sir Earle Page, leader of the Country Party in the federal parliament for many years, and Treasurer 1923-29. A government backbencher, Sir Henry Gullett, once attacked him as 'the most tragic Treasurer that Australia had ever known'.

better people is the familiar tautology that they are 'conditioned to second-rate political representation'.

Other people have attributed the poor quality of politicians to the absence of an educated class, or alternatively to the failure of the educated classes to take an interest in politics. As we noted in Chapter 6, Bryce criticised professional people for identifying themselves with the 'mercantile class', which had the unfortunate distinction of not realising 'how much thinking is needed if the problems before Australia are to be solved.'[11] Another British observer, J. D. Pringle, recorded a similar observation forty years later. Politicians were of poor quality because they represented the appallingly naked character of economic interest. To some extent, he concedes, the politics of interest dominate parties in all democracies, but in Australia this is particularly noticeable 'because of the lack of an educated class, which, even if it is only rationalising its baser appetites, discusses politics in terms of principles and ideas.' Pringle also gives us an eloquent picture of the kind of Labor politician whose pre-eminent role as a 'fixer' makes it unlikely that policies based on general ideas will play a larger part in the Labor movement.

. . . a tough, shrewd opportunist, a master of the more disreputable political arts, but utterly ignorant and contemptuous of wider horizons. The son of working-class parents, he . . . appreciates all the more the comforts and privileges—and sometimes the temptations—of power and office. . . . You see him at the races or drinking in a hotel bar surrounded by his cronies, red-faced, big-bellied, hard-eyed, the image of Tammany all the world over.[12]

The strength of public denigration of politicians is demonstrated periodically whenever an increase in the remuneration of members of parliament is in the offing. In 1951, the Federal government set up a committee of inquiry into parliamentary salaries under the chairmanship of Mr. Justice Nicholas of the NSW Supreme Court. In its report, the Nicholas committee described the flood of letters which it had received, opposing any increase in parliamentary salaries on the grounds that politicans were already overpaid and that in any case they were not worth the money.[13] The report of a similar committee in 1959 was the occasion of an avalanche of correspondence in the press, attacking the proposed increases. An analysis[14] of 711 letters published in seventeen newspapers found that over 60 per cent of the arguments by the 'antis' revolved around the poor qualities and misdemeanours of politicians, e.g.:

11 Bryce, *Modern Democracies*, vol. 2, pp. 268-71
12 J. D. Pringle, *Australian Accent*, pp. 47, 52
13 *Report on Salaries and Allowances of Members of the National Parliament*, 1952, p. 13
14 H. Mayer, P. Loveday, P. Westerway, 'Images of Politics', *Australian Journal of Political History*, vol. 6, no. 2, 1960

[There is] over-government by a bureaucratic political aristocracy
Parliament [is full] of professional politicians, time servers and place seekers
A bar-fly, a Domain magsman, or any yes-man can become a politician without any qualifications for the job
A Cabinet Minister's post [should require] an Honours pass in one foreign language, political science, economics, history, geography and good manners
We—spineless jellyfish—allow a privileged group to be born within our equality
Our politicians have demonstrated how elected leaders can abuse their privileges and display the most blatant contempt for public opinion
Party pre-selection methods, which mostly entail intensive manoeuvring, lobbying and general skullduggery, [make it] fairly obvious why men of education and quality do not always appear in Parliament

Other letter-writers spoke of a conspiracy among politicians of all parties against the people, the elevation of politicians into a race apart, the need for some kind of popular referendum or initiative to veto the pay 'grab', and in the last resort direct action was advocated, such as refusing to pay tax, a general strike, or even that 'the Diggers should take up arms.'

The analysis highlights the prevalence of 'managerial' thinking and its relation to latent contradictions in the populist conception of democracy. Both the [relatively few] supporters of the pay increases and the much more numerous opponents shared the assumption that governing Australia was an occupation similar to running a big business. Whereas the 'pros' were then led to deduce that appropriately high salaries should be paid, the 'antis' seemed to feel *both* that the managers were not doing their job properly *and* that the ultimate authority of the people had been filched from them. There were, however, very few references to 'leaders' or 'leadership', these terms being replaced by 'managers', 'executives' and 'directors'.

The authors of this study note that such letters cannot be taken as a sample of public opinion, since they come from people who feel much more intensely about politics than the relatively apathetic majority. On the other hand, a series of public opinion polls between 1947 and 1959 showed a fairly consistent average of over 60 per cent who were strongly opposed to salary increases for politicians. Their conclusion is that the publication of the 1959 report did not widen the ranks of the 'extreme antis', but intensified the feelings of this latent and permanent majority.

Davies, in a penetrating study of five contrasting types of political activists, detects a similar pejorative attitude even among those who are deeply involved in the political struggle. 'Mrs. Fenton', a sixty-three-year-old widow, a Liberal Party organiser for many years, is distinguished by her strong feeling that too many of the chaps who are in politics are bad chaps, and that this personal failure is more important than their policies. The credit squeeze imposed by the Menzies government in 1960-61, which had an adverse effect on many Liberal voters, was to be attributed to a moral collapse on Menzies' part. Politicians were unfitted for their task and should be properly trained. The Liberal Party 'fails to attract the cream of the professions, or even the utilitarian support of business talent, and is thus in constant danger of being clogged up with rejects from commerce and industry and lower-middle class *arrivistes*.' Her conversation is shot through with 'remorseless depreciation of professional politicians (those of her own party in particular).' Among other things they are called timid, overbearing, smug, inept, badly qualified, lazy and uncreative, drunkards, social climbers, 'terrible little men'.[15]

Mrs Fenton's views are, however, paralleled by 'Leonard East', an unsuccessful DLP candidate for parliament, who distrusts and dislikes all politicians, including his own leaders, and by 'Allan Isles', a Labor supporter, who treats all political and public leaders as 'somewhat weak and lacking in mana.' In Isles' estimation, notes Davies, 'few political figures rise to the average, and even the most praised (Chifley) gets his corrective slight.'[16]

Political Leadership

It is not surprising that, in such a climate of opinion, it is difficult to isolate a reasonably consistent and acceptable notion of leadership. One might think that Gilbert's Duke of Plaza Toro, who led from behind, would fit the bill, but it is soon evident that this is not what people want.

One way in which popular attitudes to political leaders may be gauged is from their reflection in works of fiction. The political novel is a recognised genre. As Butterfield has written, political and historical novels are valuable because they create personalities of flesh and blood where the social scientist sees only abstractions; they focus the important ideas and happenings of a period through the lens of an individual life-history.[17] The lens has proved singularly opaque in Australia. Such political novels as exist are few in number and unimpressive in quality. A number of them are loosely bound together by a common theme which may be described as that of the upright man too good for the dirty game of politics.[18] The central figures of these stories, after attaining office, are constrained to surrender it with their great aims unfulfilled. Either they are cut down by some cruel blow of fate, or alienated by a distaste for the sordidness of parliamentary intrigue, or a combination of both. In every case, their political aims remain vague. The most recent attempt was that of the late Vance Palmer, with his novels *Golconda*, *Seedtime*, and *The Big Fellow*. These form a trilogy based on the life of E. G. Theodore, who was first a union organiser in Queensland, then State Premier from 1919 to 1924, and Federal Treasurer from 1929 to 1931. Palmer's hero, though perhaps not as upright as he might be, otherwise follows the pattern already described. The actual content of his politics remains shadowy, and his

15 A. F. Davies, *Private Politics*, pp. 244-51
16 ibid., p. 45
17 Herbert Butterfield, *The Historical Novel: An Essay*, London, 1924
18 S. Encel, 'Political Novels in Australia', *Historical Studies*, no. 27, 1956

public career is disturbed less by political than by private incidents. An earlier example is the novel written by the wife of W. A. Holman, whose central character, one 'Ivo Kimber', is portrayed as a fine character forced to act unworthily by the exigencies of the political game. We are told that he is genuinely radical, but his beliefs are vague in the extreme. He 'stood out mentally and physically from the commonplace identities with whom he was grouped', but he is none the less cynical (or 'realistic') about politics. 'The most valuable lesson a politician can learn is that the people can always be taken in by the right kind of bluff.' His cynicism is justified by the political oblivion that descends on him as soon as his (wholly innocent) involvement in a murder trial occurs. 'Any dereliction on the part of public men is seized upon with joy by the multitude. . . . His enemies gloated with their "I told you so's" . . . his supporters were kept busy explaining how the exigencies of party foisted the wrong-doer upon them.'   There is a similar lack of contact with political reality in another novel of the same period by Frank Fox, for years a journalist on the *Bulletin* and the *Lone Hand*, whose hero, 'Henry Trent', is a thinly camouflaged version of Alfred Deakin. Trent is a great statesman, a colossus among pigmies, but the only hint we are given about his politics is that he is a leading supporter of White Australia. His views about democracy reciprocate the democratic suspicion of leadership: 'Democracy does not love distinction. It suspects courage and the power to stand alone. It has the instincts of the flock and would have us all huddle. A lonely man, now, may be a wolf in disguise with ravening designs on the flock. Dangerous certainly. Let us have for leaders, democracy prays, comfortable bellwethers who will lead us orderly to the pasturage—and to the shearing.'

The tale of the upright man forced out of politics by his own disillusion or by a catastrophic event has only the most tenuous foundation in fact. The difficulties of our authors stem rather from the absence of a suitable conception of political leadership to serve as a frame of reference. In a community that refuses to accept politicians as 'leaders', the absence of such a framework is self-evident. Canada, with its traditional emphasis on the role of the political chieftain, provides an instructive contrast. The genius of Australian politics finds its typical expression in recurrent attempts, throughout the history of party politics since the 1890's, to enforce the accountability of party leaders to their party, both inside and outside parliament. Labor spokesmen, in particular, have repeatedly asserted that the party in parliament is, or should be, no more than a 'reflex' of the industrial movement. The Labor movement, said a famous editorial in the Sydney *Worker* in 1914, had no use for leaders, and was 'infinitely in advance of the days when the workers had to be "led".'[19] A Queensland party official declared in 1907 that Labor MP's could not be trusted. 'Once you allow the politician to boss the show, he will give away everything to save himself, because he believes himself indispensable to

---

[19] Quoted by H. V. Evatt, *Australian Labour Leader*, Sydney, 1940, p. 340

the show, and in fact ends by becoming the show himself, and making a holy show of the rest of us.'[20] But a similar philosophy is embodied in the rules of the Country Party, and although the Liberal Party is less explicit, its history is also studded with attempts, successful and unsuccessful, to achieve the same general object.[21] Sir Robert Menzies, despite his record term as Prime Minister, had occasion during his career to experience the intensity of this distrust, and once remarked plaintively that he could not understand why Australians should so dislike their politicians. The ALP can claim the virtue of originality, but the other parties have paid it the compliment of emulation.

The absence of any significant body of biographical literature is more interesting and more important for our argument than the poverty of fictional accounts. Although biographies and autobiographies of a sort have appeared regularly since the 1890's, the first to claim any serious attention is Walter Murdoch's *Alfred Deakin* (London, 1923). This has the merits of a graceful style and of considerable insight into Deakin's remarkable personality. Yet it fails in one of the principal tasks of political biography—to add to our understanding of politics by telling us something of the relation between men and events. As a dominant figure in the federal movement and in the first ten years of federation, Deakin had to make a number of political choices which were of lasting significance, but Murdoch's book tells us little about them, and gives only a sketchy account of Deakin as a Prime Minister. Here again the absence of a suitable frame of reference makes itself felt.

A different case is that of Dr H. V. Evatt's massive biography of W. A. Holman (1940). This book is marred by a rambling, loose-jointed mode of presentation and a surfeit of detail, but its more important defect is the ambiguity of its attitude to Holman, reflecting in its turn the basic ambiguity of the relations between Holman and his party. The author patently admired Holman, who was indeed a man of outstanding attainments and great personal charm (including a quixotic attachment to his friends). It is clear also that Holman's opponents within the party organisation and the Australian Workers' Union were actuated by motives other than devotion to the ideals of the Labor movement.[22] Evatt oscillates between several explanations of Holman's rupture with his party which are not all compatible. He maintains, severally, that Holman made errors of political judgment; that he became dictatorial; that he was undermined by

[20] Presidential address by Matthew Reid at the 1907 Labor convention in Brisbane; quoted, Childe, *How Labour Governs*, p. 25
[21] For a full discussion see S. Encel, *Cabinet Government in Australia*, part 4, Melbourne, 1962; James Jupp, *Australian Party Politics*, chs. 3, 6-7; Katharine West, *Power in the Liberal Party*, passim; U. R. Ellis, *The Country Party*, Sydney, 1958, passim
[22] H. V. Evatt, op. cit., esp. pp. 339-82; V. G. Childe, *How Labour Governs*, ch. 2; D. W. Rawson, 'The Organisation of the Australian Labor Party 1916-41', Ph.D. thesis, University of Melbourne, 1954, ch. 1; S. Encel, op. cit., pp. 133-55

his opponents; that he was unlucky to be caught in the struggle over conscription during the 1914-18 war; that he allowed loyalty to friends to influence him in opposition to the party. On the one hand, he argues that Holman was a genuine socialist, unlike most of his Labor contemporaries, and regarded the political machine as 'a means for achieving socialist ends'. As time went on, he came 'to regard the means as a separate and independent end in itself.' He came to regard the Labor member as 'almost entitled to immunity from strong criticism at the hands of the rank and file. . . . During the period when the control of Labor's Party machine tightened, Holman raised little objection so long as he was the director of the machine . . . if a contradiction arose, he concluded too easily that the organisation was wrong.'[23]

These ambiguities may be avoided by attributing Holman's failings to the inevitable degeneration that besets Labor in office, as Michels might have done, or by adopting the more cynical view that politics is a continuing struggle for power between contending groups. Childe's writings are representative of the first viewpoint; Miller expresses the second when he writes that 'dictatorial authority in the Labor Party has always been exercised in the name of the Movement . . . a series of Trade Union and Party cliques has at various stages of Australian political history used these arguments to destroy its rivals and in turn to be destroyed by them.'[24] The first of these interpretations rests on the assumption of a golden age whose virtue has since departed, and implies also that there is a radical alternative to the 'sickness of Laborism'.[25] Both assumptions are patently improbable. The second interpretation leaves little room for the ideologue who would rather split the party than yield his position, nor for a successful reformer like the last Labor Prime Minister, J. B. Chifley.

L. F. Crisp's life of Chifley is undoubtedly the most important political biography to date, and constitutes a major contribution to the literature of politics as a whole. Chifley's career was the great success story of the Labor movement, in which he has become an archetypal figure. With great care, his biographer analyses the reasons for Chifley's remarkable ascendency within the Labor movement—an ascendency which a parliamentary press correspondent once called the 'Chifley hypnosis'. The reason for his remarkable success—apart from his good fortune in being Prime Minister at the right moment in history—was due to his ability to reconcile the principle of rank-and-file sovereignty with the requirements of strong government. In Crisp's words:

These two principles can in practice be reconciled only by a man whose detached, penetrating reflection about a long experience of politics has afforded him a quite clear-sighted grasp of how the machinery of modern

[23] op. cit., pp. 568-73
[24] J. D. B. Miller, 'Party Discipline in Australia', *Political Science*, vol. 5, 1953, nos. 1-2
[25] Ralph Miliband, *Parliamentary Socialism*, London, 1962

democratic politics actually works. Chifley thoroughly appreciated that the Government must be determined to govern—and disconcertingly, sometimes bluntly, said so. But the Labor Party myth had become part of his very being and he instinctively knew when and how far substantial concessions—and how far merely ritual obeisances—must be made to the general membership.[26]

This broad conclusion is filled in with many detailed strokes. Chifley was a 'master of party managers' (p. 145). In parliament, he operated a 'smooth procedure with such a seemingly off-hand air that most of his colleagues had little idea how firmly they were being organised as a team' (p. 216). He had a 'capacity for letting beaten antagonists down without loss of dignity' (p. 233). His ingenuity in handling troublesome caucus meetings left members 'somewhat fretful yet amazed at the manner and completeness of Chifley's achievement' (p. 235). His dominance over Cabinet was illustrated by the 'outstanding, unhesitating unanimity' (p. 328) with which its members backed him over the crucial matter of bank nationalisation in 1947.

Crisp's account may be criticised on two grounds. It exaggerates the extent to which Chifley's predominance was due to his success in applying *Labor* dogma about party leadership. Gladstone, whose personal views were different and who operated in a very different party context, is credited with similar qualities by J. A. Spender, who attributes the Grand Old Man's commanding stature in politics to his great loyalty to his colleagues, his moral posture, and his care for collective responsibility. Spender notes that 'he drew a sharp line between permissible opinions which he or others might hold as private individuals, and opinions which he could pronounce *ex cathedra* AS LEADER OF THE PARTY. His remarkable success in keeping extremists and moderates within the one fold of the Liberal Party was due largely to this theory of party leadership.'[27] Crisp, speaking of Chifley's troubles with members of his own Cabinet, notably E. J. Ward, who publicly opposed government policy, writes:

Chifley never directly or by name publicly rebuked Ward for pressing openly views and attitudes contrary to his or to Government policy. . . . Chifley stated: 'Ministers speak not on behalf of the Government but to express their personal views. The views of the Government are expressed by its Leader.' This interesting gloss on the constitutional convention of collective responsibility carried also as a corollary Chifley's scrupulously observed practice of explaining when he himself was speaking personally rather than *ex cathedra*.[28]

Another British writer, Ernest Barker, argues that emphasis on solidarity and teamwork is a characteristic of *British* politics. 'The fact of the group, and of group opinion and action, is the essential unit of British statesman-

[26] *Ben Chifley*, Melbourne, 1961, p. 237
[27] J. A. Spender, *The Public Life*, London, 1928, vol. 1, p. 72
[28] op. cit., pp. 238-39

ship . . . [which] is in the direction not of the solitary duellist, but of the team; and the general tradition has been the tradition of collegiate loyalty.'[29]

It could plausibly be argued, then, that Chifley's achievement was that of imposing the theory and practice of Cabinet government on a party whose history, despite loud and frequent emphasis on solidarity and group loyalty, has been marked by apparently endless splits, faction fights, and personal vendettas. And this brings us to the second and major deficiency in Crisp's account. It was not Chifley's personal qualities alone that made him pre-eminent, but the strength of the Prime Minister's position in the modern state—in particular, his control of the administrative apparatus. The period since 1939 has seen a great expansion of the importance of the federal government in national politics, whose concrete embodiment is the spectacular growth of the Commonwealth administrative machine. 'The rapidly mounting ascendency of the Commonwealth over the States, together with the many steps which Chifley and his colleagues took to advance the welfare state in Australia, required a permanent revolution at once in the size, the calibre, the philosophy and the significance of the [Commonwealth Public] Service.'[30] The policies adopted by Chifley's government often bore little relation to party policy. In some cases, there was no party policy; in others, government policy ran counter to strongly held party tradition. First as Treasurer, and later as both Treasurer and Prime Minister, Chifley learnt to mobilise the resources of a bureaucratic machine of unprecedented power. The most important 'team' that he led was the remarkable 'official family' of advisers[31] which was the real power-house of ideas and policy during the Labor administrations of 1941-49. As chief executive, Chifley made policy in consultation with his advisers; as party manager, he secured acceptance of this policy. In other words, he was an example of the exceptional political leader who is able to seize the future while it is molten[32] and pour it into a new mould. As Franklin Roosevelt's biographer, James Burns, has written, the political leader must normally play the role which is made for him by the situation, but an outstanding leader can disrupt the existing system and set up a new one in which there are different roles. He may bring about lasting change by 'altering the channels in which the stream of events takes place.'[33]

The great enlargement in the scope of the bureaucratic ascendency, which is Chifley's long-term contribution to Australian politics, provides the essential link between him and his record-breaking successor, Sir Robert Menzies. Just as Chifley's actions had little direct relation to Labor

---

[29] Ernest Barker, *Essays on Government*, London, 1940, pp. 32, 46
[30] Crisp, op. cit., p. 254
[31] ibid., pp. 255-59; Canberra Research Group, 'Commonwealth Policy Co-ordination', *Public Administration*, Aust., vol. 14, no. 4, 1955
[32] Lloyd George is said to have used this phrase in a conversation with the leaders of the British Labour Party in 1917.
[33] J. McGregor Burns, epilogue to *Roosevelt: The Lion and the Fox*, New York, 1956

policy, neither can the policies followed under Menzies be attributed to his own political outlook or to his party, whose record until 1949 was one of opposition, sometimes virulent, to virtually every major act of policy undertaken by the two Labor governments. On the other hand, these same policies provided the basis for nearly every constructive act of the Liberal-Country Party governments after 1949. Donald Horne's vitriolic sketch, perhaps the best thing in his book, observes that none of the characteristics of the 'age of Menzies' are the kind of thing that Menzies could be said to have stood for, and that some of them are indeed the opposite of what he said he hoped for when he was in opposition.

His great talent is to preside over events and look as if he knows what they are all about. His few active interventions have been mainly failures . . . with policy-making slowing down and sometimes stopping the permanent heads of the government departments getting on with the job of administering their departments in a way that will not cause trouble. It is one of the ironies of political life that in the 1940's some of these men were the instruments of Labor's new deal; but they became attached to Menzies and increasingly he regards them, rather than his Ministers, as his agents in running the nation.[34]

Similar things were said about Sir Robert Menzies a few years earlier by Pringle, who summed him up as a 'supremely skilful politician—ruthless, adroit, cunning—whose special device is to pose always as a statesman.'[35] Although both of these commentators note Menzies' love of power for its own sake, they are concerned with it only as a personal trait. In the present context, it is an important piece of evidence which belies the conventional wisdom about the place of politicians in the Australian community and testifies to the hollowness of the egalitarian myth. For it is precisely this arrogant, ruthless, power-loving individual who dominated the politics of his country so completely and so long as to give his term the nickname of 'the Ming dynasty'. It was remarked that Sir Alec Douglas-Home, during his brief and uncomfortable period as British Prime Minister, used to envy Sir Robert—a fellow-member of the Order of the Thistle—his complete ascendency over his party and his parliament. As well he might, for in aristocratic Britain it would be hard to imagine a personal autocracy such as can be achieved in egalitarian Australia.

Sir Robert Menzies' case is not, moreover, unique. Similar things have been said about a record-breaking state Premier, Sir Thomas Playford, who ran the government of South Australia as a one-man band for the astonishing period of twenty-seven years, 1938 to 1965. As one observer notes, his primary preoccupation was always to keep himself in power, and his attitude to the South Australian upper class resembled Bismarck's to the Junkers. Like Menzies, his ascendency depended heavily on a close alliance with senior government officials, another respect in which he

[34] op. cit., pp. 153-54
[35] op. cit., p. 65

contradicted the popular stereotype of the Liberal politician. The collective voice of his party became no more than an amplification of his own, and he was 'so often right that his followers seldom had the confidence to insist that on rare occasions he had been wrong.'[36] In the neighbouring state of Victoria, the late Sir Albert Dunstan performed the feat of remaining Premier for ten years, seven of them as head of a minority Country Party government. In this period, he gained the reputation of having double-crossed all his political allies at some point in his career; but in spite of this, and in spite of his obvious determination to retain power at all costs, his grip on Victorian politics was almost unchallenged from 1935 to 1945.[37] A few years earlier, the Labor Premier of NSW, J. T. Lang, gave a remarkable demonstration of the way in which Labor's traditions of 'solidarity' could be manipulated to give him almost absolute power within the party. In Hancock's words, the Labor movement's strenuous attempts to control the party leadership aggravate the very evil they are designed to cure, and Lang exploited this situation to win 'a power which no other Australian Premier has ever possessed. His own followers, his own ministers, became his slaves. Parliament became a machine for ratifying his decrees.'[38] Hancock compared Lang to Mussolini. One of Lang's henchmen, J. S. Garden, outdid him with the slogan 'Lang is greater than Lenin', and a minister in his cabinet, Mark Gosling, declared that the Lang ministry had no policy but its leader's. 'As soon as he announces it, we know where we stand. We do not seek to know what he is going to do, and are prepared to surrender our judgment, if necessary, in advance.'[39]

Our conclusion, then, is one that would have appealed to de Tocqueville. Egalitarian suspicion and denigration of politicians does not preclude the emergence of autocratic, dominating leaders, nor does it provide an effective defence against their abuse of their position. It has a depressing effect on the kind of individual independence of mind which is the essential requirement for effective criticism. The traditions of solidarity which it encourages are readily manipulated to suppress the contumacious individual, although they may assist the organised group. Its greatest positive virtue is that it places fairly narrow limits on the sphere within which the powerful individual can operate; on the other hand, it puts a premium on the advancement of mediocrities and nonentities who can exploit group loyalties to gain for them what their positive qualities could never achieve. If the Australian community is burdened with a second- or third-rate political elite, then the burden is self-imposed.

36 Katharine West, 'Playford and the Liberal and Country League of South Australia', *Australian Journal of Politics and History*, vol. 9, no. 2, 1963
37 J. B. Paul, 'The Premiership of Sir Albert Dunstan', M.A. thesis, University of Melbourne, 1961
38 W. K. Hancock, *Politics in Pitcairn*, London, 1947, p. 75
39 The full story of Lang has yet to be written. For a discussion of some aspects see Crisp, op. cit., ch. 6; S. Encel, op. cit., pp. 132-36, 140, 156-61; D. W. Rawson, 'The Organisation of the Australian Labor Party 1916-41' loc. cit.

12: The Political Class (2):
The Called and the Chosen

'What *is* a Caucus-race?' said Alice.
'Why', said the Dodo, 'the best way to explain it is to do it.' When they
had been running half an hour or so, the Dodo suddenly called out 'The
race is over! . . . *Everybody* has won, and all must have prizes.' . . . The
whole party at once crowded round Alice, calling out in a confused way,
'Prizes! Prizes!'

The Aspirants

The first stage of the political selection process—the endorsement of
parliamentary candidates—is inherently difficult to investigate, and varies
considerably from one state to another. Despite the steady centralisation of
Australian politics during the past generation, each major party remains
little more than a loose confederation of state political machines, all of
which are free to fix their own rules about the selection of candidates both
for state and federal parliaments. Differences in the political situation may
lead to considerable variations in the selection procedure. In South
Australia, for instance, the Country Party has no separate organisation, but
has been merged since 1930 in the Liberal-Country League. The agreement by which this body was set up includes understandings about the
selection of parliamentary candidates, and enables Federal members to
identify themselves either with the Liberal Party or the Country Party in
the Commonwealth parliament. In NSW, on the other hand, the Country
Party permits multiple endorsements for large rural electorates. Through
the exchange of preferences, this often has the effect of magnifying the
total Country Party vote.[1]

In the Liberal Party, the most interesting development in recent years
has been in NSW. In the 1930's and early forties, the United Australia
Party (forerunner of the present Liberal Party) was frequently accused of
being dominated by financial interests which constituted a 'background
organisation' with undue influence on policy and on the selection of party
leaders. Following upon the formation of the Liberal Party in 1944, the
NSW branch adopted a number of organisational methods which were

[1] See, e.g., Henry Mayer and Joan Rydon, *The Gwydir By-Election 1953*, Melbourne,
1954

aimed to free it from such domination. Notable among these is a system of pre-selection of parliamentary candidates which is unique in Australia. Aspiring candidates are required to submit a *curriculum vitae* on a pre-scribed form, which is circulated to the members of selection committees specially appointed for the occasion. In the case of selections for the House of Representatives, these committees comprise thirty members chosen by the appropriate Federal Electorate Conference, together with twenty members of the state executive and/or state council of the party, who are chosen by the state executive. For the Senate, a single selection committee is set up, comprising all members of the state executive plus one represen-tative of each Federal Electorate Council in the state; the committee must have at least thirty members. Candidates make personal appearances before these bodies, and are sometimes 'grilled' by them for considerable periods.

By inspecting the forms completed by these candidates, it is possible to gain some idea of the social characteristics of this group of aspirants to political office, who may be regarded as a fairly typical sample of Liberal Party activists.[2] Altogether, information was obtained concerning eighty-nine separate individuals (including seventeen sitting members) who were involved in pre-selection ballots for the Federal elections of 1955 and 1958. As regards age, fifty-seven were aged between forty-one and sixty; twenty-eight were forty or less; and four were over sixty. More than one-quarter had received some form of tertiary education, twenty-one being university graduates, and eight having attended other tertiary institutions. Nine had received no more than a primary education. Twenty-two had attended private secondary schools affiliated with the Headmasters' Conference.

An analysis of the candidates' occupations gave the following results:[3]

Table 12·1 Aspirants for Liberal Pre-Selection in NSW, 1955-58

Farmer or grazier	8	
Professional or semi-professional	26	(10 lawyers)
Company director or manager	19	
Small business	21	
Clerical	9	
Other	6	

These candidates for pre-selection had a record of considerable political activity. In addition to the seventeen sitting members, twenty-two had previously been candidates for parliament, and six others had unsuccess-fully contested earlier pre-selection ballots. Of the entire group forty-nine

2 I am indebted to Mr J. L. Carrick, secretary of the NSW division of the Liberal Party, for access to these records.
3 Candidates' descriptions of their own occupations are not wholly reliable, but some allowance has been made for this by checking against the other information available.

had held posts of some consequence in the party organisation. Twenty-two had held positions on local government bodies, and a further five had unsuccessfully contested municipal elections. Unfortunately, most of them gave little or no information about their reasons for entering politics, which they were invited to do at the end of the form. One, however, struck the authentic High Tory note of public service: 'I decided while still of school age that representing my fellow men in Parliament and serving my country in Parliament would be the most noble and satisfying career to which I could aspire.' Another wrote that he had become a Liberal because of his experiences in Britain, where he saw a 'great nation which had defied the German bombs brought to its knees by the subtle poison of Socialism.' Similarly, an ex-ALP man wrote that he could no longer subscribe to the 'communistic and socialistic policy that the Labor Party now stands for.' Five of the candidates came from political families. Only three were women, one of whom was the niece of a former MLA and cousin of a one-time Speaker of the Legislative Assembly.

Professional men were represented even more strongly on the state executive of the NSW Liberal Party.[4] Of a group of thirty-six office-bearers during the period 1945-60, thirteen were professional men, including eleven lawyers. Another thirteen were businessmen, though only one of them, a director of a large retail firm, could be described as an important figure in the business world. Seventeen of them had attended private schools of the Headmasters' Conference type. Only three were Roman Catholics, and only four were women, although a much larger proportion of the state council are women. In theory, the party does not discriminate against Catholics or women, and its leader has publicly appealed for Catholic support.[5]

The largest study of aspiring Liberal politicians in NSW has been made by West, who analysed the occupations of all candidates who contested pre-selection ballots for general and by-elections for the Legislative Assembly from 1950 to 1959.[6] Table 12·2 is based on her figures. If we collapse these categories under the occupational headings used by the Commonwealth Statistician, we find that the two largest groups are professional and semi-professional (31 per cent) and commercial and clerical (30 per cent).

Although no similarly detailed analysis of the ALP is available, several studies have been made which illustrate, in detail, the predominance of trade union officials at various levels of party organisation. The Labor Party arose as a means of putting working men in parliament, and its traditional solidarity was built on the principle of class loyalty. Working

---

[4] These results are based on a questionnaire survey of members of the state executive and other important committees of the NSW division of the Liberal Party who held office between 1945 and 1960. Names were kindly made available by Mr J. L. Carrick. Out of fifty individuals to whom questionnaires were sent, thirty-six replied.
[5] R. W. Askin, in *Sydney Morning Herald*, 4 August 1959
[6] Katharine West, *Power in the Liberal Party*, ch. 2

class origin and a trade union background were, and still largely remain, concrete evidence of the class allegiance which was supposed to guarantee adherence to Labor policy in parliament.[7] Throughout the history of the Labor movement, union leaders have expressed the view that the ALP was simply a 'reflex' of the industrial movement. The composition of party conferences testifies to the strength of the union influence. From 1921 to 1951, the attendance of union officials at Federal party conferences fluctuated between two-thirds and three-quarters.[8] The thirty-six delegates to the federal conference of 1963 included twenty union officials, nine parliamentarians, and five party officials.[9] A similar situation applies at the state level. In 1960, two-thirds of the delegates to the NSW state conference were from unions, which also provided 80 per cent of affiliation fees. In 1961, seven-eighths of delegates to the state conference were from unions, which contributed more than 90 per cent of affiliation fees. In Queensland, more than half of affiliation fees come from the Australian Workers' Union alone. The Queensland Central Executive, which has sometimes shown itself stronger than a Labor government, includes direct nominees of the unions, and for most of this century it has been dominated by the AWU.

Table 12·2 Aspirants for Liberal Pre-Selection in NSW, 1950-59

Occupation		*Total*	*Successful*	*Unsuccessful*
1	Small businessmen	127	50	77
2	Rural proprietors	63	25	38
3	Company directors n.e.i.	38	4	34
4	Accountants	50	11	39
5	Estate agents and auctioneers	27	13	14
6	Clerks, salesmen, and 'executives'	151	37	114
7	Lawyers and industrial advocates	56	6	50
8	Doctors, dentists, etc.	21	5	16
9	Engineers	37	2	35
10	Teachers	34	4	30
11	Journalists	19	2	17
12	Manual workers	41	9	32
13	'Politicians'	8	7	1
14	Housewives	8	3	5
15	Retired or unemployed	13	4	9
16	Miscellaneous	20	9	11
Total		713	191	522

On the other hand, these relationships have their ups and downs. During the postwar decade, control of the Labor movement in Victoria passed into the hands of the ALP 'industrial groups', whose strength was derived from

[7] Childe (op. cit., pp. 59-60) notes both the large number of manual workers in the NSW Labor governments of 1910-16, and the comparative irrelevance of the fact to government policy.
[8] L. F. Crisp, *The Australian Federal Labour Party*, London, 1956, Appendix H, pp. 327-29; L. F. Crisp and S. P. Bennett, ALP *Federal Personnel 1901-54* (typescript)
[9] James Jupp, *Australian Party Politics*, pp. 203-4

the 'Catholic Social Movement' organised and led by Mr B. A. Santamaria. As a result, the state executive of the ALP came to include a high proportion of parliamentarians, most of them linked with the 'movement'. The split in the party in 1955 re-established the predominance of the unions, especially those belonging to the Trade Union Defence Committee which had led the moves to unseat the 'groupers'. Between 1954 and 1962, the proportion of union officials on the executive rose from 28 per cent to 60 per cent, and that of parliamentarians dropped from 32 per cent to 8 per cent. In 1965, after a considerable upheaval at the state conference, the executive included fourteen union officials, three party officials, two parliamentarians, and eleven others belonging to a variety of occupational groups.[10]

The only study of social differences at the party branch level was made by Rawson and Holtzinger in the rural electorate of Eden-Monaro. They found that more than half of ALP branch members were wage-earners, compared with about 7 per cent of Liberal branch members. One-quarter of Liberal branch officials were graziers.[11]

The Parliamentarians

At the parliamentary level, the class differences which appear to exist between party activists are less sharp. Parliaments and cabinets are much more middle class in social composition. This was true also in the nineteenth century, as Martin has shown in a study of the NSW colonial legislature before Federation.[12] Until the 1890's, men of independent means almost monopolised parliamentary representation. Payment of members, introduced in 1889, helped to change this; so did the advent of the Labor Party, which first contested an election in 1891. Middle class members from Sydney and from the country towns were responsible for checking and later defeating the influence of the pastoralists. The decline in the political power of the latter is shown by the trend of their representation. In the Legislative Assembly of fifty-four elected in 1856, there were twenty-three pastoralists; in the seventy-two-man Assembly of 1877, the number had dropped to fourteen. By the end of the century, only 10 per cent of members were pastoralists. Martin goes on to argue that the composition of the Assembly, and the nature of the decisions made during the period, suggest a far greater role for the middle classes in society and politics than the 'Whig' version of Australian history has been willing to allow them. *Mutatis mutandis*, Martin's analysis may be taken as typical of nineteenth century parliaments.

If we convert Martin's figures into categories approximating to those of

---

10 ibid., pp. 65-6; *Nation*, 10 July 1965
11 D. W. Rawson and Susan Holtzinger, *Politics in Eden-Monaro*, Melbourne, 1954, p. 49
12 A. W. Martin, 'The Legislative Assembly of NSW 1856-1900', *Australian Journal of Politics and History*, vol. 2, no. 1, 1956

the occupational census of 1947, we arrive at the following breakdown of numbers who sat in the Assembly in the 1890's (embracing four parliaments).

Table 12·3 Occupations of NSW Parliamentarians, 1891-98

	%
Rural Proprietors	12
Professional and Semi-professional	32
Administrative and business	12
Commercial and clerical	20
Skilled/unskilled workers	13
Other	11
	100

NB The relatively high proportion of 'other' contains men of private means and those whose occupations were unidentified.

A more recent analysis of state parliamentarians shows considerable similarity. Davies[13] examined the occupational background of members elected to the Legislative Assembly of Victoria in 1952 and 1955. Despite the fact that the first of these had a Labor, and the second a Liberal majority, there was little difference in social composition between them, so far as occupation is an index. A composite analysis gives the results shown.

Table 12·4 Occupations of Victorian Parliamentarians, 1952-58

	%
Rural Proprietors	28
Professional and semi-professional	23
Administrative, commercial, clerical	37
Skilled/unskilled workers	11
Unstated	1
	100

The only notable difference between the two tables is the increase in the proportion of rural proprietors, which is chiefly due to the emergence of the Country Party as a separate political force in the second decade of this century. Its gains have been made largely at the expense of the professional men who figured more prominently before Federation. White-collar workers are another group whose representation in all parties has advanced as their numbers in the community have risen.

It should be noticed also that the state upper houses have a somewhat different composition, partly because all but one (Victoria) have a restricted franchise, and partly because the low level of activity in the chamber attracts people who are not 'professional politicians', but who

13 A. F. Davies, 'Victoria' in S. R. Davis (ed.), *The Government of the Australian States*, Melbourne, 1960, pp. 226-27

use the Legislative Council as a means of political representation for the special interests with which they are connected. Only in state upper houses do we find directors of really large and important companies. In recent years, Liberal members of the NSW Legislative Council[14] have included Sir Edward Warren, chairman of Coal and Allied Industries Ltd; Sir Thomas Playfair, chairman of a large meat processing firm and a director of the Australian Mutual Provident Co. and the Perpetual Trustee Co.; Sir Norman Kater, a director of the Colonial Sugar Refining Co; and Sir Harold Clayton, chairman of Australian Guarantee Corporation. In Victoria, Sir Arthur Warner, chairman of Electronic Industries Ltd, entered the Council in 1947 and was a minister in two Liberal governments. In South Australia, Sir Walter Duncan, a director of the BHP Co. and many other firms, was a member of the Council from 1918 to 1962; and Sir Arthur Rymill, chairman of the Bank of Adelaide, from 1956 to 1963. An analysis of the twenty-seven non-Labor members of the NSW upper house in 1959 showed that twenty were businessmen; of the fifteen Country Party members, four were graziers and the remainder 'Pitt Street farmers'. A somewhat similar pattern was to be found in the ALP, whose thirty-three councillors included sixteen union officials and four party officials.[15]

In the Commonwealth Parliament, the social differences between parties have been strongly marked ever since Federation, although a number of changes have taken place over the period. One of these is the decline in the proportion of manual workers in the ALP. At the NSW election of 1891, when seventeen Labor men were elected to the colonial parliament, three-quarters of them were manual workers. In the federal parliamentary party over the whole period from 1901 to 1951, 41 per cent of all members were manual workers. Between 1919 and 1934, the proportion in each parliament fluctuated around the 50 per cent mark; at the general election of 1934, it dropped below this level and has declined gradually ever since. In the parliament of 1958-61, it was only 12 per cent. The proportion of trade union officials, on the other hand, has not shown any long-term secular decline. In the whole period since Federation, it has rarely fallen below one-half of the parliamentary party, divided almost equally between salaried and honorary officers. This appears to confirm the widely-held view that union officials have a lien on safe seats, especially as most of those entering parliament tend to stay there for a long time. The prolonged terms of office common in this century had the effect of diluting the manual worker and trade union element in Labor governments. Labor was continuously in office in New South Wales from 1941 to 1965. In the original ministry of fifteen, five were prominent union officials, and five others had some union background. Up to 1965, an additional nineteen ministers had

14 Notionally, there are no Liberal MLC's in NSW, since the Liberal Party officially regards the upper house as a non-party chamber, and the ALP returns the compliment by not admitting MLC's to its parliamentary caucus. In practice, party allegiances are well-known.
15 Katharine West, op. cit.

held office, only one of whom had been a union official of any importance. In the federal parliament, the proportion of union officials drawn from clerical and 'white-collar' groups has risen, in parallel with a general increase in white-collar representation. Up to the 1940 general election, less than 10 per cent of the parliamentary party were white-collar workers. One vocational group whose representation has increased strikingly is that of teachers,[16] who constituted 15 per cent of the parliamentary Labor Party in the 1958-61 parliament. In 1949-51, the *total* number of teachers in the federal parliament was six; since then, it has risen continuously. In 1958-61, it reached fifteen.

We can make these comparisons sharper by examining the differences between two parliaments, separated by half a century. In the federal parliament of 1910-13, there were sixty-eight Labor members (out of a total of 111); in the parliament of 1958-61 there were seventy-five (out of a total of 183 in the enlarged parliament).[17]

Table 12·5 Occupations of Federal Labor Members

	1910–13	1958–61
Farmers	6	4
Shopkeepers	6	5
White-collar employees	1	17
Manual workers	24	9
Union officials (i.e. full-time)	16	20
Lawyers	4	3
Teachers	3	10
Journalists	7	5
Other	1	2
	68	75

A similar comparison between the occupations of non-Labor parliamentarians at various periods shows a more stable pattern. Three parliaments have been chosen in this case, to show the effect of the emergence of the Country Party as a major force at the general election of 1922. This has meant a permanent enlargement in rural representation. Otherwise, the three groups showing a significant increase are businessmen, shopkeepers and white-collar workers. Because of the relatively small number of

16 This includes 'teachers' from all levels of education. In the 1958-61 parliament, there were three former academics, who are included in these figures.
17 For the sake of simplicity, this analysis was based on the members elected at the general elections of 1910 and 1958, and excludes those who entered as the result of by-elections. Where changes of occupation took place, reference is made only to the occupation followed immediately before the dates of the parliament in question. This means, for example, that the proportion of men classified as 'manual workers' is understated, as the majority of those classified as 'trade union officials' had been manual workers. The same applies, to a lesser extent, to those classified as 'white-collar employees'. The two DLP senators have been treated as 'Labor' men for the purpose of this analysis.

Country Party members, and the close relationships between the two non-Labor parties, they are treated together in this analysis.

Table 12·6 Occupations of Federal Non-Labor Members

	1910–13	*1922–25*	*1958–61*
Pastoralists	6	5	22
Other Rural Proprietors	1	13	18
Business and Administrative	7	11	24
Commercial and Clerical	2	7	15
Manual workers	2	5	—
Union officials	—	2	—
Lawyers	14	13	18
Teachers	—	1	5
Journalists	2	1	2
Housewives	—	—	3
Other	6	11	3
	40	69	110

One minor and one major feature of the above table may be briefly mentioned. The manual workers and union officials who were in the Nationalist Party in 1922 are the residue of the Labor men who crossed the floor over the conscription issue in 1916. More significant is the sharp rise in the number of pastoralists, who constituted 12 per cent of all parliamentarians in 1958, compared with less than 5 per cent in 1922. This is partly due to the enlargement of the federal parliament in 1949, and particularly of the Senate, where ten out of the twenty-two pastoralists sat in 1958; but a deeper reason may be the unparalleled prosperity of the wool industry since the Second World War and its growing involvement in politics.

One occupational group deserving of a brief mention is the medical profession, which has been represented among all parties. Since 1923 at least thirty state and federal parliamentarians have been medical practitioners, and ten have held various portfolios. One of them (Sir Earle Page) was Prime Minister for a short time in 1939, and another (Sir Stanley Argyle) was Premier of Victoria from 1932 to 1935.

Women are another group worthy of note for their comparative rarity. As MacKenzie has computed in his study of *Women in Australia*, there were twelve women members of parliament in 1960, out of a total of 701 seats in all parliaments. Up to the end of 1965, thirty-two women had been elected to state or federal parliaments. The first woman ever elected was Mrs Edith Cowan in Western Australia in 1921. Only three women have held ministerial posts—Dame Florence Cardell-Oliver in Western Australia from 1947 to 1953; Dame Enid Lyons, widow of a former Prime Minister, in the Commonwealth from 1949 to 1951; Dame Annabel Rankin, also in the federal government, from 1964. As MacKenzie observes, 'the conviction that politics is essentially man's business in Australia dies hard.' He notes the importance of the trade-union influence in the ALP, which creates a strongly masculine climate of party activity. On the other hand, although the Liberal Party in some states (notably NSW and South Australia) makes considerable use of women workers at branch level, it shows no great anxiety to select them for parliamentary candidacy. It is evident that the women themselves are aware of the situation, as the number of female candidates for party pre-selection is not large.

Religion has for many years been a clear distinguishing factor between the parties. As Crisp shows, the proportion of Catholics in the ALP jumped sharply after the conflict over conscription in 1916, which led to the secession of twenty-four members of the federal parliamentary party, only three of whom were Catholics. Since the election of 1917, the proportion of Catholics in the parliamentary party has been roughly half. The high-water mark was reached in 1931 (54 per cent). In 1951, and again in 1961, it was 50 per cent. The Catholic religion has gone hand in hand with Irish extraction, which hovered around 40 per cent from the early 1920's to the late 1950's, when it began to show a slight decline. The non-Labor parties have been overwhelmingly Protestant by contrast. In 1910 the parliamentary Liberal Party included twenty-eight Protestants, two Catholics, and eleven of unknown faith; in 1922, fifty-one Protestants, three Catholics, and twelve unknown; and in 1958, eighty-nine Protestants, seven Catholics, and twelve unknown.

Politics runs in the family in Australia as it does elsewhere. On the non-Labor side, Sir Robert Menzies is the son of a member of the Victorian state parliament, and his wife was the daughter of a senator. Other members of the family have been prominent in public life; a brother was Crown Solicitor of Victoria, and a cousin became a High Court judge. Three generations of Fairbairns have served in the Federal parliament, one of them in the first Menzies ministry (1939-40) and one in a subsequent Menzies ministry (from 1964). Sir Alec Downer, a minister under Menzies from 1959 to 1964, was the scion of a family well known in South Australian public life. His father, Sir John Downer, was Premier of South Australia, became a 'father of Federation', and sat in the federal parliament. By contrast, the grandson of another South Australian founding father, Senator Playford, became Premier of the state for a record term of nearly twenty-seven years. The Abbott family, with widespread pastoral interests in northern NSW and Southern Queensland, sent a number of members to the Federal and NSW parliaments; one of them, C. L. A. Abbott, became Administrator of the Northern Territory after holding a federal portfolio. A father and son, E. B. C. Corser and B. H. Corser, succeeded one another as representatives of the Queensland constituency of Wide Bay in the House of Representatives. The old-established South Australian families of Bonython and Duncan, with large commercial and banking interests, have been represented on many occasions in both state and federal parliaments. Sir Henry Gullett, a Victorian member of the federal parliament in the 1920's and 1930's and a minister in several governments, was succeeded in 1946 by his son, H. B. S. Gullett, who became ambassador to Greece in 1965. Sir Neville Howse, vc, a minister in the Bruce government and member of a well-known family in the Orange district of nsw, was followed in federal parliament by his son, J. B. Howse, who sat from 1946 to 1960. When H. L. Anthony, for many years a Country Party mhr and a minister in the Menzies government, died in 1957, his seat was occupied by his son, J. D. Anthony, who became a minister in 1964. The Drake-Brockman family, one of the 'old families' of Western Australia, has been represented in both state and federal parliaments by several members, one of whom also became Chief Judge of the Arbitration Court. There are also a number of examples of prominent families whose activity has been restricted to the state sphere, especially in the more 'remote' states of Western Australia, South Australia, Tasmania, and Queensland.

On the Labor side, family involvement in politics is just as marked. Perhaps the outstanding example is that of the Watkins dynasty which held the Newcastle seat in the House of Representatives for almost fifty-eight years without a break. David Watkins, a miner, entered the federal parliament in 1901 and sat until his death in 1935; his son, David Oliver Watkins, succeeded him and sat until his retirement in 1958. Another miner, Rowley James, was for many years member for Hunter, also in the Newcastle district. He retired from politics in 1958 to make way for Dr H. V. Evatt, then federal parliamentary leader of the alp, who held the seat until he resigned to become Chief Justice of nsw, and was replaced by his predecessor's son, A. W. James, a former policeman. Another dynastic case was that of the Guy family in Tasmania. James Guy, general secretary of the alp in Tasmania, became state member for Bass in 1909, and senator for Tasmania from 1914 to 1920. His place as member for Bass was taken by his son, James Allan Guy, who became Chief Secretary in the state government of J. A. Lyons and entered federal parliament in 1929. With Lyons, he crossed the floor in 1931, and was a member of the Lyons government until 1934, when he lost his seat. (He was re-elected on two subsequent occasions.) Lyons himself was succeeded in the House of Representatives by his widow, Dame Enid, who sat from 1943 to 1951. His son, Kevin, later became prominent in state Liberal politics, and was deputy leader of the state parliamentary party for several years until he broke away to form a new party. Another Tasmanian case is that of the Barnard family. H. C. Barnard, a prominent figure in the trade union movement and the party organisation, was elected for the federal seat of Bass in 1934, and was a minister from 1946 to 1949, when he lost his seat. However, he gained a seat in the state parliament in the following year. His son, L. H. Barnard, was elected for Bass in 1954, and became deputy federal leader in 1967.

In Victoria, John Lemmon was a member of the Legislative Assembly for so long that he was known as the 'father of the House'. His son, Nelson Lemmon, became a farmer in Western Australia and was elected to the House of Representatives in 1943. He was a minister from 1946 to 1949, when he lost his seat; he was re-elected briefly from 1954 to 1955 for the NSW seat of St George. The Northern Territory seat in the House of Representatives has also descended from father to son. From 1922 to 1934 it was held by H. G. Nelson, for many years secretary of the North Australian Workers' Union, who lost it to an independent in 1934. It was regained in 1949 by his son, J. N. Nelson, who had business and pastoral interests in the Territory, and held the seat continuously until 1966.

Cabinet Ministers

Disraeli, meeting the venerable prophet of free trade, John Bright, in the lobby of the House of Commons, helped the old gentleman on with his overcoat and murmured in his ear, 'Ambition, Mr Bright—that is what brings us both here.' It is only a few, like Disraeli, who can seriously imagine that they will reach the top of the greasy pole, but there are many ambitious enough to see themselves as Cabinet ministers. In the succeeding pages, I shall attempt a collective portrait.[18]

The first federal parliament met in May 1901; the twenty-fifth parliament was dissolved in November 1961. Between these two dates, 196 ministers held office. They were distributed among the six states as shown in Table 12·7.

Table 12·7 Distribution of MP's and Ministers, 1901-61

State	Seats in Parliament %	Ministerial posts %
NSW	31	31
Vic.	24	28
Qld	14	12
SA	11·5	11
WA	10	8
Tas.	9·5	10
	100	100

Federalism, combined with interstate rivalry, has produced a fairly even geographical spread. With the exception of Tasmania, however, the more remote states have been under-represented, and Victoria has been correspondingly over-represented. This is partly historical. From 1901 to 1927, the federal parliament sat in Melbourne, and during that period 30 per cent of ministers were Victorians, as many as from NSW and Queensland put together. Since then, the balance has gradually been redressed, but the effect of the earlier period is still evident.

[18] For other analyses of factors related to the choice of ministers, see S. Encel, *Cabinet Government in Australia*, pp. 110-20, 141-45, 184-85, 244-56, and 'The Political Elite in Australia', *Political Studies*, vol. 9, no. 1, 1961.

The representation of states varies markedly between the parties, as Table 12·8 shows.

Table 12·8 Ministers by Parties and States

State	Liberal and CP Ministers %	Labor Ministers %
NSW	36	26
Vic.	30	22
Qld	10	14
SA	9	14
WA	8	13
Tas.	7	11
	100 (n = 120)	100 (n = 76)

The practice of electing Labor ministers by exhaustive ballot of the parliamentary caucus obviously leads to a more even spread between states. The Labor system has one remarkable bias, namely against NSW. During the sixty-year period, members from NSW constituencies held 33 per cent of all Labor seats, as compared with twenty-six per cent of ministerial posts in Labor ministries. Western Australia and Tasmania, on the other hand, have had more than their share of ministerial posts in relation to parliamentary seats (13 per cent as against 10 per cent in the case of WA, 11 per cent as against 9 per cent in that of Tasmania). In the Liberal and Country Parties, NSW and Victoria are both over-represented by comparison with the smaller states. The choice of Prime Ministers also illustrates the greater spread to be found in the Labor Party. Of its seven Prime Ministers since Federation, three were from NSW, two from Queensland, one from Victoria, and one from Western Australia. In the Liberal-Country combination, only one of the twelve Prime Ministers (until 1969) has not come from either NSW or Victoria, and this exceptional case (Lyons) was an ex-Labor man.

Social differences between the parties emerge clearly from data concerning occupation, education and religion. Father's occupation provides a useful index of social mobility between generations. On this point, information was available for 147 individuals. Some of this came from replies to a postal questionnaire returned by ninety-one men and women who had held ministerial office (both state and federal) between 1945 and 1958; the rest from published data. Altogether, sixty-three state and eighty-four federal ministers who had held office in this century were covered.[19]

It will occasion no surprise that more Labor ministers should be of working class origin than non-Labor ministers. It is remarkable, nevertheless, that the largest single group among the fathers of Labor ministers is

---

[19] Where ministers changed their party, they are classified in these tables according to the party under which they *originally* held office.

the 'commercial and clerical' category, which may be described roughly as 'lower-middle class'. Twenty of the eighty-nine non-Labor ministers were drawn from the Country Party, and of these twelve were the sons of farmers or graziers. Eight of those classified as 'professional and semi-professional' were men who were members of parliament long enough to make it their major occupation, although some of those listed under other headings had also been politically active. Ten clergymen were also included in this category. Six of the Labor ministers whose fathers were classified as 'other' were in fact orphaned in childhood. Whether the proportion is significant it is impossible to say because of the size of the sample. A careful study of these cases, if it were possible, might bear upon speculations about the effect of upbringing in a mother-centred family, which leads the son to seek power—or identity—in later life.

Table 12·9 Occupations of Fathers of Cabinet Ministers

Occupational Group	Total	Liberal-CP	Labor
1 Rural proprietors	40	29	11
2 Professional and semi-professional	33	22	11
3 Administrative and business	20	18	2
4 Commercial and clerical	25	10	15
5 Manual workers	20	8	12
6 Other	9	2	7
Total	147	89	58

The occupations of Cabinet ministers before they entered parliament also indicate a clear-cut divergence between the parties. Table 12·10 gives particulars for a total of 259 ministers, 63 state and 196 federal, who held office between 1901 and 1961. The 1947 census is again used for purposes of comparison.

Table 12·10 Previous Occupations of Ministers

Occupational group	1947 census— all breadwinners (%)	All ministers (%) (n=259)	Liberal CP (%) (n=148)	Labor (%) (n=111)
Rural proprietors	8·5	21	26	11
Professional and semi-professional	5·1	37	46	26
Administrative and business	5·4	16	25	5
Commercial and clerical	21·4	8	2	16
Manual workers	47·8	18	1	42
Other	11·8	—	—	—
Total	100·0	100	100	100

The 'manual workers' in the Labor Party were nearly all trade union officials, as were some of the white-collar workers in the 'commercial and clerical' category. Altogether, forty-eight of the 111 Labor ministers were trade union officials before entering parliament, and most of these were full-time officials. The majority of them had held one of the leading offices at state or federal level; twelve of the federal ministers had been national president or secretary of their union. Another feature is the number of lawyers in the 'professional' group. Out of ninety-six individuals, no less than fifty were lawyers, thirty-six of them in the non-Labor parties, fourteen in the Labor Party. However, only three of the Labor men had gone straight into the legal profession after completing their education; the rest had qualified as lawyers by part-time study while working as trade union officials or clerical employees. Some of the trade union officials, therefore, are included in the professional group, and not classified as manual workers.

Though farmers and graziers (i.e. 'rural proprietors') are obviously the major group within the Country Party, it is of greater interest to observe the proportion of non-farmers, especially among ministers, of whom more than one-third came from non-rural occupations, including three lawyers. Page, the second federal leader, was a doctor, and his successor, Fadden, an accountant. Half of the 'rural proprietors' in the non-Labor group have been Liberals, indicating that the political importance of the farming community spans all the parties. The Labor Party has always included a sizeable farming group, whose actual strength has oscillated in response to Labor's popularity in the wheat-growing areas. In 1941 the proportion of farmers in the federal parliamentary Labor Party reached a peak of 18 per cent, after a decade of agricultural depression. The division of rural proprietors among the three parties reflects the divisions within the rural community itself, but it is also politically advantageous to farmers and graziers aspiring to office. The two main parties are constantly interested in weakening the CP's hold on the rural vote, and one way is to offer ministerial posts to members from rural constituencies.

In addition, a number of CP ministers have combined farming with other occupations. Some have been directors of pastoral companies or food processing firms, others have operated small businesses in country towns, e.g. stock and station agents. Entry into parliament sometimes means a complete abandonment of farming even as an avocation, as we have already seen in the case of the NSW upper house. A long-time leader of the parliamentary CP in Victoria, Sir Herbert Hyland, came under increasing criticism from his party for this reason and finally lost his position. Few of the CP ministers in this analysis had returned to farming pursuits after vacating their ministerial posts or parliamentary seats.

The occupational differences shown in Table 12·10 correspond closely to educational differences.[20]

---

[20] As far as possible, the occupations given in the analysis are those followed for the five years immediately before entering parliament. Where this is inapplicable, the major occupation in the ten years before entering parliament is given.

Table 12·11 Education of Cabinet Ministers

Educational Level attained	Total %	Lib-CP %	Labor %
Primary	24	7	51
Secondary	31	34	25
University	26	36	10
Other Tertiary	11	13	9
N/A	8	10	5
	100	100	100

Not only the educational level, but the type of school attended, provides a sharp differentiation. At the primary level, this is largely a distinction between state and Catholic schools. The proportion of Catholics among Labor men is reflected in the fact that thirty-six of the 111 Labor ministers had attended Catholic primary schools, out of thirty-nine who could positively be identified as Catholics.[21] Out of seventy-six Labor ministers who held Federal office between 1904 and 1949, twenty-five were Catholics (as against thirty-six Protestants, three free-thinkers and twelve for whom no information was available).

At the secondary level, where information was available for all but twelve, we find that eighty-five of the 148 non-Labor ministers had been educated at private secondary schools. Sixty-two of these had attended schools affiliated with the Headmasters' Conference of Australia, among which a handful of the most important ones again played an outstanding role. Out of the sixty-two, twenty-two were educated at the four leading 'Associated Public' schools in Victoria—Melbourne Grammar School (eight), Scotch College (six), Wesley College (four), Geelong Grammar School (four). Another fourteen had attended a group of leading Sydney schools—Sydney Grammar School (seven), Sydney CEGS, or 'Shore' (three), Newington College (two), The King's School (two). Altogether, eleven leading private schools accounted for forty-two men in the non-Labor group—Melbourne Grammar School, Sydney Grammar School, Scotch College, Brisbane Grammar School, Prince Alfred College (Adelaide), Geelong Grammar School, Wesley College, Sydney CEGS, Launceston Grammar School, The King's School, and Newington College —in descending order of numerical importance.

Among Labor ministers, sixteen had been educated at Catholic secondary schools, six of them affiliated with the Headmasters' Conference. Another four had attended Protestant schools of this type. Most of tne remainder attended state high schools.

In federal politics, these social differences have shown considerable stability over the sixty-year period. The year 1923 provides the most convenient point of division for purposes of contrast. The earlier prepon-

[21] These figures undoubtedly understate the proportion of Catholics in state Labor governments. A check of state Labor ministers not included in these data suggests that a majority of them were Catholics.

derance of NSW and Victoria has changed in more ways than one. Up to 1923, forty-two out of seventy-five ministers had come from the two largest states, twenty-two from Victoria, twenty from NSW. From 1923 to 1961, the figures were seventy-four out of 121—forty-two from NSW, thirty-two from Victoria. Mobility between state and federal parliaments was markedly less after 1923 and has continued to decline. The representation of farmers and graziers in both cabinet and parliament rose sharply in response to the emergence of the CP as a permanent third party (it rose by only a negligible 2 per cent among ministers of the other two parties). The proportion of Catholics in Labor ministries rose significantly, as a result of the great schism over conscription in 1916. In the earlier period, nineteen out of thirty Labor ministers were Protestants, and four were Catholics (no information was available about the other seven). In the latter period, twenty-one out of forty-six were Catholics, seventeen were Protestants, three were free-thinkers, and information was unavailable about five. In the three Scullin cabinets (1929-32), there were twelve Catholics out of nineteen ministers, and in the Chifley government of 1946 there were eleven out of nineteen. There was a general rise in the standard of education, manifested principally by a threefold increase in the numbers of men educated at state high schools. A training in the law ceased to be the only form of tertiary education represented among ministers. Before 1923, there had been twenty-eight lawyers in various cabinets. From 1923 to 1961, there were twenty-four lawyers, fourteen other university graduates, and fifteen other men with some form of tertiary education who sat in cabinet. The rise of educational standards coincides with a decline in working-class representation in the parliamentary Labor Party.

What of those who, in Disraeli's words, reach the top of the greasy pole? From 1901 to 1969 there were nineteen Prime Ministers, if we include the three who acted as 'caretakers' in 1939, 1945 and 1967-68 following the deaths of the incumbents. They were a heterogeneous lot, whose diverse careers and personalities serve to remind us of the fickleness of fortune.[22] On the Liberal side, nevertheless, the role of the Bar remains outstanding. Barton, Deakin, Reid and Menzies were all barristers of repute, and to these may be added Hughes, who left the ALP in 1916 and continued as Prime Minister of a non-Labor government for a further six years. Harold Holt (1966-67) was a solicitor. Two other non-lawyers were also former Labor men—Cook, who had been a coalminer, and Lyons, a schoolteacher. Bruce was a merchant, the scion of an old-established commercial family in Melbourne, who had been educated at Cambridge. John Gorton, who became Prime Minister in 1968, went to Oxford.

Labor Prime Ministers, by contrast, have had little in common but their working class background. The Labor man is required to run a more testing race. Watson, Prime Minister in 1904, was a compositor, and moved to federal politics from the NSW colonial parliament. Fisher, his

[22] For a brief account, see S. Encel, op. cit., pp. 251-56.

successor, was a coalminer who also moved from colonial to federal parliament. Hughes, named by his father after William Morris, was a trade union organiser and builder of the Waterside Workers' Federation, who studied law at night and became one of the most notable orators and pamphleteers of his day. A Melbourne paper called him the 'Mirabeau of the proletariat'. His legal talents were of less consequence than the fact that he was a law unto himself, whether he was leading a Labor government, a Nationalist government, or sniping from the sidelines. Scullin, the next Labor Prime Minister, had been an organiser for the AWU and ran a grocer's shop. He was also a leading Catholic layman. Curtin had also been born a Catholic, but renounced his faith and became an active member of the Rationalist Association (a fellow-member was J. G. Latham, later Liberal Attorney-General and then Chief Justice of the High Court). After some years as a union organiser, Curtin became a journalist before entering federal parliament. F. M. Forde, who succeeded him briefly when Curtin died in office, was trained as an electrician and also worked as a schoolteacher before entering the Queensland state parliament. Chifley, an errant Catholic who married a Presbyterian, was a locomotive engine driver who also had business interests in Bathurst.

It remains to mention the three Country Party leaders who served briefly as Prime Ministers—Page for three weeks, Fadden for six, McEwen for three. Neither Fadden nor Page could be regarded as a countryman. Page was a surgeon, and Fadden an accountant. Page was, however, a member of a family well-known in the Clarence River district centred on the town of Grafton (his practice was in this area), and also became a considerable landowner. His loyalties were intensely local and rural.[23] Fadden, whose tastes and outlook were wholly urban, had close ties with the Queensland sugar industry, and in the context of Queensland politics this normally means association with the Country Party. McEwen, a Victorian farmer, is discussed in Chapter 19.

Diversity of careers is even more marked if we move to state politics. From 1923 to 1961 inclusive, forty-nine separate men held the office of Premier in the six states. Their previous occupations had varied widely, including fourteen manual workers, twelve farmers, six lawyers, three schoolteachers, three shopkeepers, three state government officials, two journalists, one doctor, one pharmacist, one merchant and one bank manager. Rural occupations predominated on the non-Labor side—seven of the nineteen Liberal Premiers, and all four of the Country Party Premiers—followed by the law, which accounted for five of the Liberals. Thirteen of the twenty-six Labor Premiers were manual workers, and twelve of them had been trade union officials of consequence, whether salaried or honorary officers. Irrespective of party, almost half of the Premiers were the sons of farmers or graziers. Fifteen of the Labor Premiers were Catholics; all the non-Labor men were Protestants. Edu-

---

[23] Earle Page, *Truant Surgeon*, Sydney, 1962, chs. 1-7

cational differences reflected those of religion and occupation. Only four of the Labor men had any form of tertiary education, two of them being law graduates. Most of the Labor men with a secondary education had attended state schools. Nine of the Liberals had attended private schools affiliated with the Headmasters' Conference.

It may be concluded that the system works to give each party a social profile which is strikingly 'representative' of the social groups that support it. In other words, the facts confirm the basic unreality of popular complaints about the poor quality of politicians. When the critics go on, as they frequently do, to praise the politicians of other countries by comparison with those of Australia, they are virtually praising them for being 'un-representative' of their constituents. It is a sobering thought that our politicians may indeed be representative of their fellow-citizens. Perhaps the secret of finding political leaders is to be able to select the right kinds of un-representative individuals.

13: The Bureaucratic Structure (1)

The myth of egalitarianism adheres strongly to the public services of Australia. Its effects were depicted mordantly a generation ago by Hancock:

Since the State has insisted on tackling the most formidable of Australia's problems, one would have imagined that it would have eagerly sought after the most promising Australian brains. Since its activities have been so extensively economic, one would have expected it to search for administrators capable of unravelling economic causes and imagining economic effects. But the Australians have always assumed that economic problems are simple, and have resented those classifications and rewards which suggest that some men have a higher class of intelligence than that of the majority. Democratic sentiment applauds the sound argument that every office boy should have a chance to become a manager, and perverts it into a practical rule that no one should become a manager who has not been an office boy.[1]

Hancock's words reflect a deep-rooted public attitude towards the government service. But similar criticisms have been made from the inside, especially as the result of inquiries into the structure of the system. In 1959, Professor R. S. Parker, a member of a committee of inquiry into recruitment in the Commonwealth Public Service, asserted that

One of the most serious deterrents to high quality recruitment is the belief that it requires no great merit to enter the public service at the bottom, that those who do so are motivated by a mere desire for security rather than by ambition, and that once in the service, they insist on being protected from undue personal competition either from inside the service or from outside.

The elaborate statutory provisions which protect the established public servant from 'undue competition' suggest, to members of the public, a 'preoccupation with security and a determination to protect mediocrity and discourage exceptional ability.'[2] Two royal commissioners, forty years earlier, made very similar observations. The former Commonwealth Public

[1] W. K. Hancock, *Australia*, p. 118
[2] R. S. Parker, 'Recruitment—Aims, Methods and Problems', *Public Administration*, vol. 18, no. 1, 1959

Service Commissioner, D. C. McLachlan, wrote in 1918 that the service was characterised by 'a dead level of mediocrity'.[3] Similarly, G. M. Allard, investigating the NSW Public Service as a royal commissioner, described the recruitment system as a 'pretentious portico of entrance by academic test', which in fact offered only 'an attractive shelter to mediocrity. It offers advancement and promotion by the means that mediocrity cherishes, that is seniority before merit to the point of reducing the efficiency of the meritorious.'[4]

On the face of it, the structure of the government service conforms with two assumptions characteristic of the egalitarian tradition. The first is that the public service is, or ought to be, a career open to talent, in which every telegraph messenger can aspire to become Director-General. Such a view was explicitly stated in the eighth annual report by McLachlan in 1910. (The odd thing is that McLachlan, far from being egalitarian, was a rigid authoritarian who spoke of individual advancement in the language of Samuel Smiles.) The second assumption is that nothing fits a man for higher responsibilities so much as long experience and seniority in the organisation. In 1945, the secretary of the Clerical Association in the NSW public service declared that 'training within the service of younger members of the staff, together with the study required to pass the grade examination, equips them for the performance of administrative duties . . . too much emphasis has been laid on the term "routine work". The performance of much of the so-called routine work forms a most important part in the training of juniors and gives them a knowledge of detail which is invaluable to them as they progress in the service.'[5] These assumptions are entrenched in the legislative framework of the government services, established in the thirty years preceding the 1914-18 war. The statutes which embodied these assumptions rejected the social distinctions built into the hierarchical structure of the British Civil Service, while simultaneously ignoring the basic assumption of that service which, since the Northcote-Trevelyan report of 1854, has regarded broad intellectual culture as the essential element in the make-up of an administrator. For example, the first Commonwealth Public Service Act of 1902 provided for entry into the service at an elementary level of education, with university degrees recognised only as certificates of professional competence required by architects, chemists, engineers, lawyers and medical practitioners employed as public officials. This Act took over principles already found in the legislation setting up the existing public services of the six colonies.[6]

[3] *Report of the Royal Commission on Commonwealth Public Service Administration*, Melbourne, 1918, p. 19
[4] *First Sectional Report of the Royal Commission on the NSW Public Service*, Sydney, 1918, p. 60
[5] F. L. Hedges, in *Public Administration*, vol. 5, no. 8, 1945
[6] For an extended discussion, see S. Encel, 'The Commonwealth Public Service and Outside Recruitment', *Public Administration*, vol. 14, no. 1, 1955; R. S. Parker, *Public Service Recruitment in Australia*, Melbourne, 1942; P. W. E. Curtin, 'Recruitment', in R. N. Spann (ed.), *Public Administration in Australia*, Sydney, 1959.

Although these provisions were a recognition of necessity in a colonial society which had no chance of emulating the institutions of its parent culture, they were also, to an important extent, the result of ideological predisposition. In place of special qualifications and intellectual excellence, the system provided for seniority, the embodiment of long and faithful service, as the main criterion for advancement and appointment to high office. It was assumed that length of experience and acquaintance with all the routine duties of a department was the quality above all others which made a good administrator. This criterion is unexceptionably egalitarian. All entrants start at the bottom of the ladder, without benefit of advantages gained outside.

To some extent, the system also reflected the popular suspicion of bureaucracy which we have examined in a previous chapter. For many years, the accepted convention has been that government officials are not concerned with policy. The convention is still maintained that all policy emanates from the minister, and that the task of the public servant is merely to carry out his instructions as loyally and efficiently as possible. It was this received view which made a constitutional lawyer write that, in Australia, administration was nothing more complex than 'clerical service under a political head'.[7]

It is not surprising that the application of such principles would create the impression that the public service was a sphere where youth, originality and enterprise were at a discount. Conformity with the outlook of one's superiors would naturally be the surest way of promotion, and the cardinal sin against the system would be promotion 'out of turn'. Writing of New Zealand, Lipson remarked some years ago that the policy of selecting permanent heads only from those who started as office boys meant that the New Zealand Public Service had not yet succeeded in training the needed type of administrator because it would involve the 'undemocratic' practice of promoting able men out of turn. Under these circumstances, the headship of a department would be regarded not as an opportunity to make policy and exercise influence, but simply as a prize to which no man is entitled to cling for too long. Officials would therefore become heads of departments only in the last few years of their careers, in order not to obstruct the chances of the next man in line to occupy the position for a short time before he retired.[8]

Although Ludwig von Mises was not thinking of Australia and New Zealand when he wrote his swingeing attack on bureaucracy, his description is extraordinarily apt.

In a properly arranged civil service system the promotion to higher ranks depends primarily on seniority. The Heads of the Bureaux are for the most part old men who know that after a few years they will be retired. Having

---

[7] Sir W. Harrison Moore, in M. Atkinson (ed.), *Australia: Economic and Political Studies*, Melbourne, 1920, p. 89
[8] Leslie Lipson, *The Politics of Equality*, Chicago, 1949, p. 490

spent the greater part of their lives in subordinate positions, they have lost vigour and initiative. They shun innovations and improvements. They look on every project for reform as a disturbance of their quiet. Their rigid conservatism frustrates all endeavours of a Cabinet Minister to adjust the service to changed conditions.[9]

One of the consequences of this attitude to promotion is a deliberate confusion of promotion—i.e. movement from one class of the service to another—with advancement, i.e. automatic movement by annual increments within the same class. As a result of this, public services in Australia have had great difficulty in formulating any principles regarding fitness for promotion, perhaps because it involves making judgments about one man being better than another. Automatic advancement, where such decisions are either unnecessary or comparatively simple to make, fits into the system much better. The pressure to provide as many opportunities for advancement as possible expresses itself particularly through the arbitration system. The cumulative effect of arbitration awards is generally to multiply the number of narrow, overlapping salary classifications which make it possible for officials to move frequently within the system.[10] The steady growth of arbitration as a method of dealing with internal questions of organisation has been characteristic of all Australian public services in the twentieth century.

A particularly interesting example of the pervasive influence of arbitral methods is their extension into the system of appeals against promotions. Since the beginning of the century, one of the major aims of public service unionism has been to cut down the discretionary powers of departmental heads in the making of promotions. As a result, some form of procedure enabling disgruntled individuals to appeal to a tribunal is to be found in all Australian public services.[11] The most elaborate provisions operate in the two largest services, those of the state of New South Wales and the Commonwealth. After years of negotiation, the NSW government introduced a system of promotion committees in 1929. Under Section 49A of the state Public Service Act, any promotion involving a public servant who is not in line for it because of seniority must be referred *automatically* to a three-man committee, including a departmental representative and a representative appointed by the staff association to which the official belongs. The law requires the committee to investigate the claims for promotion of *every* official who might be passed over.

Promotion committees apply only to the minority of government employees who are, technically, 'public servants'. In 1944, however, the appeal procedure was extended to a much wider range of officials with the

[9] L. von Mises, *Bureaucracy*, New York, 1945, p. 55

[10] On the confused relation between promotion and advancement, see, e.g. V. A. Subramaniam and B. B. Schaffer, in *Public Administration*, vol. 19, no. 1, 1960.

[11] V. A. Subramaniam, 'Promotion in the Commonwealth, NSW and Victorian Public Services', Ph.D. thesis, Australian National University, 1959, esp. ch. 13, pp. 354-58, 373-79

establishment of the Crown Employees Appeal Board, whose decisions can override those of the promoting authority. The Board consists of a chairman, usually a judge of the state Industrial Commission, one representative of the official side and one of the staff side.

In the Commonwealth, both responsibility for promotions and the nature of the appeal system have changed several times since Federation. The present system of appeal committees was introduced in 1945. It provides for a chairman (who, in the larger metropolitan centres, is a specially appointed official of quasi-judicial status), an official representative and a staff representative. In its first year of operation, nearly one-half of all promotions were appealed against, and in recent years the proportion has fluctuated around 30 per cent.

Australia is not, of course, unique in these matters. In a number of European countries, even more elaborate provisions exist to protect officials against dismissal, victimisation, or political bias. In France, the *Conseil d'Etat* can override the decision of a minister of state, as it did in the famous case where three officials alleged, successfully, that they had been excluded from the National School of Administration on political grounds. In France, also, departments are required to take into account the advice of committees, on which staff associations are represented, before promotions are made.[12] In Britain, the Civil Service Arbitration Tribunal was established in 1925 to fix salaries and conditions, up to a certain level, by arbitral means. But there is no real counterpart to the remarkable scope of the arbitral principle in Australia, and the extent to which its operation supersedes both the discretionary powers of high officials and the authority of a central controlling agency to determine the structure of the system. The importance of arbitration has also strengthened the role of the public service staff associations, whose interest has naturally been to play up the egalitarian features of the system and to resist tendencies towards greater stratification and diversification within it. A recent student of unionism in the Commonwealth Public Service writes that 'able leadership and a variety of tactics has given the staff associations profound influence on the course of events though they have never been completely united. Indeed, sometimes they have been united only in abusing the official side and for no other purpose.'

He goes on to note the influence of association officials in public service management.

The staff associations have been able to call upon very able leaders, men who might have had a promising career in the Service had they not opted for full-time association work. . . . Between 1915 and 1950 a dozen association career men figured prominently in the affairs of the Service personnel system and came to be consulted by Cabinets. Their ability was demonstrated as arbitration advocates, in planning High Court action, in pressure group strategy, and in outside academic and business success.

12 P. Chatenet, in W. A. Robson (ed.), *The Civil Service in Britain and France*, London, 1952, pp. 165-68

They were appointed to Royal Commissions and committees of inquiry not necessarily connected with the Service: one of them became a Commonwealth Public Service Commissioner and two others became conciliation commissioners. They were innovators, ready and willing to assist and losing no opportunity to publicise what they thought was right.[13]

Lest we become too impressed by the success of these men (whose careers can be paralleled by those of officials in various state services), we should remember that similar things have occurred in Britain, where union officials like W. J. Brown and Douglas Houghton rose to political prominence through their work in civil service union affairs. However, the scope and importance of union activity in Australia, the opportunities it has offered to able and ambitious men, and in particular its direct impact on the actual management of the administrative system, go well beyond the British comparison.

A significant result of the ability of the public service unions to exploit the arbitration system has been the entrenchment of the principle of 'work value' as the cornerstone of the public service classification system. The use of the notion appears to originate with the reclassification of the NSW public service undertaken by the first Public Service Board in 1896. It was applied to the Commonwealth service by its first commissioner, McLachlan, who had been a departmental head in NSW before Federation. The principle meant that the salary paid must be rigidly separated from any personal characteristics of the occupant. It went much further than the simple notion of the same payment for the same work; among other things, it gave promise of a reliable method of measuring 'efficiency', which would serve as an impartial method of personnel management.[14] The concept of work value, applied in its full rigour, provides the intellectual basis for the attempt to banish the phenomena of authority, status and personal discretion from the bureaucratic structure, and to replace them with the purely objective and economic concept of different jobs paid at different rates. The hierarchical features of bureaucratic organisation are pushed into the background.

The characteristics of the system, as described briefly above, have been analysed in some detail by students of public administration. However, they do not represent the whole story—perhaps no more than half of it. Administrative history illustrates not simply the working out of egalitarian principles in the public bureaucracies, but rather the way in which egalitarian pressures, generated by the environment, have forced inherent bureaucratic tendencies towards hierarchy and status distinction to take special forms which are characteristically Australian. In this respect, the bureaucratic structure is almost a paradigm of the relations between class, status and authority within the social structure as a whole. Indeed,

[13] G. E. Caiden, *Career Service*, Melbourne, 1965, pp. 10-13
[14] V. A. Subramaniam, 'The Evolution of Classification Practices', *Public Administration*, vol. 19, no. 4, 1960

egalitarian pressure, by its special demands, has resulted both in the enhancement of bureaucratic influence throughout society in general, and in the development of some particularly rigid hierarchical forms within the bureaucratic structure. Because of the strength of union pressure, the public service authorities have often found it necessary to be devious and furtive in their pursuit of rational methods of organisation. Before the advent of arbitration, the concept of economy in administration went no further than the ancient Gladstonian principle of 'saving candle-ends'. This concept had little chance of standing up to examination in an arbitration tribunal, where demands for wage-justice could not be countered by bald assertions that public servants had no right to higher pay. One of the 'iron men' of the Commonwealth service, W. J. Skewes, advocated Victorian standards of thrift and abstinence in a famous exchange with Mr Justice Powers in the Arbitration Court in 1918. He suggested that meatless days should be enforced in Australia, and pointed to the value of oatmeal for the Scots. Mr Justice Powers retorted that oatmeal was suitable only for Scotland.[15] In a small way, the relationship between the two sides reproduces the pattern of 'initiative-resistance' in party politics, and in this case also it is confined to the limited sphere in which union interests operate. Thus, the real innovations in Australian public service practice have been concerned not with management, but with the protection of the rights of the subordinate official. The paradoxical result is a special kind of rigidity and conservatism with special emphasis on seniority.

This fundamental ambiguity was recognised by Weber, who observed that democratic sentiments are suspicious of the merit system in the public service and the use of special examinations for recruitment and promotion because they may create privileged groups. Democracy, he remarked, 'takes an ambivalent stand in the face of specialised examinations, as it does in the face of all the phenomena of bureaucracy—but democracy itself promotes these developments.'[16]

In Australia, this ambiguity has been manifest for many years, in the recognition that methods would have to be found for circumventing the results of egalitarian pressure. For instance, the Commonwealth Public Service Act of 1902 followed the example of existing colonial legislation by providing that appointments could be made from outside the service, under suitable safeguards, to administrative and professional posts. The debate on this clause of the Act showed general agreement among members of parliament, many of whom had been ministers in colonial governments, on the necessity for such a provision. Various speakers agreed that the system made it difficult to put men of administrative ability into senior posts. One member asserted that officials who had been engaged on clerical work for a long time became 'fossils' by the time they were middle-aged. He declared that the head of a department must be 'a man of large general

---

[15] Quoted by Caiden, op. cit., pp. 135-36
[16] Max Weber, 'Bureaucracy', in Gerth and Mills (eds.), *From Max Weber*, p. 240

information, business capacity, and knowledge of the world'. Moreover, such an individual must have his own views about policy and be able to meet his minister on equal terms. He added that the provision was 'not a weakness, but a necessity, and it may possibly have to be exercised very often in the interests of the public.'[17]

The most interesting speech in this debate was made by Henry Bournes Higgins, who later became President of the Arbitration Court and an outstanding spokesman for social justice. Higgins saw no contradiction in supporting this clause. Ministers, he said, 'ought to be able to get for their departments the very best talent available, and they ought to be allowed to put into responsible positions brilliant young men with other experience than that of the civil service—men who have seen something of outside life, and who have not been brought up in the groove of the department.' He admitted the danger of favouritism, but went on: 'If we say we will not go outside a department for special talent, we run the risk of a still greater danger. That greater danger is that the civil servant will become wooden and incompetent and lose all initiative . . . if a man enters a public department when he is young, the tendency is for him to do whatever work he is told to do by a superior and to trust the improvement of his position to getting increments periodically, and to getting into his superior's shoes.'[18]

The same problem was touched on in McLachlan's Royal Commission report, where he criticised the low standards of education required for entry, and deplored the fact that a youth who took the trouble to gain further qualifications derived no benefit from them in his career. There was, he observed, 'no doubt that the services of many brilliant youths are lost to the Government owing to the shortsighted policy of failing to provide for entrance at a later stage and with advanced educational qualifications.' The provisions for special recruitment of qualified people were necessary for this reason, and 'a much wider field will be afforded the government for the recruitment of the service by the appointment of persons with special and distinctive qualifications.'[19]

The Predominance of the Expert

The character of the bureaucratic system is marked by the results of the struggle between egalitarian and hierarchical pressures, leading on the one hand to a rigid and authoritarian tone in the hierarchy, and on the other to the elaboration of devices to evade the effects of egalitarianism in recruitment and promotion. In addition, however, we find one generally recognised and strongly based form of hierarchical differentiation: the exaltation of the expert. In the colonial bureaucracies, the superior status of the professional man was recognised from an early date. The very first

[17] Sir William McMillan, in *Commonwealth Parliamentary Debates*, vol. 2, 1901, p. 1092
[18] ibid., p. 1100
[19] op. cit., pp. 35-36

colonial Public Service Act, passed in Victoria in 1862, created Professional and Ordinary divisions, with no separate class for departmental heads. In 1883, a further Act did create a First Division, but the Premier assured an MP who questioned this that 'the status of the permanent head of a department was not above that of the chief professional officers in that department, some of whom were in receipt of higher salaries.'[20] In the Commonwealth Public Service, professional officers have enjoyed high status since 1918. In that year, after an early period in which these officers were treated as little better than clerks, an epoch-making decision by Mr Justice Higgins established the right of professional men to claim an 'extra reward which induces men to face the drudgery of study and close application.'[21] In 1939 the highest paid officials in the Commonwealth Public Service were still professional officers. In 1961, the decision of the Commonwealth Arbitration Commission in the *Professional Engineers Case* showed how far an industrial tribunal was prepared to go in accepting the special character of professional occupations and their right to correspondingly high pay and social status. Some such recognition has been implicit in the decisions of various tribunals for many years.[22]

Somewhat similar forces have been at work in the United States. As Hofstadter notes, the passion for equality is associated with a pervasive anti-intellectualism. Society's demand for trained intelligence is therefore rationalised by equating it with professional skill. Businessmen and trade unionists alike, who disagree on many basic questions, are united on this one, and they share an outlook which emphasises 'practical culture' and exalts the 'expert' rather than the 'intellectual'. In Australia, this has often come to mean that professionally trained men have a pre-emptive right to those positions which demand higher education. Hancock's remarks have been paraphrased by a more recent student with a significantly different meaning. 'The Australian public services recruit their clerical officers at about school leaving age, when the best and even the second best go on to the universities. On the other hand, they recruit professional officers, with university degrees, thus getting back some of the best material that escaped them earlier. In consequence, many high administrative positions are "hogged" by professional officers of competence and seniority based on salary, leaving behind many ill-equipped clericals. The grotesque result is that public services have to swallow the right men with the wrong training (for administration) as the price for recruiting the wrong men to get the right training.'[23]

To some extent, this is due to the great importance of developmental and welfare functions in Australian government, and especially in the

[20] *Victorian Parliamentary Debates*, vol. 44, p. 1263
[21] Quoted by Caiden, op. cit., pp. 129-30
[22] J. R. Kerr, 'Work Value', and S. Encel, 'Social Implications of the Engineers Cases', in *Journal of Industrial Relations*, vol. 6, no. 1, 1964
[23] V. A. Subramaniam, 'Specialists and the Administrative Career—A Comment', *Public Administration*, vol. 22, no. 1, 1963

states. But it is also due to ideology, for in other countries developmental and welfare organisations have, as often as not, been run by laymen and not by experts. In state governments, writes S. R. Davis, the trend is 'towards the professionalisation of the State service, and this class of official forms a great proportion of State employees. Almost the entire incentives towards higher qualification and recruitment of the "professional" through full-time university fellowships and study grants in the State services have been in this sector. It is the engineer, the architect, the biochemist, the geologist, the agronomist, the surveyor, the teacher, in short, all the technologists required to develop a community's essential services—the building of roads, the surveying of land, the designing of dams and bridges, the prevention of disease, the exploration of mineral resources—who are, in the very nature of State functions, characteristic of the State service.'[24] Even in the Commonwealth service, where these developmental functions are not of such great importance, the preponderance of professional officers in the higher levels of the service is striking. In 1962, out of 798 senior Commonwealth public servants, 535 were graduates. Of these, 313 had professional qualifications, especially in engineering and medicine. A further ninety-three were graduates in economics, and fifty-nine in law. Only seventy were Arts graduates. In 1965, the Deputy Leader of the Opposition asked the Prime Minister for an analysis of the qualifications of officers in the Second Division of the Commonwealth Public Service. This showed, once again, a preponderance of professional qualifications. Out of 370 graduates, a total of 165 had graduated in science, engineering, law, or medicine.[25] These figures indicate that the situation has not changed greatly since the early years of the century. In 1907, 48 per cent of higher positions in the Commonwealth Public Service were occupied by professionals, and in 1922 this rose to 72 per cent.[26]

The management of postal services is a good illustration of the predominance of the professional. There is an instructive contrast here with Great Britain, where there was for many years a struggle to assert the right of specialists and professional officers in the Post Office to make policy and to have access to the Postmaster-General. The Institution of Professional Civil Servants, in its evidence before the Royal Commission on the Civil Service of 1929-31, gave numerous instances of the subordination of the expert to the administrative officer. The Institution pointed out in its evidence that technical questions always had to go through the 'administrative side', which had small understanding of the technical problems concerned, and was able to deny the expert the opportunity to influence policy by presenting his case directly to the Minister. In 1932, the Bridgeman committee of investigation into Post Office administration

[24] S. R. Davis (ed.), *The Government of the Australian States*, Melbourne, 1960, p. 697
[25] *Commonwealth Parliamentary Debates*, 14 Eliz. II, H. of R., p. 786
[26] V. A. Subramaniam, in *Public Administration*, vol. 22, no. 1, 1963

reported that no technician had ever been promoted to an administrative position. Its report drew attention to the fact that newly appointed Assistant Principals in the administrative class were not given any opportunity to learn something about the technical side of post office work by being sent first to provincial centres. Instead, they were placed directly in positions where they were required to supervise the work of a highly technical department. The result was 'an autocratic isolation of the secretariat' from the technical staff and a 'narrow and specialised meaning attached to the word administrative'. Nevertheless, even as sympathetic an observer as Harold Laski was not disposed to accept the claims of specialists to a larger share in higher administration. Laski was expressing a view generally held in Britsh adminstration when he wrote: 'The wisdom that is needed for the direction of affairs is not an expert technique but a balanced equilibrium. It is a knowledge of how to use men, a faculty of judgment about the practicability of principles. It consists not in the possession of specialised knowledge, but in a power to utilise its results, at the right moment, and in the right direction.'[27] Almost the exact reverse is the case in Australia and New Zealand. A typical criticism of the role of the expert in postal administration was given a few years ago by a former New Zealand Postmaster-General, Mr T. P. Shand. He noted the overweening influence of engineers in his former department, where they were the only ones to be classed as experts. This was largely due to the reluctance of the specialist officer to recognise that administration 'is itself a form of expertise with not only its own expert procedures, but with its own professional viewpoint'. Mr Shand noted that experience in Australia had been very similar.[28] Indeed, an analysis of permanent heads of the Australian Postal Department from 1923 to 1968 shows that seven out of nine were engineers. Even in recent reorganisations of the Post Office hierarchy, an engineering background retains its pre-eminence. (This may help to explain the remarkable dullness and grotesquely bad design of Australian postage stamps for so many years.) Professional men have been able to assert their right to dominance in the administrative field, even when they have long ceased to be making decisions of a professional character. Thus, a senior medical officer in the Commonwealth Public Service writes that 'in dealing with purely professional matters and in administering a predominantly professional department (i.e. in respect of its major substantive purpose) the expert has an unchallengeable place, as administrative knowledge grafted on to professional ability and aptitude for leadership will provide an ideal type of official for such a set of circumstances. In the administration of a service which is being provided by an entire profession, nothing could be more logical than to have a member of that profession in charge.' He goes on to argue that if the

27 H. J. Laski, *The Limitations of the Expert*, Fabian Tract, no. 235, 1931
28 N. C. Angus (ed.), *The Expert and Administration in New Zealand*, Wellington, 1958, pp. 63-86, passim

expert were to be denied the right to run his own department, then 'the only type of professional man who would be likely to enter administration would be second or third rate individuals whose main object in life would be to secure a safe, sheltered and not too onerous berth.'[29] This assertion is difficult to sustain in the face of the obvious fact that departments which are dominated by professional men, and especially doctors, are often badly administered, partly because it is extremely difficult to recruit administrative talent into them.

It is not only the high professional content of so much Australian public administration which accounts for the predominance of the professional man, but also an ideology which is powerful in perpetuating it. One of the contributors to Davis' book, writing about South Australia, notes how this is likely to cause permanent difficulties in recruiting capable officials to administrative posts in the state public service. The increase in the number of professional officers, he suggests, will make it more unlikely that senior posts in the public service would be occupied by Arts graduates. 'Indeed, any suggestions that a "broad" education might have an important place in the sphere of administration seemed bound to meet with a lukewarm reception from a service containing such a high percentage of professional men. It would appear likely, therefore, that a career in the public service of South Australia will continue to have few attractions for the good Arts graduate, and that the pattern of recruitment will remain very much the mixture as before.' The role of the professional man, wedded to a specialised technique and practising it in a restricted field, accentuates rigidity and resistance to change.[30]

The predominance of professional officers helps to create a species of elite group. Two New Zealand writers note the difficulty of asserting that administration is a profession in a service where professionalism is restricted to the expert. Instead, there is a series of closed systems. 'The career ladders of special occupational groups stand virtually isolated each from the others.' Experts tend to think of themselves as a race apart, to claim that eminence in their own field constitutes a right to special attention for their views in other fields, and that it gives special assistance to their capacity for general administration. As a result, the possession of a training in some professional field is often a deciding factor in promotion to top executive positions.[31] Davis makes much the same point when he notes the paradox by which the state public services close their doors to the ambitious youth who has chosen the opportunity of a higher general education, instead of undertaking professional training under some system of cadetship or other method which the states employ in order to recruit future specialist officials. A leading state official notes somewhat the same

[29] A. Johnson, 'The Expert: On Tap or on Top?', *Public Administration*, vol. 16, no. 3, 1957
[30] L. C. Blair, in Davis, op. cit., p. 391
[31] N. C. Angus, op. cit., pp. 106-13

phenomenon. 'One of the most notable characteristics of large numbers of specialists is the failure, refusal or inability to recognise administration as a process.' Many specialists 'do not see their activities of planning, organising, coordinating, directing, controlling and the like as administration but simply as the practice of their respective specialties.' The specialist is reluctant to recognise that there is 'an administrative element in his activities, for which he should be trained, just as he has been trained in his specialty.' He is also reluctant to recognise that 'at a certain point in his upward progress, his duties change so that his specialty commences to give way to administration as the more important subject matter of his activities . . . at higher levels, the specialist will need, for example, to be shown how to judge when political, financial, administrative, humane or other criteria should override technical criteria in solving a problem, making a decision, or advising on policy.' There is a natural tendency, he goes on, for groups of persons engaged in the same specialty to develop a feeling of exclusiveness and even superiority over other groups. Specialist groups may even 'develop the attitude that the whole organisation centres around their own particular specialty.'[32] This can take a special form in what Schaffer and Knight have described as 'ideologies of promotion'. Every public service, they suggest, employs a distinctive ideology of promotion to the elite groups in the service. 'This ideology, propagated and expressed in part by myth, is a major criterion of bureaucratic typology.'[33] In Australia, it is strongly influenced by the predominance of the professional. In Queensland, the appointment of a lay administrator as chief executive of a technical organisation called forth great protests from the engineering profession. In countries like the United States, on the other hand, the successful operation of great public works enterprises like the TVA can largely be traced to the administrative and political skills of the laymen who were appointed to head them.[34]

In the Commonwealth Public Service, this ideology takes the special form of a mystique attaching to training in economics as the ideal preparation for higher administrative office. In 1947, Commonwealth Government departments were asked by the Public Service Board to provide estimates of the number of graduates they required within the next few years. The returns indicated a total of 290 positions for which departments wished to recruit graduates. Out of this total number, departments asked for 157 graduates with qualifications in economics.[35] The economists who worked for the government during the war have testified to the great

[32] A. J. A. Gardner, 'Specialists and the Administrative Career', *Public Administration*, vol. 22, no. 1, 1963

[33] B. B. Schaffer and K. W. Knight, *Top Public Servants in Two States*, Brisbane, 1963, pp. 34-36

[34] See, e.g. Philip Selznick, TVA *and the Grassroots*, New York, 1953, and R. S. Avery, *Experiment in Management*, Alabama University Press, 1956

[35] S. Encel, 'The Commonwealth Public Service', unpublished M.A. thesis, University of Melbourne, 1952

stress placed on economic training. One such economist wrote that 'the building of the war time administrative machine fell very largely to economists. . . . Economists were responsible not merely for advice on economic policy, but also for much of its day to day execution, and even for the construction of organisations to administer controls. . . . Economists of all grades in the service found themselves charged increasingly with executive duties, for both the permanent public servants and the business-men bureaucrats appeared to have little appreciation of the use that could be made of economic advisers as distinct from administrators.'[36] The suggestion that the use of economists had relatively little to do with specialised functions of economic analysis is confirmed by the late Professor Giblin, who was associated with the Commonwealth as an economic adviser for many years. 'The role of the economist in practical matters has generally little to do with economic theory. What they contribute is commonsense judgment based on a fairly objective and complete appreciation of the facts. It is for an appreciation of the facts that economists are required; otherwise their place might almost as well be filled by classical scholars or natural scientists.'[37] The economist, in other words, is highly regarded because he possesses qualities which, in a famous definition, were held to be those of the first-class administrator, i.e. the ability to 'extract the essential points quickly from a mass of material, to present them clearly and concisely, to weigh against each other the various factors in the problem . . . and to form a sound and balanced judgment of the situation as a whole.'[38] It is not only employers in the public service who regard training in economics as being specially valuable for this purpose. Some years ago, a survey by the University of Sydney inquired into the employment of graduates in economics. The answers revealed that, to many employers, the value of training in economics lay in the fact that it was held to give 'training in logical thought', and the ability 'to see all sides of a question'.[39]

This case would appear to bear out Hofstadter's view that a society in which anti-intellectualism is a prominent feature will rationalise its need for trained minds by emphasising the value of the expert as against that of the intellectual. Economists themselves, when they try to have things both ways, express this ideology. Sir John Crawford, one of the most notable of economist-administrators, recently wrote that the 'economic adviser in the Service is of most value when he has the qualities of a good general policy adviser. This is true, but it does not mean that the specialised training an adviser may have in economics is of no use to him. In many situations it

---

[36] E. R. Walker, *The Australian Economy in War and Reconstruction*, Melbourne, 1947, p. 128
[37] L. F. Giblin, *The Growth of a Central Bank*, Melbourne, 1951, p. 262n
[38] Royal Commission on the (British) Civil Service, 1931, Minutes of Evidence, memorandum by the Association of First Division Civil Servants
[39] Report of survey by Faculty of Economics, University of Sydney, 1950

is essential and, in any case, is rarely a handicap. This is the real implication of Professor Giblin's observation.'[40]

Professional Syndicalism

The dominance of professional men is expressed also in a kind of
syndicalism which has the effect of dividing government functions roughly
according to the type of professional man employed in them. Davis
describes the relations of state governments with professional groups as
'informed by a genial pluralism'.[41] Subramaniam, writing about NSW,
observed that the status of professional officers was particularly high and
that in the Professional Division of the state public service, there were
special agreements between professional groups and the Public Service
Board providing separate salary ranges, gradings and standards of
advancement. These arrangements, which strengthen an already dominant
position, make it extremely difficult to realise the recurrent proposals for
recruiting non-specialist graduates as an administrative cadre, and
encourage professional 'affectation' among those graduates who are not
specialists.[42]

The development of self-contained professional groups reinforces existing tendencies to fragmentation. Fragmentation, in its turn, creates serious
difficulties through inbreeding of staff, and the development of narrow and
rigid attitudes towards the responsibilities of government. An American
firm of management consultants, called in to advise on the organisation of
the NSW Department of Railways, wrote that 'there is a lack of training of
the type necessary to produce administrative officers with a broad knowledge of the Department's operation as a whole. Under the present form of
organisation the various branches operate as self contained units and junior
and senior officers lack the opportunity to acquire an overall knowledge
of the system's operation.'[43] State government sometimes appears as a
collection of satrapies, within each of which the internal structure is rigid
and authoritarian. This impression is strengthened by the long list of state
government functions and the enormous range of large and small bodies
concerned to carry them out. Parker estimated a few years ago that there
were at least 500 non-departmental statutory authorities operating in NSW,
all having the common characteristic that the whole of their constitutions,
powers and functions were conferred on them directly by Act of Parliament.[44] The predominance of public utility corporations in state administration, each of them ferociously jealous of their own independence, adds to

[40] Sir John Crawford, 'The Economist in the Public Service', *Public Administration*,
vol. 22, no. 1, 1963
[41] Davis, op. cit., p. 128n
[42] V. A. Subramaniam, 'Promotion', ch. 13
[43] Report by Ebasco Services Incorporated on the Dept. of Railways and the Dept.
of Government Transport, Sydney, 1957, p. 21
[44] Davis, op. cit., p. 146

the general picture. State agencies for conservation and development 'overshadow the rest of the State administration not only as spenders or employers, but also by the intrinsic political liveliness of their work.'[45]

Syndicalism is further encouraged by the activities of trade unions within state government instrumentalities. There are entire unions, operating on a national scale, whose history is solely one of dealing with public employers. Not only does this intensify the importance of syndicalism (both in the general sense already used and in the strict sense), but it also breeds a strongly anti-authoritarian bias in unions of this kind. The Australian Railways Union, the largest of them, has been distinguished for its Left-wing militancy in several states, particularly Victoria and Queensland.[46] The same applies to the Tramways Union, which has been dominated by left-wing officials in Victoria and Western Australia for many years. The Amalgamated Postal Workers Union, the largest of public service staff associations, has an active record of industrial action. The NSW Teachers' Federation, especially since its affiliation to the NSW Labor Council in 1943, is an intensely political body and many of its members have been associated with strongly anti-authoritarian political movements.

Conclusion

Rigid hierarchies based on seniority, rigid preference for the professional man, rigid forms of centralisation, rigid systems of promotion and appeal —the same adjective springs irresistibly and repeatedly to mind on contemplating the history of bureaucratic institutions in Australia. Dislike of bureaucracy is closely bound up with this image of rigidity; and resistance to bureaucratic influence at the present day, although it is a response to specifically modern aspects of bureaucratisation and authoritarianism, rests solidly on a foundation of antipathy rooted in a century of Australian social development.

[45] A. F. Davies, 'Victoria', in ibid., p. 182
[46] L. J. Louis, *Trade Unions and the Depression*, Canberra, 1968

14: The Bureaucratic Structure (2): The Rise of the Meritocracy

The bureaucratic revolution which began in 1939 was of prime importance in altering the nature of political relationships in Australia. Its major impact, as we have seen, was on the Commonwealth, and one of its most interesting aspects was the transformation of the Commonwealth public service from a small and simple institution into a very large and complex one. This transformation was a long and tortuous process in which old-established traditions, values and methods gradually gave way to the principle of meritocracy and its many implications.

The Public Service Personnel System

In the Commonwealth Public Service, as elsewhere, the strength of egalitarian sentiment has been expressed through trade unionism, which in its turn found a potent instrument in the arbitration system. Union pressure was responsible for the introduction of arbitration in 1911, and for its growth into the major locus of decisions about personnel management—a situation which was bitterly and constantly criticised by the first Public Service Commissioner, D. C. McLachlan. McLachlan's successors, though less outspoken, nevertheless found themselves engaged in a constant struggle to assert the views of the central personnel agency—a Commissioner from 1902 to 1922, and a three-man Board thereafter—against the decisions of arbitral tribunals.[1] As Caiden writes, the 'staff associations' in the CPS have achieved a degree of success which has few parallels, especially in attaining full political rights, the almost universal application of arbitration and conciliation, and direct participation in personnel administration. They were able to call upon the services of able leaders, who gave up the prospect of advancement in the official hierarchy to become full-time union officials. In a number of crucial negotiations, they showed more grasp and imagination than their opposite numbers on the official side, and their influence on public service organisation was con-

---

[1] A full account of the tug-of-war between staff associations, arbitrators, Commissioners and Boards is given by G. E. Caiden, *Career Service*, Melbourne, 1965, esp. chs. 4, 5, 7-11, 15-19.

siderable.[2] The Public Service Board, for its part, was unable to assert much authority because its decisions on classification, salaries and conditions were always subject to appeal to the Public Service Arbitrator and, since 1953, to the Commonwealth Arbitration Commission. The introduction, in 1945, of special committees to deal with appeals against promotions means that almost every important aspect of personnel management, except recruitment, was covered by some kind of arbitral tribunal.[3]

The dominant role of arbitration was one of the influences which accounted for the fact that, when war broke out in 1939, the methods of recruiting and promoting officials were still largely the same as those provided in the original Public Service Act of 1902. Under this statute, and its successor Act passed in 1922, recruitment was, on the whole, to be open only to youths who made it their career choice and met the prescribed educational qualifications (which were not unduly high). The framers of the original Act deliberately eschewed any attempt to emulate selective or 'differential' recruitment for senior positions, on the British or French example. In the political and social circumstances at the beginning of the century, this policy was natural enough. By 1939, however, despite a number of minor changes, it did not correspond to the needs of a country struggling with the problems of economic crisis and impending war. Attempts to deal with the problem were largely frustrated by the inertia of the conservative governments which, with one brief interruption, were in power during the inter-war period. As a British mission which visited Australia in 1928 observed in its report, 'our enquiries lead us gravely to doubt whether the system followed in Australia sets out to attract the best available talent.'[4]

At the same time, both the 1902 and 1922 Acts provided for recruitment at higher levels, under the supervision of the Public Board or Commissioner, of persons with special qualifications. In 1920, an outspoken critic of the recruitment system had written that it became more inadequate every year with the growth of administrative functions, but went on to add that 'its defects would be more glaring than they are if the greater freedom of choice allowed for filling technical or professional positions did not furnish a means of introducing into the Service some men of education and proved talent who are then often put into responsible administrative posts.'[5] He was referring to the provisions used for the admission of specialist professional officers for whom the normal system of entry requiring an elementary education did not provide; but in those early days,

[2] ibid., pp. 10-13
[3] For the promotions appeal system, see Caiden, op. cit., ch. 13, and V. A. Subramaniam, 'Promotion in the Commonwealth, NSW and Victorian Public Services', Ph.D. thesis, Australian National University, 1959.
[4] *Report of the British Economic Mission*, Canberra, 1929
[5] Sir W. Harrison Moore, in M. Atkinson (ed.), *Australia: Economic and Political Studies*, Melbourne, 1920, p. 89

as later, their superiority over most of the routine public servants had caused them to be transferred quite soon to purely administrative positions. The first Public Service Commissioner, McLachlan, acknowledged much the same in his 1918 report as a royal commissioner. Although stressing the 'exceptional' character of these methods, he admitted that 'the interests of the service have benefited by this provision . . . a much wider field will be afforded the government for the recruitment of the service by the appointment of persons with special and distinctive qualifications.'[6]

The extent to which senior officials of the CPS were recruited in this way is shown in a study by Scarrow. Between 1901 and 1939, less than half of the men appointed to senior positions had been recruited through the regular examination channels. As a result of lateral appointments, he concluded, 'the higher Public Service was drawn from a broader base than might have been anticipated from the design of the controlling legislation. Nor was it as closed a group as one might have expected, since approximately a third of the lateral recruits were appointed directly to the senior ranks without prior experience in the Commonwealth Service.'[7]

The recruitment system which still operates in the Commonwealth Public Service is geared to a quadripartite divisional structure.[8] The First Division consists of departmental heads and the Second of professional, managerial and policy-advising positions immediately below that level. The total membership of these two divisions was 634 in 1967. The Third Division, with 52,200 members, included not only the bulk of clerical-administrative staff but also professional and technical personnel of all kinds. The Fourth, with 150,000 members, included junior clerical staff, tradesmen, technicians, typists, attendants, etc. Most postal employees belong to this division. Recruitment takes place mostly to the basic grades of the Third and Fourth Divisions, through competitive or qualifying examination. Professional and technical staff, however, are recruited directly on the basis of academic or other qualifications. Until 1933, there was no provision for the recruitment of administrative staff at higher levels. These methods were insufficient to deal with the critical conditions of war and post-war reconstruction, and relief was provided by three sections[9] of

[6] *Report of the Royal Commission on Public Service Administration*, Melbourne, 1918, pp. 35-36

[7] For detailed accounts of the development of recruitment policy and its relation to the organisational structure of the service, see Caiden, op. cit., chs. 2, 5, 8, 11-13, 19; P. W. E. Curtin, 'Recruitment', in Spann, op. cit.; S. Encel, 'The Recruitment of University Graduates to the Commonwealth Public Service', *Public Administration*, London, vol. 32, no. 3, 1954, and 'The CPS and Outside Recruitment', *Public Administration*, vol. 14, no. 1, 1955; R. S. Parker, *Public Service Recruitment in Australia*, Melbourne, 1942; H. A. Scarrow, *The Higher Public Service of the Commonwealth of Australia*, Duke University Press, 1957, chs. 2-4; Subramaniam, op. cit.

[8] Scarrow, op. cit., pp. 100-104

[9] As explained below, an extensive amendment of the Act in 1960 involved the replacement of the clauses listed here.

the Public Service Act, each of them originally designed to deal only with 'exceptional' cases. These were:

(a) Section 47, which provided for 'outside' or 'lateral' appointments, i.e. to positions above the basic grade. The normal provisions for examination, probation and appeal did not apply. Although the clause was inserted chiefly to provide a method of recruiting professional and other specialised personnel, the scope of its use has always been somewhat wider.

(b) Section 44, which had similar provisions, but related specifically to former state government officials.

(c) Section 36A, a clause inserted in 1933 following pressure from the universities for the admission of graduates to the public service. It enabled the appointment of graduates to the basic grade of the Third Division, but at a point close to the top of the long salary range provided for this grade. Up to 1941, it had only been used sparingly, 80 graduates being appointed out of more than 200 applicants.

During the war, normal recruitment was suspended and most appointments were made on a temporary basis. After the end of hostilities, many of the temporary officials who had come from the professions, private business, the universities and state government were appointed permanently through extensive use of Sections 44 and 47. As shown in Scarrow's study, 35 per cent of the 315 officers appointed to senior positions between 1939 and 1952 were 'lateral' recruits, and 14 of them were pre-war recruits under Section 36A. Among the permanent heads of departments, more than 40 per cent were 'lateral' appointees.[10]

These provisions for lateral recruitment alone provided the machinery for admitting to the service the large number of officers with special qualifications demanded by the expansion of Commonwealth government activities. The fact that this method, designed originally for 'exceptional' circumstances, had to be used for large-scale recruitment, evoked a repetition of the criticisms made in the inter-war years. Articles and books on post-war reconstruction made much of this point. L. F. Giblin, a long-time adviser to the Commonwealth government, declared that 'the pre-war policy of keeping all senior jobs in the Government departments as a close preserve for men who have spent all their lives in the service—i.e. permanent officers who may, perhaps, have very few qualifications beyond a familiarity with routine—will have to be abandoned.'[11] Professor Eric Ashby wrote with some bitterness that 'graduates have been drafted wholesale into Commonwealth departments. It was found that their training equipped them to deal with situations requiring foresight and judgment. The "professors" in Government offices became a great joke for the newspapers. Every distasteful decision was laid at their door. Every fantastic regulation was written up against them. When the history of this war comes to be written it will be found that they averted many a crisis.

---

[10] op. cit., pp. 111-12
[11] *Sydney Morning Herald*, 19 September 1944

But they came into the Public Service too late. Some of the crises would never have occurred if the public had listened to the counsels of the professors and had seen the need for graduates in the Public Service before the war.'[12]

For their part, the public service trade unions also reacted strongly to these developments, and pressed repeatedly for guarantees that the rights of permanent officials who had entered the service by traditional methods would be upheld. The official organ of the Commonwealth Public Service Clerical Association asserted in 1948 that 'not only the academic gentlemen who advise the Government, and plan the post-war Australia, are most outspoken in their contempt of permanent officers, but certain Cabinet Ministers who have fallen under the spell of these economic "witch doctors", are addicted to the wholesale appointment of outsiders to selected positions in the Service. . . . The professors, economists, theorists, planners and experts were transported to high government places straight from their universities, books, graphs and diagrams. From there they commenced a campaign designed to discredit the permanent public servant.'[13] Three years later, with a different party in power, whose avowed aim was to reduce administrative costs, the same complaint was heard: 'Because the Service is not efficiently administered, because outside appointees, temporaries, long-hairs, professors, authors, psychologists, advisers and economic witch-doctors have gained control of the Service organisation, the cost of government has become so high that it is now a political issue.'[14] In 1949, a mass meeting of clerical officers was held in Melbourne to protest against the excessive appointment of 'outsiders' and in 1951 a deputation waited on the new Prime Minister, R. G. Menzies, with a similar protest.

The first serious consideration to be given to the possibility of recruiting university graduates as potential members of an 'administrative grade' occurred in New South Wales. In 1911, draft regulations for this purpose were prepared by the state Public Service Board for consideration by the government.[15] In 1918, a royal commissioner, Mr G. M. Allard, revived the proposal, urging that provision be made for graduates who, as soon as they demonstrated their fitness and a proper grasp of their duties, should reach 'a status in accordance with their higher qualifications'.[16] Nothing came of these proposals. In 1925, the universities inaugurated the campaign which culminated in the insertion of Section 36A in the Public Service Act. Sir John Monash, Vice-Chancellor of the University of Melbourne and

---

12 Eric Ashby, *Universities in Australia*, Melbourne, 1943, pp. 31-2
13 *Federal Public Service Journal*, June 1948
14 ibid., August 1951
15 The man responsible was R. F. Irvine, then a senior member of the Board's staff, who later occupied the first chair of economics to be established at an Australian university. See Bruce McFarlane, 'Professor Irvine's Economics in Australian Labor History', monograph of the Australian Society for the Study of Labor History, Canberra, 1966.
16 *Royal Commission on the* NSW *Public Service*, First Report, Sydney, 1918, p. 67

chairman of the Standing Advisory Committee of Universities (later the Australian Vice-Chancellors' Committee), wrote to the Public Service Board in the name of the committee, pointing out the desirability of university education for the higher positions in the CPS.[17] But beyond this one limited amendment, no real changes had been made until, in 1957, the Commonwealth government announced the appointment of a committee of inquiry to examine recruitment standards and processes.[18] Sir Richard Boyer, chairman of the Australian Broadcasting Commission, was appointed to head the committee. One of its members was Professor R. S. Parker, who had argued the case for an 'administrative cadre' in a book published fifteen years earlier.[19]

An International Perspective

The appointment of this committee, even with its limited terms of reference, was a long overdue step. Before considering its recommendations and their subsequent history, it may be helpful to put these developments in broader perspective. The great increase of government responsibilities, experienced by all modern industrialised communities since 1930, has contributed to the growth of the higher levels of the public bureaucracy as one of the 'strategic elites' of modern society.[20] The process puts a strain on established ideas and methods. Moreover, the same general tendency results in organisational forms which are unique to each country. The growth of a bureaucratic elite, itself a form of social differentiation, makes use of established (and developing) patterns of social differentiation, which vary from country to country. Though all large-scale organisations make similar demands, methods of satisfying them differ considerably. The result is a unique blend of organisational and social requirements, which makes the character of public bureaucracies a remarkably good index of the social structure of the communities within which they operate.

In Britain, for example, the principles laid down by the Northcote-Trevelyan report of 1854 have remained operative to this day. The philosophy of this report had its outcome in the 'administrative class' of the British civil service which, until 1968, retained its pre-eminent position despite all the shocks and changes of the last two generations. The

[17] Curtin, loc. cit., gives an account of these moves. It is of some interest that Monash was the former commander of the Australian army corps in France, and C. B. Brudenell White, Chairman of the Public Service Board at the time, had previously been chief of the general staff.

[18] The appointment of this committee came after a succession of demands for a general inquiry into the structure of the CPS. These demands were stimulated by the Hoover report on US machinery of government in 1955, and in 1956 the Parliamentary Public Accounts Committee recommended a 'Hoover-type' investigation. The Board advised against this, but subsequently requested the government for an inquiry into recruitment only.

[19] *Public Service Recruitment in Australia*, ch. 11

[20] Suzanne Keller, *Beyond the Ruling Class*, New York, 1963, chs. 2-3

administrative grades were, from the outset, taken to be part of the governing classes, and their duties regarded as a vocation, not merely a profession. A list of the qualities required of an assistant secretary makes this clear. Officials at this level have always been regarded as advisers to ministers on policy. This entailed ability on the part of the individual official to analyse 'the most important general questions and problems arising out of the work of his branch; seeing their implications for the future as well as for the present, and for the country as a whole as well as for the Department; formulating practicable, and if necessary, detailed proposals for action; foreseeing the probable results of such proposals, including their effect on public opinion; taking responsibility, when required, for their adoption, and organising and supervising their execution'. In the light of these tasks, the personal qualities looked for were: (i) intellectual ability; (ii) businesslike character; (iii) constructive imagination; (iv) clarity of expression; (v) honesty and integrity of convictions; (vi) interest in people and sociability; (vii) vitality and enthusiasm; (viii) flexible mind; (ix) responsibility, loyalty, etc.[21]

Duties, responsibilities and capacities as lofty as these are beyond merely professional requirements, recalling as they do the standards Plato desired in his 'guardians'. The decline of Britain's imperial position, and the chronic problems of the British economy, led to an ever-growing chorus of demand for reform. The Priestley Royal Commission on the civil service (1953-55) called for a new concept of a 'higher civil service'. This could be defined by drawing a 'horizontal management line' across the vertical structure of all the important classes in the service, above which all officials were required to assume 'responsibilities which place them distinctly in the policy-making group.'[22] Only one-third of the 3,000 positions above the line drawn by the commission were filled by members of the administrative class; the rest were mainly professional officers—scientists, engineers, doctors, lawyers.[23]

Since then, various critical analyses of the system have proposed a higher civil service with a mixture of skills of this kind.[24] The Fulton Royal Commission, appointed in 1966, was presented with a number of such proposals, including one from no less a source than the Treasury, based on the concept of 'general management' rather than the traditional notion of administration. The report of the commission, published in June 1968, accepted this philosophy. Its major proposals, adopted by the government,

[21] *Memorandum by the Civil Service Commissioners on the Use of the Civil Service Selection Board in the Reconstruction Competitions*, HMSO, London, 1951. The methods used to test these qualities are also discussed in Cmnd 232, *Recruitment to the Administrative Class of the Home Civil Service*, London, 1958. The best historical account is probably that of Herman Finer, *The British Civil Service*, London, 1937.
[22] Report of the Royal Commission on the Civil Service, London, 1955, para. 358
[23] W. J. M. Mackenzie, 'The Royal Commission on the Civil Service', *Political Quarterly*, vol. 27, no. 2, 1956
[24] e.g. *The Administrators*, Fabian Society, London, 1964; Peter Shore, *Entitled to Know*, London, 1966; Hugh Thomas (ed.), *Crisis in the Civil Service*, London, 1968

included the abolition of the administrative class as a separate entity and its merger with the executive class, i.e. the fusion of 'administrative' and 'managerial' functions. 'The structure and practices of the Service', said the commission, 'have not kept up with the changing tasks.' The remedy was 'to replace the "all-rounder" as he has been called by his champions, or "amateur" as he has been called by his critics', with a much more professional administrator, highly skilled in his job and rigorously trained for it. A staff college was needed with an intensive one-year course in the social sciences, and careful provision should be made to draw specialists into general administration, from which the pre-eminence of the administrative class had largely excluded them.

The United States, with an utterly different civil service tradition, has nevertheless found itself pushed and pulled by similar exigencies. The size and complexity of the US governmental system have produced a loose federation of bureaucratic empires, some of them larger than the entire Commonwealth Public Service. Each major bureau, agency or department is something of a law unto itself, and looks mainly for the peculiar expertise required in its area of operations. The administrative 'generalist', corner-stone of the British tradition, has only a vague and uncertain status as compared with the specialist. The absence of a stratum of such officials became recognised as a serious defect in the system during the New Deal, and from 1934 onwards a series of attempts was made to introduce a method of recruitment and advancement for 'generalists' which would procure for the Americans the advantages of the British administrative class.[25] The most determined attempt to move in this direction arose from the report of the second Hoover Commission of 1953-55. Partly because of the great heterogeneity of the US civil service, the Hoover commission argued that the functions of general administration and co-ordination were correspondingly important. However, the system tended to over-emphasise specialisation to the point where it was an obstacle to efficiency. 'The extension to higher posts of concepts and procedures which were designed for large numbers of standardised positions has been awkward . . . some new concepts, policies and procedures are needed which are designed specifically to supply career administrators at the higher levels.'[26] To meet the case, it recommended the creation of a 'Senior Civil Service', which would encompass the three highest levels, 'super-grades', of the 18-grade American classification system and provide a cadre of senior officials who could readily be moved to various positions as the need arose. This proposal was strongly defended by ex-President Hoover himself, who declared that he would be prepared to see all the other recommendations of the

[25] For an account of these attempts see Paul van Riper, *History of the* US *Civil Service*, Princeton, 1956.
[26] Commission on the Reorganisation of the Executive Branch, Report of the Task Force on Personnel and Civil Service, Washington, 1955

Commission go by the board provided this one was implemented.[27] The scheme was just as strongly resisted, however, by politicians who saw in it a threat to their patronage, and by serving officials anxious to maintain the pre-eminence of the specialist in the system. As C. Wright Mills has pointed out, the structure of power in the United States does not provide for a permanent cadre of senior civil servants, whose presence would obstruct the working of the 'power elite' which he described.[28] The Hoover Commission's proposal, renamed the 'Career Executive Program', was entrusted to a Career Executive Board, which led an uneasy existence until it was finally extinguished in 1960 without achieving anything.

The gap described by the Hoover report remains unfilled, at least by this method. Successive American governments have, however, relied on two other means for recruiting 'generalist' advisers, both of them in the American tradition. One method is denoted by the vast expansion of the White House staff, starting under the New Deal.[29] Franklin D. Roosevelt's 'brain trust' introduced the principle of a large circle of policy consultants occupying administrative positions in Washington, and although the principle suffered a setback under Truman and Eisenhower, it reasserted itself even more strongly under John F. Kennedy and his successors. In 1937, the Brownlow Committee on Administrative Management proposed the appointment of six Presidential special assistants with a 'passion for anonymity'. From this modest proposal has grown the enormous White House staff which provoked much criticism under Eisenhower, but nevertheless continued to grow under his successors. The second means has been the remarkable partnership between the federal government on the one hand, and universities and research institutes on the other. This partnership has led to the growth of a kind of 'external bureaucracy' whose members serve the government as advisers and consultants without actually becoming civil servants, although a number of them have served for limited periods in government agencies.[30] The system has, of course,

[27] The Hoover Commission proposals are discussed by Leonard White, *Introduction to Public Administration*, 4th ed., New York, 1955, chs. 21-25; Paul van Riper, 'The Senior Civil Service and the Career System', *Public Administration Review*, vol. 18, no. 3, 1958; W. Pincus, 'Opposition to the Senior Civil Service', ibid., no. 4, 1958.
[28] C. Wright Mills, *The Power Elite*, London, 1956, pp. 237-40
[29] Accounts of American governmental history since 1933 are legion. An outstanding analysis of the whole period from Roosevelt to Johnson is given by Louis Heren, *The New American Commonwealth*, New York, 1968. Special interest attaches to Louis A. Brownlow's autobiography, *A Passion for Politics* and *A Passion for Anonymity*, Chicago, 1955 and 1958; A. M. Schlesinger's *The Coming of the New Deal*, New York, 1960; Marian D. Irish, 'The Organisation Man in the Presidency', *Journal of Politics*, vol. 20, no. 2, 1958; and Theodore Sorensen, *Kennedy*, New York, 1965.
[30] C. F. Alger, 'The External Bureaucracy in US Foreign Affairs', *Administrative Science Quarterly*, vol. 6, no. 1, 1962, describes one aspect of this system. Another aspect, science policy, is described by J. S. Dupré and S. A. Lakoff, *Science and the Nation*, Boston, 1962, and by R. Gilpin and C. Wright (eds.), *Scientists and National Policy Making*, New York, 1964.

aroused a good deal of hostility and suspicion, mostly from academics,[31] but not exclusively. Ex-President Eisenhower was clearly referring to it when, in his farewell speech in 1961, he warned his countrymen against the influence of the 'scientific-technological elite'.

The United States, like Britain, has tried to adapt its traditional institutions to the special needs of the present era. A similar process has taken place in France, another country with a long and distinctive tradition of public administration. The French administrative system, whose essential lines were laid down in the Napoleonic era, has always operated through a series of specialised *corps*, each constituting a virtually closed system, and linked with the *grandes écoles*, also dating from the eighteenth century, of which the two most important are the *Ecole Normale Supérieure* and the *Ecole Polytechnique*. Another major source of recruitment into the higher civil service was the *Ecole Libre des Sciences Politiques* (*'Sciences Po'*), a private institution established in Paris in 1874. Three of the *corps*— *Conseil d'Etat, Cour des Comptes* and *Inspection des Finances*—have been known collectively as the *grands corps d'état* since the beginning of the century. Their members were drawn overwhelmingly from this small group of elite educational institutions, which in turn drew their students largely from the Parisian upper-middle classes. Again, the inner circle of senior officials—e.g. the staffs of the personal ministerial offices or *cabinets* which are a key part of the French governmental system—are drawn largely from the three *grands corps*; under the Fourth Republic, the proportion was about two-thirds.[32]

The reforms initiated in 1945 represented a simultaneous attempt to break down the segmented character of French administration and to democratise recruitment into the higher civil service, whose undemocratic character has been a staple topic of social criticism in France as in Britain. Two new classes of 'generalist' officials were introduced, patterned on the British model and called *administrateurs civils* and *executifs*. The *Ecole Libre des Sciences Politiques* was nationalised and became part of the University of Paris; similar institutes were also set up at major provincial universities. A national academy for higher administration, the *Ecole Nationale d'Administration*, was established, with recruitment open both to serving officials and new recruits. The aim of the ENA was to provide a central system of recruitment and training for higher administration, and its elaborate three-year training program is the most rigorous of its kind in the world.

In France, as in USA, the entrenched characteristics of the system have resisted this kind of logical reform. Entry into the ENA is still dominated by *Sciences Po*, under its new title of *Institut des Etudes Politiques*, and the students of *Sciences Po* are still drawn mainly from the Parisian middle

[31] See, e.g., Loren Baritz, *The Servants of Power*, New York, 1958, and I. L. Horowitz, *The Rise and Fall of Project Camelot*, Boston, 1967.
[32] A. D. de Lamothe, 'Ministerial Cabinets in France', *Public Administration,* London, vol. 43, no. 4, 1965

classes. Although the *grands corps* no longer recruit their own higher officials, the best graduates of ENA still elect to join the corps, and the government continues to select departmental heads (not to mention, under the Fifth Republic, a large number of ministers) from members of the corps. The 'ENA man' has become recognised as an up-to-date type of technocrat, attuned to the needs of the planned economy; in this sense, he represents a continuation of the established way of doing things.[33]

The Triumph of Meritocracy

The appointment of the Boyer committee on recruitment to the CPS was the first important step in a succession of moves which have gradually brought about a radical change in the structure of higher administration. It was also the first systematic attempt to deal with the Topsy-like situation which had become increasingly confused since 1939.

The expansion of the service from 1939 onwards had led to a proliferation of new grades which were grafted into the old framework, often with confusing results. A notable example was the category of 'research officer', introduced shortly before the war and used extensively during the war and post-war periods. In theory, this designation was to apply to non-technical university graduates, recruited through Section 36A of the Public Service Act or some similar method. (About 700 were so recruited between 1948 and 1960, when the Act was extensively amended.) Research officers were supposed to collect information related to policy and generally to raise the intellectual tone of the service. In practice, the designation was used for a wide variety of jobs filled by people with widely varying qualifications and experience. It also turned out to be a convenient way of promoting (or sidetracking) individual officials when the traditional hierarchy created difficulties. Another device used repeatedly was the reclassification of positions in entire departments or sections of departments, which led to a bewildering range of slightly different descriptions and salary ranges for similar jobs. On the professional side, for example, there were no less than fourteen grades of engineer before the Commonwealth Arbitration Commission handed down the professional engineers' award of 1961; subsequently, the Public Service Board was able to consolidate them into six.

The drawbacks of this situation were well known to the Board, which made several attempts to deal with them during the 1950's. The appointment of the Boyer committee came at a time when recruitment problems

---

[33] Various aspects of French administrative history since 1945 are examined by Roger Grégoire, *La Fonction Publique*, Paris, 1954; Philip Williams, *Crisis and Compromise*, 3rd ed., London, 1964; T. Feyzioglu, 'The Reforms of the French Higher Civil Service', *Public Administration*, London, vol. 33, nos. 1 and 2, 1955; Henry Parris, 'Twenty Years of l'Ecole Nationale D'Administration', ibid., vol. 43, no. 4, 1965. A comprehensive picture is given by F. Ridley and J. Blondel, *Public Administration in France*, London, 1964.

were particularly acute also for demographic reasons.[34] The committee's report, published in November 1958, analysed the growth in size and complexity of the service, pointed out the discrepancies between its actual structure and the formal statutory framework, unchanged since 1922, and recommended the rationalisation or abolition of many of the expedients which had passed for policy since 1939. It paid special attention to the problems of higher administration. The report doubted whether the Service was geared to obtain its fair share of administrative talent. 'If the Commonwealth Service is to obtain its proper share of such people, it will require an energetic, co-ordinated, courageous and continuous policy of recruitment and staff development . . . we are not satisfied that existing legislation, traditions and practices enable the Service to attract enough of the best brains or to make in all cases the best use of them' (paras. 120, 121). One danger of the existing situation was that 'because of uneven levels of ability among its senior advisers, the Government is forced to depend disproportionately on a few officials who are outstandingly able, but necessarily represent a limited range of opinion and outlook' (para. 111).

The committee's remedy was to make recruitment more attractive and advancement more systematic. The Second Division was to be transformed into an administrative division, much along the lines of the administrative class of the British civil service. It was to include officials who were 'required to exercise administrative or executive functions in the more important offices of the Service, and officers in training to exercise such functions' (para. 130). Administration, in its turn, was defined as consisting of 'policy-advising' and 'managerial' functions (para. 107). Recruitment into this new Second Division was to be largely by competitive examination of the 'house party' type[35] open to both internal and external candidates. Thus, instead of being 'end on' to the Third Division, and accessible by promotion, the Second Division would become a parallel but much more exclusive hierarchy. It was this feature of the proposal, with its obvious affinities to the British civil service, that aroused great resistance within the Service. It is ironical, in retrospect, that the committee should

[34] The post-depression years, 1930 to 1940, caused a sharp kink in the Australian population structure, due to the combined effect of a fall in the birthrate and the virtual cessation of immigration. In addition, the CPS suffered from governmental economies, including cuts in recruitment and the abandonment of long-term policies formulated by the Board in the 1920's. The decade 1950-60 was one of great difficulty in recruiting school leavers. In general, the dislocations of the inter-war period produced an unbalanced age structure in the CPS whose effects were expected to last well into the 1980's (32nd Report of the Public Service Board, 1955-6).

[35] The nickname of 'house party' arose from the methods used in Britain after 1945 by the Civil Service Selection Board, involving psychological tests and simulated work situations as well as conventional written papers. Until 1950, the tests were actually held at a country house at Stoke d'Abernon, in Surrey. For details of the CISSB system, see reference 21 above.

have lavished such praise on the British system just a decade before the British decided to abandon it.

The committee also proposed that recruitment to the Third Division should become more competitive, and that a public service selection test should be introduced to discriminate between entrants 'according to intellectual ability, specific aptitude and potential capacity for undertaking the higher classes of work in the Third Division' (para. 149). The various provisions for 'lateral' entry were to be recast, and separated from the recruitment of professional and technical staff. Fourth Division recruitment standards were also to be raised. The committee also, in passing, recommended the abolition of the marriage bar which meant that women officials automatically lost their permanent status and prospects of advancement on marriage.

The general response to this part of the report was a mixture of lukewarmness and hostility—lukewarmness on the part of the government, the Public Service Board and the Treasury, outright hostility on the part of the public service staff associations.[36] The Professional Officers' Association, in a memorandum to the Board, opposed the formation of a new administrative division because professional officers, on whose advice policy depended, would be downgraded and their promotion opportunities restricted. The Administrative and Clerical Officers' Association was more florid in its criticisms. Its official statement declared that 'a close study of the report discloses no evidence that the present system of recruitment to clerical and administrative positions in the Service have [sic] failed or are inadequate.' The proposal reflected 'an imported philosophy of administration which can be blamed for many of the national disasters now occurring in other continents. . . . The whole idea of an administrative class of bureaucrats is an anathema to Australians.'[37] The ACOA's New South Wales branch declared that the report was the work of 'snobs, politicians, titled gentry, university professors, big business magnates and the like', and its secretary declared in a press interview that the proposal would fill the CPS with 'pukka sahibs'.[38]

After two years' delay, the Menzies government finally introduced a Public Service Bill which became law in December, 1960. Sections 33 to 47A of the 1922 Act were repealed and replaced by a totally new set of clauses dealing with recruitment. The proposal for a new administrative division was rejected in the Prime Minister's second reading speech, and action on a number of other recommendations was suspended.[39] Sir Robert Menzies declared briefly that although the government supported the Boyer committee's objectives, its methods 'would not be suitable in the present circumstances of the Australian civil service'.

It was not long, however, before the whole matter was reopened, from

---

[36] G. E. Caiden, *Career Service*, pp. 419-21
[37] *Federal Public Service Journal*, April, 1959
[38] *Sydney Morning Herald*, 21 February 1959
[39] The marriage bar, for instance, remained until 1966.

a source unexpected at the time but utterly traditional—namely, an arbitration tribunal. In 1961 and 1962, the Commonwealth Arbitration Commission handed down awards in the two Professional Engineers' cases, which between them disrupted the entire structure of pay, classification and promotion in the Second and Third divisions of the CPS.[40] The Commission decided that engineering was a learned profession and that engineers should be paid accordingly. The resulting salary increase destroyed the relativities of engineers with other professional groups such as scientists, legal officers, architects and medical officers; it meant that engineers in senior grades were now paid more than their administrative superiors (also engineers by training); and it gave engineers in the Second Division higher salaries than most other Second Division officials.

These events occurred shortly after a change of leadership in the Public Service Board. Sir William Dunk, who had been chairman since 1947, retired in 1960 and made way for a very different man, F. H. (now Sir Frederick) Wheeler, who returned from an international post to take the position.[41] Dunk's period of office, although it had seen a number of improvements in the organisation of the CPS, was marked on the whole by inability to cope with basic questions like those examined in the Boyer report. His contribution lay in 'unobtrusive unspectacular advances on all fronts against heavy odds achieved by a consummate skill in balancing conflicting pressures. Formally he was nobody's friend and everybody's enemy, torn between the desirable and the attainable. . . . What finally emerged was based on compromises dictated by expediency.'[42] His successor was a very different man, with intellectual attainments of a high order, a tough and patient negotiator, attached to first principles, and with a great deal of sophistication about industrial relations and personnel management gained during his years at Geneva. Whereas Dunk had been lukewarm about the Boyer report, foreseeing only the difficulties, Wheeler persuaded his colleagues to accept its principles, and a revision of the structure (indicated in PSB circular no. 35 of 1961) had already begun before the first Engineers' case was decided. The Board now redoubled its efforts and enlisted the aid of academic students of public administration, who wrote several memoranda supplementing the arguments of the Boyer committee, and drawing attention to overseas developments such as the report of the Priestley commission. The Board's acceptance of these arguments was denoted in a further circular (PSB Information

---

[40] S. Encel, 'Social Implications of the Engineers' Cases', *Journal of Industrial Relations*, vol. 6, no. 1, 1964
[41] Wheeler, an economist by training, joined the Treasury as a research officer in 1939. During the 1939-45 war and the reconstruction period, he was one of the most influential figures at the Treasury, and was particularly close to J. B. Chifley, Treasurer from 1941 to 1949. In 1952, he took leave from the CPS and became Treasurer of the ILO in Geneva. See L. F. Crisp, *Ben Chifley*, Melbourne, 1961, chs. 14, 17-20.
[42] Caiden, op. cit., p. 423

Bulletin no. 5, 1962), which declared that all positions above a certain level have a managerial or policy-making character.

Following the second engineers' award in 1962, a third case was scheduled to deal with 'executive engineers' in the Second Division. In May 1963, the Board applied for this case to be joined with a general hearing concerning all positions in the Second Division. In its application, the Board declared:

Policy advising and top management is a distinctive and integrated function and even where a top management job does have professional or technical content the choice of appointees should in high degree be on the basis of administrative and managerial abilities.

The Second Division case opened before a full Bench of the Arbitration Commission in November 1963. In March 1964, the Bench accepted the Board's proposals, involving the reduction of the existing seventeen salary levels to six. It agreed that the new situation called for a new structure, with markedly different lines of responsibility, and with salaries fixed on the basis of 'broad-banding'.[43] The Commission, with only a slight change of syntax, accepted the Board's view that 'policy advising and top management are a distinctive and integrated function.'[44] The Board, applauding this decision, declared that the time had come to 'develop the Second Division more fully and more positively as an integral part of top administration and management . . . [and] to increase the awareness of Second Division officers of their corporate identity and of their corporate role in contributing to the processes of government.' There was 'an evolutionary process towards crystallising the Second Division as a corps of top administrators and/or managers.'[45] A year later, the Board referred again to its 'philosophy of the Second Division as an integrated corps of the top administrators and/or managers.'[46]

In a public address given in May 1964, Wheeler himself repeated these statements and glossed them by declaring that 'even where a Second Division position has professional or technical content, the choice of appointees should, in high degree, be on the basis of administrative and managerial abilities. . . . It is our hope that the more explicit and systematic recognition of the Second Division as a "top administration and/or management" team will emphasise the common element in the working environment of senior administrators.'[47]

[43] Broad-banding, a term used in Britain since the second world war and sanctified by the Priestley commission, entails wide salary ranges covering the same official position, giving flexibility in recruitment and transfer. In the CPS, by contrast, a multiplicity of narrow, overlapping ranges has been customary for many years.
[44] 40th Report of the Public Service Board, 1963-64, p. 10
[45] ibid., p. 9
[46] 41st Report of the PSB, 1964-5, p. 11
[47] F. H. Wheeler, 'The Responsibilities of the Administrator in the Public Service', *Public Administration*, vol. 23, no. 4, 1964. The corporate identity of the Second Division was reinforced by the formation of a Second Division Association in 1966.

The quantitative effects of this redefinition of 'administrative and/or managerial' functions have been considerable. At the outbreak of the 1939-45 war, the First and Second Divisions totalled 126 men, in a service of 47,000. The Second Division, with 114, consisted mostly of professional and managerial positions, and the highest paid officers were all professional men; the five most senior professional officers in the Second Division were paid more than most permanent heads. The number of officials with 'policy advising' responsibilities was no more than 25. At the time of the engineers' cases (i.e. 30 June 1962) there were 362 positions in the two highest divisions (337 in the Second), which was a slight proportionate *decrease* over 1939, reflecting the discrepancy between the formal structure and the actual division of responsibilities. By 1964, the number of positions in the Second Division had grown to 513, and in 1967 to 591. In proportion, the Second Division was 0·24 per cent of the CPS in 1939, compared with 0·4 per cent in 1967, and perhaps one-third of its members were in 'policy advising' positions at the latter date.

The proposal of the Boyer committee that there should be direct recruitment into the Second Division has not been realised, nor is it likely to be. Nevertheless, the influence of Wheeler has also been felt in this sphere. In 1963, the Board introduced a new scheme for recruiting 'administrative trainees'.[48] The scheme, according to the official account, is 'planned to give graduates seeking generalist careers in administration a broad outlook in their approach to their careers and to prepare them for accelerated assimilation into the normal work of the Service.'[49] The annual intake is approximately twenty, chosen by examination and interview from all over Australia. They are appointed to the commencing clerical grade, but with allowances for their degrees in addition to the basic salary. Following a preparatory course of lectures and discussions in Canberra, they are employed in rotation through various departments, and in the third phase are posted on personal attachment to a senior officer, usually of Second Division status, for at least five months. (Sir Frederick Wheeler has made a point of acting as mentor to one or two trainees during this last period.)

The scheme has succeeded in attracting trainees of considerable intellectual quality. Of the 1965 intake, nine were honours graduates. Thirteen were graduates in Arts, six in Economics, and two in Science. The 'understudy' phase of the training scheme means that they come to the notice of senior officials at an early stage, and a sizeable proportion of each intake are regularly offered promotions within the departments to which they are posted. Most of those who complete the one-year training program are promoted soon afterwards. It is reasonable to assume that a high proportion of them will become attached to 'policy advising' officials in the Second Division and in due course will be strongly represented in such

---

[48] J. C. Conway, 'Training for Generalist Graduates by the Public Service Board', *Public Administration*, vol. 22, no. 4, 1963
[49] Public Service Board, *Graduate Training Programme*, Canberra, 1965

positions. One or two departments, such as Trade and Industry, operate similar departmental schemes, but the long term likelihood is that they will be absorbed into the central program. Finally, the Board has given greater stress to university education by providing special allowances for graduates employed on clerical/administrative duties. In February 1966, differential rates were fixed giving a pass graduate a salary of $3,000 and a first-class honours graduate $3,390.

Thus, the bureaucratic revolution has bred its counterpart in the bureaucratic career structure, the principle of meritocracy. If the establishment of the principle has been a long and tortuous process, beset with paradoxes and conflicts, these are readily ascribed to the reluctance of a self-consciously egalitarian and individualist society to accept the need for hierarchies of authority, status and skill in its midst. In particular, we may note the recession of egalitarian influence; the challenge to the supremacy of the expert, itself related indirectly to egalitarian assumptions; the growth of education as an indicator of social status; and the exploitation of arbitration as a method of establishing and entrenching occupational and social differentials. These factors have contributed to the gradual emergence of an elaborate hierarchy within a system permeated by a spirit of opposition to the growth of hierarchical tendencies, and as such they provide a virtual paradigm for the processes of social change in Australia since 1939.

15: The Bureaucratic Structure (3): The New Elite

Recruitment and Careers

The effects of the bureaucratic revolution just described may be seen in the personnel of the 'higher public service' which had its beginnings in the 1939-45 war and has developed steadily ever since. The data reported in this chapter are the results of two surveys of senior Commonwealth public servants conducted in 1956 and 1961.[1] In the latter year there were, altogether, 363 officials in the First and Second Divisions of the CPS. The survey yielded 278 replies, i.e. 77 per cent. The survey group of 363 included some senior men then classified as Third Division officers (a situation changed by the Second Division reorganisation of 1964), but it omitted some members of the diplomatic service who had never held positions of administrative responsibility.

An analysis of geographical origins recalls, firstly, the long-standing historical connection between Commonwealth administration and the city of Melbourne. Because of interstate jealousy at the time of federation, the centre of Commonwealth government was originally established at Melbourne, until the constitutional requirement of a new federal capital inside the state of NSW, but more than 150 miles from Sydney, could be fulfilled. Canberra, officially chosen in 1913, did not become the seat of the federal parliament until 1927, and even then some departments remained in Melbourne. Depression and war postponed their transfer still further, and during the 1939-45 war the importance of Melbourne continued to grow because new wartime departments were established there. In 1961, eight out of twenty-four departments still had their head offices in Melbourne. Victoria is consequently over-represented in Table 15·1, which compares the distribution of birthplaces among our sample with the distribution of population at the census of 1911, which is the date corresponding to the median age of the sample.

Compared with the earlier survey carried out in 1956, the importance of Victoria has declined; at the earlier date 49 per cent of senior officials were born there. This decline has continued since 1961, as shown by the recruitment of university graduates from whom the great majority of senior

---

1 The results of the earlier survey are reported in S. Encel, 'Recruitment and Careers of Higher Officials', *Public Administration*, vol. 18, no. 1, 1959.

officials of the future will be drawn. Since the middle 1950's, a disproportionately large number of these graduate recruits have come from NSW.
Between them, these two largest states will continue to dominate the higher
ranks of the service, as they do those of private industry. Unlike the USA,
mobility between urban centres is relatively uncommon, and the Sydney-
Canberra-Melbourne axis is correspondingly important, especially as the
two state capitals are the largest centres of administrative activity outside
Canberra.

Table 15·1 Geographical Origins of Public Servants

	% of sample	Population in 1911 (%)
New South Wales	22·2	29
Victoria	42·0	37
Other states and territories	27·4	34
Overseas	8·4	—
	100·0	100

An urban/rural bias is also apparent. In 1911, 55 per cent of the population lived in 'urban' areas, i.e. local government areas with a population
of 3,000 or more. Within this urban majority the largest group were
'metropolitan' residents, i.e. 38 per cent of the total population. By comparison, 70 per cent of our public servants were born in urban, and 52
per cent in metropolitan districts. Since then, urbanisation has increased so
that the 1966 census showed 58 per cent of the population living in
metropolitan areas, but the recruitment of graduates from metropolitan
districts appears to have increased even faster.

The geographical bias towards the larger states is considerably greater
than in the United States and Canada, both federations which are spread
over a huge geographical area. Bendix found that higher officials of the
US civil service came overwhelmingly from small or medium-sized towns;
41 per cent were born in towns with less than 2,500 inhabitants. A similar
pattern, though less marked, was found in a later study by Warner and his
collaborators.[2] In Canada, Porter found that Ontario was over-represented,
Quebec and the more remote provinces under-represented, although not
for the same reasons in each case.[3] In Canada, the demographic imbalance
is deliberately corrected by lateral appointment or 'jobbing in', which is
much more difficult under Australian conditions.

The rapid expansion of the CPS since 1939 and mobility within the
system are reflected in the comparatively youthful character of the sample
shown in Table 15·2.

[2] R. Bendix, *The Higher Civil Service in American Society*, Boulder, Colorado,
1949; W. L. Warner, et al., *The American Federal Executive*, New York, 1964
[3] John Porter, *The Vertical Mosaic*, Toronto, 1965

Table 15·2 Ages of Public Servants

	1956 %	1961 %
Under 41	14	10
41-45	16	19
46-50	11	25
51-55	13	15
56-60	25	15
61-65	21	16
	100	100

The 1956 distribution reflects both the pre-war age structure and the recruitment of a large number of men in their thirties and forties into the service during the war, whereas the 1961 distribution is much more indicative of the post-war situation, with 54 per cent of the sample aged 50 or less, and only 31 per cent aged fifty-six or over, compared with 46 per cent in 1956. Among the 1961 group, 45 per cent had been appointed to the Second Division below the age of forty, compared with 31 per cent of the 1956 group.

We have already remarked that the archetypal public service career of telegraphic messenger to Director-General, which always contained a large element of myth, has become further and further removed from the truth. This shows in Table 15·3, which classifies the methods by which members of our sample were recruited to the CPS. I have distinguished between recruitment at the telegraph messenger level (i.e. Junior Postal Officer), the recruitment of graduates under the former Section 36A of the Public Service Act, the 'lateral' recruitment of people in other occupations, and the two principal levels of recruitment at the lower end of the administrative hierarchy, i.e. the Third and Fourth Divisions. The last column shows the normal incidence of recruitment at these levels to the CPS in a typical year (1956-57 was used).

Table 15·3 Recruitment of Higher Public Servants

	1956 %	1961 %	Normal recruitment
Junior Postal Officer	14	10	} 78
Fourth Division	3	3	
Third Division	25	23	7·2
'Lateral'	48	49	4·2
Section 36A	7	8	0·1
Other	3	7	10·5
	100	100	100·0

An incidental result of this recruitment pattern is the distribution of ages among new recruits to the CPS. The normal pattern means that 85 per cent of recruits to the service enter it between the ages of fourteen and seventeen, whereas over 40 per cent of the 'higher public service' entered it over the age of twenty-one. In 1956, 27 per cent of the sample entered the service between the ages of twenty-one and thirty, and in 1961, 20 per cent. With the passage of time and the retirement of the large number of officials recruited during the war and post-war reconstruction periods, the 21-30 age group will undoubtedly predominate at the recruitment level.

The recruitment pattern is linked with occupational history before entry to the CPS. Nearly one-third of our sample, eighty-four in all, were recruited after pursuing professional careers for some years. The largest group represented were lawyers (nineteen), followed by engineers (seventeen), academics (fifteen), scientific workers (twelve), medical practitioners (nine) and journalists (six). Some of these had been professional officers in the states or in the United Kingdom. Seventeen had had careers in private industry, and six in the armed services; eight were former schoolteachers. This occupational pattern is reflected in educational background on recruitment. In 1961, 52 per cent of the sample had university degrees on entering the CPS, compared with 50 per cent in 1956. If former state officials are excluded, the proportions are 47 per cent in 1961 and 40 per cent in 1956. Another 5 per cent, in 1961, had other tertiary qualifications on recruitment. Among those with degrees on entry to the service, the largest number were Arts graduates (thirty-seven), followed by law (twenty-four), engineering (nineteen), economics or commerce (nineteen), science (thirteen), medicine (eleven). As compared with 1956, there was an upward trend of Arts graduates (twenty-six in 1956, out of a total sample of 280). There was also an upward trend in the number taking university courses after entry to the service (58 in the 1961 group compared with 44 in the 1956 group). At the other end of the educational scale, there was a decline in the proportion of those who entered the CPS with no more than a primary education; from 14 per cent in 1956 to 8 per cent in 1961.

Table 15·4 Social Origin of Higher Public Servants

Father's Occupational Group	1947 census %	Graduate recruits %	Rest of sample %	Total sample %
Rural	17·9	5·0	13·0	10·0
Professional, semi-professional, administrative and business	9·1	50·0	13·0	27·0
Commercial and clerical	16·4	37·0	38·0	35·0
Domestic and protective	6·4	—	6·0	6·0
Craftsmen	20·0	4·0	20·0	16·0
Operatives and labourers	27·2	4·0	10·0	6·0
Other	3·0	—	—	—
	100·0	100·0	100·0	100·0

The relation between education and social background has been discussed at length in earlier chapters, and is exemplified here in terms of father's occupation, private schooling, and university education, which are highly correlated. Table 15·4 shows the relation between the census breakdown of occupations, the occupations of the fathers of the men in our sample, and the occupations of those who entered government service as graduates.

These figures are virtually identical with a similar breakdown for the 1956 survey. Both surveys, of course, reflect the pre-war pattern of socio-educational differentiation, and by 1980, when the post-1939 situation is clearly in evidence, it may be expected that a different table would be obtained. So far, the role of government employment as an avenue of social mobility is clearly restricted to the white-collar occupations. It is relevant to note that 19 per cent of the sample were sons of government employees, most of them in minor clerical positions.

Schooling follows a similar pattern. Among the 131 men who were graduates at the point of recruitment, two-thirds had been educated at private secondary schools, and one-half had attended private schools at both the primary and secondary levels (excluding Catholic schools, which are separately considered at the end of this chapter). Among the group as a whole, 23 per cent had received their entire education, and 48 per cent their secondary education, at Protestant private schools. By comparison, 5 per cent of the school population at the last pre-war census, in 1933, had been attending schools of this kind. The 1956 survey showed a similar pattern, with a slightly higher proportion whose entire education had been private (27 per cent). Predictably, HMC schools were strongly represented. In 1956, seventy-two of the total sample of 280 had attended HMC schools, compared with seventy-nine of the 1961 group. In both cases, a small group of leading schools stood out. In 1956, six schools accounted for forty-two of the seventy-two HMC pupils—Wesley College, Melbourne (thirteen); Scotch College, Melbourne (twelve); Melbourne Grammar School (five); Brisbane Grammar School (four); Geelong Grammar School (four); Sydney Grammar School (four). In 1961, the rank order had changed, with six schools accounting for fifty-seven of the seventy-nine HMC pupils—Scotch College (twelve); Wesley College (ten); Brisbane Grammar (eight); Melbourne Grammar (seven); Geelong Grammar (five); Trinity Grammar School, Melbourne (five).

Special interest attaches to the educational background of recruits to the diplomatic service (which includes the senior administrative staff of the Department of External Affairs). In the 1961 sample, eleven were Rhodes scholars, of whom seven were in the diplomatic service. According to the recruitment records of the Department, a total of fourteen Rhodes scholars was recruited in the period 1942-62. Among 201 entrants to the diplomatic service in that period, fifty came from private schools.[4] Geelong

---

4 I am indebted to Sir Arthur Tange, formerly secretary of the Department of External Affairs, for these details. In the United States, McCamy has shown the disproportionate influence of the big north-eastern universities in the Foreign Service (J. L. McCamy, *The Administration of American Foreign Affairs*, New York, 1950, ch. 8).

Grammar School led the field with twenty-two recruits, followed by Melbourne Grammar (eleven), Sydney CEGS (Shore) with eight, and Scotch College, Melbourne, also with eight. The differences between the various state educational systems are clearly reflected. Of seventy recruits from Victoria, sixty-two were from private schools; out of sixty-five from NSW, only just over half (thirty-five) were from private schools, and the two largest groups came from state schools—Sydney Boys High School (eleven) and North Sydney Boys High School (nine). The leading role of Geelong Grammar is partly a reflection of the incidence of applications to join the diplomatic service, and partly an indication that this school appears to have particular success in producing the characteristics which the Department seeks among its applicants.

The New Elite

The growth of the new bureaucratic elite highlights one of the major areas of social change in Australia since 1939. As in other countries, the development of this elite has not occurred in a social vacuum but has multiple links with the existing structure of class, status and power. Comparisons with studies made in the United States, Britain, France and Sweden show a similar picture. Australia contrasts with them only in the extent to which the sons of white-collar workers and craftsmen have been able to enter the higher public service, although it differs little from Sweden in this respect.[5]

The growth of the new elite means, among other things, a qualitative change in the structure of political power and influence, making it more centralised, more bureaucratic (*ipso facto*) and vastly more dependent on expert advice and official opinion. It is still possible for a Prime Minister to treat senior officials in an off-hand fashion which would be unlikely to occur in Britain or Western Europe,[6] but would raise no eyebrows in the United States or Canada. Nevertheless, the days are long past when a minister would publicly refer to officials by the contemptuous title of 'gilt spurred roosters', as did the eccentric Mr King O'Malley, Minister for Home Affairs in the Labor government of 1910-13.

A notable forcing house for individuals who later occupied positions of influence in other spheres was the Department of Post-War Reconstruction, already mentioned in an earlier chapter. The presiding genius of this

[5] Warner, et al., op. cit.; R. K. Kelsall, *Higher Civil Servants in Britain*, London, 1955; T. B. Bottomore, 'La Mobilité Sociale dans la Haute Administration Française', *Cahiers Internationaux de Sociologie*, vol. 13, 1952; I. D. Dick, 'Graduates in Administration', *NZ Journal of Public Administration*, September 1957; Olof Loefberg, 'The Recruitment of Civil Servants in the Swedish Administration', *International Review of Administrative Sciences*, vol. 23, no. 4, 1957
[6] The *Australian*, 12 March 1968, describes the cavalier treatment by the new Prime Minister, Mr Gorton, of the head of his own department, Sir John Bunting. For a detailed discussion of the political role of senior Commonwealth officials, see G. E. Caiden, *The Commonwealth Bureaucracy*, ch. 8.

remarkable agency, which existed from 1942 to 1950, was Dr H. C. Coombs, whose influence on economic and social policy flowed from one of the most remarkable bureaucratic careers in Australian history. Born in Western Australia in 1905, he worked as schoolteacher and wharf labourer during the depression years, became an economist with the Commonwealth Bank and in 1942 was appointed Director of Rationing. In 1943, he moved to Post-War Reconstruction, where he remained until his appointment as Governor of the Commonwealth Bank in 1949, a position which he retained for nineteen years. In 1954, he was largely responsible for the establishment of the Australian Elizabethan Theatre Trust, a project which had originated in the Department of Post-War Reconstruction. On his retirement from the Reserve Bank in 1968, he took up two new positions, as head of a council on the performing arts and of a council on aboriginal affairs. Dr Coombs' influence on public affairs has been deep and wide, and will doubtless be appreciated only when his biography comes to be written.

One of Dr Coombs' principal subordinates at the Department of Post-War Reconstruction, Sir John Crawford, had a career scarcely less notable than that of his ex-boss. The son of a coalminer, Crawford was first a schoolteacher and then an economist on the staff of the Rural Bank of NSW. Like so many others, he joined the service of the Commonwealth government after 1939, and after working at Post-War Reconstruction became the first director of the Bureau of Agricultural Economics. He was then appointed head of the Department of Commerce and Agriculture and its successor, the Department of Trade, which he left in 1960 to go into academic life as Director of the Research School of Pacific Studies at the Australian National University, of which he became vice-chancellor in 1967. Among other things, he was the architect of the new trading relationship between Australia and Japan which was ushered in by the trade treaty of 1957, and he was actively concerned with the development of relations with other Asian countries, notably India and Indonesia.

Other members of the department who went on to make their mark included various professors, including L. F. Crisp (political science) and T. W. Swan and G. G. Firth (economics). Ten became permanent heads of other Commonwealth departments, including Sir Allen Brown (Prime Minister's), J. W. Burton (External Affairs—later a teacher of international relations at University College, London), and A. C. B. Maiden (Primary Industry—later director of the International Wool Secretariat).

The Bureaucratic Elite in the States

The development of the CPS since 1939 has given it a character very different from the government services of the states. This may be brought out by a comparison of recruitment, career patterns and social background. In addition, state officials remain an important part of the authority structure of the community, and some analysis of their collective characteristics has its own intrinsic interest.

The following data are based on a survey carried out in January 1956, at the same time as the first survey of Commonwealth officials already described.

The selection of respondents presented certain problems. To include only those people who are, in the technical sense, 'public servants' would have been to sample a very small area of state administration, where organisations like the railways employ a far larger number of people than those covered by the Public Service Acts. The selection process involved a number of steps. In the first place, a line was drawn eliminating all officers below a certain salary classification. Above this line there remained, however, a heterogeneous group, including a very high proportion of professional officers and a number of persons temporarily appointed for reasons such as political influence, or as representatives of various interested parties. It was necessary to eliminate the latter and to thin out the ranks of the professional officers, an excess of whom would have altered the whole character of the study. Those finally selected included only individuals who were judged to occupy positions of considerable administrative responsibility. Naturally, such a choice must be somewhat arbitrary, but no ready-made criterion presented itself. Similarly, all persons whose employment with the particular authority could be regarded as temporary were excluded. In the upshot, 165 questionnaires were sent to New South Wales Government officials, of which 113 were finally returned (i.e. 70 per cent), and 132 were sent to Victorian Government officials, of which 100 were finally returned (i.e. 76 per cent).

Table 15·5 State Officials: Place of Birth

	NSW officials %	Victorian officials %
1 Born in same State (country area)	29	39
2 Born in same State (capital city)	50	49
3 Elsewhere in Australia	15	8
4 Overseas	6	4
	100	100

Table 15·5 shows, as might be expected, that state officials are overwhelmingly recruited locally. It also illustrates the rural/urban imbalance we have already noted. At the 1911 census, to maintain the previous comparison, 57 per cent of the population of NSW, and 50 per cent of the population of Victoria, lived in country districts.

Ages in the state services were relatively high, and promotion relatively slow. The median age of the NSW officials was fifty-four, and that of the Victorians fifty-eight, compared with fifty-two for the Commonwealth officials (reduced to forty-eight in 1961); 30 per cent of the Commonwealth officials were under forty-five, compared with 9 per cent in NSW and 6 per cent in Victoria. In 1956, promotion rates were comparable: 31 per cent of Commonwealth officials had been appointed to the Second Division by the age of forty-five, corresponding state figures being 35 per cent in NSW and 29 per cent in Victoria, but by 1961 the Commonwealth figure had shot up to 65 per cent, whereas an inspection of state government personnel lists indicates only a minor upward trend in the same period.

The structure of state administration, where public utility corporations and welfare services predominate, entails a corresponding demand for professionally trained men. Hence, it is not surprising that they predominate among senior officials. In NSW, 47 per cent of the sample were graduates and 17 per cent had other tertiary qualifications; 36 per cent had a tertiary education on entering government service. In Victoria, 48 per cent were graduates and 3 per cent had other tertiary qualifications; 30 per cent had a tertiary education on entering the government service. In both cases, the bulk of those who had a tertiary education on entry were professionally qualified in law, medicine, engineering, agricultural science, architecture and forestry. Taking the two states together, 75 per cent of those who entered the service as graduates were qualified in these fields (i.e. forty-five out of sixty). The pattern of schooling, however, showed some interesting differences. In Victoria, of the twenty-seven graduates, twenty had attended private schools, of which two predominated: Wesley College with seven and Scotch College with five. Of the thirty-three graduate entrants in NSW, thirteen had attended private schools and there was no predominance by any particular school or schools. This reflects the much greater role played by private schools in Victorian education, and conversely, the much greater willingness of successive governments in NSW to spend money on state education.

In terms of social background, the state officials present a similar picture to the Commonwealth sample.

Table 15·6 Social Origin of Senior State Officials

Father's Occupational Group	1947 census %	NSW & Victorian officials %
1 Rural	17·9	10
2 Professional, semi-professional, administrative and business	9·1	30
3 Commercial and clerical	16·4	32
4 Domestic and protective	6·4	3
5 Craftsmen	20·0	15
6 Operatives and labourers	27·2	7
7 Others	3·0	3
	100·0	100

The profile shown in Table 15·6 is very similar to that of the Commonwealth officials in Table 15·4; if anything, it is biased even more towards the upper-middle class occupations comprising Group 2.

Religion and the Public Service

The role of the Catholic religion in the public services is one aspect of the perennial question of Catholic influence in the community at large. A common contention in discussions of this influence is that there is a disproportionately large number of Catholics in government employment. There are certain *prima facie* reasons why this might be true. Catholics are not prominent in the business world, partly because their religious culture does not seem to encourage it, partly because of discrimination. There is also some hostility to Catholics in the professions. Neither of these considerations is particularly important in the public service. There is also evidence that, perhaps because of the relative openness of the public service, some Catholic schools, and certainly a number of individual Catholic teachers, have encouraged their pupils to enter the public service as a career.[7] An anonymous Catholic public servant gives us this wry description:

The public service guaranteed both in theory and in fact freedom of entry, security and hope of promotion. The sons of wealthier Catholics entered the professions—meaning law or medicine—or inherited their fathers' hotels or grazing properties. (One remembers the school magazines containing photographs of successful 'old boys' smiling out from beneath their birettas, barristers' wigs or mortar boards. The clerkly type, even if he achieved the status of an Under-Secretary, rarely rated a mention.)[8]

One definite source of information about the proportion of Catholics is provided by the demography of Canberra. At the post-war censuses, the Catholic population of Canberra has fluctuated between 30 per cent and 35 per cent, which is significantly higher than the national urban average of Catholics in the same period. (The higher Catholic proportion seems to exist largely at the expense of the Methodists, who are substantially under-represented in the Canberra population.) Since an overwhelming proportion of the work force of Canberra are Commonwealth public servants (roughly two-thirds) the significance of these figures is apparent. Indeed, our anonymous Catholic observer suggests that the proportion of Catholics in the public service in Canberra may be more than 40 per cent.

Within the government service itself, there is a concentration within particular departments. To quote the same source, speaking of the NSW state government service:

[There is] a concentration of Catholics in particular areas, with similar movements of Protestants and Masons in other directions. Heavy concen-

7 R. S. Parker, *Public Service Recruitment in Australia*, pp. 131-32
8 Anon, 'Catholics in the Public Service', *Australian Quarterly*, vol. 32, no. 3, 1960

trations of Catholics were to be found in the 'legal' departments, particularly the Registrar-General's Department and the Public Trust Office. The police force was, and I think still is, an acknowledged stamping ground for Masons. The Education Department had a long tradition of Methodism. The Treasury, at least in the policy sections, was a poor ground for Catholics. In the Rural Bank forces were fairly evenly divided.

In the Commonwealth, there is some evidence that the proportion of Catholics is highest in three departments—Customs, Taxation and the Post Office. The reasons for this stem directly from the socio-educational pattern already described. In all three departments, the bulk of recruitment is at a fairly low educational level, advancement is heavily weighted by seniority and experience, and higher education is of relatively little importance. In the Attorney-General's Department, there is evidence (as in the state services) of a relatively high proportion of Catholics among legal officers. The reasons for this appear to be twofold. Catholics are poorly represented in some professions. Engineering is a particular case, so that the high proportion of engineers among senior officials means a correspondingly low proportion of Catholics. Catholics have tended to enter law and medicine, but even here the strongly Protestant and Masonic flavour of the two ancient professions means that a large number of Catholic lawyers and doctors find it easier to enter public employment rather than private practice. As the law is a traditionally suitable profession for Catholics, a considerable number of young men who enter the public service improve themselves by gaining legal qualifications.

This analysis is supported by examining details about the Catholics included in our two surveys of senior Commonwealth officials. In the 1956 group, fifty were positively identified as Catholics, i.e. 18 per cent of the sample. It can be assumed that not less than 30 per cent of the entire service are Catholics, so they are clearly under-represented at the higher levels. In addition, fourteen of the group—i.e. more than 25 per cent— were in two departments, Customs and Taxation.

The Catholics in our group present a different profile in several other respects. Twenty (i.e. 40 per cent) were recruited by 'special' methods, compared with 58 per cent of the total group. Fifteen (i.e. 30 per cent) had degrees on entry to the service, compared with 50 per cent for the total group. With regard to social origin, the Catholic group differs substantially as regards one category. Whereas the group as a whole contained 27 per cent whose fathers were in professional and managerial occupations, the proportion for the Catholic group was 13 per cent. These figures are too small to be significant, but the disproportions are nevertheless great enough to be suggestive.

The 1961 survey gave a similar picture. In this case there were 278 respondents, of whom forty-one were identified as Catholics, i.e. 15 per cent. There was considerable overlap between the two groups, owing to the closeness of the surveys; ninety were men who had been promoted into the higher public service in the intervening five years. During the interim, nineteen of the Catholics in the 1956 survey had retired, but only ten were represented among the ninety new respondents. The distribution among departments was similar. The fall in the number of Catholics may be related to the increasing importance of higher education as a criterion for entry into the bureaucratic elite.

The concentration of Catholics in particular departments naturally leads to allegations regarding preference to co-religionists. The reciprocal allegation is that Masonic groups operate to combat Catholic influence and to ensure the preferment of their own members or, at least, non-Catholics. There is no doubt that leading public servants have been Masons, and it is conceivable that they have not looked with special favour on Catholics. The first Commonwealth Public Service Commissioner, McLachlan, was a leading Mason in NSW. He held all offices in Craft and Mark-master masonry, and was the founder and first president of the Masonic Club in Sydney in 1899.[9] In more recent years, there have been signs of a strong Masonic colouring in departments like the Attorney-General's. In the Post Office, allegations are made of the existence of both Catholic and Masonic groups.[10] The late Sir Frederic Eggleston, who worked for the Commonwealth government during the war, noted the operation of Catholic preference in the Department of Commerce.

Commerce has some very energetic and able heads, like Murphy[11] and McCarthy. . . . Murphy was quite uninhibited in making Catholic preference throughout his department. I have been told that Catholic officers in the department have been called in by him, when they failed to attend Mass, and told that their advance in the department was dependent on their performing their religious duties.[12]

Somewhat similar occurrences have been reported in the Customs Department, where the concentration of Catholics is alleged to be a contributory factor in the censorship of imported books. On one occasion a Catholic Comptroller-General of Customs, on assuming office, reshuffled the headquarters staff by posting several senior officials to the position of Collector of Customs (the chief officer of each state branch of the department) and transferring some of the Collectors (who are often Catholics) to head office.

Accusations of sectarian influence were contained in a famous annual report of the CPS Clerical Association (now the Administrative and Clerical Officers' Association) in 1950. The secretary of the Canberra branch of

9 G. E. Caiden, 'The Early Career of D. C. McLachlan', *Public Administration*, vol. 22, no. 2, 1963

10 An acquaintance who entered the Post Office on leaving school recounts that the first question he was asked was whether he kicked off with the right or the left foot —a symbolic reference to religious affiliation, like the nickname of 'knucklecrushers' derived from the Masonic handshake.

11 J. F. Murphy, secretary of the Department of Commerce from 1934 to 1942

12 Eggleston Papers, library of the Australian National University

the Association, in his report, entitled ominously 'Quis Custodiet Ipsos Custodes?' alleged that personal and sectarian influences were being abused in the service. Although asked by the federal executive of the association to withdraw these accusations, he refused, and in the following year reiterated that public servants had a duty to say these things publicly.[13]

A picturesque instance of allegations of sectarian influence arose in the case of an inquiry into promotions in the Post Office in 1944. A postmaster, with a long record of unsuccessfully appealing against promotions, wrote to his union secretary in Brisbane asserting that 'sectarianism was rampant in the administration branches'. He went on to allege that a postal inspector, who had fined him for a breach of regulations, had told a relative: 'I have nothing against your brother, but the reason he was fined was because his wife was taking too much interest in the damned Catholic Church.' He alleged, further, that the inspector was a Mason, and that, with three other postal officials who were Masons, he had conspired against the writer. The solicitor who was handling his case had died before completing it. 'I have often wondered if the Freemasons, having got wind of E.'s intentions, put him out of their way. . . . I could fill a dozen pages like this one with instances of subversive activities, both in and out of this department, against Catholics. . . . Freemasonry has a stranglehold on this department. . . . They are the strongest Union in the world. It is not necessary for a Mason to possess merit to get a position. . . . Mr B. deals with appointments to vacant positions and no doubt would not dare to risk dismissal by order of the Grand Master for daring to promote a Catholic.' If the Masons were not got rid of, the end would be strikes and the burning down of Masonic lodges. The writer concluded: 'If you are a Mason, you have my sympathy, and advice to take a tumble and get out of the Lodge before it gets you down as it has got others down.'[14]

Rumblings such as these will no doubt continue as long as religion remains a source of social differentiation. That sectarian affiliations have a significant effect on *policy* within the bureaucracy is much more difficult to establish, and much less likely. Catholic views on social and political questions are expressed, continuously and vigorously, in the political arena, though it may be assumed that details of the execution of policy are affected by religious affiliations. But the important point appears to be that, within the restricted sphere of the public service, Catholicism and anti-Catholicism contribute to a continuing pattern of social stratification.

Night on Black Mountain

The growth of the new bureaucratic elite is epitomised by the development of Canberra. Until the 1950's, the federal capital was something of a joke

---

[13] Annual Reports of the ACT Branch of the CPSCA, 1949-50, and 1950-51. The writer was the late W. J. Lind, later assistant secretary of the Department of the Interior from 1954 to 1960.

[14] I am indebted to Dr G. E. Caiden for drawing my attention to this letter.

to most Australians—the 'bush capital' or 'good sheep paddocks spoiled'; later, it became 'a plan without a city', and then 'six suburbs in search of a city'. Canberra was officially inaugurated in 1913, but did not become the seat of government until 1927. For the next thirty years, it was little more than a sleepy country town which happened to include the federal parliament and a number of governmental institutions. In 1947, its population was no more than 17,000; half of the departmental head offices were still in Melbourne; and the ambitious city plan drawn up by Walter Burley Griffin in 1912 was largely on paper.[15] Rapid growth began about 1950. By 1959, when the transfer of departmental head offices was resumed, the population had reached 50,000. In 1969, it was 120,000, and twenty of the twenty-six departments had their headquarters in Canberra. The main features of the Griffin plan had been put into effect by the National Capital Development Commission, established in 1957 to supervise the growth of the city; indeed, Canberra had grown far beyond the original estimate and the work of the NCDC was premised on a city of 250,000 people by the year 1985.

This concentration of bureaucratic activity has stimulated various subsidiary growths. Until 1960, only a few national pressure group organisations had bothered to set up their own offices in Canberra. In that year, the Associated Chambers of Manufactures (ACMA), one of Australia's largest lobbies, opened their own building, Industry House, which now accommodates a number of other lobbyists' offices. Other organisations have since followed suit, and more and more of them have found it expedient to recruit former government officials into their service. A number of them now hold their annual conventions in Canberra, and their example is followed by many other professional, business and cultural bodies. The first important step towards the development of Canberra as a cultural centre was the establishment of the Australian National University (ANU) in 1946, but progress was slow thereafter until the late 1950's. By 1969, Canberra not only possessed the ANU but a range of other establishments in the fields of higher education, scientific research, drama, music, the plastic arts and libraries. It was well on the way to becoming a mini-Washington, without the slums but with similar problems of discontent about the absence of self-government, which remains denied to the citizens of Canberra despite forty years of intermittent agitation.

Self-government apart, the residents of Canberra enjoy a privileged existence. Two-thirds of the work force in the Australian Capital Territory are employed by the government, giving them a remarkable degree of security and affluence. A professor at the ANU remarked in 1952 that the concentration of highly placed officials helps to give Canberra 'about twice the national average in income per capita, birth rate, consumption of alcohol, and IQ'.[16] The paternal Commonwealth government, with greater

[15] For an account of the tangled history of Canberra from 1900 to 1963 see Lionel Wigmore, *The Long View*, Melbourne, 1963.

resources and fewer responsibilities than the state governments, is able to provide a significantly higher standard of public services than is to be found anywhere else in Australia. As the local cliché puts it, Canberra is a wonderful place to bring up children. Griffin's plan was for a garden city built around a lake. The lake (appropriately named after him) did not come into being until 1963, with the damming of the Molonglo river, but the concept of the garden city has been faithfully adhered to since the beginning. Canberra has at least as many trees as it has people, and comes very close to the Australian dream of a house and garden for every family. Its garden character is maintained by the absence of manufacturing industry and the virtual absence of a working class. Unlike Washington, where acute class tensions revolve around the position of the depressed black majority, Canberra is an almost perfectly middle class community. As a result, the pattern of stratification has some unusual features. In particular, gradations within the middle class itself are more refined than usual. One of the traditional over-simplifications about Canberra is that public servants live in a strict pecking order in which those on the same rung of the official hierarchy reside in the same suburb and mix socially. Canberra was never really like this, and the old pattern was in any case disrupted by the rapid expansion which has gone on unbrokenly since 1950. Residence, education, occupation, income, tastes and social connections are more closely correlated in Canberra than anywhere else in Australia; however, this takes in not only public servants but academics and other professional people, diplomats, journalists and full-time lobbyists. It is a mixture of these people whom one is likely to meet at a social gathering in the federal capital.

Canberra lies in a valley dominated by three hills—Mt Ainslie to the east, Black Mountain to the west, and Mt Mugga Mugga to the south. The lookout on Black Mountain provides the most dramatic view of the city and the surrounding countryside. At night, the lights on the two bridges across the lake show up the basic outlines of Griffin's plan—an irregular amphitheatre, flanked by the surrounding hills, with two major axes running south-west from Mt Ainslie and south-east from Black Mountain, and a central zone of government buildings linked by two great avenues running from the bridges to meet at Capital Hill, where a building representing the 'sentimental and spiritual head' of government was to be erected.[17] The view is an impressive one; it is also a reminder that the growth of a national capital inhabited mainly by bureaucrats is an index of the power and privileges accruing to bureaucracy in Australian society. At the same time, the suburban character of Canberra is also a reminder of the strength of middle class values in Australia, here encouraged to flourish as nowhere else. The monumental character of Canberra's layout and its official architecture blend with its suburban prettiness to make it the fine flower of the bureaucratic ascendency.

[16] Quoted, ibid., p. 162
[17] The Griffin plan is discussed at length in ibid., pp. 66-79.

Part Four
Economy and Society

16: Broad Acres

The cattlemen of the High Plains care not for your accent; or how many brewery shares you hold, or if you go to Government House. They have a simple confidence in themselves and a pride in their heritage. They, and their kind, are the breed that made Australia and continue to make it. They, not the moneyed commercial barons, are Australia's aristocracy.

Inscription in the visitors' book, dated April 1944,
Roper's Hut, Bogong High Plains, Victoria

The legend of the man on the land, the rural backbone of the nation, has dominated the image of Australia for most of its history. In a romantic-aristocratic form, it has permeated Australian literature since Henry Kingsley's novel *The Recollections of Geoffrey Hamlyn* was first published in 1859; in a romantic-proletarian form, it was first propagated by the 'bush' school of writers associated with the Sydney weekly the *Bulletin* whose leading exponent, Henry Lawson, gave a perfect literary expression to the bush creed of 'mateship' in his earlier short stories. 'Australia', wrote an English visitor in 1911, 'has no more picturesque figure than the pioneer squatter . . . merryhearted and of undaunted courage, he was partly driven, and partly he set himself, to find out unconquered lands in the wild.'[1] In 1964, an advertisement in the London *Observer*, inviting British investors to put their money into a new Australian unit trust, was graced with the picture of a tall, rangy man in a slouch hat, although the attractive investments offered were in mining and manufacturing.

The legend of the man on the land retains its influence partly because of ignorance of Australian social conditions; partly because it reflects the reality of a vast, empty country whose population lives mainly in coastal cities but whose consciousness is dominated by the great outback. The novelist Patrick White, himself a descendant of a pioneer landed family in the New England district of New South Wales, has given an imaginative account of the fascination exercised by this great loneliness in *Voss*; in another novel, *The Tree of Man*, he describes the lure of empty lands for the immigrant settlers of the nineteenth century. For the non-Australian town dweller, the picture of great open spaces inhabited by sheep, kangaroos and men on horseback is much more satisfyingly romantic than

---

[1] James Collier, *The Pastoral Age in Australia*, London, 1911, p. 77

the prosaic urban reality of Australian society, and the 'real Australia' is the sunburnt country of Dorothea Mackellar's verses. But there is also a solid economic reality behind these romantic preferences. Although only 16 per cent of the population live in rural areas, and rural production accounted for only 8 per cent of GNP in 1965 (compared with more than 20 per cent in 1950), Australia's prosperity still depends heavily on export income from rural commodities, which accounted for more than three-quarters of the value of exports in 1965. Wool, in particular, accounted for 40 per cent of total exports and made up 30 per cent of the value of rural output. Post-1945 industrialisation has transformed the sources of national income, and the mining boom of the 1960's altered the balance of exports, but the dependence on rural products has remained.[2] In this sense, the man on the land remains the backbone of economic prosperity, and the structure of rural society is (or should be) of compelling interest to the sociologist, in a way which distinguishes Australia from other industrial, urban communities. In this chapter, we shall not be attempting to draw a detailed picture of rural life, but to show how the rural community makes its distinctive contribution to the general pattern of class, status and power in Australia.

A Pastoral Aristocracy

The 'pastoral ascendency' which dominated politics and society in eastern Australia until the end of the nineteenth century originated, as every schoolboy knows, with the introduction of merino sheep by John Macarthur, the stormy petrel of early colonial days (after Sir Joseph Banks had advised against a 'mere theoretical speculation'). Between 1814 and 1820, the annual export of wool to Britain varied from 60,000 to 90,000 lbs and in the 1820's and 1830's companies were formed in London 'to seize, on a large scale, the great chance that had so long gone begging at the Antipodes.'[3] The Australian Agricultural Company established itself in New South Wales in 1825. In 1829 a German sheep breeder, Frederick Brecker, came to Queensland with 200 pedigree Saxon merinos from the Esterhazy flock in Silesia; one of his rams is regarded as the founder of the Queensland merino stock. Donald Gunn, who emigrated from the Scottish Highlands in 1840, acquired a flock of 5,000 stud rams descended from these sheep, and the Gunn family became one of the largest land-owning groups in Queensland.[4] In 1845, John Dunmore Lang noted the patriarchal way of life established by the shepherd kings of the period, which made it possible for a respectable family to settle in the bush near Moreton Bay, in Queensland, 'with comparatively moderate means and exertion, with all their flocks and herds around them, like the patriarchs

[2] L. J. Hume, 'Wool in the Australian Economy 1946-58' in Alan Barnard (ed.), *The Simple Fleece*, Melbourne, 1962, esp. at pp. 620-23

[3] Edward Shann, *An Economic History of Australia*, London, 1930, p. 96

[4] Donald Gunn, *Links with the Past*, Brisbane, 1937

Abraham, Isaac and Jacob.'⁵ North of Moreton Bay, William Archer, head of one of the pioneer landed families of Queensland, wrote in 1860 that the town of Rockhampton had developed a definite social structure in which the landowners played a distinctive and leading role. After them came an 'upper-middle class' of government officials, bankers, lawyers, doctors and agents; then the large shopkeepers and employers; and finally a class of small shopkeepers, mechanics and manual labourers.⁶

In Victoria, a well-established 'squattocracy'⁷ had come into existence in the fertile basalt country of the Western District of the colony by the middle of the century. An early observer, writing of the Western District squatters in the 1840's, remarked on the curious notions which townsfolk already entertained about the squatter. He was supposed to be able to ride fifty miles at a gallop every day, to be immune from fatigue in the saddle, while 'some sense . . . enabled him to find his way in the most unerring manner through trackless forests and waterless wastes.' From observation of the squatter in town, on the other hand, they had learnt that he was 'lavish in his expenditure, affected tandem driving, had a decided penchant for beer and brandy, and was not as a rule over-punctual in his payments.'⁸

The first family to establish itself in the Western District was that of Henty, a yeoman family from Sussex, where it still has a branch. Thomas Henty, who also raised merinos from the royal flock whence Macarthur had obtained his original sheep, left England in 1829 after becoming convinced that sheep-raising would not pay in England. After trying the Swan River colony in Western Australia and the settlement at Launceston, in Tasmania, the family established themselves at Portland Bay, in the south-western corner of Victoria, in 1834. On their property at Muntham, inland from Portland, Edward Henty, who succeeded Thomas as head of the family, 'was not only a squatter but a squire as well . . . he was a master who could show each man his particular task . . . [and create] an easy-going edition of the social life he had seen among the Sussex estate-owners as a boy.' The estate was run on a lavish scale, with 'herds of roan Durhams, the magnificent Suffolk Punches, the stable full of glorious saddle-horses and handsome carriage horses, perfectly matched; the five

---

⁵ Quoted by C. M. H. Clark, *Select Documents in Australian History*, vol. 1, p. 277
⁶ B. H. Crew, 'History of the Walker and Archer Families in Australia', unpublished M.A. thesis, Australian National University, 1963, p. 216
⁷ The term 'squatter' originated in North America to denote a settler occupying a tract of land not yet surveyed or allocated by the Government. It became current in Australia in the 1830's, and its social prestige rose with the prosperity of the squatter class. The explorer Leichhardt, in 1847, described his squatter hosts as 'young men of good education, gentlemanly habits, and high principles'. The term 'squattocracy' was in use in the 1840's. E. E. Morris, in his book, *Austral English*, noted the phrase 'squattocratic impudence' used in a Melbourne newspaper in 1854. The *Saturday Review*, London, noted in 1864 that landed proprietors had been 'designated by the ingenious colonial title of a squattocracy'.
⁸ E. M. Curr, quoted by Clark, op. cit., p. 287

acres of gardens, with their natural springs and rich chocolate soil; the comfortable house, set against the steep downs, where the high-spirited "Colonial experiencers" lived in more than comfort, cared for by the indoor staff always kept there . . . [it was] essentially England: Rockingham china and fluted tea-caddy were in daily use, papier-mache work box rested on mahogany and walnut beside volumes describing travels in Italy and Greece.'[9] This account was written by one such 'colonial experiencer', i.e. a young man from an English county family sent to Australia to try his luck, usually on a sheep station. These men worked as 'jackeroos'[10], i.e. cadet station managers, and sometimes married the daughters of the station families. They were regarded with a degree of amused tolerance by the rural workers, reflected in the words of the popular song 'Click Go the Shears':

The colonial experienced man
He is there of course,
With his shiny leggings
Just off his horse

and passing himself off as a 'real connoisseur' of the standard of shearing.

The development of the squatter ascendency in the Western District has been traced at length in a notable history by the late Margaret Kiddle, herself a descendant of a squatter family.[11] Two-thirds of the pioneer settlers, she notes, were Scottish Lowland farmers, a fact reflected in the names of prominent families to this day. 'It has been said, with pardonable exaggeration, that the Scots own all the land in Australia, while the Irish own all the public-houses.'[12] The labour required to develop their sheep runs was provided for a number of years by assigned convicts and ex-convicts from Van Diemen's Land, where a number of the settlers had tried their luck before crossing Bass Strait to the new colony of Victoria. By the 1840's, there were nearly 300 sheep runs in the Western District. Most of the lease-holders of these runs had no aspiration to become country gentlemen like the Hentys; their aim was to make their pile and get out. 'Every season', writes Kiddle, 'was a gamble to men who had not sufficient capital to establish themselves as squatters and supply the world wool markets . . . in most cases their object was to make money, not to make a home . . . they intended to leave when they had made their fortunes . . . neither were they concerned with the developing life of the towns, for they were used only as depots by the Western District settlers.'[13] However, the squatters who

[9] Marnie Bassett, *The Hentys*, London, 1954, pp. 531-33
[10] The term jackeroo ('jackaroo' was the preferred spelling in the nineteenth century) is first recorded in the 1880's, and appears to be a compound of the words Jack and kangaroo. Rolf Boldrewood, in *A Colonial Reformer*, 1891, speaks of a young man 'going jackerooing'.
[11] Margaret Kiddle, *Men of Yesterday*, Melbourne, 1961
[12] Collier, op. cit., p. 81
[13] Kiddle, op. cit., pp. 45, 115, 143

survived the early hardships of a difficult environment, and the economic crises which made farming and wool-growing precarious, became men of substance and authority. Their social and political leadership was established in the 1840's, when they 'dominated, so to speak, the nature, the quality, the social reality of Victoria.'[14] The constitution of the colony, framed in the 1850's, established an upper house with a restrictive property qualification which favoured the squatters until the end of the century, and this predominance led to an interminable series of political crises.

With the granting of self-government in 1855, and the great social and economic changes brought about by the gold rushes of the 1850's, the Western District squatters found that they were increasingly influenced by the growth of an urban metropolis in Melbourne. They established permanent houses in the city, and the growth of absentee landlordism and the development of pastoral companies produced radical changes in the structure of land ownership. The squatters formed the centre of the urban social elite, and the 'Collins Street farmer' (in Sydney, the 'Pitt Street grazier') became a byword. 'The towns and villages arranged themselves as a social hierarchy. In this the squatter was at the apex, for though he did not live in the town he provided local storekeepers, doctors, bankers and lawyers with their most reliable business and his influence was important in shire and municipal councils. . . . Beneath the squatters in a series of delicate gradations devised by wives were the parson, priest and minister, the bank manager, the doctor, the lawyer and the newspaper owner.'[15]

The way of life established at this period has persisted into contemporary Australia, and seems likely to remain, with some changes, so long as woolgrowing retains its importance in the economy. Jean Martin, herself of country origin, describes it in these words:

They spent their money in characteristic ways: in sending their children to the highest status non-government schools; in travelling to visit friends and relatives scattered throughout their State and beyond; and to take part in the picnic races, the country shows, the city weddings and other events through which their identity as a group is maintained; they also spend their money on maintaining large establishments, sometimes in both country and city, and in observing the ritual and formality they regard as appropriate to a gracious life. Although these families do not form a leisured class—the men usually running their own properties or businesses—they are expected to take a leading part in occupational organisations like the Graziers' Association, and in service groups like the Red Cross and the Victoria League.[16]

Partly for geographical and partly for social reasons, the squatters stand somewhat outside the urban social system although they have numerous

---

[14] ibid., p. 151

[15] ibid., p. 430

[16] Jean Martin, 'Marriage, the Family and Class' in A. P. Elkin (ed.), *Marriage and the Family in Australia*, Sydney, 1957, pp. 36-37

links with it, and their strength as a group makes an important contribution to the status dimension of social inequality. As Pringle has remarked, egalitarian Australia is almost the last stronghold of this form of social differentiation. 'Throughout history the man who could ride round his broad acres and watch his beasts graze was held to be superior to the man who had to get down from his horse and dig with his hands. . . . The grazier is a natural aristocrat, a man who lives on his own property where he is lord and master . . . he is the true *caballero*, even if, as is quite likely today in Australia, he generally drives a jeep or a Land Rover . . . he fits in very ill with the general democratic character of Australia, and the tensions caused by this conflict are evident among the Australian graziers today.'[17]

Pringle also comments on the comparative reluctance of the grazing community to involve itself in politics or wider public affairs. They refuse, he asserts, 'to take their part in public life and local government. They do little or nothing for the country towns which, in spite of the enormous wealth around them, are often little better than country slums—dreary, hideous, unspeakably dull. They grumble about politics and politicians, but only rarely enter politics themselves, though many of them are in an excellent position to do so.'[18] The same point was made independently by Martin, who declared that graziers act as leaders 'only in their own communities or in promoting the interests of particular groups such as the primary producers; they seldom take office in local government or in parliament.' The complaint is not a new one. The Victorian Western District pioneer, Niel Black, regretted in his letters that the squatters were not playing their proper role in governing the country and attributed this to their isolation from urban life.[19] Isolation is, indeed, a factor in the situation. Another cause is to be found in Martin's remark that squatters are not a leisured class; certainly, the most active and intelligent individuals are likely to prefer the management of their affairs to the life of politics, for which their upbringing in many cases unfits them. The uncertainty of farming and grazing in the unfriendly Australian countryside, the succession of problems caused by natural hazards and price fluctuations, leave comparatively little time and energy for political pursuits. Rural political activity is, in fact, more common among small farmers, whose demands for government assistance are endless and are expressed through a bewildering variety of organised interest groups. In spite of all this, graziers are more active in politics (especially in times of prosperity) than the remarks of Martin, Pringle and many other critics of the squattocracy would suggest. In 1968, the newly chosen Prime Minister, John Gorton, appointed three members of well-known pastoral families to his government—Fraser (Victorian Western District), Fairbairn (NSW Riverina district) and Kelly

[17] J. D. Pringle, *Australian Accent*, pp. 105-6
[18] ibid., p. 108
[19] Kiddle, op cit., p. 227

(South Australia). At the local government level, graziers are well represented, and also in the upper houses of state parliaments, especially South Australia and Tasmania. Lack of public spirit is more evident in the relative failure of the grazing community to contribute to the cultural and educational life of Australia. The late Professor A. J. Marshall, one of Australia's leading biologists, sharply attacked the failure of graziers to support scientific research on the sheep industry.[20]

One of the outstanding social characteristics of the squatter community is its strong link with England, and its identification with the outlook, values and way of life of the England of the shires, the Court Circular, Ascot and the London season. Hancock writes: 'The squatters and their allies were not, like the great mass of immigrant settlers and their children, compelled by circumstances to break their connections with England and accept Australia as their only home. They went to and from one hemisphere to another; often they ended their days in England and sometimes they sent their sons to Oxford or Cambridge; behind them stood the powerful financial houses, controlled from London and controlling the economy of Australia; they were welcome at Government House, and met there officers of Her Majesty's Navy.'[21] Collier, in 1911, saw the squatter as 'almost always a gentleman immigrant, often a man of education and culture, "Glover of Corpus" accidentally foregathering with "Hallett of Oriel".'[22] The novelist Rolf Boldrewood, author of *Robbery Under Arms*, glorified the squatters as 'splendid fellows . . . all gentlemen by birth and education', who had furnished Australia with 'pattern country gentlemen'. More recently, Pringle has remarked that visiting pastoral properties is 'a curious, as well as a pleasant, experience, for it is exactly like visiting an English "county" family fifty years ago.' The squatters, he declared, 'are generally quite English in manner and outlook, and often regard Sydney or Melbourne as the Duke of Devonshire would regard Bakewell—as a place to buy the groceries. They send their sons to Oxford and Cambridge, visit London every other year and behave as if Australia had not yet been granted self-government.'[23]

These statements are permeated by the exaggeration which seems to mark all accounts of the squatter elite. It is not true that squatter families are generally offshoots of English county families. Many of the squatters were of Scottish farming origin; others were self-made men with no family pretensions; and a large proportion of present-day graziers are first-generation settlers. The extent to which English landed families are represented among the squatters may be judged from *Burke's Colonial Gentry*, many of whose entries describe families which no longer have any

[20] A. J. Marshall, *Australia Limited*, Sydney, 1942
[21] W. K. Hancock, *Australia*, p. 60. One of these naval officers, Captain A. W. Onslow, married into the Macarthur family and gave it the name of Macarthur-Onslow which it has since borne.
[22] Collier, op. cit., p. 77
[23] Pringle, op. cit., p. 107

significant connection with the land.[24] Again, it is not true that graziers generally behave like English gentlemen; some of the leading representatives of the squatter community are well-known as roughnecks, whose manners were learnt in the shearing shed or the mustering paddock rather than the junior common room. Finally, although a number of graziers were sent by their families to be educated in England, these were a minority, and the practice has declined since the 1939-45 war. But the attachment to England—Edwardian England—is real and persistent, although it has been badly shaken by the decay of the Empire and a succession of Labor governments. An index of changing attitudes may be derived from an opinion poll taken in 1962 on the question of a governor-general for Australia to replace the aristocratic Lord De L'Isle. Respondents were asked whether the new incumbent should be an Englishman or an Australian. Two-thirds of the respondents preferred an Australian. Among occupational groups, 63 per cent of farm proprietors preferred an Australian, 29 per cent an Englishman, and 8 per cent gave other replies. This result was not significantly different from the general picture, and the only group where there was no clear majority for an Australian were 'professionals, executives, and owners of large businesses.'[25] It is safe to infer that the graziers' vote would be different from that of farm owners as a whole (especially wheat farmers, among whom political radicalism is endemic), but it is also safe to infer that there was no clear preference among them for an English governor-general. The appointment by a conservative government of an Australian, Lord Casey (who had strong links with the squattocracy), to succeed Lord De L'Isle in 1965 was another step away from the colonial pattern.

The social life of the squatter community, although a favourite topic for everyday comment, has received little serious attention, and the information that follows, based on two surveys, represents only a first step towards the construction of a detailed social profile. In 1958, a postal questionnaire was sent to 120 'leaders' of the rural community. For this purpose, all elected presidents, vice-presidents and past presidents of the more significant producers' organisations set up on federal, state or regional lines, and elected producer representatives on the large number of Commonwealth government commodity marketing boards, were treated as leaders.[26] Replies were received from eighty-seven individuals. To this was added an analysis of entries from *Who's Who in Australia* for 1959. The criteria used by the latter publication include wealth (especially size of holdings), social prestige, official honours conferred, and political prominence, giving a list which overlapped only to a minor extent with the 1958 survey. The total number of distinct individuals thus obtained was 214, out of whom

[24] Sir John Bernard Burke, *A Genealogical and Heraldic History of the Colonial Gentry*, etc. London, 1891
[25] APOP *Bulletin*, June 1962
[26] I am indebted to the Commonwealth Department of Primary Industry for its assistance in compiling this list.

121 could be described unambiguously as 'graziers'. Another fourteen were 'mixed farmers', which means that most of them ran sheep and cattle on their properties; sixteen were 'wheat farmers' many of whom also ran cattle and sheep; and thirty-four were involved in 'processing', of whom a number were connected with grazing either through family ties or previous occupation. As farming is traditionally an activity with manifold and fluctuating aspects, it is difficult to select a 'pure' sample of graziers. The difficulty is intensified by distinctions between sheep-raising, cattle-raising and animal breeding, and reflected in the looseness with which the words 'farmer' and 'grazier' are used. What we have, therefore, is a sample of the rural elite which is dominated by pastoralists, or alternatively a sample of the pastoral elite diluted by other branches of farming. The nature of the dilution is, however, obvious in most areas of the analysis, e.g. education. In the 1958 survey, full details were available about sixty-three men, twenty-five from graziers' associations, thirty-eight from other farmers' organisations. Of the twenty-five graziers, twenty-four had completed secondary school, and all of these had attended private schools; four were university graduates. Among the thirty-eight farmers, only nineteen— exactly half—had a secondary education, and eight of these had been to private schools. None were graduates.

Like the other groups analysed in this book, our rural elite shows some geographical imbalance, but in this case it is South Australia which is over-represented at the expense of Queensland. This is shown in Table 16·1.

Table 16·1 Geographical Origin of the Rural Elite

Place of Birth	Number	%
NSW	56	26
Victoria	53	25
South Australia	48	22·5
Queensland	15	7
Western Australia	14	6·5
Tasmania	10	4·5
United Kingdom	14	6·5
New Zealand	2	1
N.A.	2	1
	214	100·0

One reason for the over-representation of South Australia, the fourth state in terms of population, is the relatively large number of smaller farmers (especially orchardists) from that region; another is the prominence of rural industries by comparison with the industrialised states of the east; and a third is that the grazing industry in Queensland is dominated by absentee landlords in the shape of big pastoral companies, Australian, British and American.

The geographical pattern also helps to account for a pattern of schooling which is markedly different from the business and bureaucratic elites examined in other chapters. One hundred and eighty-two men had had at least a secondary education, 142 at private schools. Of the latter, 120 had attended HMC schools, and two were at English 'public' schools. The most important HMC school was Geelong Grammar School, attended by twenty. As explained in an earlier chapter, Geelong's natural hinterland is the Western District of Victoria, but it also attracts the sons of graziers from NSW and South Australia. It was followed by St Peter's College, Adelaide, with fifteen; Prince Alfred College, Adelaide, contributed seven. Melbourne Grammar School was represented by eleven individuals. The others of any significance were The King's School, Parramatta (seven), which has the oldest tradition of educating the landed gentry; Scotch College, Melbourne (seven); Sydney Grammar School (six); Sydney CEGS ('Shore'), with four; Hale School, Perth (four); Guildford Grammar School, Perth (four); and Cranbrook School, Sydney (three). Forty-six men had graduated from university, of whom forty were graziers, three were professional men connected with farmers' organisations as officials, and three were connected with processing but had never worked on the land. Twenty-two of the graduates had attended Cambridge (nineteen) and Oxford (three). At least seven of the Cambridge men had been at Jesus College. Sixteen had received other forms of tertiary training, usually at agricultural colleges.

The connection with Cambridge reflects a particular link between Jesus College and Geelong Grammar School. The link was established in the 1870's, evidently under the influence of an early headmaster, John Bracebridge Wilson, who was a Cambridge man. It was strongly fostered by a later headmaster, L. H. Lindon (1896-1911), who had been at Jesus College. Family connections with the college, once established, have persisted over the generations.[27]

The history of land settlement would lead one to expect a great predominance of Protestants among the graziers, so the results of the survey hardly came as a surprise. Of the entire group of 214, only seven could positively be identified as Catholics, and only one of these was a grazier. Like the businessmen examined in a later chapter, the rural elite has an overwhelming WASP complexion.

Graziers, again like businessmen, are members of 'exclusive' clubs on a large scale, and the early history of some of the clubs is connected, as we have seen, with the emergence of the 'squattocracy'. Ninety-three men in the survey gave details of club membership. The Australian Club, Sydney (twenty-five) and the Melbourne Club (twenty-four) had pride of place, followed closely by the Adelaide Club (nineteen) and the Australian Club, Melbourne (also nineteen). In Sydney, the other clubs preferred by graziers were the Union (fifteen) and Royal Sydney Golf

[27] I am indebted to Mr M. D. C. Persse, senior history master and archivist of Geelong Grammar School, for information on this point.

(thirteen). In Brisbane, the Queensland Club had fifteen members. In Perth, allegiance was divided between the Weld (six) and the West Australian (four). By contrast with businessmen, graziers seem to congregate in a smaller range of clubs, and they also have a military tincture which is not evident among the businessmen; seven of them were members of the Naval and Military Club (Melbourne) and six of the Imperial Service Club (Sydney). They were also strongly represented in racing clubs. Twelve were members of the Victoria Racing Club, six of them holding official positions, and eight of the Australian Jockey Club (Sydney), where three held official positions; ten were members of Tattersall's Club, Sydney.

Since the latter part of the nineteenth century, pastoral wealth and industrial wealth have become more and more closely connected. Squatters invested in the gold rushes of the 1850's, and later in the mining boom touched off by the discoveries at Broken Hill in the 1880's. Two of the large private shareholdings in the iron and steel monopoly, BHP Co. Ltd, are in the hands of the old-established (and inter-related) pastoral families of Maple-Brown and Faithfull (NSW). In Victoria, the Manifold family, one of the pioneer families of the Western District, has large shareholdings in the Electrolytic Zinc Co., Australian Consolidated Industries, Commonwealth Industrial Gases, Olympic Consolidated Industries (rubber) and Repco Ltd (automotive parts). In NSW, the Hordern family is a large shareholder in the Commercial Banking Co. of Sydney, the MLC Assurance Co., Tooth's Brewery, and Yarra Falls Ltd (woollen mills). Other leading pastoral families with large shareholdings and/or directorships in big companies include those of Law-Smith, Angas, Barr Smith, Bonython and Duncan in South Australia, Mackinnon in Victoria, Kater and Waddell in NSW. Altogether, fifty-five men in our group of 214 held directorships in 108 companies which were not directly connected with primary production, including such branches as insurance (twenty-three companies), banking and finance (thirteen), manufacturing (fifteen), trading (thirteen), transport (eight), newspapers (eight), brewing (five) and oil exploration (four). Seventy-five men were directors of companies concerned with the processing or sale of primary products, and another thirty-seven were directors of both types of company.

At the time of the survey, thirty-nine men in the sample were, or had been, members of parliament, and of these twenty-five were graziers. Ten graziers were federal parliamentarians, fifteen state parliamentarians; four had been federal Ministers, and five in state governments. Thirty had been shire councillors, and ten had held municipal office. These figures do not suggest a very high level of political activity, but neither do they bear out the strictures quoted above (especially when one takes account of unsuccessful candidates who do not appear in these figures).

The Family Nexus

Schumpeter's observation that the history of social classes is the history of families is nowhere borne out more clearly than in the case of the landed gentry. The ownership of land, the need to preserve estates and the desire to add to existing holdings, have always been a powerful force in securing alliances between landed families. In Australia, the nexus of family relations among the landed gentry is close and intricate. Only a sample can be given here to illustrate its ramifications.[28] We may begin with the descendants of the original ruling class. Philip Gidley King, governor of NSW from 1800 to 1806, had a daughter called Anna Maria who married Hannibal Hawkins Macarthur, nephew of John Macarthur, the pioneer of the sheep industry and a member of the New South Wales Corps which effectively governed the colony for the first twenty years of its existence. Their daughter Elizabeth married Philip Gidley King, the son of Philip Parker King and grandson of his namesake the governor. Philip Parker King's wife was Harriet Lethbridge, whose brother had married Governor King's second daughter Mary. Altogether, four marriages took place between the King and Lethbridge families, but the King surname faded out after the fourth generation. One of Governor King's great-grandsons, George Bartholomew (d. 1910) had six daughters, three of whom married three brothers named Willsallen, sons of the landed proprietor Thomas Polk Willsallen. Nancy, the daughter of P. S. Willsallen and Adeline King, married M. L. Baillieu, scion of the remarkable business dynasty of that name (see below, Chapter 19). P. S. Willsallen was, in 1965, a director of the pastoral firm of Elder Smith Goldsbrough Mort and a large shareholder in BHP and Australian Consolidated Industries. The Lethbridge family also formed a connection with the Blaxlands, another name dating from the establishment of the colony of NSW. Gregory Blaxland was one of the three explorers who found a route across the Blue Mountains from Sydney to the western slopes and plains of NSW in 1813. Gregory Blaxland's great-great-grandson, Francis, married Josephine Lethbridge, a descendant of the marriage between R. C. Lethbridge and Mary King.

The Fairbairn family provides a convenient focus for another important set of kinship connections.[29] The founder of the family, George Fairbairn (b. 1810) emigrated to Australia in 1839 and acquired extensive holdings in NSW and Queensland, running both sheep and cattle. His biggest holding was Peak Downs in Queensland, one of the most notable cattle stations in Australia. In 1880 he established one of the early factories to freeze meat for export. He had six sons, most of whom followed him on to the land. Four of them also followed an established family pattern of education at Geelong Grammar School and Jesus College, Cambridge, where all rowed in the university crew against Oxford. The eldest, George (later

---

28 Major bibliographical sources include P. C. Mowle, *Pioneer Families of Australia*, 2nd ed., Sydney, 1941; *Burke's Colonial Gentry*; A. Henderson, *Early Australian Families*, Melbourne, 1941; *The Australian Dictionary of Biography*, vol. 1, Melbourne, 1966; and successive editions of *Who's Who in Australia*. Mowle uses the term 'pioneer' to denote families established in Australia within 50 years of the foundation of the first colony in 1788.
29 Stephen Fairbairn, *Fairbairn of Jesus*, London, 1931

knighted), stroked the Cambridge crew but spent only two years at college, because he knew no Greek. Only Stephen (1862-1938), the youngest, took a degree after attending college for six years, and later became a barrister. He was the man of whom it was later said that he 'taught Jesus to row'. At Cambridge he rowed in many winning teams, introduced the 'Fairbairn system', and coached many crews after settling permanently in London in 1904. The London *Times* wrote, years later, that he had done more for rowing in England than any other single person.[30] The Fairbairn family has a long association with right-wing politics. Sir George Fairbairn (d. 1943) was a Liberal member of the Victorian state parliament, later a Senator, and president of the National Union of the United Australia Party. He also served as president of the Central Council of Employers of Australia. His nephew, J. V. Fairbairn, was a Liberal member of the Federal parliament and a Minister in 1939-40. (He was killed in an air crash at Canberra in 1940.) Sir George's grandson, D. E. Fairbairn, also became a Liberal member of federal parliament, and a Minister in 1962. Sir George's brother Charles was one of the employers' leaders in the great Queensland shearers' strike of 1891. D. E. Fairbairn's cousin, Geoffrey, a lecturer in history at the Australian National University, was one of the leading intellectual apologists for the Australian government's support of American policy in South-East Asia, including participation in the Vietnam war, in the late 1960's. The family has extensive business interests apart from its landholdings. Sir George Fairbairn was chairman of the local board of the large pastoral firm of Dalgety's (whose head office is in London) and of the Union Trustee Co., a director of the AMP, Australia's largest life assurance office, and a local director of the Union Bank. Stephen Fairbairn was a director of Dalgety's, and J. V. Fairbairn of the Union Trustee Co. and the Commercial Banking Co. of Sydney.

The Fairbairns are allied with the NSW pastoral family of Prell, owners of one of the leading studs for breeding Corriedale sheep. The stud was established at Gundowringa, near Goulburn, by C. E. Prell (1865-1946) and was being managed in 1969 by his daughters and his grandsons. C. E. Prell's sister Jessie married Sir George Fairbairn. Another alliance was with the Armytage family of the Victorian Western District, whose name is almost synonymous with 'squattocracy' in Victoria. Thomas Armytage crossed from Van Diemen's Land to Victoria in the 1830's and settled on the Barwon river near Winchelsea, now a seaside resort accessible from Geelong. He died after only a few years and was succeeded by his brother George (1795-1862), who had six sons. One of these, Charles, did pioneer work on the use of eucalyptus oil and bought the mansion of 'Como' at South Yarra, Melbourne, which has been preserved by the family as a historical building. George Armytage's grandson, George Francis, was the first Australian to row in the Cambridge crew against Oxford in 1874.

---

[30] ibid., ch. 4. The Fairbairn system involved the use of the legs to give additional thrust, and was described in several books.

Another grandson, Frank, married Sir George Fairbairn's daughter; their son Trevor was the first pupil at Geelong Grammar School whose grand-fathers had both attended that institution.

The most spectacular example of an extended kinship system may be traced by following the ramifications of the two families of Cox and Faith-full. William Cox, another pioneer of the Western District, was among the first to bring merino sheep to Australia, and his work was carried on by five sons, one of whom married the daughter of another pioneer family, that of Mackenzie. Various descendants intermarried with the landed families of Baylis, Bettington, Lamb, Bell and Blomfield. Through these connections arise other connections. Mary M. Lamb, whose aunt was a Cox, married E. W. Fairfax, a scion of the wealthy Fairfax newspaper-owning family of Sydney (see below, Chapter 19). The Lamb family also intermarried with the pastoral family of Dangar on at least two separate occasions. The connection between the Cox and Faithfull families arises from the fact that both intermarried with the Bells. The original William Faithfull arrived in Sydney in 1791 as a private soldier in the NSW Corps. When he left the Corps, having married Marie Bell, his company com-mander, Captain Foveaux, helped him to settle in the Hawkesbury River district. His son, W. P. Faithfull, became a successful sheep breeder at Springfield, in the Goulburn district of NSW, and the property remained in the family until its current owner, the granddaughter of W. P. Faithfull, married into the Maple-Brown family, who also have pastoral holdings in this part of NSW. Another granddaughter, Mrs J. Wilkinson, died in 1963 at the age of eighty, having lived as a recluse on the Isle of Man for seven years, and left an estate of £720,000, most of it invested in Australia.[31] The Faithfulls are also connected with the landed family of Gibson. Alice, daughter of William Faithfull, married Andrew Gibson; their grand-daughter Jessie married Robert, the son of W. P. Faithfull.

The Dangar family, just mentioned, were among the first to take up land in the Hunter River valley north of Sydney. Henry Dangar's great-granddaughter married a scion of the Giblin family, one of the oldest-established family groups in Tasmania, whose best-known member was the late Professor L. F. Giblin, for many years professor of economics at the University of Melbourne and economic adviser to the Commonwealth government.

Apart from the intricate web of intermarriage, the importance of family holdings and family influence remains great, and some of the strongest family groups are also the oldest. An example is that of the Angas family in South Australia, founded by George Fife Angas (1789-1879), son of a prosperous merchant and shipowner in Newcastle-on-Tyne, and descended from the Earls of Angus, whose interests include pastoral properties and industrial firms. Another is the Falkiner family of NSW, founded by F. S. Falkiner (1835-1909). In 1878 he bought Boonoke stud

[31] *Sun-Herald*, Sydney, 11 August 1963

in the Riverina, and his four sons enlarged the family interests until they constituted the largest family freeholding in Australia. The eldest son, F. B. S. Falkiner, purchased the world-famous merino stud farm of Haddon Rig, near Warren, on the rich black soil country of central NSW. His younger brother, Ralph, a man of parts, patented the first mechanical sugarcane harvester in Australia in 1921, prototype of the commercially successful machines which came into use more than thirty years later. His son, G. B. S. Falkiner, who died of cancer in 1961, became one of the most influential graziers and animal breeders in Australia, and at his death was president of the Association of Stud Merino Breeders. Apart from its property holdings, the Falkiner family also has extensive business interests, including the manufacture of air-conditioning and refrigerating equipment. In Queensland, the best-known figure in the pastoral industry is Sir William Gunn, chairman in 1969 of the Australian Wool Board and the International Wool Secretariat, and descendant of the pioneer settler Donald Gunn, who took up his first sheep-run in 1843. In addition to large property holdings, Sir William Gunn is also a director of companies such as Rothmans Ltd and the National Mutual Life Assurance Co., and of various pastoral companies.

The largest of all family sheep holdings in Australian history was that of Sir Samuel McCaughey (1835-1919), known as the 'wool lord', whose holdings at one time covered 7,000 square miles and included fifteen separate properties.[32] The establishment of the McCaughey estate was a family affair. The four Wilson brothers, Samuel, John, Alexander and Charles, of a large and old-established Ulster Protestant family, migrated to Australia in the 1830's and 1840's, and acquired a number of sheep stations. Their nephew, Samuel McCaughey, joined them in 1856 and with their assistance began to accumulate his enormous estates. He was an energetic innovator, and introduced mechanical shearing, irrigation of pasture, electric light in shearing sheds, new sheep strains (such as the American Vermont breed), and artesian bores. At the age of seventy he began selling off his properties, and as his uncles had done before him, he assisted his nephews to acquire them. He left Coonong station, in the Riverina, one of the show places of rural Australia, to his nephew, now Sir Roy McCaughey. He died leaving an estate of £1¾ millions, most of it bequeathed for philanthropic and educational purposes.

Pastoral Empires

The ownership and control of land, animals and crops has always been a mixture of family capitalism and corporate capitalism. In particular, pastoral companies have been a major factor in providing investment capital for land use, animal husbandry, food processing and transport. Some companies are locally based, others overseas based (mostly British,

[32] Patricia McCaughey, *Samuel McCaughey*, Sydney, 1955

but with some American interests), and the role of the latter has always been a fertile source of controversy about the actions of overseas capital in plundering the agricultural wealth of Australia. A recent critic of government policy in northern Australia writes that 'the history of occupancy of the cattle lands of the remote regions of northern Australia is largely one of primitive animal husbandry; of inefficient, low-investment production on low rental, inadequately improved leaseholds; of an outmoded, open-range system of cattle-grazing in some parts to the lasting detriment of the native pasturage', and he blames this on the rapacity of overseas companies, with Australian participation serving as a front to enable easier penetration by overseas capital.[33]

In cattle-raising, the main object of these and similar strictures is the British firm of Vesteys, an enormous international concern with an astonishing range of activities which it prefers to veil under a variety of names and corporate identities. The Vesteys enterprise is almost entirely controlled by the family, the biggest company in the group being Union International Ltd. Along with pastoral properties in Australia, Argentina and North America, Vesteys are involved in killing works, meat-packing plants, cold storage facilities, wholesale butcheries (under the name of W. Weddel and Co.), retail shops (under the name of Dewhurst and others), ice cream manufacture, frozen foods, knitting wools, perfumes and the Blue Star shipping line. A board of inquiry in 1937 was told that Vesteys had 3,000 butchers' shops and 40,000 employees in England alone.[34] At that time they controlled eleven cattle stations in the Northern Territory, covering 25,000 square miles, under the name of Northern Agency Ltd. (Another large British firm, Bovril Estates, controlled two stations with 12,000 square miles, and an Australian company, Connor Doherty and Durack, three stations over 8,000 square miles.) Their current holdings are similar in size.

Vesteys' activities in the Northern Territory date from 1912, when they were invited to lease large tracts of land for cattle raising. Sir William (later Lord) Vestey came to Australia and decided to build a meatworks at Darwin, which operated for several years under the name of North Australian Meat Co. In 1934, the family increased its Australian interests very substantially by taking over most of the business of William Angliss, Australia's largest butcher and 'cattle king'.[35] Angliss (1865-1957) was a self-made tycoon in the mould of the Victorian era. Born in Devon, he started work as a butcher in London, and came to Australia in 1884. He entered the meat export trade during the South African War, and opened offices in London and Liverpool in 1909. In 1912, the company of William Angliss and Co. Pty Ltd was formed, and in 1922 it became William Angliss and Co. (Australia). The company was effectively controlled by

[33] J. H. Kelly, *Struggle for the North*, Melbourne, 1966, p. 20
[34] Report of the Board of Inquiry into the Land and Land Industries of the Northern Territory (the Payne-Fletcher Report), Canberra, 1937
[35] Jacobina Angliss, *The Life Story of Sir William Angliss*, Melbourne, 1960

the Angliss family; in 1965, its chairman was Reginald Angliss, one of the founder's nephews, and another nephew, W. A. Angliss, was managing director of its pastoral properties, held through Pastoral Interests Pty Ltd. From 1914 onwards, the Angliss interests acquired, jointly with the South Australian 'cattle king', Sidney Kidman, a number of large sheep stations in NSW and South Australia, and several large cattle holdings in Queensland. In 1929, the latter totalled more than 15,000 square miles with about 220,000 head of cattle.

In 1934, after the Ottawa agreement on imperial preference had improved the prospects of the meat trade following the great depression, Vesteys, in the shape of Weddel and Co., offered to buy the Angliss concern. Sir Edmund Vestey telephoned Angliss from London, an act more dramatic in 1934 than it would be a generation later. The deal was concluded for £1½ millions and the *Daily Express* described it as 'the greatest meat merger in the history of the British Empire'.[36] Angliss retained his chairmanship of the company, and his family retained substantial holdings in its various concerns, which are channelled through a family investment company, Investors Pty Ltd. Indeed, given the love of privacy shown by both parties, it is not possible to discover the extent to which the Angliss family still exercises influence over the business. It is indisputable, however, that Angliss left an estate of £4 millions, and that the family interests include pastoral companies, refrigeration, quarrying, cement, retail stores, insurance and textiles as well as meat.

Sidney Kidman (1857-1935) started, unlike Angliss, as a drover and rouseabout.[37] He was the youngest of four brothers who all went droving. Kidman started trading in horses and contracting for transport by bullock team. When the copper mining centre of Cobar was developed, he set up as butcher. In company with his brothers, he bought and sold stock, speculated in properties, and ran a mail coach service between Adelaide and Broken Hill. He realised at an early stage of his career that the problem of long distances must be solved, and set out to acquire a chain of stations ranging from the far north all the way to the shipping terminals, so that stock could be moved gradually from one station to the next without losing too much condition during the overlanding process. In the days before motor transport eased the problem of movement, he made extensive use of the telegraph so that he could start moving stock in advance of demand. Originally interested in horses to supply coach transport, he gradually widened his interest to cattle and then to sheep. Many of the properties he bought outright, others were acquired in partnership with friends and relatives, notably the Angliss interests. In 1914, Angliss and Kidman bought a sheep property of 500,000 acres at Salisbury Downs, NSW. In 1923, they acquired two properties in South Australia, controlled by a

[36] ibid., p. 211
[37] A highly coloured version of Kidman's career is given by Ion L. Idriess, *The Cattle King*, Sydney, 1936.

company directed by Angliss, Kidman and Sydney Reid, Kidman's son-in-law. Later, Angliss and several members of the Kidman family jointly acquired two cattle stations near the Gulf of Carpentaria, Rutland Plains and Iffley Downs. At his peak, Kidman was owner or part-owner of lands whose extent has been variously estimated from 85,000 to 107,000 square miles. Kidman's interests were inherited by his son, W. S. P. Kidman, his three daughters and sons-in-law. In 1965, W. S. P. Kidman was a director of twenty pastoral companies; his cousin, A. S. Kidman (d. 1961) was also active in the business.

The first use of the London capital market to finance pastoral development in Australia came with the formation of the Australian Agricultural Co. in 1825. In return for a grant of one million acres near Port Stephens, north of the Hunter River, the company undertook to raise flocks of sheep and to produce fine wool for export. The floating of the company was initiated by the Macarthur family. Another kind of relationship between a local pastoralist and a British company is illustrated by the story of Niel Black, a pioneer of the Western District of Victoria. Niel Black and Co. was formed in Scotland by four partners in 1839, and Black himself went to Australia as managing partner. The accounts were kept by a firm in Liverpool, where proceeds from sheep-raising were credited, station requirements were bought and dispatched, and arrangements were made for the sending of Scottish shepherds to Australia and for their payment.[38]

As a result of mergers between pastoral companies since 1945, activity in the sheep and wool industry has been dominated since 1962 by four large companies—Dalgety-New Zealand Loan, Elder Smith Goldsbrough Mort, Australian Mercantile Land and Finance Co., and the Australian Estates Co., in order of importance. Of these four, only the second is based in Australia, and the others reflect the curious relationship between Britain and Australia which forms part of the special economic and social character of the pastoral industry and pastoral society. The biggest firm, Dalgety-NZL, dates from the arrival in Australia of F. G. Dalgety, yet another Scottish immigrant, in 1833. Dalgety worked for various merchants in Sydney and Melbourne and went into business on his own account in the 1840's. The Dalgety organisation began as a general importing firm in Melbourne, but wool exporting soon became its principal activity. In 1884, the various partnerships established by Dalgety were incorporated into a limited liability company with its head office in London. The activities of Dalgety's, and its network of associated companies, encompass a tremendous variety including woolgrowing, woolbroking, shipping, wholesale and retail trading, textiles, insurance, banking, mining, chemicals and fertilisers, meat packing, dairy farming, pharmaceutical products, urban real estate, stevedoring and aerial crop spraying. From its Australian origins, the company has spread to embrace a wide range of interests in Britain, Canada, the United States, East Africa, Germany and New Zealand. Its

[38] Alan Barnard, *The Australian Wool Market 1840-1900*, Melbourne, 1958, p. 136

directors in London included Stephen Fairbairn, two members of the Glyn family of bankers, S. R. Livingstone-Learmonth, of the Western District pastoral family of Learmonth, and Lord Gowrie, Governor-General of Australia from 1936 to 1946. The local board of Dalgety's in Australia included Sir George Fairbairn; R. O. Blackwood (also a director of BHP); and various members of the Wittenoom family, prominent in both primary and secondary industry and in politics in Western Australia.

The Australian Mercantile Land and Finance Co. (AML & F) was established in 1863 to take over the Melbourne firm of Gibbs Ronald and Co., formed in the mid-fifties to undertake wool consignments to the parent firm of Richard Gibbs and Co. in London. The New Zealand Loan and Mercantile Agency was formed in the following year to invest in pastoral activity in New Zealand and export pastoral produce. It extended its business to Victoria in 1874 and to NSW in 1876. The Australian Estates Co. was established to take over the business of the Union Mortgage and Agency Co., formed in 1884. The UMA, which had absorbed several other private firms in the wool trade, was a principal source of funds for investment in the pastoral industry in the 1880's. In 1887, the UMA transferred its domicile to London, and in 1905 was taken over by the Australian Estates Co., which has a number of properties in Queensland, NSW and Victoria, including sugar as well as pastoral activities among its interests. One of its board members in 1965 was Sir Keith Officer, scion of an old-established landed family, who was appointed a director in 1957 after retiring from the Australian diplomatic service in 1955; he was also a director of the English Scottish and Australian Bank. His cousin, V. W. Officer, was for many years secretary of the Graziers' Association of Victoria.

The firm of Elder, Smith & Co. originated in 1839 in South Australia with the mercantile partnership of A. L. and Thomas Elder, who merged in 1863 with the business of the Barr Smith family. The firm soon acquired extensive pastoral interests through purchase or marriage. Throughout its history, the company has been closely connected with the fortunes of several landed families, especially that of Barr Smith. Other families, prominent in both business and politics in South Australia, include those of Murray, Downer, McBride, Melrose, Cudmore and Dumas. The growth of Elder Smith is closely linked with the history of copper mining in South Australia and Tasmania, and through interlocking relationships it was connected with a number of manufacturing, mining, shipping and trading concerns. The firm of Goldsbrough Mort embodied the names of the two men who founded it. Thomas Mort (d. 1878) set up as an auctioneer in Sydney in 1843, but soon graduated to wool selling and then woolgrowing. Richard Goldsbrough (d. 1886), trained in the woollen industry in Bradford, started business in Melbourne in 1848. These two men were largely responsible for shaping the structure of the wool market and for the establishment of the auction system which remains its key institution and one of the most familiar features of commercial life in Australia.[39] Goldsbrough concentrated on the wool industry, while Mort's interests were widespread and included the development of refrigerated shipping (to which he made important technological contributions), railway promotion, gold mining, engineering and ship-building. His breadth of vision and imagination were remarkable; in 1870, for instance, he attempted to operate a joint ownership scheme with the workmen in his ship-repairing enterprise. Also in the 1870's, Mort and his collaborator Nicolle marketed a small household refrigerator, using the same principles as the ship refrigeration plant which they had already designed. This was perhaps the first domestic refrigerator ever constructed.

In 1888, the two companies merged and the firm of Goldsbrough, Mort and Co. came into being. The subsequent history of pastoral companies is one of merger and consolidation, as family firms gave way to limited liability companies. By 1961, the business was dominated by no more than seven firms, and further consolidation reduced the number to five. In that year Dalgety's made a successful takeover bid for NZL & M. The new concern, Dalgety-NZL, which was established with a capital of nearly £12 millions, became the largest pastoral company in the world.[40] A director of the merged concern (until his death in 1967) was Lord Baillieu, senior member of that family, and a member of the Australian board, in 1965, was his relative J. M. Baillieu. This merger soon touched off a parallel amalgamation between the two Australian firms of Elder Smith and Goldsbrough Mort[41] to form the new concern of Elder Smith Goldsbrough Mort Ltd, with a nominal capital of £25 millions. Chairman of the merged company, in 1965, was Sir Philip McBride, former chairman of Elder Smith, a former federal Cabinet minister, and for several years federal president of the Liberal Party (see below, Chapter 18). Its deputy chairman, Sir Colin York Syme (see below, Chapter 21), was the former chairman of Goldsbrough Mort and also chairman of BHP. Each of these two pastoral giants handles about one-quarter of the annual wool clip.

These events run parallel with the general trend towards the replacement of the family holding by the large company-owned estate. An American commentator has observed that while the 'revolution of science, mechanics and heavy capital investment . . . has not as yet done away with the family farm, it has gone a long way toward getting rid of the farm family . . . eventually the era of the small family homestead will appear brief. With its demise any influence which widespread security in land ownership may have had upon the American psyche will cease to exist.'[42] The process has not gone nearly so far in Australia, but signs of it undeniably exist. In addition to the factors mentioned, company ownership

---

[39] ibid., ch. 7. Mort's numerous interests are described by the same author in a biography, *Visions and Profits*, Melbourne, 1961.
[40] *Sydney Morning Herald*, 12 September 1961
[41] ibid., 24 February 1962
[42] E. Higbee, *Farms and Farmers in an Urban Age*, New York, 1963, pp. 8-9

is spreading as a result of rising costs, a long-term decline in the price of wool, and a trend towards beef-raising, which demands large capital assets. Taxation concessions available to primary producers have also encouraged wealthy individuals and business firms to buy properties.

The influence of pastoral companies, banks and insurance companies as property owners was already perceptible at the end of the nineteenth century, although exaggerated by earlier writers.[43] The role of companies accounts largely for the highly concentrated character of the ownership of sheep and cattle. According to a census of holdings taken by the Bureau of Agricultural Economics in 1956, less than 14 per cent of holdings accounted for 54 per cent of all sheep, and 6 per cent of holdings for 28 per cent of sheep. An article in the *Sydney Morning Herald* in 1968 gave some details about large holdings in NSW.[44] The largest single property, Delilah Downs (668,000 acres) was owned by Dalgety-NZL, who also owned one of the largest wheat farms in the world, Gurley Station, near Moree in northern NSW. The two companies with the largest holdings were the NZ and Australian Land Co. Ltd and the Scottish-Australian Land Co. Ltd, both British firms, each owning thirteen stations. The Australian Agricultural Co. owned six large properties totalling 200,000 acres, and AML and F had five. The British Tobacco Co., which has diversified into many fields since cigarette smoking came to be regarded as a dangerous activity, had acquired three large stations, including the famous Mungadal stud of 105,000 acres formerly owned by the Hordern family.[45] The big real estate firm of L. J. Hooker Ltd entered the pastoral industry through a subsidiary company in the 1960's and acquired the Bovril estates in the Northern Territory, as well as eight sheep and cattle stations in NSW totalling 135,000 acres.

A possible indication of the shape of things to come was the launching in 1967 of the Tipperary Land Corporation by a group of American businessmen with ambitious plans for land development in the Northern Territory. The company raised $6·5 millions (US) on the New York stock exchange and also borrowed $800,000 from the Bank of NSW. Its plan was to farm a tract of more than two million acres on the Daly River by growing sorghum which would be exported to Japan and also used as fodder for cattle raised in the area, and at a later stage to grow maize and use it for feeding pigs.[46] The movement of American capital into Australian land development, of which there have been a number of instances, has aroused concern about domination by foreign investors. In September 1968, the general manager of the Australian Resources Development Bank, established in 1967 under federal legislation by a consortium of all the trading

[43] For a discussion of the role of company ownership, see Alan Barnard (ed.), *The Simple Fleece*, chs. 23, 26.
[44] Joe Glascott, 'Build-up of Giant Pastoral Empires', *Sydney Morning Herald*, 29 May 1968
[45] *Sydney Morning Herald*, 23 September 1963
[46] *Australian*, 5 June 1968

banks, foreshadowed the possibility of action to restrain this trend.[47] In the foreseeable future, however, it appears that land ownership in Australia will continue to be a mixture, as in the past, of family capitalism and corporate capitalism, interwoven by a web of personal and institutional linkages.

Land and Politics

Farming and politics seem to go hand in hand, especially since governments in industrial societies accepted responsibility for broad economic policy. Farmers have long appeared to be particularly adept and active in organising themselves to put pressure on governments through a multitude of associations, and governments have responded by setting up a great range of boards and committees. Farmers, who pride themselves on being individualists, are paradoxically prepared to accept the most rigorous forms of *Gleichschaltung* so long as they are imposed by farmer-dominated regulatory bodies and not by city slickers. The paradox is expressed in a quaint (and perhaps unwitting) choice of words by Digby, who describes agricultural regulation as based on the idea of 'compulsory co-operation' and the 'absolute control of the product by the producer'.[48]

The complex structure of farmers' and graziers' organisations may be viewed from the top downwards by examining the relations of the four 'peak associations' of primary producers. The largest and most important is the Australian Woolgrowers' and Graziers' Council, formed in 1960 by a merger of two old-established bodies, the Australian Woolgrowers' Council and the Graziers' Federal Council. The AWGC is made up of ten constituent associations from all states and the Northern Territory, and represents the large graziers, woolgrowers and companies. Parallel and competing with it is the Australian Wool and Meat Producers' Federation, made up of five constituent bodies from the mainland states. Both federations were represented on the National Farmers' Union, which aspired for some years to speak for all men on the land. The NFU was formed in 1949 by the amalgamation of two national bodies established during the 1939-45 war—the Australian Primary Producers' Council formed in 1943 to bring together the national organisations of woolgrowers, wheatgrowers and dairy farmers, and the Australian Council of Agricultural Societies, set up in 1944 as a federation of various state-wide agricultural bodies. The fourth of the peak associations is the Australian Primary Producers' Union, whose main strength comes from small farmers, orchardists, apiarists etc. in Victoria, South Australia and Tasmania. The AWGC, the AWMPF and the APPU are all represented on the Australian Wool Industry Conference, which acts as a so-called 'parliament' of the industry and nominates six members to the Australian Wool Board. The Board, which is also the

---

[47] *Australian*, 25 September 1968
[48] Margaret Digby, *Agricultural Co-operation in the Commonwealth*, Oxford, 1951, p. 57

main body represented on the International Wool Secretariat in London, works through four committees concerned with marketing, testing and research.

Unity among primary producers has never been easy to achieve, and the principal conflict is between the large woolgrowers and the rest of the farming community. The majority of farmers support government action in the form of subsidies, bounties, organised marketing and price stabilisation. The large woolgrowers are strongly opposed to government intervention in their affairs, and their support of *laissez-faire* breeds a generally conservative outlook on politics. In 1965, after a conflict of opinion within the NFU, the AWGC withdrew from it. Such conflicts also account for the fact that while the majority of smaller farmers and graziers support the Country Party, which acts as the political arm of their peak associations, the large woolgrowers and graziers are to be found in the Liberal Party, of which they constitute one of the most conservative sections.

The NSW Graziers' Association is perhaps the pre-eminent organisation of large pastoralists. Most of its leaders are members of the pastoral aristocracy, with similar personal histories—descendant of a prominent squatting family, owner of a large property, educated at an HMC school and sometimes a university graduate, and spent some time in early manhood working as a jackeroo or with a wool firm. Since the establishment of the Association in 1890, there has been a recurring pattern of family groups active in it, and presidents tend to be sons of former presidents. Although the Association is probably as democratic as any other farmers' body, this hereditary influence among its councillors leads to periodic allegations that it is ruled by a self-perpetuating coterie of wealthy graziers working hand-in-hand with the wool brokers. The Association has a substantial income which has enabled it to buy its own office building in Sydney and to employ a large and competent staff.[49]

The policies of graziers' associations derive from two basic attitudes. In the first place, as wool and meat have to compete in an open world export market, graziers are constantly preoccupied with costs, and this places them in a position of constant antagonism to trade unions and to any policy that is likely to increase wages. The result is a kind of 'class struggle in the countryside' which has had a far-reaching influence both on the history of the Labor movement and on the political posture of the graziers. 'Pastoralists', wrote one of them in 1890, 'must be persuaded to make a determined effort rather than let this union yoke be fitted on their necks.' And he urged the sheep-owner to 'keep firmly in his own hands the right of judging whether the class of work given by the workman is sufficiently good or not.'[50] As Graham notes, the graziers expected every Labor government to legislate against their interests, and were always prone to

[49] G. S. Harman, 'The Graziers' Association of NSW', seminar paper, Dept. of Political Science, Australian National University, 1966
[50] R. A. Gollan, 'Industrial Relations in the Pastoral Industry', in Barnard (ed.), *The Simple Fleece*, pp. 604-5

exaggerate the influence of communists and 'agitators' within the Labor Party and to cherish fears of revolution. In 1925, during a waterfront strike, the secretary of the NSW Graziers' Association declared hysterically that 'foreign elements' were aiming at the destruction of the British mercantile marine, and that the strike leaders intended to overthrow democracy and establish a Soviet system.[51]

The second basic political attitude is the fear of government intervention, which is seen as the thin end of the wedge of government control. This attitude is a major factor in the opposition of the large graziers, both individually and through their organisations, to schemes for price and market stabilisation in the wool industry. In this, the pastoralists see eye to eye with the wool brokers, who regard a stabilisation scheme as a threat to their interests. Marketing schemes have been projected ever since the experience of the British-Australian Wool Realisation Association (BAWRA) which handled the entire wool clip during the 1914-18 war. The graziers' associations have steadfastly opposed these proposals. In 1929, at the onset of the great depression, a delegation representing the smaller woolgrowers waited on the Labor Prime Minister, Mr Scullin, to suggest a stabilisation scheme, but the proposal was so strongly opposed by another delegation from the Graziers' Federal Council and the Woolgrowers' Council that Scullin decided to do nothing.[52] Again in 1949, fearing a fall in wool prices, growers' organisations in South Africa and New Zealand as well as Australia supported a marketing scheme, but the boom caused by the Korean war brought a sharp change of attitude and when the proposal was put to a referendum of growers in 1951 it was defeated.

The subject was again aired following the establishment of a committee of inquiry on a wool marketing (reserve price) scheme by the federal government in 1960. The committee made some cautious recommendations in favour of a marketing scheme, and the chairman of the Australian Wool Board, Sir William Gunn, former president of the United Graziers' Association of Queensland, became its apostle and carried out a vigorous propaganda campaign in its favour.[53] The campaign was marked by spectacular incidents such as the throwing of a tomato at Sir William during a speech at a growers' meeting in Victoria. The NSW Graziers' Association opposed the scheme, as did the woolbroking firms and a number of large pastoral companies, and a violent press attack against it was carried on by the Sydney *Daily Telegraph*. The smaller growers' organisations, such as the United Farmers' and Woolgrowers' Association of NSW, campaigned strongly in favour of the scheme, which was ultimately defeated in a growers' referendum. The subject is almost certain to recur, and in the long run Australia may, like New Zealand and South Africa,

---

[51] B. D. Graham, 'Graziers in Politics', in ibid., pp. 593-94
[52] J. A. Morey, *The Role of the Statutory Marketing Board in Organised Marketing*, M.Ec. thesis, University of Sydney, 1959, pp. 109-14
[53] The marketing scheme is discussed in *Nation*, 22 April 1961 and 6 May 1961, and again in the issue of 25 July 1964.

adopt a marketing system, which could have profound effects on the social and political role of the wool industry, hitherto the great exception in the highly regulated structure of primary production.

This highly regulated structure makes its own special contribution to the bureaucratic character of Australian social and political life. The position of farmers is strengthened by some circumstances peculiar to this country. The political strength of rural interests has been fortified in state politics by the gerrymandering of electorates, as in South Australia and until recently in Victoria, and in federal politics by the disproportionate weight given to rural votes in the distribution of seats—a softened and disguised form of gerrymander. The ability of the Country Party, with the aid of the preferential voting system, to hold the balance of power in state and federal parliament, has meant that farmers' representatives are frequently able to hold ministerial portfolios which enable them to advance the interests of farmers by direct administrative action. The report of an inquiry into the dairy industry in 1961, presented to a Country Party Minister for Primary Industry, was quietly pigeonholed because the dairying organisations were opposed to its recommendations. In the following year, the report of a committee on the sugar industry was suppressed by the same minister. The influence of the Country Party has also been important in establishing the practice by which most decisions affecting rural industries are in effect taken by the producers themselves, either through a vote or by the operation of marketing boards which consist almost entirely of producers' representatives. In primary industry, pressure group activity has evolved into more formal bureaucratic machinery than in any other area of social life.

17: Capitalism in Australia (1)

The Australian community, like most other 'advanced societies', is a product of industrial capitalism. The special character of the relations between economy and society in Australia arises from the way in which capitalist structures are moderated and modified by a number of influences. We may divide these influences roughly into two kinds—structural characteristics deriving from the interaction of history and geography, and values or ideologies which both govern and reflect the relation between economic institutions and the rest of the social system.

Structural characteristics fall under seven headings:

(1) A plantation or colonial economy;

(2) A high level of dependence on government, through public enterprise, regulation, protection and incentives;

(3) A high level of overseas investment and ownership;

(4) The dependence of prosperity on export income from primary products, i.e. farm products and minerals;

(5) A high standard of living, protected by a wide variety of politico-legal devices;

(6) Industrial activity characterised by small and medium-sized enterprises;

(7) A high level of concentration of ownership and control of industry and finance.

To this list may be added an almost equal number of prevailing values and ideologies:

(1) The ideology of 'development', of 'Australia unlimited', and the filling up of vast open spaces;

(2) The concept of a 'free enterprise' economy;

(3) A 'ring fence of protection' for industry;

(4) Acceptance of the continuing need for foreign investment, with its counterpart, suspicion of exploitation by overseas interests;

(5) The economic role of the industrial arbitration system;

(6) The need for equal progress among the six states.

These structural and ideological features may be distinguished for analytical purposes, but in practice they overlap a great deal, and in the ensuing discussion they will not be systematically separated except where it is convenient to do so.

Government Intervention and 'Free Enterprise'

The origin of European society in Australia lies in the plantation of a colony, and its development in a continuous history of immigration. The industrial structure, for its part, is also the result of the introduction of European technology and of a continuous importation of techniques, of labour, of capital and of managerial skills. In a relatively small, isolated community, the industrial economy has remained dependent on its overseas sources, on the state of the export market for primary products, and above all on governmental encouragement for this implanted structure. The resultant characteristics are dealt with at length in the literature of economics, and what follows is largely a restatement of familiar themes, outlined briefly to support generalisations not about economics, but about the relation between economy and society, and in particular about the contribution of economic factors to the structure of class, status and power.

In an earlier chapter on the 'bureaucratic ascendency' which shapes so many areas of organised social life, we noted the extent to which government has been the most important single contributor to economic activity in Australia from the earliest years. Government enterprise, intervention, regulation and protection have been, for more than a century, the dominant factors in the growth of industry. Tariff protection was introduced in the colony of Victoria in the 1860's, became the settled policy of the whole country after the federation of the six colonies and has remained of tremendous importance ever since. Manufactured goods produced behind the tariff barrier are directed mainly at the small domestic market. This makes possible the existence of a large number of comparatively small and comparatively inefficient firms, depending on the protective system for their survival. The chronic shortage of investment capital also encourages the growth of monopolies or oligopolies in areas where large amounts of capital are required, and the development of these monopolies is frequently assisted by government action or even guaranteed by it, as in the case of sugar refining. Protective tariffs, taxation policies and other devices have also encouraged overseas investment as a means of overcoming the shortage of capital, so that industrial concentration frequently coincides with foreign ownership and control. The role of overseas firms in manufacturing industry has only been possible because of tariff protection.

The policy of protection, justified by traditional arguments for a century, received a new twist in the 1950's when Australian representatives at international trade conferences began to advance the view that Australia was a 'semi-developed' or 'intermediate' economy, qualitatively different from the 'developed' industrial economies of North America and Western Europe. This notion is supported by the British economist Maizels, who classifies a number of countries according to their level of industrial development. Group 1 of his classification comprises fully industrialised economies. In this group he places Canada, a country with which Australia has a number of affinities. Admittedly, he treats Canada as a borderline case. But there is no difficulty, on Maizels' criteria, in placing Australia clearly within Group 2, the 'semi-industrial' economies. The group comprises countries which, in 1955, produced over us$75 and not more than us$350 net value of manufactured goods per head, and where exports of finished manufactures accounted for less than 15 per cent of total exports. Apart from Australia and New Zealand, it includes Argentina, Israel and Yugoslavia. Except for the last-named, all the members of Group 2 are countries of recent settlement. 'The degree of industrialisation achieved by Australia and New Zealand, on the criteria used here, is as great as many of the advanced countries of Western Europe but, unlike the latter, they still depend predominantly on primary products for the great bulk of their export earnings.'[1]

Maizels also makes use of the extent to which manufacturing depends on the use of partly-finished imported goods:

As industries develop, a definite sequence of processes tends to be adopted. In the earlier stages, manufacturing may depend to a considerable extent on imported parts and components, or on imported semi-processed goods (such as yarns) whereas at a later stage, when labour skills are more developed and the home market is more extensive, complete production from the raw material to the final product may be introduced. This general sequence may, of course, apply more to some industries or countries than to others. Insofar, however, as it has any general application among industrialising countries it is likely to reinforce the tendency for the pattern of imports of manufactures to shift towards intermediate products in the earlier phases of the industrialisation process, though not perhaps in the latter.[2]

On this argument, the character of much industrial production in Australia also helps to place it in the semi-industrial category.

In the sphere of international trade, similar notions have been employed at least since 1955 to justify a continuing high level of government intervention to protect Australian manufacturing industries. In that year, a review of the General Agreement on Tariffs and Trade (GATT) took place in Geneva. The Australian delegation argued successfully that this country was in a midway situation which entitled it to special consideration regarding tariff policy. The responsible Minister, Mr John McEwen, restated the midway doctrine in his report to the federal parliament on the Geneva conference, and declared:

[1] A. Maizels, *Industrial Growth and World Trade*, London, 1963, p. 62. In recent years, about 12 per cent of Australia's exports have consisted of manufactured goods.
[2] ibid., p. 69

We had it accepted, not as an abstract principle, but as a practical feature governing Australia's position in many fields, that Australia was in a category almost of its own. . . . The Australian economy is a rapidly growing one, but still dependent on a few major exports for overseas funds.[3]

In 1965, when negotiations to amend GATT were again in progress, the Australian delegation once more emphasised the special midway position of their country. Under the amendments, developed countries were to agree not to impose new tariffs or other restrictions on manufactured products 'currently or potentially of particular export interest to less-developed countries' and gradually to eliminate existing tariffs and other restrictions on such products. Australia declared herself unable, as a country 'which is in neither of the categories specified in the articles' to accept the amendments as they stood. The leader of the Australian delegation, Mr A. T. Carmody, refused to commit Australia to a general policy of lowering tariffs:

In effect we are being asked to contract out of using the tariff to develop segments of industry which might be of interest to less-developed countries. Most of those industries are already developed in the industrial countries of the world, and it is those countries which would probably receive the main benefit from any such concessions. . . . It is inevitable that Australia will, on occasions, find it necessary to introduce protective duties on products of interest to less-developed countries. Usually these duties will be required only to protect our industries against imports from the highly industrialised countries.[4]

As might be expected from the above, the tariff has its most direct influence on those industries whose products compete with imported goods —which means the bulk of secondary industry. Something like 60 per cent of people employed in secondary industry work in fields whose economic viability depends on tariffs, especially machinery, motor vehicles, light to medium engineering products, paper, textiles, electrical apparatus and chemicals. The average duty for those goods protected by the tariff has been calculated as 30 per cent *ad valorem*, but in specific cases it is much higher, e.g. in clothing and textiles, and also in motor cars.[5] Under the influence of John McEwen, Minister for Trade since 1956, the policy of industrial growth became closely interwoven with the policy of 'protection all round', by which virtually any industry which could claim that it was competing with imported goods was able to obtain a measure of tariff protection.[6]

[3] Quoted by H. W. Arndt in the *Economic Record*, vol. 40, no. 95, 1965
[4] ibid.
[5] W. M. Corden, 'The Tariff' in A. Hunter (ed.), *The Economics of Australian Industry*, Melbourne, 1963
[6] M. Newton, 'The Economy' in A. F. Davies and S. Encel (eds.), *Australian Society*, Melbourne, 1965. Mr Newton, one of Australia's leading financial journalists, has been the foremost critic of Mr McEwen's indiscriminate protectionism.

The tariff, though its role is fundamental, is only one dimension of government economic intervention. The regulation of markets for agricultural and pastoral products is a major force—probably the most important single force—in the determination of prices, investment and output in this sector, where tax policies also have a great effect. Transport is either carried on by government enterprises or closely regulated by government. In the case of domestic air transport, the 'two-airline policy' provides a truly remarkable instance of fusion of the two policies. In the field of banking and credit, there is a system of detailed and complicated control by the Federal government and its agencies. Here too, direct government enterprise is of great significance, ever since Governor Macquarie was responsible for the establishment of the first bank in 1817. The largest providers of goods and services are in the public sector, which, because of its size and diversity, has an important influence on prices and output in many industries which deal with it either as customers or suppliers. Into any analysis of economic institutions in Australia, there must be inserted a consideration of the role of governments before any approximation to the true balance of forces governing economic behaviour can be reached. Leaving the rural sector aside, the Australian economy might be accurately described as a system of monopoly capitalism, operating through a highly regulated structure of output, prices and wages, which is interlocked with and maintained by an extensive system of government activity.

Paradoxically, the ideology of free enterprise and *laissez-faire* can be maintained under these circumstances. It is not surprising that businessmen should subscribe to this ideology, since its provides them with a *raison d'etre* and with a base from which to attack government 'interference'. A leading business spokesman declared in 1966 that the 'gigantic development projects visible around Australia today bear witness to the speed with which free enterprise is shaping Australia's future and the standard of living of its people.'[7] At the same time he noted that prosperity required efficient monetary, transport and communication facilities, and an atmosphere of political stability, law and order, and rewards for enterprise and skill—none of which would be possible without government action on a large scale. He also omitted to recognise that most of the 'gigantic development projects' are government projects. A more defensive note was struck at the first annual conference of the Institute of Directors in Sydney in 1966. 'There is an inbuilt resistance to free enterprise by those who have not the enterprise to be free. . . . Thousands of otherwise intelligent people are convinced that the free enterprise system is some sort of gigantic racket perpetuated by those who have a vested interest in its survival. . . . If directors themselves cannot see the point of speaking up

[7] F. G. May, president of the Associated Chambers of Commerce of Australia, *Sydney Morning Herald*, 8 July 1966

for themselves, and the system by which they survive, we might as well join in a chorus singing *The Red Flag*.'[8]

It is even more striking that this ideology should also be propagated from official sources. The annual economic survey published by the Commonwealth Treasury describes the system as 'a preponderantly free enterprise economy, in which the great bulk of goods and services are provided in response to demand, local or foreign. . . . The underlying assumption is that, given the right facilities and economic climate, private enterprise will advance growth further, and along lines more acceptable to the community, than any alternative system would.' However, the report is somewhat less than whole-hearted about the matter, because it emphasises in the same paragraph that governments go a long way to 'encourage and assist private enterprise in particular directions, through, for example, tariff protection, bounties and subsidies, tax concessions, overseas trade promotion, special developmental works and the like.'[9]

Even among economists, the dogmas of private enterprise retain a firm grip. It is true that, especially since Keynes, the role of government activity has been more effectively assimilated into the literature of economics, and theoretical models to explain the effects of governmental regulatory activities have formed an important part of academic economic discussion in the last three decades. Nevertheless, most attention has been paid to explaining how deviations from the 'competitive norm' operate in the business sector, with the conventional analyses of imperfect competition, oligopoly, monopoly and so forth. A widely-read textbook published in 1962 states that its object is to 'examine the Australian economy with the special task of determining the extent to which it diverges from the competitive *laissez-faire* model, both with respect to market organisation and to the activities of government.'[10] This orthodox stance also explains why economists have made so few attempts to explore the economics of state enterprises, even though their performance has a great effect on the economy as a whole and on public finance in particular. Although a pioneering attempt was made by Brigden in 1927,[11] there were few others for many years; one exception was the largely propagandist effort of the economic historian Brian Fitzpatrick, *Public Enterprise Does Pay* (Melbourne, 1945). It was not until 1968 that a sustained attempt was made by an academic economist to examine the Australian economy in the light of

[8] Sir Richard Powell, director-general of the Institute, reported in the *Canberra Times*, 26 February 1966

[9] *The Australian Economy, 1962*, Treasury Report to Parliament, Government Printer, Canberra

[10] P. H. Karmel and Maureen Brunt, *The Structure of the Australian Economy*, Melbourne, 1962, p. 4

[11] J. B. Brigden, 'State Enterprises in Australia', *International Labour Review*, July 1927, pp. 26-49

government intervention and to subject the working of state enterprises to detailed economic analysis.[12]

The terminological ambiguity which links 'free enterprise' and 'private enterprise' denotes a deeper ambiguity of meaning. It could be argued that the Australian economy is largely 'private', but not that it is free. The concept of free enterprise, dating from Adam Smith and the Physiocrats, can be applied to the growth of capitalism in Western Europe and North America, although with reservations which have been increasingly recognised by economic historians. These reservations become overwhelming in the case of colonial economies such as Australia, whose economic history only makes sense if government action is put at the centre of the picture.[13] The term 'private' is justified in the sense that three-quarters of the work force is employed in the private sector, and that manufacturing industry is privately owned, but not in other senses. It is much nearer the truth to conceive of the Australian economy as having been dependent, throughout its history, on government action and government regulation. 'Within the private sector', write Karmel and Brunt, 'there is as passionate a belief in "private enterprise" as can be found elsewhere, but it is a belief in a free enterprise which emphasises freedom from government intervention and public scrutiny. It is a belief in *private* enterprise in a very literal sense.'[14]

Nevertheless, the ideology of private enterprise remains strong and pervasive and it is important to explore the reasons for this strength and persistence. In the first place, although the economy is highly regulated, most of this regulation is haphazard, determined not by conscious planning but by a constant tussle between sectional interests for more or less regulation in the furtherance of their own objectives. Regulatory measures often result from *ad hoc* political pressures, including wars, depressions, balance of payments crises, or the failure of private enterprise in particular fields. The result is a patchwork which bears no resemblance to a planned economy.[15] The wide scope which the system allows for pressure-group activity gives colour to the notion of free competition, though perhaps not in the nineteenth century sense. In addition, the framework of legal regulation of business activity is in some ways remarkably light. The tone is set by Section 92 of the Federal Constitution, which provides that trade, commerce and intercourse between the states shall be 'absolutely free'—a deliberate piece of layman's language which has proved a goldmine to the

[12] Bruce McFarlane, *Economic Policy in Australia—The Case for Reform*, Melbourne, 1968, ch. 6. Studies of government enterprise are also included in Hunter, op. cit.

[13] This has been done by economic historians like Noel Butlin; e.g. 'The Shape of the Australian Economy 1856-1900', *Economic Record*, vol. 34, no. 67, 1958 and 'Colonial Socialism in Australia' in H. G. J. Aitken (ed.), *The State and Economic Growth*, New York, 1959.

[14] Karmel and Brunt, op. cit., p. 143

[15] Newton, loc. cit.; McFarlane, op. cit., ch. 5

legal profession and has enabled various schemes of government regulation to be invalidated by judges with obvious sympathies on the side of private business.[16] Provisions for disclosure of information are relatively sketchy, except in the special case of banking, where detailed requirements were imposed on the private banks during the 1939-45 war and have remained since. A crop of company failures following the credit squeeze of 1960 revealed how little legal protection was available to the investor, and uniform company legislation was agreed upon by the several states in 1961. Even then, the conservative government of South Australia refused to follow suit, until it was replaced by a Labor administration.

The lightweight regulation of company affairs is often justified on the grounds that it helps to attract foreign capital, and that tightening of the law would discourage overseas firms. This is highly arguable, to say the least. What can be said positively is that overseas firms are able to set up subsidiaries which require no local participation, about whose affairs there is very little information, and can remit all their profits overseas if they so desire.[17] Underlying public discontent with this situation comes to the surface periodically, especially when the annual report of General Motors-Holden's, the Australian subsidiary of the American automobile colossus, is published, showing large profits remitted to the United States.

The significance of rural industry, where the small producer remains important, is another factor in preserving the ideology of free enterprise, which plays a considerable part in the political rhetoric of the Country Party. Yet here we encounter a further paradox, for the Country Party also believes in a high level of government activity to benefit the farming community—agrarian socialism as it is sometimes called, or 'wheat pool socialism' as it was once derided by the Labor leader, J. H. Scullin.[18] This is only one of many paradoxes about the Country Party, whose curious character is amply documented in the literature of Australian politics. For our present purpose, it is sufficient that the Country Party is a major influence in support of the ideology of private enterprise, and that it finds it possible to reconcile this stance with other contradictory postures. Thus, it can at once favour the sale of wheat to China while being vociferously anti-Communist; attack the Labor movement while being hostile to big business; support free trade simultaneously with high tariffs and embargoes on the import of farm products; and demand lower taxes while supporting higher public expenditure (in country areas). Pointing out these paradoxes about the Country Party is a favourite game with both Liberal and Labor parties; as often happens, the players observe the mote in the other man's eye and ignore the beam in their own. The Liberals, for instance, find it possible to reconcile their support for free enterprise with a strong emphasis

16 Geoffrey Sawer, 'Constitutional Issues', in A. F. Davies and A. G. Serle, *Policies for Progress*, Melbourne, 1954
17 For an extensive discussion see E. L. Wheelwright and Brian Fitzpatrick, *The Highest Bidder*, Melbourne, 1965.
18 *Commonwealth Parliamentary Debates*, vol. 102, 1923, p. 100

on public enterprise,[19] and to praise the closely regulated two-airline system as an example of 'competition'. A. F. Davies has written that the 'shy appearance of a plank, "prevention of monopolies", in the Liberal Party's first Federal programme provoked one of the genuine belly-laughs of Australian politics.'[20] The ALP has, on various occasions, found it possible to prefer private enterprise to government enterprise and to support 'state interests' (which are often private interests) at the expense of national interests.[21] Jockeying for position among the states, and between the states and the Commonwealth, is a major political contribution towards sustaining the ideology of private enterprise, especially as it occurs irrespective of party.

Finally, it should be added that the ALP's attempt to nationalise banking in 1947-49 gave a great stimulus to 'free enterprise' propaganda.[22] The events of this period left a deep impress on national politics for a number of years and revived the image of the 'socialist tiger' first exploited by George Reid in 1905.

Ownership and Control

The legend of free enterprise makes particularly little sense in view of the remarkably high degree of concentration of ownership which has existed since the beginning of the century. From 1905 to 1919, a succession of attempts was made to restrict monopoly and cartelisation. With the rapid growth of urbanisation and industrialisation in the last years of the nineteenth century, there took place a shift of wealth and power from the pastoral aristocracy of the preceding period to the newer group of industrial entrepreneurs. The Labor Party, only recently organised, made the struggle against monopoly one of its foremost planks. Public opinion became alarmed at the rapid formation of cartels and trusts in industries such as tobacco, sugar, coalmining and shipping, and 'trust-busting' policies received wide support.[23] In 1906, the Federal government led by Deakin (under an alliance with Labor) brought down the Australian Industries Preservation Act, with provisions copied directly from the US Sherman Act. The statute was designed to prevent combinations in restraint of trade, which by unfair competition would injure Australian industry. It prohibited

[19] A useful discussion of Liberal attitudes to public enterprise is to be found in A. C. Garnett, *Freedom and Planning in Australia*, Wisconsin, 1949; a review of recent policies is given by Roger Wettenhall in the *Political Quarterly*, vol. 36, no. 4, 1965.
[20] Davies and Serle, op. cit., p. 65
[21] Examples of the twists and turns of ALP policy are to be found in D. Carboch and A. Wildavsky, *Studies in Australian Politics*, Melbourne, 1958; D. W. Rawson, 'Labour, Socialism and the Working Class', *Australian Journal of Politics and History*, vol. 7, no. 1, 1961; H. V. Evatt, *Australian Labour Leader*, Sydney, 1940, chs. 41-42.
[22] Crisp, op. cit., pp. 338-42, 368-74, gives details of this campaign.
[23] H. L. Wilkinson, *The Trust Movement in Australia*, Melbourne, 1914, esp. chs. 3-12, 14-19

monopolies and rings, and gave the government power to examine the books of companies against whom action was taken. One (unsuccessful) prosecution was launched under this measure, the Coal Vend case of 1912, in which the High Court of Australia and the Privy Council, on appeal, found against the Commonwealth.[24]

Until the 1950's, studies of industrial concentration were the province of left-wing pamphleteering, of which Wilkinson's 1914 volume was an early example. The general tendency of these studies has been to emphasise the existence of a small number of interconnected family groups owning large tracts of industry and commerce. In the 1930's, Rawling, Fitzpatrick and others were able to list an 'exclusive clique of wealthy families', about fifty in number, who formed an interlocking directorate controlling nearly one-half of Australia's total wealth, with links between activities such as woolgrowing, mining, sugar refining, brewing, iron and steel, papermaking, banking and shipping. Fitzpatrick also showed that, in 1939, 61 per cent of total investment in public companies was in 91 firms with capital exceeding one million pounds, and in particular that the group of companies linked with the iron and steel combine, BHP, controlled more than one-quarter of all shareholders' funds invested in public companies. In sixty companies belonging to the BHP group, forty-two men held nearly one-half of more than 300 directorships. Almost every profitable industry, concluded Fitzpatrick, was dominated by monopolistic organisations.[25]

This kind of pamphleteering has continued into the post-war period. J. Moss, *Monopoly Owns South Australia* (Adelaide, 1961), produced evidence that ownership of industry in that state was divided among twenty families with major shares in over 100 companies valued at not less than 580 million pounds. E. W. Campbell, *The Sixty Families Who Own Australia* (Sydney, 1964) brought the pre-war studies up to date. However, since the 1950's the study of industrial concentration has become part of the normal subject matter of economics, and there are now a number of analyses of the structure of ownership which go far beyond the resources of pamphleteering. Generally speaking, the more elaborate studies now available show that within the greatly expanded industrial sector of the economy since 1940, the pattern of concentration has remained broadly similar. Penrose, in an early study of this kind, estimated that the seventy-five largest manufacturing concerns owned, in 1955, more than 40 per cent of all fixed assets in manufacturing industry.[26] Hall, in 1956, analysed the financial structure of public companies in terms of total assets shown

---

[24] ibid. The Newcastle Coal Vend was a cartel arrangement between shipowners and colliery proprietors.
[25] J. N. Rawling, *Who Owns Australia?* Sydney, 1937; *Monopoly*, Left Book Club, Sydney, 1941; Brian Fitzpatrick, *A Critical Analysis of Australian Industrial Institutions*, Melbourne, 1941, and *The Rich Get Richer*, Melbourne, 1944
[26] Edith T. Penrose, 'Foreign Investment and the Growth of the Firm', *Economic Journal*, vol. 66, no. 262, 1956

in published balance sheets.[27] On this basis, he found that 100 of the largest companies accounted for 20 per cent of total employment in commerce and manufacturing, and for 30 per cent of total plant, equipment and buildings used in secondary industry. In selected industries, the degree of concentration was much higher. In iron and steel, the companies listed by Hall accounted for 100 per cent of employment; in brewing and in gas manufacture, 90 per cent and in rubber, 80 per cent.

Karmel and Brunt, in the volume already referred to,[28] devote their longest sections to the concentration of ownership and control. A few examples from their long and detailed analysis may be quoted.

Banking Six private banks held over 75 per cent of total assets.
Life insurance Five offices did 90 per cent of the business.
Hire purchase Eight firms handled 90 per cent of business.
Manufacturing The ten largest listed public companies accounted for 18 per cent of fixed assets in manufacturing; for various reasons, this is an understatement of the degree of concentration, especially as some of the biggest concerns are not listed.
Mining The four largest mining firms produced 40 per cent of the value of mining output; 20 per cent was produced by the BHP group, and 15 per cent by the 'Collins House' group.
Share values In 1960, the first 27 quoted public companies accounted for 42 per cent of total market value of ordinary shares quoted on the stock exchanges.
Mass media In 1960, 43 per cent of daily newspaper circulation was controlled by one firm, Herald & Weekly Times Ltd; the leading four enterprises handled 75 per cent of total daily circulation, owned 8 of the 16 metropolitan TV stations, and dominated the magazine market.

A more recent analysis of concentration in manufacturing industry is provided by Newton, on the basis of data available in 1964. In each case, a small group of firms controlled more than half of the output of the industry concerned:
Plastics—3
Soap and detergents—2
Motor cars—5 (85 per cent of the market)
Rubber—5 (80 per cent of the market)
Beer—5 (80 per cent of the market)
Copper extraction—3
Lead and zinc smelting—3
Aluminium extraction—2
Tobacco—4 (90 per cent of the market)
Pulp, paper and board—4 (75 per cent of the market)
In the case of iron and steel, flat steel products, steel tubes and sugar refining, the market was dominated or monopolised by a single firm.[29]

[27] A. R. Hall, *Australian Company Finance 1945-55*, Canberra, 1956
[28] *The Structure of the Australian Economy*, pp. 27-33, 55-60. Most of these figures apply to the period 1959-60.
[29] loc. cit., pp. 237-38

Karmel and Brunt's conclusion is that the degree of concentration is outstandingly high in Australia. One-third of manufacturing industry is 'highly concentrated', i.e. the four largest firms in the industry account for at least 50 per cent of employment, and one-half is at least 'fairly concentrated', i.e. with the largest eight firms in a corresponding position. By comparison with USA, monopolistic and near-monopolistic practices were 'overwhelmingly more important' and by comparison with Canada and the UK, 'significantly more important'. Not only that, but 'old-fashioned monopoly', regarded in the textbooks as virtually non-existent, existed in fourteen important cases, all of them basic industries, accounting for more than 5 per cent of employment and 8 per cent of value added in manufacturing.[30] It is interesting, they reflect, that the power exercised by a small number of men in this situation has been relatively unexplored. 'This may be largely because the dominance of a small number of men ("leaders of the business community" is the usual Australian phrase) both in economic decision-making and political bargaining is so obvious as to be taken for granted. And partly too it may be because paternalism in government and paternalism in business are part of the Australian tradition: the Australian is less of a rugged individualist than might be imagined.'[31]

A study of interlocking directorates by Rolfe, using data for 1963, gives a fine-grained picture of concentration in major business areas. Rolfe examined fifty of the largest Australian public companies. In brewing, she found three leading firms interlocked with forty-seven other companies, including six of her group of fifty, so that they were also indirectly interlocked with one another. In coal and gas production, the two largest producers were linked with nine other major firms in shipping, insurance, electrical manufacture and steelmaking. Electrical manufacturing itself was dominated by three firms, two of them interlocked, and linked also with the 'Collins House' group of metal companies. The food and tobacco group revealed interlocks between its largest member, the Colonial Sugar Refining Co. and another of Australia's largest firms, Australian Consolidated Industries; CSR was also interlocked with the textile firm of Courtaulds. In the manufacture of industrial gases and drugs, there were links with Collins House; with BHP, the steel monopoly; with three banks; with insurance; and with Mt Isa Mines. The Grimwade and Stewart families were responsible for a number of these interlocks. The Collins House group itself was linked with paper making, metal manufacturing, chemicals (ICIANZ), steel fabrication, insurance, pipemaking, cement and oil refining. The paper industry had a remarkable series of interlocks, partly due to overlapping interests and partly to historical and personal connections, which included packaging, chemicals, mining, insurance, cement, gasmaking, oil refining, glassmaking, pipemaking and the pastoral industry. The rubber industry (through Dunlop Rubber) had a variety of

[30] op. cit., pp. 78-87
[31] ibid., p. 63

links for a similar mixture of reasons, including radio manufacture, textiles, die casting, agricultural machinery and mining. Australian Consolidated Industries (ACI) had perhaps the most remarkable series of links—with BHP, ICIANZ, CSR, AMP (insurance), Carlton and United Breweries and the pastoral firm of Elder Smith Goldsbrough Mort.[32]

We have, then, an economy which is closely dominated by no more than two hundred firms, whose leading members have established themselves in impregnable positions in a number of strategic industries. Moreover, despite post-war industrial expansion and diversification, it is largely the old-established giants which retain this dominant position. 'If we ask how today's leading firms achieved both their large absolute size and their position of market dominance, the answer is largely that they were established early and grew with their markets. . . . It is a fact of greatest significance in Australian industrial organisation that the high concentration of economic power is largely a reflection of the high degree of market concentration. . . . In Australia over the last twenty-five years Big Business and positions of market dominance have gone hand in hand. The one has served to reinforce the other.'[33]

These points become clearer if we look at the top of the 'league table'. There were, in 1967, sixteen manufacturing or trading companies with shareholders' funds in excess of $75 millions.[34]

Table 17·1 The Top Sixteen Companies, 1967 (1)

1	Broken Hill Proprietary Co. Ltd (iron and steel monopoly, established 1885)
2	Imperial Chemical Industries of Australia and NZ (established 1928)
3	General Motors-Holden's (dating from 1926)
4	Colonial Sugar Refining Co. (sugar refining monopoly, established 1855)
5	Mt Isa Mines Ltd (established 1920)
6	Conzinc-Rio Tinto of Australia (CRA), established 1962, but dating back to 1905
7	Australian Consolidated Industries (glassmaking monopoly, established 1920, but dating from the 1870's)
8	British Petroleum (established in Australia in 1920)
9	Myer Emporium Ltd (retail trader, established 1930)
10	Australian Paper Manufacturers (established 1900)
11	Ampol Petroleum (established 1935)
12	G. J. Coles Ltd (retail trader, established 1920)
13	Woolworths Ltd (retail trader, established 1920)
14	Carlton and United Breweries (established 1920, but dating from the 1870's)
15	Dalgety-New Zealand Loan (pastoral, shipping and trading combine, established 1963 by merger of two firms dating back to 1845)
16	British Tobacco (Aust.) Ltd (established 1904)

If employment and other criteria are taken into account, the story is much the same. In Table 17·2, ranking by shareholders' funds is compared with rankings under three other headings indicating levels of activity.

[32] Hylda A. Rolfe, *The Controllers*, Melbourne, 1967, ch. 5
[33] Karmel and Brunt, op. cit., pp. 57, 89
[34] These details are drawn from the *Delfin Digest*, Sydney, 1968.

Table 17·2 The Top Sixteen Companies, 1967 (2)

Firm		Total Assets	Net Profit	Employment
1	BHP	1	1	1
2	ICIANZ	2	7	10
3	GMH	5	2	5
4	CSR	3	5	9
5	MIM	10	3	31
6	CRA	4	4	30
7	ACI	13	8	6
8	BP	6	20	32
9	Myers	12	6	3
10	APM	15	12	25
11	Ampol	8	14	72
12	G. J. Coles	14	9	4
13	Woolworths	9	10	2
14	C. & U.B.	18	13	38
15	Dalgety-NZL	7	15	35
16	British Tobacco	11	11	8

These rankings show, inter alia, that the two oldest monopolies in Australia, BHP and CSR, have retained their pre-eminent position. The predominance of BHP over other large companies has, if anything, become more marked as a result of post-war industrial expansion. In 1967, BHP's shareholders' funds amounted to $574 millions, compared with its nearest rivals, ICIANZ ($196 millions), GMH ($191 millions), and CSR ($186 millions). Four other companies—MIM, CRA, ACI and BP—had shareholders' funds in excess of $100 millions. BHP's total assets were $870 millions, compared with ICIANZ ($364 millions), CSR ($302 millions) and CRA ($299 millions). Its net profit was $36 millions, compared with $22 millions for GMH, $21 millions for MIM, $13 millions for CRA, $12·9 millions for CSR, and $11 millions for the Myer Emporium. It employed a total of 48,000 people, almost twice as many as the next largest employer, Woolworths; only three other firms, Myers, G. J. Coles and GMH employed over 20,000 people.

As is well known, the remarkable role of BHP in Australian industry (and its corresponding place in the pantheon, or pandemonium, of monopoly) is due to its complete vertical monopoly of iron and steel production and its dominant position in many fields of steel fabrication, including structural steel, tubes, containers, wire, shipbuilding and toolmaking. In addition, the company has large interests in non-ferrous minerals and metals, shipping, fertilisers, chemicals (it is a large shareholder in ICIANZ), papermaking and aircraft manufacture.[35] Through its investments in other companies, and through large-scale holdings in BHP by banks, investment companies and unit trusts, its ramifications are vast. Its most recent act of diversification was to go into the petroleum business in partnership with Esso-Standard Oil.

[35] For a detailed history of BHP see Helen Hughes, *The Australian Iron and Steel Industry, 1848-1962*, Melbourne, 1964.

The second largest monopoly firm, CSR, has a much narrower base and its post-war growth has been due very largely to diversification and investment in other areas. CSR's interests now include activities as remote from sugar as road metal, concrete, iron ore, television, building materials, chemicals, aluminium smelting, plastics and mineral insulating materials.

Mergers and Takeovers

The merger movement in Australian industry and commerce has been even more active than in other countries, stimulated by the fact that much of Australian industry operates through small firms with small capital resources. In 1956, Hall suggested that capital shortage was the major reason for mergers among firms worth less than £200,000.[36] Bushnell, in a detailed study of mergers and takeovers, gave a variety of reasons for the merger movement: taxes, rapid industrial expansion, rapid technological change, capital shortage, shortage of qualified managers and technical personnel, import restrictions, over-full employment, movement of firms into interstate markets, entry of overseas firms into the Australian market. 'Advanced technology and the increased size of the Australian economy demanded a revolution in the organisation of some industries to enable production by large firms using complicated production lines backed by greatly expanded research and engineering.'[37] Bushnell estimated that, between 1947 and 1955, there were twice as many mergers per 1,000 firms in Australia as in the United States.[38] He also concluded that a substantial part of the growth of large companies was due to mergers; 40 of the 103 largest firms engaged in take-overs during the period he studied, and these contributed between 14 per cent and 18 per cent of the total growth of these 103 companies.[39] The most significant effect of mergers was to increase concentration in areas where oligopoly already existed, and Bushnell noted eighteen of these, including banking, newspaper publishing, air transport, chemicals, brewing, papermaking, pastoral companies, textiles, rubber and tobacco.[40] A similar conclusion is reached by Karmel and Brunt, who suggested that 'the merger movement has been a force making for increased concentration.'[41]

Restrictive Practices

Heavy concentration of ownership and control is one side of the story; the other side is the continued importance of the small firm whose role is protected by government action (especially tariffs) and by an extensive

[36] A. R. Hall, op. cit.
[37] J. A. Bushnell, *Australian Company Mergers 1945-59*, Melbourne, 1961, p. 94
[38] ibid., p. 83
[39] ibid., pp. 120-21
[40] ibid., pp. 163, 210
[41] op. cit., p. 91

network of self-regulation in the form of restrictive practices, which flourish with tropical luxuriance in Australia. Restrictive practices contribute largely to the 'regulated economy' where, as Newton observes, 'the danger of cosy little arrangements, benefiting small groups of producers at the expense of the community at large, is an ever-present problem.'[42] Restrictive practices, as H. W. Arndt observed some years ago, are characteristic of those industries 'where numerous small and medium-sized firms have banded together in trade associations. It is here that we get the explicit agreements for price maintenance, buttressed by restrictive-entry practices, such as exclusive dealing, collective boycotts, aggregate rebates, etc. which do most damage to the efficiency of business.' As he went on to comment, the extent of restrictive practices in Australia is probably greater than in either Britain or America, but is very difficult to verify because of the lack of information and the lack of legal provisions or administrative machinery for finding out. 'The economist who wants to investigate the prevalence of monopolistic practices in Australia comes up against insuperable barriers of business secrecy, misleading accounts and the law of libel. . . . Analysis of published accounts . . . is of little use so long as profits are arbitrarily understated by one or more of various well-known devices and essential information such as turnover figures (which any self-respecting American corporation publishes as a matter of course) withheld.'[43]

Acceptance by both business and governments of the existence of restrictive practices is widespread and long-established, and attempts to deal with them have been sporadic and limited. In the period 1910-20, a number of state enterprises were set up by Labor governments in New South Wales and Queensland, largely to counteract monopolistic practices and high prices in fields such as building materials, insurance and food supply. A good deal of evidence about restrictive practices was collected by the Tariff Board during its hearings of applications for tariff protection,[44] and the tariff has occasionally been used against monopoly. But the general degree of acceptance of restrictive practices is indicated by the fact that NSW legislation on the subject has never been enforced. It was not until 1957 that a royal commission was set up by the West Australian government to investigate the matter. The remarkable construction placed by businessmen on the words 'free enterprise' is indicated in the following exchange:

Question: Can you indicate why you are not in favour of government

---

[42] Newton, loc. cit., p. 252

[43] H. W. Arndt, 'The Dangers of Big Business', *Australian Quarterly*, vol. 29, no. 4, 1957

[44] An analysis of material presented to Tariff Board hearings in the 1930's is made in a paper on monopolistic practices written in 1947 by Dr L. J. Hume of the Australian National University. This paper has unfortunately remained unpublished. Particular instances examined by Dr Hume include automotive parts and petroleum products.

control and yet in favour of private control in regard to price fixation? *Witness*: Yes, because firstly, we stand primarily for free enterprise and the voluntary conducting of our affairs without being bound by a statute.[45]

An illustration of relations in the hardware trade is given by Hunter, who has specialised in the study of restrictive practices and monopolies. At the end of 1959, representatives of the firm of John Lysaght (Aust.) Pty Ltd, which has a monopoly of the manufacture of galvanised iron, met the leaders of the trade association concerned at a conference in Sydney. 'Interstate delegates were entertained by Lysaghts at luncheon at the Hotel Australia, and appreciation was expressed for the manufacturers' hospitality, for their co-operation, and support in the orderly and efficient marketing of galvanised iron. The success of the conference provides further evidence of the cordiality and goodwill that exists between the manufacturers and their Australian distributors and the growing understanding of each others' problems by a closer merchant-manufacturer relationship.'[46] Thus, Hunter observes dryly, do 'our business men, apparently with a high degree of unanimity and in an atmosphere of good cheer, formulate the prices and competitive conditions which they consider best suited for the Australian public.'[47]

In a detailed analysis of the extent of restrictive practices, Hunter estimated that there were approximately 600 state and federal associations, of which about two-thirds operated restrictive agreements, and that tied contracts and collusive tendering were significantly more common in Australia than elsewhere. He cites agreements dealing with pharmaceutical products, confectionery, tobacco and cigarettes, automotive parts, tyres and tubes, petroleum products, paper products, rope and cordage, electric batteries, cement, footwear, electrical goods, building materials, bread, timber, milk, etc. etc. By any standards, he concludes, Australia is 'handsomely endowed' with restrictive practices.

Two remarkable examples of restrictive practices in the fields of automotive spare parts and timber supplies were analysed in detail in 1963 by the fortnightly review *Nation*. In the first case, operations were controlled in the state of NSW by the Wholesale Automotive Supplies and Parts Association (WASPA), consisting of nine firms which were responsible for ninety per cent of the business in the state. WASPA operated through an agreement with the Automotive Parts Manufacturers of Australia which provided that non-members of WASPA would not be supplied with goods. The biggest maker of spare parts, Repco Ltd, was a member of both associations, and could exert sanctions on both sides of the relationship. If a manufacturer infringed the agreement, he would be blackballed by the

---

[45] *Report of the Royal Commission on Restrictive Trade Practices and Legislation*, Perth, 1958
[46] *The Federated Hardware News*, Sydney, no. 30, December 1959; quoted by Alex Hunter, 'Restrictive Practices and Monopolies in Australia' in H. W. Arndt and W. M. Corden (eds.), *The Australian Economy*, Melbourne, 1963, p. 301
[47] Hunter, ibid.

member firms of WASPA. In 1962, a distributing firm which was a non-member submitted a statement to the Tariff Board alleging that they had been unable to buy locally manufactured parts. Timber marketing was controlled by two associations, one concerned with local distribution and one with importation. An inquiry in 1955 by a judge of the NSW Industrial Commission, Mr Justice Richards, revealed an array of sanctions, including fines for breaches of secrecy administered by these two bodies. He concluded that the cartel arrangements operated 'in such a way and to such an extent as in the circumstances to prevent or destroy all reasonably effective competition. They may be said to have stifled or struck down effective competition which stands between them and the community at large.'[48]

It is only fair to add that in 1963 the Commonwealth Attorney-General, prompted by evidence of public dissatisfaction, introduced a Bill into Federal Parliament to provide for registration and regulation of trade agreements. After considerable lobbying by business interests against the legislation and the translation of the Attorney-General, Sir Garfield Barwick, to the High Court, a watered-down version of the original Bill was finally passed in 1967. This was the first piece of federal legislation since the abortive Industries Preservation Act of 1906.

Overseas Ownership

From its colonial origins, the growth of white society in Australia has depended on the inflow of men, money and materials. Periods of economic expansion have coincided with the large-scale flow of capital from overseas. Hall has demonstrated that the rapid growth of urbanisation at the end of the nineteenth century was made possible by British investment, just as the railway boom of the 1870's and 1880's was fed by British capital.[49]

This dependence on overseas investment has, throughout the twentieth century, given rise to mixed if not contradictory feelings. The 'free enterprise' philosophy expressed by businessmen and by the Liberal Party sees overseas investment as an almost unmitigated gain. The late Mr Harold Holt, then Treasurer, stated in 1965:

The Government has consistently encouraged capital inflow, believing it to be vital to Australia's growth and the strengthening of national security . . . the Commonwealth has never wavered in its view that the advantages far outweigh the disadvantages.

This favourable view diminishes as one moves leftwards across the political spectrum. The Country Party's leading spokesman, Mr John McEwen, Minister for Trade and Industry, stated in 1963:

[48] 'Masters of Restraint', *Nation*, 9 March 1963
[49] A. R. Hall, *The London Capital Market and the Flow of Capital to Australia 1870-1914*, Canberra, 1964, pp. 180-89

I support the inflow of capital whether borrowed by the Government or
. . . brought in by private enterprise. . . . But that does not mean that I
necessarily believe in the unlimited or indiscriminate inflow of capital.

The leader of the ALP, Mr A. A. Calwell, declared that his party welcomed overseas investment:

when it genuinely contributes to the growth and prosperity of this nation.
We do not applaud investment that merely takes over control of existing
well-established Australian industries. . . . We believe that the control of
basic Australian industries should remain in Australian hands. We believe
that the present restrictions on exports imposed on Australian subsidiaries
by British, American and other foreign companies must be abolished.[50]

Opinion among economists, whatever their political colour, is that
official policies of encouraging overseas investment in the name of
'development' are short-sighted and uncritical, especially because of their
implications for the balance of payments. The consensus of economic
opinion was expressed in the report of the Vernon Committee, set up by
the Federal government in 1963:

Once an economy has a substantial body of overseas investment it is in a
sense 'on the tiger's back' unless the trade balance is improving sufficiently
to meet the additional income payable overseas. The continuation of capital
inflow becomes seemingly more and more desirable as a means of off-
setting the increasing payments on the latter account . . . [and] the
immediate consequences of an interruption of the capital inflow . . .
become more and more serious.[51]

McFarlane[52] has listed nine other disadvantages arising from dependence
on foreign capital:

1 Foreign control of growth points in the economy;
2 Control over capital assets;
3 Foreign-owned firms can evade government fiscal controls;
4 Dampening effect on shares of local firms;
5 Increased concentration, both by foreign ownership and by local
   mergers to compete with foreign firms;
6 Wasteful competition in new fields of production, e.g. motor cars;
7 Depressing effect on local research and development;
8 Restriction on exports by local subsidiaries;
9 Political influence (e.g. a US veto on trade with Communist countries).

However, other left-wing economists are inclined to discount some of the
more extreme objections. Newton, for instance, writes that 'the invasion
of the Australian economy by foreign companies in recent years has had

[50] These three statements are quoted by R. A. Irish in *Growth*, no. 10, 1966 (Committee for Economic Development of Australia), pp. 37-38.
[51] *Report of the Committee of Economic Inquiry*, Canberra, 1965, vol. 1, para 11.47
[52] McFarlane, *Economic Policy in Australia*, pp. 151-53

a salutary effect by helping to break down local restrictive practices and by bringing in a new range of improved management and technology . . . foreign participation does provide at least the potentiality of increasing competition in a regulated economy.'[53] An English economist, W. B. Reddaway, whose acquaintance with the Australian economy goes back to the 1930's, suggests that 'the more emotive arguments used on this topic seem to rest on a false identification of "foreign owned" with "owned by a foreign government".'[54]

Traditionally, foreign ownership was British ownership, and hostility to overseas investment has been strongly coloured by resentment of British dominance in Australian affairs. British ownership has predominated for many years in the following areas:

Chemicals (ICI)
Paints
Matches (Bryant & May)
Soap (Unilever)
Petroleum products (Shell and BP)
Cable making
Tobacco (Imperial Tobacco Co.)
Rubber (Dunlop Rubber)
Cement (Associated Portland Cement Manufacturers)
Mining (RTZ and others)
Electrical appliances (AEI, General Electric)
Woollen yarn (Patons & Baldwins)
Synthetic fibres (ICI, Courtaulds)
Cocoa and chocolate (Cadbury's)
Pastoral production (Dalgety's, Australian Agricultural Co., Australian Estates Co., Vesteys, AML & F Co.)
Shipping (P & O and the Australian conference lines)

These interests have traditional links with the City of London. Two of the major private banks, the Australia and New Zealand Bank and the English, Scottish and Australian Bank, have their head offices in London. Both are closely linked with the merchant banking firm of Antony Gibbs & Sons. In 1965 Lord Aldenham (Walter Gibbs), chairman of Gibbs and a director of the Westminster Bank, was a director of the ES & A Bank; Sir Geoffrey Gibbs was chairman of the ANZ Bank. The Hon. D. F. Brand, chairman of Lazards, was a director of Barclays Bank, the National Provincial Bank, the Midland Bank, Glyn Mills, De Stein's merchant bank, and chairman of the ES & A Bank. The AML & F (Australian Mercantile Loan and Finance Co.) had directors from the ES & A, the merchant banks of Lazards, Helbert Wagg and Arbuthnot Latham, and Lloyds Bank.

---

[53] Newton, loc. cit., pp. 248-52
[54] W. B. Reddaway, 'The Australian Economy, 1937 and 1965', *Australian Journal of Science*, vol. 28, no. 8, 1965, p. 301

Newton, in an analysis of industries where foreign companies are important, distinguished those areas which were 'dominated' and those which were 'heavily infiltrated' by foreign companies. In the first category are agricultural machinery, motor vehicles, chemicals, paints, aluminium extraction and fabrication, oil refining, matches, soap and detergents, telephone equipment, cable making and pharmaceutical products. In the second are food, rubber, cement, non-ferrous metals other than aluminium, electrical appliances, automotive parts, woollen and synthetic yarns.[55]

Until the 1950's, overseas investment was overwhelmingly British. American investment first became significant in 1949-50 and thereafter climbed steadily until in 1961-62 it actually surpassed the British figure. According to an official survey, the total figure for the postwar period up to 1964 was £1,967 millions ($3,934 millions), of which 54·4 per cent came from Britain, 34·3 per cent from USA, and 11·3 per cent from other countries.[56] Another official survey found that in 1965 the book value of business assets owned in Australia by foreign companies was $4,730 millions, of which the US share was $1,789 millions.[57]

There is some dispute as to the actual proportion of Australian industry which is under overseas control. The official figures give the impression that 25 per cent of manufacturing industry is owned overseas. The most detailed calculations on this point have been made by Wheelwright. In 1967, Wheelwright published his most recent analysis, based on 300 of the largest manufacturing companies. He examined the largest twenty shareholdings in each of these firms and concluded that 36 per cent of their equity was owned overseas. The main reason for the high level of concentration of ownership was large holdings by companies, which accounted for almost three-quarters of the total held by the twenty largest shareholders. Australian firms held only £128 million ($256 millions) out of this company-owned equity, the remaining £746 million ($1,492 millions) accruing to overseas firms. Nearly all this foreign equity was held in 193 companies, of which 108 were British-owned (forty-five wholly British), seventy-four American (forty wholly American) and the remaining eleven were divided between Swiss, Dutch, German and French corporations. British capital was concentrated in petroleum, chemicals, non-ferrous metals, iron and steel, food processing, textiles and electrical engineering; American in motor vehicles, petroleum, chemicals, non-ferrous metals, agricultural equipment and food processing.[58]

Wheelwright found that the twenty largest shareholdings, when aggregated, accounted for 57·7 per cent of total shareholders' funds; there

[55] Newton, loc. cit., pp. 249-51
[56] Commonwealth Treasury, *Aspects of Overseas Investment*, Canberra, 1965
[57] Department of Trade and Industry, *Overseas Investment in Australian Industry*, Canberra, 1966
[58] E. L. Wheelwright and Judith Miskelly, *Anatomy of Australian Manufacturing Industry*, Sydney, 1967, p. 3

were 3,683 such holdings out of a total of 800,000. The 299 largest holdings alone accounted for 40 per cent of all holdings and the major reason for this heavy concentration was the extent of overseas ownership.[59] Overseas control, he argues further, is an important factor in the advance of the managerial revolution. 'Over two-thirds of these key manufacturing companies, and over four-fifths of their assets were controlled by managers of one kind or another . . . for nearly half the companies and over half the assets, the managers are selected by the management of overseas corporations.'[60]

Wheelwright's investigations give a picture far removed from the traditional left-wing theme of the 'sixty families who own Australia' (to which he himself gave some support in an earlier version of this study[61]). 'The category most deserving of the title of the dominant owners of the large concentrations of capital in these key manufacturing companies is not rich Australians but overseas corporations.'[62] Nevertheless, as he himself shows, there remains a solid core of family shareholdings, accounting for about 10 per cent of total equity, of which he identifies 84 separate holdings of $500,000 or more held by one person or a small group of persons.[63] Most, but not all of these, were established in the early days of industrialisation. The extent of this family influence and its continued predominance at the directorial and executive level, is examined in detail in later chapters. Although post-1945 industrial expansion has been financed to an enormous extent by overseas capital, the local agents and beneficiaries of this expansion continue to be the established economic elite.

[59] ibid., p. 18
[60] ibid., p. 8
[61] E. L. Wheelwright, *Ownership and Control of Australian Industry*, Sydney, 1957
[62] op. cit., p. 4
[63] ibid., p. 44

18: Capitalism in Australia (2): Wealth and Power

'Democracy for the few, democracy for the rich: that is the democracy of capitalist society'—so wrote Lenin in *The State and Revolution*. Or, as the American sociologist Robert Lynd put it more temperately, a Liberal democracy is one which yokes together a professedly democratic social structure and political system with a capitalist economy.[1] The principles of social and political equality implicit in one sphere are periodically in conflict with the principles of individual enrichment and the private ownership of the means of production on which the other is based, and from this tension are formed the politico-economic relations typical of a capitalist democracy.

According to Finer, the political power of private capital in a democratic polity may be classified under five headings:

(i) The possession of wealth and its concomitant social advantages;
(ii) Organisation, in the form of large enterprises and 'peak associations' of industrial groups;
(iii) Special access to government;
(iv) Patronage—the power to hire, fire and intimidate;
(v) Surrogateship—i.e. the power to take over some of the functions of government through the principle of 'self-government in industry'.[2]

A comprehensive discussion of these phenomena would require not one but several books. The literature of Australian politics, industrial relations and economic history is in any case replete with examples of the way in which private capital has used its power to gain both short- and long-term advantages through its financial connections with conservative political parties, the manipulation of public opinion, the operation of a multitude of lobbying organisations, tax concessions and protective tariffs, and the work of the numerous 'organs of syndical satisfaction' as J. D. B. Miller has aptly called them in his book *Australian Government and Politics*. In this chapter and in the following one we shall be concerned merely to select examples of politico-economic relationships which illustrate the

[1] Robert S. Lynd, 'Power in American Society' in A. W. Kornhauser (ed.), *Problems of Power in American Democracy*, Detroit, 1957, p. 6
[2] S. E. Finer, 'The Political Power of Private Capital', *Sociological Review*, vol. 3, no. 2, 1955

distribution of class, status and power in the Australian community; the way this distribution is reflected in the attitudes of political organisations and social groups; the organisational structures and policies of business pressure groups; and the interlocking of business, political and administrative hierarchies as manifested in the careers of individuals. The present chapter deals with the long-established resentment of 'money power' which has been the dominant strain in anti-capitalist ideology; stresses and strains within the parties of 'town and country capital', as L. F. Crisp describes them in his standard textbook, *Australian National Government*; the financial links between big business and the Liberal Party; and the structure of the major business pressure groups. The subsequent chapter goes into some detail about interlocking hierarchies and the final chapters in this part of the book examine the social characteristics of the business elite.

The Attack on 'Money Power'

Pamphleteering attacks on the power of private capital have a long history in Australia, but the diversity of private ownership has led to a corresponding diversity of objects for these criticisms. At various times, the attack has fluctuated between private fortunes as against trusts and monopolies, local capital as against overseas capital, manufacturers as against bankers, restrictive practices as against inadequate protection for local producers. However, the most persistent form of attack has been on 'money power', a mode which in Australia, as in North America, appeals to farmers and small shopkeepers as well as the radical sections of the working class. The anti-trust movement, which attracted the support of these diverse groups in the USA from the 1880's, has also had some influence on public policy in Australia.

From an early stage of its history, the Labor movement made a number of attempts to resist the growth of concentration, either by supporting legislation like the Industries Preservation Act of 1906, by advocating public ownership in its platform, or by using public enterprise to counteract restrictive practices and excessively high prices. The failure of the Industries Preservation Act in the courts led to attempts at constitutional amendments designed to give the Commonwealth parliament power to control monopolies and combinations in restraint of trade. Three constitutional referenda for this purpose were submitted to the electorate, and rejected, in 1911, 1913 and 1919.[3] In addition, various royal commissions have inquired into monopoly in oil, sugar and iron and steel. An early Labor attack on the trusts was mounted by W. M. Hughes, later Prime Minister, in a series of articles published in the Sydney *Daily Telegraph* and republished in book form in 1908 as *The Case for Labor*. A radical journalist of the same period, H. I. Jensen, claimed that 'instead of an irresponsible and callous aris tocracy of birth claiming all the good things of life, whilst doing nothing, we have an aristocracy of money lords claiming everything and discarding all responsibility.' Jensen's main complaint was against domination by British capital: 'The system swindles and impoverishes us, and unduly enriches the British moneylender.' He ridiculed the Liberal politicians of the day who 'delighted to see the result of Australian industry flowing to London to pay interest', and tried to frighten voters away from the Labor Party by telling them that capital would be 'humping its bluey out of the country, and of the disaster which will befall us when it has left.' Jensen made an economic point of significance when he noted that both Australia and New Zealand were suffering from the decline in commodity prices, which had the effect of increasing the amount of interest on debts owed to Britain, and anticipated the later policies of J. T. Lang by calling for the abolition of the gold standard and its replacement by an exchange standard based on the average price of commodities. His peroration injected an anti-Semitic note which is familiar in the literature of money power: New Zealand, he declared, was 'allowing herself to be fleeced wholesale by British capitalism; in other words, by hooknosed moneylenders.'[4]

A politico-religious overtone of a different character was struck a few years later by the Labor publicist and MP, Frank Anstey. 'Under the guise of the freest democracy', he wrote, 'the most odious oligarchy holds unbroken dominion. . . . In secrecy and silence has been built up a Black Masonic Order of Plutocracy, cemented in all its parts by the lust of power and the cohesive power of plunder.'[5]

Hostility to overseas money power was effectively exploited by the Labor Premier of Queensland, E. G. Theodore, during a political crisis in 1920. The crisis had arisen over three separate issues: the appointment of a new Governor, an attempt by Theodore to raise a loan for developmental works while on a visit to London, and an Act of Parliament to abolish the upper house of the state legislature. Among other actions, the Theodore government had nationalised the privately owned tramways in Brisbane. At a meeting of pastoral and commercial interests, a 'constitutional defence committee' of three members was chosen, headed by a leading Queensland businessman and former Premier, Sir Robert Philp. This committee went to London shortly before Theodore was due to do so, petitioned the Colonial Secretary, Lord Milner, to appoint a new Governor and used its influence in the City to prevent Theodore from obtaining a loan. The financial press of London advised its readers that lending would be dangerous unless the state government gave assurances to investors against confiscation. A Brisbane newspaper echoed these sentiments by alleging that the Labor government was setting up a dictatorship. Queensland was controlled by a junta which

H. I. Jensen, *The Rising Tide*, Sydney, 1909, pp. 53-66

Frank Anstey, *Money Power*, Melbourne, 1921. Anstey's diatribe against the ___ons recalls a familiar theme of Catholic political rhetoric. Although Anstey ___ thinker, he came from an Irish Catholic family.

had seized the organs of the state. Only a delegation of solid citizens could undo the damage by advising a policy of caution until 'responsible government' was restored by the return of the Nationalist Party. Theodore failed to obtain his loan, and on returning to Queensland obtained a dissolution of parliament and campaigned on a policy of 'self-determination'. Financial interests in London, he declared, were trying to run Queensland by insisting on the repeal of state legislation. British capitalists were 'digging their claws into the industries and businesses of Queensland and gorging themselves on the life blood of the people. . . . The Tories here talk of the junta of the Trades Hall. Why, we know nothing about outside influence or the power of a secret junta. We have to go to London to learn what that means.'[6] Theodore's rhetoric clearly touched responsive chords among the electorate, because his government was returned with a comfortable majority.

The great depression which began in 1929 brought large-scale unemployment among the working class and the collapse of markets for primary products. Monetary theories grew thickly in that underworld of economics from which, as Keynes admitted, many valuable ideas nevertheless emerged. The Commonwealth Bank, controlled by a board made up of businessmen, insisted that the Scullin Labor government pursue orthodox deflationary policies, and the Commonwealth Arbitration Court cut the national basic wage by 10 per cent. At this point a state Labor government was elected in New South Wales under the leadership of J. T. Lang. Lang, whose economics were of a primitive Keynesian variety, revived the demand for the abolition of the gold standard and its replacement by a 'goods standard', and also tried to suspend debt payments to overseas bondholders. This brought him into conflict with the federal government (by now a non-Labor administration), which pushed through an Act of Parliament sequestrating the state government's finances. Lang attempted to evade this, and for his pains was dismissed by the state Governor, Sir Philip Game.[7] In his book *Why I Fight* (1936), Lang blamed the crisis on a bankers' ramp, as various Labor men in Britain had done, and gave particular attention to the personal role of Sir Montagu Norman, governor of the Bank of England. According to Lang's account, the two directors of the Bank of England, Niemeyer and Gregory, who visited Australia on a special mission in 1930, had come at Norman's behest to conspire with the Australian banks against the Federal Labor government.[8] A similar viewpoint was put by E. G. Theodore, now Federal Treasurer, in a public

---

6 S. Encel, *Cabinet Government in Australia*, Melbourne, 1962, pp. 95-96, 107
7 For the history of this period see, e.g. F. O. Shann and D. B. Copland, *The Battle of the Plans*, Sydney, 1931; W. R. Maclaurin, *Economic Planning in Australia 1929-36*, New York, 1937; L. F. Crisp, *Ben Chifley*, Melbourne, 1961, chs. 5-6; S. Encel, op. cit., pp. 65-67; Bethia Foott, *Dismissal of a Premier*, Sydney, 1968.
8 Sir Otto Niemeyer came from one of the Anglo-German families who have figured in English banking history. He was wrongly believed to be a Jew, and this helped to feed the theory of an international Jewish bankers' conspiracy.

speech: 'The powers of the organised banks in Australia are used to dictate the Government's economic policies, financial policy and even its industrial policy. These great financial institutions have arrogated to themselves a political power that should not be in their possession. They have no mandate from the people to wield the power which they have wielded.'[9]

The most picturesque account of the situation was given in a report by the Australian correspondent of the London weekly *The New Age*,[10] while Lang was still in office. The Australian Loan Council and the Premiers' Conference, which Lang was defying, represented 'the political and financial wings of the Private Financial Autocracy which effectively rules Australia behind the veil of the Federal Government's nominal rulership.' This 'Directorate' had bought the newspapers, and it had also helped to set up the New Guard,[11] a para-military organisation opposed to Lang, which the journal called the 'Niemeyer Nazis'. There was, the correspondent continued, 'an illimitable amount of credit ready to be mobilised in every important capital of the world and flung in to support the banks' Australian agents. Seeing that the banks are already nursing practically the whole of the world's mercantile marine, the addition of a tiny little suckling like a group of Australian newspapers would not trouble them. The Old Sow of Finance has a tit for every tout.'[12]

The practical outcome of this hostility to the 'money power' was the setting up in 1935 of a royal commission on banking and monetary policy by the conservative Lyons government, responding tardily to the strength of public feeling. One of the members of the commission was J. B. Chifley, a former member of the Scullin government, later to become Treasurer and Prime Minister. In a minority report, Chifley advocated the nationalisation of all private banking. Banking, he declared, 'differs from any other form of business, because any action, good or bad, by a banking system affects almost every phase of national life. A banking policy should have one aim—service for the general good of the community. The making of profit is not necessary to such a policy . . . there is no possibility of the objectives [of the commission's report] being reached, or of any well-ordered progress being made in the community, under a system in which there are privately-owned trading banks which have been established for the purpose of making profit.'[13]

In 1947, Chifley attempted to put these views into effect. The bank

---

9 Crisp, op. cit., p. 55
10 *The New Age*, established by A. R. Orage (1873-1934) in 1907, was a leading radical weekly for a number of years. In 1918, Orage became converted to the monetary theories of C. H. Douglas, and *The New Age* was for some time a vehicle for Social Credit propaganda.
11 See below, ch. 26
12 *The New Age*, 24 March 1932
13 Chifley's role on the commission is described by Crisp, op. cit., pp. 166-72. The work of the commission and the fate of its recommendations are examined by L. F. Giblin, *The Growth of a Central Bank*, Melbourne, 1951.

nationalisation legislation of that year was seen by him and his colleagues as 'the ultimate challenge to the heart of the economic system whose weaknesses and injustices most of them had campaigned against for a lifetime.'[14] In his second reading speech, Chifley echoed his words as a royal commissioner ten years earlier: '[A nationalised banking system] will be free from the cramping limitations of sectional private ownership which bid the private banks to serve this interest but not that interest, and to judge all business from the narrow standpoint of maximum profits for the smallest outlay. . . . Full public ownership of the banks will ensure control of banking in the public interest.'[15]

The bank nationalisation legislation was adjudged unconstitutional by the High Court in 1948, in a judgment which showed considerable ingenuity on the part of the judges in protecting private enterprise against governmental action. The High Court decision was upheld a year later by the Privy Council. These events represented the culmination of efforts by the Labor movement, starting in 1911, to bring private industry and commerce under public ownership. Since then, the nationalisation objective which became official Labor policy in 1921 has been pushed out of sight and was finally dropped in 1963. However, the Labor movement gained its objectives to a great degree in the sense that central government control over banking, as recommended by the royal commission on which Chifley sat, has become the settled policy of the country since 1941, despite threats to reverse the policy from the non-Labor parties and some modifications in the system of control introduced in 1959 after prolonged lobbying by the private banks.[16] The banking system has for many years been under effective regulation by the Reserve Bank and the Commonwealth Treasury and there is no prospect that this control will be abandoned. To that extent, 'money power' has been effectively curbed. As a result, the particular style of rhetoric associated with this mode of attack on private capital has virtually disappeared from Australian political dialogue. Perhaps the last important occasion when it made a public appearance was during the dispute within the Chifley government over ratification of the Bretton Woods agreement setting up the International Monetary Fund.[17] As Crisp observes, 'to many Labor stalwarts it smelt of international financiers, "the Money Power"—the ultimate forces of capitalistic evil which Labor had felt itself to be fighting right down the years.' One of Chifley's ministerial colleagues, E. J. Ward, who had entered Federal Parliament in 1931 as a protege of J. T. Lang, opposed govern-

[14] Crisp., op. cit., p. 327
[15] Quoted, ibid., p. 330
[16] For a full discussion of central banking, see H. W. Arndt, *The Australian Trading Banks*, Melbourne, 3rd ed., 1965, ch. 8; and H. C. Coombs, *Conditions of Monetary Policy in Australia*, the R. C. Mills Memorial Lecture, 1958.
[17] An account of this dispute is given by Crisp, op. cit., ch. 14; J. D. B. Miller, 'The Bretton Woods Controversy', *Australian Outlook*, vol. 1, no. 3, 1947; S. Encel, op. cit., pp. 188-90.

ment policy in public. In a radio broadcast in March 1946, Ward declared that 'whilst our men and women were making tremendous sacrifices to prevent the establishment of a world dictatorship, the International Financial Interests were working out the details of a plan—more insidious because they laboured unseen—whereby the whole world would come under their domination . . . the Agreement will enthrone a World Dictatorship of private finance, more complete and terrible than any Hitlerite dream. . . . World collaboration of private financial interests can only mean mass unemployment, slavery, misery, degradation and final destruction.'

Ward's rhetoric was echoed by his erstwhile patron, Lang, who had entered Federal Parliament in 1946. The agreement, declared Lang in the second reading debate in March 1947, 'hands control [of Australia's credit] over to an international organisation—an international financial cartel, a financial oligarchy. . . . We shall revert to the gold standard; we shall lose control of our own exchange; we shall not be able to defend our industries against dumping from abroad. . . . The Fund, and not this Parliament, will control Australia.'

In an age of full employment and rapid economic growth, this florid rhetoric is at a discount. Statements of economic and monetary policy now bear the stamp of the technocrat rather than the ideologue, the commissar rather than the yogi. In a managed economy it is the managerial tone of voice, rather than the moral indignation of attacks on the money power, which commands attention. Moreover, the attack on the banks was the culmination of demands for some vague objective of nationalisation, expressed by Labor conferences in various forms from 1905 onwards. Rawson has asserted that bank nationalisation was the only real piece of socialisation which had ever been of serious concern to the Australian Labor Party, as shown by agreement between a wide range of Labor leaders like Anstey, Lang, Chifley and J. Forgan Smith (the conservative Labor premier of Queensland from 1932 to 1942). With the failure of bank nationalisation as a practical policy, party conferences had been constrained to tinker with the socialisation objective of 1921 until they reduced it 'from ambiguity to fatuity' before its final disappearance.[18] Since 1956, especially, when Professor H. W. Arndt delivered a celebrated Chifley Memorial Lecture on 'Labor and Economic Policy', statements by Labor spokesmen and sympathisers have emphasised planning, control and efficiency rather than the need to destroy the money power.

Capitalism and the Middle Classes

The congruence of economic, social and political structures in Australia manifests itself particularly in the nature of the party system. The ALP has been, throughout its history, overwhelmingly the instrument of the

[18] D. W. Rawson, 'Labour, Socialism and the Working Class', *Australian Journal of Politics and History*, vol. 7, no. 1, 1961

trade union movement, the Country Party of small and medium farmers, and the Liberal Party (in its successive incarnations) of urban capital and the urban middle classes. Radical millionaires, Tory trade unionists and agrarian socialists are almost equally absent from the Australian scene. But it is too facile to extend this analysis beyond a certain point and at various periods of political stress the complexity of the social structure reveals itself in violent cross-currents which disrupt the calm surface of this political reflecting pool. Attacks on the 'money power' can evoke a positive response from sections of the middle classes and it is not only the Labor movement which cherishes a deep distrust of foreign capital. Within the Liberal Party, there is a persistent strain of lower-middle class hostility towards the dominance of big business interests and this is complemented by the rural-urban antagonism which colours relations between Liberal and Country parties. Internal conflicts in the Liberal Party are frequently accompanied by accusations about the undue influence of big business on Liberal policy and party organisation. Usually, these accusations are couched in general terms referring to 'outside interests' or 'background organisations';[19] occasionally, however, names are named. In 1925, the Prime Minister, S. M. Bruce, was alleged to be acting at the behest of a leading merchant in Melbourne, Sir William McBeath, who was president of the National Union—a shadowy body whose functions approximated those of a federal council of the Nationalist Party.[20] In 1941, after a national political crisis had led to the downfall of the coalition ministry led first by R. G. Menzies and then by A. W. Fadden and the advent of a Labor administration under John Curtin, the *Age* newspaper attacked the influence of a 'Collins Street junta' in Federal politics.[21] The junta had helped to identify itself a few days earlier when the late Mr Staniforth Ricketson, chairman of the old-established stockbroking firm of J. B. Were and Son, told a royal commission that he and his friends had been active in promoting Mr Menzies' political career.[22]

The Country Party, whose *raison d'etre* is the protection of the small farmer, represents a particular form of antagonism to the business interests supporting its long-term Liberal ally. In 1921, Dr Earle Page, Federal

[19] The role of 'outside interests' is discussed, *inter alia*, by Crisp, *Australian National Government*, Melbourne, 1965, pp. 205-11; B. D. Graham, 'The Place of Finance Committees in Non-Labour Politics 1910-1930', *Australian Journal of Politics and History*, vol. 6, no. 1, 1960; D. Carboch and A. Wildavsky, *Studies in Australian Politics*, Melbourne, 1958; Sir Frederic Eggleston, *Reflections of an Australian Liberal*, Melbourne, 1952; Encel, op. cit., chs. 16-17. Events since 1945 are analysed in detail by Katharine West, *Power in the Liberal Party*, Melbourne, 1966.
[20] Graham, loc. cit.
[21] *Age*, Melbourne, 11 November 1941
[22] Evidence to the Royal Commission on Secret Funds, reported *Sydney Morning Herald*, 16 October 1941. The office of J. B. Were is in Capel Court, Collins Street, Melbourne, close to the Stock Exchange. R. G. Menzies was a director of the firm before entering Federal politics, and a cousin, F. G. Menzies, became a director in 1955.

Parliamentary leader of the Country Party, described the Nationalists as a party of 'looters and burglars', and other Country Party spokesmen echoed him by calling them profiteers and spendthrifts. These attitudes, naturally, dropped out of sight when the Nationalists and the Country Party formed a composite ministry in 1923. In 1932, however, they reappeared when the United Australia Party (as the Nationalists had renamed themselves) refused to take the Country Party into a new coalition. Page attacked the UAP for being dominated by the Associated Chambers of Manufactures and alleged that ACMA had declared the Country Party 'black'.[23] A few years later Page's lieutenant, A. W. Fadden, made a violent attack on the business interests backing the UAP, at a time when a UAP-CP coalition had actually been formed. The UAP, he declared, 'gives its allegiance to the big financial and manufacturing interests of the cities, and to the middlemen and monopolists . . . who suck the life-blood from the countryside . . . preference [is] extended by the United Australia Party so that city importers—the men behind the United Australia Party—should reap a harvest.'[24] Again, in 1950, as Treasurer in a Liberal-Country Party coalition, Fadden declared his opposition to business interests which were pressing for a revaluation of the Australian pound to parity with sterling and declared that revaluation would take place 'only over his dead body'.

Other tensions between the Liberal and Country parties continued to afflict the tenor of government policy in the long-lived Liberal-Country Party coalition which took office under R. G. Menzies in 1949. Strangely enough, although the former is traditionally a high-tariff party and the latter a low-tariff party, these tensions arose largely because of the protectionist, interventionist policies pursued with great energy and persistence by the leader of the Country Party, Mr John McEwen. As Maxwell Newton has observed, the key to this otherwise paradoxical conflict of policies may be found in the determination of the Country Party leader to use political processes to assist the 'little man'—not only the man on the land and in the outback, but the small manufacturer demanding tariff protection. With this goes opposition to 'open door' policies on imports, to 'dear money' fiscal policies, and to complete freedom for foreign investors, couched in nationalist, activist terms which portray the development of Australia's economic resources as the prime function of government.[25] By a curious and sometimes inconsistent development, the internal tensions of upper class, upper-middle class and lower-middle class groups thus continued to find political expression within the governing coalition, and to justify, in a somewhat unexpected way, the contention of some political scientists that the Country Party plays a separate role alongside the ALP and the Liberal Party.[26]

23 Encel, op. cit., pp. 230-31
24 Quoted by Crisp, op. cit., p. 217
25 M. Newton, 'Jack-in-the Box', *Nation*, 17 April 1965
26 This view is expressed by D. Aitkin in H. Mayer (ed.), *Australian Politics*, Melbourne, 1966, ch. 26. The contrary view is strongly argued by Crisp, op. cit., ch. 7.

Money and Politics

Conservative parties, observes Finer, are aligned with industrial organisations, preferably in the form of 'peak associations' which claim to speak for industry and business as a whole, or through specialised propaganda bodies for private capital, which act as the vertex of a triangle linking the parties and the business world. The industrial and commercial organisations act, in Finer's words, as 'the armature of party policy.'[27] Examples of specialised bodies which have had such triangular relationships include the Institute of Public Affairs, The Australian Constitutional League and the Consultative Council of the Nationalist Party and UAP in New South Wales.[28]

The connections between the Liberal Party and the business world are close, but unlike some other English-speaking countries, they rarely take the form of overlapping membership between the political and business elites, except at the state level, where leading businessmen can be found in the upper house of parliament but rarely in the cabinet.[29] In Britain, however, numerous directorships are held by members of both houses of parliament[30] and members of the government have regularly been drawn from industry—perhaps the most famous being W. H. Smith, the millionaire bookseller and publisher, who was the subject of W. S. Gilbert's satire as 'the ruler of the Queen's Navee' in HMS *Pinafore*. In Canada, remarks Porter, the dominant Liberal Party has never had any hesitation about inviting members of the corporate elite to join the federal cabinet, and a ministerial post has on many occasions served as an 'interstitial' stage in a business career.[31] In Australia, there have been a few such cases. One was Sir Walter Massy-Greene, a minister in the Hughes government from 1917 to 1923, who later became a director of many large companies (at one stage he held forty directorships, probably the Australian record).[32] Another was E. G. Theodore, who, after a spectacular career in both state and federal politics turned to business and became a mining magnate and a newspaper proprietor. In more recent years, some Liberal politicians have gone into business following defeat or retirement, but rarely in an important capacity. The case of Sir Arthur Warner, a leading figure in Victorian state politics, is described below.

Liberal Party finance committees, as might be expected, are largely

[27] Finer, op. cit., part 2, *Sociological Review*, vol. 4, no. 1, 1956

[28] The activities of these bodies are described *inter alia*, by Louise Overacker, *The Australian Party System*, New York, 1952; Crisp, op. cit., ch. 7. The director of the Institute of Public Affairs, C. D. Kemp, has given a slightly mystifying account of its activities in a volume of biographical sketches, *Big Businessmen*, Melbourne, 1964.

[29] See above, ch. 9

[30] Details on this point are given by Simon Haxey, *Tory* M.P., London, 1939 and Andrew Roth, *The Business Background of Members of Parliament*, 3rd ed., London, 1967.

[31] John Porter, *The Vertical Mosaic*, Toronto, 1965, pp. 398, 402

[32] Massy-Greene's career is described by Kemp, op. cit.

made up of businessmen, drawn heavily from the commercial and financial worlds, notably retail trading and insurance, rather than manufacturing industry. In the state of Victoria, they have included Sir Ian Potter, one of Australia's leading stockbrokers; Sir Maurice Nathan, chairman of the furniture retailing firm of Patersons Ltd; Sir George Coles, founder and director of the retail chain of G. J. Coles and Co.; Herbert Taylor, chartered accountant, company director and a past president of the Associated Chambers of Commerce of Australia; F. E. Lampe, former president of the Australian Council of Retailers; H. G. Brain, chairman of T & G Life Assurance Co.; K. A. Taylor, a former president of the Fire & Accident Underwriters' Association of Victoria; W. Kirkhope, chartered accountant and company director and chairman of the committee for twelve years; J. M. Anderson, an importer, chairman of the committee for four years and also chairman of the state council of the party for four years. Apart from Anderson, other party presidents during a twenty-year period included three graziers, an architect and one accountant and company director (another Anderson—Sir William Anderson, who also held office as Federal president of the party from 1951 to 1956). In NSW, perhaps because the party was out of office for twenty-four years, there were few prominent businessmen willing to associate themselves with it. Leading figures on the state executive and finance committee included L. H. Moore, for many years president of the Real Estate & Stock Institute; R. C. Cotton, a country retailer and timber merchant; R. H. Honner, a solicitor; Brigadier J. E. Pagan, a retailer and director of a small life assurance company; the late Sir William Spooner, for many years also a member of the Senate, who was a chartered accountant; S. F. Utz, a stockbroker; J. C. Maddison, another solicitor, who was treasurer from 1959 to 1965; and J. A. Clough, a public accountant.

A case of special interest is that of South Australia, where the coalescence of Liberal politics, private business, family connections and social status is so close that one may accurately speak of an 'Establishment'. Even the antagonism between town and country capital was submerged by a party merger in 1932 to form the Liberal-Country League (LCL), which operates as a single unit in state politics and as a coalition in federal politics. The late Sir Walter Duncan, head of one of the 'twenty families who own South Australia',[33] was for many years a director of the BHP group, president of the LCL from 1932 to 1944 and a member of the upper house of the state parliament from 1918 to 1962. He played a king-making role in 1938 when he helped to promote Sir Thomas Playford (a member of another old family and grandson of a former Premier) to the Premiership, which he held for the record term of 27 years until his government was defeated in 1965. Sir Arthur Rymill, head of another leading family and a lawyer by profession, was Lord Mayor of Adelaide

---

[33] See above, ch. 16. Most of the information in these paragraphs is based on West, op. cit.

from 1950 to 1954, president of the LCL from 1953 to 1955, a member of the upper house from 1956 to 1963, and chairman of the Bank of Adelaide from 1952 onwards. Other leading figures included I. D. Hayward, a company director, president of the LCL from 1961 to 1964; J. K. Angas, a leading pastoralist and a descendant of an early pioneer family, who was chairman from 1947 to 1950; W. G. Gerard, chairman from 1961 to 1964, company director, former president of ACMA, and a member of the federal government's Manufacturing Industries Advisory Council. Angas, Rymill, Hayward and Gerard had also served as chairmen of the party's finance committee.

One of the most notable of South Australian Liberal politicians was Sir Philip McBride, member of a leading pastoral family and chairman for many years of the big pastoral firm of Elder Smith & Co. (which merged in 1962 with another leading pastoral firm, Goldsbrough Mort & Co., to become Elder Smith Goldsbrough Mort Ltd, one of the two biggest concerns in the field, still under Sir Philip's chairmanship in 1965). On becoming a minister in the federal Cabinet in 1949, he was obliged to resign no fewer than thirty-three directorships at the request of the Prime Minister. Sir Philip's career was mainly in federal politics, where he was a member of both houses of parliament from 1931 to 1958, with a short break from 1944 to 1946. He was a minister under Sir Robert Menzies from 1940 to 1941, and again from 1949 to 1958. From 1960 to 1965 he was federal president of the Liberal Party.[34] Throughout his career he was also a member of a small, select group of advisers to the state LCL, which also included Duncan and Rymill.

Close links between business and government can become scandalously close and Australian political history is replete with incidents where business firms or wealthy individuals have used their political connections to direct personal advantage. A number of these incidents became the subject of official inquiries which throw an unflattering light on the personal ethics of businessmen and politicians who are loud in their praise of 'free enterprise'.[35] In the affluent society of post-war Australia, the most notable example was afforded by the activities of the late Sir Arthur Warner, one of the few politicians who has combined business management with ministerial office. Throughout his ministerial career in successive Victorian state governments (1947-50 and 1955-62), Warner was the central figure in a succession of incidents where he had obviously used his political position to advance his business interests.[36]

The Lobbyists

The interlocking of business and government in the twentieth century has been marked, above all, by the rise of the organised pressure group or

[34] J. Ransome, 'Man in Faraway House', *Nation*, 7 May 1962
[35] A number of these cases are discussed by S. Encel, op. cit., pp. 293-302.
[36] 'The Soft Drink Vendor,' *Nation*, 22 November 1958; West, op. cit., ch. 1

lobby whose structure and activities give it a quasi-governmental character. The interaction between government and business pressure groups is one of the most important aspects of the growth of the 'power elite' which exists, in varying forms, in all advanced industrial communities. The political activities of business groups operate both through the giant firm and the 'peak associations' representing industry groups. Brady has argued that the peak association, with its ideology of 'self-government in industry', is the characteristic form of organised business power. The great extension of government intervention in business affairs which took place during the 1914-18 war led businessmen to accept it as unavoidable. Peak associations developed both as a defensive measure and also as a means of claiming delegated authority in the name of business self-government. The first real interlocking of government and peak associations took place at this time, especially in Germany and the United States.[37] The great depression of the 1930's, followed by the 1939-45 war, gave enormous impetus to the movement. As Mills has written, 'the bureaucracies of business tend to duplicate the regulatory agencies of the federal hierarchy, to place their members within the governmental commissions and agencies, to hire officials away from government, and to develop elaborate mazes within which are hidden the official secrets of business operations.'[38] As we shall see, these processes are well developed in Australia.

The original motive for the setting up of peak associations on a national scale was the demand for protective tariffs. According to Brady, it was the force behind the establishment of the National Association of Manufacturers (USA), the Reichsverband der Deutschen Industrie, the Confédération Générale du Patronat Français and the Federation (now Confederation) of British Industries. With time, he observes, 'tariff walls have been heightened and generalised to meet the needs of every organised interest group; the forms of protection and aid have been multiplied to meet every particular need; the whole of the network of national protection and aid has gradually been articulated.'[39] This description applies with particular aptness to Australia. The oldest and strongest of peak associations is the Associated Chambers of Manufactures of Australia (ACMA), which was formally established in 1903 at the fourth conference of state chambers. The oldest of these was the South Australian chamber, established in 1869; Queensland was the last, in 1911. The name ACMA was adopted in 1908, and the head office was transferred from Melbourne to Canberra in 1936.[40]

[37] Robert A. Brady, *Business as a System of Power*, New York, 1943, introduction
[38] C. Wright Mills, *White Collar*, London, 1951, p. 79
[39] Brady, op. cit., p. 253
[40] The following paragraphs are based mainly on two sources: *A Brief History of ACMA*, written by its federal director, R. W. C. Anderson, Canberra, 1960, and a research essay by one of my former students at the Australian National University, Miss M. E. Ainsworth.

The interests of ACMA are indicated in a list of major policies adopted by it between 1904 and 1918.

1904 Branding of imported goods
Decimal coinage and the metric system
1906 Uniform quarantine laws
'Buy Australian' campaign
1911 Establishment of a Tariff Board
Establishment of a Trade Commissioner Service
1918 Incentive payments in industry.

The membership of ACMA comprises the six state chambers, which have autonomous powers within their own states. Until 1962, it also included the Metal Trades Employers' Association, which was affiliated nationally but not in every state. This covers some 18,000 companies employing well over one million people. Industry divisions are separately organised (eight in all) but work through the state chambers. At its headquarters, 'Industry House' (completed in 1960), ACMA publishes a monthly bulletin, the *Canberra Letter*, which is directly aimed at the dissemination of its views, together with political, economic and statistical information on current issues of interest both to government and industry. This newsletter is distributed to all members of parliament, state chambers, government departments, industrialists and other interested bodies.

Another important area of activity is the conduct of industrial case-work. Most of this is located in Melbourne, where a policy and consultative committee of ACMA, consisting of the presidents of over forty major employer organisations under the leadership of the president of ACMA meets to discuss cases as they arise and determine a suitable course of action. They appoint a working party for each case including a representative of ACMA and various counsel. The collection of evidence and securing of witnesses is done by ACMA staff, working in conjunction with counsel appointed for the case.

Tariff policy remains, however, the heart of ACMA's activities, and its staff are continuously occupied with negotiations on this score within ACMA, between ACMA and other industrial associations, between ACMA and the government, and with the preparation of submissions to the Tariff Board. A good example of ACMA in action was provided by the Japan-Australia trade treaty concluded in 1957, which gave Japanese manufacturers considerably greater access to the Australian market. Exploratory talks between the two governments began early in 1956, and in July the Department of Trade organised a confidential meeting with ACMA and other employers' associations to acquaint them with the general outline of the draft treaty. ACMA's immediate reaction was to oppose the treaty, and failing that to demand direct quantitative restrictions on Japanese imports.

Immediately before the signing of the agreement, ACMA and state Chambers of Manufactures, the Australian Industries Development Association, the Textile Workers' Union and other bodies published statements criticising the proposals. It was claimed that the lack of adequate tariff and licensing restrictions against Japanese goods would mean heavy reductions in local manufacture of textiles, light metals and light engineering, toys, etc. with consequent problems of unemployment, loss of capital and a deterioration of shareholders' funds. Correspondence and discussions on a ministerial and departmental level were used to urge the provision of adequate safeguards in the agreement; several press statements were issued and members of parliament were pressured. The official spokesmen of ACMA claim that, as a result, an atmosphere of 'logical fear' was created to such a degree that before the ratification of the treaty, Mr McEwen, Minister for Trade, announced that a system of continuous consultation between his department and industry groups would be arranged. This system, which was devised by the Department of Trade in conjunction with ACMA, took the form of Industry Panels which manufacturers have established for the purpose of making representations as to the damage caused or likely to be caused to their industry by a flow of imports from Japan. These panels are on a national basis, sponsored by ACMA, which is officially responsible for the accuracy of the statistical data produced by any panel.

These arrangements were attacked at the time as providing for 'direct intervention by manufacturers in the import control process for the protection of their own interests'.[41] However, nearly all such applications have been refused and where the Minister for Trade has acted to restrict imports from Japan (as in the notable case of motor car manufacture), the decision appears to have come from his own assessment of the situation. The demands of the new situation, plus the abolition of import licensing in 1960, apparently produced a realisation among the leaders of ACMA that a more sophisticated style of organisation was necessary. Since the trade agreement of 1957, ACMA has built up its head office and recruited a steady trickle of officials from government departments on the 'poacher-turned-gamekeeper' principle. An early recruit (in 1959) was Mr G. R. Bain, deputy assistant secretary in the Department of Trade, as assistant director; when he was appointed director of the NSW state chamber, his place was taken by Mr L. N. Cottle, also recruited from the Department of Trade, and Mr Cottle's successor as chief tariff officer was Mr J. L. McNamara, who came from the Department of Customs and Excise. Mr McNamara, in his turn, was replaced by Mr K. Cremean, again from the Department of Trade. In 1966, ACMA appointed Mr J. McMahon, of the Department of Trade, as an economist. The result, as one journal sardonically observed, is that 'two sets of specialists furnish each other with work to do. Take any public servant on the middle to senior level with a flow of bright ideas; what better support than a submission from an outside body, which, while differing from his own scheme sufficiently, will yet urge its essentials? And who better to do the job than a former colleague who

41 *Sydney Morning Herald*, 12 October 1957

knows the style of the Department and keeps up with the current scale of priorities?'[42]

ACMA is, of course, merely the most important specimen of a numerous breed.[43] It has been estimated that there are about 1,250 trade associations in Australia. However, concentration is as important here as in industry. In Victoria, for example, six associations accounted for 17 per cent of the total membership in that state, and four for 11 per cent.[44] The largest business organisation representing a viewpoint contrary to the protectionism of ACMA is the Associated Chambers of Commerce of Australia (ACCA), established in 1901. It is a much less effective and active body than ACMA, but in recent years it has revamped its organisation in a similar way. In 1962, ACCA appointed Mr R. P. Thorman, formerly a senior finance officer at the Commonwealth Treasury, as its director (he had previously been assistant director). In 1967, ACCA built its own headquarters in Canberra ('Commerce House') and has recruited a trained staff, including— inevitably—a former official of the Department of Trade.[45] Another body with interests parallel to those of ACCA is the Australian British Trade Association (ABTA), previously known as the Australian Association of British Manufacturers. ACMA and ABTA are both represented on the Tariff Advisory Committee of the Department of Trade. In recent years, there has been some movement towards specialisation of interests. In 1962, the metal trades employers set up their own association, the Australian Metal Industries Association, although many metal manufacturing firms also belong, individually, to ACMA and its state constituents. The chemical industry set up its own council in 1965, at a time when a Tariff Board inquiry into the industry was pending. Specialisation of interest also seems to lie behind the recent expansion of the Australian Industries Development Association (AIDA), initially established in 1921 as the Australian Industries Protection League. Renamed in 1951, the AIDA was originally concerned with 'Made in Australia' advertising campaigns and representations to the Tariff Board. In 1968 it was announced that its head office was to be moved from Melbourne to Canberra, and Mr W. Callaghan, deputy secretary of the Department of Trade, would become its director.[46] This move is apparently supported by some of Australia's major industrial firms, like BHP and ICIANZ, who feel the need for a more sophisticated organisation to deal with their particular interests.

Another important group of bodies are the employers' federations which exist in all states, nationally associated in the Australian Council of

[42] 'The Lobbying Bureaucracy', *Nation*, 12 February 1963
[43] A general discussion of pressure groups is Trevor Matthews, 'Pressure Groups in Australia', in H. Mayer (ed.), *Australian Politics*. Crisp, op. cit., pp. 130-37, examines the influence of pressure groups in federal politics.
[44] R. D. Freeman, 'Trade Associations in the Australian Economy', *Public Administration*, Sydney, vol. 24, no. 4, 1965
[45] Maxwell Newton, 'Lobby and Anti-Lobby', *Nation*, 11 June 1966
[46] *Australian*, 15 May 1968

Employers' Federations (ACEF).[47] State federations were established in Victoria, NSW and Queensland in 1903 and a Central Council of Employers of Australia (CCEA) was set up in 1904 (which became the ACEF in 1942). The main objectives of these bodies were to campaign against industrial legislation and to support parliamentary candidates. As the secretary of the Council said, employers would 'come out in the open and take an offensive attitude towards these political bodies which dared to control their hours, money and methods of work.' Similarly, the Victorian Employers' Federation declared in 1904 that it was the first which had 'openly proclaimed its determination to fight socialism as the one issue before Australia.'

In practice, the CCEA, the ACEF and their constituent state bodies have mostly attracted small employers, especially in the building and construction industries, and their major service to these is in the field of industrial arbitration, where they regularly represent their members. The main employers' organisations—ACMA, AMIA, ACEF and the Australian Woolgrowers' and Graziers' Council—have, since 1961, established a regular system of co-operation through the National Employers' Policy Committee and the National Employers' Industrial Committee—one consisting of the presidents of the four bodies concerned, the other made up of staff members. The functions of these twin committees are to co-ordinate and present national wage cases before the Commonwealth Arbitration Commission. Employers' organisations frequently bewail the disunity that exists among them. However, when it comes to basic questions about the relation between capital and labour, the employers speak with one voice.

[47] Trevor Matthews, 'The Political Activities of Australian Employers' Federations', unpublished paper, Australian Political Studies Association conference, Canberra, 1964. The quotations which follow are drawn from this paper.

19: Capitalism in Australia (3): Feet under the Table

Across the bargaining tables of power, the bureaucracies of business and government face one another, and under the tables their myriad feet are interlocked in wonderfully complex ways.

C. Wright Mills, *White Collar*

Government and Business

The ideology of business enterprise towards government activity in Australia is purely instrumental: activity which helps business and industry is desirable, activity which restricts them is undesirable. The authors of a well-known study of American business ideologies distinguish between the 'classical' and 'managerial' versions: the former regards government intervention as an unmitigated evil, the latter as a necessary evil which may even be turned to good account.[1] In Australia, the classical view has never had much influence. Eighty years ago, a Free Trade politician protested against the collectivist, protectionist version of liberalism which was becoming dominant as a corruption of the pure milk of *laissez-faire*, but his was a lone voice.[2] As already noted, the dependence of local capitalism on governmental patronage, assistance and regulation is a key feature of the relation between economy and society, which in turn largely determines the structure of class, status and power. In this chapter, we shall be concerned with some significant examples of the relationship and in particular with its development in the past thirty years.

The nurturing role of government, although it had been present from the earliest days of settlement, assumed its most characteristic aspect with the introduction of protective tariffs in the 1860's. With the growth of industry under the shelter of the tariff, the role of government also extended. The Commonwealth government became actively involved in the affairs of industry as a result of the First World War. In Australia, the Commonwealth was responsible for a major reorganisation of metalliferous mining and smelting, for the introduction of organised marketing of primary products, especially wheat and wool, and for the encouragement of local manufacturing in a number of fields. The ebullient wartime Prime Minister, W. M.

[1] F. X. Sutton, et al., *The American Business Creed*, New York, 2nd ed., 1962, pp. 192-207
[2] Bruce Smith, *Liberty and Liberalism*, Melbourne, 1887, ch. 1

Hughes, was full of schemes for industrial development, including a system of industrial cartels or syndicates.[3] This notion, as Brady has shown, became popular in a number of countries where the affairs of government and industry had become interlocked as a result of the new problems of war production, and the theory of 'self-government in business' through government-sponsored cartels was propagated by business spokesmen.[4]

With the end of fighting in 1918 came the end of the war boom and tariffs were hastily raised to protect the new industries which had grown up with governmental encouragement. In 1921, the Tariff Board was established to provide a regular institutional method of dealing with applications for protection. At the same period, Hughes was also responsible for the establishment of two new industries, oil refining and radio manufacture. Both were accomplished by setting up mixed companies in which the government had a half share, Commonwealth Oil Refineries (in partnership with the then Anglo-Iranian Oil Company) and Amalgamated Wireless (Australia) Ltd.[5] Hughes, like his successors, also tried unsuccessfully to have a motor vehicle industry set up in Australia. In 1939 and 1940, the Federal parliament passed two Acts, giving effect to an agreement between the Menzies government and Australian Consolidated Industries Ltd by which the latter would undertake the manufacture of motor vehicles in return for a bounty and a monopoly of the market. The scheme never went into action, partly because the blatancy of the favour shown to a single company was too much for many of the Prime Minister's own supporters.[6] It was the Labor government of J. B. Chifley which finally induced General Motors-Holden's Ltd, the Australian branch of the American automobile colossus, to start making cars in 1948.[7]

Throughout the world, the pattern of relationships between government and industry in the two world wars followed a similar course. Following a temporary upsurge of government intervention in the 1914-18 war, there was a quest for 'normalcy' and a general dismantling of wartime apparatus. The 1939-45 war, following on the heels of the depression of the 1930's, brought a permanent shift in the relation between the public and private sectors. In Australia, the needs of total war brought about a virtual industrial revolution under government sponsorship. Munitions production, previously restricted to the manufacture of small arms and ammunition, expanded enormously and stimulated the growth of numerous ancillary industries. Shipbuilding, aircraft construction, chemicals, aluminium

---

[3] Hughes convened a conference representing government, business and the trade unions in June 1918 to discuss the scheme, but no action was ever taken.

[4] Robert A. Brady, *Business as a System of Power*, New York, 1943, introduction

[5] The governmental share in both of these undertakings was liquidated in 1952, the oil refining enterprise becoming BP (Australia) Ltd.

[6] S. Encel, *Cabinet Government in Australia*, Melbourne, 1962, pp. 239-40

[7] L. F. Crisp, *Ben Chifley*, Melbourne, 1961, p. 239. A highly personal account of these events is given by the former managing director of GMH Ltd, Mr L. J. Hartnett, in his autobiography, *Big Wheels and Little Wheels*, Melbourne, 1964.

refining, heavy electrical manufacture and many other fields of heavy and light engineering were either established or greatly expanded.[8] Money and banking came under detailed federal government controls, many of which survived into the postwar period. Concern with the structure, capacity and efficiency of manufacturing industry became a permanent function of government. A wide range of organised marketing and stabilisation schemes for rural products, many of which had been previously frustrated by constitutional limitations on the powers of the federal government, were set up under wartime powers conferred by the National Security Act and became permanent by the use of extra-constitutional devices after the war. Much of the industrial plant and facilities created for wartime purposes formed the basis for industrial development in the post-war period. The post-war mining boom was made possible through the work of the Bureau of Mineral Resources, established in 1940.

On the personal level, wartime experience and contacts had an important influence on the character of the post-war business elite. Many businessmen served as temporary public servants in wartime agencies, and many others found themselves working in collaboration with government departments. One of the typical figures of post-war industrial growth is the skilled craftsman who ran a struggling business in the depressed 1930's, became a key man in a war factory or ancillary industry, and moved into the 'big time' after the war. Again, many of the businessmen who sat on government boards and committees in the post-war period gained their first insight into government affairs as temporary public servants. The flow of government officials into private industry, discussed later in this chapter, had its roots in the personal relationship established during wartime administration.

One notable departure from the latter trend, involving absorption from the private sector into permanent government service, involves the careers of a group of officials from the Bank of New South Wales, Australia's largest private bank.[9] These men were all officials of the economic research department of the bank, established by its general manager, the late Sir Alfred Davidson, in the early 1930's. Davidson, for many years the dominant personality in Australian banking, saw the need for expert economic advice when the 1929 depression hit the country, and he built up a large staff of young economists (eighteen at one point). They were soon nicknamed 'Davidson's kindergarten', an allusion to the more famous kindergarten established in South Africa by Lord Milner after the South African War. (Davidson was a friend and admirer of Lionel Curtis, one of Milner's proteges.) When war broke out, a number of these young men were recruited into the Commonwealth service, and some remained permanently. They included the permanent head of the Department of

---

[8] E. R. Walker, *The Australian Economy in War and Reconstruction*, New York, 1947; S. J. Butlin, *War Economy*, Canberra, 1955, series 4, vol. 3, of the *Official History of the 1939-45 War*; D. P. Mellor, *The Role of Science and Industry*, Canberra, 1958, series 4, vol. 5 of the *Official History*
[9] 'Unique Era in Australian Banking', *Australian Financial Review*, 5 February 1965

External Affairs, Sir James Plimsoll; his predecessor, Sir Arthur Tange, who became High Commissioner to India; Dr R. S. Mendelsohn, deputy secretary of the Department of Housing; Mr B. Fleming, a senior official of the Treasury; Mr Walter Ives, a member of the Executive of CSIRO; Mr R. B. McMillan, who was for a number of years chief executive officer of the Australian Wool Board; and Mr Leslie Holmes, senior trade commissioner in India. Others graduated from the Commonwealth service into international administration: Mr Peter Reid to the World Bank and Mr Leslie Bury to the International Monetary Fund. Mr Bury became the most famous of the troupe when he resigned his position to enter politics in 1956, holding various ministerial portfolios from 1961 onwards.

During the war, government departments such as Munitions, Supply, War Organisation of Industry, and Labour and National Service became intimately involved in the affairs of industrial firms and gradually accumulated a repository of information about investment problems, capital equipment needs, efficiency, productivity, industrial training, industrial relations and the like. Personal contacts and organisational relationships built up in this way were of major importance during the postwar reconstruction period. The return of Mr R. G. (later Sir Robert) Menzies to power in 1949 at the head of a Liberal ministry strongly committed to 'free enterprise' led to a sharp decline in these activities, but did not destroy them and from the middle 1950's the trend of government opinion began to swing back towards the interventionist philosophy of the war years— tempered by the ideological peculiarities of the governing coalition. The main focus for these new developments was the Department of Trade, under the political guidance of Mr John McEwen, who became parliamentary leader of the Country Party in 1958 and the second most important figure in the government. From a predominant concern with overseas trade, the department grew more and more involved in questions related to manufacturing industry, and in 1964 was renamed Trade and Industry. The existing Secondary Industries Division became part of the Office of Secondary Industry, with a total headquarters staff of 150.[10] In 1962, the former division had introduced an ambitious system of collecting information on private firms and by 1968 detailed files had been established on more than 25,000 companies. Each firm is surveyed annually, with information obtained personally from a senior member of the management. Information is collected on commodities handled, export activity, franchise restrictions, value of output, affiliations with overseas and other Australian companies, and export marketing arrangements.

The activities carried out by the Office of Secondary Industry were started during the war by the Secondary Industries Commission, which later became the Division of Industrial Development and then the Industries Division of the Department of Trade. The results of their inquiries were published periodically in the form of glossy pamphlets giving details about

[10] This was the figure at 30 June 1968.

overseas investment in Australian industry, franchise and licensing arrangements and 'gaps' in industrial capacity. Under the OSI, this information was extended to deal with inter-firm and inter-industry comparisons. This requires companies to disclose details of their profits, assets, sales, costs and technical processes at all stages of production and distribution. The firms supplying this information obtain summaries which do not identify individual enterprises, while the OSI retains the original material. Political influence of the Department of Trade and the personal influence of its hard-driving Minister have clearly become very great as a result of these activities.

The role of Mr McEwen was one of the major political phenomena of the 1950's and 1960's. In 1969, he was the only survivor of the original Menzies government of 1949; he had been Deputy Prime Minister for ten years; and he had acted as Prime Minister for a total of close on two years. (The latter covers a number of short periods as Acting Prime Minister and a period of three weeks as 'caretaker' Prime Minister following the death of Mr Harold Holt in December, 1967. In government circles, he was sometimes referred to satirically as the 'associate Prime Minister' or the 'second Prime Minister'. His political influence was built largely on the intimate connections between his department and private industry. As one of his most persistent critics, Mr Maxwell Newton, has written, Mr McEwen's policy of 'protection all round' meant a series of special measures for special groups and the close meshing of government policy with a wide range of private economic interests. This meant that the Office of Secondary Industry was to be a 'clearing house and ginger group for manufacturing industry, encouraging and overseeing improvements through mergers, co-operation in manufacturing, joint production with overseas firms and the like.' In addition, by giving clear directions to the Tariff Board as to what its findings should be through the technique of 'writing the policy into the reference', Mr McEwen was using his power over the tariff to move into a form of industry economic planning, one of whose major aims was that of placing restrictions on overseas corporations for the benefit of Australian firms.[11]

This interlocking of government and business interests is manifested in the establishment of a wide range of advisory boards and committees, where business and government find their feet entwined in the many ways suggested by Wright Mills' striking phrase. The Department of Trade was responsible for the setting up of bodies such as the Manufacturing Industries Advisory Council (MIAC) and the Export Development Council; the Department of Supply for a range of twelve committees, with eighty representatives of industry, dealing with defence production.[12] The right

[11] M. Newton, 'Jack-in-the-Box', *Nation*, 17 April 1965
[12] The work of the industry advisory committees of the Department of Supply is discussed by Peter Robinson, *Australian Financial Review*, 29 March 1966 and by the Minister for Supply, Mr Fairhall, *House of Representatives Debates*, 10 May 1966.

of organised business to advise the government directly was forthrightly stated by a prominent member of this committee establishment, the late Sir John Allison, whose connection with government originated during the war. Organised groups of businessmen, he declared in a public lecture in 1960, 'must concern themselves increasingly with policy issues . . . and increasingly take the initiative in making representations as occasion demands. If this right is acknowledged, we should require government to provide systematic machinery for encouraging and registering such representations.' Ministers should be guided not only by their official advisers, but by the advice of business interests. 'The Public Service occupies, by default of others, too much of this advisory field. . . . We in business want less of this from the Public Service and more of it from ourselves and other relevant groups. . . . Current practice allows the departments too free a hand in imposing views on aspects which they themselves are not always competent to judge. . . . We want a situation where the Public Service is not the final arbiter on recommendations to go to a Minister, but is only one party, among others, to such recommendations.' Organised businessmen, he added, voicing the 'solidarist' philosophy of the Associated Chambers of Manufactures, were expressing the national interest, and the public service did not have a monopoly in this sphere.[13]

A smoother and more 'managerial' version of these attitudes was expressed some years later by another prominent businessman, Mr R. A. Irish, chairman of MIAC. Government and business, he observed, must work in partnership, 'each serving the other and each depending on the other. There is no question that Government is intruding more and more into business, and how it does this and where it does it are very important issues. . . . One cannot visualise a successful partnership where partners do not confer and do not have an amity of feeling. . . . I believe that the great danger facing free enterprise stems from an "unapproachable bureaucracy" . . . danger can lurk in the Administration, where so many ideas and policies germinate before they grow into political reality. . . . One of the main responsibilities of the Administration is to know and understand its partner. It should seek honest opinions and advice from business leaders and others competent to give them, and . . . it should not lightly ease them aside in favour of is own preconceived ideas.'[14]

Business spokesmen are apparently able to perform, without discomfort, the mental acrobatics required to reconcile this notion of 'partnership' with the rather different notion of representative democracy. Others find the disjunction more alarming. The dangers of big business, Professor H. W. Arndt has observed, arise from the concentration of economic power, the ability to make enormous profits, the distorting effects of monopoly and the inequality of incomes and living standards which big business both

13 Sir John Allison, 'The Businessman's Part in the Art of Democracy', 8th Queale Memorial Lecture, SA Chamber of Manufactures, 1960
14 R. A. Irish, 'A Businessman's Views on the Administration', Robert Garran Memorial Oration, Royal Institute of Public Administration, Canberra, 1966

perpetuates and aggravates. They also lie in the 'power to ensure, through control of the nation's finance, press and even Government policies, the maintenance of a capitalist system and of the privileges of big business and its capitalist owners.' Big business, he continues, makes decisions of great national importance and is accountable to no one (as when the iron and steel monopoly, BHP, decided in 1956 to finance a large expansion program and did so by raising the price of steel—a purely internal decision but with implications for the entire economy). Because so much private investment is now financed from undistributed profits, 'a disproportionate share of the nation's savings is at the discretionary disposal of the largest companies. Much of this may be invested in the best interest of the nation; some of it is used to multiply service stations. In either case important decisions affecting the economic development of the nation are taken by a handful of individuals responsible to no one. . . . One answer to this charge of unaccountability . . . is that big business executives know best what is in the nation's interest and can be relied upon to act in the national interest—an answer difficult to reconcile with democratic principles.'[15]

Moreover, Professor Arndt concludes, if it is argued that business interests are in practice unable to act without government control or at least consultation, the notion of 'partnership' becomes simply a euphemism for the existence of a power elite. 'Are we in danger', he asks, 'of allowing our lives to be controlled by a narrow class of "managers"—more or less benevolent, able, expert, powerful business executives, acting in concert with more or less benevolent, able, expert, powerful heads of government departments, public corporations, trade unions, primary producers' organisations, professions? If you look around you, particularly at Canberra where few important decisions are made without consultation and negotiation between senior public servants and senior representatives of private interests, you can convince yourself that this is the most serious threat to democracy in Australia.'[16]

Perhaps the most striking example of 'partnership' between government and business established by the Liberal government of Sir Robert Menzies was in relation to air transport.[17] In 1946, following an unsuccessful attempt to nationalise internal airlines, the Chifley Labor government established a publicly-owned domestic air service, Trans-Australia Airlines. By 1952, the major private airline, Australian National Airways, was feeling the pinch of competition and was faced with heavy costs for re-equipment. The company approached the Liberal government with a request to liquidate TAA. Although the majority of the Cabinet was probably sympa-

---

[15] H. W. Arndt, 'The Dangers of Big Business', *Australian Quarterly*, vol. 29, no. 4, 1957
[16] ibid.
[17] For a detailed analysis of the development of airline policy see D. M. Hocking and C. P. Haddon-Cave, *Air Transport in Australia*, Melbourne, 1952; D. C. Corbett, *Politics and the Airlines*, London, 1965; Stanley Brogden, *Australia's Two-Airline Policy*, Melbourne, 1967.

thetic to this request, dissension among the governing parties made it politically impossible to grant. Instead, the government gave financial assistance to ANA and introduced a system of 'rationalisation' or 'controlled competition' between the two enterprises—as Shakespeare might have called it, hot ice or wondrous strange snow. By 1957, ANA was again in difficulties and this time a private capitalist stepped in. This was Mr R. M. Ansett, founder and head of Ansett Transport Industries, which then operated a relatively minor airline service. ANA was taken over by ATI and rechristened Ansett-ANA. Mr Ansett, a self-made businessman of the 1930's, well-endowed with the brash, tough ruthlessness of his type, used the existing rationalisation agreement to extract every ounce of advantage from the situation. The result, as Karmel and Brunt dryly observe, is a system of 'fair and active competition . . . so fair, it seems, as to guarantee the existence of the leading private operator; so active as to allow the consumer a choice of air hostesses.'[18] The system is, in fact, the antithesis of competition: 'market sharing, investment control and rationalising of fares, services and timetables.'[19] In Franklin Street, Melbourne, where both airlines have their head offices, it is said that even the movement of the lifts in the two buildings is synchronised. Mr Ansett, in the words of the leader of the Labor Party, follows Danton's advice: *toujours l'audace*, and was frank enough to admit in 1961 that government action had guaranteed him a 50 per cent share of the industry's revenue, which in that year was $72 millions,[20] and has grown enormously since.

'Pantouflage'

The managerial attitude expressed by business spokesmen like Allison and Irish is not, of course, the whole story, and even in their lectures, quoted above, there is a degree of ambivalence towards the public service and public servants. In less sophisticated circles, the 'classical' attitude of hostility towards the public service is expressed more nakedly. In 1958, for example, ACMA and seven other employers' associations sent a deputation to the Prime Minister to complain about the size, expense and inefficiency of the public service, and suggested that they might 'assist' the government to make it more efficient.[21] They would have agreed with the financial editor of the *New York Times*, who wrote indignantly in 1950 that the American people were being asked 'to believe that a little group of bureaucrats in Washington can run the economy better than it has been run for a century and three-quarters under the free-enterprise system.'[22]

---

18 Karmel and Brunt, op. cit., p. 137
19 ibid., p. 112
20 The Hon. E. G. Whitlam, *House of Representatives Debates*, 23 April 1964, p. 1403
21 G. E. Caiden, *Career Service*, Melbourne, 1965, describes this and similar criticisms in the period 1957-58, pp. 404-8.
22 Quoted, Sutton et al., *The American Business Creed*, p. 206

One interesting test of the businessman's attitude towards public servants is his willingness to employ them in his own enterprises, and ambivalence becomes particularly evident on this score. In Australia, as in some other countries, the closeness of the relationship between government and business has been marked by a growing exodus of senior public servants into executive positions in the private sector. The London *Observer*, a few years ago, described the 'gold rush' from the civil service into industry, and Mr Peter Shore, now a British Labour MP, noted that senior civil servants were becoming frequent targets for tempting offers from private industry.[23] (Some of Shore's examples are of special interest to Australia. Sir Paul Chambers, once of the Inland Revenue, became Chairman of ICI and a director of its Australian affiliate, ICIANZ. Sir Eric Speed, permanent head of the War Office, joined the Anglo-Australian Corporation. Sir William Strath, a senior Treasury official, became managing director of British Aluminium, which has large Australian interests.)

In Britain, industry has been particularly concerned to attract Treasury or Inland Revenue officials, with special knowledge of finance or taxation and an intimate acquaintance with the Whitehall network.[24] In France, on the other hand, where the flow of officials to industry is an old-established custom, the biggest demand is for the professional and managerial skills of the engineer. An American student who carried out a survey of large public companies in 1958 found that more than 80 per cent of their senior executives were graduates of the three great national engineering schools, *Polytechnique*, *Centrale* and *Mines*, and that a majority of these had served from ten to twenty years in government departments and in the armed services.[25] There is also a keen demand for members of the corps of *inspecteurs de finances*, one of the elite groups of the French government service. In 1958, there were 316 inspectors and ex-inspectors living of whom about one-third were in private employment.[26] The French, as might be expected, have a word for it: *pantouflage*, a slang term current since 1880, originally applied to graduates of the *Ecole Polytechnique* who declined to enter the government service; hence *pantouflard*, someone who prefers the home comforts of a *bourgeois* existence (the literal meaning of 'pantoufles' is slippers).

The situation in France has certain affinities with Australia. For many years, French industry has been characterised by the family-controlled firm, small or medium-sized, with only a limited role for the salaried manager. Careers in industry have carried relatively little social prestige, whereas the *grands corps* of the government service have been fed by the intellectual cream of the nation, educated at the *grandes écoles* like *Polytechnique*

23 *Observer*, 18 June 1961; Peter Shore, 'The Rewards of Affluence', *New Statesman*, 7 April 1961
24 Anthony Sampson, *Anatomy of Britain*, London, 1961, pp. 286-87
25 David Granick, *The European Executive*, London, 1962, pp. 72-76
26 Henry W. Ehrmann, 'Pressures in a divided France', *World Politics*, vol. 11, no. 1, 1958

and *Normale Supérieure,* and since 1945 also at the National School of Administration (ENA). The engineering profession has grown up very largely under government patronage since the formation of a corps of civil engineers was first suggested in the seventeenth century by the great military engineer, Vauban. In later life, however, intellectual achievement and social prestige often succumb to the attractions of money.[27]

In Australia, large-scale enterprise is found predominantly in developmental works and public utilities operated by governments. It is in these fields, rather than most of private industry, that the need for specialised managerial skills is evident and that steps have been taken to develop them. The extent of this cross-traffic, even before the war, was greater than it was generally known or admitted to be. Since the war, it has increased sharply, reflecting both the greater range of government activities and the growth in the size and complexity of industrial and business operations, calling for managerial and administrative abilities which have many affinities with the work of government agencies.

As in France, engineers stand out as the most important group. Railway engineers may be taken first. Mr A. D. J. Forster joined the NSW railways as an engineer in 1915, became a commissioner in 1925, was a member of the Tariff Board from 1932 to 1934 and in 1935 became managing director of Clyde Engineering Co., a major manufacturer of rolling stock. Subsequently, he was a director of the agricultural machinery firm of H. V. McKay-Massey Harris, chairman of Volkswagen Distributors Pty Ltd, chairman of the Emu Bay Railway Co., and a director of Lakes Oil Ltd. Mr J. A. Ellis, commissioner for railways in Western Australia from 1934 to 1949, became Chairman of Western Collieries Ltd and of Gwalia Gold Mine Ltd and a director of Tomlinson Steel Ltd. Mr O. G. Meyer, a railway engineer since 1932 and a Victorian commissioner from 1950 to 1958, resigned to become chairman and managing director of Australian Carbon Black Pty Ltd. Mr P. J. Hannaberry, Commonwealth Railways Commissioner from 1948 to 1960, resigned to become deputy chairman of Clyde Engineering Co., a director of Fruehauf Trailers and of other transport companies. A case of a man who moved in both directions was that of W. J. Cleary, who was an engineer on the staff of the brewing firm of Tooth and Co. for many years before being appointed Chief Commissioner of Railways in NSW in 1929, and chairman of the Australian Broadcasting Commission from 1934 to 1943. Subsequently, he held various directorships, including the post of chairman of the department store of Mark Foy's.

The Post Office is another notable source of engineers (and others) who have gone into private business. Sir Harry Brown, Director-General of Posts and Telegraphs from 1923 to 1940, retired at the optional age of sixty to become chairman and joint managing director of the British General Electric Co. His successor, Sir Daniel McVey, resigned from the

[27] Granick, op. cit., ch. 2

public service in 1946 to become chairman and managing director of Standard Telephones and Cables Pty Ltd and subsequently chairman of Dunlop Rubber, managing director of Metal Manufactures Ltd, a director of ICIANZ, John Darling & Son and other companies. Sir Giles Chippindall, Director-General from 1949 to 1958, retired to become a director of Dunlop Rubber, deputy chairman of Pyrox Ltd, chairman of a firm of newspaper publishers in Tasmania, and a director of Plessey Pacific Pty Ltd. His successor, Mr M. R. C. Stradwick, resigned after two years in the job to become vice-president in the Far East for the International Telephone and Telegraph Co. Mr C. G. Friend, Director of Posts and Telegraphs in WA, retired in 1957 to become a director of the television company TVW Ltd. His counterpart in Queensland, Mr Claude Faragher, also retired in 1957 and became a director of Brisbane TV Ltd and other companies. Sir Stanley Jones was an engineer with the Post Office for sixteen years, served as a signals officer in the Middle East from 1940 to 1942 and became director of radio and signal supplies in the Department of Munitions. In 1945, he joined Philips Electrical Industries as technical manager, and in 1961 became managing director of STC Pty Ltd. Mr N. W. Strange retired in 1957 as Director of Posts and Telegraphs in Victoria, to become a director of Siddons Industries Ltd and of Stanhill Holdings Ltd—a post which was to cause him a great deal of public and private embarrassment when the Stanhill group of companies crashed spectacularly in 1962.

Munitions production is another branch of government industrial enterprise with a record of supplying engineers and industrial managers to private industry. This includes three successive holders of the post of Controller-General of Munitions. Mr N. K. S. Brodribb (retired 1951) became a director of Clyde Industries and the Mt Lyell Mining and Railway Co.; Mr M. M. O'Loughlin (retired 1952) became deputy chairman of Pacific Oxygen Ltd and a director of Overseas Corporation; Mr R. H. Doyle (retired 1958) became a director of Borg-Warner (Aust.) Pty Ltd, H. P. Gregory & Co., and other companies. Sir John Jensen, secretary of the Departments of Munitions and Supply from 1941 to 1949, became chairman of British Automatic Telephone and Electric Pty Ltd and a director of Pacific Oxygen, Pyrox Ltd and other companies. Mr A. S. V. Smith, permanent head of the Department of Supply and Shipping from 1942 to 1945, resigned to become a director of Associated Electrical Industries, Emmco Pty Ltd, John Vicars and Co., and Buckinghams Ltd. Sir Jack Stevens, for many years a Post Office engineer and later a major-general, was secretary of the Supply Department from 1951 to 1952 and then chairman of the Atomic Energy Commission. He retired in 1956 at the optional age of sixty to become the chairman of Associated Electrical Industries, a director of Mt Isa Mines, Commonwealth Industrial Gases, Vickers (Aust.) Pty Ltd, and chairman of Development Underwriting Ltd. Mr H. C. Green, assistant secretary of the Munitions Department during the 1939-45 war, resigned to become chairman and managing director of Sydney Cooke Ltd and a director of Australian Titan Products Pty Ltd and of the United Insurance Company. Mr V. F. Letcher, assistant secretary in charge of aircraft production and subsequently representative of the Supply Department in London from 1952 to 1957, became Australian agent for the French aircraft industry, and reputedly played a major part in the negotiations by which the Commonwealth government decided to buy the Mirage jet fighter plane.

The armed services have also contributed engineers to industry. Rear-Admiral C. C. Clark was Third Naval Member and Chief of Naval Construction from 1953 to 1959; on his retirement, he became a director of the BHP Co., which has large shipbuilding interests. His predecessor, Rear-Admiral A. B. Doyle, retired in 1948 to become a director of Federated British Engineers (NSW) Ltd. Captain G. I. D. Hutcheson, formerly director of engineering in the RAN, retired in 1947 to become managing director of Cockatoo Docks & Engineering Co. Pty Ltd, and from 1953-55 president of the Chamber of Manufactures in NSW. Captain A. C. Weeks, RAN, left the service in 1946 to become chief mechanical engineer of Australian Paper Manufacturers Ltd and later its personnel manager. Brigadier J. W. A. O'Brien, DSO, was deputy Master-General of Ordnance, chief of the scientific and technical division of SCAP, Tokyo, from 1946 to 1951, and military supply representative in Washington, 1951 to 1954; he resigned to enter industry and became managing director of Howard Industries Pty Ltd, makers of agricultural machinery. Air Vice-Marshal J. E. Hewitt, Air Member for Supply and Equipment from 1951 to 1956, became manager in charge of technical training for the International Harvester Co. Major-General L. E. Beavis, who was Master-General of Ordnance from 1942 to 1946, and later held administrative and diplomatic posts, retired in 1954 and became a director of Rubbertex Industries and other companies.

Finally, there is a miscellaneous category of engineers whose professional careers have embodied a variety of moves between private and public employment. Mr L. R. Benjamin worked as a chemical engineer with the Institute of Science and Industry (which became, in 1926, the Council for Scientific and Industrial Research) from 1919 to 1928, and then entered the papermaking industry. Sir John Butters, one of the best known of all Australian engineers, was general manager of the Hydro-Electric Commission of Tasmania from 1914 to 1924, and chairman from 1925 to 1929 of the Federal Capital Commission, which was responsible for the original construction and administration of Canberra; he subsequently became chairman of a string of large companies, including Associated Newspapers, North Shore Gas Co., Hadfields Ltd, and the Royal Insurance Co. and a director of many others. Mr H. G. Carter, DSO, resigned in 1929 from the Public Works Department of NSW after working on the Burrinjuck hydro-electric scheme, to become chairman of Sydney Cold Stores and Australia Silknit Co., and a director of Carrier Air Conditioning Co., Claude Neon Industries and Concrete Industries. Mr G. D. Balsille, director of public works in Tasmania for twenty years until his retirement in 1949, became a director of Industrial Sales & Service Ltd, makers of earth-moving equipment. Sir Russell Dumas, head of the Public Works department in Western Australia and a former chairman of the State Electricity Commission, retired in 1953 to become a director of Hadfields (wa) Ltd, Kiernan Transport Ltd, and Western Collieries Ltd. Mr R. A. Hunt, dso, chairman of the State Electricity Commission of Victoria from 1949 to 1956, became deputy chairman of the engineering firm of Malcolm Moore Industries Ltd, and a director of Haunstrup Constructions Ltd. Mr G. R. Goffin, chief engineer of the Brisbane City Council, resigned in 1955 to become chief engineer of Humes Ltd, Australia's largest maker of concrete pipes. Mr H. J. Brown was an electrical engineer with the Tasmanian Hydro-Electric Commission before the war; worked with csir during the war; was professor of electrical engineering at the nsw University of Technology (now the University of nsw), and controller of the Weapons Research Establishment, South Australia, from 1955 to 1958. He resigned to become technical director of the Rola Co., radio manufacturers, and later technical director of Philips Electrical Pty Ltd.

Another electrical engineer, Mr F. C. Edmondson, who succeeded Sir Russell Dumas as chairman of the Electricity Commission in Western Australia, resigned in 1956 to become general manager of email Ltd, one of Australia's largest makers of electrical equipment. Mr A. G. Langton, who entered government service as an aircraft engineer during the war, was subsequently in charge of management training at the School of Mines, Adelaide, and then director of industrial development for the Tasmanian government from 1953 to 1958 before going into private industry. Mr D. L. McLarty, an engineer in private industry for some years, became director of the nsw state dockyard in 1941 and a member of the Electricity Commission in 1950, returning to private industry after his retirement in 1957.

These forty cases have been cited not in order to provide an exhaustive list, but to illustrate the scope and extent of mobility in this field— engineering and industrial management—from the public to the private sector. It is evident that the tendency has been established for many years and on a wide scale. Until fairly recent years, the commonest pattern was for retired public employees to be appointed as directors of private firms on the grounds of either special experience or social prestige. The latter applies particularly to 'top brass' in the armed services. Before the war, three former chiefs of the army general staff became directors of private firms on their retirement: Sir Julius Bruche, Sir Harry Chauvel and Sir C. B. Brudenell White. The expansion of the armed services during and after the war led to an increase in the number of senior officers, and correspondingly more were to be found on boards of directors after their retirement. They included several admirals—Bracegirdle, Farquhar-Smith, Harries; three chiefs of the general staff, Sturdee, Rowell, Wells, and a number of other generals (Berryman, Bridgeford, King, Northcott,

Robertson, Dyke, Lloyd, Smart); and a sprinkling of air-marshals (Jones, Cole, McCauley).

The practice of appointing retired civil officials to directorships has also grown apace since the war, but just as significant is the extent to which industry has actively sought to obtain the services of senior officials at an earlier stage of their careers by inducing them to resign and accept executive posts in private firms. Peter Shore, noting the growing similarity between business management and public administration, wrote: 'In the vast, stable and permanent establishments of modern industry, far removed from the vulgar higglings of the market, the newly recruited civil servant may well find an atmosphere hardly to be distinguished from the one he has just left. . . .'[28] Balogh has also drawn attention to the changed post-war situation. Before the war, he writes, 'the employment by private firms of civil servants could be of little *direct* advantage to anyone, i.e. due to the personal influence of a civil servant with his late colleagues.' Because of much closer links betwen government and industry, the bureaucratic skills of the civil servant have become an asset. 'State policy decisions have become more vitally important and the decision can easily be influenced one way and another by judicious summing up.'[29] Another recent British observer, Anthony Sampson, believes that personal links remain important when public servants go into industry, and that informal lobbying may reach the point where it 'becomes in the end a sort of like-mindedness in which it may not be clear who is the persuader and who the persuaded.' Industrialists, he suggests, appreciate both the patient, analytical intellects of Whitehall and the fact that civil servants know their way around Whitehall.[30]

In postwar Australia, these recurrent changes of status from gamekeeper to poacher have become part of the normal pattern of relationships between government and industry. Financial expertise is an outstanding reason. Mr W. C. Balmford, for many years Commonwealth Actuary and Insurance Commissioner, retired in 1957 to become a director of Australia's largest group of investment companies, the Capel Court group, associated with the old-established Melbourne sharebroking firm of J. B. Were. Mr J. W. R. Hughes, Deputy Commissioner of Taxation in NSW from 1942 to 1955, became a director of Rothmans Ltd and of Electrical and Musical Industries (EMI). Mr H. T. Armitage, Governor of the Commonwealth Bank until 1948, became a director of Legal and General Assurance Co., Australian United Acceptance Pty Ltd, and United Discount Co. of Australia Pty Ltd. Sir Patrick McGovern, Commissioner of Taxation from 1951 to 1963, became a director of various companies registered in the Australian Capital Territory (where the tax laws were for many years less exacting than elsewhere in Australia). Mr A. N. Armstrong, deputy

[28] Shore, loc. cit.
[29] Thomas Balogh, 'The Apotheosis of the Dilettante' in Hugh Thomas (ed.), *The Establishment*, p. 94, London, 1959
[30] Sampson, op. cit., pp. 61, 287

managing director of the Commonwealth Banking Corporation until 1964, became a director of J. A. Gilbert (Holdings) Ltd. Mr Cecil Gostelow, NSW government actuary until his retirement in 1956, became a director of W. G. Watson Holdings Ltd. Sir Fred Drew, Under-Treasurer of South Australia from 1946 to 1960, became a director of the Adelaide Steamship Co. and also of South Australian Unit Trusts, the latter having already acquired the services of Mr E. S. Williams, general manager of the South Australian government savings bank from 1953 to 1959. Mr C. R. McKerihan, for many years chairman of the Rural Bank of NSW, remained in the financial world after his retirement in 1963 as a consultant to the Sydney sharebroking firm of Roland Walton and Co. Sir Arthur Smithers, Director of Finance for the Victorian government from 1937 to 1959, became a director of Australian Capital Fund Incorporated, an investment company linked with the sharebroking firm of Ian Potter and Co., and also acted as financial adviser to a large American-Australian hotel enterprise in Melbourne. Mr J. V. Ratcliffe, a senior taxation official of the NSW government, resigned after the war to become chairman of Bond's Industries, a director of Consolidated Press Holdings, and various other companies. Mr P. F. Jones, a senior finance officer in the Commonwealth Treasury, resigned in 1951 to go to the Herald and Weekly Times Ltd, Australia's largest newspaper chain, of which he became general manager. Mr R. P. Thorman left a similar position in 1959 to take the position of assistant federal director of the Associated Chambers of Commerce; he became director in 1962.

Other forms of expertise or of special contacts have also been in demand. Dr A. J. Metcalfe, Director-General of the Commonwealth Health Department until 1960, became a consultant to the pharmaceutical firm of Lederle Laboratories, a division of the vast US Cyanamid Corporation. Mr C. H. McFadyen, a secretary of the Department of Shipping and Transport until 1957, remained in the shipping business as chairman and managing director of the Port Phillip Stevedoring Company. Sir William Dunk, chairman of the Public Service Board from 1947 to 1960, and a member of the Commonwealth Immigration Advisory Council, became a director of Navcot Pty Ltd, a shipping firm with interests in the operation of immigrant ships between Europe and Australia. The great expansion of the mining and metal industries has been reflected in the movement of government officials between the private and public sectors. Mr S. F. Cochran, chairman of the Joint Coal Board from 1950 to 1963, retired to become a director of Thiess Holdings Ltd, a firm with large coal interests in Queensland. Sir Harold Raggatt, secretary of the Department of National Development from 1952 to 1965 and a major figure in oil geology, became a director of Ampol Exploration Ltd, a leading oil search company. Mr K. H. Herde, an assistant secretary in the Prime Minister's Department, who was actively concerned with negotiations over the exploitation of the vast bauxite field at Weipa, in Queensland, resigned in 1965 to join Conzinc-Rio Tinto of Australia Ltd. Mr A. E. Warburton, assistant under-secretary in the NSW Treasury Department and a member of the Joint Coal Board for ten years, resigned in 1956 to become assistant general manager of Coal and Allied Industries Ltd. Mr D. J. Hibberd, first assistant secretary in the Commonwealth Treasury and government representative on the Australian Aluminium Production Commission, entered the metal industry in 1956 and became managing director of Comalco Ltd and a director of the Southern Aluminium Co. Mr G. P. Phillips, deputy secretary of the Department of Trade, resigned in 1968 to become chief executive officer of the Australian Mining Industry Council. Mr C. A. Kneipp, director of industry services in the Office of Secondary Industry, became executive director of the Aluminium Development Council in 1967. Mr J. A. Back, an assistant secretary in the same department, left it in 1968 to become chief excutive officer of the Australian Metal Industries Association. Mr Harold Amos, an assistant secretary in the Department of External Territories, resigned in 1968 to become finance director of Western Mining Corporation. The mining industry has also recruited geologists on a large scale from the Commonwealth Bureau of Mineral Resources; in 1965, for instance, a senior geologist with the Bureau, Mr B. P. Walpole, left it to set up as Australian consultant to the Anaconda Copper Co. and recruited a number of his colleagues to join him.

Officials concerned with overseas trade, either in relation to tariff administration or general trade policy are also in demand. An early instance was that of Mr A. C. Moore, Assistant Comptroller-General of Customs and Director of the wartime Division of Import Procurement, who resigned to become managing director of the Coca-Cola Bottling Corporation and subsequently general manager of the *Daily Mirror* newspaper. Sir Frank Meere, Comptroller-General of Customs until 1960, became a director of Pope Industries Ltd and Philips Pty Ltd. Mr J. W. Brophy, Collector of Customs for Victoria until 1955, became a director of Oliver-Davey Glass Industries Ltd. Since 1960, the cross-traffic has swollen significantly. Mr R. W. Brack, first assistant Comptroller-General of Customs, became commercial manager of Australian Consolidated Industries in 1964. In the seven years 1961 to 1968, the Department of Trade and Industry lost nine Second Division officers. The first of these was Mr Eric McClintock, first assistant secretary, who joined the Development Finance Corporation in 1961. Others included Mr W. S. Lowe, who was recruited in 1962 by a firm of management consultants, J. P. Young & Co., to run their new export development branch; Mr J. P. Kemp, secretary of the Tariff Board, who became general manager of British-Australian Tobacco in 1963; and Mr J. H. Willis, first assistant secretary, who went into private business in New York. Mr B. R. Barry, secretary of MIAC, resigned to join a firm of chartered accountants, Irish & Michelmore, whose principal, Mr R. A. Irish, was chairman of MIAC and also of Rothmans Ltd. Mr A. J. Campbell, deputy secretary of Trade, became director of export marketing for Colonial Sugar Refining Ltd in 1968.[31] A number of Trade officials have joined the staffs of major industry pressure groups. Mr G. R. Bain, deputy assistant secretary in the department, became assistant director of the NSW division of the Associated Chambers of Manufactures in 1959 and director in 1960. He was replaced as assistant director by Mr L. N. Cottle, also from Trade, who in turn became director in 1964 when Mr Bain took up a senior executive position with the newspaper firm of John Fairfax Ltd. Mr W. Callaghan, deputy secretary of Trade and head of the Office of Secondary Industry, and formerly deputy chairman of the Tariff Board, resigned in 1968 to become director of the Australian Industries Development Association, an industry lobby concerned largely with tariff protection.

Commenting on this flow of officials to key positions in industry, the *Australian* noted in 1968 that movement out of the Department of Trade had been particularly active at the deputy assistant secretary level (i.e. the senior ranges in the Third Division), where more than a dozen officials had left in the course of a few years. 'The department has lost even more people at a slightly junior level to this, but who rank among its most experienced officers. Private industry has been following a conscious policy of recruiting from the bright young men in the senior ranks of the department.'[32] The same newspaper also noted the scale of financial inducements offered to government officials, ranging up to $10,000 in excess of their public service salaries.[33] Other inducements include houses, cars, shares and private school fees for children.

Last, but by no means least in the gamekeeper-turned-poacher category, are two significant moves from the service of the Commonwealth into that of Ansett Transport Industries. Mr Harold Poulton, a lawyer by training, entered the Commonwealth Public Service in 1941 and remained there for twenty-three years. He was the framer of the 'two-airline' policy already described and as Assistant Director-General of Civil Aviation from 1956 to 1964 bore a major responsibility for the administration of the policy. In 1964 he resigned to join the Ansett enterprise. In 1965 he was followed by the public relations officer of the Department, Mr R. Alexander, who moved to a similar job with the Ansett airline.

In a highly organised, bureaucratic society, mobility between 'strategic elites' is a normal phenomenon, and has certain beneficial consequences. But it is equally natural for people to become alarmed when movement takes place on the scale described above. It is not necessary to adopt the vulgar Marxist view that 'the civil service in our society is in the hands of men who step freely from the civil service into the direct service of

---

[31] Some of these details are contained in an answer to a parliamentary question by Mr McEwen, *House of Representatives Debates*, 30 May 1968, p. 1881.
[32] *Australian*, 25 May 1968
[33] ibid., 29 June 1968

monopoly and vice versa.'[34] The danger is rather, as Balogh suggests, that if such mobility becomes a normal expectation for a successful public servant in middle life, the standards of public service will themselves be endangered, especially where decisions have to be taken which affect the interests of private business. What counts is 'the reaction of those men (or at least the general average of those men) who remain in the Service, who will also wish to do well and will therefore be—in most cases quite unconsciously—inclined to take a general view of things not awkward to large private interests.'[35] It is essential, as a British official report declared in 1937, that 'public confidence in the disinterestedness and integrity of the Crown Services should be maintained . . . there should be no possibility of a suggestion . . . that members of those Services might be influenced in the course of their official relations with business concerns by hopes or offers of future employment in any of those concerns.'[36] The report recommended what has become the official British practice, that the acceptance of an appointment within two years of resignation or retirement with a firm having business relationships with the government, should require the consent of the responsible Minister of the Crown and of the Treasury.[37] In France, similarly, no former *inspecteur de finances* may be personally involved in negotiations with the *Inspection Générale de Finances* for three years after his resignation.

It is the absence of any such formal safeguards in Australia which has excited public comment on the operations of *pantouflage* in recent years. The matter was referred to in the Federal parliament in 1961 by Mr E. G. Whitlam, then Deputy Leader of the Opposition, who asked the Minister for Health whether he had approved the appointment of Dr A. J. Metcalfe, the former Director-General of Health, as a consultant to the pharmaceutical firm of Lederle Laboratories. Mr Whitlam noted that pharmaceutical benefits were paid in respect of drugs placed on the 'free list' on the advice of the Pharmaceutical Benefits Advisory Committee. He continued:

On 3rd May last year the Minister told the honourable member for Yarra (Mr Cairns) that it has never been policy to publicise the names of the gentlemen who serve on the Pharmaceutical Benefits Advisory Committee,

[34] E. F. Hill, in the *Communist Review*, May 1958. See also John Playford, *Neo-Capitalism in Australia*, Melbourne, 1969
[35] op. cit., p. 96
[36] *Memorandum on the Acceptance of Business Appointments by Crown Officers*, Cmnd. 5517, 1937
[37] The 1937 report arose out of the case in which Sir Christopher Bullock, permanent head of the Air Ministry, approached Imperial Airways Ltd about the possibility of his appointment as a director. The affair was examined by a board of inquiry and Bullock was censured and relieved of his position. In its report (Cmnd. 5254, 1936), the board of inquiry restated the code laid down in a Treasury circular of 1928, which declared that the public expects from civil servants 'a standard of integrity and conduct not only inflexible but fastidious'.

who are all eminent practitioners in their respective spheres. Publication of their names, the Minister said, might well result in their being subjected to unfair and unwelcome pressure from various sources. . . . On the 28th of last month, the Minister told me that he had not answered to the public or revealed to the drug companies the names of members of any committees he has appointed. In these circumstances, it is all the more deplorable that the recently retired Director-General of Health should have become a consultant to one of the largest firms whose drugs are approved by the department as pharmaceutical benefits. The Minister admitted to me on 12th September that, when the Director-General retired, he did not seek or receive the Minister's approval. . . . It is obvious that the former Director-General is in a position to [disclose the membership of these committees to the company]. . . . He has broken no statute or contract, however unethically and improperly he may have acted in accepting such a position. His is only the latest of many cases where senior public servants and officers of the armed forces have resigned or retired and have forthwith accepted positions in which their confidential knowledge would seem to be of material interest to their new employers or principals.[38]

The Minister for Health, replying to this speech, merely accused Mr Whitlam of damaging the reputation of a distinguished public servant, and ignored the wider question of principle, as it has been consistently ignored by all governments. As Max Beloff has argued, even the safeguards imposed in Britain reflect Victorian standards of public rectitude which are not really helpful in the second half of the twentieth century, when the relations between government and industry rest on quite other factors. If, he writes, 'the seepage of top civil servants into industry becomes accepted as normal in mid-career, another basic change in our Victorian institutional pattern will have to be faced.'[39] In Australia, the character of the bureaucratic ascendency was formed in the late-Victorian era, when the scale of bureaucratic institutions was relatively small and that of private business even smaller. Since then, both have grown into large, complex and stratified domains and mobility between them reflects the general growth of stratification within the Australian community.

[38] *House of Representatives Debates*, 4 October 1961, pp. 1648-9
[39] *Encounter*, November 1962

20: The Business Elite (1): Family Affairs

It is doubtful whether Australians have any clear 'image' of business men. Individual figures have impressed themselves on the public at various times, but mostly in relation to some specific incident, often of a sensational character. Even businessmen themselves, when queried, rarely have an inclusive picture of the business community, although they can point to current trends, such as the rising importance of higher education in a business career. One reason for this lack is that the businessman is not a folk hero. The literary and the popular culture both have examples of enterprise, daring and inventiveness, all qualities associated with the successful entrepreneur, but the individuals to whom they are attributed are likely to be rural pioneers, soldiers, explorers, 'battlers' or even bushrangers rather than businessmen. Making money evidently does not command attention as a feat worthy of admiration or emulation, and if a businessman does attract these sentiments it is likely to be for some other reason, such as being a sporting champion in his youth.

The role of the businessman is, of course, quite different in the two major English-speaking countries, the USA and Great Britain. For many years, the popular legend of the American businessman was based on the 'rags to riches' stories whose most famous exponent was Horatio Alger. The 'robber barons' of the Gilded Age following the Civil War were the outstanding examples of the species. Their achievements were supposed to be an illustration of equality of opportunity. Studies by American historians since 1945 have done much to expose the mythical character of these beliefs. Far from starting life in circumstances of abysmal poverty, it seems that the majority of the great entrepreneurs came from families which, if not wealthy, were at least sufficiently well off to give their sons a good start.[1] Moreover, as Wright Mills has pointed out, the importance of family ownership remains greater than the widely accepted theory of the 'managerial revolution' allows for.[2]

In England, the tradition is rather different. The typical entrepreneur of

[1] See, e.g., William Miller (ed.), *Men in Business*, Cambridge, Mass., 1952; ibid., 'The Recruitment of the American Business Elite', *Quarterly Journal of Economics*, vol. 64, no. 2, 1950; Mabel Newcomer, *The Big Business Executive*, New York, 1956
[2] C. Wright Mills, *The Power Elite*, New York, 1956, chs. 5-7

the eighteenth and nineteenth centuries was a man who had his own small business and was astute enough to seize the opportunities made available by technological change to enlarge his plant or start an entirely new enterprise. In this case there is a tradition of hard work, self-denial, the ploughing back of profits and the gradual building up of small firms into large ones. Ruthlessness towards competitors and ferocious resistance to trade unions were much less evident than in the United States, but in common with the American tradition, the leaders in British industrial expansion were taken to be self-made men, whose hagiographer in this case was Samuel Smiles.

In both cases, the image is a flattering one. In Australia, the absence of such an image may be traced to the characteristics of the Australian economy described in Chapter 17 above. Businessmen, apart from isolated individuals, are not generally regarded as having contributed prominently to the 'development' of Australia. These attitudes are generally shared by scholars, so that the writing of business history was virtually unknown until the late 1950's.[3]

The social changes attending upon rapid industrial growth since the early 1940's have already produced some re-evaluation of the businessman's role in society, and it is certain that the process will go much further. In this chapter, we shall present some evidence of the character of the business elite in the 1950's and 1960's, but the historical development of this group cannot as yet be traced in detail. One unpublished study of manufacturers in Victoria, the leading industrial state in the year 1900, does suggest a very substantial change in the character of the business community since that period.[4] This group, 282 in all, covered a wide range of industrial production, including food and drink, boots and shoes, brewing, chemicals, clothing and textiles, glass and pottery, leather goods, timber, metal manufacturing, ropes and canvas, rubber, tobacco, vehicles and instruments of various kinds. More than 70 per cent of the group were immigrants. Of the entire number, 36 per cent came from England, 11 per cent from Scotland, 5 per cent from Ireland and 4 per cent from Germany. The largest number had started their businesses as comparatively young men, 41 per cent below the age of 40, 29 per cent before they were 30. Nearly one-half had worked in other trades before going into business and a similar proportion had established their enterprises single-handed, without partners or family backing; only 14 per cent had bought their businesses. Although information is incomplete, it is probable that well over half had no more than a primary education (the actual figure obtained being 45

---

[3] The work of Geoffrey Blainey is the first substantial contribution in this field, with special emphasis on the mining industry: *The Peaks of Lyell, Mines in the Spinifex* and *The Rush that Never Ended*.

[4] The material that follows is drawn from an unpublished study kindly given to me by Dr A. R. Hall of the Australian National University. The information was obtained from a number of contemporary business directories and biographical dictionaries.

per cent of the two-thirds for whom information was available). Religion was unknown in most cases, but 13·5 per cent of the group were known to be Masons; as information about lodge membership was only available for 27 per cent of the group, it is likely that the actual proportion was higher. Twelve per cent were active in local government.

The picture emerges of a group very like the image of the nineteenth century British businessman, starting in this case as an immigrant with a few shillings in his pocket and improving himself by thrift and hard work; a pillar of the community, active in public affairs and a conscientious member of the Anglican or Nonconformist churches. This conforms with our general knowledge of the period. Although such men continue to be represented in the business elite, they are not typical. It is noteworthy that of the 282 men in the group, only 20 names can be identified with industries of any consequence in the period since 1950. In the intervening half century, the establishment of industrial enterprises required capital on a scale which placed a premium on family connections.[5] It is to the great influence of family groups that we now turn.

The First Family

As noted in Chapter 17, pre-war studies indicated that almost one-half of industrial investment was owned by about fifty family groups. In the 1960's, according to E. W. Campbell, the number of family groups had increased to sixty (although one suspects that his choice of this number was influenced by the title of Ferdinand Lundberg's famous book of the 1920's, *America's Sixty Families*). Business history in the twentieth century is, to a large extent, the history of these family fortunes. A comprehensive account of their growth would be beyond the scope of this book and much more detailed information would in any case be necessary before it could be written. Here, we shall be concerned with the contribution that major family groups have made to the directorship and management of particular areas of industry and business, as a background to the more general analysis of the composition of the business elite.

Beyond question, the premier business family of Australia is that of Baillieu. According to family records, its founder was a lacemaker in the Belgian city of Liège, one Jean-Baptiste Baillieux, who died in 1744.[6] His grandson, Etienne Lambert Baillieux, settled in Bristol, England, during the French Revolution and opened a dancing academy in 1797. The family soon dropped the last letter from its surname and changed its religion to Anglicanism, but retained the given name of Lambert in subsequent generations (St Lambert was a seventh century bishop who was murdered in Liège). James G. Baillieu migrated to Australia in 1851 from

---

[5] An important section of this period is examined by C. A. Forster, *Industrial Development in Australia 1920-30*, Canberra, 1964.

[6] I am indebted for much information about the Baillieu family to Mr Geoffrey Tebbutt, of the Melbourne *Herald*.

Pembrokeshire, and after a spell on the goldfields became an official of the customs and health departments of the colony of Victoria. Later, he owned a hotel at Queenscliff, at the entrance to Port Phillip Bay, where many members of the family are buried. He had sixteen children, of whom the youngest, M. H. L. Baillieu, died in 1961. The size of the family and its strong sense of kinship have helped to spread its ramifications through a remarkable range of industrial and commercial activity, including mining, smelting, iron and steel, brewing, papermaking, banking, retailing, cattle raising, textiles, sharebroking, pastoral trading, rubber and woollen clothing. Other prominent business families with whom the Baillieus have intermarried include those of Darling (iron and steel), Myer (retail trading), Stewart (mining and chemicals), Hordern (retail trading and pastoral properties), Law-Smith (pastoral properties, banking and agricultural machinery), Vicars (brewing and textiles), Knox (electrical manufacture), Cuming (chemicals and fertilisers), and Robinson (mining and metals).

Several of J. G. Baillieu's sons became prominent in business, but by far the most important of them was William Laurence (1859-1936), who enjoyed a reputation in his lifetime as a financial wizard. He was largely unschooled and went to work for the Bank of Victoria at the age of fourteen. During the land boom of the 1880's, he went into business as an auctioneer in partnership with one Donald Munro, son of a leading colonial politician, and made a fortune from land transactions. In 1892, after the boom had collapsed leaving a trail of bankruptcies, bank failures and mass unemployment, W. L. Baillieu set up his own firm of real estate agents, which became Baillieu Allard and Co. in 1899, and remains one of the principal firms in the business in Victoria. In 1887, the family acquired an interest in the largest brewing concern in Australia, Carlton & United Breweries, when he married the daughter of its founder, Edward Latham. (The story goes that he was waiting for Bertha Latham on the pilot boat at Queenscliff when she returned from a trip to England with her father.) All six children of the marriage were given the middle name of Latham and there has been a Baillieu on the board of Carlton & United Breweries ever since. The alliance was cemented even more firmly when Edward Latham married for the second time by taking W. L. Baillieu's sister Emma as his bride.[7]

The collapse of the land boom in the early 1890's found the Baillieus at the centre of the financial crisis. One of W. L. Baillieu's contemporaries, W. G. Meudell,[8] gives an unflattering picture of his activities at this period:

[7] In the artless words of Mr M. H. L. Baillieu, as recorded by Geoffrey Tebbutt, 'the sustained link with Carlton and United Breweries recalls a romantic episode that also marked a turning point in the Baillieu family fortunes.'

[8] W. G. Meudell, *The Pleasant Career of a Spendthrift*, London, 1929. Meudell was a well-known stockbroker and man-about-town in Melbourne. When the book was published, it caused great indignation among the Baillieus, who are said to have done their best to buy up the entire edition. Meudell was also threatened with legal

The spectacular fortune made recently in Victoria belongs to W. L. Baillieu, *a* hero of the ancient land boom, if not *the* hero. W. L. made a coup and a separate fortune by amalgamating the London Chartered Bank, of which he was the local director, with the ES and A Bank. If W. L. Baillieu is not worth £5 millions it is a shame, a very great shame, for he ought to be.[9]

Concerning Baillieu's role in the land boom, Meudell wrote:

W. L. Baillieu was the outstanding figure of the cranky march of the citizens to nearly universal insolvency. Strong, able, self-controlled, a born money spinner, a natural gambler in land lots and scrip certificates, W. L. Baillieu is incomparably the cleverest financier in Australia. He burst for a million pounds and will die double that.[10]

Meudell goes on to describe the financial disaster that overtook the Federal Bank, in which various members of the Baillieu family were involved. The head of the bank was James Munro, a prominent colonial politician and a leading figure in the temperance movement. Meudell writes:

The downfall of the Federal Bank was the most disgraceful climacteric of the disastrous banking and land boom. . . . The head and front of the whole offending was the late James Munro . . . [who] used his position and his building society business to push his politics.[11]

The affairs of the Federal Bank were analysed in detail by a popular weekly paper, *Table Talk*. Munro and his associates had borrowed the entire capital of the bank (£500,000) and most of its deposits. Donald Munro had nine overdrafts amounting to more than £160,000 and paid 6d. in the £1 to his creditors after his bankruptcy. The Baillieus had overdrafts amounting to more than £150,000 out of a total overdraft account of £565,000.[12]

Having settled with his creditors, W. L. Baillieu established a share-

action. In a subsequent edition, *The Pleasant Career of a Spendthrift and his Later Reflections*, London, 1936, the sections dealing with W. L. Baillieu were either omitted or rewritten. It is worth noting that Baillieu left a personal estate of no more than £60,000.

[9] ibid., p. 131. This passage was omitted from the second edition.

[10] ibid., p. 256. This passage is replaced in the second edition by a section which begins: 'Here is one of Melbourne's most enterprising and successful men, who profited by the experiences of his feverish years before the depression.', p. 217.

[11] ibid., p. 63 (omitted from the second edition). James Munro (1832-1908), was reputed to be a millionaire on the strength of his land dealings and used his reputation to raise large amounts in England. In 1890 he became Premier and Treasurer of the colony and in 1892 went to London as Agent-General for Victoria. In the following year, he was recalled because of the banking crisis, which ruined him. His son, Donald Munro, was W. L. Baillieu's partner in real estate.

[12] Quoted by Meudell, pp. 64-5 (Omitted from the second edition)

broking firm, E. L. and C. Baillieu.[13] Under his leadership, the family's interests extended into the Dunlop Rubber Co., several mining companies at Broken Hill, the Melbourne *Herald* newspaper (now the centre of the largest newspaper empire in Australia), the ES & A Bank, the Commercial Bank of Australia, and pastoral properties in Queensland. During the 1914-18 war W. L. Baillieu, in conjunction with W. S. Robinson and Sir Colin Fraser, a leading mining engineer, was responsible for setting up, with strong prompting from the Commonwealth government, the Broken Hill Associated Smelters at Port Pirie, in South Australia and the Electrolytic Zinc works at Risdon, Tasmania. From 1901 to 1922 he was a member of the upper house of the Victorian state parliament and held various ministerial posts between 1909 and 1917. He was a leading figure in negotiations with the miners' unions in the 1920's which led to the introduction of the 'lead bonus' at Broken Hill, a rare example of the profit-sharing principle in Australian industry. When he retired in 1930 at the age of seventy, he was chairman of Broken Hill Associated Smelters, North Broken Hill, Electrolytic Zinc Co., and a director of many other companies. In 1910, he and his five surviving brothers built Collins House at 360 Collins Street, Melbourne, which remains the headquarters of the 'Collins House Group'—synonymous 'in and out of politics and commerce with deeply entrenched financial and industrial power and business acumen.'[14]

W. L. Baillieu had many connections in England and was regarded in the City of London as the most important single representative of Australian financial interests. This role was taken over by his son Clive (d. 1967), who settled in England after the 1914-18 war. He attended Magdalen College, rowed in the Oxford eight and became a barrister of the Inner Temple. He became a director of Dunlop Rubber in 1929, chairman in 1949 and president in 1957. (The family are major shareholders in the Australian branch of the company and there has been a Baillieu on the board for many years.) Clive Baillieu was also a director of Dalgety-NZL, the ES & A Bank, the Midland Bank, and Rio Tinto-Zinc (previously Consolidated Zinc). From 1945 to 1947 he was chairman of the Federation of British Industries. In 1953 he was raised to the peerage, thus becoming a perfect symbol of a classic type of British-Australian relationship, with a kangaroo in his coat of arms and a painting of the old family cottage at Queenscliff on the walls of the baronial mansion in Surrey.

As already noted, dynastic marriages are a key to the extraordinary ramifications of this first family of Australian business. Among the children of W. L. Baillieu, Clive (Lord) Baillieu married Ruby Clark, daughter of William Clark, partner in the sharebroking firm of L. Robinson, Clark

---

[13] There is an apparently well-attested story among veteran members of the Melbourne Stock Exchange that the firm was originally denied membership of the Exchange because of W. L. Baillieu's financial operations in the 1890's.
[14] Geoffrey Tebbutt, loc. cit.

and Co. and Harry, his brother, married Margaret Christie Robinson, daughter of W. S. Robinson, younger brother of L. Robinson and a partner in the same firm. Their father, A. B. Robinson, was a speculator in mining shares and was associated with W. L. Baillieu in several enterprises in the 1890's. W. S. Robinson (of whom more below) was an even more important figure in the mining industry than Baillieu, and the significance of the relationship would be difficult to exaggerate. One of W. L. Baillieu's youngest daughters, Claire, married R. J. Vicars, chairman for many years of Tooth's Brewing Co., the largest brewing concern in NSW, and director of many other companies including a family textile and clothing concern.

W. L. Baillieu's great-niece, Margery Merlyn, became the second wife of Sidney Myer, founder of the vast retail empire Myer Emporium Ltd. Meudell, with his usual charity, describes how Myer,[15] a Polish-Jewish immigrant, 'travelled with a pedlar's pack of haberdashery to the thinly peopled Mallee district of Victoria selling pins, buttons, needles and thread at profit ranging from one to two thousand per cent . . . [after putting a rival firm out of business in the town of Bendigo] he came to town and picked a foothold in Bourke Street. . . . Sid Myer is a human octopus with as many tentacles as a centipede has legs. Rapidly he has created a departmental store bigger than the Magasin de Louvre etc. . . . He has crippled all his big rivals in the city and smothered dozens of small shops in the suburbs. What will be the end of this gigantic wen nobody can foresee.'[16] The son of Sidney Myer and Merlyn Baillieu, Kenneth Baillieu Myer, was deputy chairman of the Myer Emporium Ltd in 1965, and his uncle, R. F. Baillieu, was a director.

The family has intermarried no less than three times with the old-established NSW family of Hordern, owners of one of the oldest retail businesses in Sydney and of various pastoral properties. W. L. Baillieu's niece June married Sir Samuel Hordern and his grandson Peter married Edwina Hordern. In 1963 Kenneth Myer's son married Sir Samuel Hordern's daughter Sarah. Peter Baillieu has been active in the pastoral industry as a director of Queensland National Pastoral Co. and of King Ranch (Aust.) Pty Ltd. The latter enterprise, devoted to the introduction to Australia of the Santa Gertrudis cattle breed developed at the famous King Ranch in Texas, was promoted largely by his other grandfather, W. S. Robinson. Another Baillieu marriage of significance in an entirely different sphere was that of Miss Sunday Baillieu to the Adelaide art collector and publisher, John Reed. Apart from their other services to

[15] Sidney Myer (Simcha Meyer Baevski, 1878-1934), immigrated to Australia in 1897. He and his brother, E. B. Myer, established a store in the gold-mining town of Bendigo and bought their first property in Melbourne in 1911. The firm now owns stores in every major city and a number of provincial towns. Myer left an estate of almost £1 million. Alan Marshall, *The Gay Provider*, Melbourne, 1961.

[16] op. cit., p. 253. This page was omitted from the second edition and replaced by a section which begins: 'This young Russian immigrant was the brightest commercial genius who has ever built up a first-class business out of nothing.', p. 227.

Australian art, Mr and Mrs Reed were early patrons of the painter Sidney Nolan and his supporters over a considerable period.

The Baillieus and their connections are one of the principal groups of shareholders in Australia's biggest enterprise, the BHP Co. Ltd, but they have never played a directing part in its activities. The family which has figured on the board of BHP continuously since the 1890's is the Darling family, of Adelaide, with whom the Baillieus have, however, intermarried. In view of this connection, it is convenient to treat the Darlings at this point.

The founder of the family in Australia was John Darling, a Scottish metalworker who emigrated to Adelaide in 1855. He established himself as a grain dealer in 1864. The gold rushes in Victoria and later in Western Australia created a demand for flour and the company exported flour and wheat on a large scale, helping to establish the Adelaide Steamship Company for the purpose. Profits from the grain and flour business were invested in copper mining in South Australia and in the production of fertilisers from by-products of copper smelting. John Darling and his son, John junior, also invested in the Broken Hill mines in the 1880's. For reasons which are not entirely clear, John Darling jr. was made a director of the BHP Co. in 1892, and became its chairman in 1907 until his death in 1914. In 1897 he also became sole proprietor of the grain firm, which has continued to develop as a separate interest, becoming a public company in 1958 under the title of John Darling & Son (Aust.) Ltd. Its subsidiaries include a number of private companies in the wheat, flour and baking fields. The family is also (since 1934) represented on the board of the National Bank of Australia, in which they are major shareholders. The connection goes back to the last century when the bank extended large credits to the family and its enterprises.

Harold G. Darling, the most important member of the family, succeeded his father as a director of BHP in 1914 and was chairman from 1923 until he died in 1950. At the time of his death, he was also chairman of Stewarts and Lloyds (Aust.) Pty Ltd, Rylands Bros (Aust.) Pty Ltd, and Commonwealth Aircraft Corporation, a director of the National Bank and of ICIANZ. His brother Leonard was also a director of BHP and related companies and Leonard's son, L. G. Darling, became a director after his uncle's death. H. G. Darling's son, John, held a number of directorships in 1965, but none associated with BHP.

Apart from their directorships, the Darling family are major shareholders in John Darling and Son Ltd and its subsidiaries, in BHP, the National Bank, Western Mining Corporation and the pastoral firm of Elder Smith Goldsbrough Mort (of which John Darling III is a director). The connection with the Baillieus arises from the marriage of Elizabeth, daughter of Harold Darling, to J. M. Baillieu, nephew of W. L. Baillieu and grandson of a former Chief Justice of Victoria, Sir John Madden. This marriage also establishes another chain of family business links. J. M. Baillieu's sister Beatrice married A. W. Stewart, son of Sir Alexander Stewart, a mining engineer who was prominent in the Collins House Group. Sir Alexander Stewart, in his turn, married Grace, daughter of James Cuming. The Cuming family's extensive interests in chemicals and fertiliser manufacture were involved in the series of mergers that led to the establishment of ICIANZ in 1928 and the family has been represented on the board of the company ever since, as well as being important shareholders. They are also represented on the board of BHP. A. W. Stewart and his brother, J. Cuming Stewart, are large shareholders in Australian Consolidated Industries, Commonwealth Industrial Gases and directors of Australian Pulp and Paper Mills, Broken Hill South, Metal Manufactures Ltd, Mt Lyell Mining Co., and Commonwealth Industrial Gases.

Through their direct holdings, directorships and direct or indirect links, the Baillieu family is connected with no fewer than seven of the sixteen top companies listed in Chapter 14, as well as with many others not so large or under other headings. The full story of the family and its role in Australian economic and social history remains to be written. For the present, we may close this short survey of its fortunes by quoting Geoffrey Tebbutt again:

The family lived well, without extravagance or ostentation, always with an eye to durable values and to productive investment, always looking to higher standards for themselves and those associated with them, and believing devoutly in a somewhat paternal version of capitalism. The wealth accumulated by the family has never been used ostentatiously, nor has it served as an excuse for idleness. The sons of J. G. Baillieu never forgot, when they themselves became patriarchs of finance, the struggle their father had to give them a start. The Baillieus may understandably have come to believe that what was good for them was also good for Australia; and this must often have been true. At any rate, they and their enterprises have become symbols of wealth and solid worth.[17]

As *envoi* for the story of a capitalist family animated by the Protestant ethic, this could hardly be bettered.

Other Family Groups

The closeness of the link between the Baillieu and Robinson families has already been mentioned. W. S. Robinson (1876-1963), the most notable member of the Robinson family, was a figure of quite remarkable influence in Australian business history, not only in the metal industry which was his main concern, but in a number of other important spheres.[18] A. B.

---

[17] loc. cit. Mr Tebbutt's words are a paraphrase of an interview in 1955 with the late M. H. L. Baillieu.

[18] Details of Robinson's life may be found in Geoffrey Blainey (ed.), *If I Remember Rightly: The Memoirs of W. S. Robinson*, Melbourne, 1967. Blainey also deals with the history of the mining firms in which the Baillieus and Robinsons were associated in *The Peaks of Lyell*, Cambridge, 1959 and *The Rush that Never Ended*, Cambridge, 1963.

Robinson, his father, was commercial editor of the Melbourne *Age* and in Blainey's words, an 'impetuous mining speculator'. He married Harriet, sister of Edmund Barton, later first Prime Minister of Australia, and had five sons. His association with W. L. Baillieu began during the land and mining boom of the 1880's and 1890's.

A. B. Robinson's eldest son, Lionel, was a stockbroker in Melbourne; after failing during the crash of the 1890's, he joined the Adelaide Stock Exchange and later set up a broking firm in London. His partner in London was William Clark, who had been a member of the Melbourne and Adelaide stock exchanges, and they traded as L. Robinson, Clark and Co. Clark, whose daughter Ruby married Clive (later Lord) Baillieu, became a director of many large companies in London. The firm made its fortune by specialising in Western Australian gold shares. In London, Lionel Robinson became intimate with a number of American mining magnates and financiers, notably Herbert Hoover (President of the USA, 1929-32), J. P. Morgan, Bernard Baruch and E. H. Harriman. Hoover was then in London as a partner in the American firm of Bewick, Moreing and Co. and travelled to Australia at Robinson's suggestion. The result of this visit was the establishment of the Zinc Corporation in 1905 (of which W. L. Baillieu was first chairman); in addition, Hoover and Baillieu took out an extensive lease on the brown coal deposits at Morwell, in eastern Victoria, which later became the basis for electricity generation by the State Electricity Commission of Victoria.

A. B. Robinson's third son, Sir Arthur Robinson (1872-1945), became a solicitor and founded the law firm of Arthur Robinson and Co., whose partners are to be found on the boards of a number of important firms. The pattern was set by its founder, who held fifteen directorships at one time, including the Bank of Adelaide, the AMP Society (Australia's largest life assurance office), the Ford Motor Co., and BALM Ltd (the biggest paint firm in Australia, largely owned by ICIANZ). Robinson was active in both state and federal politics from 1900 to 1925 and held various portfolios in the Victorian state government between 1915 and 1924. He was a leading figure in the Victorian Chamber of Manufactures and led a campaign in opposition to the Commonwealth government's attempt to gain full control of industrial arbitration by a constitutional referendum in 1926. This campaign was supported by a manufacturers' pressure group called the Single Purpose League, whose leading figures included the general manager of BHP, G. D. Delprat and H. V. McKay, head of the largest agricultural machinery firm in Australia. Robinson was also for many years chairman of the council of one of Australia's leading private schools, Scotch College.

The youngest son, William Sydney Robinson, was trained for a farming life, but became a journalist instead and at the early age of twenty-three succeeded his father as commercial editor of the *Age* newspaper. David Syme, its proprietor, perhaps the outstanding figure in Australian newspaper history, was one of his patrons, together with his elder brother

Lionel and W. L. Baillieu. In 1906, Robinson became a partner in his brother's sharebroking firm in London and although he returned to Australia before the 1914-18 war he remained, throughout his life, an international figure in the mining industry and in other fields, mostly in his preferred role of grey eminence. As a reviewer observed about his memoirs, 'he lived most of his life in a back room, as it were, which nevertheless abutted the most important international corridors of financial and political power.'[19] He played an influential role in the motor vehicle industry both in England and Australia and was instrumental in persuading General Motors to set up car manufacture in this country. He was one of the earliest backers of Frank Whittle, designer of jet engines, and a prime mover in the establishment of aircraft manufacture in Australia. He was largely responsible for the establishment of smelting of non-ferrous metals during the First World War. During the First World War, he also helped to establish the manufacture of fine woollen materials for clothing by the firm of Yarra Falls Ltd, of which his nephew Norman was managing director for a number of years. (Major shareholders in this firm include the Baillieu, Knox and McKay families.) Robinson personally negotiated with the King Ranch interests in Texas for the introduction of the Santa Gertrudis breed of cattle (specially adapted to the hot conditions prevailing in northern Australia) in the 1950's.

Robinson's business contacts included many politicians in Australia, Britain and the USA and he carried out various missions on behalf of governments. He was a personal friend of Sir Winston Churchill and was a frequent guest at Chequers when Churchill was Prime Minister. True to his character, however, he refused many offers of titles and honours. During the 1939-45 war, he was a constant adviser to the Commonwealth government and a member of various missions; on one of these, accompanying the Minister for External Affairs, Dr H. V. Evatt, he was instrumental in obtaining from the British government two squadrons of Spitfire fighters for the Royal Australian Air Force for use against the Japanese. He became personally intimate with the Labor leader, J. B. Chifley, to whom he rendered a number of services.[20]

Although Robinson retired from his directorships in 1951 and took up farming, he retained his influence in the mining world and was instrumental in the merger in 1962 of Consolidated Zinc Corporation Ltd with the Rio Tinto interests to form the Rio Tinto-Zinc (RTZ) group of companies, one of the largest mining combines in the world. His contacts with the mining business were maintained partly through his son, L. B. Robinson (d. 1961), who resided in London and was chairman of Consolidated Zinc, Zinc Corporation Ltd, New Broken Hill Ltd, Imperial Smelting Corporation, and a director of Broken Hill Associated Smelters and Electrolytic Zinc Co. With the death of W. S. Robinson and his son, the

[19] Clement Semmler, *Sydney Morning Herald*, 29 June 1968
[20] Chifley's tributes to Robinson are quoted by Crisp, *Ben Chifley*, passim.

family's distinctive contribution to Australian economic history appears to have ended.

Another family firm with Anglo-Australian connections is that of Lysaght. John Lysaght (Aust.) Ltd has a monopoly of the production of sheet steel and a predominant share in other branches of steel fabrication. Since the entry of BHP into iron and steel production, the two companies have been closely linked. The Lysaght family has a long connection with the iron and steel industry in Britain, particularly with the GKN group (Guest Keen and Nettlefolds).[21] The founder of the firm, John Lysaght, was the youngest son of a landowner in Ireland, William Lysaght. The son migrated to Bristol in 1857, established a small galvanising works, and was joined there by two nephews who succeeded him in the Welsh branch of the business when John Lysaght moved to Wolverhampton in 1880. In 1879, he decided to exploit the growing market for galvanised iron in Australia and opened an agency in Melbourne. In 1884 a third nephew, Henry Royse Lysaght, born in Bristol in 1862, was sent to Sydney to work in the Australian branch and became its manager in 1899. In 1914, the company bought land at Newcastle, near the site of the projected BHP steelworks, and in 1920 the company, now known as John Lysaght (Aust.) Pty Ltd, began manufacturing in Australia. H. R. Lysaght was chairman of this firm and a director of BHP, Australian Iron and Steel Ltd, the Commonwealth Rolling Mill Co., Anthony Hordern and Co., and the Australian Bank of Commerce. His son, D. R. Lysaght, born in Australia in 1896, was (in 1965) a director of John Lysaght (Australia) which became a public company in 1960, chairman of the Commercial Banking Co. of Sydney, and a director of GKN-Lysaght Pty Ltd. His two sons, E. C. Lysaght and J. C. F. Lysaght, were also directors of the family firm.

Two other notable business dynasties are worth special mention—the Fairfax and Knox families.[22] The Fairfaxes trace their descent back to Robert Fairfax of Barford Manor, Warwickshire, in the sixteenth century, and claim a collateral relationship with the Yorkshire Fairfaxes who fought on the Parliamentary side in the civil war of the seventeenth century. John Fairfax (1804-77) was a printer and publisher in Leamington, who went bankrupt as a result of a libel action and emigrated to Australia in 1838. In 1841 he bought the *Sydney Morning Herald* with a partner and in 1853 became sole proprietor. John Fairfax and his wife Sarah were among the pioneer 'settlers' in the high-class residential areas of Sydney's eastern suburbs, along the southern shore of Sydney Harbour. In 1858 they built a mansion, 'Ginahgulla', on a ridge called Bellevue Hill, overlooking both the harbour and the Pacific Ocean to the east. This neighbourhood became, in the 1960's, the location of the most expensive residential sites in Australia.

[21] Charlotte Erickson, *British Industrialists,* London, 1959 and personal communication
[22] J. F. Fairfax, *The Story of John Fairfax,* Sydney, 1941; A. G. Lowndes (ed.), *South Pacific Enterprise,* Sydney, 1956

John Fairfax's successors as head of the *Herald* and its associated enterprises were his second son, Sir James R. Fairfax (1834-1919); his grandsons, Sir James O. Fairfax (1863-1928) and Geoffrey Fairfax (1861-1930); and his great-grandson, Sir Warwick Fairfax (born 1901) who also became a director of the London *Times* in 1961. In 1961 a public company, John Fairfax Ltd was formed, whose directors in 1965 included Warwick Fairfax, his son J. O. F. Fairfax and his cousin Vincent Fairfax. This is the holding company for a number of operating enterprises covering newspapers, radio, television, printing, real estate and newsprint manufacture. In addition, successive generations have held a traditional circle of directorships, including the AMP Society (of which the first John Fairfax was an original director), the Bank of NSW, the Australian Gas Light Co., the Commercial Banking Co. of Sydney and the Perpetual Trustee Co. Another family pattern is the education of its sons at Oxford, beginning with the sons of Sir James R. Fairfax, and yet another is a leading role in philanthropic and cultural activities, including art collecting. The Fairfaxes have accumulated great wealth (Sir Warwick Fairfax is undoubtedly one of the wealthiest individuals in Australia), but it has not been derived from the kinds of productive enterprises with which other business families are associated.

The Knox family is inseparably connected with the history of Australia's second largest monopoly, the Colonial Sugar Refining Co. Edward Knox (1819-1901) born in Denmark, came to Australia in 1839, and in 1842 was appointed manager of the Australian Sugar Co., one of several firms engaged in sugar refining. In 1855, he was the moving force in the establishment of CSR, which absorbed virtually all its competitors in the 1880's and established a remarkable relationship with both the Commonwealth and Queensland state governments by which the price of sugar is fixed. Edward Knox was also chairman for many years of the Commercial Banking Co. of Sydney, sometimes referred to as the 'sugar bank'. His son, Edward William Knox, became general manager of CSR in 1880 and was the moving force behind the mergers of the 1880's. E. W. Knox's brothers included T. F. Knox, who became managing director of Dalgety's Ltd and Sir Adrian Knox, Chief Justice of Australia from 1919 to 1930. The dynastic succession was continued by his son, Sir Edward Ritchie Knox, who became chairman of both CSR and the CBCS in 1940, and retired in 1961. Sir Edward Knox's retirement broke the family succession and marks the advent of managerial control of the enterprise, although the family remains a major shareholder in CSR and in a number of other companies, including British Tobacco, Tooth's Brewing Co., BHP, Dunlop Rubber, Felt and Textiles Ltd, Olympic Consolidated Industries and Yarra Falls Ltd.

It would be possible to enlarge almost indefinitely upon the role of family interests, but we may content ourselves here with a brief list of industries where family interests have predominated over a long period. In retail trading, the role of the Myer-Baillieu family group is paralleled by the history of the Coles and Lloyd Jones families. George Coles, a country storekeeper in Victoria, had four sons who founded the firm of G. J. Coles and Co. in 1921 and made it one of the largest retail chains in the country. Three of their sons were directors in 1965. David Lloyd Jones, a Welsh migrant, founded the firm of David Jones in Sydney in 1838 and his direct descendants have been at the head of the firm almost unbrokenly since. The old-established retailing, trading and shipping firm of Burns Philp and Co. Ltd was founded in Brisbane in 1875 by a Scottish migrant, James Burns, in partnership with Robert Philp, later Premier of Queensland.[23] Philp withdrew from active participation in 1892 and James Burns remained chairman until 1923 when his son took over, retiring in 1967, at the age of 85, to give way to his son, James David Burns.

Family groups have figured prominently in coal mining and coal transport. The Howard Smith family became important in these fields and remains so, but one of the most spectacular stories of the coal industry, as yet unwritten, is that of the Brown family. James and Alexander Brown were Scottish migrants in the 1840's who played a leading part in developing the northern coalfields of NSW and made Newcastle into a major exporting centre, sending coal to Europe, USA and the Far East. James Brown's son, John, became the head of the firm in 1887 and remained so until he died in 1930. One of the toughest and most ruthless capitalists in Australian history, he was a principal figure in the *Coal Vend* case of 1912, in a bitter and protracted lawsuit with his relatives over the inheritance, and in the Rothbury incident of 1929 when striking miners were shot by police. Known as the 'Coal King' and the 'Coal Baron', he also owned hundreds of racehorses, some of which he raced under the pseudonym of Mr Baron. When he died in 1930, a large part of his estate was bequeathed to Sir Adrian Knox, Chief Justice of the High Court, who had been senior counsel for John Brown in the family lawsuit. Knox resigned to enjoy the bequest, but died in 1932. The rest of Brown's estate went to his estranged brother Stephen, who had lived the life of a playboy on the French Riviera since 1918, and who returned to Australia to become chairman of the company (now known as Coal and Allied Industries).

One may also mention the Grimwade family, connected with the pharmaceutical and glass industries since the 1870's; the Brookes family, with papermaking; the Michaelis and Hallenstein families, with the leather industry; and the McKay family, with agricultural machinery. And there are, of course, many other groups of less importance which continue to make family influence a major factor in the character of Australian capitalism and the composition of its owners and controllers.

[23] H. C. Perry, *Memoirs of Sir Robert Philp*, Brisbane, 1923

21: The Business Elite (2): Directors and Managers

Family connections are, of course, only one factor in determining individual access to positions of wealth and authority within the industrial system. In the present chapter, we shall be concerned with other aspects of social stratification which influence this access and shape the character of the business elite. Apart from inheritance, these factors include geography, education, religion and established status in another sphere of employment.

The Men on the Boards

In 1961, a survey was made of the directors of a number of public and private companies with the object of discovering common social character-istics among those who sat on a number of boards and formed the 'inter-locking directorate' of a highly concentrated system of ownership and control. This survey took in 270 men, holding a total of 1,328 director-ships in 330 companies. A number of these companies were small, but the list includes all the largest concerns in the main industrial and commercial groups—manufacturing, trading, banking, insurance, transport and the press. The selection of individuals was made in several phases. Initially, men holding three or more directorships were selected, provided that at least one place was on the board of a large firm (i.e. employing at least 1,000 people). This gave a list of 193 men. Of the other 77, 43 held two directorships in large firms and the remaining 34 all had places on the boards of one of the 100 leading companies listed by Hall.[1] Private firms were included mainly to encompass local subsidiaries of big overseas companies.

The 270 men in the survey fell into seven categories, whose respective contributions to the picture were as shown in Table 21·1.

The extent of family influence is indicated by the fact that Group 1, the 'scions' of business families, constituted 40 per cent of the individuals and

[1] A. R. Hall, *Sources of Australian Company Finance 1945-55*, Canberra, 1956. Other information came from the 'Digest' *Yearbook of Public Companies*, 1960 ed., the annual reports of eighty-seven private companies registered in Melbourne and Sydney, the annual reports of eighteen legal firms in the same two cities, and the 1959 edition of *Who's Who in Australia*.

Table 21.1 Directors of Australian Companies, 1960

Classification*		Number of Individuals		Number of Directorships	
			%		%
1	Scions	108	40	477	36
2	Lawyers	52	19·5	237	18
3	Technicians	29	11	131	10
4	Accountants	28	10	237	17·5
5	Organisation Men	28	10	123	9
6	Public Servants	16	6	90	7
7	Generals	9	3·5	33	2·5
		270	100·0	1328	100·0

* As there is some overlap between categories, a few individuals have been assigned to one category rather than another.

held 36 per cent of the directorships. This may be compared with Copeman's finding that 60 per cent of directors in a British sample of 1,200 had family connections, nearly one-half of them being in the family business.[2] As Copeman's sample was selected on a rather different basis, it is probable that the actual difference between the two countries is even smaller. The scions were drawn from fifty-six family groups, almost the number of E. W. Campbell's 'sixty families who own Australia'. Fourteen family groups were represented by three or more individuals, as shown in Table 21·2.

Table 21·2 Family Groups and Directorships, 1960

Family Name*	Number of Individuals	Number of Places
Baillieu (and close connections)	15	58
Coles	5	17
Carpenter	4	13
Darling	3	16
Fairfax	3	7
Gillespie	3	5
Knox (and close connections)	3	15
Lysaght	3	7
Michaelis	3	10
Myer	3	4
Nicholas	3	6
Robinson	3	9
Vicars	3	13
York Syme	3	12
	57	192

* Since the survey was made, there has been some change in the list of important families; in particular, the Knox and Robinson families have faded out.

The interests of most of the family groups listed in Table 21·2 were described in the preceding chapter. Those not included there were the

2 G. H. Copeman, *Leaders of British Industry,* London, 1955

Carpenter family, long established in shipping and trading, especially in the South Pacific;[3] the Gillespie family, also long established in flour milling and baking; the Nicholas family, in pharmaceuticals;[4] and the York Syme family, in a variety of fields including the BHP group.

There was a marked concentration of 'scions' on the boards of some of the largest companies. Four firms had six scions on their boards: BHP, the AMP Society (Australia's largest life office), Australian Iron and Steel Co., and the Perpetual Trustee Co. Six firms had five on their boards: Cuming Smith and Co. (chemicals and fertilisers), Goldsbrough Mort Ltd (pastoral and shipping), G. J. Coles Ltd, National Bank of Australasia, Commercial Banking Co. of Sydney, and Broken Hill Associated Smelters. Another six had four scions as directors: Myer Emporium Ltd, Colonial Sugar Refining Co., Metal Manufactures Ltd, John Darling and Son, Commonwealth Fertilisers and Chemicals, and Atlas Assurance Co.

It is hardly surprising that the second largest group in Table 21·1 should be lawyers. The importance of legal advice for a large firm is obvious and in Australia is accentuated by the complexities of a federal system and the judicial character of wage-fixing. During the expansion of the Australian economy since 1945, legal advice has also become of increased importance because of large transactions involving land and the problems created by mergers and takeovers. International corporations setting up business in Australia find it convenient to appoint their legal representatives to the board of the local subsidiary.

The role of the legal profession in industry is epitomised by the history of the Melbourne firm of solicitors, Hedderwick Fookes and Alston, whose partners held, in 1965, an impressive string of directorships covering BHP, Australian Consolidated Industries, ICIANZ, the National Bank, the Herald and Weekly Times, Drug Houses of Australia and Elder Smith Goldsbrough Mort. Sir Colin York Syme, a senior partner of the firm and scion of a leading business family, was chairman of both the first and last-named companies and his partner J. A. Forrest was chairman of ACI and the National Bank. The firm became prominent in the business world as administrator of the Felton Trust, a large estate left by the nineteenth century Melbourne businessman and philanthropist, Alfred Felton, founder

---

[3] The firm of W. R. Carpenter is well known throughout the islands of Melanesia and Polynesia, where for many years it has supplied trade goods to stores run by the missions. Hence the irreverent translation of its initials as 'We Rob Christ'. For good measure, the initials of their main competitor, Burns Philp, are rendered as 'Bloody Pirates'.

[4] G. R. Nicholas, a suburban pharmacist in Melbourne, won a prize of £10,000 offered by the Commonwealth government in 1915 for a local process to manufacture aspirin, supplies of which were previously imported from Germany. The trade name, 'Aspro', is a household word in many countries. A branch, Aspro-Nicholas Ltd, was set up in the United Kingdom in 1925 and a section of the family established itself in England. In 1968 the Australian firm, Nicholas Pty. Ltd., became a public company and acquired control of Aspro-Nicholas. G. R. Nicholas died in 1963 leaving more than £4 million.

of the glassmaking firm which became ACI and of the pharmaceutical firm which became Drug Houses of Australia. In the 1930's and 1940's the senior partner of the firm, T. C. Alston, had become a director of ACI, the National Bank and the Melbourne Steamship Co. (with which the York Syme family has a long connection). The following commentary is worth quoting at length:

If this single legal firm directs a great swathe of Australian key industry, their species directs even more. Messrs Syme and Forrest represent a new type of company chairman. . . . Usually a lawyer but occasionally an accountant . . . he has been appointed from outside as a part-time director but early enough in his life to be far more of a working director, a controller of detail in policy, than the traditional outside chairman. . . . This new ascendency of boardroom control follows the passing out of the generation of industrial pioneers . . . strong managing directors who had mastered the organisation from the workbench up. Inheritors of well-moated monopolistic castles, the new men are more cultivated and less intense. . . . Part of their opportunity springs from the indifference or decadence, in a business-administrative sense, of the third generation of wealthy inheritors like the Baillieus and Grimwades, families which are happy to delegate their responsibilities. Though this pattern is not universal, it is spreading.[5]

In other words, the impact of the managerial revolution is being felt in Australia as elsewhere. However, it is not taking the form of replacing capitalists by technicians on boards of directors, as Table 21·1 indicates. The growing importance of the lawyer is not, moreover, a movement towards the American pattern of the corporation lawyer; very few companies in Australia have their own legal departments, and the rise of the legal man as a director involves a change in the work of the legal firm rather than a trend towards the recruitment of legally trained men into business firms. Although Hedderwick Fookes and Alston is the most notable, there are at least a dozen other legal firms in a comparable situation. They include Arthur Robinson and Co. (Melbourne), established by the late Sir Arthur Robinson and having close links with the Collins House group of metal companies. Another Melbourne firm with important business links is that of Blake and Riggall. A former partner, William Riggall, was closely connected with the Victorian Employers' Federation in the early years of the century and was chairman for some years of a body called the Constitutional Union which raised funds for the Liberal and Nationalist parties. In Sydney, the old-established firms of Allen, Allen and Hemsley, and Minter, Simpson and Co. play a similar role in business, and both have strong political connections.

The growth of lawyers on company boards has taken place partly at the

---

[5] 'The Big Outsider', *Nation*, 8 April 1961. The York Syme connection with both BHP and Goldsbrough Mort has some historical background. The Hon. John Lewis, father of Essington Lewis, one of the leading figures in the history of BHP, sold his pastoral firm to Goldsbrough Mort in 1925.

expense of family proprietors, but partly also at the expense of accountants. Before the 1939-45 war, much of Australian industry was permeated by the cautious, unimaginative outlook of the accountant and his
preoccupation with balancing the books. Pre-eminent among them was
Sir Walter Massy-Greene (d. 1953), who at one time held the
phenomenal number of forty directorships, including the Collins House
group, ICIANZ and the National Bank.[6] A few accountants continue to
occupy positions of major importance. Among them, in 1965, were
Raymont Moore of Sydney, a director of many companies; R. A. Irish,
also of Sydney, chairman of Rothmans Ltd; Sir Raymond Purves, director
of many companies and an underwriting member of Lloyds; A. B. Taylor,
managing director of the large electrical manufacturing firm of Email Ltd;
and H. W. Rowden, managing director of Felt and Textiles Ltd. Only six
of the twenty-eight accountants in our list were university graduates,
another old-world touch, as the movement in the accounting profession
is strongly towards higher education and the mastery of modern information systems. Accountants, like lawyers, have tended to gravitate to the
boards of companies for whom they performed professional services. In
future, it is more likely that the accountant who becomes a director will be
a highly trained technician promoted from within the firm.

The increasing role of former public servants in business has already
been discussed in Chapter 18 and some of the individuals mentioned there
appear among the sixteen ex-government officials included in this survey
(Table 21·1). So rapid has been this trend, however, that the numbers
are certain to have risen significantly since the original analysis was made.
Group 7, 'generals', has also grown since 1960. In the latter year, six
military and three naval men fell within the scope of the survey.

The category of 'technicians' refers to men with some form of specialised
technical training, usually undertaken before they entered an industrial
firm. Ten had degrees in engineering and seven in science; eight had
engineering diplomas; four had diplomas in unspecified fields. They had
attended a wide range of institutions, including the universities of
Melbourne, Sydney, Western Australia, Queensland, Leeds, London,
Columbia, Minnesota and Yale; technical colleges in New York,
Manchester, Michigan, Birmingham, Melbourne, Sydney, Broken
Hill, Woolwich and the US Naval Academy. Five were Americans.
As might be expected, they were heavily concentrated in mining,
chemicals and metal manufacturing. The twenty-eight 'organisation men'
comprised those who had started their business career without either
specialised qualifications or family connections and had been promoted
through various levels of responsibility. Some had started 'at the bottom'
as clerks, messengers, or workmen; others had entered large firms after
pursuing other occupations; nine had undertaken specialised training in

[6] Massy-Greene's career is described by C. D. Kemp, *Big Businessmen*, Melbourne,
1964.

the course of their careers. Fourteen of the twenty-eight were in manufacturing industry and the other half were evenly distributed between banking, retailing and the press. Ten were connected with British or American companies and had been sent to Australia by the firm.

We may now look briefly at the social background of these men. In terms of geographical origin, they reflect the economic predominance of the city of Melbourne, referred to in a previous chapter.

Table 21·3 Directors of Australian Companies, 1960

Place of Birth	Number	%
New South Wales	59	22
Victoria	90	33·5
Queensland	8	3
South Australia	21	7·5
Western Australia	5	2
Tasmania	1	0·5
United Kingdom	21	7·5
North America	7	2·5
Other	5	2
No information	53	19·5
	270	100·0

The distribution as between birthplaces was similar for all seven groups; in other words, the concentration of ownership in Melbourne produced similar effects in all our categories (with the minor exception of the ex-military men). In terms of education, however, there was considerable diversity between the seven categories given in Table 21·1. Most of the scions and the lawyers had attended private secondary schools of the Headmasters' Conference, unlike the other five groups.

Table 21·4 Company Directors, 1960—Schools Attended

	Private School	State School	No Information
Scions (108)	74	14	20
Lawyers (52)	24	7	21
Others (110)	40	51	19
	138	72	60

Of the seventy-four scions who had attended private schools, sixty-nine had been at schools of the Headmasters' Conference: eighteen at Melbourne Grammar School, ten at Sydney Grammar School, six at St Peter's College, Adelaide, nine at Geelong Grammar School, six at Scotch College, Melbourne, and three at Wesley College, Melbourne. Five had attended English public schools (Eton, Malvern, Repton, Stowe). The lawyers were much more evenly divided: the only schools represented by more than one individual were Sydney Grammar School (three), St Peter's College (three) and Barker College, Sydney (two). The lawyers also had, as might be expected, the highest proportion of university graduates—thirty-four out of fifty-two, divided proportionately to birthplace (twelve at Melbourne, nine at Sydney, five at Adelaide). However, the scions were close behind with 54 out of 108—exactly one-half. An interesting reflection on the character of traditional upper class education is provided by the fact that ten were graduates of Cambridge and seven of Oxford; otherwise the geographical proportions were followed (Melbourne fifteen, Sydney seven, Adelaide four).

With regard to religion, there were only two individuals among the entire 270 who could be positively identified as Catholics. There were probably a few others among these for whom no information was available, but even on the most generous assumptions it is safe to conclude that the proportion of Catholics was no more than one or two per cent. In no other social group is the predominance of the WASPS so complete.

Our group of directors were great clubmen, and the list of clubs represented provides an index of the relation between clubmanship and social position which was discussed in general terms in Chapter 7. Information was available for just over 200 of the total group of 270, and for this number there were 338 separate club memberships. The largest number belonged to the Melbourne Club (54), in which all seven groups were represented in varying proportions, from one-third of the scions and one-quarter of the lawyers to one-seventh of the organisation men. The Union Club, Sydney, followed with forty, but was much more selective. One-quarter of the scions and of the lawyers were members, but the next in proportion were the organisation men with only one-tenth. The Australian Club, Melbourne, had thirty-eight memberships evenly spread between the groups, with the interesting exception of the lawyers, who were thinly represented (only one-tenth). The exception is particularly interesting because the club's premises, which are located near the Law Courts, are patronised by many members of the legal profession who have offices in the neighbourhood. The Australian Club, Sydney, had thirty-two memberships, with the two best represented groups being scions (one-sixth), lawyers (one-sixth) and technicians (one-fifth). The other clubs of some significance were Royal Sydney Golf (thirty-one), Athenaeum, Melbourne (thirty), Royal Melbourne Golf (twenty-seven), and Adelaide (fifteen). As might be expected, the most notable clubmen were the scions, with an average of two memberships each, including eleven in London clubs.

A parallel analysis of directors is made by Hylda A. Rolfe, who examined the fifty largest companies in 1962, chosen on the basis of net profit and shareholders' funds.[7] There were 348 directorships held by 302 individuals, of whom 12 per cent held 24 per cent of all places. In addition, the same 302 men held a further 402 places on the boards of an additional 275

[7] Hylda A. Rolfe, *The Controllers*, Melbourne, 1967. The quotations that follow are drawn from chs. 6-7 of Mrs Rolfe's study.

companies. This suggests a somewhat lower level of concentration of directorships than is given by the 1961 survey just described; the difference is largely accounted for by Mrs Rolfe's method of selection, which is confined to listed Australian public companies. In the 1961 survey, there was an average of five places per man; in Mrs Rolfe's the ration was 2·5. However, the concentration of multiple directorships was remarkably similar. In Mrs Rolfe's study, 14·5 per cent of the men held 42 per cent of 750 directorships; in the 1961 survey, 16 per cent of the men held 44·2 per cent of 1,328 directorships. She also showed that the incidence of multiple directorships was particularly high among those men who were directors of banks and life offices. More than half the bank directors held more than three places each and 59 per cent of life office directors were in the same position. After comparing the Australian pattern with the United Kingdom, the United States and India, she concludes that the Australian pattern resembles most closely the pattern found among smaller British and American companies, whose need for capital and directorial ability prompts them, like most Australian firms, to look outside for board members.

Mrs Rolfe notes the extent to which men holding multiple directorships tend to be members of family groups. 'Over 40 per cent of all the interlocking directors were on the boards of the largest financial institutions, and almost all of these directors were members of the so-called "ruling families".' Intermarriage, she observes with a touch of irony, 'whilst undoubtedly always for love, was also related to advancement in a few instances. Predictably, these were notable in the ambit of the Collins House directors.'[8] Its economic significance, she suggests, is due to the value of interlocking directorates as a useful way of protecting and extending family fortunes. Linkages between companies in which family interests are important reflect the inter-dependence of family fortunes. 'Family alliances can be taken to some degree as reflecting the direction of capital into the expanding industrial base of Australia. Ownership and control in these basic industries have gradually become a little less synonymous in the face of increased participation of institutional investors in the financing of industry; there remains, however, a solid core of family shareholdings to accompany the traditions of directorial participation which were established at the outset of the industrialisation of the Australian economy.'[9]

Managers and Executives

The business elite does not, of course, consist only of members of boards of directors. The notion that real control of modern industry is vested in professional managers has been familiar since Berle and Means wrote *The Modern Corporation and Private Property* forty years ago. The postwar expansion of industry in Australia has led to a great growth in the tasks

[8] ibid., p. 89
[9] ibid., p. 90

of management and a correspondingly greater concern with recruitment and training. The following pages are concerned with the results of two surveys of recruitment, careers and social background of managers and executives—one carried out by the author in 1957-58, the other by C. S. Beed in 1966.[10]

There is naturally an overlap between the functions of director and manager. As companies grow larger, more complex and more bureaucratic, boards of directors are increasingly recruited from the executive staffs of the firm itself.[11] A study by a public-relations firm concludes that 40 per cent of public company directors were executives of the company and the remaining sixty per cent were 'outside' directors.[12] The evidence of the studies quoted in this chapter suggests that 40 per cent is an overestimate. In the 1961 survey, the proportion of respondents who were executives of their companies was 24 per cent.[13]

The 1958 survey was carried out by sending 750 copies of a postal questionnaire to a total of 230 firms, public and private, in the fields of manufacturing, retail and wholesale trading, shipping and transport, banking and insurance and newspaper publishing. The selection included all managing directors and assistant managing directors; general managers and assistant general managers; and any executive directors not covered by the former categories. In the larger firms, categories such as technical director, sales director and secretary were also included. The aim was to provide a balanced group rather than to concentrate on the top 100 Australian companies, although all the latter were included. To them were added all the banks, all the major life offices, twenty-five large unlisted subsidiaries of overseas firms and a number of large or medium-sized manufacturing, trading and transport concerns. The 366 respondents were distributed among 195 separate firms, comprising 135 manufacturing concerns, six banks, eleven insurance companies, eight newspaper publishers and thirty-five trading and transport companies. The respondents were divided among general management (251), secretarial and/or accounting functions (54), production management (36) and sales management (25). Forty-nine firms out of the total of 195 were represented by more than one respondent. Nineteen firms were unlisted overseas subsidiaries. Thirty per cent of the group were also directors of their own and/or other companies.

The distribution of birthplaces among members of the group may be

[10] C. S. Beed, 'Career Structures of Australian Company Directors', M.Com. thesis, University of Melbourne, 1967

[11] British and American practice on this point is examined by P. S. Florence, *Ownership, Control and Success of Large Companies,* London, 1961.

[12] Beckingsale and Co., *The Australian Board of Directors,* Melbourne, 1964

[13] As the questionnaires were anonymous, it is not possible to state precisely how many of the 1958 survey were included in the 1961 survey of directors already described. Internal exidence suggests that the number was between sixty and eighty, so that the overlap between the two surveys is not of major significance.

compared with the results for the 1961 directors' survey given in Table 21·3 above.

Table 21·5 Australian Managers, 1958—Place of Birth

State or Country	Number	%
New South Wales	115	31
Victoria	149	41
Queensland	13	4
South Australia	22	5·5
Western Australia	7	2
Tasmania	7	2
United Kingdom	32	9
New Zealand	7	2
North America	9	2·5
Other	5	1
	366	100·0

As compared with Table 21·3, the predominance of Victoria is more striking, and the combined predominance of Victoria and NSW, which account for almost three-quarters of the whole group, more striking still.

Age structure of the group had an oddly kinked character. Sixty per cent of the group were between the ages of forty-one and fifty-five, but seventy (19 per cent) were between forty-one and forty-five, sixty-nine (also 19 per cent) between forty-six and fifty, and seventy-six (20·8 per cent) between fifty-one and fifty-five years. This distribution probably reflects the chequered economic history of the period since 1918, with the industrial expansion of the 1920's followed by the depressed years of the 1930's, and these followed in turn by the industrial expansion which started during the 1939-45 war and has continued ever since. The influence of postwar expansion is also shown by the large number who were appointed to executive positions (i.e. those within the ambit of the survey) below the age of forty. The number was 223, i.e. two-thirds of the total group, compared with 113 (31 per cent) appointed to this level between the ages of forty and fifty. As might be expected, the ages of the directors were much higher, as illustrated in the next table.

Table 21·6 Ages of Directors and Managers

Age Group	Directors %	Managers %
Under 41	3	13
41—45	1	19
46—50	8	19
51—55	11	21
56—60	15	12
61—65	20	7
Over 65	32	9
No information	10	—
	100	100

Even allowing for the two-year discrepancy between the two studies, the difference is remarkable. The concentration of 'old men' on boards of directors is a regular subject for comment by economic journalists.[14] A survey of 1000 top companies published by the *Australian* in 1964 found that one-quarter of their directors were over the age of seventy. The oldest director in the 1958 survey was eighty-four, and there were a number in their late seventies and early eighties. There have been a number of remarkable individual cases. In 1965, the press noted the retirement of Mr A. W. Palfreyman, chairman of Australia's largest food canning company, Henry Jones Ltd, in his nineties, having been head of the firm for forty years. He was replaced by the deputy chairman, Mr Peacock, who was in his mid-seventies.[15] In 1967, Mr James Burns, aged eighty-eight, retired as managing director of Burns Philp and Co. after forty-four years, but remained as chairman.[16] The heavy weighting of 'scions' among directors is a factor in this age distribution, but not the only one; in effect, about half of all categories of directors, apart from 'technicians' and 'organisation men', were over sixty. The reasons for this age weighting have been frequently discussed in the financial press, the most favoured theory being the general shortage of men with directorial ability.[17] By comparison, British studies show that 31 per cent of directors and 10 per cent of managers were over sixty; the average age of managers was fifty, of directors fifty-five.[18] In Australia, the median age of managers was forty-nine, but for directors it was sixty-two.

Managerial status was achieved by a variety of methods, which have been reduced to six for purposes of classification:

1   Scion
2   Outside status
3   Technician or expert
4   White-collar worker
5   Factory worker
6   Founder of business

These categories may be compared with the six devised by Clements in his study of managers and directors in England.[19] Clements distinguished the following groups:

1   Crown princes
2   Managerial trainees
3   Experts trained outside industry

---

[14] See, e.g., Michael Baume, 'The Grey Men of Business', *Quadrant*, April-May 1964.
[15] J. B. Hood in the *Canberra Times*, 23 January 1965
[16] *Australian*, 28 February 1967
[17] e.g. *Australian Financial Review*, 20 January 1964; Baume, loc. cit.; *Sydney Morning Herald*, 22 August 1964; *Australian*, 29 July 1964; Rolfe, op. cit., chs. 1, 8-9
[18] R. Lewis and R. Stewart, *The Boss*, London, 1961, p. 101
[19] R. V. Clements, *Managers: A Study of their Career in Industry*, London, 1958, chs. 3-8

4   Special entrants (e.g. sales trainees)
5   Risen from the bottom:
   (a) Later school leavers (usually clerks)
   (b) Early school leavers (usually factory workers)

These two classifications are obviously similar. The term 'scion' has been retained for the purpose of comparison with the directorial group, but in this context it is clearly the same as Clements' 'crown prince'. There were no managerial trainees in the Australian survey; these are a comparatively recent development in Australian industry and would not yet be apparent in a survey completed in 1958. 'Outside status' in the Australian survey refers to men who had already attained a degree of professional or executive responsibility outside industry, including lawyers, accountants, public servants and small businessmen who joined large corporations. Thus, fourteen respondents changed their jobs permanently by moving from a professional position to a managerial job in industry. Most of these were members of accounting firms who became company secretaries. Eight others became managers through a combination of professional training and family influence. Eight were previously in other businesses, six having been on the land and two in retail trading. Some changed their occupation after an interruption due to war service. The third category, 'technician or expert', comprises men who entered industry after completing specialised training, sometimes as company cadets (BHP was the first firm to introduce cadet schemes for technicians in the 1930's). It is similar to Clements' third category, although he also includes in it some examples of our second category. Clements' fourth category has no real parallel in the Australian survey; it includes premium apprentices (i.e. those whose parents paid for their apprenticeships) and sales trainees. His fifth and sixth categories, however, correspond to the fourth and fifth items in our 1958 classification.

In Table 21·7, the distribution of these categories among the managers in the 1958 survey is shown. The figures for directors are shown alongside.

Table 21·7 Career Patterns of Directors and Managers

Managers			*Directors*		
1 Scions	62	(17%)	1 Scions	108	(40%)
2 Outside status	43	(12%)	2 Lawyers	52	(19·5%)
3 Experts or technicians	70	(19%)	3 Technicians	29	(11%)
4 White-collar workers	157	(42%)	4 Accountants	28	(10%)
5 Factory workers	17	(5%)	5 Organisation Men	28	(10%)
6 Founders of business	17	(5%)	6 Public Servants	16	(6%)
			7 Generals	9	(3·5%)
	366	(100%)		270	(100%)

The striking differences between the two groups require little comment. If we group lawyers, public servants, generals and (say) half of the accountants in the directorial group under the heading of 'outside status', they amount to 44 per cent of all directors, compared with 12 per cent of managers. The 'organisation men' among the directors correspond to categories four and five among the managers, giving a proportion of 10 per cent as against 47 per cent. However, family connections are more important among managers, and also more complex, than would appear from Table 21·7. Of the sixty-two 'scions' who entered family firms, forty-nine (14 per cent) were the sons of directors of the same firm.[20] In the other thirteen cases, the son went into the father's business and developed it into a larger concern, or started another undertaking in a related field, or amalgamated a small concern with a larger one. The same occurred in a further eight cases where the individuals in question are not classified as scions because of other attributes which appear to be more significant.

Family connections do not, of course, stop there. There were a further twenty-seven instances where the man in question was the son of a company director and started his business career with this advantage. Most of these men entered the same firms as their fathers. Similarly, twenty-four men entered firms where their fathers were managers. The effect of family connections may be extended, therefore, to a total of 121 individuals, which gives a proportion of 32 per cent as compared with the 17 per cent who were straightforward 'crown princes'. A similar point may also be made about some directors in other categories, since family connections played a role in their appointment, e.g. lawyers (at least eight cases, notably that of Sir Colin York Syme).

As the figures in Table 21·7 refer to a wide variety of business undertakings, they cannot be compared directly with Clements' figures, which relate only to manufacturing industry. We can make this comparison by extracting the 200 cases which were drawn from manufacturing industry in the 1958 survey. The main difference from the total survey, as might be expected, lies in the role of the white-collar worker, who is correspondingly less important in manufacturing industry.

Table 21·8 Career Patterns of British and Australian Managers

1958 Survey			*Clements*		
		%			%
1	Scions	20·5	1	Crown Princes	4
2	Outside status	10·5	2	Managerial trainees	10
3	Technicians or experts	30·5	3	Experts	20
4	White-collar workers	25·0	4	Special entrants	12
5	Factory workers	6.5	5	From the bottom	
6	Founders of business	7·0		(a) Clerical workers	} 54
				(b) Factory workers	
		100·0			100·0

[20] By comparison, Copeman found that 18 per cent of his respondents were sons of directors of the same firm.

At the managerial level, therefore, it appears that British industry is rather more 'democratic' than Australian industry. Whereas 54 per cent of Clements' sample (646 in all) started at the bottom, the corresponding figure for the Australian survey was 31.5 per cent. The differences are much less at the director level. Almost 30 per cent of Clements' directors were crown princes, compared with 40 per cent in the Australian survey of directors, and if one adds to his figure those with family connections who were classified under other headings, the difference between the two proportions is further reduced.

These statistics encompass a wide variety of life histories which reflect the impact of depression, war and postwar boom on the development of business and industry. Some of the most interesting come from the self-made men who make up a significant proportion of the group. One of these learnt his engineering skills on the farm. His father was a farmer who was very clever with tools and blacksmithing and undertook most local machinery repair jobs. The son inherited these talents, reading books while sitting at the wheel of a tractor between farming operations. 'All that I have ever learnt about mass production engineering, all types of machine tools including automatics, turret engine lathes, millers, grinders etc. have been self-taught from textbooks and experience. I slowly and gradually built up a business in mass production engineering . . . wholly owned by the family.' Another self-made man left Russia as a youth in 1922 and entered a textile mill, rising to become merchandising director of the firm. Others found that the depression years of the 1930's were a stimulus to find new ways of making a living. It was during this period that skilled tradesmen, out of work or on short time, went into business on their own in order to make a living, especially in light engineering. The industrial demands of the war effort gave them opportunities to expand their businesses, to learn new techniques and skills, and to make contacts which were of great importance. With postwar industrial growth, many of them have become leaders of industry.

The effects of the depression were, however, more varied. In one case, a man with a brilliant academic record in engineering and a promising practice as a civil engineer was forced out of his profession to assist his father in the family packaging and printing business, of which he became managing director, and never returned to engineering. Another man, the son of a government official, was trained as a professional draftsman but appeared in the survey because he was investment manager of a large financial institution. He remarked laconically on his survey form that in explanation of this drastic shift of occupations, 'I can only offer the suggestion that the financial training afforded to the eldest son of a civil servant during the depression years is an admirable background.'

The combination of higher education with a father in a professional or managerial occupation carries a strong guarantee of success in industry. One instance is that of the son of an actuary, educated at Melbourne Grammar School and Cambridge, who became a stockbroker and attained the rank of colonel during the 1939-45 war. After the war, he left the Stock Exchange to enter industry on the engineering side and was deputy managing director of a large company at the time of the survey. A second example, the son of a professor, also attended Melbourne Grammar School, won a Rhodes scholarship, attended the Technische Hochschule at Charlottenburg, and at the time of the survey was assistant managing director of one of the largest metal firms in Australia. Another Melbourne Grammar schoolboy, the son of a chartered accountant, was a brilliant classical scholar and took a law degree. He entered the company of which his father was secretary and became assistant general manager. A fourth case was the scion of a family flour-milling concern, educated this time at Scotch College, Melbourne, where he was dux, who then took an engineering degree, entered BHP as a cadet and became one of its senior executives.

From these individual cases, we may turn to the general influence of schooling and education on the managerial career. Of our total group of 366, 202 (55 per cent) had their secondary education at private schools and 107 (29 per cent) attended private schools at both primary and secondary levels. Schools of the Headmasters' Conference accounted for 181 individuals, almost exactly one-half of the group. A small group of HMC schools predominated, although the rank order was not the same as for the directors. Of our 181, thirty-one had attended Melbourne Grammar School; thirty, Scotch College, Melbourne; eleven, Sydney Grammar School; eleven, Sydney CEGS ('Shore'); eleven, Wesley College, Melbourne; ten, St Peter's College, Adelaide; and five, Geelong Grammar School.[21] The list of schools reflects the predominance of Victorians (41 per cent); the predominant role of private schools within the Victorian educational system; and the predominance of a small number of schools within that private sector. Out of 149 men born in Victoria, 100 attended private schools; of these, eighty-five attended a total of eight schools belonging to the Headmasters' Conference; of these, seventy-seven went to four leading HMC schools; and of these, sixty-one attended two schools in almost equal numbers. Expressed in percentage terms, this means that 41 per cent of the Victorians attended two schools, Melbourne Grammar School and Scotch College, and that these two schools also accounted for 17 per cent of the entire group. By comparison, 19 per cent of the 210 directors for whom we have information also attended two schools (Melbourne Grammar and Sydney Grammar), and 35 per cent attended five leading schools (Melbourne Grammar, twenty-four; Sydney Grammar, sixteen; St Peter's College, thirteen; Geelong Grammar, eleven; Scotch College, nine).

These figures may again be compared with the British studies. Copeman found that slightly over half his sample had attended private schools, but the influence of a small group of elite schools was marked, so that Eton,

---

[21] Fourteen of the managers had also attended private schools in the United Kingdom, including Aberdeen Grammar School; Clifton; Eton; Paston Grammar School; St Edward's School; Sherborne; and George Heriot's School, Edinburgh.

Harrow and Winchester contributed 8 per cent of his sample of 1,200.[22] A study by the Acton Society Trust of 400 top managers found that grammar school boys had twice the average chance of becoming managers, and 'public' school boys about ten times the average.[23] In a random sample of 100 businessmen taken from *Who's Who*, Lewis and Stewart found that nineteeen had been to Eton.[24]

At the tertiary level of education, slightly more than one-third of the managers had degrees or diplomas; 102 were graduates and nineteen were diplomates. Engineering was the most popular degree (forty-one), followed by science (thirty), economics (twenty-nine) and law (ten). There were thirteen diplomas in engineering and six in chemistry. No fewer than 127 had gained accountancy qualifications. These figures are similar to Copeman's findings; in his sample, 36 per cent were graduates and 27 per cent had some other form of tertiary training. The figures for the United States, as might be expected, are higher than for either Britain or Australia. Warner and Abegglen's study, covering more than 8,000 executives of large corporations, found that 76 per cent had 'attended' universities or colleges, and that 57 per cent had graduated.[25] This is a reflection of the greater scale and complexity of industry in the USA. In Australia, the influence of the large firm is shown by the fact that one-half of the men qualified in science or engineering were employed by a dozen large concerns, including BHP and its subsidiaries, CSR, DHA, ICIANZ and APM. Size of firm, however, was not of great significance in relation to tertiary education as a whole. This may be shown by comparing the group as a whole with the managers of large, non-banking, Australian companies (to eliminate factors due to overseas control), who numbered 150 in all. In the total group, 35 per cent had a tertiary education; in the Australian large companies, 43 per cent.

Size of firm also had relatively little influence on two other findings. Whereas 20·5 per cent of the total group were 'scions' in terms of career pattern, the proportion among the Australian companies was 24 per cent; and whereas the proportion attending schools of the HMC type was 49 per cent among the total group, it was 57 per cent among the managers of Australian companies.

It will be convenient at this point to look at the results of Beed's study of company directors, carried out in 1966. Beed made a postal survey of 1,472 directors, covering a wide range of firms, and received 445 replies. Although his data do not permit an exact computation, the proportion of executive directors appears to lie between one-half and two-thirds of his sample. By comparison, 24 per cent of the 1961 survey of directors were executive directors and 30 per cent of the 1958 survey of managers were

[22] op. cit., pp. 101-2
[23] Acton Society Trust, *Management Succession*, London, 1956
[24] op. cit., p. 99
[25] W. L. Warner and J. G. Abegglen, *Occupational Mobility in American Business and Industry*, Minneapolis, 1955

also directors. Even compared with the estimate that 40 per cent of public company directors are executives, quoted above, Beed's survey is clearly biased towards the executive director,[26] and is therefore drawing on a somewhat different universe than either of the other two studies. Nevertheless, most of his conclusions about social background of directors are similar. Beed found that 53 per cent of his sample had obtained most of their secondary schooling at private schools, compared with 55 per cent in the 1958 survey of managers and 65 per cent in the 1961 survey of directors. He observed a considerable age differential, in that only 50 per cent of men under forty-five had been educated at private secondary schools, but the proportion rose steadily with age to 63 per cent among those aged sixty-five and over. This reflects both the expansion of state education and the expansion of opportunities in industry.

Beed also found that 36 per cent of his group had been to private primary as well as secondary schools, compared with 29 per cent of the 1958 survey. Out of 204 private school boys, 168 had attended schools belonging to the Headmasters' Conference, with the same pattern of predominance of five major schools—Melbourne Grammar, twenty; Scotch College, nineteen; Sydney Grammar, sixteen; St Peter's College, nine; Wesley College, eight. These five schools accounted for 16 per cent of the whole group and for nearly 50 per cent of all HMC school boys. Thirty-five per cent were university graduates, which compares with 45 per cent of the 1961 directors' survey and 27 per cent of the 1958 managers' survey. As with the managers, engineering was the most popular degree, followed by science, law and Arts. By contrast, among the 1961 directors' group the most popular field was law, followed by Arts, engineering, science and economics.

In view of the great influence of family connections, it is not surprising to find that a large proportion of the managers were the sons of businessmen. Compared with the 20·5 per cent of managers in the 1958 survey who were 'scions', 35 per cent were the sons of directors, company secretaries or managers. In Table 21·9, fathers' occupations are analysed and compared with the proportions of male breadwinners given by the Commonwealth census of 1947. This was the first census since Federation to provide a breakdown of occupations, and therefore the closest to the period when the bulk of our sample would have started work. (The questionnaire specified that each one should state his father's occupation at the time the respondent entered regular employment.) The only significant change in the occupational structure which would be unrepresented in the census figures is the decline in rural employment since the end of the first world war.

In the 'administrative and business' category, eighty-one (out of 129) were the sons of company directors. Most of those in the 'clerical' category

[26] Experience suggests that this type of person is more likely to be responsive to a survey questionnaire.

were government officials. Eight of those classed as 'professional' were clergymen. In Table 21·10, we reproduce Beed's findings regarding father's occupation, which are not strictly comparable with Table 21·9 because he has used different occupational categories.

Table 21·9 Occupations of Fathers of Managers, 1958

Father's Occupational Group		1947 Census (Male Breadwinners) %	1958 Survey of Managers %
1	Rural	17·9	7
2	Professional and semi-professional	3·5	17
3	Administrative and business	5·6	35
4	Commercial	7·4	19
5	Clerical	9·0	8
6	Domestic and protective	6·4	1
7	Craftsmen	20·0	9
8	Operatives and labourers	27·2	2
9	Other	3·0	2
		100·0	100·0

Although Beed's categories are different, the profile is similar. In Table 21·9, categories 6, 7 and 8 amount to 12 per cent; the comparable figure of 14 per cent is obtained by adding Beed's categories 6 to 9. Beed's first category is comparable to category 3 in Table 21·9, i.e. 39 per cent as against 35 per cent. His general conclusions on the social background of his sample are that the younger men are better educated than the older men, that education and father's occupation are closely correlated among all age groups, and that there is no evidence for an increase in upward social mobility through the business world.[27] Of those whose fathers belonged to Beed's first category, 36 per cent had a university degree at the time of starting work, compared with an average figure of 28 per cent.

Table 21·10 Occupations of Fathers of Directors, 1966

Father's Occupational Group		%
1	Administrative, executive or professional position in business	39
2	Proprietors	14
3	'Semi-administrative' (business)	10
4	Administrative and semi-administrative (non-business)	8
5	Clerical and sales	7
6	Craftsmen	6
7	Operatives	3
8	Service workers	4
9	Labourers	1
10	Farmers	8
		100

[27] Beed, op. cit., pp. 133-35

The comparisons already made with other countries suggest that although opportunities to rise in the business world are somewhat higher in Australia, the influence of inherited economic and social position is the most important single factor in all cases, not excluding Australia. The situation in Australia is undoubtedly very different from that in Europe. A French survey carried out in 1960, for instance, found that 70 per cent of executives were the sons of business or professional men, and only 4 per cent of manual workers or farmers. A Dutch study found that family connections were important in the careers of more than two-thirds of directors and managers in Holland.[28] By comparison with Great Britain and North America, however, the Australian pattern does not diverge markedly. In Table 21·11, the findings of the 1958 survey are compared with two other studies carried out in the 1950's—Copeman's for Britain, and Warner and Abegglen's for the United States.

Table 21·11 Occupations of Fathers of Businessmen in Three Countries

Father's Occupational Group	*Australia*	*Great Britain*	*USA*
	%	%	%
1 Rural	7	2	9
2 Professional	17	15	14
3 Administrative (non-business)	2	7	—
4 Administrative (business)	33	34	41
5 Commercial	19	16	11
6 Clerical	8	} 8	8
7 Manual worker	11		15
8 Other	3	18	2
	100	100	100

There are, of course, certain difficulties in equating the categories used in the three surveys. In Copeman's rather large 'other' category, one-half are described as 'retired', which obviously includes former businessmen, senior civil servants and officers of the armed services. To reclassify these would involve increases in categories 3 and 4; in particular, the numbers in category 4 are probably closer to the American figure than shown by Copeman's tabulation. Again, Warner and Abegglen make no provision for senior government officials, and it is reasonable to assume that some of their 'professionals' and 'white-collar workers' could fit into category 3. With these cautions borne in mind, it appears that Australia does not differ greatly from the other English-speaking capitalist democracies. (In Canada, Porter has estimated that over 30 per cent of the economic elite come from business families.)[29]

Finally, we may note the very small representation of minority groups among both managers and directors. In the 1961 survey of directors, only

[28] N. Delefortrie-Soubeyroux, *Les Dirigeants de l'Industrie Francaise*, Paris, 1961; R. A. Hendriks, 'Vertical Social Mobility of the Chief Executive Groups in the Netherlands', *Sociologia Neerlandica*, vol. 2, no. 1, 1964
[29] John Porter, *The Vertical Mosaic*, Toronto, 1965, pp. 291-93

two could be positively identified as Catholics. Among the managers, the proportion was slightly higher—fifteen out of 366, i.e. 4 per cent. Nearly all of these had entered business firms as clerks, on the conventional Catholic pattern. Another ten were Jews, most of them immigrants following another classic pattern described at length by Warner and Abegglen. Only two of the respondents were women, both of them executives in family concerns, and one was quite explicit that her position as secretary of a manufacturing firm was an accident of kinship.[30]

The Stock Exchange

Access to capital is obviously a key matter in business, and the problems of raising money on the Australian capital market are a major factor in the highly concentrated structure of ownership and control. As Mrs Rolfe points out, bankers and stockbrokers are relatively common on boards of directors.[31] It will be recalled that the Baillieu fortune began with the activities of W. L. Baillieu as a stockbroker and that the early history of the Robinson family fortune also hinged on speculation in mining shares. Appropriately, a leading part in the postwar mining boom has been played by the broking firm of Ian Potter and Co. The career of Sir Ian Potter, its founder, is one of the success stories of Australian business. No account of the character of the business elite would be complete without some attention to the Stock Exchange.

In 1963, the largest of the stock exchanges were in Melbourne (54 firms, 166 members) and Sydney (61 firms, 138 members); smaller exchanges operated in Adelaide and Brisbane. A recent account of their activities notes the exclusive character of membership:

The stock exchanges have sometimes been criticised on the ground that they tend to operate as exclusive clubs, candidates for membership being blackballed for religious or other reasons which are unrelated to their functions. . . . At the same time, candidates for membership are not required to pass professional examinations or otherwise to prove their competence in the same way as prospective members of most other professional bodies. . . . Members of a stock exchange are in a position to exert considerable influence not only on the securities market but on the economy in general, and the view has been expressed that power such as this should not be exercised by a self-regulating body.[32]

The social exclusiveness of the stock exchanges may be gauged from a study of members of the Melbourne exchange in 1961. Details were available for eighty members, representing two-thirds of the membership

[30] For a discussion of the restricted opportunities open to women in business, see Norman MacKenzie, *Women in Australia*, Melbourne, 1962.
[31] op. cit., pp. 2, 80, 84
[32] Russell Mathews, 'The Stock Exchange', in R. R. Hirst and R. H. Wallace (eds.), *Studies in the Australian Capital Market*, Melbourne, 1964, p. 4

at that time.[33] They represented a wide spectrum of age groups: twenty-one were under thirty-five, twenty-eight between thirty-five and forty-nine years, twelve in their fifties and nineteen aged sixty or over. Three-quarters were born in Victoria. Twenty-six were university graduates, nineteen of them in economics or commerce; twenty-three (some of them graduates) were qualified in accountancy. Details about schooling were available for seventy-five individuals, of whom fifty-six (i.e. seventy-five per cent) had attended HMC schools. As might be expected, Melbourne Grammar School headed the list with eighteen, followed by Geelong Grammar (ten), Scotch College (nine), and Wesley College (six). The largest number were sons of brokers (sixteen), followed by sons of directors or managers (ten) and professional men (ten). The administrative (non-business) group also contributed ten. Only seven out of a total of fifty-three for whom information was available had fathers in other occupations.

The combination of father's occupation with schooling makes the degree of social selectivity clearer still. For the fifty-three about whom we have complete information, all but two of the brokers' sons had attended one of the four leading HMC schools; ten had been to Melbourne Grammar School alone. Of the forty-three men who had attended these four schools, all but five were the sons of brokers or other businessmen. With the passage of time, social selectivity becomes even more marked as the role of inheritance grows. Eight of the sixteen whose fathers were brokers were under thirty-five, and of these all attended either Melbourne Grammar or Geelong Grammar. Scotch College, whose strongest links are with the professions, was unrepresented in this age group.[34]

It is noteworthy that, despite the tradition of social exclusiveness, the Melbourne exchange has for a number of years refrained from discriminating against Roman Catholics. Three of the eighty members surveyed had attended Xavier College, the leading Catholic school in Victoria and a foundation member of the Headmasters' Conference; six had attended other Catholic schools. By contrast, the Sydney Stock Exchange did not admit Catholics until after the 1939-45 war, and then only under strong political pressure, but Jews have been admitted to membership for a number of years. In Melbourne, however, the nomination of a Jewish broker for membership was turned down by the committee of the exchange a few years ago, amid a blaze of publicity.[35] The public reaction was so great that the exchange finally admitted a Jewish member, but not the

[33] I am indebted for the basic information to Dr A. R. Hall of the Australian National University, who carried out a survey of the membership of the exchange while collecting material for an official history, *The Stock Exchange of Melbourne and the Victorian Economy, 1852-1900*, Canberra, 1968.

[34] By comparison, a British study of City of London financiers involved in the Bank Rate inquiry of 1958 found that one-third were old Etonians; T. Lupton and C. S. Wilson, 'The Social Background and Connections of Top Decision Makers', *Manchester School*, vol. 27, no. 1, 1959.

[35] 'A Gentile Rialto', *Nation*, 9 April 1960

original applicant. The strongly traditional character of the Melbourne exchange is reflected in the history of its leading firm, J. B. Were and Son, the oldest broking firm in the country.[36] Jonathan Were, its founder, came to Melbourne in 1839 and became founder and first chairman of the Melbourne Stock Exchange. After his death in 1885, his son Francis became head of the firm and the pattern continued down to Staniforth Ricketson (d. 1968), great-grandson of J. B. Were, who was elected chairman of the stock exchange in 1942 and held the position for many years. Two of his sons became members of the firm in due course. J. B. Were is the centre of a group of eight investment companies, the Capel Court group, with extensive financial ramifications. Six directors of this group figured in the 1961 survey of directors. The late Staniforth Ricketson was, in his lifetime, a pillar of financial and political conservatism; it was said that he regarded the adventurous activities of his major competitor, Sir Ian Potter, with considerable disfavour. The firm had close links with the former Prime Minister, Sir Robert Menzies, who was a director of the Capel Court group from 1929 to 1938; his brother, F. G. Menzies, became a director in 1955 after his retirement from the post of Crown Solicitor for Victoria.

On the Sydney exchange, by contrast, the 1950's and 1960's saw the hereditary principle overlaid by the recruitment of bright young men from various sources, including the financial press. The firm of Ord Minnett–T. J. Thompson received particular publicity for its 'kindergarten' in the 1960's, but at least four other leading firms of brokers followed this example, recruiting among others the financial editors of the *Age* (Melbourne), the *Sun-Herald* and the *Daily Mirror* (Sydney). Another departure from the conservative traditions of stockbroking was the appointment by the firm of J. and J. North of women as investment counsellors (specialising in advice to elderly widows).

The Business Way of Life

As Porter has observed, the economic elite appears as a complex network of small groups interlocked by a high degree of cross-membership; kinship, the private school, the club, the philanthropic institution and the activities featured on the 'social pages' of newspapers all contribute to the essential fabric provided by the interlocking directorates of companies.[37] The social world of the businessman has been explored by a number of writers in the United States, Canada and Britain. William H. Whyte gives a half-sympathetic, half-acid portrayal of the new suburbia inhabited by American corporation executives and their families. Three Canadian sociologists have anatomised the life of an upper-middle class suburb in Toronto. In Britain, Erickson, Shore and Samuel have observed the social role of the business-

[36] An official history of the firm on its centenary was published under the title *The House of Were*, Melbourne, 1954.
[37] op. cit., pp. 304-5

man from various viewpoints.[38] Novelists, particularly Americans, have provided a number of fictional portraits (e.g. J. P. Marquand in novels like *Wickford Point* and *Sincerely Willis Wayde*), and an Australian novel of interest on this theme is John McGhee's *Walls of Time*.

An opportunity to collect some information on this theme was provided by a survey carried out in Sydney in 1960.[39] Of the 100 men interviewed, forty-three worked for manufacturing concerns, twenty-five in retailing or trading companies, ten in banking, insurance or finance and the rest in a variety of undertakings. Sixty-six were directors or general managers, thirteen were in sales management, nine in secretarial or accounting positions, eight in production management and the rest were unspecified. They were evenly distributed by age. Only sixty-two had been born in NSW. Thirty-three were proprietors or managing directors of their firms; fourteen were employed by overseas concerns. The general pattern of schooling, tertiary education, business career, father's occupation and so forth was similar to the data already presented, though with some differences as almost one-half were employed by medium-sized private companies. What we shall be concerned with here are matters of a more personal kind which the survey was designed to elicit.

What kind of families do businessmen have? Marriage is customarily the first step. Forty of our Sydney businessmen were the sons of company directors or managers, eighteen of small proprietors and eleven were the sons of professional men, but twenty-two had married the daughters of professional men, almost exactly the same number as those who married the daughters of directors or managers. Two were unmarried, one was twice married. Only two wives were the daughters of manual workers, both of them skilled tradesmen. The family background of respondents was fairly average; twenty-nine came from families of five or more children, sixty-four from families of two to four children and seven were only sons. Place in the family was also evenly distributed; twenty-six were eldest and twenty-two youngest sons. The two-child family was the predominant pattern in their own households; forty-one had two children, twenty had one child, thirty-one had more than two and eight had none.

The educational intentions of parents for their children reflect a period of social mobility with strong emphasis on education. Only eight of the group had university degrees, but their plans for their children were rather different. Seventeen sons were already attending university and another thirty-two were intended for university by their parents, making a total of

---

[38] W. H. Whyte, *The Organisation Man*, New York, 1956, pt. 7; J. R. Seeley, R. A. Sim and E. W. Loosley, *Crestwood Heights*, Toronto, 1956; Peter Shore in Norman MacKenzie (ed.), *Conviction*, London, 1958; Ralph Samuel in Norman Birnbaum (ed.), *Out of Apathy*, London, 1960; Charlotte Erickson, *British Industrialists*, London, 1959

[39] The survey was carried out in co-operation with the Beacon Research Company, whose staff conducted 100 interviews with a sample of businessmen living in residential suburbs of Sydney.

forty-nine out of 108 boys. More interesting, perhaps, were their plans for their daughters, of whom twenty-one out of 112 were at university or were intended to go. Schooling shows a similar pattern of social mobility: thirty-three fathers had attended HMC schools, but sixty-five sons were doing so, mostly in Sydney. However, five men who had attended Scotch College, Melbourne, were also sending their sons to the *alma mater*. A few of the respondents admitted that the quality of education at most private schools was inferior to the standard of state education. One of them, who had sent his daughters to state school and his son to a private school, explained that he felt the boy was intellectually below average and therefore needed the 'polish' conferred by a private school. Educational and occupational aspirations for children were obviously related. The majority of those who were willing to commit themselves about the future of their sons indicated that they wanted them to enter the professions rather than business. In the meantime, fifteen boys from twelve households were either in the father's firm or intended to enter it. Their aspirations for daughters were, however, exceedingly modest and conventional: secretarial work, teaching and nursing were the only careers specifically mentioned.

In a community where personal housing absorbs a strikingly high proportion of investment, the quality of a family's house and garden becomes a matter of major concern. To this can be attributed the remarkably high level of mobility found among the group; seven respondents had moved house within Sydney on six or more occasions, two of them nine times. Improving one's dwelling, or moving to a more select district, is of course not the sole reason for a businessman having to change his private address, but thirty-four out of the sixty-eight respondents who had moved three or more times had done so only within Sydney. Sixty respondents owned their own houses and thirty were paying them off. It is not surprising that gardening was the main hobby mentioned by respondents, although the list is so wide that it is impossible to resist quoting from it. Among the twenty-seven separate hobbies listed, special mention may be made of farming (five), flying (two), engineering (two), collecting antiques, astronomy, geology, prospecting, and, most remarkable of all, 'Christianity'.

As compared with Whyte's organisation men, this group was essentially one of 'non-joiners'. Eighteen of them belonged to clubs like the Australian, NSW, University and Imperial Service Clubs; ten were Rotarians; thirty belonged to some kind of civic, philanthropic, cultural or political association. The largest single group belonging to one association were Masons, with twenty-three current members (one had resigned). What difference Masonry made to their lives would, in the nature of the case, be difficult to discover; objectively, the only apparent difference between the Masons and the rest was that one-half of them were engaged in public activities of some kind. Apart from membership of a masonic order, the most important single influence on public activities related to children's welfare or education, such as the respondent who was active on behalf of the deaf because he had a deaf child. There is little evident drive towards community leadership here, and Professor Parker's comment on the political apathy of business-men seems apposite: 'Since what they mainly want from government is to be left unmolested and untaxed, the real leaders of business, finance and the professions have been content to pull perfunctory financial strings from behind the scenes, leaving politics to "lesser men" who are public spirited enough to undertake the thankless chores of party hackwork.'[40]

Lack of drive was also manifested in answers to questions about the careers of respondents, their estimation of the qualities needed to make a successful manager and their future plans. A number of the respondents were candid about the fact that family connections were a major influence on their careers and were even inclined to be apologetic about it. One said he had no alternative but to go into business. The most frequently men-tioned character trait required for an executive was that he should be 'responsible' (twenty-seven mentions); ability, experience and hard work ran far behind (eight, seven and six respectively). One respondent observed that 'the old hard bosses have gone', but whether with regret or satisfaction is not clear. Few of them had any clear response to a question about the way future executives should be trained, although one believed firmly in the Protestant ethic: 'A hard apprenticeship, the harder the better. Instil into the young people an appreciation of their opportunities.' Suitably, he was a Lutheran, aged forty-two and the proprietor of his firm. When asked about their future plans, almost none gave a strong impression that they wished to rise further in the business hierarchy, as if they had not really committed themselves to being managers. Some spoke of retirement, but in a tepid fashion; some of travel, perhaps as a symbolic way of giving up their present existence, or as something which provides the illusion of meaningful activity at a crucial time.

These attitudes are crystallised in some representative statements:

Having got there, I'm afraid there isn't such a great deal in it after all. (Aged 60, making £8,000, proprietor)
I'd like to be able to make a worthwhile contribution to the underprivileged and needy while I have the opportunity. I will retire soon so that I can give my full time to this. (Aged 54, Congregationalist, earning £8,000)
Something must be done in industry to overcome the disruption that is often caused by an over-ambitious member of a team. (Aged 54, proprietor of own company)
Moderation in all things, avoiding extremes in domestic, social and business life. (Anglican, aged 70, five children, earning £5,000, proprietor)
Happiness in the home is number one! (Aged 30)
If I had my life over again I don't think I would go into the family business but would very much like to become a doctor.
Lead a good healthy life, honouring Almighty God, and seeking his guidance. (Baptist, aged 68)
I was a poor scholar, but the bright boys have become nothing. Maybe bright boys burn themselves up early—others conserve energy. (Aged 55, Congregationalist, earning £10,000, proprietor)

[40] R. S. Parker in S. R. Davis (ed.), *The Government of the Australian States,* Melbourne, 1960, p. 89

Executives are not trained to cope with human personalities. You virtually have to leave your technical training behind you when you become an executive. (Catholic, aged 34, earning £5,000)

A sample of this kind may or may not be typical of the business elite. But its generally low-powered character, the pervasive feeling that given the chance many would have preferred to do something different and perhaps more 'creative', squares with the frequent complaints of economists and financial journalists that the business world is a place for cosy, remunerative relationships rather than a dynamic force in Australian society. Businessmen themselves complain about the lack of capable directors with an interest in economic growth. The managing director of a large and successful engineering firm, interviewed by the author in 1963, observed that it was very hard to get the right type of people. 'The sort of man who has been a production engineer doesn't want to become a director when he retires. There are professional directors who are younger but they are often not much use. Too many directors are interested in the corporate requirements of an organisation without being interested in development.' An economist asks a similar question: 'Is the labyrinth of interlocking directors . . . the most efficient way of organising the strategic areas of the Australian economy? . . . the system . . . of interlocking directorships keeps as its paramount objective the preservation and extension of capital values.'[41] Michael Baume is touching on a similar point when he describes business as 'the most poorly serviced vocation in Australia . . . [made up from] the left-overs of the professions. . . . Australia's prosperity at the present seems to depend on good luck rather than on any inspired entrepreneurial activity.'[42] Perhaps, as in the case of politicians, a country so comfortably assured of its own egalitarian virtues will get the businessmen that it deserves.

[41] E. L. Wheelwright, introduction to Rolfe, *The Controllers*, p. xvi
[42] Baume, loc. cit.

Part Five
Nationalism, Imperialism and Militarism

22: Australia and the Outside World

Class, status and power are all influenced by the role of force in social relationships. Power, in particular, is readily defined in terms of the ability to dispose of force, and Weber distinguished the political power of the state as depending on a monopoly of the legitimate use of force. The social sciences have, until recently, paid little attention to the role of force and violence in society, perhaps because the professional ideology of the social scientist is dominated by middle class liberal values. The cataclysmic events of the twentieth century have undermined the optimistic estimate of human nature on which the social sciences were largely founded and no account of social differentiation can overlook the role of force as a determinant of the social order, or of militarism as an aspect of social relations.[1]

This subject can be divided under four main heads:

1 The part played by violence, or the threat of violence, in the community as a whole; the development of values and attitudes in response to it; and the extent to which coercion forms part of the structure of legitimate authority.

2 The accepted pattern of civil-military relations, including the degree of 'politicisation' of the army and the extent to which military chiefs will accept, without resistance, the directions of a civilian political head.

3 The part played by military rank in the prestige hierarchy. This includes the extent of deference to military rank by civilians, the attitude to commissioned rank within the armed forces themselves, and the degree of public recognition given to the ex-soldier. It is *prima facie* likely that a country in which civilians defer to an officer in uniform will be militaristic in character, but the situation is much more complex and subtle than this simple example would suggest.

4 The social origins of the officer corps, which constitute part of the general structure of class and status.

Militarism exists in Australia, as in the other Anglo-American societies, because of the fear of external attack rather than internal violence and its influence is to be understood in terms of the quality of these fears.

---

[1] A shorter version of the material in these chapters is to be found in J. A. A. van Doorn (ed.), *Armed Forces and Society*, The Hague, 1968.

Historically, Australia's attitudes may be understood as the product of a local nationalism which grew up in the shade of British imperialism, and both nationalism and imperialism have contributed strongly to the development of social consciousness.

Australian attitudes towards the outside world, especially as they affect defence policy, have been dominated by at least three outstanding considerations. The first of these arises from the obvious physical fact that the Australian continent, with its long and exposed coastline, cannot be defended by its own population. Its foreign and defence policies require it to have, in the phrase much favoured by Sir Robert Menzies, 'great and powerful friends'. Until the signature of the ANZUS pact in 1951, Australian defence policy was a reflex of British imperial strategy; since then, it has become little more than an appendage of United States strategy in the Pacific area. Secondly, the feeling that Australia, as a British outpost, owed a moral obligation to rally to the defence of the mother country has been a powerful psychological influence, matched by the feeling that Britain also had a moral responsibility concerning the defence of Australia. This consciousness of British identity has frequently been at odds with the third factor, i.e. the problem of our relationship to Asia, which for two generations has been the source of real or imagined threats to Australia's security. This relationship is responsible for a complex interplay of attitudes into which defence, foreign policy, coloured immigration and the imperial connection, among others, have entered.

Politicians of all parties have given utterance to sentiments of patriotic fervour towards Britain in times of international danger. During the federal election campaign of July 1914, which coincided with the crisis following the assassination of the Archduke Franz Ferdinand, the Prime Minister, Joseph Cook, declared: 'If there is to be a war, you and I shall be in it. We must be in it. If the old country is at war, so are we.' One of his leading supporters, Sir John Forrest, went further: 'If Britain goes to her Armageddon, we will go with her. Our fate and hers, for good and ill, are as woven threads.' Not to be outdone, Andrew Fisher, the Labor leader, who had said in 1911 that he would not hesitate to haul down the Union Jack if Australia's interests required it, now declared in a famous phrase: 'Should the worst happen, after everything has been done that honour will permit, Australians will stand beside the mother country to help and defend her to our last man and our last shilling.'[2] These sentiments were not confined to politicians, who were carried along by a wave of popular feeling, itself reflecting the intensity of pro-war emotion in Britain. A young man named J. D. Burns, later killed in France, wrote an idealistic poem which recalls Brooke's 'The Soldier':

[2] C. E. W. Bean, *The Story of Anzac*, Official History of Australia in the War of 1914-18, vol. 1, Sydney, 1923, pp. 16-17

The bugles of England were calling o'er the sea,
As they had called a thousand years, were calling now to me;
They woke me from dreaming in the dawning of the day,
England, oh England, how could I stay?

The Country Party, which appeared on the political scene during the 1914-18 war, has been characterised by a particularly exuberant brand of sentimental patriotism focused on 'old England', the monarchy and the empire. During the Chanak crisis of 1922, when acrimonious exchanges took place between the British and Australian governments because of the failure of the former to inform the latter,[3] the Country Party leader, Dr Earle Page, roundly declared in parliament that 'if Great Britain thinks it necessary to go to war we believe that Australia, as part of the great British Empire, should always be ready to come to her assistance.'[4] In 1914, a declaration of war by the British government automatically committed Australia, and again in 1939. In his broadcast speech on 4 September 1939, the Prime Minister, R. G. Menzies, told his audience: 'It is my melancholy duty to inform you officially that, in consequence of a persistence by Germany in the invasion of Poland, Great Britain has declared war upon her and that, as a result, Australia is also at war. . . . There can be no doubt that where Great Britain stands there stand the people of the entire British world.'[5] Constitutionally speaking, the prerogative of declaring war still resides in the British Crown. Although the executive power of the Commonwealth of Australia is vested in the Governor-General, neither the letters patent nor the instructions issued to him by the monarch confer authority to declare war, and no legislation exists for this purpose.[6] On the other hand, the Labor government which took office in October 1941 was concerned, throughout its term, to stress Australia's independent role in world affairs and upon the outbreak of war against Japan in December 1941 it took steps to enable the Governor-General, Lord Gowrie, to make a separate declaration. Arrangements were made for the issue of a special authority by King George VI under the great seal of the realm, empowering the Governor-General on the advice of his ministers to proclaim a state of war between Australia and Japan.[7]

The determination of the Labor Party to assert that Australia's strategic interests were not necessarily the same as those of Britain was underlined a few days after this incident when the Prime Minister, John Curtin, published a statement which produced an even greater effect than Curtin (or his speechwriter) intended. 'We refuse', the article stated flatly, 'to accept the dictum that the Pacific struggle must be treated as a subordinate segment

---

[3] W. M. Hughes, *The Splendid Adventure*, London, 1929
[4] *Commonwealth Parliamentary Debates*, vol. 100, p. 2355
[5] Paul Hasluck, *The Government and the People 1939-41*, Official History of the 1939-45 War, series 4, vol. 1, Canberra, 1953, p. 152
[6] W. A. Wynes, *Legislative, Executive and Judicial Powers in Australia*, Sydney, 3rd ed., 1962, p. 115
[7] *Commonwealth Parliamentary Debates*, vol. 169, pp. 1078-81

of the general conflict.' This was clearly aimed at Britain and its policy of 'beat Hitler first', and Winston Churchill responded angrily; according to his own account, he considered making a direct broadcast to the Australian public.[8] The article, however, went further. It declared that the Pacific struggle was one that concerned the United States and Australia, rather than Britain. 'Without any inhibitions of any kind, I make it quite clear that Australia looks to America, free of any pangs as to our traditional links or kinship with the United Kingdom. . . . Australia can go and Britain can still hold on. We are, therefore, determined that Australia shall not go, and shall exert all our energies towards the shaping of a plan, with the United States as its keystone, which will give to our country some confidence of being able to hold out.'[9]

The movement of Australia into the American strategic orbit did not, in fact, take effect until a decade later, and it happened more gradually and with greater 'pangs' than Curtin's wartime rhetoric suggested. Although his words now appear prophetic, they were probably influenced more at the time by echoes of the past than by thought of the future. The consequences of being a mere cog in the British defence machine had been starkly brought home during the 1914-18 war, when 60,000 Australians were killed, most of them in the futile offensives of the Western front. In 1916, the British government had called for increased recruitment to meet an alleged manpower shortage in France, and the Federal Labor government led by W. M. Hughes had attempted to introduce conscription for this reason. The result was a great split within the Labor movement, and within the community at large, whose effects were felt for many years. Curtin himself had been a leading propagandist on the anti-conscription side. As accounts of politico-military relationships in Britain at the time have since revealed, the military chiefs had misled the British government about the manpower situation. The bitterness and mistrust left by these events pervaded the outlook of the Labor movement until after the second world war.[10]

Australia and Japan

Disagreements betweeen Britain and Australia over strategy rested on a deeper conflict of views arising from Australian fears about aggression in the Pacific.[11] As one observer wrote in 1940, 'Australians have always felt themselves threatened by a menace of some sort. In the early days it was the French, and later on it was, at various times, the Russians, the French

[8] Winston S. Churchill, *The History of the Second World War*, vol. 4, London, 1948, p. 8. A further dispute over the return of Australian troops from the Middle East is described in ibid., pp. 136-45, and by L. G. Wigmore, *The Japanese Thrust*, Official History of the 1939-45 War, vol. 4, series 1, Canberra, 1958.
[9] Melbourne *Herald*, 27 December 1941
[10] Roy Forward and Bob Reece, *Conscription in Australia*, Brisbane, 1968, esp. chs. 2 and 4
[11] S. Encel, 'Defence and the World Outside', *Australian Outlook*, vol. 17, no. 2, 1963

again, the Germans.'[12] Historically, the growth of militarism is commonly the result of an external menace, real or imaginary. The feeling of isolation and vulnerability is a powerful influence in moulding Australian consciousness of the outside world, and the extent to which social norms and social organisation are tinged by militarism may be traced to this influence, especially as manifested in anti-Asian xenophobia and the 'White Australia' policy. From the Sino-Japanese war of 1895, Japan was the focus of concern, and for many years the Australian outlook on defence was dominated by the conviction that Britain was incapable of understanding the extent of the Japanese threat. It was almost impossible, wrote the Premier of Queensland when on a visit to London in 1920, 'for a person who has resided only in this country to appreciate the real significance of Australian sentiment on this burning question.'[13]

The profound influence of Australia's apprehensions about Japan was noted some years ago by an American student who remarked that 'Australia's interest in her defence has fluctuated as her relations with Japan have become better or worse.'[14] These fluctuations are clearly observable during the six periods into which Japanese-Australian relations may be roughly divided. During the first period, beginning with the Sino-Japanese war of 1895, Japan was seen not as a menace, but as a possible trading partner. Indeed, the *Bulletin*, apostle of 'Australia for the white man', pooh-poohed the 'Japanese bogy' as a device for perpetuating British imperialism in the Pacific.[15] Official doctrine was that the British navy could adequately protect Australia, and the military establishment was actually cut between 1900 and 1905. Even the Japanese victory over the Russians in 1905 brought no more than scattered reactions, and a leading conservative politician, Joseph Cook, suggested that in view of Japan's military strength the White Australia policy should be modified to avoid provoking her.[16]

The second period, dating from 1907, reflected the growing international crisis in Europe, and the fear that the British fleet might be pinned down by the rapidly increasing naval power of Germany. Between 1907 and 1914, 'fears of Japan became acute and widespread, finding expression in great increases in naval and military expenditure, in apprehensive ministerial statements, in numerous allegations of Japanese espionage and in invasion as a popular theme in imaginative literature.'[17] W. M. Hughes achieved fame at this time as an advocate of compulsory military training. He

---

[12] J. Shepherd, *Australia's Interests and Policies in the Far East*, Melbourne, 1940, p. 7
[13] E. G. Theodore in *Review of Reviews*, June 1920
[14] Irving Friedman, 'Australia and Japan', *Political Science Quarterly*, vol. 52, no. 3, 1937
[15] Quoted by D. C. S. Sissons, *Attitudes to Japan and Defence 1890-1923*, M.A. thesis, University of Melbourne, 1956
[16] *Commonwealth Parliamentary Debates*, vol. 30, pp. 6308-10
[17] Sissons, op. cit., p. 48

reminded Australians that they lived only 'a few days' steaming distance from countries inhabited by nearly 1,000 million of coloured people.'[18] His colleague George Pearce, later to be Minister for Defence for a total of thirteen years, told the Senate that 'our White Australian legislation is so much waste paper unless we have rifles to back it up'[19] and that Australia needed 'twenty million standing behind the guns.'[20]

During the First World War, Hughes became increasingly concerned with the possibility of Japanese expansion because of British withdrawal from the Pacific. In July 1916, on returning from Britain, he declared in a florid speeech that 'we have nailed the flag of White Australia to the top-most minarets of our national edifice',[21] and at a secret session of parliament on 31 August he spoke of the need for defence against the coloured hordes, especially the Japanese.[22] The ALP, even after the split on conscription, agreed with him about this. A Labor newspaper wrote that Australia had unfortunately allied herself with 'bloodthirsty, barbarous Asiatics',[23] and the Japanese menace was discussed at length by the ALP conference of 1918. Hughes' determined stand at the Versailles peace conference on Australia's right to annex the former German possessions south of the Equator made him internationally famous, and brought him into sharp conflict with Woodrow Wilson and also with Lloyd George. In the end, a compromise proposal was worked out, largely through the efforts of Maurice Hankey, secretary of the empire delegation, and J. G. Latham,[24] the Australian assistant secretary, which provided for the extension of the 'mandate' system originally suggested by Smuts to the Pacific territories.[25]

Hughes remained in power for nearly four years after Versailles, and Australian defence policy continued to be dominated by fear of Japanese expansion. The government took steps to improve the level of information about the Far East in Australia. Major E. L. Piesse, previously Director of Military Intelligence, was appointed head of a Pacific Branch of the Prime Minister's Department. This office was, in effect, a successor to the Department of External Affairs, which had been suspended during the war. A chair of Oriental Studies was established at the University of Sydney, financed partly by the Defence Department on condition that the professor also gave lectures at the Royal Military College. Selected graduates of the RMC were sent to Japan after receiving intensive courses in the Japanese language and in Far Eastern history. Japanese language teaching was introduced at several metropolitan secondary schools in Sydney. A

[18] *Commonwealth Parliamentary Debates,* vol. 37, p. 1289
[19] ibid., vol. 41, p. 5679
[20] Sissons, op. cit., p. 55
[21] ibid., p. 79
[22] ibid., ch. 3
[23] *Labor Call,* Melbourne, 6 April 1917
[24] Later Sir John Latham, Attorney-General and Chief Justice
[25] Ernest Scott, *Australia During the War,* Official History of the 1914-18 War, vol. 11, Sydney, 1940, pp. 747-801

committee of six senior generals prepared a scheme for an army of 180,000 men, which they estimated would be needed to prevent Japanese forces from capturing the densely populated areas of south-eastern Australia until help arrived from Britain.[26]

But conditions were against such policies. There was strong political pressure for cuts in government expenditure. A royal commission commented unfavourably upon 'a desire in some quarters to maintain the military spirit and permanently saddle the country with an expenditure on defence which would be exceedingly onerous.'[27] The ALP was in a strongly anti-militarist mood, and during the Budget debate of 1921, a Labor motion proposed the deletion of the entire army vote from the estimates.[28] Frank Anstey, a leading left-wing member, accused the government of using Japan as a bogy in order to build up a military caste.[29] The Washington naval treaties of 1922 removed the external incentive for a vigorous defence policy. Early in 1923, Hughes resigned and his ministry was replaced by the economy-minded Bruce government. During 1922-23, defence expenditure was cut sharply, and the Pacific Branch of the Prime Minister's Department was wound up.

These events ushered in the third phase of Australian relations with Japan, which lasted until 1936. Consciousness of the Japanese menace receded, and defence expenditure, such as it was, concentrated on the navy. With the slump of 1929, trade between Australia and Japan expanded rapidly. Japan became one of Australia's best customers for wool and wheat and in return, cheap Japanese textiles were imported in large quantities. The resulting upsurge of friendly feelings towards Japan, reminiscent of the first phase of Australian-Japanese relations before 1907, in both cases derived from economic interest. Japanese aggression in Manchuria in 1931 was played down in the press,[30] and a goodwill mission visited Japan in 1934.

The fourth period was an interlude of growing suspicion and hostility, stimulated by the growth of Japanese militarism, and culminating in the attack on Pearl Harbour. It may be dated from the 'trade diversion policy' of 1936, which was aimed principally against Japan.[31] Although its ostensible purpose was to protect Australian industry against cheap imported manufactures, Shepherd argues that it sprang ultimately from traditional fears about national security. The policy, and the public controversy that accompanied it, revealed once more 'the persistence of the conflicting hopes and fears that have influenced public opinion and official policy on this subject ever since the 'nineties, when Australians first realised

---

[26] Sissons, op. cit., pp. 109-10
[27] Royal Commission on Federal Economies, First Progress Report, Melbourne, 1919
[28] *Commonwealth Parliamentary Debates*, vol. 97, p. 12025
[29] ibid., vol. 93, p. 4919
[30] W. M. Ball (ed.), *Press, Radio and World Affairs*, Melbourne, 1938, pp. 44-48
[31] Shepherd, op. cit., pp. 43-66

that Japan had risen to a position of political and commercial importance which must have a vital effect upon Australia's own development.'[32]

Fifty years of fear and suspicion attained their climax in the Pacific war of 1941-45. The invasion of New Guinea, the bombing of Darwin and Townsville, the midget submarine attack on Sydney, gave Australia a taste of the aggression so often portrayed in the speeches of politicians and the fictional imaginings of writers. The inhumanity of the Japanese towards their captives, as manifested in the Sandakan 'death march', the building of the Burma-Siam railway, the execution of prisoners of war (including a beheading incident in New Guinea),[33] and the maltreatment of civilian prisoners, left a deposit of hate, bitterness and distrust which is reflected in a voluminous literature of wartime reminiscences. The best known of these is probably Russell Braddon's *The Naked Island*, depicting life in the notorious Changi prison camp. In 1951, an official committee inquiring into the payment of compensation to former POWs wrote that 'in general, prisoners in Japanese hands were treated by their captors throughout the long period of their captivity with a brutality and inhumanity incapable of imagination by a civilised people.'[34]

The immediate result of the war was general insistence on a 'tough' policy towards Japan, a dramatic symbol of which was the hostile speech made by the Australian commander-in-chief, Sir Thomas Blamey, to the commander of the Japanese Second Army on Morotai when he received his surrender on 9 September 1945.[35] This attitude was carried over into the policy of non-fraternisation laid down in an uncompromisingly worded directive issued by General Northcott, the first commander of the British Commonwealth Occupation Force in Japan, a body in which Australian influence was predominant. However, attempts by Australia to assert the necessity for keeping Japan disarmed were ineffectual in the face of American determination, since 1949, to build up Japanese strength as a counter to the Communist regimes of the Soviet Union and mainland China. The signature of a peace treaty with Japan in 1951 providing for a degree of rearmament aroused considerable resentment in Australia, and stimulated a feeling that Australia was being dragged at the chariot wheels of American foreign policy, especially as represented by Mr John Foster Dulles. A public opinion poll taken at this time showed 67 per cent against ratification of the treaty. The Prime Minister, in an article published after the treaty conference at San Francisco, revealed the uneasiness of the government when he pleaded that Japanese rearmament should be confined to defensive weapons.[36] The debate on ratification manifested general

---

[32] ibid., p. 58

[33] Douglas Gillison, *Royal Australian Air Force 1939-42*, Official History of the 1939-45 War, vol. 1, series 3, 1957, p. 699

[34] *Commonwealth Parliamentary Debates*, vol. 216, p. 229

[35] John Hetherington, *Blamey*, Melbourne, 1959, p. 216

[36] R. G. Menzies, 'The Pacific Settlement Seen From Australia', *Foreign Affairs*, vol. 30, no. 2, 1952

reluctance to accept the treaty coupled with resignation at the unavoidable necessity for doing so. The Minister for External Affairs, Mr R. G. Casey, confessed he was 'by no means wholly satisfied', and was unsure that Japan could be trusted to refrain from 'the aggressive military and economic policies that have threatened our very existence in the past.' A government backbencher, Mr A. R. Downer, himself an ex-POW, refused to vote in favour of the treaty, which he called 'an act of folly, a myopic blunder'; the Dulles policy of containing Russia and China at all costs was an act of 'barefaced expediency'.[37]

The sixth and continuing phase of Australia's relations with Japan, dating from the ratification of the peace treaty, has been marked by a progressive reorientation of attitudes towards Asia. The long-standing emphasis on the benefits of economic ties reasserted itself with the trade treaty of 1957, although the signature of the treaty was marked by hostile and irrational outbursts from various quarters, including the ALP. The renewal of the treaty in 1963, however, was generally welcomed. Although a deep-seated fear of the Japanese may still lurk in the psyche of many Australians, its expression is beset by inhibitions and reservations, and by a consciousness that Australia, as a relatively wealthy nation, owes a moral obligation to less fortunate countries. The title of Russell Braddon's book *End of a Hate*, written seven years after his account of life in Changi prison camp, is symbolic. Braddon attacks the Dulles policy, which has given Australia 'Imperial Japan disguised as an ally'. On the other hand, he advocated the abandonment of the White Australia policy and the admission of Japanese to New Guinea and the Northern Territory; otherwise Japan's population problem would move her to expand aggressively again.

Australia and Indonesia

Indonesia, on the other hand, has become a major focus of interest. The Indonesian claim to West New Guinea was a source of apprehension for years until it was settled, and the settlement raised a whole new set of problems whose future development is incalculable, especially as political instability remains the one stable fact in Indonesian politics. Moreover, the Indonesian 'confrontation' policy against Malaysia and its policy of obtaining arms from the USSR aroused further fears about security in the South-West Pacific area. This irruption of Indonesia into Australian consciousness of the external world has been met with three distinct patterns of response. On the 'Left' there is the view that Indonesia would present no threat if Australia were to pursue a policy of economic, political and cultural co-operation, with the aim of ensuring Indonesia's internal stability. According to an editorial in *Nation* 'the friendship of Indonesia is a matter of life and death. A hostile Indonesia means the effective neutralisation of the SEATO bases as defence outposts.'[38] The moral, according to a subse-

[37] CPD, vol. 216, pp. 19, 290
[38] *Nation*, 11 February 1961

quent article in the same journal, is that Australians must try 'to work out common objectives and common policies with our Asian neighbours.'[39]

At the other extreme is an attitude of profound distrust, expressed by some backbench members of the Liberal Party, by some newspapers, notably the *Sydney Morning Herald*, and by sections of the ALP. In a leading article on defence policy, published shortly before the revolt in Brunei in 1962, the *Herald* declared that 'we have right at our doorstep a country whose population and armed resources are far in excess of our own. The future of Indonesian policy may be very debatable, but she has done nothing to inspire confidence in her goodwill.'[40] In this and other articles, the *Herald* repeatedly criticised the Menzies government for abdicating its responsibilities and for its fallacious reliance on the protection afforded by Australia's allies, especially the USA, which could not be counted upon to dissuade Indonesia from 'throwing overboard the principles of peace and justice'. The hostility of the *Herald* and of other critics of the government was reinforced by the contention that Indonesia was in imminent danger of a Communist takeover and that deterrence was all the more necessary in consequence.

Between these two poles, the attitudes of both the major parties wobbled in a somewhat similar fashion, though for differing reasons. For several years, Sir Robert Menzies' outlook was characterised by an apparent distaste at the probability that Australia would have to establish closer political relations with the Indonesians, as if they were one of Kipling's lesser tribes without the law. He was palpably chagrined at the Dutch decision to withdraw from West New Guinea, which seemed like letting down the side. The extravagance of Indonesian 'confrontation' tactics under the leadership of ex-President Soekarno gave support to this attitude of hostile suspicion.

The abortive coup d'etat in Indonesia in 1965 and the reorientation of Indonesian politics as a result, brought about considerable changes, especially as Sir Robert Menzies retired from politics early in 1966 and was succeeded by the late Mr Harold Holt, who was anxious to exhibit friendliness towards Asia. As a result, the Australian outlook on Indonesia came to depend upon political and strategic calculations which had little to do with the xenophobic nationalism, with its racialist undertones, which coloured Australian attitudes to Asia for two generations.

Australia and the United States

Under the Menzies government, defence policy became firmly based on the assumption that limited wars were likely to continue in South-East Asia under the shadow of the nuclear deterrent, and that Australia's defence should therefore depend upon modern conventional weapons on the one hand, and co-operation with the US in regional security arrangements on

---

[39] W. M. Ball, in *Nation*, 26 January 1963
[40] *Sydney Morning Herald*, 20 October 1962

the other. Sir Robert Menzies became Prime Minister only a few months after the final victory of the Chinese Communists over the Kuomintang in 1949, and almost from the outset of his long tenure of office his government acted on the assumption that the new danger to Australia was that of expansionist communism. This meant, first of all, a policy of assisting the containment of communism on the Asian mainland by joining regional defence arrangements such as ANZUS, ANZAM and SEATO and of pressing the United States to become deeply involved in the defence of South-East Asia against communism. The combined logic of these two lines of policy led to Australia's decision, in 1965, to support American action in the Vietnam war by sending Australian troops to fight there. The late Mr Holt took pains to show his enthusiasm for American action under President Lyndon Johnson by declaring publicly 'All the way with LBJ'. The American alliance poses many problems for Australia. Many Australians are uneasily aware that Australia is expendable in terms of American global strategy and that 'for America the costs of defending Australia and of conducting a military association with her . . . are less and perhaps considerably less than Australia's usefulness to some of America's central purposes in the Indo-Pacific region.'[41] The special links between Britain and Australia have no significance for the USA, and Britain's decline as a world power leaves no other 'great and powerful friend' to fall back upon. As a result, Australian attitudes have fluctuated violently in response to American policies. From the point of view of the present discussion, the most important results of events since 1965 have been the intensification of tendencies towards militarism and authoritarianism inside Australia, exemplified by repressive attitudes towards opposition to the Vietnam war; a renewed emergence of isolationism, marked in the speeches of Mr J. G. Gorton, who became Prime Minister in 1968, about the need to develop 'fortress Australia'; and an ideological struggle within the Labor Party.

These shifts of opinion have produced interesting reversals of posture among the political parties. The ALP, traditionally the supporter of military strength and White Australia, has moved to a position of advocating economic and social links with Asia and of keeping Australia's military commitments to a minimum. The American alliance, on this view, should be counterbalanced by closer relations with Britain, Japan and other Asian countries, and Australia's principal relationship with Asia should not be a military one. The Liberals, the traditional party of the British Empire, have come to treat Britain with suspicion. The DLP has emerged as the most intransigent party, its attitudes being a curious mixture of traditional xenophobia with intense, religiously-inspired anti-communism. This conflict of attitudes is related not only to a far more complicated external situation, but also to the growth of a more complicated, stratified society at home, and the increasing stratification of attitudes towards the external world is likely to be a feature of Australian society in the future.

---

41 H. G. Gelber, *The Australian-American Alliance*, London, 1968, p. 130

23: A Military Tradition

Militarism, according to one of its historians, is a system of ideas and values which ranks 'military institutions and ways above the ways of civilian life.'[1] Its ripest expressions are to be found, appropriately enough, in the mouths of a Prussian general and a Japanese shogun. Moltke claimed that 'the army is the most outstanding institution in every country, for it alone makes possible the existence of all civic institutions.'[2] Iyeyasu, founder of the Tokugawa dynasty, declared that 'it is the custom of the country to regard the actions of the military class as the standard of conduct for the nation.'[3]

Militarism in this sense has been relatively feeble in the English-speaking countries, where public authority presents a less forbidding aspect for its lack of militarisation. Howard observes that whereas many European countries have been characterised by a profound rift between the civil and the military interest, in Britain there is no more than a 'shallow depression'.[4] The Central European etiquette which gives social predominance to an officer in uniform, bitingly satirised in Arthur Schnitzler's story *Leutnant Gustl*, is subtly reversed, as in the custom of not wearing uniforms off duty. Huntington observes that liberalism is, on the one hand, hostile to the existence of a military establishment, but the fact of its existence arouses continuous attempts at refashioning the institutions of war to make them lose their peculiarly military characteristics. Militarism is seen as the origin of four threats to liberal society which emanate from the existence of armed forces: threats to freedom, to democracy, to prosperity (because of the economic burden of armaments) and to peace.[5] On the other hand, three forms of mitigation have been urged: first, defence is a civic responsibility, not the preserve of a clique (so there should be a maximum of public discussion); second, a democratic country should have a democratic army; and finally, if armed forces are to exist they should have some practical peacetime use—thus, the Army Engineers.

Military heroes do not figure in the liberal pantheon, except when they display the virtues of a Cincinnatus. 'The liberal hero', remarks Huntington,

---

[1] Alfred Vagts, *A History of Militarism*, New York, 1959, p. 17
[2] ibid., p. 16
[3] ibid., p. 450
[4] Michael Howard, *Soldiers and Governments*, London, 1957, p. 21
[5] S. P. Huntington, *The Soldier and the State*, Cambridge, Mass., 1957, p. 155

'is a versatile hero'—especially if he is a man of peace who leaves his trade to beat the professional military men at theirs. 'While the American people like their political candidates to be military heroes, they want their military experience to be an interlude in, or a sideline to, an otherwise civilian career.'[6]

Huntington's analysis applies, almost *a fortiori*, to the situation in Australia, where a history of citizen military effort in two world wars has further contributed to the relatively low esteem enjoyed by the professional soldier. The fact that Australia's greatest military commander, Sir John Monash, was a citizen soldier with a distinguished civilian career both before and after his service in the 1914-18 war, is another factor of some psychological importance. The popular attitude to military glory is summed up in the private soldier's wisecrack: 'The only kind of soldier I want to be is a returned soldier.'

Such attitudes, coupled with the smallness of the permanent military establishment throughout our history, can easily lead to an undervaluation of the influence of militarism in Australian life. Yet the very strength of the citizen tradition is a reason for the stress on military virtues—hierarchy, loyalty, order, patriotism—which is so frequent on public occasions. The most distinctive of all national holidays (other than Melbourne Cup Day) is Anzac Day, the anniversary of the first major battle in which Australian troops were engaged in large numbers. Official provision for the re-establishment of discharged servicemen in civil life has been remarkably extensive, including elaborate legislation providing for preference in employment, as well as schemes for housing, settlement on the land and retraining.

McCallum has suggested that militaristic tendencies are connected with the cult of manliness in Australia.[7] Private coercion has been practised by patriotic ex-soldiers' organisations as well as the police. He also sees a 'contained regard for military virtues if only in small doses.' Military training remains a school for virtues, in the tradition of Bodin, who praised the ancient Roman camp as a school of 'honour, sobriety, chastity, justice, and virtue', or Harrington, who regarded a system of universal military training as the most important guarantee for the stability of the Commonwealth.[8] Politicians, parents and teachers, says McCallum, cling to the notion that 'intelligent and potentially sensitive and percipient youth may gain certain poorly defined traits of character, backbone and moral fibre by being subjected to military training for ludicrously brief periods. Uncritical attitudes towards the special virtues of Australian military forces consort ambivalently with attitudes of criticism adopted towards militarism in the United States or in Russia.' In 1932, a Labor newspaper, deploring the

[6] ibid., p. 159. In fact, many political generals have been regular soldiers.

[7] D. M. McCallum, in P. Coleman (ed.), *Australian Civilization*, Melbourne, 1962, p. 34

[8] David C. Rapoport, 'A Comparative Theory of Military and Political Types' in S. P. Huntington (ed.), *Changing Patterns of Military Politics*, New York, 1962, pp. 71-98

activities of a semi-fascist organisation of ex-soldiers, the New Guard, found that the worst thing it could say about them was that they had 'disgraced that sacred vestment, the King's Uniform.'[9] The historian, K. S. Inglis, writing in the literary quarterly *Meanjin* (No. 1, 1965) reminds us that the 'Anzac tradition' is in many ways co-extensive with an older Australian nationalist tradition and the legend of the 'Digger' has military as well as civilian aspects. The strength of this tradition shows that one cannot, too readily, accept the view that the working class is anti-militarist and anti-war.

In an essay published more than a century ago, Friedrich Engels argued that the characteristics of the military establishment in any state are determined by the dominant political characteristics of that state. Recently, Rapoport[10] has described military and political institutions as 'mutually dependent variables'. The political function of an army is the key to its character, and both character and function depend on prevailing conceptions about the place of the army in civil society. An example of such a conception is that of the 'nation in arms', historic examples of which go back to the Greek city-states and the Roman republic; in the modern world, Switzerland and Israel are leading examples. The nation in arms is characterised by the ability to mobilise a large proportion of its population at short notice, and by emphasis on a citizen army rather than a professional one. In the armies of Switzerland and Israel, Rapoport notes, few men are appointed to high permanent military rank, giving a relatively large number of citizen officers the chance to exercise the duties of higher command.

The manner in which a concept of the nation in arms has affected the development of the military establishment in Australia will be discussed at some length in the following pages. It is exemplified in the long-standing support for compulsory military training found among groups like the Labor Party before the First World War, and the Returned Services League since then. In the case of the RSL and other self-consciously patriotic groups, moreover, compulsory training appears to be advocated at least as much on civic as on military grounds. The concept is also reflected in a distinctive military tradition, to be found in folklore, in literature, in military history, and in painting.[11]

The sources of this tradition lie partly in necessity, partly within the everyday culture which has been carried over into the brief interlude of military life, and partly in accepted myths about the qualities of the Australian soldier, which are generally notions about 'national character' transferred to a warlike setting. Well-developed examples are to be found in the work of the doyen of Australian military historians, the late Dr C. E. W. Bean. Bean ascribed the virtues of the Australian soldier to a

---

[9] *Labor Call*, Melbourne, 7 April 1932
[10] loc. cit.
[11] Even the legend of Ned Kelly, the bushranger, has military overtones and Sidney Nolan's paintings have caught some of them by using the dominant motif of a man in armour.

combination of nature and nurture, to the effect of the conditions of outback life on British stock. 'It was a fact often observed,' he remarks, 'that in a shipwreck or a bushfire one man of British stock could compass the work of several Germans; and this capacity the Australian possessed to an extreme degree.'[12] To the inherent superiority of the British race, the Australians had added qualities of initiative, resourcefulness and leadership. British soldiers, who were 'the best-natured of men, extraordinarily guileless, humble-minded to a degree, never boastful, and seldom the cause of any serious trouble, [sic] instinctively looked up to the Australian private as a leader.'[13] Bean's views were a repetition of what he had written earlier in a book about life in rural Australia. 'The up-country Australian', he wrote, 'is possibly the most capable man among Anglo-Saxons.' He possessed the outstanding virtues of being able to turn his hand to almost anything. 'That extraordinary versatility, the capacity to do anything, is in the Englishman; indeed it was from him that it came . . . it does not come to the surface until they get to places like Western America or Australia.'[14]

Others have also contributed to the picture. The British airman, Colonel Strange, who served with Australian flying squadrons in the First World War, was impressed by the Australians as 'the finest material for an attacking force in the air, just as their infantry divisions on the ground were the best that the war produced on either side.' Just as Australians have quaint views about Britain and the British army, so Strange's account of Australia becomes adulterated by the American Wild West. Australian initiative, he writes, was 'inherited from ancestors who had been cattlemen, sheep-ranchers, poachers, trappers, outriders, overland post and transport drivers . . . they were equally at home when cutting out cattle at a round-up or shooting the rapids in a canoe'. The Australian squadrons made him think of 'the sheriff and his posse going out after bushrangers.'[15]

These qualities of initiative and resource are, traditionally, accompanied by a casual if not downright hostile attitude to the hierarchical structure of the military command system. Bean noticed 'a sort of suppressed resentfulness, never very serious, but yet noticeable, of the whole system of "officers".'[16] Field-Marshal Allenby is said to have observed that he had never met troops so completely unimpressed by senior rank. A widely-held view in both world wars was that British officers, accustomed to instant and unquestioning obedience from other ranks, were unable to handle Australian troops, who did not care for the outward show of obedience, and were liable to react unfavourably to orders which were demonstrably stupid. The notorious refusal of Australian soldiers to salute British officers when off duty was the cause of numerous incidents during the First World War. Several incidents of this kind, evidently based on fact, are recounted

---

[12] Bean, *The Story of Anzac*, p. 5
[13] ibid., p. 48
[14] Bean, *On the Wool Track*, Sydney, 1910; republished 1944, pp. 31, 104
[15] L. A. Strange, *Recollections of an Airman*, London, 1933, pp. 175-78
[16] Bean, *The Story of Anzac*, p. 48

in Leonard Mann's novel of the 1914-18 war, *Flesh in Armour*. The spirit of the times was also reflected in an Australian version of the famous song, 'Fred Karno's Army', which was current in the British army at the time:

We are the Anzac Army,
The ANZAC,
We cannot shoot, we don't salute,
What bloody good are we?[17]

General Monash was gratified to see that in the Australian army, unlike the British,

there was no officer caste, no social distinction in the whole force. In not a few instances, men of humble origin and belonging to the artisan class rose, during the war, from privates to the command of battalions . . . the whole Australian army became automatically graded into leaders and followers according to the individual merits of every man, and there grew a wonderful understanding between them.[18]

The Australian attitude towards military rank may usefully be compared with that of the Americans and the British.[19] American war literature expresses widespread hostility towards rank. A man who becomes an officer automatically becomes a son-of-a-bitch and the professional soldier who is 'RA all the way' is a standing joke. Australian soldiers who served alongside Americans were struck by the rigid divisions between officers and men enforced in the American army, just as Americans were surprised by the easy-going relationships in the Australian army. In Australia, the suspicion of rank seems to rest less on hostility to the idea as such than on the feeling that too many of the men who attain command are unworthy to exercise it. A recurrent myth about the Australian army is the existence of an 'unwritten creed among officers . . . that they would never ask a man to do anything they themselves could not or would not do.'[20] This myth is sometimes used to point a contrast with British officers, who are supposed to observe different standards. An analogy from the cricket field comes from the pen of an Australian cricketer, who writes that 'West Indians and Australians play *with* a captain, and Englishmen play *under* one.'[21] Australian troops were well known for their resistance to spit-and-polish and anything that resembled 'putting on side'. However, one incident recounted by an Australian general suggests that these relationships may have their surprises. In 1918, a British colonel was posted to command an Australian company of field engineers in France. The colonel sported a monocle. One morning the company paraded, with each man wearing an identity disc in

[17] Quoted by John Laffin, *Digger*, London, 1959, p. 61
[18] Sir John Monash, *The Australian Victories in France*, Melbourne, 1923, p. 300
[19] S. Richardson, in *Administrative Science Quarterly*, vol. 1, no. 1, 1956, discusses different attitudes towards rank among British and American sailors.
[20] Laffin, op. cit., p. 171
[21] Ken Mackay, *Slasher Opens Up*, London, 1964

his left eye. The colonel, in no way disconcerted, took out his monocle, threw it in the air, caught it in his eye as it fell, and barked: 'Do that, you bastards!'[22]

A remarkable discussion of rank in fiction appears in T. A. G. Hungerford's novel, *The Ridge and the River*. The hero, Corporal Alec Shearwood, leader of a patrol in the jungle of Bougainville, has several times refused a commission. When his superior, Major Lovatt, asks him why he refuses to go to an officers' school, Shearwood replies that he cannot face the thought of ordering men to get killed. He dreads the 'responsibility of standing out from the ruck'; commissioned rank is an 'implacable Rubicon' which he does not wish to cross. Looking at Lovatt, whom he esteems, Shearwood 'felt sure that he hated his loneliness, and hated the necessity for making the men resent him.' At the climax of the book, Lovatt tells Shearwood that he has been given a commission in the field, without the need for an officer's training course, and this Shearwood at last accepts, because he feels that in this way he has earned his rank.

Necessity has played a decisive part in moulding an Australian military tradition. Because of limited resources, sparse population, incapacity to defend the country unaided, and reliance on citizen forces, the features of this tradition are bound to contrast with countries possessing large and well-equipped standing armies. Lack of material resources leads to great emphasis on the bravery and resource of the individual soldier or the small independent unit. 'Scrounging' becomes a major virtue, sometimes reaching embarrassing proportions. The skill of Australian soldiers in bartering liquor or dubious 'souvenirs' for American cigarettes, clothing and small items of military equipment during the Pacific campaign was proverbial. Air-Commodore Scherger,[23] commanding RAAF formations in New Guinea in 1944, noted that he had been compelled to order the jettisoning of a great deal of equipment collected by RAAF units through 'scrounging' and 'magpieing'. By comparison, he observed, this was unknown among American units, and concluded: 'There is little doubt in my mind that "scrounging" is a characteristic only of a Service which has been or is starved of adequate supplies for all its requirements.'[24] The manufacture of small arms has always been the predominant feature of Australian war production, and the best-known Australian contribution to military technology during the Second World War was the Owen submachine gun, a weapon of great simplicity and durability under adverse conditions.

Limited resources of manpower, and the lack of a large and elaborate general staff of professions, help to account for the relative absence of massive pitched battles in Australian military history, and an emphasis on

[22] G. Drake-Brockman, *The Turning Wheel*, Perth, 1960, p. 119
[23] Later Air-Marshal Scherger, Chief of the Air Staff and chairman of the Chiefs of Staff Committee
[24] George Odgers, *Air War Against Japan,* Official History of the 1939-45 War, vol. 2, series 3, Canberra, 1958, p. 200

tactical skill and cunning as opposed to the large-scale strategic operation
and the deployment of big battalions. Laffin makes an interesting comparison between the attitudes and methods of the Australians and those of
the British or Americans. For the British, he argues, the acme of military
performance is represented by the mass, disciplined advance in the open
against murderous fire; for the Americans, the concentration of enormous
firepower followed by a frontal attack with little regard to casualties; for
the Australians, economy in the use of men and only limited dependence
on firepower. 'The Digger has never had a hankering for fighting as a way
of getting more battle honours on the regimental colours, nor does he
place too much reliance on armour and artillery. He expects success to
follow the taking of calculated risks, plus confidence in himself, in his
mates and in his leaders.'[25] The military history of all countries is, of
course, replete with examples where success in war has been gained only
by radical departures from the accepted patterns of military performance,
but none the less such patterns remain stable over long periods, suggesting
that they depend at least as much on long-term social factors as on the
demands of war itself. The reliance of the Americans on firepower
reappears, for example, in the overproduction of weapons of mass
destruction since 1945.

The writing of military history in Australia bears some witness to the
tradition we have been discussing. Military histories are generally
concerned with strategy, with campaigns, with large battles, and with the
personalities, the attainments, and the failings of commanders. In Australia, a rather different model was set by Dr Bean, as general editor of
the official history of the 1914-18 war, and it has been closely followed
ever since. For Bean and his successors, war history is made up of the
doings of individual soldiers and of the small units which form the framework of their everyday existence. It is history written from the point of
view of the men in the field, rather than the staff at GHQ. The great
strategic decisions, the battles, the political conflicts, the personal rivalries
of generals and admirals, form no more than a backdrop to hundreds of
personal dramas drawn from regimental histories. As Inglis remarks, Bean
'believed that he was writing a history about an army which was unusually
good because of the character, and in particular the egalitarian comradeship, of its members; and he wrote a history appropriate to his belief . . .
as far as possible, the responsibility for the events described should be
attributed to the men actually responsible.'[26] It is the kind of history that
would have commended itself to Tolstoy.

[25] Laffin, op. cit., p. 178
[26] K. S. Inglis, 'The Anzac Tradition', *Meanjin Quarterly*, no. 1, 1965

24: World War and Cold War

The history of the armed services, the relations between soldiers and governments, and the conduct of particular campaigns, have all been influenced by the twists and turns of external policy.

When the century opened, British and Australian politicians alike saw Pacific defence as merely an incident of British policy. In 1901 the Colonial Defence Committee (precursor of the Committee of Imperial Defence) advised the newly-established Commonwealth government that it need have the resources only to repel a squadron of three or four cruisers which might make a raid of 'a hasty or fugitive character'. The military establishment taken over by the Commonwealth from the former colonial governments was accordingly reduced. The Defence Acts of 1903 and 1904 replaced the former colonial commands with six military districts. The 1904 legislation also made provision for a Council of Defence, a Naval Board and a Military Board. The Defence Act of 1909 provided both for compulsory training and for the establishment of the Royal Military College, which came into being in 1911. In 1910, a report by Lord Kitchener outlined a scheme which has remained the basis of the relationship between professional and citizen forces. He recommended a force of at least 80,000 trained men, recruited from cadets at the age of eighteen. This citizen force would be directed by a staff corps of professional officers. The keystone of the citizen force would be the area officer, a professional soldier responsible for the training and registration of the citizen militia. 'No social considerations,' wrote Kitchener, 'no influence, nothing but efficiency, should be allowed to affect the selection and promotion of these officers.'[1]

Two World Wars

At the outbreak of war in 1914, the army establishment comprised 3,000 permanent and 42,000 citizen soldiers, but this was swamped by the enlistment of voluntary recruits in the Australian expeditionary force. The senior professional officer in the armed services at that time was Major-General Sir William Bridges, who occupied the post of Inspector-General. Whereas it had originally been assumed that Australian contingents would be incorporated into British units, Bridges held out strongly for a national army in which Australian troops would be commanded by Australian

[1] Scott, *Australia During the War*, p. 195

officers. The son of a naval captain, whose training had been at the Royal Military College in Canada, Bridges was known as a critic of British army methods and was apprehensive about the results of putting British officers in command of Australian units. As Australian representative on the Imperial General Staff, he is reputed to have told a meeting of that body that British training manuals were 'as much use to the Australians as the cuneiform inscriptions on a Babylonian brick.'[2] Bridges' contributions to the Australian military tradition were the concept of 'Anzac' and the name 'Australian Imperial Forces' (AIF) which was a *tour de force* of patriotic synthesis.[3] The principle that Australia should have a 'national' army and should not reproduce the regional divisions of the British army had already been established by the Minister for Defence, George Pearce, at the outbreak of war. In a parliamentary debate, Pearce declared that the establishment of 'national regiments' (i.e. Scottish, Irish, Welsh units) was not compatible with building up 'a strong Australian national sentiment based on Australian tradition and associated with Australian ideals.'[4]

The latent uneasiness of the filial relationship between Britain and Australia expressed itself in peacetime disputes about strategy and in wartime disputes about operations. Between the two wars, the leading body of thought on defence policy was predicated upon the possibility of a Japanese invasion, which meant that Australia should pay special attention to aerial defence and that the central importance attached by Britain to naval defence, based on Singapore, held dangers for Australian security.[5] Critics of government policy, including the ALP (which was in opposition for most of this period), a number of senior officers of the Staff Corps and various publicists, attacked the Bruce and Lyons governments for adhering uncritically to British strategic assumptions. In 1936, the leader of the ALP, John Curtin, declared that Britain's ability to protect Australia was 'too dangerous a hazard upon which to found Australia's defence policy', and in the following year he called for a stronger air force.[6]

These arguments about policy were matched by conflicts over the disposition of Australian forces in wartime. Notable examples during the First World War included the Gallipoli campaign and the Somme and Passchendaele offensives in France. During the Second World War, the anxiety of the Australian government to procure the return of three divisions serving in the Middle East to protect Australia against the Japanese threat led to a bitter conflict between Winston Churchill and John Curtin, then Prime Minister of Australia.

The command of Australian troops by British generals was a regular cause of aggravation. The policy of Bridges, to organise Australian troops

---

[2] C. E. W. Bean, *Two Men I Knew*, Sydney, 1954, p. 15
[3] Bean, *The Story of Anzac*, pp. 30-31
[4] *Commonwealth Parliamentary Debates*, vol. 42, 29 May 1914, p. 1663
[5] Gavin Long, *To Benghazi*, Official History of the 1939-45 War, vol. 1, series 1, Canberra, 1954, ch. 1; Paul Hasluck, *The Government and the People, 1939-41*, ch. 2
[6] *Commonwealth Parliamentary Debates*, vol. 152, pp. 1547-54

in their own units under their own commanders, was continued after his death at Gallipoli by the chief staff officer of the AIF, C. B. Brudenell White. After the withdrawal from the peninsula, White was responsible for negotiating with British HQ to ensure that the Australian forces would be commanded by a general responsible to the Commonwealth government. In this he was strongly backed by General Birdwood, who had been appointed GOC Anzac corps during the Gallipoli campaign. Birdwood was an Indian Army commander who was relatively free from the arrogant prejudices of the British officers of his generation. He conceived a great affection for the Australians under his control, and on one occasion told Milner, the Secretary for War, that his experience with the Australians had convinced him of the value of citizen soldiers for important commands.[7] Haig, on the other hand, wrote about the Anzacs that 'some of their divisional generals are so ignorant and (like many Colonials) so conceited, that they cannot be trusted to work out unaided the plans of attack.'[8] At one staff conference, Haig made a sweeping condemnation of a recent operation carried out by the Australians. White, refusing to be intimidated, took pains to demonstrate in detail that almost every one of Haig's specific criticisms was mistaken. Haig then replied patronizingly, 'I dare say you are right, young man,' and noted in his diary that White was 'a very sound capable fellow, and assured me they had learned a lesson and would be more thorough in future,' apparently unaware all this time that only one of the divisional commanders he had been so scathing about was an Australian.[9]

The failure of British commanders to understand the qualities of Australian troops caused the leading Australian general of the Second World War, Sir Thomas Blamey, to complain in a letter to the Prime Minister, R. G. Menzies, of the situation 'where British leaders have control of considerable bodies of first-class Dominion troops while Dominion commanders are excluded from all responsibility in control, planning and policy.'[10] A similar note of bitterness is to be found in a letter written by John Monash to his wife from Egypt in 1916: 'I have firmly resolved not to intrigue or canvass for promotion in any way, and if Australia chooses to let her forces be exploited to find jobs for unemployed senior British officers, that is not my affair.'[11]

Blamey's determination that Australian troops should be commanded by Australians led him into several clashes with the British high command during the 1939-45 war. As commander of the second AIF, he was given a directive by the Australian government stating that sections of the force could be detached only with the consent of the GOC. In August 1940 he wrote to John Northcott, Deputy Chief of the General Staff, observing

[7] Lord Birdwood, *Khaki and Gown*, London, 1943, p. 324
[8] *The Private Papers of Douglas Haig*, London, 1930, p. 156
[9] Bean, *Two Men I Knew*, pp. 136-38
[10] John Hetherington, *Blamey*, p. 120
[11] F. M. Cutlack (ed.), *War Letters of General Monash*, Sydney, 1934, pp. 107-8

that he had had 'some trifling difficulties in educating the British staffs to an understanding that the AIF is a national force.'[12] The campaign in Greece was an outstanding illustration of Australian and New Zealand troops being employed in pursuit of a strategy for which their governments were not responsible, under the direction of British generals whose estimate of the situation differed strongly from that of their own officers.

The situation of the Australian and New Zealand commanders was rendered even more difficult by the fact that their respective Prime Ministers, R. G. Menzies and Peter Fraser, were too ready to accept official British advice on policy and strategy without previously consulting their own military advisers. 'Menzies might have been expected to consult Blamey, and Blamey to have expressed his opinion. . . . It was the duty [of the Dominion governments] to ensure that they were adequately informed on military matters, and to assert their right to swift and adequate information from London and effective consultation.'[13]

Conflicts and intrigues over command within the Australian military hierarchy have played themselves out within the framework of dependence on a big power—Britain in the First World War, Britain and America in the Second World War. The first important example occurred over the command of the Australian corps in France in 1918. Haig, whose opinion of the Australians had evidently changed, was anxious that an Australian general should command the corps, especially after the precedent of the Canadian corps, which had been led by a Canadian general, Sir Arthur Currie, since July 1917. In May 1918 Birdwood was appointed to the command of the British Fifth Army, and recommended to Pearce, the Minister for Defence, that Monash, then commanding the 3rd Division AIF, should take his place. Birdwood was influenced in this decision by the high regard in which Monash was held not only by Haig but by the other British generals under whom he had served. In his dispatch to Pearce, Birdwood informed him that the choice was clearly between Monash and White, chief of staff of the Australian corps, and that he was recommending Monash as the senior of the two. In his autobiography, Birdwood describes Monash as 'a truly great brain . . . an extremely able organiser and administrator', but adds that, in the absence of Monash, White 'would have filled the post with equal success.'[14] He proposed that White should accompany him to the Fifth Army as chief of staff, and Pearce accepted both recommendations.

Birdwood's recommendation started a train of intrigues in favour of White. A small group of senior staff officers were opposed to Monash's promotion, and their views gained the support of Bean, of Will Dyson, the celebrated newspaper cartoonist, and of the war correspondent, Keith Murdoch. To complicate the situation, Birdwood was reluctant to lose touch with the AIF, and as he had been a *protégé* of Kitchener he was not

12 Hetherington, op. cit., pp. 70-71
13 Gavin Long, *Greece, Crete and Syria,* Official History of the 1939-45 War, vol. 2, series 1, Canberra, 1956, p. 194
14 Birdwood, op. cit.

favourably regarded by the new CIGS, Sir Henry Wilson. Bean and Dyson crossed to London and persuaded Murdoch that Monash should have administrative control and that White should command in the field. Murdoch intervened both with W. M. Hughes, who was then on his way to England for the Imperial War Conference, and with Wilson. When Hughes arrived in London, Murdoch arranged a dinner party for him with Wilson, Milner and Bonar Law, the Conservative leader. However, Hughes' own inquiries among the Australian divisional commanders showed that they wanted Birdwood to continue in the administrative command, and he offered him the option of remaining in this position provided he gave up the army command. Haig advised Birdwood to accept this offer, provided it became effective from 30 November, and the problem consequently evaporated with the Armistice.

Another conflict over command in the field occurred in 1942, as the result of the incorporation of Australian troops into the South-West Pacific Area command under General Douglas MacArthur. Blamey had already been secretly recalled from Cairo by the Prime Minister, John Curtin, after a series of conflicts and intrigues over command within the army hierarchy and the government. On 18 March 1942, MacArthur landed in Australia after a secret flight from the Philippines and was appointed Supreme Commander, SWPA. Blamey landed at Fremantle five days later to take up his new post as Commander-in-Chief, Australian Military Forces. Although MacArthur was reluctant to give Blamey any special role in the Allied high command, he was pressed to do so by Washington, which was under pressure in its turn from Curtin. Blamey was accordingly made deputy to MacArthur, with the title of Commander of Allied Land Forces. In this capacity, he was soon called upon to intervene in operations in New Guinea. Under the command of Lieut-General S. F. Rowell, the AIF had retreated steadily before the Japanese. MacArthur, who had repeatedly expressed concern for the safety of Port Moresby, telephoned to Curtin from his headquarters in Brisbane on 17 September asking that Blamey should take personal command in New Guinea. (On the same day, Blamey had assured the Advisory War Council that Port Moresby would be held.) Blamey arrived in Port Moresby on 23 September, and after Rowell had refused to serve under Blamey's direction, Blamey relieved him of his command and ordered him to return to Australia. In a letter to Curtin on 1 October, Blamey accused Rowell of 'personal animus', and described him as 'most difficult and recalcitrant', when his duty had been to carry out instructions without question.[15] The rights and wrongs of this celebrated incident have been repeatedly canvassed in the past twenty-five years. It is probably fair to conclude, as Hetherington does, that while Rowell was stiffnecked and unco-operative, Blamey was harsh, rough and vindictive. His vindictiveness towards Rowell continued for the rest of the

[15] Dudley McCarthy, *South-West Pacific Area, First Year,* Official History of the 1939-45 War, vol. 4, series 1, Canberra, 1960, p. 237

war. Various attempts to find Rowell another post were vetoed by Blamey, including a request from Sir Alan Brooke, the British CIGS. Under pressure from Curtin, Blamey agreed to the appointment of Rowell as Director of Tactical Investigation at the War Office in London, but he refused to see Rowell before the latter left Australia and did not reply to a letter from him.

Relations with the Americans underlay another famous command dispute, this time in the Royal Australian Air Force. On the one hand, the Australian Air Board, headed by Air Vice-Marshal Jones, was officially responsible for both the operational and administrative control of the RAAF; on the other, the American commander of the Allied Air Forces, General Kenney, set up a formation known as 'RAAF Command, Allied Air Forces' and appointed another senior RAAF officer, Air Vice-Marshal Bostock, as its head. The fact that the Minister for Air, A. S. Drakeford, supported Jones and the Air Board, while Curtin, the Prime Minister, refrained from supporting Drakeford, only increased the tension.

This history of the armed services has been marked, in Australia as elsewhere, by conflicts over the relationship between civil and military authorities. A Federal Cabinet sub-committee declared in 1918 that there had, at all times, been a 'prolonged struggle to determine whether the final authority with regard to the administration of both Army and Navy should be civil or military.' It was unthinkable, they concluded, that Australia should depart from the British tradition that the civil authority must prevail. The occasion for this declaration was a recommendation by a royal commission that, in matters of naval policy and administration, the final say should rest with the Naval Board. As the Cabinet sub-committee pointed out, this would make the position of the responsible minister impossible. He could not, they argued, defend in Parliament an action with which he disagreed: 'no Minister can fairly be expected to answer to Parliament regarding the administration of a department over which he exercises no authority.'[16]

The only Australian general to become directly involved in conflicts at the political level was Blamey. The politician with whom he was most directly concerned with John Curtin, who supported Blamey throughout his appointment as C-in-C, and gave Blamey direct access to him in his capacity as Minister for Defence. Curtin was the only politician he respected and whom he took into his confidence. Because of Blamey's lack of faith in the other members of War Cabinet, he kept his own staff officers in ignorance of operational plans so that there was no risk of disclosure to ministers. Curtin alone would be told, either by Blamey or by MacArthur. As a result, Curtin regularly had to defend Blamey against criticism by his own colleagues. Blamey's right-wing political views were well known and disliked by the parliamentary ALP, who were constantly seeking opportunities to cut down his authority. With the death of Curtin in June 1945

[16] Report of the Royal Commission on Navy and Defence Administration, Melbourne, 1917-18, Appendix, para. 8

and the end of the war two months later, Blamey's position became untenable. In November, he was given notice. A sharp public rebuke came from the new Prime Minister, J. B. Chifley, when Blamey criticised government defence policy in the press. Chifley, visiting London for a Prime Ministers' Conference in 1946, was asked about Blamey's views, and replied with characteristic bluntness: 'We don't need stooges to speak for us. General Blamey is not the spokesman of the Australian Government.'[17]

Civilian authority over the army has been manifested more at the administrative than at the political level, especially through financial control exercised by the Treasury. In the early months of the second world war, for instance, comparatively modest proposals for expenditure on munitions and equipment were turned down by Treasury officials who were apparently 'resolved that the war should not be an excuse for undue extravagance on the part of the Services.'[18] It took four months for the Department of Supply to obtain War Cabinet assent to the manufacture of modern field artillery to replace the obsolete weapons which the AIF had brought back with it in 1919.

The battle over financial control flared up with particular intensity after Blamey's appointment as C-in-C. As Blamey had been appointed with virtually unlimited powers, some of his staff officers claimed he should have sole fiscal authority, with the right to delegate this to his subordinates. As this would have run directly counter to the British traditions of Treasury control which have never been seriously challenged in Australian public administration, the public servants concerned were not slow to take up the challenge—in particular, F. R. Sinclair, Secretary of the Army Department, who was supported by his Minister, F. M. Forde. After several disputes, Curtin called a meeting at the end of 1942, attended by Blamey, Forde and the Treasurer, J. B. Chifley, which agreed that financial authority should be vested in Sinclair. However, in October 1943, an army staff paper was issued on behalf of Blamey by Lieut-General Wynter, in charge of administration at army HQ, which declared that the army itself should be responsible for internal audit. In a memorandum to Forde, Sinclair observed that corruption and extravagance were inherent in all communities, and it was a delusion to pretend they did not exist in the army. 'I have consistently maintained that there must be independent control, under direct Ministerial authority, to ensure the regularity of the activities of the Army relating to the expenditure of public funds.'[19] Forde reported the incident to Curtin, who ruled that the 1942 agreement must stand.

Treasury control was strongly attacked in a document published a few months after the end of the war under the names of the nine senior officers of the Royal Australian Engineers.[20] Treasury officials, they declared,

---

[17] Hetherington, op. cit., p. 239
[18] Long, *To Benghazi*, p. 41
[19] Hetherington, op. cit., pp. 151-52
[20] Royal Army Engineers, *Some Lessons from the War of 1939-45*, Melbourne, 1945

'seemed unable to understand that in war the question of cost is not paramount.' The dominant factors in war production were manpower and
materials, rather than money. The procurement of stores was unduly
hindered by the need to have military requirements approved 'by a succession of civil and departmental authorities outside the army. These
authorities . . . had the power of veto and delay, and had to be convinced
that the service need existed.' Their decisions were influenced by a distrust
of military officers, so that 'generals who were responsible for the success
of operations involving the safety of the nation were not permitted to
expend money except indirectly.'

It is difficult—nay, impossible—to decide between the antagonists in
this argument. Soldiers are by nature unreasonable in their demands. The
existence of war reflects the unreasonableness of mankind. As if in
response, Treasury officials, and politicians, are inclined to treat the
demands of soldiers with suspicion; their own unreasonableness emerges
when they apply the canons of civilian life to the requirements of men
living under wholly different conditions. As Michael Howard has written:

There are no limits to the demands which the military would make on the
Treasury, if it had the chance, and there is no limit to the grants which
the Treasury could make to the military, if it had the will. In spite of all
the techniques which military analysts may perfect, the great questions of
national security will be settled, at best by rough justice based on calculated
risk, and at worst by weak administrations yielding to the strongest pressure
groups.[21]

Defence Policy Since 1945

After the 1939-45 war, a basic change in defence policy came about
through a move towards a largely professional military establishment. This
movement was inaugurated in 1947, when the Minister for Defence in
the Chifley government, Mr J. J. Dedman, announced the establishment
for the first time in Australian history of a regular army (ARA). The ARA,
to number 19,000 men of all ranks, was the main feature of a five-year defence
plan which included an expanded navy and air force, and a citizen military
force of 50,000.[22] The strength of the ARA has increased only slightly since
then; in 1959 it was 23,800, and by 1965 it had risen to 30,000.

The relative importance of the ARA and the citizen forces has moved
steadily in favour of the former. In 1957, the Prime Minister stated that
the defence program required 'a judicious balance of highly trained regular
forces possessing mobility and power, and adequate reserve forces capable
of rapid expansion in time of emergency.'[23] At this stage, the strength of
the ARA was just over 22,000, and that of the CMF was 89,600. By 1959,
it had been decided to cut the CMF to 30,000, and to integrate CMF units
into the regular army framework instead of maintaining them as separate

21 *Encounter,* September 1962
22 *Commonwealth Parliamentary Debates,* vol. 192, pp. 3335-46
23 *Commonwealth Parliamentary Debates,* 6 Eliz. II, H. of R. 14, p. 574

formations. Integration, according to the Minister for Defence, would create 'flexible, mobile and readily available forces.'[24] In 1959, national service training—the Australian euphemism for conscription—was abolished after eight years of operation, but was hastily reintroduced in 1964 for reasons which were obscure at the time, but became clearer when the federal government decided to send troops to support American action in Vietnam in 1965. The conscript troops or 'national servicemen' were incorporated into regular army formations and the Defence Act was changed to permit them to be sent overseas.

The expansion of the military establishment is limited by the twin facts that defence remains dependent upon the policies of an overwhelmingly powerful ally, and that modern weapons systems are financially beyond the reach of a small country.[25] Dependence means that certain kinds of decisions simply cannot be made; financial restriction means that civilian officials are involved in decision-making at all levels. There is no point, high or low, at which finance does not occupy a prime place in policy-making, and it becomes virtually impossible for the defence chiefs to make decisions on 'purely' military grounds. One curious result is that the traditional clash between civilian and military priorities occurs only faintly and in a narrow field.

The higher defence organisation which has developed since the war clearly reflects the dilemma of a country which is bound to follow the pattern of its powerful allies, and yet faces all kinds of inherent difficulties in doing so. Australia emerged from the 1939-45 war with a Department of Defence and three service departments, on the British model, and various joint committees have grown up within this structure, again on the British model. The most important of these is the Defence Committee, originally set up in 1926. In 1946, the Minister for Defence was given power to appoint a chairman, who is invariably the permanent head of the Defence Department, and to co-opt members. In 1956, the permanent heads of the Treasury, the Prime Minister's Department, and the Department of External Affairs were so co-opted, thereby creating a majority of civilians over the three service chiefs. In 1958, the balance was slightly redressed when the Chiefs of Staff Committee, second only in importance to the Defence Committee, was given an independent chairman who became a member of the Defence Committee. Thus Australia, after a suitable time lag, again followed its two great allies.

The key position of civilian officials is further enhanced by the relative absence of a Cabinet committee structure to parallel the official hierarchy —by contrast with both Britain and the USA. The Council of Defence, a statutory body established in 1904, was virtually replaced in 1952 by a Cabinet committee, the Defence Preparations Committee, and became

---

24 *Sydney Morning Herald*, 25 October 1962
25 The ensuing paragraphs are indebted to B. B. Schaffer, 'Policy and System in Defence: the Australian Case', *World Politics*, vol. 15, no. 2, 1963.

dormant; the Defence Preparations Committee[26] lapsed in its turn in 1958, when the Prime Minister announced that the authority of the Minister of Defence would be strengthened.[27] With the build-up of the Indonesian policy of 'confrontation' towards Malaysia in the early 1960's, the Menzies government found it expedient to set up yet another Cabinet committee, this time combining the functions of defence and foreign affairs.

Australia, like other countries, has found the problem of defence organisation intractable and the history of defence policy and administration has been one of continuous reorganisation and reshuffle in response to successive crises and wars in Korea, Malaya and Vietnam.[28] Each of these reshuffles may reasonably be described as the result of failure to evolve a system of military organisation and administration suited to the problems of Australian external and defence policy in a period of cold war and 'limited' land wars in South and East Asia. These failures are largely the result of political conservatism and incompetence, resulting in blindness to the fact that Australia's relations with South-East Asia in the post-1945 period demand a reorientation of policy and a need to develop institutions relevant to it. Australian defence policy, instead of addressing itself to fundamental questions of this kind, has been based on two considerations designed to avoid such rethinking: the concept of 'forward defence', which assumes that the real defence frontier is on the Asian continent and that Australia should participate in regional defence arrangements in Asia, either by sending troops or adhering to treaties; and the related policy of depending on 'great and powerful friends', which since 1950 has meant the United States.[29] The lack of interest shown by politicians in the subject has been reflected in the lack of interest shown by civilian public servants, so that the committee designed to draw them into decision-making has failed to operate because of their dilettante attitude. Successive governments have also failed to appreciate that a military tradition based on the concept of the nation in arms in response to an emergency makes little sense in a world where crises are unceasing. Canada, whose military problems have affinities with those of Australia, decided in the early 1960's that a 'middle' power must think in terms of relatively small, but compact and highly professional armed services which are fully unified. Whether Canada's policy is correct remains to be seen, but it represents the application of thought and determination which were noticeably lacking in Australia, at least until the Vietnam war produced a major crisis in the role of the armed forces in Australian society.

[26] The work of the Defence Preparations Committee is described in the 29th Report of the Parliamentary Public Accounts Committee, Canberra, 1956.

[27] *Commonwealth Parliamentary Debates*, 1958, 7 Eliz. II, H. of R. 18, pp. 433-37

[28] For discussion of these questions see J. Wilkes (ed.), *Australia's Defence and Foreign Policy*, Sydney, 1964, especially the papers by B. D. Beddie and T. B. Millar; T. B. Millar, *Australia's Defence*, Melbourne, 1965; T. B. Millar, *Australian Foreign Policy*, Melbourne, 1968.

[29] H. G. Gelber, *The Australian-American Alliance*, London, 1968

25: The Officer Corps

In terms of both numbers and influence, citizen soldiers have been predominant in Australian military history. Out of the forty-three senior officers of the Australian corps in France in 1918, twenty-five were citizen soldiers.[1] A similar proportion was to be found during the Second World War, when posts at this level were filled in the approximate ratio of eighty citizen officers to fifty regular officers.

The role of the citizen soldier is epitomised in the career of General Sir John Monash, the only Australian to be recognised outside his own country as an outstanding military leader. Monash's history renders him an archetypal figure, all the more compelling because his victories in peace were as notable as those in war, and because his civilian accomplishments can so readily be linked with his military successes. It is strange that no life of this remarkable and complex man, whose personal idiosyncrasies alone would be a rich quarry for the biographer, has yet been written, although several short accounts are extant.[2]

Monash, the son of a Russian-Jewish immigrant, was educated at Scotch College, Melbourne, where he was dux. He trained as a civil engineer at the University of Melbourne, and later qualified as a lawyer and patent attorney. While a student, he joined the university company of the Victorian Rifles, and in 1908 he was promoted to lieutenant-colonel and placed in command of the Australian Intelligence Corps, a body composed of professional men like himself, which was the precursor of the general staff. He was familiar with both French and German, in which languages he read both military history and engineering literature. As a result, he became familiar with the use of reinforced concrete, and was one of its pioneers in Australia, going into business in 1901 to make monier pipes. He also had an extensive practice as expert witness and arbitrator in litigation involving engineering works. In 1912, he was elected president of the Victorian branch of the Institution of Engineers (Australia). His greatest achievement in civil life was as chairman and general manager of

[1] Monash, *The Australian Victories in France*, p. 323, gives a list comprising divisional commanders, their chief staff officers, and brigade commanders.
[2] Warren Perry, 'General Sir John Monash,' *Proceedings of the Australian Jewish Historical Society*, vol. 4, pt. 6, 1957; J. A. Hetherington, *Sir John Monash*, Melbourne, 1962

the State Electricity Commission of Victoria. His achievements in this capacity were not only technical and administrative, but also political, in a period of chronic political instability which had damaging effects on other public enterprises. In 1924, for example, he made a successful direct appeal to the upper house of the Victorian parliament not to obstruct the passage of a Bill taking over the Melbourne Electric Supply Company and transferring its activities to the SEC.

Monash was also appointed Vice-Chancellor of the University of Melbourne in 1923, an office he retained until his death in 1931, and he became chairman of the Australian Universities' Standing Committee (later the Vice-Chancellors' Committee). In this capacity, he was instrumental in persuading the Commonwealth government to recruit university graduates to the Commonwealth Public Service.[3] His interest in Jewish affairs was manifested by the fact that he became the first president of the Zionist Federation of Australia and New Zealand when it was established in 1926.

This career would, by itself, be sufficient to make Monash one of the leading public figures of his generation. When coupled with the military achievements which led Lloyd George to describe him as 'the most resourceful general in the whole of the British Army', or Liddell Hart to write in his *Times* obituary that Monash 'had the greatest capacity for command in modern war among all those who held command', the combined effect is overwhelming.

The appointment of Monash to command the Australian corps in 1918 was not, of course, entirely to the liking of his regular army comrades. Lloyd George wrote sourly in his memoirs that the greatness of Monash's abilities was not brought to the attention of Cabinet in any dispatches from the front. 'Professional soldiers could hardly be expected to advertise that the greatest strategist in the Army was a civilian when war began.' Monash himself was aware of the crosscurrents of intrigue that eddied about his appointment. In a letter to his family dated 25 June 1918, he refers to 'rumours and intrigues' against himself and Birdwood. 'As the only excuse for getting rid of Birdwood is that they wish to separate the functions of corps commander from those of GOC, AIF, their first problem is to displace me from the corps. In order to bring this about they have started an attempt to attack my capacity to command the corps, and are putting about propaganda that Brudenell White, being a permanent soldier, would be better fitted for this job.'[4] Monash's capacity was questioned, says Bean, because he was suspected of not being physically brave. His 'reputation as a front-line soldier was poor'[5] and he lacked 'the physical audacity that Australian troops were thought to require in their leaders.'[6] He was regarded as a 'showman', who would go to great lengths to impress

3 See chapter 14
4 F. M. Cutlack (ed.), *War Letters of General Monash*, p. 249
5 Bean, *Two Men I Knew*, p. 171
6 Bean, *The AIF in France in 1918,* Official History of the 1914-18 War, vol. 4, 195

his superiors; he had 'an almost Napoleonic skill in transmitting the impression of his capacity.'[7] On the other hand, one of Monash's comrades-in-arms, Major-General Drake-Brockman, gives an admiring portrait of him, citing his analytical ability, his capacity for detail, his readiness to listen to even the most junior officer and his lack of interest in spit-and-polish. 'He looked more like a professor than a soldier; sartorially, in his old and ruckled top-boots, he might have been a lieutenant in charge of transport.' Drake-Brockman also praises the remarkable job done by Monash as director of demobilisation for the AIF; he issued 'a series of masterly instructions [which] supplied an answer to almost every problem that arose.'[8]

The fact that Monash was a Jew gave a special edge to these criticisms. A hint of anti-Semitic prejudice peeps out even from the balanced prose of Bean. 'Major-General Monash was the last man to use, or permit the use of, rough and ready methods of training or of treatment. His Jewish blood gave him an outstanding capacity for tirelessly careful organisation. . . . Questions that others might consider trifling would be included—as to the movements of the YMCA representative and his coffee stall, the provision of a cinema show, or of a special system of inspection of the cooking arrangements.'[9] Bean admits that because Monash was prepared to go to 'any extreme of mental or bodily effort' to achieve efficiency, his staff work was particularly well done, officers and NCO's took special care of the men, and the crime rate in his division was low, but it is obvious that his personality made him an odd man out among his fellow commanders. A historian of the 1914-18 war, Barrie Pitt, says flatly that 'Monash was a Jew—and it is indicative of his ability that despite the prejudice which existed both in military circles and in the Dominion against members of his race, he had risen to the rank he then held.'[10]

Pitt argues that Monash was a successful soldier precisely because he was not a professional. He possessed 'the "Big Business" type of brain which the vast complex of the modern army has made necessary for successful command.'[11] This is an echo of Monash's own words. In a letter from the front to his friend, Dr Felix Meyer, he declared that the only way to command was 'to deal with every task and every situation on the basis of simple business propositions, differing in no way from the problems of civil life, except that they are governed by a special technique. The main thing is always to have a plan; if it is not the best plan, it is at least better than no plan at all.'[12] In his book *The Australian Victories in France in 1918*, Monash described his successes as due to the application of engineering principles, and on this basis he presented the work as a thesis for the

---

[7] ibid., p. 196
[8] G. Drake-Brockman, *The Turning Wheel*, pp. 117, 131
[9] Bean, *The AIF in France in 1917*, Official History of the 1914-18 War, vol. 3, p. 562
[10] Barrie Pitt, *1918—The Last Act*, London, 1962, p. 171
[11] ibid.
[12] *War Letters of General Monash*, p. 245

degree of Doctor of Engineering Science. His tactics, involving the effective use of tanks, aircraft and motor vehicles, were far in advance of contemporary practice, and foreshadowed the 'combined operations' of the 1939-45 war.

The significance of the Australian victories at Hamel and at Mont St Quentin in July and August 1918 was that, together with the Canadian victory at Cambrai, they indicated that the German line could be broken. Hamel was a battle where 'everything went according to programme, the first forecast of the overwhelming victories that were to come in the late summer.'[13] The result was the Allied decision to attack the Hindenburg Line, which was breached in September, although the original policy of waiting until American strength in France had been built up could well have prolonged the war until 1919. In addition, GHQ published a special pamphlet for Allied commanders describing the battle plan at Hamel and the new tactics developed by Monash. The latter, never one to hide his light under a bushel, wrote that the activities of his corps were 'by far the biggest factor in the reversal of the fortunes of the Allies,' and he had 'no doubt at all' that it was the victory of Hamel which encouraged Foch to undertake the counter-blow of 18 July, which pushed the Germans back from the Marne and led to the successful crossing of the Somme and the assault on the Hindenburg Line.[14]

The Regular Army

In short in matters vegetable, animal and mineral,
I am the very model of a modern major-general.

W. S. Gilbert

With the growth of national armies, the officer corps has become one of the most thorough-going attempts to create a deliberately chosen and specially trained elite, with an ethos reaching back beyond the national state to the traditions of aristocracy and chivalry. The professional officer, William Windham wrote in 1760, was 'a class of man set apart from the general mass of the community, trained to particular uses, formed to particular notions, governed by peculiar laws, marked by peculiar distinctions.'[15] Two centuries later, an ex-regular officer found that the purpose of the quasi-moral imperatives instilled into British officer candidates was precisely to convince them that they were members of an elite. 'To all intents they come to resemble a feudal class in their confirmed sense of status.'[16]

In egalitarian communities like those of North America and Australia, such feudal attitudes are unlikely to be tolerated. The necessity for the

---

[13] *Times History of the War*, London, 1919, vol. 20, p. 243
[14] op. cit., p. 274
[15] William Windham, *A Plan of Discipline*, London, 1760
[16] Simon Raven, 'Perish by the Sword', in Hugh Thomas (ed.), *The Establishment*, London, 1959

existence of an officer corps is softened by playing down its separateness and by emphasising the technical content of officer training. Even so, the sense of belonging to something like a feudal estate, in a society suspicious of rank and privilege, is bound to engender strains in the individual. When General Robert E. Lee left the army, he is said to have declared that the greatest mistake of his life had been to take a military education.

Janowitz suggests that the traditional military code has four components —gentlemanly conduct, personal fealty to superior officers, membership of a self-regulating fraternity, and the pursuit of glory. In a democratic society, however, 'it is highly inappropriate for honour to be the sole, or even the dominant, value of the professional military cadre.'[17] Military men are required, rather, to think of themselves as technicians in a technological society. The increasing professionalisation of military life has accentuated the shift from traditional discipline to authority based on 'persuasion, explanation and expertise', especially as the military establishment comes to be staffed more and more by technical specialists. Janowitz estimates that, in the American Civil War, 93·2 per cent of US army officers had 'purely' military occupations; this proportion had fallen to 28·8 per cent after the Korean war, and was lower still in the navy and air force.

In Australia, as in America, the social role of the officer corps is anomalous. Regular soldiers, complains Hetherington, 'were treated by their Government and by the Australian public as more or less of an unnecessary evil.'[18] Even citizen service has never been exactly popular. 'An Australian who made the militia a hobby was likely to be regarded by his acquaintances as a peculiar fellow with an eccentric taste for uniforms and the exercise of petty authority.'[19] The social problem is accentuated by the small size of the military establishment and the unimportance of Australia as a military power, which means that the exercise of professional skills is severely hampered. For most regular officers, the common form of employment between the wars was that of area commandant in charge of a drill hall, an activity which was hardly calculated to stimulate imagination or flexibility of outlook. The unattractiveness of the profession was accentuated by its low pay. In 1938, the maximum salary paid to a lieutenant-colonel was £779; the comparable maximum for an official of the Commonwealth Public Service would have been £912, and for a British lieutenant-colonel, £1,204. Both the civilian official and the British officer were also entitled to much more generous superannuation. (Since 1945, both pay and superannuation have been assimilated more closely to CPS conditions.)

The professional military model embraces features such as early recruitment, the specialised training of cadets in a separate college, careful career

[17] Morris Janowitz, *The Professional Soldier*, New York, 1960, p. 225
[18] John Hetherington, *Australians—Nine Profiles*, Melbourne, 1963, p. 4
[19] Long, *To Benghazi*, pp. 11-12

planning, and post-graduate work in a staff college. Normal as these are in the military profession, they are unusual in Australia, especially when compared with civilian branches of public employment. The career of a military or naval officer is more 'professional' in character than the typical public service career, where there is much less emphasis on all-round training and varied experience. The Australian military pattern has been deliberately created on the basis of a general professional model, whose applicability to the Australian defence situation is open to doubt. This is manifested also on the administrative side of military duties. The ideal regular officer is an administrative 'generalist', a notion which has never been popular in the public services, where advancement, when it does not depend on seniority, is usually tied to specialised skill in some particular sphere. The whole process of advancement in the army is rigidly controlled and maintained on a strict hierarchical pattern, by which the officer is consciously prepared through education and experience for promotion to a rank at least two levels above that which he currently holds. The military rule (laid down in the Defence Act) that promotion to major and lieutenant-colonel depends upon courses of instruction and the passing of examinations would be inconceivable in the public services. This fact, and the predominance of Royal Military College graduates conscious of their role as a *corps d'élite*, make the officer corps approximate much more closely to the administrative class of the British civil service than to the Commonwealth Public Service. The Australian system, concludes Schaffer, is seeking 'an image which is inherently paradoxical and especially difficult for Australia to meet. . . . We have had here a continual effort to introduce an overseas model which does not fit easily into Australia and has not so far found normal times in which to operate.'[20]

The heart of the officer corps is the Royal Military College at Duntroon, in the Australian Capital Territory.[21] Until the opening of the RMC in 1911, appointments to the permanent forces were made either from Australians who had gained commissions in the British army, or on the basis of examinations held at irregular intervals when vacancies arose. Although recommendations for the establishment of a college had been made on several occasions since the 1880's, it was Kitchener's report of 1910 which led to its foundation. Bridges, then a colonel, was instructed to investigate training methods in England, the United States and Canada, and on his return to Australia was appointed first commandant with the rank of brigadier-general. Kitchener's report had advocated an institution along the lines of West Point, and Bridges' report was in the same vein, especially as regards discipline and the teaching of civil subjects.[22] A three-year course was prescribed, and the college was officially opened at the end of June 1911. Out of 110 eligible candidates, forty-two were admitted,

[20] B. B. Schaffer, 'Policy and System in Defence', *World Politics*, vol. 15, no. 2, 1963
[21] J. E. Lee, *Duntroon*, Canberra, 1952
[22] ibid., pp. 195-201

including ten from New Zealand, which supported the RMC from its inception and has regularly accounted for a proportion of the cadets. The first class had not yet graduated when war broke out, and they were forthwith commissioned and posted on active service. One hundred and fifty-eight Duntroon graduates served in the 1914-18 war, and forty-two were killed. Between the two world wars, graduates were normally posted for one year to a British Army unit in India or the British Isles. On their return, they were appointed as adjutants or quartermasters to militia units, or as regimental officers with units of the permanent forces. At the outbreak of war in 1939, there were 233 on the active list out of 406 graduates. Of the rest, sixty-four had resigned or become reserve officers, fifty-eight had died, twenty-seven had transferred to the British or Indian armies, and twenty-four had joined the RAAF.[23]

The importance of Duntroon as a source of officers has been muted by the traditional preponderance of citizen forces in the Australian military system, both in peace and in war. There are neither rules nor conventions barring the appointment of militia officers to even the highest ranks. The symbolic case is again that of Monash, who became a corps commander and a full general. Even in the ARA, because of its short history, RMC graduates have provided less than one-third of officers with long service commissions. In 1959, out of a total of 2,284 such officers, 631 had graduated from Duntroon, as compared with 305 who had passed through the Officer Candidate School at Portsea (established in 1951), and the rest from various sources.[24] Ultimately, it is planned that one-half of the entry should be via the RMC.

Parsimonious treatment of the army between the wars contributed to this situation. In 1922, the regular staff corps of 300 (established in 1920) was reduced by seventy-two enforced retirements, and promotion slowed down to a snail's pace. The result was a 'sense of injustice and frustration. . . . Not until 1935 and 1936 had most of the senior Duntroon graduates regained in the peacetime army the substantive rank and the pay they had won in the AIF. A number of their most enterprising members had resigned and had joined the British or Indian armies where they had gained more rapid promotion than those who remained in Australia. Promotion of militia officers had been relatively rapid so that some had risen from the ranks to lieutenant-colonels in ten years, while it had been usual for a staff corps officer, after having spent eight years as a lieutenant, to remain in the rank of captain for ten or perhaps twelve.'[25]

The sense of isolation and unfairness accentuated the solidarity of the senior members of the officer corps and helped to turn them into the 'closed corporation' whose existence was strongly resented by their citizen force comrades during the Second World War. One aspect of the retrenchment of

[23] ibid., p. 181
[24] Schaffer, loc. cit.
[25] Long, op. cit., p. 45

1922 was that entry into the staff corps was reserved for RMC graduates. In 1947, all serving members of the staff corps, except for one lieutenant-general and one major-general, were Duntroon men. In 1961, there were 304 regular officers above the rank of major; 151 were RMC graduates. Of thirty-eight generals and brigadiers, thirty-two were RMC men. The relative advantage of Duntroon graduates at higher levels is also shown by the structure of promotions in the calendar year 1958. All those promoted to the rank of colonel and above were RMC men; at lieutenant-colonel, the proportion was 85 per cent, at major 50 per cent, at captain 49 per cent, and at lieutenant 42 per cent.[26]

The starvation of the regular army between the wars meant that on the outbreak of war in 1939 a large number of officers on the active list were citizen officers. When the 'Second AIF' was formed, the Prime Minister, Mr Menzies, announced that commands in the new 6th Division would go to militia officers, an announcement that caused chagrin throughout the whole staff corps.[27] Uneasiness in the relation between regular and citizen generals persisted during the war. A notable instance was that of Lieut-General Gordon Bennett, one of the most senior citizen officers, who was known as an inveterate hater of 'blimps'. His definition of a blimp was 'more apt to be generous in the width of its ambit than in charity. Generically he rated all regulars as blimps . . . generally speaking, all citizen soldiers were *not* blimps, unless they specifically proved otherwise. He was especially down on British regulars, and his association with Australian regulars in high places were not exactly heartwarming.'[28]

Bennett made himself especially unpopular by writing a series of newspaper articles on defence in 1937, where he asserted that 'experience has proved that citizen officers can handle our citizen army more efficiently than permanent officers. Our permanent officers are trained as staff officers and not as active soldiers.' When the series was suspended because the Military Board forbade Bennett to write for the press, Bennett wrote to a friend that the regular officers on the Board regarded it as 'sacrilege' for a citizen soldier to criticise defence policy, and added: 'The Military Board, which had never forgiven me for my promotion . . . and which could not abide any criticism from a civilian . . . now turned on me the full force of its fury.'[29]

Another citizen soldier, Drake-Brockman, expresses the same scepticism about the abilities of regular soldiers. In peacetime, he writes, 'regular soldiers have to undergo years of boresome routine, probably with only half a job, and often enough in a limited circle of military social snobbery. . . . When war breaks out again [they] become senior staff officers and generals. Many of them will have grown old without ever having had real

[26] Schaffer, loc. cit.
[27] Long, op. cit., p. 45
[28] Obituary in the *Bulletin*, 11 August 1962
[29] Frank Legg, *The Gordon Bennett Story*, Sydney, 1965, p. 153

authority or responsibility, and without adequate training for top-level planning.' By contrast, he argues, citizen officers have a far wider range of experience and contacts, and the isolation of the regular officer should be minimised by better academic training and the opportunity to pursue civilian occupations.[30]

In 1944, the senior regular officers decided that they would prevent the shabby treatment meted out to them after 1918, when many regulars were deprived of the ranks they had gained through wartime promotions and reverted to the ranks they had held before the war, or would have attained by the normal operation of seniority. A special section was established in the Adjutant-General's Department (later in the office of the Military Secretary) to ensure that command postings after the war went to regular officers of the staff corps.

The effects of this determination by the regular officers to assert their position are evident from several sets of figures. To demonstrate trends in senior appointments, I examined the careers of forty senior officers who were on the retired list in 1956. All had served in both world wars, and comprised thirteen lieutenant-generals, nineteen major-generals and eight brigadiers. Eleven of them had been appointed to the permanent forces before the Royal Military College opened in 1911; another twenty-four were Duntroon graduates. This is in marked contrast to another group of forty-eight senior officers who were on the active list in 1956. In this case, details were obtained about thirty-six generals and brigadiers (out of a possible forty-four) and twelve of the twenty most senior colonels. Of this group, no fewer than forty were Duntroon graduates. The relative advantage of Duntroon graduates at higher levels is also shown by the structure of promotions in the calendar year 1958, noted above.[31]

This pattern shows an interesting affinity with the United States, where, as in Australia, the ratio of regular to citizen officers has risen steadily. Before the 1939-45 war, a large majority of general officers came from the National Guard. During the war, however, more than 57 per cent of all commands from division upwards were held by West Point graduates. Eleven army commanders (out of twenty), seven army group commanders (out of nine) and all three supreme commanders had come through West Point. Since the war, although less than 3 per cent of officers commissioned by the US army have come from military schools, about one-half of officers from the rank of major-general upwards have been West Point graduates—in 1950, the number was eighty out of 166.[32]

Other social characteristics of the first generation of senior officers can be demonstrated through a biographical study of the forty retired generals and brigadiers just mentioned. As in the case of the Commonwealth Public

[30] Drake-Brockman, op. cit., pp. 92-94. Drake-Brockman's views may be compared with those of his relative, Major-General J. W. Hackett, in *The Profession of Arms*, London, 1963
[31] Schaffer, loc. cit.
[32] Janowitz, op. cit., pp. 54-60

Service, geographical origin shows a strong bias towards Victoria, where eighteen of the forty were born (and educated); the reasons for the bias are presumably also similar. The importance of Queensland, on the other hand, may be traced to the greater sensitivity of Queenslanders to the 'threat from the north'. The predominance of Victoria is still evident, though less markedly, in the group of forty-eight senior officers on the active list in 1956.

Table 25·1 Birthplace of Senior Officers, 1956

Birthplace	Retired List 1956	Active List 1956
Victoria	18	19
New South Wales	8	14
Queensland	9	4
South Australia	3	2
Other states and territories	1	6
Great Britain	–	1
Other overseas	1	2
	40	48

The Royal Australian Naval College was established in 1913 at Geelong, Victoria, and moved to its chosen site at Jervis Bay, an enclave of Federal territory on the coast of NSW, in the following year. As an economy measure during the depression, it was moved to the Flinders naval depot on the south coast of Victoria in 1930, and did not return to Jervis Bay until 1958. From the start, its curriculum and methods have been modelled closely on the Royal Navy training college at Dartmouth. As with other navies, it is the most 'professional' of the three services, and its officers have, in consequence, largely been drawn from graduates of its own training establishment. The RAAF, on the other hand, possessed no training establishment other than a flying school until the Second World War, and the majority of its senior officers in 1939 had originally been recruited to the Australian Flying Corps of 1915-19, or had served in the Royal Flying Corps. Some had been trained at the RMC, or had entered the RAAF with professional qualifications. The policy in the RAAF (as in the RAF) has always been to appoint a number of officers on short-service commissions, so that there is always a high proportion of young men. Until 1939, many of the permanent officers had been trained at No. 1 Flying Training School, Point Cook, Victoria. It was not until 1946 that the RAAF set up its own college at Point Cook to train new entrants, in addition to its staff college (set up during the 1939-45 war) for advanced training. The expansion of the RAAF during and after the war meant that a number of permanent commissions were given to men who were originally short-service officers. The RAAF College was renamed the RAAF Academy in 1960 and operates under the aegis of the University of Melbourne; its function is now described as training airmen for the 'space age'. They graduate with a B.Sc. degree.

The figures in Table 25·2 are derived from surveys of the senior officers of all three services made at the end of 1956.[33] Table 25·2 shows variations in geographical origin.

Table 25·2 Geographical Origins of Senior Officers, All Services, 1956

Place of Birth	Army	Navy	Air Force	Total
Victoria	19	12	24	55
New South Wales	14	13	10	37
Queensland	4	4	4	12
Western Australia	4	2	2	8
Other Aust.	4	3	3	10
Great Britain	1	3	2	6
Other overseas	2	1	1	4
	48	38	46	132

If we turn now to methods of entry into the officer corps, the preponderance of training college graduates in the army and navy contrasts strongly with the more varied character of the air force. The difference will undoubtedly diminish as the postwar pattern becomes the dominant one in the RAAF.

Table 25·3 Recruitment of Senior Officers, 1956

Method of Entry	Army	Navy	Air Force	Total
1 Direct commission in peacetime	—	5	23	28
2 Training college	40	28	8	76
3 Permanent appointment after war service	7	1	6	14
4 Specialist commission	1	4	9	14
	48	38	46	132

The eight members of the RAAF who passed through training college were Duntroon graduates who had transferred from the army, except for one who had trained in England with the RAF.

If we take education as an indicator of social status, then the navy emerges as the most socially selective of the three services, and the air force as the least. Among our total group of 132, seventy-six were educated at state secondary schools as against fifty-six who attended private schools. In the RAAF, however, the proportions were thirty state school pupils as against sixteen private school pupils; in the navy, eighteen as against twenty; in the army, twenty-eight as against twenty. Fifteen of the naval men, moreover, attended private schools at both the primary and secondary levels. Forty of the fifty-six who were educated at private schools

---

[33] These surveys were carried out by postal questionnaire with the permission and co-operation of the three services. The ranks surveyed were: RAN, commander and above; army, colonel and above; RAAF, group-captain and above. Coverage was virtually complete in the navy and air force, and 75 per cent in the case of the army.

attended schools affiliated with the Headmasters' Conference. As in other cases, the three leading schools in Melbourne stand out. Between them, they accounted for eighteen members of our group—Melbourne Grammar School took seven, Wesley College six, and Scotch College five. A similar pattern may be found among the group of forty retired army officers, twenty-two of whom attended schools belonging to the Headmasters' Conference; eight went to Melbourne Grammar School and Wesley College.

The prominence of Wesley College is related to the personal influence of its long-time headmaster, L. A. Adamson, who held firmly to the British tradition that a public school should produce men who would devote their lives to the service of their country. Accordingly, he provided special coaching for boys wishing to enter the RMC, and five out of the thirty cadets admitted in 1930 were from Wesley. A notable instance of a boy who was influenced by Adamson was Major-General George Vasey, leader of the Australians on the Kokoda Trail in 1942.[34]

School attendance also provides some guidance as to religious affiliation. Seven members of the group received their secondary education at Catholic denominational schools. Even allowing for an equal number of Catholics educated at state schools, we may assume that no more than fifteen of the group were Catholics. Other biographical data suggest that the actual number was less, so the proportion in the total group may be estimated as between 5 per cent and 10 per cent. This figure is in accord with Janowitz's data, which show that 91 per cent of all generals in the US Army between 1898 and 1940 were Protestants. In 1950, the proportions were still similar: among senior officers in the navy, 90 per cent were Protestants, in the army, 89 per cent, and in the air force, 84 per cent.[35]

A study of fathers' occupations reveals a diversity of social origins. The numbers of those who attended independent schools are closely matched by the number of those whose fathers were business or professional men. The predominant group were in 'lower-middle class' occupations, i.e. small business men ('commercial'), schoolteachers and clerks, but they were

Table 25·4 Social Origins of Senior Officers, 1956

Father's Occupation	Army	Navy	Air Force	Total
1 Rural	5	6	6	17
2 Professional	8	12	7	27
3 Schoolteachers	4	3	6	13
4 Business (directors and managers)	6	6	8	20
5 Armed Forces (officers)	9	1	–	10
6 Commercial	8	6	12	26
7 Clerical	6	2	2	10
8 Manual workers	2	2	3	7
9 Other	–	–	2	2
	48	38	46	132

[34] Hetherington, op. cit.; Felix Meyer, *Adamson of Wesley*, Melbourne, 1933
[35] op. cit., ch. 5

closely followed by professional men, company directors and managers and the like.

Perhaps the most interesting feature of the above table is the high proportion of sons of schoolteachers, who make up 10 per cent of the total. If teachers are regarded as a 'professional' category, the combined contribution of the professional and managerial group, including service officers, amounts to just over 50 per cent of the whole. This is again in line with the investigations of Janowitz, who found that 'professional and managerial' groups had consistently made the largest contributions to the US officer corps. In 1950, the proportions were 45 per cent in the army, and 38 per cent in both the navy and air force. Teachers and clergymen were outstanding. The link between the military and teaching professions in Australia was also evident at an early stage. In the first eight years of the Royal Military College, seventeen out of sixty-six entrants were the sons of schoolteachers, and six of clergymen.[36] A number of generals began their careers as teachers, including six of our group of forty retired officers, not to mention the late Field-Marshal Sir Thomas Blamey.

Applicants for admission to Duntroon are required to state their fathers' occupations on their application forms. From 1911 to 1961, 2,088 cadets entered the college. Although the details given on their forms are subject to errors of description, the main tendencies are unmistakable.[37]

Table 25·5 RMC Cadets, 1911-61

Father's Occupation	Cadets	%
Armed services	210	10·06
Government officials	196	9·39
'Managers'	140	6·70
Schoolteachers and school inspectors	118	5·65
Farmers	90	4·31
Clerks	85	4·07
Accountants	73	3·50
Others*	848	40·61
Not stated	328	15·71
	2,088	100·00

*All other occupations given in the RMC records account for less than 5 per cent of the total.

As a social group, the citizen soldiers differ from the regular officers. The following analyses refer to sixty citizen soldiers who attained the ranks of brigadier or above during the 1914-18 war, and to a similar group of eighty during the 1939-45 war. In terms of geographical origin, they were much more evenly divided than the regular soldiers.

36 Bean, *The Story of Anzac*, p. 56
37 A list of occupations entered on application forms was kindly supplied by Major-General C. H. Finlay, former commandant of RMC.

Table 25·6 Birthplace of Citizen Soldiers

Place of Birth	1914-18 group	1939-45 group
New South Wales	20	30
Victoria	18	29
Queensland	7	4
South Australia	2	4
Western Australia	4	6
Tasmania	2	3
Great Britain	7	4
	60	80

Educationally, the 1939-45 group varied from its predecessor. There was a rise in the proportion of those who attended state schools (from 25 per cent to 40 per cent), but this may reflect the expansion of state secondary schools rather than any general 'democratisation' of education. In each case, there was a group of private schools which contributed a relatively large share. In the earlier group, out of twenty-four who attended sixteen schools belonging to the Headmasters' Conference, twelve went to four schools—Melbourne Grammar, Sydney Grammar, Scotch College (Melbourne), and Brisbane Grammar. In the 1939-45 group, twenty-nine former pupils of seventeen Headmasters' Conference schools were included; of these, fifteen attended a group of five schools—Melbourne Grammar, Sydney CEGS ('Shore'), Sydney Grammar, the Hale School (Perth) and St Peter's College. There was also an appreciable rise in the number of those with tertiary education. The 1914-18 group contained eleven university graduates and five with other tertiary qualifications; in the later group, there were twenty-one graduates and twenty-seven with other tertiary qualifications.

An analysis of civilian occupations shows a predominance of professional men in both cases. The only striking difference is the sharp fall in the number of those who came from rural occupations, which is related to the importance of the Light Horse brigades in the 1914-18 war. Also, the depression of the 1930's meant that many citizen officers in rural occupations could not afford the time and expense of military operations.

Table 25·7 Civilian Occupations of Senior Officers

Civilian Occupation	1914-18 group	1939-45 group
1 Professional (including teachers)	26	39
2 Business (directors and managers)	14	23
3 Farmers and graziers	14	4
4 Government officials	6	8
5 Other	–	6
	60	80

High military rank frequently goes with family connections, or with prominence in business, politics, public administration and the like.

Australia's most famous pastoral family, the Macarthur-Onslows, have contributed soldiers over several generations. Captain A. A. W. Onslow, RN, married Elizabeth, the granddaughter of John Macarthur, in 1867. His eldest son was Major-General the Hon. J. W. Macarthur-Onslow, who served in India, South Africa and France. A younger son, Brigadier-General G. M. Macarthur-Onslow, was a Light Horse commander at Gallipoli and in the Palestine campaign. Their nephew, Major-General Denzil Macarthur-Onslow, a man of many and varied enterprises, joined the artillery in 1924 at the age of twenty, served in the Middle East during the 1939-45 war, and in 1965 was the most senior citizen officer on the active list. (His younger brother, who served in the RAAF, was killed on active service.)

Another pioneering landed family, the Gellibrands of Tasmania, was represented by Major-General Sir John Gellibrand, a divisional commander in France. His grandfather came to Van Diemen's Land as its first Attorney-General in 1824, and assisted John Batman in the settlement of Port Phillip; his uncle, W. A. Gellibrand, was President of the Legislative Council. The grandson was educated at Sandhurst, where he was first in the entrance examination, first in the final examination and gained almost every prize available.[38] He had a brilliant record also at the Staff College, Camberley, in 1907. After serving as a regular officer in Britain, he returned to farming in Tasmania when his regiment was disbanded under Haldane's reorganisation scheme in 1912, and held militia commands after 1918. A well-known pioneering family of Western Australia was represented by E. A. Drake-Brockman, who commanded a brigade in France in 1918 with the rank of brevet colonel, and was promoted major-general in 1937. Previously, he had been a judge of the Commonwealth Arbitration Court, and was recalled to the Bench as Chief Justice in 1942. His brother, G. Drake-Brockman, an engineer by profession, also became a major-general in the 1939-45 war. A relative, J. W. Hackett, joined the British army and also became a major-general. From another pastoral family in NSW came Major-General Sir Granville Ryrie, who served in South Africa as well as in the 1914-18 war, and had a political career of some note; his son, Colonel A. D. Ryrie, was a regular officer in 1965.

Major-General H. W. Grimwade, who commanded the artillery of the Australian corps in 1918, belonged to a family with extensive interests in the glass, chemical and pharmaceutical industries. Business families were, however, better represented in the Second World War. The Knox family of Melbourne, with interests in insurance and various branches of the electrical and engineering industries, was represented by Brigadier Sir George Knox; the Cullen family, of Sydney, with interests in the Australian Gas Light Co. and in various investment companies, by Brigadier Paul

---

[38] It may be relevant to mention that Douglas Haig failed the Sandhurst entrance examination and was able to enter only through the influence of the Duke of Cambridge.

Cullen; the Playfair family, also of Sydney, and well known in the food industry, by Brigadier Sir Thomas Playfair. The name of Wills, long prominent in the mercantile life of Adelaide, was represented by Brigadier Sir Kenneth Wills. Brigadier R. L. Sandover came of an Anglo-Australian family with mercantile interests in England and in Western Australia. An Englishman by birth, he transferred to the militia from the British Territorial Army in 1936, and served in the second AIF, returning to England after the war. His cousin, A. E. Sandover, was also an officer in the second AIF, and in 1965 was a director of Swan Portland Cement Co. and the West Australian Trustee Executor and Agency Co.

From a well-known legal family in NSW comes Major-General Sir Victor Windeyer, who commanded an infantry battalion at the siege of Tobruk, and was a senior officer of the CMF until he retired in 1957. He gained considerable notoriety as counsel to the Royal Commission on Espionage in 1954, appointed following the defection of the Russian diplomat Vladimir Petrov. He married the daughter of a leading Sydney industrialist, Mr R. J. Vicars, in 1934, and was himself a director of the Colonial Sugar Refining Co. and the MLC Assurance Co. In 1958, he was appointed a Justice of the High Court.

The Armed Services Since 1945

Like all military establishments, the Australian armed services are in a state of flux because of the demands of a vastly different world situation. The profession of arms, or, as Harold Lasswell has called it, the management of violence, is becoming subject to the processes of specialisation and professionalisation which have affected many other occupations. The militarisation of society which has become part of the social pattern of the twentieth century involves a number of changes in the traditional relations between the armed forces and the rest of the community. The institutionalisation of violence, and the growth of elaborate bureaucratic means of managing it, constitute a major modification of the social structure of the capitalist democracies of which Australia is a representative example. The growth of a professional military establishment means the introduction of new kinds of hierarchical relationships, which are not part of the traditional social structure, and have often been regarded as alien or repellent.

In consequence, much of the analysis already presented relates to a period which is passing. The military establishment of the 1970's will differ considerably from that of the 1950's and 1960's, although it will continue to operate within the framework set by history, and in particular the strong public feeling in favour of voluntary enlistment and voluntary service.[39] The move towards professionalism, already noted, will continue. It will be influenced by the fact that officers with war experience are now to be found in the permanent forces rather than the citizen forces. The succession of

[39] Examples of public attitudes to conscription and the use of conscripts in Vietnam are cited in R. K. Forward and Bob Reece (eds.), *Conscription in Australia*.

two world wars and the lack of employment of professional soldiers between them meant that a high proportion of senior officers in 1939-45 were citizen soldiers with experience in the 1914-18 war. By 1965, most of the experienced senior officers in the citizen forces had retired, and there was a growing number of regular officers who had followed up their experience in the 1939-45 war with service in Korea, Malaya and Vietnam. In 1967, the Military Board took an important step towards greater professionalism by giving the RMC full academic status. Under an agreement concluded with the University of New South Wales, the RMC's teaching activities were reorganised to provide for degrees of B.A.(Mil.) and B.SC.(Mil.) to be awarded under the supervision of the University. The army thus followed in the path already established by the RAAF in 1960.

26: Cincinnatus at Home

We have already noted the relatively large number of regular soldiers who were sons of schoolteachers, as well as those who were teachers before they joined the permanent forces. Apart from the obvious affinity between the disciplinary aspects of schooling and the relation between an officer and his men, certain social influences have conspired to make the link much stronger. In the First World War, particularly, the necessity to recruit a large number of officers in a short time placed a premium on school-teachers, with their relatively high educational standard and their experience of shepherding large groups of turbulent youths. Many of the successful citizen officers of both world wars had been schoolteachers in civilian life. In the period between the wars, many of them were prominent in the militia. School holidays provided opportunities for training, and the Education Departments of the state governments were normally well disposed to make special arrangements for leave where this was necessary. The link was further strengthened by returned soldier preference (discussed below), which operates in connection with both recruitment and pro-motion. An opportunity for continued practice of certain military skills was provided, furthermore, by the importance attached by the army authorities to the existence of school cadet corps, many of which were conducted by staff teachers who were citizen officers. Biographical evidence suggests that most of the regular officers in our surveys who were sons of schoolteachers had fathers who were active in the militia, and that this is an important source of hereditary influence.

A few outstanding cases may be quoted to illustrate the connection between military rank and the administration of education. Perhaps the leading instance is that of Major-General Sir Alan Ramsay, Director of Education in Victoria from 1948 to 1960, and subsequently chairman of two committees of inquiry on education, who was an officer in both world wars. Another ex-soldier who became Director of Education in South Australia was Mr Evan Mander-Jones. Lieut-General Sir Iven Mackay, also an officer in both wars, was headmaster of Cranbrook, one of the best-known private schools in Sydney, from 1933 to 1940. Major-General Ivan Dougherty, director of civil defence in NSW since 1955, was previously an inspector in the NSW Education Department, and became Deputy Chancellor of Sydney University in 1958. Major W. H. Ellwood, who had a distinguished record in the 1914-18 war, was chief inspector of primary schools in Victoria and became first chairman of the Victorian Teachers' Tribunal in 1946. Brigadier W. E. Cremor, an artilleryman in both world wars, was a teacher in the Victorian Education Department and became government representative on the Teachers' Tribunal in 1949. Brigadier G. F. Langley, a Light Horse commander in the first AIF and an infantryman in the second AIF, was headmaster of various state high schools in Victoria from 1920 until he retired in 1955. A soldier whose influence on his sons seems to have been profound was Brigadier-General Sir Walter McNicoll, who was a teacher in the Victorian state service until 1914, and headmaster of Presbyterian Ladies' College, Goulburn, from 1921 to 1931. One son entered the navy and one the army; at the end of 1965, one was Chief of the Naval Staff and the other a major-general. (The third son became a well-known journalist in Sydney.)

The prominence of ex-servicemen and citizen soldiers in the teaching profession could hardly fail to act as an influence on education. It is to be found, for example, in the role of state as well as private schools in propagating the military virtues, and in helping to encourage a generally authoritarian pattern of relationships, both within the school and within the departmental system. Anzac Day is an important ceremonial occasion in all schools, and the presence of staff members in uniform helps to provide an appropriate atmosphere for extolling the value of patriotism, loyalty and order,

... the precepts which taught
the heroes of old to be hardy and bold,
and the men who at Marathon fought.[1]

Sir Brudenell White was a soldier who considered it his public duty to deplore, like Aristophanes, the unfortunate contrast between the generations of war and of peace. In a speech to the Fathers' Association in 1920, he regretted that Australians were not maintaining the character of the fine stock they came from, but eating, drinking and playing too much. In an address at Ararat, Victoria, in 1931, he declared that democracy could only function if men learnt the need for 'service, sacrifice, fellowship and unselfishness.'[2] Twenty years later, one of the prominent signatories of the *Call to the Nation*, a document appealing for the revival of similar virtues, was Lieut-General Sir Edmund Herring, an officer in both world wars who was appointed Chief Justice of the Supreme Court of Victoria in 1944.

Military service has affinities, not only with education, but even more obviously with police work. Soldiers have played their part in the Australian police forces. Although the numbers are not large (six out of thirty-three police commissioners appointed since 1901)[3] their influence has been

---

[1] Aristophanes, *The Clouds*
[2] Bean, *Two Men I Knew*, pp. 185, 226
[3] R. W. Whitrod, 'Thoughts on a Police Administrative Grade', *Public Administration*, vol. 19, no. 2, 1960

considerable. In particular, military men have been appointed to head police forces at critical periods, when reorganisation was necessary because of low morale, corruption or the absence of suitable officers for promotion from within. Three such appointments followed one another in rapid succession in Victoria, where the police force had notoriously failed to improve its standards since a royal commission in 1880, appointed after the capture of the Kelly gang of bushrangers, made scathing comments on police capacity, morale and organisation. In 1919, Lieut-Colonel Sir George Steward was appointed to 'clean up' the force, but died in the following year. He was replaced by Major-General Gellibrand, who left the post of Public Service Commissioner in Tasmania to accept the assignment, but resigned in 1922 because a parsimonious government refused to appoint 200 extra men required to bring the force up to strength.[4] The disastrous police strike of 1923 followed. In 1925 a new government, on the advice of the Chief of the General Staff, Sir Harry Chauvel, appointed Blamey at the then unprecedented salary of £1,500.[5] Blamey's career as commissioner, which was punctuated by a variety of incidents, lasted until 1936, when he resigned after a scandal involving a senior police officer.

In 1954, the Victorian government again appointed a citizen soldier, Major-General S. H. Porter, as commissioner. Porter's term of office was marked by some notable measures to modernise and improve police work, such as the institution of a seven-month training course for commissioned police officers, modelled on the British police training college at Ryton.

The only other state with a record of military appointments is South Australia. Brigadier-General Sir Raymond Leane, of a noted military family, was commissioner from 1920 to 1944, after a business career. In 1957 another 'outsider', Brigadier J. G. McKinna, an engineer by profession, was appointed commissioner after a brief period as deputy commissioner. In Queensland, after some military appointments, a policy of selecting from the ranks was established in 1921, but was broken between 1934 and 1949 when C. J. Carroll, a former schoolteacher and captain in the AIF, served as commissioner. The longest tenure on record was that of Colonel J. E. Lord, who served as Tasmanian commissioner from 1906 to 1940.

Soldiers have also figured in a number of other public capacities. Some held diplomatic posts, like Sir William Glasgow and Sir Granville Ryrie, both citizen soldiers of the 1914-18 war. The former was High Commissioner to Canada from 1940 to 1945, and the latter High Commissioner in London from 1927 to 1932. Sir Iven Mackay was High Commissioner in India from 1944 to 1948. Three regular soldiers of the 1939-45 war also served as diplomats—Lieut-General E. K. Smart, Consul-General in the US from 1946 to 1954; Major-General L. E. Beavis, High Commissioner to Pakistan from 1952 to 1954; Sir Walter Cawthorn,

[4] G. M. O'Brien, *The Australian Police Forces*, Sydney, 1961, p. 64
[5] John Hetherington, *Blamey*, ch. 6

High Commissioner to Pakistan and then to Canada. Other citizen soldiers holding public positions of importance were Brigadier Warren McDonald, an engineer and director of construction companies, who was appointed a member of the Australian National Airlines Commission in 1952, was its chairman from 1957 to 1959, and became chairman of the Commonwealth Banking Corporation in 1959; Major-General R. J. H. Risson, chairman of the Melbourne and Metropolitan Tramways Board; Brigadier J. Field, general superintendent at the Yallourn works of the Victorian State Electricity Commission; Brigadier-General Sir Walter McNicoll, Administrator of the mandated territory of New Guinea from 1934 to 1941. Brigadier Sir Donald Cleland, a lawyer by profession, was director of the Federal secretariat of the Liberal Party from 1945 to 1951. During the war, he had been an officer of the military administration of Papua-New Guinea, and in 1953 he became Administrator of the territory. Major-General J. R. Stevenson became Clerk of the NSW Parliament in 1954. Brigadier D. D. Paine was chairman of the Public Service Board of Victoria from 1944 to 1957.

An important factor contributing to the relative prominence of ex-soldiers in public administration has been the operation of preference for ex-servicemen in government employment. Although preference is supposd to operate in all spheres, it has always played a much greater part in public than in private spheres. The Commonwealth Public Service Act was amended in 1915 to provide that war service would count towards length of employment in the CPS, and entrance examinations were suspended. This soon caused serious problems, and the government finally agreed to resume examinations, but giving absolute preference to any returned soldier who took an examination within a year of discharge. In 1917, the Act was again amended, restricting all examinations to returned soldiers and making a variety of other concessions. Efforts were also made to secure preference in promotion, and this was an item in the platform of the Returned Services National Party. The former Public Service Commissioner, D. C. McLachlan, advised against it, observing tactfully that he believed returned servicemen would not trade on their patriotism, but would 'be ready to stake their future advancement upon their qualifications and capacity . . . under the regular conditions . . . and not by means of undue preference.'[6] The government accepted McLachlan's advice, but in practice the promotion system was heavily loaded in favour of ex-servicemen. By 1927, abuses of the promotion system had become so substantial that the Public Service Board (which was chaired by a general, Brudenell White, and had another military officer, Brigadier J. P. McGlinn, as a member) abolished all internal preference. The Board was then bombarded with letters and deputations from ex-servicemen's organisations.[7]

[6] *Report of the Royal Commission on Public Service Administration*, Melbourne, 1918, pp. 78-79
[7] V. A. Subramaniam, *Promotion in the Commonwealth, N.S.W. and Victorian Public Services*, Ph.D. thesis, Australian National University, 1959, pp. 133-34, 247

In Victoria, the Public Service Act was similarly amended in 1915, and again in 1919 to give preference in promotion as well as recruitment. In practice, the Public Service Commissioner decided to simplify his problems by giving a flat-rate addition of two years' seniority to all returned service-men.[8] Other states, with the exception of Queensland, introduced similar provisions. In NSW, a preference Act of 1919 contained stringent clauses which enabled several successful legal actions against employers.

The situation after the Second World War was rather different. The Commonwealth Public Service Act was amended in 1945, providing that the age limit for ex-service appointments should be fixed at fifty-one years. In 1957, 58 per cent of Commonwealth public servants were ex-service-men, compared with 30 per cent in the work force as a whole.[9]

The influence of preference may be seen in the higher ranks of the public services. In a survey of 120 senior government officials in NSW in 1956, forty-five were ex-soldiers. In Victoria, the proportion was forty out of 100. In the Commonwealth Public Service, the figures are similar. In a survey of 325 senior officials made in 1956, 40 per cent were found to be ex-servicemen. Out of twenty-four permanent heads of Commonwealth departments at the end of 1962, ten were ex-servicemen.

The role of ex-servicemen in the Commonwealth Public Service is marked by some outstanding individual cases. Thus, Sir Brudenell White, after a term as CGS, was chairman of the Public Service Board from 1923 to 1928 after it had been constituted under the new Public Service Act of 1922. Under his chairmanship, the Board recommended sweeping changes in the classification of the service, which were bitterly criticised both by staff unions in the service and by Labor members of the Federal parliament, who regarded White as a leading figure in the 'military caste'. Hostility to the Board on the grounds of military influence was strengthened by the fact that one of White's colleagues was a citizen soldier, Brigadier-General J. P. McGlinn, who had previously been an official of the Post Office.

The only high-ranking regular officer to hold a senior public service appointment after the 1939-45 war was Air-Marshal Sir Richard Williams, Chief of the Air Staff from 1921 to 1938, who was Director-General of Civil Aviation from 1946 to 1955. Several citizen soldiers of high rank, however, have been appointed heads of Commonwealth departments, like Major-General Sir Jack Stevens, who was originally a Post Office technician and served in both world wars. In 1945 he was appointed an assistant commissioner of the Public Service Board, and subsequently headed, successively, the Overseas Telecommunications Commission, the Departments of National Development and Supply and the Atomic Energy Commission. Major-General Sir George Wootten, a Duntroon graduate,

[8] ibid., pp. 264-66
[9] Report of the Committee on Public Service Recruitment (Canberra, 1958), pp. 47-49

left the regular army between the wars and became a solicitor, returning to active service in 1939. In 1945 he became chairman of the Repatriation Commission, in which capacity he was succeeded in 1958 by another lawyer, Brigadier F. O. Chilton, who had served in various capacities in the Defence Department since the war. Major-General W. D. Refshauge, who was a lieutenant-colonel in the Australian Army Medical Corps, later became Director-General of army medical services and in 1960 was appointed permanent head of the Health Department. Mr A. B. McFarlane, also a lawyer, rose to the rank of Group-Captain in the RAAF, from which he transferred to the Department of Civil Aviation and then to the Department of Air, of which he was appointed secretary in 1956. Mr R. Kingsland, a regular officer of the RAAF, transferred to the Commonwealth Public Service after holding several administrative posts in the air force. In 1963, he became secretary of the Department of the Interior.

The role of ex-soldiers in civilian life, and the workings of preference in particular, are inseparable from the history of the Returned Services League, one of the best-known of all voluntary associations in Australia, and one of the most successful of ex-service organisations anywhere. A former Governor-General, Field-Marshal Sir William Slim, told the 1953 national conference of the RSL that although he had seen ex-service bodies elsewhere, 'I do not think that anywhere have I been has the organisation been so vigorous or played so large a part in the ordinary affairs of the nation as it does in Australia.'[10]

The RSL grew out of separate associations in four states, formed during 1915 and 1916 to assist soldiers invalided home from Egypt and Gallipoli. A national meeting was held in Melbourne in June 1916, but it was not until two years later that the RSL became effectively nation-wide. Its early years were troubled by disputes whether the League should act as a 'pressure group', dealing with specific grievances in relation to the repatriation policy of the Commonwealth government, or set itself up as a political party based on the comradeship of the trenches. A similar conflict took place at about the same time in the American Legion, which was founded in 1919, with the express encouragement of the army high command, as an anti-Communist organisation. 'Anti-Bolshevism', wrote Dixon Wecter, 'was the cement which held the early Legion together'.[11] The cohesiveness based on anti-Communism was soon replaced by the use of the Legion as a machine for gaining benefits from Congress, and its political purpose was reduced to vestiges like the annual motion opposing recognition of the Soviet Union, or the attempt to introduce 'Americanism Day' on the last Friday in April as a counter to May Day. In the case of the RSL, there was a strong move in its early years for entry into politics as a 'non-party' organisation. The problem was solved by a decision that, while the League itself would be 'non-party and non-

[10] Annual Report of the Returned Services League for 1953
[11] Dixon Wecter, *When Johnny Comes Marching Home*, Boston, 1944, p. 429

sectarian',[12] individual members were free to take part in politics wherever 'national' issues were concerned.

The enforcement of this policy by the national governing body of the RSL was only possible after considerable struggles. A number of returned soldier parties were formed in the period 1917-19, with which RSL members were prominently associated. The national executive was responsible for an official memorandum sent to all League branches from the head office of the RSL in May 1918, which attacked 'the curse of the party system', and declared that the time had arrived when the League should become a political organisation with its own parliamentary candidates, pledged to hold the League's platform paramount, but free to support other parties on matters outside the platform. The memorandum also proposed that the League should support candidates of other parties if they were pledged to support the RSL program. Apart from matters directly affecting returned soldiers, the proposed platform contained a few items regularly associated with 'non-party' movements, including proportional representation and elective ministries.

The nature of the political relations between the RSL and the Nationalist government of W. M. Hughes appears to have had great practical significance. In September 1917 the Minister for Repatriation, Senator E. D. Millen, addressed the central council and invited the League to make direct representations to him. He also promised financial help to the League, which was chronically short of funds during its early years.[13] In October 1918, the Minister for Defence issued an order to all Commonwealth departments notifying them that the League was to be recognised as the official representative body of returned soldiers.[14] This was a compromise with the original request to the government, in 1916, that the RSL be granted a charter giving it exclusive rights to the term 'returned soldier.'[15]

The main concern of the RSL since its formation has been to influence policy and administration in regard to the repatriation and re-establishment of returned servicemen, and its success in these aims has been quite remarkable.[16] A repatriation scheme under voluntary auspices was started in 1915. In the following year, an Act was passed establishing the Australian Soldiers' Repatriation Fund, and setting up a board of honorary trustees which, among other things, was given the sole right to the use of the word 'Anzac'. In 1917, after representations both from the trustees and from the RSL, a further Act was passed setting up a Repatriation Department. The Department started operations in April 1918, with a board of seven honorary commissioners under the chairmanship of the

12 G. L. Kristianson, *The Politics of Patriotism*, Canberra, 1966
13 ibid.
14 *Herald*, Melbourne, 23 March 1919
15 *Commonwealth Parliamentary Debates*, vol. 87, p. 8342
16 The early history of repatriation policy is given by Ernest Scott, *Australia During the War*, pp. 828-46; Loftus Hills and Arundel Dene, *The RSSILA*, Melbourne, 1938.

Minister, Senator Millen. This was not to the liking of the RSL, whose views were publicised unremittingly by its president, Senator W. K. Bolton, both in the press and in parliament. Criticising the Repatriation Bill of 1917, Bolton objected to honorary boards and committees because they had 'neither souls to be saved nor bodies to be kicked.'[17] In November 1918, he moved the adjournment of the Senate to ask for a change in the Act by which an executive commission of three would be appointed, one of them to be a representative of the RSL.

Faced with an election at the end of 1919, Hughes finally gave way to RSL pressure, and promised that new legislation would be introduced. In 1920, a Bill was brought down providing for a board of three full-time commissioners and for a Repatriation Board in each State. The Bill did not provide directly for RSL representation, stating merely that 'an organisation representing returned soldiers throughout the Commonwealth may submit to the Minister a list containing the names of not less than three persons . . .' to be considered for appointment. The RSL waged an unrelenting battle on the exact meaning of this clause, and in October 1920 Hughes agreed that the RSL would have one representative on each board of three within the departmental machinery. Similar provision for representation is made in the sections of the Act dealing with the state Repatriation Boards, with the Pensions Entitlement Appeal Tribunals, and so on throughout the system. The relationship between the League and the Repatriation Department (which the RSL always refers to as the 'Commission') has become thoroughly institutionalised. Since 1935, appointment as a member of the Commission has been the natural culmination of the career of the national secretary of the RSL; four successive secretaries have replaced one another in this way. Virtually all employees of the Department are returned soldiers, and until 1947, when personnel management was brought under the control of the Public Service Board, the Commission had complete authority over its own staffing arrangements. Even now, the members of the Commission are not subject to the Public Service Act. As a result, the standard of recruitment to the Department has been significantly lower than in the Commonwealth Public Service as a whole, and its standard of operations was correspondingly low. Ernest Scott commented that most of the early recruits to the department 'had everything to learn about administrative work'.[18]

On grounds of economy and efficiency, there is little justification for the existence of a separate department to deal with ex-service pensions, medical services and the like, which could be dealt with by the Commonwealth Departments of Health and Social Services. In particular, the large hospitals controlled by the Repatriation Department could be used more economically if their facilities became part of the general stock of hospital accommodation. However, as the continued existence of the Repatriation

---

[17] *Commonwealth Parliamentary Debates*, vol. 82, p. 275
[18] Scott, op. cit., p. 834

Department is an obvious vested interest of the RSL, it may be expected to remain for a long time. There can be few cases of what David B. Truman describes as the 'functional attachment' of interest groups to the machinery of government which are as smoothly articulated as this one.[19]

The influence of the RSL on appointments and promotions at the state government level is also considerable. In 1946, the League was instrumental in the establishment of a special agency, the Soldier Settlement Commission, to administer the Victorian state government's side of the joint federal-state scheme of War Service Land Settlement (in other cases this was normally done through the state Lands Department). Throughout the life of the Commission, the RSL has had a major influence on its policy and on staff appointments. Its interest has also extended to other spheres of state administration. Thus, when the Victorian government set up a new Licensing Court in 1954, there were complaints that no returned servicemen had been included in the initial appointments.

The outstanding instance of the ability of the RSL to influence government policy occurred in 1931, when the Commonwealth and state governments agreed on the 'Premiers' Plan' to meet the economic dislocation caused by the world depression. One item of this plan called for a cut in pensions, including war pensions. The federal president of the RSL, Gilbert Dyett, who led the organisation continuously from 1919 to 1946 with great tact and patience, asked for permission to address the Premiers' Conference in opposition to this proposal. As a result, a committee was set up on which various ex-service organisations were represented. The committee produced a scheme involving a significantly smaller reduction in pension rates, which was accepted by the Prime Minister, J. H. Scullin.

It is sometimes argued that the patriotic functions of ex-service organisations are of little importance beside their operations as pressure groups working for the special interests of ex-servicemen. An American writer accuses veterans' organisations of being 'emotional slobs' on the subject of patriotism, which is used to give their other activities an aura of national importance.[20] It would, however, be an error to regard the RSL's activity in this direction as merely a veneer. While its strength depends on its great success as an interest group, it is this very strength which enables it to be taken seriously as the hierophant of the patriotic virtues. The most important symbol of its role is in connection with Anzac Day, whose celebration as a distinctive national holiday is due largely to the RSL. At its national congress in 1922, the League decided to press for

---

[19] David B. Truman, *The Governmental Process*, New York, 1953, pp. 52-53. The influence of the American Legion on the Veterans' Administration is comparable but is not based on the same kind of formal recognition (Justin Gray, *The Inside Story of the Legion*, New York, 1948). A detailed exposure of health rackets in Repatriation Department hospitals is made by a former medical officer, Dr John Whiting in *Be In It Mate!*, Adelaide, 1970.

[20] W. E. Davies, *Patriotism on Parade*, Cambridge, Mass., 1952, p. 355

the universal observance of the landing on Gallipoli as a day of remembrance, and within six years the necessary legislation had been gazetted by all states and the Commonwealth. In the words of the League's official historian, the Gallipoli landing denoted 'the irresistible entry of Australia among the nations of the world—an entrance welcomed with admiration by other great nations, and sanctified by the lives of those who made the great sacrifice . . . in the evolution and sustaining of a national pride and consciousness, a national day is essential as a crystallising point'.[21]

The public image of Anzac Day became clouded in the years since the Second World War, as it increasingly turned into an occasion for, at the best, conviviality, and at the worst, exhibitions of riotous drunkenness. This problem is not, of course, confined to Australia; in Canada, for instance, a magazine writer suggested a few years ago that membership of the Canadian Legion was regarded by the public as an excuse to drink beer and play bingo, both of which had proved lucrative for Legion branches.[22] Restrictive drinking laws in most Australian states have similarly encouraged the growth of licensed clubs, of which the largest single number are operated by RSL sub-branches. The social norms represented by the RSL have increasingly been the object of criticism, for instance by the satirical stage comedian Barry Humphries, in Sumner Locke-Elliot's play, *Rusty Bugles*, and in Alan Seymour's play, *The One Day of the Year*. In the latter work, the pretence and the actuality of Anzac Day observance are laid bare, and given an extra dramatic turn by linking them to the conflict of generations within a family. The climax of the play comes in the third act, when the father, Alf Cook, tells his son Hugh, whose life as a student is rapidly alienating him from his parents, that Anzac Day gives 'the ordinary bloke a right to feel a bit proud of himself for once'. The son retorts that all he ever saw, year after year, when his father dragged him through the crowds on Anzac Day, was 'a screaming tribe of great, stupid, drunken no-hopers', and gives a derisive imitation of a platform orator delivering the traditional speech about Anzac Day as the occasion on which Australian reached national maturity. The playwright has shown, among other things, that the vainglory attached to this notion can be made to look ridiculous by self-parody, simply by using the same words with a satiric edge. His moral seems to be that Australia is an unimportant country which has contributed little or nothing of a distinctive character to the world, and that Anzac Day is a spurious occasion because it is based on a spurious notion of Australia's real place in the scheme of things.

Seymour's moral reflects a mood widespread in Australian literature of the last twenty years—most poignantly, perhaps, in the poetry of A. D. Hope. This mood represents the challenge of a sophisticated urban intelligentsia to the values symbolised by the RSL, which belong to a provincial, small-town culture.

[21] Loftus Hills, op. cit., p. 57
[22] *Maclean's Magazine*, 15 February 1958

Like other ex-servicemen's organisations throughout the world, the RSL's politics are intensely conservative. As Alfred Vagts observes, the majority of ex-servicemen are unwilling to join organisations, and those who do are the more conservative ones. Like generals, their outlook is coloured by memories of the last war, and their influence on military thinking, if any, is backward-looking.[23] The late President Kennedy once remarked of the American Legion that they had not had a new idea since 1919. The RSL has been a principal agency in keeping alive the concept of the British Empire long after it had effectively disintegrated. It was not until 1965 that the word 'Imperial' was dropped from its full title (Returned Sailors, Soldiers and Airmen's Imperial League of Australia), and it became the Returned Services League. Its political posture is marked by recurrent acts of strident 'patriotism'. In 1962, the South Australian branch of the RSL persuaded the state government that the teaching service was honeycombed with Communists who were subverting youth. The government carried out an inquiry, discovered that a few teachers were Communists, but no evidence of subversion. Nothing daunted, the state president of the League, Brigadier T. C. Eastick, accused the federal government of 'ineptitude' in dealing with communism.[24] Again like other ex-service organisations, the League is highly sensitive to criticism. In August 1963, the Australian Broadcasting Commission's weekly TV program 'Four Corners' broadcast a discussion about the RSL in which a few critical remarks were uttered, although the major speaker was the deputy federal president of the League, Sir Raymond Huish. As a result, there was a public outcry from the RSL about an unfair presentation, and the ABC bowed before the storm by removing some of the responsible production staff from the program.[25] The reintroduction of conscription in 1964, and the sending of conscripts to Vietnam, led the RSL to exert pressure on the ABC and the newspapers not to use these terms but to substitute 'national service' and 'national servicemen'. In 1968, the executive of the NSW branch of the RSL, headed by the outstanding fire-eater among the League's spokesmen, Sir William Yeo, expelled two of its members for association with an anti-war movement. The action was probably *ultra vires*, and was acutely embarrassing to the national executive, which has been trying for some years to alter the 'image' of the RSL.[26] After considerable pressure from the national leadership, the NSW branch agreed to lift the suspensions. Sir William Yeo was again in the news in 1968 when he told the state congress of the RSL that Australia should not be required to defend a multi-racial Commonwealth composed of 'wogs, bogs, logs and dogs'.

The RSL represents the major channel for the political activities of

[23] Vagts, *A History of Militarism*, pp. 355-59
[24] *Age*, Melbourne, 30 October 1964
[25] The incident is discussed by G. L. Kristianson and P. B. Westerway in the *Australian Quarterly*, vol. 36, nos. 1 and 2, 1964.
[26] The RSL's federal president, Sir Arthur Lee, discusses the search for a new image in an interview published in the *Australian*, 4 August 1965.

ex-servicemen, although occasionally it has taken more direct forms, as in the violent clashes between ex-servicemen and trade unionists in Brisbane in 1918-19, and similar disturbances in Sydney at the same period.[27] During the police strike in Melbourne in 1923, many special constables were sworn in to keep the peace, most of them ex-servicemen. The strike was accompanied by considerable looting, hooliganism and damage to property, which caused dismay among the wealthier sections of the community, and led to the formation of a secret association, the White Guard, dedicated to the preservation of law and order. Its leader was Sir Brudenell White, from whom the name of the organisation was derived. More notable, and much more far-reaching in its impact, was the 'New Guard', formed in the depths of the depression in 1931 as a counter to the policies of the Lang Labor government in NSW. The doings of the New Guard constitute the only real parallel in Australian history to the activities of the right-wing, proto-Fascist organisations of ex-soldiers in the troubled Europe of the 1920's and 30's.[28]

Lang's policy speeches during the state election campaign, and his victory at the election in November 1930, greatly alarmed the owners of property. Lang and his supporters were calling for the repudiation of overseas debts, the nationalisation of the banks, the abolition of the gold standard, and for other measures which sounded like Red revolution, especially when Lang's lieutenant, J. S. Garden, declared that 'Lang is greater than Lenin!' Soon after Lang had become Premier, some leading ex-servicemen organised a body for the defence of property, which was known simply as 'the Movement'. Its treasurer, Philip Goldfinch, was general manager of the Colonial Sugar Refining Company. The 'Movement' was supported by 'respectable' people, and its aims were restricted to the provision of an auxiliary police force. As the economic situation grew worse, and Lang's speeches became more extreme, an organisation with more extensive aims —the New Guard—was formed at a meeting at the Imperial Service Club, Sydney, in February 1931. Its leader was Lieut-Colonel Eric Campbell, a solicitor and company director. Although Campbell attended a conference called by the 'Movement' in March, he soon broke away from it and in July 1931 he publicly announced that the New Guard was in existence. The New Guard was markedly less 'respectable' than its parent movement, and so were its activities, which included the use of physical violence for breaking up Labor and Communist political meetings and demonstrations of the unemployed. Like other para-military bodies, the Guard imitated military forms of organisation and was divided into zones and special corps, including a 'shock brigade' and an engineering corps. It was apparently well-informed about official arms stores in NSW, and encouraged

[27] D. W. Rawson, 'Violence in Australian Politics', *Dissent*, Melbourne, autumn 1968
[28] The story of the New Guard is told by its leader, Eric Campbell, in *The Rallying Point*, Melbourne, 1965. A critical version of its doings is given by J. R. H. James in *Nation*, 11 March 1961 and in a lengthy review of Campbell's book in *Nation*, 2 October 1965.

its members to buy arms and ammunition. A record number of pistol licences was in force in NSW in 1932. At the height of its activity, the Guard claimed to have 100,000 members. Its general meetings were crowded, and its sympathies were underlined by the Fascist salute given by all members when Campbell entered the gathering.

In February 1932, Campbell was indicted—for vagrancy, and for insulting language about the Premier. He was convicted, but the conviction was later quashed. A few weeks later, on 19 March, the most celebrated incident connected with the Guard took place at the official opening of the Sydney Harbour Bridge. Before Lang could cut the ceremonial ribbon, a leading Guardsman, F. E. de Groot, rode up on horseback and slashed the ribbon with a sword. De Groot was taken to the Reception House for mentally deranged persons, and charged with being insane. After the charge was dismissed by a magistrate, he was convicted and fined for offensive behaviour.

The dismissal of Lang by the Governor, Sir Philip Game, on 13 May, and the subsequent election victory by the conservative United Australia Party, removed the Guard's *raison d'etre*, only a few days after the police had prepared charges against seven of the Guard's leaders following a raid on its offices which was prompted by an assault on J. S. Garden in his home. The presence of a UAP government deflected the interests of the men of property who had supported the Guard and the 'Movement', although the Guard continued to exist until 1934. During the election campaign, it carried out propaganda for the UAP, and in October 1932 Campbell declared that this was the Guard's main purpose. In 1933, he went for a trip to Europe, where he met Sir Oswald Mosley. His last political activity was to stand as a 'Centre' candidate for the state election of 1935.

A recent commentator, J. R. James, concludes that the Guard was prepared to use force to prevent socialism, and that their ability to do so on the orders of a private council constituted the real danger. 'Any private military body in a democracy is liable to destroy the delicate public trust in law so essential to our way of life.'[29]

A number of high-ranking officers have been active in politics in a more orthodox way, generally in the interests of conservative parties.[30] Most of them were citizen soldiers, but a few were retired permanent officers. Blamey was an unsuccessful candidate for electoral endorsement in 1937; Air Vice-Marshal Bostock (see above, Chapter 24) was a Liberal MP from 1949 to 1958; Air-Marshal Sir George Jones, a unique case, was an unsuccessful ALP candidate in the federal election of 1961. Among senior officers (Generals, Flag Officers, Air Officers) twelve were members of the federal Parliament between 1901 and 1961; six of state parliaments; seven stood unsuccessfully as parliamentary candidates; and three tried unsuccess-

---

29 ibid.
30 John Playford, 'Top Brass in Australian Politics', APSA *News*, vol. 7, no. 1, 1962

fully for party endorsement. Major-General Sir Newton Moore became Premier of Western Australia and later a British MP; three were ministers in federal governments in the 1920's (Sir William Glasgow, Sir Granville Ryrie, Sir Neville Howse); one was briefly Minister for Defence in 1904-5 (Sir James McCay). At the level of brigadier, nine became state MP's, six were Federal members, and six were unsuccessful parliamentary candidates. One of them, G. A. Street, became Minister for Defence, and later Minister for the Army at the outbreak of war; he was killed in an air crash at Canberra in 1940.

Senior officers have, with few exceptions, played no part in the affairs of ex-servicemen's organisations, especially those with political functions like the RSL, whose leadership is drawn almost entirely from junior officers or NCO's. A distinctive outlet for senior officers was provided by the establishment of the Legacy Club in 1925 by Major-General Sir John Gellibrand, who saw it as an indigenous counterpart of the Rotary movement with the special task of caring for the widows and orphans of deceased soldiers. The leading spirit in the Legacy movement for many years was Lieut-General Sir Stanley Savige (d. 1960), who built up its welfare activities to a considerable volume.[31] The work of Legacy and its associated women's auxiliary, 'Torchbearers for Legacy', has become an activity with considerable social *cachet,* and election as an office-bearer is keenly sought after. Thus do the hierarchical patterns of the military life become intertwined with suburban patterns of social status.

[31] The history of Legacy is given in a biography of Savige by I. Russell, *There Goes a Man*, Melbourne, 1962.

Index

Aborigines 54-55, 137-38
Accountants 394
Adams, Francis 49, 81, 186
Adamson, L. A. 160, 458
  see also Wesley College
Adelaide Club 133, 135, 302, 396
Administrative class (British civil
  service) 263-64
  see also Northcote-Trevelyan Re-
  port
Airline policy 363-64
  see also Ansett Transport
  Industries
Alford, R. R. 44, 182
Allard, G. M. 243, 262
  see also royal commissions
Allingham, J. D. 121
Allison, Sir John 362
American Legion 469
Anderson, John 202
Anglican Church 152-53, 165
Angliss, Sir William 308-10
  see also Vesteys
Ansett, Sir Reginald 364
Ansett Transport Industries 364,
  373
  see also airline policy
Anstey, F. 140, 342, 425
Anti-intellectualism 52-53
Anti-Semitism 132, 140, 307, 342,
  449
Anzac 432, 434, 438, 470
  Day 160, 431, 465, 473
ANZUS 420, 429

Arbitration Commission, Common-
  wealth 60-62, 76, 122, 138, 248-
  50, 271-72
Arbitration, industrial 59-60, 76-77,
  199-200, 245-46, 258-59
Archer, W. 295
Armytage, W. H. G. 144
Arndt, H. W. 333, 346, 362-63
Ashby, Sir Eric 261
Asia 55-56, 420
Associated Chambers of Commerce
  of Australia 355
Associated Chambers of Manufac-
  tures of Australia 288, 348, 352-
  55, 362, 364
Associated Headmistresses of Aus-
  tralia 158, 176
Associated Public Schools 158
Athenaeum Club 132, 134
Australian Agricultural Company,
  294, 310, 313
Australian Broadcasting Commis-
  sion 92, 141, 474
Australian Club 132-34, 302, 396
Australian Consolidated Industries
  329-30, 358
  see also concentration of owner-
  ship, directorships
Australian Council for Educational
  Research 145, 147-48, 150
Australian Council of Employers'
  Federations 355-56
Australian Imperial Forces (AIF)
  438-41, 448-49, 453-54

Australian Industries Development Association 353, 355
Australian Industries Preservation Act 326-27, 341
see also trust-busting
Australian Labor Party 55, 70, 85, 97, 99, 129, 198-201, 206, 217, 225-27, 235-37, 326, 346, 421, 424-25, 428-29, 438
industrial groups 181, 227
see also Chifley, J. B., Curtin, J., Labor movement, political parties, trade unions
Australian Metal Industries Association 355
Australian National University 281, 288
Australian Primary Producers' Union 314
Australian Regular Army (ARA) 444-45, 453
Australian Vice-Chancellors' Committee 263
Australian Wool Board 307, 314-16
Australian Wool Industry Conference 314
Australian Wool & Meat Producers' Federation 314
Australian Woolgrowers & Graziers' Council 314-15, 356
see also Graziers' Federal Council, NSW Graziers' Association
Australian Workers' Union (AWU) 133, 217, 226
Authoritarianism 78-79
in education 143-45
among schoolboys 160-61

Bagehot, Walter 191-92
Baillieu, family 304, 312, 378-84, 391-93, 409
Balogh, T. 370, 374
Baltzell, E. D. 130, 132, 191-92
Bank nationalisation 344-45
Banking 322, 325-28, 343-46

Banton, M. 45
Barber, B. 43, 131-32
Barker, Sir Ernest 220
Barton, Sir Edmund 55-56, 237
Basic wage 50
Bassett, G. W. 148, 150
Bathurst, Lord 152
Baume, M. 415
BAWRA 316
Bean, C. E. W. 161-62, 163-64, 432-33, 436, 449
Beed, C. S. 111, 405-407
Beer, Samuel 192
Bell, D. 43
Bendix, R. 51-52, 123, 276
Bennett, General 454
Bentley, A. F. 201
Bentley, Eric 209
Berdie, R. F. 148
Bergonzi, B. 170-71, 176
Berlin, Isaiah 56
Berry, Graham 133
Bingham, Alfred 24
Birdwood, Lord 439-41, 448
Black, N. 298, 310
Blamey, Sir Thomas 426, 439-43, 459, 466, 476
Blumer, H. H. 45
Boldrewood, Rolf 296, 299
Bolton, G. C. 188
Bott, Elizabeth 28-29
Bourgeoisie 14, 16, 56, 124-25
Boyd, Martin 158, 161, 186-88
Boyer committee 263, 268-71, 273
Braddon, R. 426-27
Brady, R. A. 352, 358
Bridges, General 437-38, 452
Brisbane Grammar School 279, 460
Britain 35, 128, 184-89, 191, 243, 246, 299-300, 337-38, 342, 420-24, 438
Broken Hill Proprietary Company (BHP) 303, 304, 327, 330-31, 383, 401, 404-405
Broom, Leonard 89-92, 100, 115, 121-22

Broughton, Bishop 152
Bruce, Lord 156, 239, 347
Bryce, Lord 81-83, 198, 213
Bulletin, The 55-56, 128, 140, 293, 423
Bureaucracy 8, 21, 57, 58-62, 65-66, 73-74, 78-79, 205-207, 209, 220-21, 244, 247-48, 289
Burnham, James 24
Burns, C. L., 182-83
Burns, J. D. 420-21
Burns, J. M. 172, 220
Bury, Leslie 360
Bushnell, J. A. 332
Butlin, N. G. 62-63, 71
Butterfield, H. 198, 215
Butts, R. F. 145, 151

Cadet corps 160, 464
Caiden, G. E. 246-48, 258, 271
'Call to the Nation' 141, 465
Calwell, A. A. 336
Cambridge University 302, 396, 403
Campbell, Eric 475-76
Campbell, E. W. 327, 391
Canada 49, 59, 124, 190-91, 194, 200, 216, 276, 320, 349, 408, 411-12, 446, 473
  see also Porter, John
Canberra 275, 284, 287-89, 363
Capital 7, 22, 27
Capitalism 7, 22, 62, 318
Carlton and United Breweries Ltd 330, 379
Casey, Lord 300, 427
Catholic Action 181
Catholic priests 170
  religion 167, 169, 177
  schools 146-47, 158, 167, 172-78
  Social Movement 181, 225
Catholics, anti-intellectualism of 53
  class-consciousness of 52, 168, 181-83
  discrimination against 132-33,
168-69, 174-75, 178, 180, 287
  in business 396, 409-10
  in federal parliament 232, 238-39
  in the armed forces 458
  in the farming community 302
  influence on censorship 78
  Irish influence on 166-69
  role in government departments 284-87
  role in the Labor movement 178-79, 181-83
  role in the Liberal Party 223
  social status of 167, 177-78
Censorship 5, 77-78
Centers, R. 93
Centralisation, in education 144-47
Charles, Prince 163-64
Chartism 50-51
Chifley, J. B. 3, 67, 125, 172, 215, 218-20, 240, 344-45, 358, 386, 443
  see also Australian Labor Party, bank nationalisation, Prime Minister
Childe, V. G. 199, 218
Churchill, Winston 422, 438
Citizen soldiers 447, 454-63, 464-65
Civil - military relations 442-46
Civil Service Selection Board 264, 269
Clark, C. M. H. 53-55, 169-70
Class 7-10, 12-15, 27-32
  and education 151-52
  and family 43-44
  and occupation 119-21
  and religion 45, 164-66
  consciousness 14-15, 25, 31, 42; among skilled workers 92-93, 105-106, 120-21; false 25, 37; in Australia 81-84, 86, 88-101
  identification 89-90, 96-101
  lower-middle 20-22
  models 28, 94, 101
  political 16, 210

relation to status and power 31-41

ruling 16

upper 16-19, 86

upper-middle 18, 23

see also Dahrendorf, Gordon, Halbwachs, Lockwood, Marx, Mayer K., middle classes, Prandy, Rose, status, stratification, Svalastoga, working class, Warner, Weber

Clements, R. V. 400-403

Coal Vend case 327, 389

Cockburn, Claud 141

Coghlan, T. A. 55

Cole, G. D. H. 24

Coles, G. J. & Company Ltd 330-31, 350

Collins House group 329, 381, 393-94, 397

Colonial Office 185

Colonial society 188-89, 191

Colonial Sugar Refining Co. Ltd 329-32, 475

Colonialism 56

Commonwealth Bank 343

government 67-69, 275

Public Service 66, 242-48, 258, 260-63, 268-73, 275-81, 467-68

Statistician 116

Communist Manifesto 16

Concentration of ownership 326-32

Conflict 10-11

Congalton, A. A. 54, 91, 118-19

Connell, W. F. 145

Conscription 200, 208, 422, 445, 462, 474

Conseil d'Etat 246

Constant, B. 192

Constructs 29-31

Cook, Joseph 238, 420, 423

Coombs, H. C. 70, 281

Copeman, G. H. 391, 404-405, 408

Corporate schools 153

Corwin, E. S. 74

Cosgrove, Sir Robert 129

Country Party 200, 217, 223, 228, 230, 235-37, 315, 317, 325, 347-48, 421

Cox, O. C. 44-45

Crawford, Sir John 255-56, 281

Crick, B. 201

Crisp, L. F. 218-20, 231, 281, 341, 345

Crown princes 400-403

Crown, the 186, 421

Curtin, John 67, 240, 347, 421-22, 438, 441

Customs Department, censorship activities 77-78

Dahrendorf, Ralf 6, 10, 27

Dalgety-NZL Ltd 310-13

Dalley, J. 198

D'Alton, S. O. 199-202

Dark, Eleanor 208

Davidson, Sir Alfred 359

Davies, A. F. 59, 93-95, 115, 183, 205-207, 214-15, 228, 326

Davis, S. R. 251, 253, 256

Deakin, Alfred 216-17, 239, 326

Defence administration 445-46

Committee 445

policy 423-25, 437, 444-46

Deferential noters 191

De Groot, F. E. 476

Democratic Labor Party 181-83, 429

Denmark 89

Dicey, A. V. 74

Dickens, Charles 106

Dilke, Sir C. 81, 186

Diplomats 131

Directorships, interlocking 329, 390-92, 396-97, 415

Disraeli, B. 234, 239

Dixon, Sir Owen 75

Dogan, M. 44

Douglas-Home, Sir Alec 221

Dowling, R. E. 14-15, 29, 203

Downer, family 144, 159, 232

Drake-Brockman, G. 435, 449, 454-55
Dual system, in education 143, 146
Duffy, Charles Gavan 174-75
Duncan, family 229, 232, 350-51
Dunk, Sir William 271
Dulles, John F. 426-27
Dunstan, Sir Albert 222
Durkheim, E. 116

Ecole Nationale d'Administration 246, 267-68, 366
Economists 72-73, 254-55, 262
Egalitarianism 49, 50, 52-53, 54, 85, 242, 247-48
Eggleston, Sir Frederic 58, 62, 286
Eighteenth Brumaire of Louis Bonaparte 13-14
Eisenhower, President 266-67
Eisenstadt, S. N. 33, 65
Elder Smith Goldsbrough Mort Ltd 310-12, 330, 351
Elites 3-4, 16, 39, 46, 51
Embourgeoisement 92
Engels, F. 6, 16, 19, 37, 135, 432
Engineers 252, 366-69
Equality 6, 56-57, 82
'Establishment', the 140-42
Eton 394, 404-405
Evaluated Participation 12
Evatt, H. V. 75, 217-18, 233, 386
Experts, in the public service 250-54
Ex-servicemen, in education 475, in politics 476-77
    preference in employment 467-69
External Affairs, Department of 279-80

Fadden, Sir Arthur 126, 237, 239, 347-48
Fairbairn, family 232, 304-305, 311
Fairbridge, Kingsley 187
Fairlie, H. 140-41

Family groups
Angas 306, 351
Angliss 308-309
Armytage 305-306
Baillieu 304, 312, 378-84, 409
Barr Smith 303, 311
Blaxland 304
Brookes 389
Brown 389
Burns 389, 400
Carpenter 391-92
Cohen 136
Cohen (Cullen) 136, 461-62
Coles 389, 391
Cox 306
Cuming 384
Dangar 306
Darling 383-84, 391
Downer 141, 154, 227
Drake-Brockman 228, 461
Duncan 224, 227, 350-51
Fairbairn 232, 304-305, 311
Fairfax 306, 387-88
Faithfull 303, 306
Falkiner 306-307
Giblin 306
Gillespie 391-92
Grimwade 329, 389, 461
Gunn 294, 307
Henty 295-96
Hordern 303, 382
Howard Smith 389
Kidman 310
King 304
Knox 388, 391
Lethbridge 304
Lloyd Jones 389
Lysaght 387, 391
Macarthur (Macarthur-Onslow) 304, 310, 461
McBride 311-12, 351
McKay 385-86, 389
Manifold 303
Maple-Brown 303, 306

Michaelis 139, 389, 391
Myer 382
Nicholas 391-92
Officer 311
Playfair 350, 462
Prell 305
Robinson 379, 385, 391
Rymill 229, 350-51
Ryrie 461
Sandover 462
Stewart 329, 383-84
Vicars 383, 391, 462
Were 411
White 293
Willsallen 304
Windeyer 462
York Syme 391-93, 402
Family influence
in business 327, 339, 390-93,
397, 401-404
in politics 227-29
in rural life 304-307, 309-14
Family, relation to social class 43-
44
Farmers 237, 298, 301, 314-15,
317
Fensham, P. J. 150
Finer, S. E. 340, 349
Fisher, Andrew 420
Fitzpatrick, Brian 211-12, 323, 327
Forde, F. M. 443
Forrest, John 420
Fox, F. 193, 211
Frayn, Michael 17
France 65, 71, 246, 263-64, 365-
66, 408
Frederick William, Elector of
Prussia 65
Free enterprise 322-26, 333-34
French, E. L. 153
Froude, J. A. 186
Full employment, policy of 70, 73
Functionalism 11-13
Furphy, Joseph 50

Gair, V. C. 133
Gallipoli 438-39, 472-73
Gallup Poll, Australian 88-89, 119
Game, Sir Philip 343, 476
Garden, J. S. 222, 475-76
GATT 320-21
Geelong Grammar School 153, 154,
155, 160-62, 163-64, 238, 279-
80, 302, 304, 395, 404, 410
Geiger, T. 37, 41
Gellibrand, Sir John 461, 466, 477
General Motors-Holden's 325, 330-
31, 358
General will, the 202-204
German Ideology, The 7, 16, 22
Germany 101
Gerth, H. H. 20, 24
Giblin, L. F. 142, 255, 261, 306
Ginsberg, M. 42
Glass, David 3
Gold standard 342-43
Goldsbrough, R. 311
Gollan, R. A. 185
Gordon, M. M. 36-37
Gorton, J. G. 157, 189, 239, 298,
429
Governing consensus 4, 204
Government, economic intervention
by 319-20, 322-23, 357-59
Governor-General 300, 421
Grammar Schools Act (Queensland)
153
Gramsci, Antonio 4, 60
Grandes Ecoles 267, 365-66
Grands Corps 267-68, 365
Grattan, C. H. 80
Graziers 110-12, 133-34, 227, 229,
238, 298-303, 314-16
Graziers' Federal Council 314, 316
Greater Public Schools 158
Griffin, W. B. 288-89
Group theory, in politics 202-204
Gunn, family 294, 307
Gunn, Sir William 307, 316

Habakkuk, H. J. 43
Haig, Lord 439-41
Halbwachs, M. 25
Hale School, The 153, 156, 157, 302, 460
Hall, A. R. 326-27, 332, 335
Hall-Jones scale 17
Hamel, battle of 450
Hammond, S. B. 87-88, 93
Hancock, Sir Keith 50, 58, 66, 197, 222, 242, 299
Hartshorne, R. 63
Hartz, Louis 50-51, 194
Harvester Judgment 60, 62
Headmasters' Conference of Australia 157, 162, 224, 239, 279, 395, 404, 406, 410, 460
Healey, C. O. 159, 162, 163
Hearn, W. E. 142
Hedderwick Fookes and Alston 392-93
Hempel, C. G. 30, 31
Henty, family 295-96
Herald and Weekly Times Ltd 130
Hetherington, J. A. 439-41, 451
Hiatt, L. R. 137-38
Higgins, H. B. 60, 61, 248-50
High Court of Australia 69, 75, 345
Higher public service 275, 278
Higinbotham, George 207
Hindenburg Line 450
Hofstadter, R. 52-53, 250, 255
Hoggart, R. 185
Holland 408
Hollingshead, A. B. 90-91
Holman, W. A. 105, 204, 216, 217-18
Holt, H. E. 428-29
Hoover Commission (USA) 263, 265-66
Hoover, Herbert 266, 385
Horne, Donald 169, 211, 221
'House party' 269
Howard, M. 430, 444
Hughes, Helen 117

Hughes, W. M. 67, 180, 239-40, 341, 357-58, 422, 423-25, 441, 470-71
Hungerford, T. A. G. 435
Hunter, A. 334
Huntington, S. P. 430-31
Husserl, E. 29

Immigration, from Britain 184, policy 70
Imperial Chemical Industries of Australia and New Zealand 329-31
Imperial Service Club 134, 303, 475
Income distribution 109-11, 114-15, 117
  of businessmen 111-12
  of government officials 113
  of profesional men 112-13
Income, factor 110
Index of Social Position 90
  of Social Rank 90-92
  of Status Characteristics (ISC) 12, 90
Inequality 6, 8, 11, 27, 31, 33, 39, 42, 49, 203
Inglis, K. S. 432, 436
Interest groups 201-206
International Wool Secretariat 281, 307, 315
Irish influence in Australia 169-72, 296
  see also Catholics
Irish, R. A. 362, 372
Irvine, R. F. 142, 262
Isaacs, Sir Isaac 55, 132, 139

Jackson, J. A. 39
Jackeroos 296
Jacobson, Dan 142
James, J. R. H., 475-76
Janowitz, M. 451, 458-59
Japan 353-54, 421-27

Jensen, H. I. 341-42
Jesus College, Cambridge 302, 304-305
Jews 132, 139-40, 409, 410-11, 448-49
Jones, F. L. 91, 121
Jose, A. W. 58-59, 84
Judges 74-76

Kahl, J. A. 28, 191
Karmel, P. H. 323-24, 328-29, 364
Keating, M. S. 110
Kelly, Ned 52
Keynes, Lord 323, 343
Kiddle, Margaret 296
Kidman, Sir Sidney 309-10
King's School 152, 154, 156-57, 238, 302
Kitchener, Lord 437, 452
Knighthoods 125-27
Kolko, G. 114
Korsch, Karl 19

Labor movement 49-50, 55, 198-99, 216, 217-19, 220-22, 315, 341
Labor Party, Aust., *see* Australian Labor Party
Labouchere, Henry 128
Laffin, J. 434, 436
Lafitte, P. 92-93
Lang, J. D. 294
Lang, J. T. 222-23, 342-46, 475-76
Laski, H. J. 65, 252
Lasswell, H. D. 16, 20, 462
Lasswell, T. E. 28-29
La Trobe election survey 88
Lawrence, D. H. 49, 86
Lawson, Henry 49-50, 105, 293
Lawyers 75-76, 111-12, 123, 237, 392-96
Legacy Club 477
Legion of Honour 124
Legislative Council 229

Lenin, V. I. 7, 340
Lenski, G. E. 13-14, 33, 45
Liberal Party 70, 97, 99, 200, 208, 215-16, 217, 223-26, 315, 325-26, 347-51, 428-29
Liddell Hart, B. H. 448
Light Horse 460-61
Lindon, L. H. 302
Lipset, S. M. 51, 54, 59, 189-90, 193-94
Lipson, L. 244
Littlejohn, W. S. 155
Lloyd George, D., 448
Lockwood, D. 21, 25, 26, 37-38, 60-61, 92-93
Lydall, H. F., 114
Lyons, J. A. 67, 233, 239
Lysaght Ltd., John 334, 387

MacArthur, General Douglas 441-42
Macarthur, John 294-95
McBride, Sir Philip 311-12, 351
McCallum, D. M. 78, 431
McCaughey, Sir Samuel 307
McCoy, C. A. 182
McEwen, J. 240, 320-21, 348, 354, 360-61
McFarlane, B. 63, 336
McGlinn, J. P. 467-68
McGregor, C. 77, 92-93
Machajski, V. 8
MacKenzie, J. 86-87
MacKenzie, N. 231
McLachlan, D. C. 243, 247, 249, 258, 260, 286, 467
McLaren, J. 53, 144, 151, 162-63
Macpherson, C. B. 36-37
Macrossan, J. M. 133
Maizels, A. 319-20
Malaysia 427, 446
Man, Henri de 199
Mannix, Archbishop 173, 180-81
Manual workers, role in politics 224-25, 236

Manufacturing Industries' Advisory Council 351, 361-62
Market situation 34, 37
Marshall, A. J. 212-13
Marshall, T. H. 10-11, 14-16, 35-36, 42
Martin, A. W. 227
Martin, Jean 297-98
Marx, Karl 6-7, 9-10, 14, 16, 19, 22, 25, 27, 35-37, 44, 116, 135
Marxism 9-10, 11, 17, 24
Masonic Order 168, 174, 284-87, 342, 413
Massy Greene, W. 349
Mateship 54, 85, 185, 190
Mathews, R. L. 58-59
Matriculation 146-47
Matthew principle 150
Mayer, H. 197, 199
Mayer, K. 8, 12, 80-81, 86, 114
Mechanisation 22-23
Medical profession, in politics 231
  incomes 112-13
  power 122-23
  prestige 119, 125-27, 131
Melbourne 275, 395
  Club 132-34, 302, 396
  Grammar School 153, 155, 238, 279-80, 395, 403-404, 406, 410, 458, 460
Melbourne, Lord 125
Menzies, Sir Robert 5, 125, 156, 162, 177, 189, 214, 217, 220-21, 232, 239, 262, 270, 347-48, 351, 360, 411, 420-21, 428, 439-40, 454
Merleau-Ponty, M. 19-20
Merton, R. K. 150
Metal Trades Employers' Association 353
Methodists 153, 164-66, 168
Métin, A. 54, 56, 200-201
Michels, R. 16, 18, 199, 218
Middle classes 17-23, 82-83, 124-25, 227
Migrants 138-39

Miliband, R. 199, 218
Militarism 419, 423, 429, 430-32
Military administration 442-44
  Board 437, 454, 463
  see also civil-military relations
Miller, J. D. B. 59, 195, 198, 202, 216, 340
Mills, C. Wright 3-4, 16, 21, 24, 46, 130, 140-41, 194, 204, 208, 266, 352, 357, 361, 376
'Ming dynasty' 221
Ministers, education of 238
  selection of 235
Mises, L. von 244
Mitford, Nancy 96, 129
Mobility, social 51, 121-22
Models 28
Moellendorf, W. 23
Mol, J. J. 167, 175, 181
Monash, Sir John 262-63, 431, 434, 439-41, 447-50, 453
Monk, A. 129
Monopoly 322, 327-35, 341
Moran, Cardinal 199
Moran, H. M. 170, 178, 180-81
Morrison, family 154
Mort, T. S. 311-12
Mosca, G 16, 18, 208
Moynihan, D. P. 172
Murdoch, K. 440-41
Murdoch, W. 217
Musil, Robert 141
Myer Emporium Ltd 330-31, 382
Myer, Sidney 139, 382
Myrdal, G. 54, 61

Nagel, E. 29-30
Napoleon 124
National Civic Council 181
National Farmers' Union 314-15
Nationalism 21, 184
New Deal 69, 265
New Guard 344, 432, 475-77
New South Wales 71-72, 223-24, 245, 275-76, 280, 283, 350, 399

New South Wales Graziers' Association 315-16
New Zealand 91, 190, 201, 244, 251, 316, 342
Newton, M. 328, 333, 336-37, 338, 348, 361
Nicholas, Mr Justice 213
Nicklin, G. F. 133
Niemeyer, Sir Otto 343
Nietzsche, Friedrich 6
Northcote-Trevelyan Report 65, 243, 263
Northcott, C. H. 83-84
Northcott, General 426, 439
Norman, Montagu 343

Occupations, classification 117, 119-21
  mobility between 121-22
  prestige of 118-19
  relation to class 116, 119-21
  trends 117-18
Office of Secondary Industry 360-61
O'Malley, K. 280
Order of the British Empire 125, 127
Order of St Michael and St George 128
O'Rell, M. 184
Orwell, George 106, 193
Ossowski, S. 15
Oxford University 187-88, 396

Pacific, strategy in the 420-26, 437-38
Packer, Sir Frank 128
Page, Sir Earle 240, 347-48, 421
Paine, T. 123-24, 142
Palmer, Vance 215
Pareto, V. 9, 16, 18
Parker, R. S. 203, 242, 256, 263, 414
Parkes, Sir Henry 84, 173-74

Parsons, T. 10, 11-12, 44, 190
Parties, policy on immigration 70
  political 197-201, 205-206, 207, 346-48
  selection of parliamentary candidates 223-26
Partridge, P. H. 203-204
Pastoral ascendency 294
Pastoralists 227, 231, 315-16
Patriotism 420-21, 431-32, 472, 474
Pattern variables 190
Peak associations 349, 352
Pearce, Sir George 424, 438, 440
Penrose, E. T. 327
Pfeffer, K. H. 84-85, 132, 168
Philistinism 53, 141, 186
Phillips, A. A. 162
Philp, Sir Robert 342, 389
Pike, R. M. 146, 148-49
Pitt, B. 449
Pitt, William 211
Pius IX 172-73
Playboy 78
Playford, J. 75
Playford, Sir Thomas 221-22, 232, 350
Plutocracy 50, 192
Police 77-78, 465-66
Politicians, occupational background of 227-31
  status of 191, 210-14
Populism 211, 214
Porter, John 49, 190, 194, 276, 408, 411
Post Office 251-52
Post-War Reconstruction, Department of 72-73, 280-81
Potter, Sir Ian 350, 409, 411
Poverty 115
Poverty of Philosophy, The 7, 14
Power 3-5, 7-9, 14, 16, 31-33, 39, 40-42
Power elite 3, 4, 16, 352, 363
Praed, Mrs Campbell 128
Prandy, K. 38

Premiers, state 240-41
Premiers' Plan 472
Presbyterians 153-54, 164-66
Prestige 9, 15, 28, 33, 43
Prime Minister 217-21, 235, 239-40
Pringle, J. D. 86, 168-69, 179, 213, 221, 298-99
Private enterprise 324
Private schools, fees 161-62
    government aid for 162, 173, 177, 179, 183
    religious function 159-60, 163
    training of leaders 158-59
    terminology 146
Privilege 13-14, 15, 52
Professional Engineers' Cases 122, 250, 268, 271
Professional men, in the public service 251-54, 256
    status of 122-23
Professionalism 23-25
Professors, status of 54
Promotion, in the public service 245-46, 253-54
Protection 319-23, 348
Protestant ethic 384, 414
Protestants 164-70, 176, 178, 181
Proudhon, P. J. 44
Public enterprise 63-65, 256-57, 322-24, 333
Public expenditure 63-64
Public interest, the 203-205
Public rank 43, 46
Public servants 71-74
    as advisers 362
    ex-servicemen 468-69
    in politics 73
    in private industry 366-75
Public service, recruitment to 259-63, 268-70, 277-78
Public Service Board 247, 254, 258-59, 262-63, 268-73, 467-68
Public Service Clerical Association 262, 270, 286-87
Purple Heart 124

Quanta Cura 172
Queensland 133-34, 301, 342-43, 456
    Club 133-34, 303

Racial origin 44-46
Racialism 55-56, 138, 207-208
Rank, in armed services 434-35
Rapoport, D. C. 431-32
Ratchford, B. U. 64
Rathenau, W. 23
Rawson, D. W. 117, 196-97, 227
Reddaway, W. B. 337
Reeves, W. P. 61-62, 203
Reference groups 28-29
Reiss, A. J. 118
Reissman, L. 7, 11-12, 34, 116, 191
Relative deprivation 25-26, 33
Religion, link with class 44, 164-66
    link with education 152-53, 159-60, 167, 172-73, 175-76
    link with voting 166
    see also Catholics, Jews, Masonic Order, Methodists, Presbyterians, Protestants, WASP's
Repatriation 470-72
Returned Services League (RSL) 432, 469-74, 477
Rex, John 10
Rhodes, Cecil 187
    scholarships 187-88, 279, 404
Ricketson, S. 347, 411
Riesman, D. 107
Rigidity, in education 145
Robbins report 147
Robinson, Sir Arthur 385, 393
Robinson, W. S. 384-87
Rolfe, Hylda 329-30, 396-97, 409
Rolph, C. H. 77
Roosevelt, F. D. 218, 266
Rose, A. 116
Rothman, S. 203
Rousseau, J. J. 6, 46
Rowell, General S. F. 441-42

Rowland, P. F. 80, 83, 186
Royal Australian Air Force (RAAF) 442, 456-57, 461, 463, 469
Royal Australian Navy 456
Royal commissions 60, 76, 247-48, 260, 264-65, 344, 425, 442, 462
Royal Military College (Duntroon) 424, 437, 452-55, 457-59, 463
Runciman, W. G. 7-8, 25-26, 32-33, 38-39
Rymill, Sir Arthur 229, 350-51

Santamaria, B. A. 181, 227
St John, E. H. 207
St Peter's College 152, 156-57, 187, 302, 395, 404, 406, 460
Scarrow, H. A. 260-61
'Scavenger's daughter' 174
Schaffer, B. B. 254, 445-46, 452
Scherger, Sir Frederick 435
Schmoller, G. 13
Schumpeter, J. A. 8, 11, 43
Schutz, Alfred 29-32
Sciences Po 267
Scions 390-91, 395-96, 400-402
    see also family influence
Schoolteachers 144-47, 464-65
    social background of 148-49
Scotch College (Melbourne) 152-56, 187, 238, 279-80, 283, 302, 395, 404, 406, 410, 413, 447, 458, 460
Scots 248, 296, 299, 310
Scott, E. 424, 470-71
Scott, Rev. T. 152
Scullin, J. H. 239-40, 316, 325, 343, 472
SEATO 427, 429
Seeley, Sir John 184
Seniority, in the public service 244
Sexual attitudes 167, 170-71
Seymour, A. 473
Shand, T. P. 252
Shaw, G. B. 35, 192
Shepherd, J. 422-23, 425-26

Shils, E. A. 45-46, 124, 193
Shore, P. 364, 370
Siegfried, A. 80, 201
Simmel, G. 108
Simpson, Helen 178
Sinclair, F. R. 443
Single Purpose League 385
Skewes, W. J. 248
Skilled workers, class consciousness of 92-93, 105-106
Snobbery 96
Social Register 130
Socialism 62-63, 199-201, 218, 225, 356
Socio-economic status 41, 90
Sombart, W. 38
Sorel, G. 19
South Africa 189-90, 205-208
South Australia 72, 133, 135, 301, 350-51
Soviet Union 4, 22, 35, 40-41, 124
Spann, R. N. 182
Spender, J. A. 219
Spiro, H. J. 46
Squatters 132, 134, 154, 293, 295-300
Staff corps 453-55
States, administration in 251, 253, 256, 282-83
Status 7-8, 12, 22, 31, 32-42
Stevens, Sir Bertram 72
Stevens, Sir Jack 367, 468
Stock Exchange 140, 404
Stockbrokers 409-11
Strange, L. A. 433
Stratification 11-12, 16
Students, social background of 148-50
Subramaniam, V. A. 250, 256, 467
Subsidies, to church schools 146, 153, 173, 177
Svalastoga, K. 36, 89, 92
Sydney Boys' High School 158, 280
Sydney Church of England Grammar School ('Shore') 153, 156-57, 238, 280, 302, 404, 460